THE CLAY SANSKRIT LIBRARY

FOUNDED BY JOHN & JENNIFER CLAY

EDITED BY

RICHARD GOMBRICH

WWW.CLAYSANSKRITLIBRARY.ORG
WWW.NYUPRESS.ORG

Artwork by Robert Beer.
Cover design by Isabelle Onians.
Layout & typesetting by Somadeva Vasudeva.
Typeset in Adobe Garamond at 10.25 : 12.3+pt.
Printed and Bound in Great Britain by
TJ Books Limited, Cornwall on acid free paper

WHAT TEN YOUNG MEN DID

BY DAṆḌIN

TRANSLATED BY
ISABELLE ONIANS

NEW YORK UNIVERSITY PRESS
JJC FOUNDATION
2005

First Edition 2005

ISBN 978-0-8147-6206-6

The Clay Sanskrit Library is co-published by
New York University Press
and the JJC Foundation.

Further information about this volume
and the rest of the Clay Sanskrit Library
is available on the following websites:
www.claysanskritlibrary.org
www.nyupress.org

Library of Congress Cataloging-in-Publication Data
Daṇḍin, 7th cent.
[Dasakumāracarita. English]
What ten young men did / by Dandin ;
translated by Isabelle Onians.
p. cm. – (The Clay Sanskrit library)
Prose literature.
In English and Sanskrit;
translated from Sanskrit.
Includes bibliographical references and index.
ISBN 978-0-8147-6206-6
I. Title: What 10 young men did.
II. Onians, Isabelle, 1971- III. Title. IV. Series.
PK3794.D4D213 2005
891'.21–dc22 2004028985

CONTENTS

A *sandhi* grid is printed on the inside of the back cover

SANSKRIT ALPHABETICAL ORDER

Vowels:	*a ā i ī u ū ṛ ṝ ḷ ḹ e ai o au ṃ ḥ*
Gutturals:	*k kh g gh ṅ*
Palatals:	*c ch j jh ñ*
Retroflex:	*ṭ ṭh ḍ ḍh ṇ*
Labials:	*p ph b bh m*
Semivowels:	*y r l v*
Spirants:	*ś ṣ s h*

GUIDE TO SANSKRIT PRONUNCIATION

a	b*u*t
ā, â	r*a*ther
i	s*i*t
ī, î	f*ee*
u	p*u*t
ū, û	b*oo*
ṛ	vocalic *r*, American p*ur*dy or English p*re*tty
ṝ	lengthened *ṛ*
ḷ	vocalic *l*, ab*le*
e, ê, ē	m*a*de, esp. in Welsh pronunciation
ai	b*i*te
o, ô, ō	r*o*pe, esp. Welsh pronunciation; Italian s*o*lo
au	s*ou*nd
ṃ	*anusvāra* nasalizes the preceding vowel
ḥ	*visarga*, a voiceless aspiration (resembling English *h*), or like Scottish lo*ch*, or an aspiration with a faint echoing of the preceding vowel so that *taiḥ* is pronounced *taih*^{i}
k	lu*ck*
kh	blo*ckh*ead
g	*g*o
gh	bi*gh*ead
ṅ	a*n*ger
c	*ch*ill
ch	mat*chh*ead
j	*j*og
jh	aspirated *j*, he*dgeh*og
ñ	ca*ny*on
ṭ	retroflex *t*, *t*ry (with the tip of tongue turned up to touch the hard palate)
ṭh	same as the preceding but aspirated
ḍ	retroflex *d* (with the tip of tongue turned up to touch the hard palate)
ḍh	same as the preceding but aspirated
ṇ	retroflex *n* (with the tip of tongue turned up to touch the hard palate)
t	French *t*out
th	ten*t h*ook

d	*d*inner	*r*	trilled, resembling the Italian pronunciation of *r*
dh	guil*dh*all	*l*	*l*inger
n	*n*ow	*v*	*w*ord
p	*p*ill	*ś*	*sh*ore
ph	u*ph*eaval	*ṣ*	retroflex *sh* (with the tip of the tongue turned up to touch the hard palate)
b	*b*efore	*s*	hi*ss*
bh	a*bh*orrent	*h*	*h*ood
m	*m*ind		
y	*y*es		

CSL PUNCTUATION OF ENGLISH

The acute accent on Sanskrit words when they occur outside of the Sanskrit text itself, marks stress, e.g. Ramáyana. It is not part of traditional Sanskrit orthography, transliteration or transcription, but we supply it here to guide readers in the pronunciation of these unfamiliar words. Since no Sanskrit word is accented on the last syllable it is not necessary to accent disyllables, e.g. Rama.

The second CSL innovation designed to assist the reader in the pronunciation of lengthy unfamiliar words is to insert an unobtrusive middle dot between semantic word breaks in compound names (provided the word break does not fall on a vowel resulting from the fusion of two vowels), e.g. Maha·bhárata, but Ramáyana (not Rama·áyana). Our dot echoes the punctuating middle dot (·) found in the oldest surviving forms of written Sanskrit, the Ashókan inscriptions of the third century BCE.

The deep layering of Sanskrit narrative has also dictated that we use quotation marks only to announce the beginning and end of every direct speech, and not at the beginning of every paragraph.

CSL PUNCTUATION OF SANSKRIT

The Sanskrit text is also punctuated, in accordance with the punctuation of the English translation. In mid-verse, the punctuation will not alter the *sandhi* or the scansion. Proper names are capitalized, as are the initial words of verses (or paragraphs in prose texts). Most Sanskrit metres have four "feet" *(pāda):* where possible we print the common *śloka* metre on two lines. The capitalization of verse beginnings makes it easy for the reader to recognize longer metres where it is necessary to print the four metrical feet over four or eight lines. In the Sanskrit text, we use French *Guillemets* (e.g. *«kva saṃcicīrṣuḥ?»*) instead of English quotation marks (e.g. "Where are you off to?") to avoid confusion with the apostrophes used for vowel elision in *sandhi*.

Sanskrit presents the learner with a challenge: *sandhi* ("euphonic combination"). *Sandhi* means that when two words are joined in connected speech or writing (which in Sanskrit reflects speech), the last letter (or even letters) of the first word often changes; compare the way we pronounce "the" in "the beginning" and "the end."

In Sanskrit the first letter of the second word may also change; and if both the last letter of the first word and the first letter of the second are vowels, they may fuse. This has a parallel in English: a nasal consonant is inserted between two vowels that would otherwise coalesce: "a pear" and "an apple." Sanskrit vowel fusion may produce ambiguity. The chart at the back of each book gives the full *sandhi* system.

Fortunately it is not necessary to know these changes in order to start reading Sanskrit. For that, what is important is to know the form of the second word without *sandhi* (pre-*sandhi*), so that it can be recognized or looked up in a dictionary. Therefore we are printing Sanskrit with a system of punctuation that will indicate, unambiguously, the original form of the second word, i.e., the form without *sandhi*. Such *sandhi* mostly concerns the fusion of two vowels.

In Sanskrit, vowels may be short or long and are written differently accordingly. We follow the general convention that a vowel with no mark above it is short. Other books mark a long vowel either with a bar called a macron (*ā*) or with a circumflex (*â*). Our system uses the macron, except that for initial vowels in *sandhi* we use a circumflex to indicate that originally the vowel was short, or the shorter of two possibilities (*e* rather than *ai*, *o* rather than *au*).

When we print initial *â*,	before *sandhi* that vowel was *a*
î or *ê*,	*i*
û or *ô*,	*u*
âi,	*e*

âu,	*o*
ā,	*ā* (i.e., the same)
ī,	*ī* (i.e., the same)
ū,	*ū* (i.e., the same)
ē,	*ī*
ō,	*ū*
āi,	*ai*
āu,	*au*

', before *sandhi* there was a vowel *a*

FURTHER HELP WITH VOWEL SANDHI

When a final short vowel (*a*, *i* or *u*) has merged into a following vowel, we print ' at the end of the word, and when a final long vowel (*ā*, *ī* or *ū*) has merged into a following vowel we print " at the end of the word. The vast majority of these cases will concern a final *a* or *ā*.

Examples:

What before *sandhi* was *atra asti* is represented as *atr' âsti*

atra āste	*atr' āste*
kanyā asti	*kany" âsti*
kanyā āste	*kany" āste*
atra iti	*atr' êti*
kanyā iti	*kany" êti*
kanyā īpsitā	*kany" ēpsitā*

Finally, three other points concerning the initial letter of the second word:

(1) A word that before *sandhi* begins with *ṛ* (vowel), after *sandhi* begins with *r* followed by a consonant: *yatha" rtu* represents pre-*sandhi* *yathā ṛtu*.

(2) When before *sandhi* the previous word ends in *t* and the following word begins with *ś*, after *sandhi* the last letter of the previous word is *c* and the following word begins with *ch*: *syāc chāstravit* represents pre-*sandhi* *syāt śāstravit*.

(3) Where a word begins with *h* and the previous word ends with a double consonant, this is our simplified spelling to show the pre-*sandhi*

form: *tad hasati* is commonly written as *tad dhasati*, but we write *tadd hasati* so that the original initial letter is obvious.

COMPOUNDS

We also punctuate the division of compounds (*samāsa*), simply by inserting a thin vertical line between words. There are words where the decision whether to regard them as compounds is arbitrary. Our principle has been to try to guide readers to the correct dictionary entries.

WORDPLAY

Classical Sanskrit literature can abound in puns *(śleṣa)*. Such paronomasia, or wordplay, is raised to a high art; rarely is it a *cliché*. Multiple meanings merge *(śliṣyanti)* into a single word or phrase. Most common are pairs of meanings, but as many as ten separate meanings are attested. To mark the parallel senses in the English, as well as the punning original in the Sanskrit, we use a *slanted* font (different from *italic*) and a triple colon *(⁝)* to separate the alternatives. E.g.

> Yuktaṃ Kādambarīṃ śrutvā kavayo maunam āśritāḥ
> *Bāṇa/dhvanāv* an|adhyāyo bhavat' îti smṛtir yataḥ.
>
> It is right that poets should fall silent upon hearing the Kádambari, for the sacred law rules that recitation must be suspended when *the sound of an arrow ⁝ the poetry of Bana* is heard.
>
> Soméshvara·deva's "Moonlight of Glory" I.15

EXAMPLE

Where the Deva·nágari script reads:

कुम्भस्थली रक्षतु वो विकीर्णसिन्दूररेणुर्द्विरदाननस्य।
प्रशान्तये विघ्नतमश्छटानां निष्ठ्यूतबालातपपल्लवेव॥

Others would print:

kumbhasthalī rakṣatu vo vikīrṇasindūrareṇur dviradānanasya /
praśāntaye vighnatamaśchaṭānāṃ niṣṭhyūtabālātapapallaveva //

We print:

Kumbha|sthalī rakṣatu vo vikīrṇa|sindūra|reṇur dvirad'|ānanasya
praśāntaye vighna|tamaś|chaṭānāṃ niṣṭhyūta|bāl'|ātapa|pallav" êva.

And in English:

"May Ganésha's domed forehead protect you! Streaked with vermilion dust, it seems to be emitting the spreading rays of the rising sun to pacify the teeming darkness of obstructions."

"Nava·sáhasanka and the Serpent Princess" I.3 by Padma·gupta

INTRODUCTION

"What Ten Young Men Did"[1] is a coming-of-age novel. Dandin's text compares readily with the modern genre known in English by its German name, the *Bildungs·roman*. Except that this is an Indian story, with the propensity to proliferation implied thereby, so that instead of a single young person's passage to maturity we have the kaleidoscopic accounts of ten young men.

The novel's form is autobiographical: each of the ten in turn narrates his adventures, on the occasion of their reunion. Even before the magical subterranean intervention that results in their separation, we learn how nine boys, five of them foundlings, came to be brought up together with their leader, Crown Prince Raja·váhana. Their rich and broad education equips them with the skills—some of them morally dubious—to manage magnificently when they find themselves isolated out in the big wide world.

As young men, their youthful instincts are vital; they seldom hesitate to enter into fights and love affairs. Indeed, their separation could have been avoided, had they had the patience to wait a while for Raja·váhana's return from his mysterious absence, rather than charging off in different directions in search of their friend. But in that case there would have been no individual exploits, no series of personal narratives to compare and contrast.

A further German term can be fruitfully applied to Dandin's plot: *Wander·lust*. The drive to travel far is an integral feature of the coming-of-age novel, with a physical journey mirroring an interior quest. Our ten heroes are no less picaresque than the much later characters of Cervantes, or of Petronius and Apuleius centuries earlier. The principal

Sanskrit root for "wander" *(bhram)* occurs forty-eight times in the text.

Yet, in the tradition of Indian amplitude again, their wanderings are iterated, since not only are they compelled to find separately their way in the world, but they had originally set out on a group "conquest of the directions" *(dig·víjaya).*

World domination, "the conquest of the directions," is a long-standing Indian royal preoccupation. In the first book of the *Maha·bhárata*, the Kuru king Pandu marches forth on his *dig·víjaya* at the head of massed forces, and receives the homage and tribute from neighboring kings which confirm his preeminent status, after which the still young king can retire to the forest *(Ādi/parvan ch.113)*; in Kali·dasa's *Raghu/vaṃśa*, King Raghu sets out with his sixfold army in the first autumn of his reign to conquer the world in each of the directions (Ragh IV.26ff.). Here, however, a gang of sixteen-year-olds are sent off to conquer the world, but without any military or material resources to back them up.

The crown prince's father had been deposed in battle. His son was born in exile, in the jungle, although surrounded by much of the apparatus of a court. A sage had predicted the child's future reconquest of all that the king had lost. Thus the youthful group leave their uncertain home with everything to gain. Their mission is to restore King Raja·hamsa to his throne, thereby winning back their own respective birthrights. The sage's infallible prediction notwithstanding, one cannot help but fear that the adolescents are being deployed on a suicide mission.

Dandin has at the outset inverted one of the mainstays of the Indian royal tradition. But he has done so with a glorious precedent, the third-century BCE Buddhist emperor of all India, Ashóka. Full of remorse at the widespread slaughter and suffering of the population caused by his violent unification of his great empire, at the close of his XIIIth rock edict Ashóka deliberately redefined true world domination as "conquest by religion" *(dharma/vijaya).*

The Art of Politics

The rod (*daṇḍa*) for which Dandin is named (albeit in his case the staff is usually understood to refer to an ascetic mendicant *sannyásin*'s walking stick) also defines statecraft, the policy of the scepter and rod *(daṇḍa/nīti)*, the enforcement of justice. Danda·niti is the theme of the famous *Artha/śāstra*, in comparison with which, in the words of MAX WEBER, MACHIAVELLI's notorious *Prince* is an "innocuous book" (1963:10-18). The teachings of the *Artha/śāstra* are echoed throughout "What Ten Young Men Did," but they are initially here trumped by the dubious ruses of our juveniles, who are thrown back on their personal resources, unassisted—and, equally, unhampered—by reinforcements.

One of the high points of the book is the concluding narrative, that of Víshruta, within which Dandin composes a virtuoso satire on the *Artha/śāstra*'s injunctions. This extensive satire's climactic position emphasizes its key function; the explicit undermining of conventional political wisdom is the denouement of a complex of parallel yet differentiated individual narratives.

Longest of all the chapters, Apahára·varman's, next after the crown prince Raja·váhana's own account, commences with a correspondingly comic device. Maríchi, paragon of renunciant values and attainments, is reduced by the prostitute Kama·máñjari to adoring submission. She had sought him out for religious instruction, but it is she who teaches him about the true relative ranking of the fundamental Indian three ends of man: piety, profit and pleasure *(dharma, artha, kāma)*—comparable to the European Latin trinity of activity for the sake of fame, money or love *(fama, pecunia, amor)*.

In both of these episodes, pleasure, or love, is elevated to the highest goal, as progenitor of profit and even piety.

The Art of Love

Every one of the ten youths has at least one major love affair, an encounter key to his ultimate attainment of royal status. The ladies in question are both objectified—they represent the Earth itself, and their conquest by a man symbolizes his mastery over territory—and portrayed as equal partners; the seduction is inevitably mutual, if not instigated and facilitated by women.

The very first female name to appear is that of Vásumati, the crown prince's mother, named after the "Wealthy" Earth. One of the book's showpieces is the animated depiction of the young princess, Kandukávati, performing a ball-dance in honor of her patron goddess. The globe she holds in her hand embodies world domination, participating in a wider Sanskritic cultural trope. Without the queen who incarnates Majesty, Shri, kingship is void.

These indispensable women are not, however, mere tokens. They actually enjoy erotic fulfillment. These are not the disdainful remote heroines of medieval European courtly love. Although their distant glance is inevitably an incurable violent wound for the man they look upon. Sight is pivotal to these relationships, but not face-to-face vision alone.

Art in Literature

The painted portrait plays a determining role in Dandin's plot, a leitmotif that recurs in many works of classical Indian literature, from *Shakúntala* onward. Other than appearances loaned from India in, for example, *The 1001 Nights*, is this prominent device unparalleled in other literatures of the world? Men and women alike are susceptible to falling in love at first sight of a likeness, which can be a self-portrait; and both are quick to sketch the object of their feelings or themselves after an encounter.

In Dandin one of these visual representations is further exploited to lure an ugly king to enter a risky ritual that promises to transform him into the handsome youth he sees depicted. Without even a visual prop, the offer of an illusory metamorphosis persuades another unattractive monarch to dive into a lake to meet his doom.

Not only are credulous leaders prepared to believe in the possibility of a non-surgical face and body lift, but the staging of a wedding masque conceals the true marriage it performs, and an acrobatic performance presents, as is universal, the opportunity to swiftly assassinate the relaxing ruler. In addition to the ball-dance referred to above, Dandin portrays other dramatic and musical entertainments aplenty.

The art of cooking too merits an in-depth description, when an impoverished young lady rises to her guest's challenge to prepare him a full dinner out of a single package of raw rice.

The Art of Words

The connoisseur of Sanskrit literature may well have been alive to the potency of the visual arts, but in this lengthy novel, words paint a thousand pictures. In a verse repeated in many an anthology and commentary, Dandin's skill is encapsulated as "felicity of expression" *(pada/lālitya; MaSuSa 7104)*. When the *Kavi/caritra* compares three preeminent Sanskrit poets—Dandin, Bhava·bhuti and Kali·dasa—Dandin's style is characterized by its jingling consonance of alliterative syllables.

Dandin's French translator Marie-Claude Porcher infers that it was his "linguistic virtuosity which so embarrassed Occidentals that they denied [the book] any coherent content and preferred to relegate it to the Hell of libraries of stories" (1995b:186). The pioneer comparative philologist William Jones, already in 1786, eulogized the "wonderful structure" of the Sanskrit language as "more perfect than the Greek, more copious than the Latin, and more exquisitely refined than either." Dandin's writing is a case in point.

Nevertheless, our novel stands apart from the majority of Sanskrit literature, which is in verse, both recreational and philosophical, in that it is composed in prose, with only a handful of key verses. Antecedent to "What Ten Young Men Did" in this exclusive category is the paradigmatic political treatise that it satirizes, the *Artha/śāstra*; Dandin's choice may thus not be coincidental.

In Dandin's other important work, the theoretical study of classical Sanskrit literary aesthetics "The Mirror of Poetic Composition" *(Kāvy'/ādarśa)*, he expresses preference for the simple, Vaidárbhi, Southern style (I.34,41–42). Never mind the fact that some of Dandin's sentences spread over several pages of the CSL edition, and Sanskrit compounds stretch over many lines. In "The Mirror of Poetic Composition," Dandin himself opined that the life and soul of prose is the presence (if not profusion, *bhūyastva*, I.80) of compounds. Rarely is sense obscured by florid elaboration.

Even Dandin's linguistic tour de force made high demands only of himself, not of the reader. The penultimate young man's narrative, "What Mantra·gupta Did," is a lipogram *(sthāna/niyama, KA III.88–91)*, of the genre that requires one or more letters of the alphabet to be excluded from a text. Mantra·gupta's lips have been so ravished with biting kisses that he is constrained to tell his story without allowing his battered lips to touch, that is, without using the sounds *m* or *p* or *b*. In an antique tradition where so much is lost to the passage of time, it is perhaps thanks to this chapter of artful circumlocutions that the book has been preserved.

The Art of Translation

The present translation is not the first, but it does seem to be the first in the long history of translations of this masterpiece that strives to reproduce the labial-free effect in the original. Readers may be amused to try a similar exercise even within their own native language: experiment with a sentence or two, translating within the preferred language into words that do not include an *m* or *p* or *b*.

Translation, the challenge runs, is like a woman: it can either be beautiful or faithful, but never both. An example of the dreaded travesty of translation that has been likened to a parrot's head on a plate is the treatment of the title of Dandin's novel, *Daśa/kumāra/carita*, here translated "What Ten *(Daśa/)* Young Men *(/kumāra/)* Did *(/carita)*." Until today the title has unanimously been rendered with reference to ten "princes," whether alluding to their "adventures," "exploits" or "history" *(/carita)*.

But our energetic unrepressed heroes are not princes, or at least, not all ten of them are. One is the crown prince, although born only after his father's fall from power; two more are brother foundling princes, recognized as such, yet brought up far from their royal parents; and the majority of the other seven are ministerial offspring, hardly deserving of regal titles. In the end, all ten do ascend each to a throne or two, but many do so directly, bypassing princely status. The problem word is */kumāra/*; it can mean "boy," "youth," "young man" or, by extension, "prince," depending, crucially, on context.

Mistranslation aside, the work's very Sanskrit title itself is contested.

Part or Whole?

The *Daśa/kumāra/carita* has not survived the centuries whole. The text here published is tripartite. The central bulk is Dandin's, sandwiched between two secondary paraphrases of the missing sections of his original work. The "front book" *(pūrva/pīṭhikā)*, here called "Postscript Beginning," is prolix (pp. 35–165, or c. 23% of the whole), while the "end book" *(uttara/pīṭhikā)*, here "Postscript Conclusion," is cursory (just pp. 553–575, or c. 4%).

These supplements may be presumed to transmit details proper to "What Ten Young Men Did," introducing, however, some discrepancies, but their respective authors' style is at odds with that of Dandin's core. The poet Kétana (c. 1250 CE) translated the book into Telugu, a Dravidian language of Andhra Pradesh, in southeastern India, several centuries after its initial composition. One plausible scenario is that the "Postscript Beginning" at least was translated back from this extant translation, with which it agrees closely, even including Telugu idioms and usages. Nor are these two the only candidates for the prosthetic appendices, although it is they that are everywhere preserved together with the headless, tailless torso in the subsequent plentiful manuscript transmission.

The problematic has been compounded since the rediscovery, at the beginning of the twentieth century, of an extensive fragment of our author's prose *Avanti/sundarī*—named for Avánti·súndari, the heroine who becomes Raja·váhana's wife—and an accompanying metrical summary *(sāra)* of the work, also incomplete, called *Avanti/sundarī/kathā/sāra*.

Reversing previous assumptions, Peter Khoroche argues, in a yet unpublished study, that the *Daśa/kumāra/carita* is merely a subsection of the far greater original *Avanti/sundarī*, the lengthiest fragment of which is almost ten times as long as the first half of the current "Postscript Beginning." The hypothetical larger whole may thus have been composed in emulation of the ambitious proportions of Dandin's more mannered and less snappy predecessor, the northerner Bana's (fl. 620–40) *Kādambarī*, whose story is indeed interpolated into both the *Avanti/sundarī* works. Hence the enduring question mark to our working title. Moreover, the perceived stylistic disjunction between the two parts of the notional whole is a continuing caveat.

Dandin in Time and Space

Dandin and his oeuvre are no different from the mass of Sanskrit literature in being but loosely contextualized on either the personal or sociohistorical plane. Few indeed are contemporary historical sources, other than inscriptions that deal mainly with matters of property and power, and the often corrupt far younger secondary manuscripts that do occasionally provide a colophon or authorial preface referring to the temporal and geographical context of the original composition.

Thus both *Avanti/sundarī* versions open with an account of Dandin's ancestors and the circumstances in which the work came to be written. His great-grandfather, Damódara, was a promising South Indian poet, we are told, initially influenced by the famous poet Bháravi (fl. c. 570–590 CE). Befriended by a sequence of three datable Deccan kings (of the Badámi Chalúkya, Mysore Gangéya and Kañchi Pállava dynasties), Damódara must have flourished at the close of the sixth century. By extrapolation, one can place Dandin, his great-grandson, at the Pállava court at Kañchi sometime in the years 690–725. Also mentioned are a number of works and authors, of whom the latest in date are Bana and Mayúra, who both flourished under the poet king Harsha of Kanauj in northern India, c. 620–40.

We are further told that Dandin was orphaned when still a child. His hometown of Kanchi·pura, in present-day Tamil Nadu, was subsequently beset by Chalúkya attack, driving the youth into exile. For twelve years he wandered from kingdom to kingdom, studying with different teachers, until peace was restored in Kanchi, when he could return. It is no coincidence, then, that his novel evidences the same *Wander·lust*.

"What Ten Young Men Did" is autobiographical in both senses. It both relates ten fictional autobiographies and could not have been written with such realism and confidence had not its author himself undergone many of the same traveler's adventures. Since in five of the narratives foundlings are finally reunited with their parents, the implication is that Dandin had himself fantasized about reunion with his dear departed parents.

The hypothesis advanced above—that the *Daśa/kumāra/carita* is but a subordinate continuing section of the *Avanti/sundarī*—notwithstanding, a persuasive chronology would assign "What Ten Young Men Did" to Dandin's early output, filled with an exuberance that was mellowed into masterful sobriety in the later *Kāvy'/ādarśa* and *Avanti/sundarī*. What is more, the colophons of these last two make their author "professor" *(ācārya)*, a qualification absent from *Daśa/kumāra/carita* signatures.

Relative Originality

Classical Sanskrit narratives exhibit a high degree of intertextuality. Dandin's novel is no exception, although most of his book appears to be totally original. We find slight and casual borrowings from earlier works, above all Gunádhya's *Bṛhat/kathā* and Buddhist játakas, but nothing wholesale.

The narrative is unprecedented both in its portrayal of people from the middle classes alongside rulers with all too human failings and in its lack of overt moralizing, in contrast to the older *Pañca/tantra*, for example. Here the unconventional pages are replete with gambling, burglary, impersonation, murder, abduction, alcoholic beverages, amorous pleasure, illicit love and spittle.

In the young men's encounters with numerous kings one would expect to find allusions to contemporary historical events and personages. But this remains a moot issue. Even certain elements of the extensive geographical information continue to elude identification. Nonetheless, we provide a simple map to enable minimum orientation.

A nineteenth-century French translation of the romance of Upahára·varman and Kalpa·súndari—mediated by the sending of the young man's self-portrait to the young queen married to a monster—inspired MALLARMÉ to write the first of his *Contes Indiens*, "Le Portrait Enchanté." Imagine if the present series of new CLAY SANSKRIT LIBRARY translations could trigger contemporary creations in twenty-first-century media!

Dedicated to the Memory of
FRIEDHELM ERNST HARDY (1953–2004),
For his Power, Love and Wisdom,
South Indianist and
Prince Among Young Men.

BIBLIOGRAPHY OF WORKS REFERRED TO[2]

TEXTS AND TRANSLATIONS

DAṆḌIN

Avanti/sundarī [fragmentary MS] ed. SASTRI, K. S. MAHADEVA. Trivandrum. 1954.

Avanti/sundarī/kathā and Avanti/sundarī/kathā/sāra [ASK & ASKS] ed. KAVI, M. R. Madras. 1924.

Avanti/sundarī/kathā/sāra [An improved edition of the anonymous ASKS, based on a better but still incomplete MS (it breaks off at Upahāravarman's intrigue with Kalpasundarī = §8.21 below)] ed. SASTRI, G. HARIHARA. Madras. 1954.

VAN BUITENEN, J. A. B. *Tales of Ancient India.* Chicago. 1959.

Daśa/kumāra/carita Ed. and tr. KALE, M. R. [Containing current PP and UP] "With Sanskrit Commentary, Various Readings, A Literal English Translation, Explanatory and Critical Notes, and an Exhaustive Introduction." Reprinted posthumous 4th "edition" of 3rd edition (Bombay. 1925; 2nd ed. had only "free" translation). Delhi. 1966.

—Telugu tr. KETANA, MULAGHATIKA Ed. 1967.

Kāvy'/ādarśa [KA] Ed. IYER, V. N. Madras. 1952.

MEYER, J. J. *Daṇḍins Daśakumāracaritam, die Abenteuer der zehn Prinzen. Ein altindischer Schelmenroman.* Leipzig. 1902.

PORCHER, M.-C. *Histoire des dix princes, par Daṇḍin. Traduit du sanscrit, présenté et annoté.* Paris. 1995a.

OTHER SANSKRIT WORKS

Artha/śāstra [ASh] of Kauṭilya. Ed. KANGLE, R. P. Bombay. 1960.

—Tr. KANGLE, R. P. Bombay. 1963.

Bṛhat/kathā/śloka/saṃgraha of Budhasvāmin. Ed. & tr. MALLINSON, J. (two volumes). CSL. New York. 2005.

Kādambarī of Bāṇa. Ed. VAIDYA, P. L. Poona. 1935.

Kāma/sūtra [KaSu] of Vātsyāyana. Ed. (with Hindi commentary) SASTRI, D. Varanasi. 1964.

—Tr. DONIGER, W. & S. KAKAR. Oxford. 2003.

Kathā/sarit/sāgara of Somadeva Bhaṭṭa. Ed. DURGAPRASAD, P. & K. PANDURANG PARAB. Bombay. 1903.

—Tr. *The ocean of story.* TAWNEY, C.H. Ed. PENZER, N.M. Delhi. 1968.

Kumāra/saṃbhava [KuSam]. Ed. & tr. SMITH, D. CSL. New York. 2005.

Mahā/subhāṣita/saṃgraha [MaSuSa] Ed. NAIR, B. Hoshiarpur. 1980.

Mālatī/mādhava of Bhavabhūti. Ed. & tr. KALE, M.R. Bombay. 1926.

Mālavik"/âgnimitra of Kālidāsa. Ed. SHASTRI, C. Lahore. 1933.

Manimekhalai of Shattan. Tr. from the Tamil by DANIÉLOU, A. with the collaboration of T. V. GOPALA IYER. London. 1993.

Mānava/dharma/śāstra [Manu]. Ed. & tr. OLIVELLE, P. New York. 2004.

Megha/dūta of Kālidāsa. Ed. & tr. MALLINSON, J. CSL. New York. 2005.

Mṛc/chakaṭika of Śūdraka. Ed. KALE, M. R. Bombay. 1962. (CSL ed. & tr., ACHARYA, D., to be published 2006).

Raghu/vaṃśa [Ragh] of Kālidāsa. Ed. GOODALL, D. & H. ISAACSON (CSL tr., GOODALL, D., to be published 2006).

Rāja/taraṅgiṇī of Kalhaṇa. Ed. SASTRI, V. Hoshiarpur. 1963–1965.

—Tr. STEIN, M.A.. Westminster. 1900.

Ratnāvalī of Harṣa. Ed. & tr. KALE, M.R. Delhi. 1984. (CSL tr., DONIGER, W., to be published 2006).

Śākuntalā [Shak] of Kālidāsa. Ed. & tr. VASUDEVA, S. D. CSL. New York. 2005.

Vetāla/pañca/viṃśati [Vetāla]. Ed. & tr. EMENEAU, M.B. New Haven. 1934.

Vikram'/ûrvaśīya [Vikr] of Kālidāsa. Ed. & tr. KARMARKAR, R. D. Poona. 1920.

Yājñavalkya/smṛti [Yaj] Ed. Bombay. 1936.

STUDIES

CHAKRAVARTY, N. "Jātaka Stories in the Daśakumāracarita." *All India Oriental Conferences*. 1922. pp.549–551.

GUPTA, D.K. *A critical study of Dandin and his works*. Delhi. 1970.

JONES, W. *Third Anniversary Discourse to the Asiatick Society*, February 2, 1786.

HARDY, F.E. *The religious culture of India: power, love and wisdom*. Cambridge. 1994.

LIENHARD, S. "Kanyākandukakrīḍā—Ballspiel junger Damen. Zur Entwicklung eines Motivs der klassischen Sanskrit-Dichtung." *Nachrichten der Akademie der Wissenschaften in Göttingen. (Philos.-his. Kl.)*. 1999, Nr. 8. pp.403–418.

MALLARMÉ, S. "Contes Indiens." *Oeuvres complètes*. Paris. 1945.

PEREC, G. *La Disparition*. Paris. 1969.

PORCHER, M.-C. "La princesse et le royaume." *Journal asiatique* cclxxiii, pp.183–206. Paris. 1995b.

RUBEN, W. *Die Erlebnisse der zehn Prinzen: eine Erzählung Dandins*. Berlin. 1952.

WEBER, M. *Le savant et le politique*. Paris, 1963.

NOTES

1 Three extended introductions to earlier translations of this work should be consulted for greater detail: M.-C. PORCHER (1995a, in French); M. R. KALE (2nd ed. 1925, in English; subsequent unchanged "editions" and reprints); and J. J. MEYER (1902, in German). For enlightening monographs, please refer to D. K. GUPTA (1970, in English) and W. RUBEN (1952, in German).

2 For a fuller bibliography please consult the CSL website.

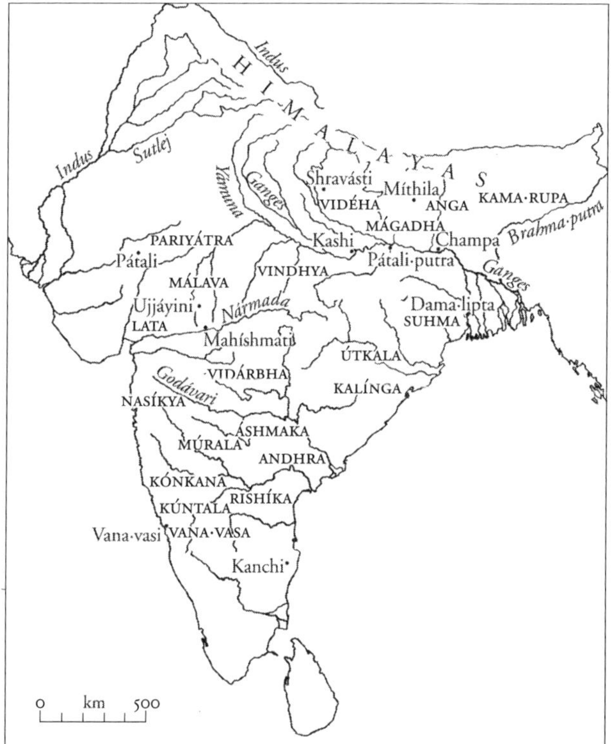

H I M A L A Y A S
Indus
Indus
Sutlej
Yámuna
Ganges
Shravásti
Míthila
VIDÉHA
ANGA
KAMA·RUPA
Brahma·putra
MÁGADHA
Kashi
Champa
Pátali·putra
Ganges
PARIYÁTRA
Pátali
VINDHYA
MÁLAVA
Ujjáyini
Nármada
LATA
Dama·lipta
SUHMA
Mahíshmati
ÚTKALA
VIDÁRBHA
Godávari
KALÍNGA
NASÍKYA
ÁSHMAKA
MÚRALA
ANDHRA
KÓNKANA
RISHÍKA
KÚNTALA
Vana·vasi
VANA·VASA
Kanchi
0 km 500

PART I:
POSTSCRIPT BEGINNING

Brahm'|âṇḍa|chatra|daṇḍaḥ
    Śata|dhṛti|bhavan'|âmbhoruho nāla|daṇḍaḥ
kṣoṇī|nau|kūpa|daṇḍaḥ
    kṣarad|amara|sarit|paṭṭikā|ketu|daṇḍaḥ
jyotiś|cakr'|âkṣa|daṇḍas
    tri|bhuvana|vijaya|stambho 'ṅghri|daṇḍaḥ
śreyas|Traivikramas te
    vitaratu vibudha|dveṣiṇāṃ kāla|daṇḍaḥ.

Postscript Beginning

Pole for the parasol-shell that is Brahma's cosmic egg,
Stem for Brahma's lotus seat,
Mast for the ship that is the earth,
Rod for the banner that is the rushing immortal river
    Ganges,
Axle rod for the rotating zodiac,
Pillar of victory over the three worlds—
May Vishnu's leg favor you with blessings—
Staff that is the leg of him who as Tri·víkrama reclaimed
    those three worlds in three steps,
Rod of time, death itself, for the demon enemies
    of the gods.*

CHAPTER ONE:
THE ORIGINS OF THE YOUNG MEN

ASTI SAMASTA|NAGARĪ|nikaṣāyamāṇā śaśvad|agaṇya|paṇya|vistārita|maṇi|gaṇ'|ādi|vastu|jāta|vyākhyāta|ratn'|ākara|māhātmyā Magadha|deśa|śekharī|bhūtā Puṣpapurī nāma nagarī.

Tatra vīra|bhaṭa|paṭal'|ôttaraṅga|turaṅga|kuñjara|makara|bhīṣaṇa|sakala|ripu|gaṇa|kaṭaka|jala|nidhi|mathana|Mandarāyamāṇa|samuddaṇḍa|bhuja|daṇḍaḥ;*

1.3 Puraṃdara|pur'|âṅgaṇa|vana|viharaṇa|parāyaṇa|gīrvāṇa|taruṇa|gaṇikā|gaṇa|jegīyamānay" âtimānayā śarad|indu|kunda|ghana|sāra|nīhāra|hāra|mṛṇāla|marāla|sura|gaja|nīra|kṣīra|Giriś'|âṭṭa|hāsa|Kailāsa|kāśa|nīkāśa|mūrtyā racita|dig|antarāla|pūrtyā kīrty" âbhitaḥ surabhitaḥ;

svar|loka|śikhar'|ôru|rucira|ratna|ratn'|ākara|velā|mekhalā|valayita|dharaṇī|ramaṇī|saubhāgya|bhoga|bhāgyavān, an|avarata|yāga|dakṣiṇā|rakṣita|śiṣṭa|viśiṣṭa|vidyā|saṃbhāra|bhāsura|bhū|sura|nikaraḥ, viracit'|ârāti|saṃtāpena pratāpena satata|tulita|viyan|madhya|haṃsaḥ, Rājahaṃso nāma ghana|darpa|Kaṃdarpa|saundarya|sodarya|hṛdya|nir|avadya|rūpo bhūpo babhūva.

THERE IS A CITY called Pushpa·puri, "Flowertown,"* the touchstone of all cities. Pushpa·puri is the crown of the land of Mágadha. By the ceaseless array of innumerable goods and collections of precious stones for sale there, it is testament to the greatness of the ocean that is known as the mine of treasures.

That city had once a king called Raja·hamsa, "Best, 'Swan' indeed, among kings."* When this king raised his massive arms it was as though the mountain Mándara was churning the primeval ocean, except that his ocean was the army of all his enemy's troops. That army was horrific, with war elephants and horses for sharks, and the massed ranks of valiant soldiers for pounding waves.

Measureless fame enveloped Raja·hamsa in its perfume, 1.3
filling with its fragrance every quarter of the globe. His fame was sung again and again by choruses of the young divine courtesans who frolic in the groves around Amarávati, "Undying," the city of Indra, king of the gods. Such fame shines spotless as the autumn moon or jasmine, bright as camphor, snow and pearls, a lotus stalk, a swan or Indra's white elephant Airávata, water, milk, Shiva's loud laughter and his mountain, Kailash, and the white *kasha* flower.*

It was the king's joy to enjoy, as though it were a lovely lady, a joyful land,* with the seashore for a girdle. True to its epithet, that sea is a mine of jewels, filled with jewels big and beautiful as those on celestial Mount Meru's peaks. His never-ending sacrificial payments provided for great numbers of learned brahmins, gods on earth in their splendid amassing of special knowledge. Like the midday sun, but day and night, his glory scorched his enemies. His beauty

Tasya Vasumatī nāma su|matī līlāvatī|kula|śekhara|maṇī ramaṇī babhūva. roṣaṇ'|ēkṣaṇena Niṭil'|ēkṣaṇena bhasmī-kṛta|cetane Makara|ketane tadā bhayen' ân|a|vadyā vanit" êti matvā;

1.6 tasyā rolamb'|āvalī keśa|jālam, prem'|ākaro rajanī|karo vijit'|âravindaṃ vadanam, jaya|dhvajāyamāno mīno jāyā|yuto 'kṣi|yugalam, sakala|sainik'|âṅga|vīro malaya|samīro niḥśvāsaḥ, pathika|hṛd|dalana|karavālaḥ pravālaś c' âdhara|bimbam;

jaya|śaṅkho bandhurā lāvaṇya|dharā kaṃ|dharā, pūrṇa|kumbhau cakravāk'|ânukārau payodharau, jyāyamāne mārdav'|âsamāne bisa|late ca bāhū, īṣat|phulla|līl"|âvataṃsa|kahlāra|korako Gaṅg"|āvarta|sa|nābhir nābhiḥ, dūrīkṛta|yogi|mano|ratho jaitra|ratho 'tighanaṃ jaghanam, jaya|stambha|bhūte saundarya|bhūte vighnita|yati|jan'|ārambhe rambhe c' ūru|yugam, ātapatra|sahasra|patraṃ pāda|dvayam, astra|bhūtāni prasūnāni tān' îtarāṇy aṅgāni ca samabhūvann iva.

too was enchanting and faultless, making him the double of Kama, proud god of love.

Raja·hamsa had a wise wife called Vásumati, "Wealthy as the Earth," the jewel in the crown of the whole class of lovely ladies. Her body had become what it was after Shiva of the third eye had turned his furious gaze on Kama, whose banner is the fish, and burned him to a cinder. Terrified, the love god's accoutrements thought they could hide in her innocent person.*

Thus her thick hair was the string of black bees from his 1.6
bow. For her face the lotus was no competition: it was the moon, the source of love. Her two eyes were the fish that acts as Kama's victory banner, together with that fish's wife. Her breath was the southern sandalwood-scented breeze that was the hero of all Kama's martial forces. The ruddy *bimba* fruit of her lower lip was the tender bud that stabs painfully at the lonely traveler's heart.

Her neck, graceful bearer of loveliness, was his victory conch. Her breasts were a pair of full jars, nestling like a couple of loving *chakra·vaka* birds.* And her arms were the two lotus shoots of incomparable tenderness which formed Kama's bowstring. Her navel, the twin of an eddy of the Ganges, was the lotus bud, just slightly opened, which he sports as an ear decoration. Her very ample buttocks were the round wheels of Kama's victory chariot, driving away a renunciate's higher desires; her two plump tapered thighs were the two plantain trunks that are the love god's victory pillars, loveliness itself and spelling defeat for an ascetic's exertions; her two feet were the thousand-petalled lotus that

Vijit'|Âmara|pure Puṣpapure nivasatā s" *Ân/anta/bhoga/ lālitā* Vasumatī Vasumat" îva Magadha|rājena yathā|sukham anvabhāvi.

1.9 Tasya rājñaḥ parama|vidheyā Dharmapāla|Padmodbhava|Sitavarma|nāma|dheyā dhīra|dhiṣaṇ'|âvadhīrita|vibudh'|ā-cārya|vicārya|kārya|sāhityāḥ kul'|âmātyās trayo 'bhūvan. teṣāṃ Sitavarmaṇaḥ Sumati|Satyavarmāṇau, Dharmapālasya Sumantra|Sumitra|Kāmapālāḥ, Padmodbhavasya Suśruta|Ratnodbhavāv iti tanayāḥ samabhūvan.

Teṣu dharma|śīlaḥ Satyavarmā saṃsār'|â|sāratāṃ buddhvā tīrtha|yātr'|âbhilāṣī deś'|ântaram agamat. viṭa|naṭa|vāra|nā-rī|parāyaṇo dur|vinītaḥ Kāmapālo janak'|âgra|janmanoḥ śāsanam atikramya bhuvaṃ babhrāma. Ratnodbhavo 'pi vāṇijya|nipuṇatayā pār'|âvāra|taraṇam akarot. itare man-tri|sūnavaḥ Puraṃdara|pur'|âtithiṣu pitṛṣu yathā|pūrvam anvatiṣṭhan.

is his parasol; and the rest of her was made of the flowers that are Kama's arrows.

Living in Pushpa·pura, unmatched even by Amarávati, the city of the immortals, the Mágadhan king enjoyed this Vásumati at his leisure. He *caressed her in endless enjoyments,* just as he did the Earth, also known as Vásumati—"The wealthy one"—*and is similarly caressed in the hoods of Anánta, the king of the serpents.**

That king had three totally dependable hereditary min- 1.9
isters, called Dharma·pala, Padmódbhava and Sita·varman, all superlative in their service. Excelling in their steady good counsel they had what it takes to carry out what would make even the pandit of the gods, Brihas·pati, stop to think. They all had sons: Sita·varman's were Súmati and Satya·varman; Dharma·pala had Sumántra, Sumítra and Kama·pala; and Padmódbhava's two were Súshruta and Ratnódbhava.

Of these young men, Satya·varman, "With truth as his armor," was religiously inclined. Awakened to the emptiness of everything he set his heart on pilgrimage to holy places, and went abroad. Kama·pala, "The protector of love," was badly behaved, and besotted by rakes, actors and vulgar women. He rebelled against the instructions of his father and elder brother and wandered the earth. Ratnódbhava, "Jewel-born," had a good head for commerce, and so he too travelled from shore to shore. The other ministerial sons did their duty in the posts they inherited once their fathers had become guests in the city of Indra, that is heaven.

Tataḥ kadā cin nānā|vidha|mahad|āyudha|naipuṇya|racit'|âgaṇya|janya|rājanya|mauli|pāli|nihita|niśita|sāyako Magadha|nāyako Mālav'|ēśvaraṃ pratyagra|saṅgrāma|ghasmaraṃ samutkaṭa|māna|sāraṃ Mānasāraṃ prati sa|helaṃ nyakkṛta|jala|dhi|nirghoṣ'|âhaṅkāreṇa bherī|jhāṅkāreṇa haṭhik'|ākarṇan'|ākrānta|bhaya|caṇḍimānaṃ dig|dantāvala|valayaṃ vighūrṇayan nija|bhara|naman|medinī|bhareṇ' āyasta|bhujaga|rāja|mastaka|balena catur|aṅga|balena saṃyutaḥ saṅgrām'|âbhilāṣeṇa roṣeṇa mahat" āviṣṭo niryayau. Mālava|nātho 'py an|ek'|ânekapa|yūtha|sa|nātho vigrahaḥ sa|vigraha iva sāgraho 'bhimukhībhūya bhūyo nirjagāma.

1.12 Tayor atha ratha|turaga|khura|kṣuṇṇa|kṣoṇī|samudbhūte kari|ghaṭā|kaṭa|sravan|mada|dhārā|dhauta|mūle navya|vallabha|varaṇ'|āgata|divya|kanyā|jana|javanikā|paṭa|maṇḍapa iva viyat|tala|vyākule dhūlī|paṭale diviṣad|adhvani dhikkṛt'|ânya|dhvani|paṭaha|dhvāna|badhirit'|âśeṣa|dig|antarālaṃ śastrā|śastri hastā|hasti paras|par'|âbhihata|sainyaṃ janyam ajani.

Now, Raja·hamsa, the Mágadhan lord, was filled with a great rage for war against Mana·sara, the lord of Málava,* a glutton for new battles and—true to his name—inordinately proud. One day Raja·hamsa marched out against Mana·sara, leading his fourfold army of elephants, cavalry, chariots and infantry. Raja·hamsa's great skill in the use of many different kinds of weapons had been perfected in innumerable battles where he had buried his sharp arrows in the heads of a string of royals. His army made the Lady Earth bow down under her burden, and she in turn weighed heavy on the strength of the serpent king's hoods. The roar of kettledrums effortlessly humiliated the ocean, arrogant about its own crashing. The roar even rocked the ring of elephants stationed at the universe's quarters, so wild was their fear at the violent sound. Then the Málavan king, too, who might have been born only for combat, marched out in force to meet the other headlong, at the head of many ranks of elephants.

The two men began their battle. Soldier struck soldier, 1.12
sword on sword, hand to hand. Chariots and horses' hooves pounded the earth, throwing up a fog of dust that filled the air above. At its base the dust cloud was washed away by the river of rut streaming from the temples of the elephant troops. It looked as though a nuptial pavilion was screening off the crowd of celestial damsels come down to choose for themselves from the fresh crop of lovers. In all directions the space was deafened by the roll of war drums, shouting down every other sound in the realm of the gods.

Tatra Magadha|rājaḥ prakṣīṇa|sakala|sainya|maṇḍalaṃ Mālava|rājaṃ jīva|grāham abhigṛhya kṛpālutayā punar api svarājye pratiṣṭhāpayām āsa.

Tataḥ sa ratn'|ākara|mekhalām ilām an|anya|śāsanāṃ śāsad an|apatyatayā Nārāyaṇaṃ sakala|lok'|âika|kāraṇaṃ nirantaram arcayām āsa. atha kadā cit tad|agra|mahiṣī devī:

1.15 «Devena kalpa|vallī|phalam āpnuh' îti.»

Prabhāta|samaye su|svapnam avalokitavatī. sā tadā dayita|manoratha|puṣpa|bhūtaṃ garbham adhatta. rāj" âpi saṃpan|nyakkṛt'|Ākhaṇḍalaḥ suhṛn|nṛpa|maṇḍalaṃ samāhūya nija|saṃpan|mano|rath'|ânurūpaṃ devyāḥ sīmant'|ôtsavaṃ vyadhatta.

Ekadā hitaiḥ suhṛn|mantri|puro|hitaiḥ sabhāyāṃ siṃh'|āsan'|āsīnaḥ guṇair a|hīno lalāṭa|taṭa|nyast'|âñjalinā dvāra|pālena vyajñāpi:

1.18 «Deva, deva|saṃdarśana|lālasa|mānasaḥ ko 'pi devena viracy"|ârcan'|ârho yatir dvāra|deśam adhyāsta iti.»

Tad|anujñātena tena sa saṃyamī nṛpa|samīpam anāyi. bhū|patir āyāntaṃ taṃ vilokya samyag|jñāta|tadīya|gūḍha|cāra|bhāvo nikhilam anucara|nikaraṃ visṛjya mantri|jana|sametaḥ praṇatam enaṃ manda|hāsam abhāṣata:

In that battle the king of Mágadha captured the king of Málava alive, once the whole array of his army had been obliterated. But then, in his mercy, Raja·hamsa reinstated Mana·sara to his kingdom.

Thereafter King Raja·hamsa ruled the earth, up to its ocean girdle, as sole ruler. But because he was childless he paid constant worship to Vishnu Naráyana, the one and only creator of all creatures. Until one day at dawn his chief queen had an auspicious dream in which she was told:

"You should harvest with your husband a fruit from the 1.15
wish-fulfilling tree."

After that she became pregnant with a child, the flower of her beloved's desires. Thereupon the king, fortunate far beyond Akhándala Indra, invited his circle of ruling friends to celebrate his queen's hair-parting pregnancy festival,* in the style befitting his personal fortune and tastes.

Some time later the king, who was not short of virtues, was sitting on his lion-throne in council with his favorite friends, ministers and family priests when the doorkeeper pressed his folded hands to his forehead and announced:

"My Lord, there is a holy man at the door who merits 1.18
Your Majesty's worshipful respect. He desires an audience with Your Majesty."

The king gave his consent, and the doorkeeper led the renunciate into the royal presence. The king studied the man as he entered, and rightly recognized him for one of his undercover agents. Dismissing the whole entourage of attendants but retaining his ministers, with a slight smile he addressed the one bowing down before him:

«Nanu, tāpasa, deśaṃ s'|âpadeśaṃ bhraman bhavāṃs tatra tatra bhavad|abhijñātaṃ kathayatv iti.»

1.21 Ten' âbhāṣi bhū|bhramaṇa|balinā pr'|âñjalinā:

«Deva, śirasi devasy' ājñām ādāy' âinaṃ nirdoṣaṃ veṣaṃ svīkṛtya Mālav'|êndra|nagaraṃ praviśya tatra gūḍhataraṃ vartamānas tasya rājñaḥ samastam udanta|jātaṃ viditvā pratyāgamam.

Mānī Mānasāraḥ sva|sainik'|āyuṣmatt"|ântarāye saṃparāye bhavataḥ parājayam anubhūya vailakṣya|lakṣya|hṛdayo vīta|dayo Mahākāla|nivāsinaṃ Kālī|vilāsinam a|naśvaraṃ Maheśvaraṃ samārādhya tapaḥ|prabhāva|saṃtuṣṭād asmād eka|vīr'|ârāti|ghnīṃ bhaya|dāṃ gadāṃ labdhv" ātmānam a|pratibhaṭaṃ manyamāno mah"|âbhimāno bhavantam abhiyoktum udyuṅkte. tataḥ paraṃ deva eva pramāṇam iti.»

1.24 Tad ālocya niścita|tat|kṛtyair amātyai rājā vijñāpito 'bhūt:

«Deva, nir|upāyena deva|sahāyena yoddhum arātir āyāti. tasmād asmākaṃ yuddhaṃ sāṃpratam a|sāṃpratam. sahasā durga|saṃśrayaḥ kārya iti.»

Tair bahudhā vijñāpito 'py a|kharveṇa garveṇa virājamāno rājā tad|vākyam akṛtyam ity an|ādṛtya pratiyoddhu|manā babhūva.

"Now, holy man, pray tell what you have uncovered here or there in your wanderings in disguise."

At this the one free to wander the world saluted him with 1.21
folded hands and began to speak:

"My Lord, your humble servant, heeding your command, I made this innocuous costume my own. I went to the city of the Málavan king, and lived there completely undercover. Having gathered all the possible intelligence about that king, I am returned.

Mana·sara is proud by name and proud by nature. After his defeat at your hands in the battle that finished his soldiers' hopes for a long life, shame pierced his heart and he became heartless. He went then to propitiate Shiva the indestructible, Kali's delight, in the Maha·kala shrine at Ujjain.* The god was pleased with the force of his fervor and gave him a formidable mace, with which to kill the most heroic enemy. So arrogant is the king now, thinking himself invincible, that he is preparing to launch an attack on you. Your lordship must now be the judge in this matter."

The ministers considered the report, decided what the 1.24
king must do, and addressed him as follows:

"Lord, the enemy who comes to fight has as his irresistible ally the god Shiva. Therefore now is not the moment for us to fight back. We must withdraw to the safety of the citadel, without delay."

They went on repeating this advice to the king, but glorying in no mean pride he rejected the plan they proposed as unworthy, and resolved to make a counterattack.

1.27 Śiti|kaṇṭha|datta|śakti|sāro Mānasāro yoddhu|manasām agrībhūya sāmagrī|sameto '|kleśaṃ Magadha|deśaṃ praviveśa.

Tadā tad ākarṇya mantriṇo bhū|mah"|êndraṃ Magadh'|êndraṃ kathaṃ cid anunīya ripubhir a|sādhye Vindhy'|âṭavī|madhye 'varodhān mūla|bala|rakṣitān niveśayām āsuḥ. Rājahaṃsas tu praśasta|vīta|dainya|sainya|sametas tīvra|gatyā nirgaty' âdhika|ruṣaṃ dviṣaṃ rurodhe.

Paras|para|baddha|vairayor etayoḥ śūrayos tadā tad|ālokana|kutūhal'|āgata|gagana|car'|āścarya|kāraṇe raṇe vartamāne jay'|ākāṅkṣī Mālava|deśa|rakṣī vividh'|āyudha|sthairya|cary"|âñcita|samara|tulit'|âmar'|ēśvarasya Magadh'|ēśvarasya tasy' ôpari purā Pur'|ârāti|dattāṃ gadāṃ prāhiṇot.

1.30 Niśita|śara|nikara|śakalīkṛt" âpi sā Paśupati|śāsanasy' âvandhyatayā sūtaṃ nihatya ratha|sthaṃ rājānaṃ mūrcchitam akārṣīt. tato vīta|pragrahā akṣata|vigrahā vāhā ratham ādāya daiva|gaty" ântaḥ|pura|śaraṇyaṃ mah"|âraṇyaṃ prāviśan.

Mālava|nātho jaya|lakṣmī|sa|nātho Magadha|rājyaṃ prājyaṃ samākramya Puṣpapuram adhyatiṣṭhat.

Mana·sara led a host determined to attack, and was equipped with supplies, but his essential strength was the power granted him by Shiva, the blue-throated one,* enabling them to march unharassed right into the land of Mágadha. 1.27

When the ministers heard this news they managed with some difficulty to persuade the king of Mágadha, a great Indra on earth, to let them install his harem,* guarded by a hereditary elite, in the middle of the Vindhyan forest, where the enemy could not penetrate. Meanwhile Raja·hamsa charged out at full speed with his choice army in good cheer, and blocked his extremely annoyed enemy.

Then began the battle of these two warriors, locked in hostility toward each other. It was a source of amazement for the gods who came out of curiosity to watch. In combat the Mágadhan lord was equal to Indra, the lord of the immortals, distinguished by his confident deployment of every type of weapon. But, hungry for victory, the protector of Málava hurled at Raja·hamsa's head the mace given him earlier by Shiva, enemy of the triple cities.

Although a flock of sharp arrows shattered the missile, 1.30
the command of Pashu·pati, the Lord of creation, cannot be in vain, and so, having slain the charioteer the missile left the king unconscious in his chariot. Thereupon the horses, released from their reins and unharmed, carried the chariot off, entering the jungle where, as luck would have it, the king's harem had taken refuge.

With the victory goddess at his side the king of Málava conquered the bountiful Mágadhan kingdom and set himself up in Pushpa·pura.

Tatra heti|tati|hati|śrāntā amātyā daiva|gaty" ân|utkrānta|jīvitā niś"|ânta|vāta|labdha|saṃjñāḥ kathaṃ cid āśvasya rājānaṃ samantād anvīkṣy' ân|avalokitavanto dainyavanto devīm avāpuḥ. Vasumatī tu tebhyo nikhila|sainya|kṣatiṃ rājño '|dṛśyatvaṃ c' ākarṇy' ôdvignā śoka|sāgara|magnā ramaṇ'|ânugamane matiṃ vyadhatta.

1.33 «Kalyāṇi, bhū|ramaṇa|maraṇam a|niścitam. kiṃ ca daiva|jña|kathito mathit'|ôddhat'|ârātiḥ sārvabhaumo 'bhirāmo bhavitā su|kumāraḥ kumāras tvad|udare vasati. tasmād adya tava maraṇam an|ucitam. iti»

bhūṣita|bhāṣitair amātya|puro|hitair anunīyamānayā tayā kṣaṇaṃ kṣaṇa|hīnayā tūṣṇīm asthāyi.

Ath' ârdha|rātre nidrā|nilīḍha|netre parijane vijane śoka|pārāvāram apāram uttartum a|śaknuvatī senā|niveśa|deśaṃ niḥśabda|leśaṃ śanair atikramya yasmin rathasya saṃsaktatayā tad|ānayana|palāyana|śrāntā gantum a|kṣamāḥ kṣamā|pati|rathyāḥ pathy|ākulāḥ pūrvam atiṣṭhaṃs tasya nikaṭa|vaṭa|taroḥ śākhāyāṃ mṛti|rekhāyām iva kva cid uttarīy'|ârdhena bandhanaṃ mṛti|sādhanaṃ viracya martu|kām" âbhirāmā vāṅ|mādhurī|virasīkṛta|kala|kaṇṭhā s'|âśru|kaṇṭhā vyalapat:

Meanwhile many weapons had beaten Raja·hamsa's ministers to exhaustion, but fortunately they had not breathed their last. At the end of the night a breeze revived them, and they managed to pluck up their spirits and started searching all around for their king. Unable to find him, they had to go with heavy hearts to the queen. Vásumati was horrified when they told her of the destruction of the whole army, and the king's disappearance. Sunk in an ocean of grief, she made up her mind to follow her beloved in death. Only the polished words of the ministers and priests dissuaded her:

"Blessed Lady, we cannot be sure whether our king, beloved 1.33
of the Earth, is dead. What is more, a tender young handsome prince lives in your womb. The astrologers have foretold that he will destroy our insolent enemy and conquer the world. Hence it would be quite inappropriate for you to die today."

She stood silent, her despair momentarily interrupted.

Yet later, at midnight, when sleep had settled on the eyes of her attendants, the queen, all alone, could not pull herself out of the unbounded ocean of her sorrow. She slowly crossed the utterly silent place where the army was camped, until she came to a banyan tree. The tree was just near where the king's horses had earlier come to a halt, unable to continue because the chariot was entangled, and exhausted by dragging it with them in their flight. Desiring death, she constructed a noose out of half of her shawl with which to hang herself, on a branch that looked like the line of death drawn on the palm of one's hand. With tears in her throat, in her sweet voice, sweeter than that of the sweet-throated dove, the beautiful woman lamented:*

1.36 «Lāvaṇy'|ôpamita|puṣpa|sāyaka, bhū|nāyaka, bhavān eva bhāviny api janmani vallabho bhavatv iti.»

Tad ākarṇya nīhāra|kara|kiraṇa|nikara|saṃparka|labdh'|âvabodho Māgadho 'gādha|rudhira|vikṣaraṇa|naṣṭa|ceṣṭo devī|vākyam eva niścinvānas tanvānaḥ priya|vacanāni śanais tām āhvayat. sā sa|saṃbhramam āgaty' â|manda|hṛday'|ānanda|saṃphulla|vadan'|âravindā tam upoṣitābhyām iv' â|nimiṣitābhyāṃ locanābhyāṃ pibantī vikasvareṇa svareṇa puro|hit'|âmātya|janam uccair āhūya tebhyas tam adarśayat. rājā niṭila|taṭa|cumbita|nija|caraṇ'|âmbujaiḥ praśaṃsita|daiva|māhātmyair amātyair abhāṇi:

«Deva, rathya|cayaḥ sārathy|apagame rathaṃ rabhasād araṇyam anayad iti.»

1.39 «Tatra nihita|sainika|grāme saṃgrāme Mālava|patin" ārādhita|Pur"|ârātinā prahitayā gadayā dayā|hīnena tāḍito mūrcchām āgaty' âtra vane niś"|ânta|pavanena bodhito 'bhavam iti» mahī|patir akathayat.

Tato viracita|mahena mantri|nivahena viracita|daiv'|ânukūlyena kālena śibiram ānīy' âpanīt'|â|śeṣa|śalyo vikasita|nij'|ânan'|âravindo rājā sahasā viropita|vraṇo 'kāri.

Virodhi|daiva|dhikkṛta|puruṣa|kāro dainya|vyāpt'|ākāro Magadh'|âdhipatir adhik'|ādhir amātya|saṃmatyā mṛdu|bhāṣitayā Vasumatyā matyā kalitayā ca samabodhi:

"O Lord of the Earth, as lovely as Kama with his flower arrows, may you again be my beloved in my next birth, too!" 1.36

The Mágadhan one himself heard her, roused to consciousness by the cool touch of a flood of moonbeams, but he could not move, because he was losing such a volume of blood. Certain that this was his own queen's voice, he called to her softly with words of love. She flew toward him, her face blooming like a lotus with the rush of joy in her heart, and drank him in with unblinking eyes starved for the sight of him. With expansive voice she called out loudly to the priest and ministers to come, and showed him to them. The ministers kissed the king's lotus-feet with their foreheads, praised the magnanimity of fate, and explained:

"Lord, after your charioteer had fallen the team of horses led the chariot headlong into the wilderness."

The king told his part of the story: "The majority of my 1.39
soldiers had been struck down in the battle, when Shiva's favorite, the king of Málava, let fly his merciless mace, and struck me. I lost consciousness, and was only revived by the dawn breeze, here in the forest."

Next the group of ministers declared a holiday and had the king carried into the encampment at the time pronounced propitious to fate. There the arrowheads were extracted from his body, his own lotus-face bloomed again, and his wounds healed rapidly.

But after the contempt that hostile fate had shown for his manliness, the Mágadhan overlord was thoroughly wretched, and became inordinately depressed. Upon the advice

1.42 «Deva, sakalasya bhū|pāla|kulasya madhye tejo|variṣṭho gariṣṭho bhavān adya Vindhya|vana|madhyaṃ nivasat' îti jala|budbuda|samānā virājamānā saṃpat taḍil|lat" êva sahas" âiv' ôdeti naśyati ca. tan nikhilaṃ daiv'|āyattam ev' âvadhāryaṃ kāryam. kiṃ ca purā Hariścandra|Rāmacandra| mukhyā a|saṃkhyā mah"|îndrā aiśvary'|ôpamita|mah"|êndrā daiva|tantraṃ duḥkha|yantraṃ samyag anubhūya paścād an|eka|kālaṃ nija|rājyam akurvan. tadvad eva bhavān bhaviṣyati. kaṃ cana kālaṃ viracita|daiva|samādhir gat'|ādhis tiṣṭhatu tāvad iti.»

Tataḥ sakala|sainya|samanvito Rājahaṃsas tapo|vibhrājamānaṃ Vāmadeva|nāmānaṃ tapo|dhanaṃ nij'|âbhilāṣ'| âvāpti|sādhanaṃ jagāma. taṃ praṇamya tena kṛt'|ātithyas tasmai kathita|kathyas tad|āśrame dūrīkṛta|śrame kaṃ cana kālam uṣitvā nija|rājy'|âbhilāṣī mita|bhāṣī soma|kul'|âvataṃso Rājahaṃso munim abhāṣata:

«Bhagavan, Mānasāraḥ prabalena daiva|balena māṃ nirjitya mad|bhogyaṃ rājyam anubhavati. tadvad aham apy ugraṃ tapo viracya tam arātim unmūlayiṣyāṃi loka|śaraṇyena

of his ministers, Vásumati, wise and thoughtful, consoled him with tender words:

“My Lord, you were the most charismatic and most im- 1.42
portant of the entire class of kings, protectors of the earth, yet today you live in the middle of the Vindhyan forest. Thus it is that success glitters like a bubble of water; like a flash of lightning it is born and then destroyed all in an instant. Therefore, we must accept that every venture is entirely in the control of destiny. Moreover, countless great kings of the past, from Harish·chandra and Rama·chandra onward,* all equal to the great lord Indra in their lordship, first fell victim to the power of fate, instrument of torture, only then to acquire again their own kingdoms, more than once. It will be like that for you, too. Reconcile yourself to your destiny. Do not worry, but simply bide your time a while.”

Later, Raja·hamsa went with all his soldiers to visit the sage Vama·deva, rich in self-deprivation, glittering with pious penance, through whom he could obtain what he desired. He bowed down to the sage, who welcomed him as a guest, and told him the whole story. After he had dwelled a while in Vama·deva's ashram,* his troubles far away, Raja·hamsa, ornament of the lunar dynasty, still desired his own kingdom, and so he addressed the holy man with measured words:

“Blessed one, Mana·sara conquered me by means of the almighty might of destiny. Now he enjoys the kingdom that should be mine to enjoy. I came to your self-controlled self thinking that your compassion for the succor of the world

bhavat|kāruṇyen' êti niyamavantaṃ bhavantaṃ prāpnavam iti.»

1.45 Tatas tri|kāla|jñas tapo|dhano rājānam avocat:

«Sakhe, śarīra|kārśya|kāriṇā tapas" âlam! Vasumatī|garbha|sthaḥ sakala|ripu|kula|mardano rāja|nandano nūnaṃ saṃbhaviṣyati, kaṃ cana kālaṃ tūṣṇīm āssv' êti.»

Gagana|cāriṇy" âpi vāṇyā:

1.48 «Satyam etad. iti»

tad" âiv' âvāci. rāj" âpi muni|vākyam aṅgīkṛty' âtiṣṭhat.

Tataḥ saṃpūrṇa|garbha|divasā Vasumatī su|muhūrte sakala|lakṣaṇa|lakṣitaṃ sutam asūta. brahma|varcasena tulita|vedhasaṃ purodhasaṃ puraskṛtya kṛtyavin mahī|patiḥ kumāraṃ su|kumāraṃ jāta|saṃskāreṇa bāl'|âlaṃkāreṇa ca virājamānaṃ Rājavāhana|nāmānaṃ vyadhatta.

1.51 Tasminn eva kāle Sumati|Sumitra|Sumantra|Suśrutānāṃ mantriṇāṃ Pramati|Mitragupta|Mantragupta|Viśrut'|ākhyā mahad|abhikhyāḥ sūnavo nav'|ôdyad|indu|rucaś cir'|āyuṣaḥ samajāyanta.

would help me uproot that enemy in turn through the performance of fierce ascetic practices like he had performed."

In response the sage, rich in self-deprivation, who knew 1.45
the three times, past, present and future, told the king:

"My friend, what need of penance to torture your body? In Vásumati's womb there is a prince, the delight of a king, who will destroy the entire band of your enemies. That is certain. So stay patient for a while."

That same moment an airborne voice said to the king:

"This is the truth." 1.48

And so the king also accepted the holy man's words, and did nothing.

At an auspicious moment, the term of pregnancy complete, Vásumati gave birth to a son marked with all the signs of distinction. Knowing due procedure, the king was guided by the royal priest, equal to Brahma in religious power, in naming the tender young prince Raja·váhana, "Bearer of royalty," as he shone with the rituals of birth and baby ornaments.

At the very same time sons were born to the ministers 1.51
Súmati, Sumítra, Sumántra and Súshruta, called, respectively, Prámati, Mitra·gupta, Mantra·gupta and Víshruta. Extremely handsome, shining like the newly rising moon, they were to be long-lived.

Rājavāhano mantri|putrair ātma|mitraiḥ saha bāla|kelīr anubhavann avardhata.

Atha kadā cid ekena tāpasena rasena rāja|lakṣaṇa|virājitaṃ kaṃ cin nayan'|ānanda|karaṃ su|kumāraṃ kumāraṃ rājñe samarpy' âvoci:

1.54 «Bhū|vallabha, kuśa|samid|ānayanāya vanaṃ gatena mayā kācid a|śaraṇyā vyakta|kārpaṇy" âśru muñcantī vanitā vilokitā.

‹Nirjane vane kiṃ|nimittaṃ rudyate tvay" êti?›

pṛṣṭvā sā kara|ruhair aśru pramṛjya sa|gadgadaṃ mām avocat:

1.57 ‹Mune, lāvaṇya|jita|puṣpa|sāyake Mithilā|nāyake kīrti|vyāpṛta|sudharmaṇi nija|suhṛdo Magadha|rājasya sīmantinī|sīmanta|mah"|ôtsavāya putra|dāra|samanvite Puṣpapuram upetya kaṃ cana kālam adhivasati samārādhita|Gir'|īśo Mālav'|âdhīśo Magadha|rājaṃ yoddhum abhyagāt.

Tatra prakhyātayor etayor a|saṃkhye saṃkhye vartamāne suhṛt|sāhāyyakaṃ kurvāṇo nija|bale sati videhe Videh'|ēśvaraḥ Prahāravarmā jayavatā ripuṇ" âbhigṛhya kāruṇyena puṇyena visṛṣṭo hat'|âvaśeṣeṇa śūnyena sainyena saha sva|pura|gamanam akarot. tato vana|mārgeṇa durgeṇa gacchann adhika|balena śabara|balena rabhasād abhihanyamāno mūla|bal'|âbhirakṣit'|âvarodhaḥ sa mahā|nirodhaḥ palāyiṣṭa.

Raja·váhana grew up with the ministers' sons as his good friends, sharing childhood games.

Then one day an ascetic came and emotionally handed over to the king an unknown tender young prince, resplendent with the marks of royalty, and a joy to behold. He explained:

"O Master of the earth, I was in the forest collecting *kusha* 1.54
grass and firewood when I saw a woman weeping. She was obviously desperate and without a refuge. I asked her:

'Why are you weeping in this desolate forest?'

She wiped away her tears with her fingers and spoke to me in sobs:

'O holy man, Prahára·varman, the lord of Míthila, was 1.57
lovelier than Kama with his flower arrows, and the assembly of the gods was full of his fame. He went with his wife and son to Pushpa·pura for the great hair-parting pregnancy festival of the pregnant queen of his personal friend, Raja·hamsa, the king of Mágadha. They had been staying there some time when the Málavan king, whose worship had won over Shiva, Lord of the mountains, came to attack the king of Mágadha.

While the two famous men waged their vast battle, Prahára·varman, lord of Vidéha and Míthila, went to the assistance of his friend. But with his own forces lost, the victorious enemy captured him. Yet out of compassion or because of his religious merit, he was released. Together with what remained from the slaughter of his listless army, he set off for his own city. Then, as they were on a remote dangerous road through the forest, they were violently attacked by a gang of savages, *shábaras*,* superior in strength. With the

Tadīy'|ârbhakayor yamayor dhātrī|bhāvena parikalpit" âhaṃ mad|duhit" âpi tīvra|gatiṃ bhū|patim anugantum a|kṣamo 'bhūva. tatra vivṛta|vadanaḥ ko 'pi rūpī kopa iva vyāghraḥ śīghraṃ mām āghrātum āgatavān. bhīt" âham udagra|grāvṇi skhalantī paryapatam. madīya|pāṇi|bhraṣṭo bālakaḥ kasy' âpi kapilā|śavasya kroḍam abhyalīyata. tac|chav'|ākarṣiṇo 'marṣiṇo vyāghrasya prāṇān bāṇo bāṇ'|āsana|yantra|mukto 'pāharat. vilol'|âlako bālako 'pi śabarair ādāya kutra cid upānīyata. kumāram aparam udvahantī mad|duhitā kutra gatā na jāne.

1.60 S" âhaṃ mohaṃ gatā ken' âpi kṛpālunā vṛṣṇa|pālena sva|kuṭīram āveśya viropita|vraṇ" âbhavam. tataḥ svasthībhūya bhūyaḥ kṣmā|bhartur antikam upatiṣṭhāsur a|sahāyatayā duhitur an|abhijñātatayā ca vyākulībhavām' îti.›

abhidadhānā:

‹Ekākiny api svāminaṃ gamiṣyām' îti.›

1.63 Sā tad" âiva niragāt.

Aham api bhavan|mitrasya Videha|nāthasya vipan|nimittaṃ viṣādam anubhavaṃs tad|anvay'|âṅkuraṃ kumāram anviṣyaṃs tad" âikaṃ Caṇḍikā|mandiraṃ sundaraṃ prāgām. tatra saṃtatam evaṃvidha|vijaya|siddhaye kumāraṃ devat"|ôpahāraṃ kariṣyantaḥ Kirātāḥ:

hereditary guard providing safe escort for his harem, the king beat a retreat from this great ambush.

My daughter and I had been appointed nurses to the king's twin baby boys, but we were unable to keep up with his fast pace. Then a tiger came rushing, fury incarnate, his jaws agape to swallow me up. Terrified, I stumbled on a rock jutting out, and fell. The baby tumbled from my arms, and clung to the belly of a dead brown cow. As the tiger was savagely dragging at that carcass, someone fired an arrow from a mechanized bow and killed him. The tribals seized the baby, his curls bouncing, and took him away, I know not where. Nor do I know where my daughter, who was carrying the other little prince, went.

Some kind shepherd carried me unconscious to his hut, 1.60
and healed my wounds. Now that I am fully recovered I want to rejoin my king. But I am friendless and do not know where my daughter is. I am so confused.'

Without a pause she said:

'Alone as I am, I must go to my master.'

And in that instant was gone. 1.63

I too was grieved by the tragedy of Your Majesty's friend, the king of Vidéha, and so I started hunting for the prince, scion of his race. I came then to a charming Chándika Durga temple.* There the *kiráta* savages were about to sacrifice the young prince to the goddess so as to ensure continual victories like the one they had just won. They were debating:

‹Mahīruha|śākh"|âvalambitam enam asi|latayā vā, saikata| tale khanana|nikṣipta|caraṇaṃ lakṣīkṛtya śita|śara|nikareṇa vā, an|eka|caraṇaiḥ palāyamānaṃ kukkura|bālakair vā daṃśayitvā saṃhaniṣyāma iti?›

1.66 bhāṣamāṇā mayā samabhyabhāṣyanta:

‹Nanu Kirāt'|ôttamāḥ, ghora|pracāre kāntāre skhalita|pathaḥ sthavira|bhū|suro 'haṃ mama putrakaṃ kva cic chāyāyāṃ nikṣipya mārg'|ânveṣaṇāya kiṃ cid antaram agaccham. sa kutra gataḥ, kena vā gṛhītaḥ, parīkṣy' âpi na vīkṣyate. tan|mukh'|âvalokanena vin" ân|ekāny ahāny atītāni. kiṃ karomi? kva yāmi? bhavadbhir na kim adarś' îti?›

‹Dvij'|ôttama, kaścid atra tiṣṭhati. kim eṣa tava nandanaḥ satyam eva? tad enaṃ gṛhāṇ' êti.›

1.69 uktvā daiv'|ânukūlyena mahyaṃ taṃ vyataran. tebhyo datt'|āśīr ahaṃ bālakam aṅgīkṛtya śiśir'|ôdak'|ādin" ôpacāreṇ' āśvāsya niḥśaṅkaṃ bhavad|aṅkaṃ samānītavān asmi. evam āyuṣmantaṃ pitṛ|rūpo bhavān abhirakṣatād! iti»

Rājā suhṛd|āpan|nimittaṃ śokaṃ tan|nandana|vilokana| sukhena kiṃ cid adharīkṛtya tam Upahāravarma|nāmn" āhūya Rājavāhanam iva puposa.

Jana|patir ekasmin puṇya|divase tīrtha|snānāya pakkaṇa| nikaṭa|mārgeṇa gacchann abalayā kayā cid upalālitam anupama|śarīraṃ kumāraṃ kaṃ cid avalokya kutūhal'|ākulas tām apṛcchat:

'How shall we slaughter him? Shall we hang him on a tree and kill him with the blade of a sword? Or bury his feet in a hole in the dirt and make him the target for a rain of sharp arrows? Or shall we let him get torn to pieces by young dogs while he tries to escape on all fours?'

I interrupted: 1.66

'Please, good *kirátas*. I am an old brahmin who lost my way in the dreary forest where it is frightening to travel. I placed my son somewhere in the shade, and went ahead a bit in search of a way out. Where has he gone? Or has someone taken him? Much as I look I cannot find him. Several days have passed since I last looked on his face. What shall I do? Where can I go? Have you gentlemen not seen anything?'

'Good brahmin, there is such a one here. Is he, in fact, your dear son? Then take him.'

With this reply they handed him over to me, thank heav- 1.69
ens! I gave them my blessing, received the little boy, and freshened him up with remedies such as cool water. Without hesitating I have brought him before you. May you protect this long-lived child like a father!"

The king's grief at his friend's tragedy was somewhat lessened by his joy at seeing that man's dear son. He named him Upahára·varman, "Protected by sacrifice," and brought him up just as he did Raja·váhana.

One auspicious day* the Lord of the people was going to the sacred ford to have a ritual bath, via an unsavory neighborhood. He noticed a little boy of incomparable loveliness being fondled by one of the weaker sex.* His curiosity aroused, he asked her:

1.72 «Bhāmini, rucira|mūrtiḥ sa|rāja|guṇa|saṃpūrtir asāv arbhako bhavad|anvaya|saṃbhavo na bhavati. kasya nayan'|ānandanaḥ? nimittena kena bhavad|adhīno jātaḥ? kathyatām yāthātathyena tvay" êti.»

Praṇatayā tayā śabaryā sa|līlam alāpi:

«Rājan, ātma|pallī|samīpe padavyāṃ vartamānasya Śakra|samānasya Mithil"|ēśvarasya sarvasvam apaharati śabara|sainye mad|dayiten' âpahṛtya kumāra eṣa mahyam arpito vyavardhat' êti.»

1.75 Tad avadhārya kārya|jño rājā muni|kathitaṃ dvitīyaṃ rāja|kumāram eva niścitya sāma|dānābhyāṃ tām anunīy' Âpahāravarm'|êty|ākhyāya devyai «vardhay' êti» samarpitavān.

Kadā cid Vāmadeva|śiṣyaḥ Somadevaśarmā nāma kaṃ cid ekaṃ bālakaṃ rājñaḥ puro nikṣipy' âbhāṣata:

«Deva, Rāma|tīrthe snātvā pratyāgacchatā mayā kānanā|vanau vanitayā kay" âpi dhāryamāṇam enam ujjval'|ākāraṃ kumāraṃ vilokya s'|ādaram abhāṇi:

1.78 ‹Sthavire, kā tvam? etasminn aṭavī|madhye bālakam udvahantī kim|artham āyāsena bhramas' îti?›

Vṛddhay" âpy abhāṣi:

‹Muni|vara, Kālayavana|nāmni dvīpe Kālagupto nāma dhan'|āḍhyo vaiśya|varaḥ kaś cid asti. tan|nandinīṃ nayan'|ānanda|kāriṇīṃ Suvṛttāṃ nām' âitasmād dvīpād āgato Magadha|nātha|mantri|saṃbhavo Ratnodbhavo nāma ra-

"Dear lady, this lovely-looking child, the fulfillment of 1.72
regal virtues, he cannot belong to your line. Joy of whose eyes is he? How did he come to be in your care? You must tell me the whole truth."

The savage bowed down to him and spoke gracefully:

"O king, once when Prahára·varman, the king of Míthila, Shakra Indra's equal, was travelling on the road near this tribal settlement, our army plundered all he had. That was when my husband carried off this young boy, and gave him to me, and I have brought him up."

The conscientious king considered a moment and was 1.75
convinced that this was the second royal child of the holy man's story. With persuasive words and with gifts* he won her over, named the boy Apahára·varman, "Protected by being taken away," and entrusted him into the queen's care to be reared.

Another day a disciple of Vama·deva, Soma·deva·sharman by name, laid an unknown baby boy before the king, with the words:

"My Lord, I was returning from my ablutions at the ford of Rama, when I saw a woman carrying this luminous little boy in the forest. Concerned, I asked her:

'Old lady, who are you? Why are you having to struggle, 1.78
wandering in the middle of this jungle carrying a child?'

And the aged woman replied:

'Good holy man, on the island of Kala·yávana* there lived an excellent merchant of enormous wealth called Kala·gupta. His daughter, Suvrítta, "Good news," a joy to set eyes on, was married by Ratnódbhava, an attractive man of business who came from the mainland, son of the king of Mágadha's

maṇīya|guṇ'|ālayo bhrānta|bhū|valayo manohārī vyavahāry upayamya su|vastu|saṃpadā śvaśureṇa saṃmānito 'bhūt. kāla|krameṇa nat'|âṅgī garbhiṇī jātā. tataḥ sodara|vilokana| kutūhalena Ratnodbhavaḥ kathaṃ cic chvaśuram anunīya capala|locanay" ânayā saha pravahaṇam āruhya Puṣpapuram abhipretasthe.

1.81 Kallola|mālik'|âbhihataḥ potaḥ samudr'|âmbhasy amajjat. garbha|bhar'|ālasāṃ tāṃ lalanāṃ dhātrī|bhāvena kalpit" âhaṃ karābhyām udvahantī phalakam ekam adhiruhya daiva|gatyā tīra|bhūmim agamam. suhṛj|jana|parivṛto Ratnodbhavas tatra nimagno vā ken' ôpāyena tīram agamad vā na jānāmi.

Kleśasya parāṃ kāṣṭhām adhigatā Suvṛtt" âsminn aṭavī| madhye 'dya sutam asūta. prasava|vedanayā vi|cetanā sā pracchāya|śītale taru|tale nivasati. vi|jane vane sthātum a|śakyatayā jana|pada|gāminaṃ mārgam anveṣṭum udyuktayā mayā vivaśāyās tasyāḥ samīpe bālakaṃ nikṣipya gantum a-n|ucitam iti kumāro 'py ānāy' îti.›

Tasminn eva kṣaṇe vanyo vāraṇaḥ kaś cid adṛśyata. taṃ vilokya bhītā sā bālakaṃ nipātya prādravat. ahaṃ samīpa|latā|gulmake praviśya parīkṣamāṇo 'tiṣṭham. nipatitaṃ bālakaṃ pallava|kavalam iv' ādadati gaja|patau kaṇṭhī|ravo bhīma|ravo mahā|graheṇa nyapatat. bhay'|ākulena dantāvalena jhaṭiti viyati samutpātyamāno bālako nyapatat.

minister. Endowed with delightful qualities, he had wandered the circumference of the earth, and now his father-in-law honored him with an abundance of fine property. In the course of time his graceful lady became pregnant. At that point Ratnódbhava developed a longing to see his brother. Having managed to persuade his father-in-law, he boarded ship with his woman of tremulous eyes and they set sail for Pushpa·pura.

Smashed up by a welter of wild waves, the vessel sank in 1.81
the ocean waters. I had been appointed to take care of the lady, slow with child, so I held her up with my two hands, and maneuvered us onto a plank that fate brought to the seashore. Whether Ratnódbhava sank there together with all his friends, or somehow managed to reach land, I do not know.

Suvrítta has experienced the ultimate in distress, and has today given birth here in the middle of the jungle to a son. Senseless with the pains of childbirth, she is resting in the cool deep shade beneath a tree. Since we could not stay in the desolate forest, I was determined to find a path to lead us to civilization. But, thinking it would be wrong to go leaving the baby with her while she is insensible, I have brought the little boy with me.'

At that very instant a wild elephant appeared. The old woman was terrified at the sight of him, and ran away, dropping the baby. I had taken cover in a nearby thicket of creepers, and stood watching to see what would happen. Just when the great elephant was picking the fallen baby up as though he were a mouthful of twigs, a lion fell on him in a great spring, with a terrible roar. The elephant was mad

1.84 Cir'|āyuṣmattayā sa c' ônnata|taru|śākhā|samāsīnena vānareṇa kena cit pakva|phala|buddhyā parigṛhya phal'|êtaratayā vitata|skandha|mūle nikṣipto 'bhūt. so 'pi markaṭaḥ kva cid agāt. bālakena sattva|saṃpannatayā sakala|kleśa|sahen' âbhāvi. kesariṇā kariṇaṃ nihatya kutra cid agāmi. latā|gṛhān nirgato 'ham api tejaḥ|puñjaṃ bālakaṃ śanair avanīruhād avatārya van'|āntare vanitām anviṣy' âviloky' âinam ānīya gurave nivedya tan|nideśena bhavan|nikaṭam ānītavān asm' îti.»

Sarveṣāṃ suhṛdām ekad" âiv' ânukūla|daiv'|âbhāvena mahad āścaryaṃ bibhrāṇo rājā Ratnodbhavaḥ katham abhavad iti cintayaṃs tan|nandanaṃ Puṣpodbhava|nāmadheyaṃ vidhāya tad|udantaṃ vyākhyāya Suśrutāya viṣāda|saṃtoṣāv anubhavaṃs tad|anujata|nayaṃ samarpitavān.

Anye|dyuḥ kaṃ cana bālakam urasi dadhatī Vasumatī vallabham abhigatā. tena:

1.87 «Kutratyo 'yam? iti»

pṛṣṭā samabhāṣat:

«Rājan, atītāyāṃ rātrau kā cana divya|vanitā mat|orataḥ kumāram ekaṃ saṃsthāpya nidrā|mudritām māṃ vibodhya vinīt" âbravīt:

with fear and immediately tossed the child up into the sky from where—down he fell.

Being destined to have a long life, the baby was caught 1.84
by a monkey sitting in the high branch of a tree, thinking here was a ripe fruit. Once he realized it was not a fruit he threw him down at the base of a broad branch. Then off the monkey also went, somewhere or other. Thanks to his innate vitality the infant survived all its sufferings. After the lion had attacked the elephant, he had also disappeared. Out I came from my creeper shelter and carefully lifted the illustrious baby down from the tree. Although I searched I could not find the woman within the forest, which is why I took him with me, informed my guru, and on his instruction have brought the boy before you."

The king was greatly amazed at the same bad luck befalling all his friends at the same time. Worrying what could have become of Ratnódbhava, he named that man's son Pushpódbhava, "Born from a flower." Then he explained to Súshruta, Ratnódbhava's elder brother, all that had happened and with mixed pain and satisfaction handed him his younger brother's son.

On another day, Vásumati came to her beloved husband bearing an unknown baby boy on her breast. He asked her:

"Where does this one come from?" 1.87

And she told him:

"O king, last night a heavenly lady placed a child before me, woke me from my sleeping state, and politely said:

1.90 ‹Devi, tvan|mantriṇo Dharmapāla|nandanasya Kāmapālasya vallabhā yakṣa|kānt" âhaṃ Tārāvalī nāma, nandinī Maṇibhadrasya. yakṣ'|ēśvar'|ânumatyā mad|ātmajam etaṃ bhavat|tanūjasy' âmbho|nidhi|valaya|veṣṭita|kṣoṇī|maṇḍal'|ēśvarasya bhāvino viśuddha|yaśo|nidhe Rājavāhanasya paricaryā|karaṇāy' ānītavaty asmi. tvam enaṃ manoja|saṃnibham abhivardhay' êti.›

Vismaya|vikasita|nayanayā mayā sa|vinayaṃ satkṛtā sv|akṣī yakṣī s" âpy a|dṛśyatām ayāsīd iti.»

Kāmapālasya yakṣa|kanyā|saṃgame vismayamāna|mānaso Rājahaṃso rañjita|mitraṃ Sumitraṃ mantriṇam āhūya tadīya|bhrātṛ|putram Arthapālaṃ vidhāya tasmai sarvaṃ vārtt'|ādikaṃ vyākhyāy' âdāt.

1.93 Tataḥ parasmin divase Vāmadev'|ântevāsī tad|āśrama|vāsī samārādhita|deva|kīrtiṃ nirbhartsita|Māra|mūrtiṃ kusuma|su|kumāraṃ kumāram ekam avagamayya nara|patim avādīt:

«Deva, tīrtha|yātrā|prasaṅgena Kāverī|tīram āgato 'haṃ vilol'|âlakaṃ bālakaṃ nij'|ôtsaṅga|tale nidhāya rudatīṃ sthavirām ekāṃ viloky' āvocam:

‹Sthavire, kā tvam? ayam arbhakaḥ kasya nayan'|ānandakaraḥ? kāntāraṃ kim artham āgatā? śoka|kāraṇaṃ kim?› iti.

1.96 Sā kara|yugena bāṣpa|jalam unmṛjya nija|śoka|śaṅk'|ûtpāṭana|kṣamam iva mām avalokya śoka|hetum avocat:

'O queen, my name is Tarávali. I am a *yakshi*, the daughter of Mani·bhadra, and the beloved wife of Kama·pala, son of your minister Dharma·pala. With the permission of Kubéra, king of the *yakshas*, I am bringing you this my baby to serve your own son, Raja·váhana, treasury of pure glory, who will be Lord of the Earth's *mándala*, encircled by its ocean girdle. Please look after this child, the image of mind-born Kama.' 1.90

My eyes wide with wonder I received the fair-eyed *yakshi* with due reverence, and then she disappeared from sight."

Raja·hamsa's mind was amazed to hear of Kama·pala's union with a *yaksha* girl. He called for his minister Sumítra, "Good friend," the delight of his friends by nature as well as by name, gave that man's brother's son the name Artha·pala, explained to him all that had happened, and gave him the child.

On yet another day, an acolyte of Vama·deva who was 1.93
living at his ashram presented the king with a baby boy, tender as a flower, blessed with divine splendor, and more beautiful than fatal Kama.* He explained:

"My Lord, I was on a pilgrimage when I came to the bank of the Kavéri River. There I saw an old woman weeping with a curly-locked baby boy in her lap, so I asked:

'Old lady, who are you? Whose is this child, so delightful to the eye? Why have you come to the dreary forest? And what makes you unhappy?'

She wiped away her tears with both hands, looked up at 1.96
me as though I could extract the dagger of her grief, and explained its origin:

‹Dvij'|ātmaja! Rājahaṃsa|mantriṇaḥ Sitavarmaṇaḥ kanīyān ātmajaḥ Satyavarmā tīrtha|yātr"|âbhilāṣeṇa deśam enam āgacchat. sa kasmiṃś cid agra|hāre Kālīṃ nāma kasya cid bhū|surasya nandinīṃ vivāhya tasyā an|apatyatayā Gaurīṃ nāma tad|bhaginīṃ kāñcana|kāntiṃ pariṇīya tasyām ekaṃ tanayam alabhata. Kālī s" âsūyam ekadā dhātryā mayā saha bālam enam ekena miṣeṇ' ānīya taṭinyām etasyām akṣipat.

Kareṇ' âikena bālam uddhṛty' âpareṇa plavamānā nadī|veg'|āgatasya kasya cit taroḥ śākhām avalambya tatra śiśuṃ nidhāya nadī|vegen' ôhyamānā kena cit taru|lagnena kāla|bhogin" âham adaṃśi. mad|avalambībhūto bhūruho 'yam asmin deśe tīram agamat. garalasy' ôddīpanatayā mayi mṛtāyām araṇye kaś cana śaraṇyo n' âst' îti mayā śocyata iti.›

1.99 Tato viṣama|viṣa|jvāl'|âvalīḍh'|âvayavā sā dharaṇī|tale nyapatat. day"|āviṣṭa|hṛdayo 'haṃ mantra|balena viṣa|vyavasthām apanetum a|kṣamaḥ samīpa|kuñjeṣv oṣadhi|viśeṣam anviṣya pratyāgato vyutkrānta|jīvitāṃ tāṃ vyalokayam. tad|anu tasyāḥ pāvaka|saṃskāraṃ viracya śok'|ākula|cetā bālam enam agatim ādāya Satyavarma|vṛtt'|ânta|śravaṇa|velāyāṃ tan|nivās'|âgrahāra|nāmadheyasy' âśrutatayā tad|anveṣaṇam aśakyam ity ālocya bhavad|amātya|tanayasya bhavān ev' âbhirakṣit' êti bhavantam enam anayam iti.»

'O son of a brahmin! Satya·varman, the younger son of Sita·varman, Raja·hamsa's minister, came to this country on a pilgrimage. In a village given by the king to brahmins to provide them with an income,* he married Kali, a brahmin's lovely daughter. But when she did not produce any children he took in marriage her younger sister, Gauri, a golden beauty, and with her got a son. Kali was jealous, so one day on some pretext she led the child with me, his nurse, to this river and threw us in.

With one hand I held the boy up, while with the other I kept afloat. Getting hold of the branch of some tree that had arrived in the flow of the river, I placed the infant there. But while the river current was carrying me along, I was bitten by a deadly black snake, attached to the tree. This is where the tree ran aground, with me clinging to it. I am grieving because once this burning poison has killed me, the child will have no protection in the forest.'

And with that she fell down to the ground, her limbs 1.99
lashed by the poison's noxious flames. Compassion flooded my heart, but my mantras were not powerful enough to counteract the working of the poison, so I went to hunt for a special remedy in the nearby thickets. When I returned I found that the life had left her body. Beside myself with grief, I performed her cremation rite. I took the helpless child but could not go in search of Satya·varman, since when she had told the story I had not heard the name of that brahmin-gifted village where he lived. Hence I have brought the baby to you, thinking that you are the sole guardian of your minister's son."

Tan niśamya Satyavarma|sthiteḥ samyag|a|niścitatayā khinna|mānaso nara|patiḥ Sumataye mantriṇe Somadattaṃ nāma tad|anuja|tanayam arpitavān. so 'pi sodaram āgatam iva manyamāno viśeṣeṇa pupoṣa.

Evaṃ militena kumāra|maṇḍalena bāla|kelīr anubhavann adhirūḍh'|ân|eka|vāhano Rājavāhano 'nukrameṇa caul'|ôpanayan'|ādi|saṃskāra|jātam alabhata.

1.102 Tataḥ sakala|lipi|jñānaṃ nikhila|deśīya|bhāṣā|pāṇḍityaṃ ṣaḍ|aṅga|sahita|Veda|samudāya|kovidatvaṃ kāvya|nāṭak'|ākhyānak'|ākhyāyik"|êtihāsa|citra|kathā|sahita|Purāṇa|gaṇa|naipuṇyaṃ dharma|śabda|jyotis|tarka|mīmāṃs"|ādi|samasta|śāstra|nikara|cāturyaṃ Kauṭilya|Kāmandakīy'|ādi|nīti|paṭala|kauśalaṃ vīṇ"|ādy|a|śeṣa|vādya|dākṣyaṃ saṃgīta|sāhitya|hāritvaṃ maṇi|mantr'|âuṣadh'|ādi|māyā|prapañca|cañcutvaṃ mātaṅga|turaṅg'|ādi|vāhan'|ārohaṇa|pāṭavaṃ vividh'|āyudha|prayoga|caṇatvaṃ caurya|durodar'|ādi|kapaṭa|kalā|prauḍhatvaṃ ca tat|tad|ācāryebhyaḥ samyag labdhvā;

The king was depressed by the story, because it was so unclear where Satya·varman was. He named the baby Soma·datta and entrusted him to his father's elder brother, the minister Súmati. Súmati, for his part, felt as if his own brother had returned, and reared the boy with special care.

That is how Raja·váhana came to meet the circle of boys with whom he played children's games and learned to ride a variety of steeds. In accord with the Vedic tradition he passed through all the life-cycle rites in order: his hair was cut leaving a tuft, he was invested with the sacred thread, and so on.

Next, the appropriate teachers taught that group of young 1.102
men well: all about different scripts and fluency in the languages of every country; the wisdom contained in the collection of Vedas together with their six auxiliaries: phonetics, meter, grammar, etymology, astrology and ritual; skill in the set of eighteen Purána epics, as well as in poetry, drama, short stories, prose composition, history and fables; complete mastery of the range of sciences: law, grammar, astronomy, logic, Mimámsa interpretation of ritual and philosophy, and so on; skill in the political traditions such as of Kautílya and Kamándaki;* dexterity on all instruments, beginning with the *vina* lute; elegance in song and public speaking; manifest facility in manifold illusions such as magic gems, mantra spells and medicinal herbs; proficiency at riding elephants, horses and so on; renown in the handling of various weapons; and confidence in the crooked arts, such as robbery and gambling.

Yauvanena vilasantaṃ kṛtyeṣv analasaṃ taṃ kumāra|nikaraṃ nirīkṣya mahī|vallabhaḥ saḥ:

«Ahaṃ śatru|jana|durlabha iti!» param'|ānandam a|mandam avindata.

iti śrī|Daṇḍinaḥ kṛtau
Daśa|kumāra|carite
Kumār'|ôtpattir
nāma
prathama ucchvāsaḥ.

The king, beloved of the earth, saw this, and how they gleamed with youth and were quick to their tasks, and he felt intensely the greatest joy, thinking:

"No enemy can beat me!"

That is the end of the first chapter of
the glorious Dandin's
What Ten Young Men Did.
It is called:
The Origins of the Young Men.

CHAPTER TWO
A FAVOR FOR THE BRAHMIN

Ath' âikadā Vāmadevaḥ sakala|kalā|kuśalena Kusuma|sāyaka|saṃśayita|saundaryeṇa kalpita|sodaryeṇa sāhas" ôpahasita|Kumāreṇa su|kumāreṇa jaya|dhvaj'|ātapa|vāraṇa|kuliś'|âṅkita|kareṇa kumāra|nikareṇa pariveṣṭitaṃ rājānam ānata|śirasaṃ samabhigamya tena tāṃ kṛtāṃ paricaryām aṅgīkṛtya nija|caraṇa|kamala|yugala|milan|madhukarāyamāṇa|kāka|pakṣaṃ vidaliṣyamāṇa|vipakṣaṃ kumāra|cayaṃ gāḍham āliṅgya mita|satya|vākyena vihit'|āśīr abhyabhāṣata:

«Bhū|vallabha, bhavadīya|mano|ratha|phalam iva samṛddha|lāvaṇyaṃ tāruṇyaṃ nuta|mitro bhavat|putro 'nubhavati. saha|cara|sametasya nūnam etasya dig|vijay'|ārambha|samaya eṣaḥ. tad asya sakala|kleśa|sahasya Rājavāhanasya dig|vijaya|prayāṇaṃ kriyatām! iti»

2.3 Kumārā mār'|âbhirāmā Rām'|ādya|pauruṣā ruṣā bhasmīkṛt'|ārayo ray'|ôpahasita|samīraṇā raṇ'|âbhiyānena yānen' âbhyuday'|āśaṃsaṃ rājānam akārṣuḥ. tat|sācivyam itareṣāṃ vidhāya samucitāṃ buddhim upadiśya śubhe muhūrte sa|parivāraṃ kumāraṃ vijayāya visasarja.

Now, one day Vama·deva approached the king, who bowed down low before the sage. The king was surrounded by the entourage of young men. These same young men were skilled in all the arts, so lovely as to be confused with flower-bowed Kama; brothers in spirit, bolder than even Skanda Karttikéya the paradigm prince,* their hands bore the auspicious regal marks of a victory banner, a parasol and *vajra* thunderbolt. After Vama·deva had acknowledged the honor done him by the king, the princely group touched their heads to his toes, their "crow-wing" side-locks settling like black bees on his two lotus-like feet. He tightly embraced these young men, destined to pulverize the enemy, and laid his blessings upon them, before addressing the king with measured frank words:

"Beloved master of the Earth, the lovely youth of your son and his commendable companions has ripened into the very fruit of your own desires. Surely now is the time for him and his fellows to start out on the conquest of the directions. Raja·váhana can cope with every affliction. Let him set off to conquer the quarters!"

The young men were as distractingly lovely as Kama the 2.3
destroyer, and heroic as the epic heroes led by Rama. Their rage was enough to reduce their enemies to ashes, and their swiftness put the wind to shame. Marching out to battle they inspired the king's confidence that their mission would be successful. Raja·hamsa appointed the other young men to minister to Raja·váhana, advised him with fitting counsel, and at the auspicious moment sent him and his entourage off on the conquest.

Rājavāhano maṅgala|sūcakaṃ śubha|śakunaṃ vilokayan deśaṃ kaṃ cid atikramya Vindhy'|âṭavī|madhyam aviśat. tatra heti|hati|kiṇ'|âṅkaṃ kāl'|āyasa|karkaśa|kāyaṃ yajñ'|ôpavīten' ânumeya|vipra|bhāvaṃ vyakta|Kirāta|prabhāvaṃ locana|paruṣaṃ kam api puruṣaṃ dadarśa. tena vihita|pūjano Rājavāhano 'bhāṣata:

«Nanu, mānava, jana|saṅga|rahite mṛga|hite ghora|pracāre kāntāre Vindhy'|âṭavī|madhye bhavān ekākī kim|iti nivasati? bhavad|aṃs'|ôpanītaṃ yajñ'|ôpavītaṃ bhū|sura|bhāvaṃ dyotayati. heti|hatibhiḥ Kirāta|rītir anumīyate. kathaya kim etad iti?»

2.6 «Tejo|mayo 'yaṃ mānuṣa|mātra|pauruṣo nūnaṃ na bhavat' îti,»

matvā sa puruṣas tad|vayasya|mukhān nāma|janane vijñāya tasmai nija|vṛtt'|ântam akathayat:

«Rāja|nandana! kecid asyām aṭavyāṃ ved'|ādi|vidy"|âbhyāsam apahāya nija|kul'|ācāraṃ dūrīkṛtya satya|śauc'|ādi|dharma|vrātaṃ parihṛtya kilbiṣam anviṣyantaḥ Pulinda|purogamās tad|annam upabhuñjānā bahavo brāhmaṇa|bruvā nivasanti.

2.9 Teṣu kasya cit putro nindā|pātra|cāritro Mātaṅgo nām' âhaṃ saha Kirāta|balena jana|padaṃ praviśya grāmeṣu dhaninaḥ strī|bāla|sahitān ānīy' âṭavyāṃ bandhane nidhāya te-

Raja·váhana had travelled a certain distance, noticing omens of good fortune that boded well—favorable birdcalls, for example—when he reached the middle of the Vindhya forest. There he saw someone rough on the eye, his body hard as iron, inscribed with the scars of weapon cuts. From his sacrificial thread one could infer that he was a brahmin, but his strength was clearly that of a *kiráta* savage. The man paid them his respects, and Raja·váhana addressed him:

"I say, my man! Why are you living all alone in the middle of the Vindhyan jungle, in this completely uninhabited dreary forest given over to wild animals and a horrible place to stay? The sacred thread hung over your shoulder marks you out as a brahmin, god on earth. The weapon scars imply a *kiráta* savage lifestyle. Tell us, what does this mean?"

The fellow thought to himself: "This splendid person 2.6
surely cannot be a mere mortal."

So he ascertained the prince's name and birth from the mouths of his friends before recounting his story:

"O king's delightful son! In this jungle there live many who are brahmins in name only. They have rejected the cultivation of Vedic and other kinds of traditional learning, and are far removed from the rituals of their own people. They have abandoned the whole culture of their religious rights and duties, from speaking the truth to ritual purity and so on. These seekers after sin are led by *pulínda* tribals, and eat their food.

I am the son of one of these so-called brahmins. Matánga 2.9
is my name.* My career is nothing to be proud of. I used to live without mercy, going to a settlement with a band of savage *kirátas* to capture the wealthy in the villages, together

ṣāṃ sakala|dhanam apaharann uddhṛtya vīta|dayo vyacaram.

Kadā cid ekasmin kāntāre madīya|sahacara|gaṇena jighāṃsyamānaṃ bhū|suram ekam avalokya day"|āyatta|citto 'bravam:

‹Nanu pāpāḥ! na hantavyo brāhmaṇa iti.›

2.12 Te roṣ'|âruṇa|nayanā māṃ bahudhā nirabhartsayan. teṣāṃ bhāṣaṇa|pāruṣyam a|sahiṣṇur aham avani|sura|rakṣaṇāya ciraṃ prayudhya tair abhihato gata|jīvito 'bhavam.

Tataḥ Pretapurīm upetya tatra deha|dhāribhiḥ puruṣaiḥ pariveṣṭitaṃ sabhā|madhye ratna|khacita|siṃh'|āsan'|āsīnaṃ Śamanaṃ vilokya tasmai daṇḍa|praṇāmam akaravam. so 'pi mām avekṣya Citraguptaṃ nāma nij'|âmātyam āhūya tam avocat:

‹Saciva, n' âiṣo 'muṣya mṛtyu|samayaḥ. nindita|carito 'py ayaṃ mahī|sura|nimittaṃ gata|jīvito 'bhūt. itaḥ prabhṛti vigalita|kalmaṣasy' âsya puṇya|karma|karaṇe rucir udeṣyati. pāpiṣṭhair anubhūyamānam atra yātanā|viśeṣaṃ vilokya punar api pūrva|śarīram anena gamyatām iti.›

2.15 Citragupto 'pi tatra tatra saṃtapteṣv āyasa|stambheṣu badhyamānān, aty|uṣṇīkṛte vitata|śarāve taile nikṣipyamāṇān, laguḍair jarjarīkṛt'|âvayavān, niśita|ṭaṅkaiḥ paritakṣyamāṇān api darśayitvā puṇya|buddhim upadiśya mām amuñcat.

with their wives and children. We would keep them prisoner in the jungle and seize all their possessions, before letting them go.

One day, in a lonely forest, I watched the gang of my fellows prepare to kill a brahmin, a god on earth. Compassion got the better of me, and I said:

'Please, you villains! You should not kill a brahmin.'

Their eyes went red with rage and they hurled all sorts of 2.12
abuse at me. I could not take their rough words, and fought long and hard to save the brahmin, a god on earth. But they struck me down, and my spirit passed away.

Then I went to Preta·puri, City of the Dead, where I saw Yama, the god of death, seated on his jewel-studded lion-throne in the middle of the assembly, surrounded by an entourage of embodied souls. I prostrated myself full-length before him. He looked down at me, before summoning his personal counsellor Chitra·gupta and saying:*

'Minister, it is not yet this man's time to die. Although he lived reprehensibly, he lost his life for the sake of a brahmin, a god on earth. Henceforward his sins have been erased, and his passion for doing good deeds will grow. Let him first look on the special tortures the worst sinners undergo here, and then he should be returned to the body he had before.'

Accordingly, Chitra·gupta showed me the different places 2.15
where people were being bound to red-hot iron pillars or thrown into huge vats of boiling oil. He showed me men whose limbs were being splintered by clubs, and others being chopped to bits by whetted axes. Finally he released me, with the recommendation that I should be good.

Tad eva pūrva|śarīram ahaṃ prāpto mah"|âṭavī|madhye śītal'|ôpacāraṃ racayatā mahī|sureṇa parīkṣyamāṇaḥ śilāyāṃ śāyitaḥ kṣaṇam atiṣṭham. tad|anu vidit'|ôdanto madīya|vaṃśa|bandhu|gaṇaḥ sahas" āgatya mandiram ānīya mām apakrānta|vraṇam akarot.

Dvi|janmā kṛta|jño mahyam a|kṣara|śikṣāṃ vidhāya vividh'|āgama|tantram ākhyāya kalmaṣa|kṣaya|kāraṇaṃ sad|ācāram upadiśya jñān'|ēkṣaṇa|gamyamānasya śaśi|khaṇḍa|śekharasya pūjā|vidhānam abhidhāya pūjāṃ mat|kṛtām aṅgīkṛtya niragāt.

2.18 Tad|ārabhy' âhaṃ Kirāta|kṛta|saṃsargaṃ bandhu|kula|vargam utsṛjya sakala|lok'|Âika|gurum indu|kal"|âvataṃsaṃ cetasi smarann asmin kānane dūrīkṛta|kalaṅko vasāmi.

Deva, bhavate vijñāpanīyaṃ rahasyaṃ kiṃ cid asti. āgamyatām iti.»

Sa vayasya|gaṇād apanīya rahasi punar enam abhāṣata:

2.21 «Rājan, atīte niśānte Gaurī|patiḥ svapna|saṃnihito nidrā|mudrita|locanaṃ vibodhya prasanna|vadana|kāntiḥ praśray'|ānataṃ mām avocat:

‹Mātaṅga, Daṇḍak'|âraṇy'|ântarāla|gāminyās taṭinyās tīra|bhūmau siddha|sādhy'|ārādhyamānasya sphaṭika|liṅgasya paścād Adri|pati|kanyā|pada|paṅkti|cihnitasy' âśmanaḥ savi-

The same second I was back in my former body in the middle of the great jungle. The brahmin was taking care of me, applying soothing remedies. For a short while I stayed there, resting on a rock. Thereupon a band of my fellow kinsmen who had heard the news came rushing up and carried me home, where they tended my wounds.

The grateful well-behaved 'twice-born' brahmin taught me my letters,* and instructed me in many kinds of scripture and tantras. He explained the correct procedure to ensure the destruction of impurity, and initiated me in the methods for worshipping Shiva of the crescent moon crest, visible only to the eye of wisdom. After accepting the respect I paid him, he left.

From then on I repudiated all my many kinsmen who 2.18
were intimates of the *kiráta* savages, and ever since I have been living here in this grove, far removed from temptation, meditating on the One Master of the universe, he who wears the digit of the moon as an ornament, Shiva.

My Lord, there is one secret about which I must inform you. Please come with me."

He led the prince away from his friends to address him in private:

"King, today at dawn Gauri's husband Shiva appeared to 2.21
me in a dream. My eyes were sealed in sleep when he woke me. I bowed down in reverence before him, so lovely with his beatific face, and he said:

'Matánga, on the bank of the river that flows through the middle of the Dándaka forest,* behind the crystal *linga* worshipped by both saintly *siddhas* and *sadhyas*, next to the stone stamped with the footprints of Párvati, the

dhe vidher ānanam iva kim api bilaṃ vidyate. tat praviśya tatra nikṣiptaṃ tāmra|śāsanaṃ śāsanaṃ vidhātur iva samādāya vidhiṃ tad|upadiṣṭaṃ diṣṭa|vijayam iva vidhāya pātāla|lok'|âdh'|īśvareṇa bhavatā bhavitavyam. bhavat|sāhāyya|karo rāja|kumāro 'dya śvo vā samāgamiṣyat' îti.›

Tad|ādeś'|ânuguṇam eva bhavad|āgamanam abhūt. sādhan'|âbhilāṣiṇo mama toṣiṇo racaya sāhāyyam iti.»

2.24 «Tath" êti» Rājavāhanaḥ sākaṃ Mātaṅgena namit'|ôttam'|âṅgena vihāy' ârdha|rātre nidrā|para|tantraṃ mitra|gaṇaṃ van'|ântaram avāpa.

Tad|anu tad|anucarāḥ kalye sākalyena rāja|kumāram an|avalokayanto viṣaṇṇa|hṛdayās teṣu teṣu vaneṣu samyag anviṣy' ân|avekṣamāṇā etad|anveṣaṇa|manīṣayā deś'|ântaraṃ cariṣṇavo 'tisahiṣṇavo niścita|punaḥ|saṃgama|saṃketa|sthānāḥ paras|paraṃ viyujya yayuḥ.

Lok'|âika|vīreṇa kumāreṇa rakṣyamāṇaḥ saṃtuṣṭ'|ântar|aṅgo Mātaṅgo 'pi bilaṃ śaśi|śekhara|kathit'|âbhijñāna|parijñātaṃ niḥśaṅkaṃ praviśya gṛhīta|tāmra|śāsano Rasātalaṃ pathā ten' âiv' ôpetya;

2.27 tatra kasya cit pattanasya nikaṭe kelī|kānana|kāsārasya vitata|sārasasya samīpe nānā|vidhen' ēśa|śāsana|vidhān'|ôpapāditena haviṣā homaṃ viracya pratyūha|parihāriṇi sa|visma-

daughter of the Lord of the mountains, there is a cave like the mouth of destiny. You must enter that cave and collect the copper-plate inscription placed there on the ground as though it were fate's own inevitable decree. Perform the ritual it prescribes, as if you were conquering destiny, and you will become the overlord of the underworld. A royal prince will arrive today or tomorrow who will be able to help you.'

Your arrival accords perfectly with his pronouncement. I am keen to succeed and would be delighted if you would help me."

Raja·váhana agreed. At midnight he forsook the group of 2.24
his friends, overpowered by sleep, and went with Matánga, who bowed down deeply before him, to another grove.

In the morning, when his companions could not find the royal prince anywhere, they were sick at heart, and searched one grove after another. Still they did not find him, and so they resolved to travel to different countries, unstoppable in their desire to find him. They fixed on a place to rendezvous, took their leave of one another, and off they set.

Meanwhile, Matánga was delighted at heart to be escorted by the prince, the world's greatest hero. He identified the cave according to the features described by moon-crested Shiva and entered fearlessly. Having picked up the copper-plate inscription, they made their way on down to the Ra-sa·tala underworld.

There, beside a pool populated with waterbirds in a plea- 2.27
sure garden near to a certain city, Matánga performed a *homa* fire sacrifice with oblations of many sorts, prepared according to the Lord's instructions. While Raja·váhana watched

yaṃ vilokayati Rājavāhane samid|ājya|samujjvalite jvalane puṇya|gehaṃ dehaṃ mantra|pūrvakam āhutīkṛtya taḍit|samāna|kāntiṃ divyāṃ tanum alabhata.

Tad|anu maṇi|maya|maṇḍana|maṇḍaka|maṇḍitā sakala|loka|lalanā|kula|lalāma|bhūta|kanyakā kā cana vinīt'|ân|eka|sakhī|jan'|ânugamyamānā kala|haṃsa|gatyā śanair āgaty' âvani|sur'|ôttamāya maṇim ekam ujjval'|ākāram upāyanīkṛtya tena;

«kā tvam iti?»

2.30 pṛṣṭā s'|ôtkaṇṭhā kala|kaṇṭha|svanena mandaṃ mandam udañjalir abhāṣata:

«Bhū|sur'|ôttama, aham asur'|ôttama|nandinī Kālindī nāma. mama pit" âsya lokāsya śāsitā mah"|ânubhāvo nija|parākram'|âsahiṣṇunā Viṣṇunā dūrīkṛt'|âmare samare Yama|nagar'|âtithir akāri. tad|viyoga|śoka|sāgara|magnaṃ mām avekṣya ko 'pi kāruṇikaḥ siddha|tāpaso 'bhāṣata:

‹Bāle, kaś cid divya|deha|dhārī mānavo navo vallabhas tava bhūtvā sakalaṃ Rasātalaṃ pālayiṣyat' îti.›

2.33 Tad|ādeśaṃ niśamya ghana|śabd'|ônmukhī cātakī varṣ'|āgamanam iva tav' ālokana|kāṅkṣiṇī ciram atiṣṭham. man|mano|ratha|phalāyamānaṃ bhavad|āgamanam avagamya mad|rājy'|âvalamba|bhūt'|āmāty'|ânumatyā Madana|kṛta|sā-

in amazement, fending off disturbances, the brahmin uttered some mantras and offered his meritorious body into the fire flaming with wood and clarified butter ghee, and obtained a divine form lovely as lightning.

That instant a girl with the graceful gait of a swan approached, accompanied by a group of demure girlfriends. Adorned with gem-set ornaments, she was herself the loveliest jewel of the very species of lovelies in all the three worlds. She presented to the best of brahmins one flashing jewel. He asked:

"Who are you?"

With her hands folded before her forehead in respect she 2.30
answered longingly and ever so gently in a voice like a sweet-voiced dove:

"O best of brahmins, god upon the earth, I am Kalíndi, the dear daughter of the best of *ásura* gods. My father was the greatly powerful ruler of this world. But Vishnu could not bear his heroism, and in a battle that routed even the immortals sent him to the City of Death.* Some compassionate accomplished ascetic, a *siddha*, noticed me sunk in the ocean of suffering at the loss of my father, and said:

'Child, a human stranger in a divine body will become your new beloved and will rule over all the Rasa·tala underworld.'

Since I heard his prediction I have been waiting a long 2.33
time, yearning to see you, just as the *chátaki* bird that drinks only raindrops waits for the coming of rain, face upturned, longing for the sound of thunder from a cloud. As soon as I realized that you were on your way, and that my desires were

rathyena manasā bhavantam āgaccham. lokasy' âsya rāja|Lakṣmīm aṅgīkṛtya māṃ tat|sapatnīṃ karotu bhavān iti.»

Mātaṅgo 'pi Rājavāhan'|ânumatyā tāṃ taruṇīṃ pariṇīya divy'|âṅganā|lābhena hṛṣṭataro Rasātala|rājyam urarīkṛtya param'|ānandam āsasāda.

Vañcayitvā vayasya|gaṇaṃ samāgato Rājavāhanas tad|avalokana|kautūhalena bhuvaṃ gamiṣṇuḥ Kālindī|dattaṃ kṣut|pipās'|ādi|kleśa|nāśanaṃ maṇiṃ sāhāyya|karaṇa|saṃtuṣṭān Mātaṅgāl labdhvā kaṃ can' âdhvānam anuvartamānaṃ taṃ visṛjya bila|pathena tena niryayau.

2.36 Tatra ca mitra|gaṇam an|avalokya bhuvaṃ babhrāma. bhramaṃś ca Viśāl"|ôpaśalye kam apy ākrīḍam āsādya tatra viśiśramiṣur āndolik"|ārūḍhaṃ ramaṇī|sahitam āpta|jana|parivṛtam udyāne samāgatam ekaṃ puruṣam apaśyat. so 'pi param'|ānandena pallavita|cetā vikasita|vadan'|âravindaḥ:

«Mama svāmī soma|kul'|âvataṃso viśuddha|yaśo|nidhī Rājavāhana eṣaḥ. mahā|bhāgyatay" âkāṇḍa ev' âsya pāda|mūlaṃ gatavān asmi. samprati mahān nayan'|ôtsavo jāta iti!»

bearing fruit, my mind was driven by maddening Love* to come and meet you, with the approval of my ministers, the pillars of my kingdom. Accept Lakshmi, the Majesty who embodies kingship over this world, and make me her co-wife."*

Then, with the approval of Raja·váhana, Matánga took the young woman as his wife. Most thrilled* to acquire a divine lady, he accepted the kingship of the Rasa·tala underworld, and found the greatest joy.

Raja·váhana had deceived his friends when he came away, but now he longed to ascend to the surface and see them again. Delighted with his assistance, Matánga gave him the jewel Kalíndi had given, which banishes torments such as hunger and thirst.* Matánga accompanied Raja·váhana part of the way until the prince took his leave and went out by the same path through the cave.

Once outside, however, he did not find his friends, but 2.36
had to wander the earth. In his wanderings he came to a certain pleasure garden in the suburbs of Ujjain the Vast.* He was about to take some rest there when he saw someone arrive in the park, seated on a palanquin, his lovely lady at his side, his intimates around him. That man jumped off his litter in a rush, the lotus of his face blooming and his mind budding with the highest joy:

"My master is here, Raja·váhana, scion of the lunar race, repository of purest glory! By great good fortune I am quite unexpectedly at his feet again. Now I can feast my eyes!"

sa|saṃbhramam āndolikāyā avatīrya sa|rabhasa|pada|vinyāsa|vilāsi|harṣ'|ôtkarṣa|caritas tri|catura|padāny udgatasya caraṇa|kamala|yugalaṃ galad|ullasan|mallik"|âvalayena maulinā pasparśa. pramod'|âśru|pūrṇo rājā pulakit'|âṅgaṃ taṃ gāḍham āliṅgya:

2.39 «Aye saumya Somadatt' êti!»

vyājahāra. tataḥ kasy' âpi Puṃ|nāga|bhūruhasya chāyā|śītale tale saṃviṣṭena Manuja|nāthena sa|praṇayam abhāṇi:

«Sakhe, kālam etāvantaṃ deśe kasmin, prakāreṇa ken' āsthāyi bhavatā? saṃprati kutra gamyate? taruṇī k" êyam? eṣa parijanaḥ saṃpāditaḥ katham? kathay' êti!»

2.42 So 'pi mitra|saṃdarśana|vyatikar'|âpagata|cintā|jvar'|âtiśayo mukulita|kara|kamalaḥ sa|vinayam ātmīya|pracāra|prakāram avocat:

iti śrī|Daṇḍinaḥ kṛtau
Daśa|kumāra|carite
Dvij'|ôpakṛtir
nāma
dvitīya ucchvāsaḥ.

Eagerly stepping forward he showed his ecstatic delight. Touching with his head the prince's two lotus-feet he dropped his crown of splendid *mállika* jasmine flowers. The royal prince had come forward three or four steps, his eyes filled with tears of joy and he held the other man's thrilled body tightly to him, crying out:

"Oh, my sweet Soma·datta!" 2.39

Then they sat down on the ground in the cool shade of a nutmeg tree and the Lord of men asked fondly:

"My friend, tell me! Where have you been all this time? What have you been doing? Where are you going now? Who is this young lady? How did you come by these attendants?"

Soma·datta had recovered from the overwhelming fever 2.42
of thoughts that had beset him at the sight of his friend. He cupped his hands like a lotus bud at his forehead in respect, and modestly told the story of his own travels:

That is the end of the second chapter of
the glorious Dandin's
What Ten Young Men Did.
It is called:
A Favor for the Brahmin.

CHAPTER THREE
WHAT SOMA·DATTA DID

«DEVA, BHAVAC|CARAṆA|KAMALA|sev"|âbhilāṣībhūto 'haṃ bhramann ekasyāṃ vanā|vanau pipās"|ākulo latā|parivṛtaṃ śītalaṃ nada|salilaṃ pibann ujjval'|ākāraṃ ratnaṃ tatr' âikam adrākṣam. tad ādāya gatvā kaṃ can' âdhvānam ambara|maṇer aty|uṣṇatayā gantum a|kṣamo vane 'sminn eva kim api devat"|āyatanaṃ praviṣṭo dīn'|ânanaṃ bahu|tanaya|sametaṃ sthavira|mahī|suram ekam avalokya kuśalam udita|dayo 'ham apṛccham. kārpaṇya|vi|varṇa|vadano mahad|āśā|pūrṇa|mānaso 'vocad agra|janmā:

‹Mahā|bhāga, sutān etān mātṛ|hīnān an|ekair upāyai rakṣann idānīm asmin ku|deśe bhaikṣyaṃ saṃpādya dadad etebhyo vasāmi Śiv'|ālaye 'sminn iti.›

3.3 ‹Bhū|deva, etat|kaṭak'|âdhipatī rājā kasya deśasya? kiṃ|nāmadheyaḥ? kim atr' āgamana|kāraṇam asy' êti?»

pṛṣṭo 'bhāṣata mahī|suraḥ:

‹Saumya, Mattakālo nāma Lāṭ'|ēśvaro deśasy' âsya pālayitur Vīraketos tanayāṃ Vāmalocanāṃ nāma taruṇī|ratnam a|samāna|lāvaṇyaṃ śrāvaṃ śrāvam avadhūta|duhitṛ|prārthanasya tasya nagarīm arautsīt. Vīraketur api bhīto mahad|upāyanam iva tanayāṃ Mattakālāy' ādāt.

3.6 Taruṇī|lābha|hṛṣṭa|cetā Lāṭa|patiḥ:

«Pariṇeyā nija|pura ev' êti,»

"My Lord, I so wanted to serve your lotus-feet. I had been roaming through some forest when, disoriented with thirst, I went to drink cool river water in a place all covered with creepers. There I saw a blazing gemstone. I took it and went. But the sky's jewel, the sun, was so extremely hot that, unable to proceed, I entered a temple in the same grove. There I saw an aged brahmin, his expression wretched, with many boys around him. My compassion roused, I asked after his well-being. Highest born,* the brahmin's face was colorless with misery, but his mind now filled with great expectation, as he said:

'Good sir, these are my motherless sons. Now I must look after them by one way and another, begging in this desperate place for food for them, and inhabiting this Shiva temple.'

I asked: 'O brahmin, the commander of the army camp 3.3
here, of which country is he king? What is his name? Why has he come to this place?'

The brahmin replied:

'Gentle sir, Matta·kala is his name. He is lord of the Latas.* He kept on hearing about the incomparable loveliness of Vama·lóchana, jewel among lovely ladies and daughter of Vira·ketu, the protector of this country. But that man rejected the request for his daughter, and so Matta·kala laid siege to his city, Pátali. Vira·ketu was thus intimidated into handing his daughter over to Matta·kala as if she were an enormous bribe.

The lord of the Latas was thrilled at heart to have won 3.6
the young woman. He decided:

"I shall marry her only in my own city."

niścitya gacchan nija|deśaṃ prati saṃprati mṛgay"|ādareṇ' âtra vane sainya|vāsam akārayat. kanyā|sāreṇa niyukto Mānapālo nāma Vīraketu|mantrī māna|dhanaś catur|aṅga|bala|samanvito 'nyatra racita|śibiras taṃ nija|nāth'|âvamāna|khinna|mānaso 'ntar bibhed' êti.›

3.9 Vipro 'sau bahu|tanayo vidvān nirdhanaḥ sthaviraś ca dāna|yogya iti tasmai karuṇā|pūrṇa|manā ratnam adām. param'|āhlāda|vikasit'|ânano 'bhihit'|ân|ek'|āśīḥ kutra cid agra|janmā jagāma. adhva|śrama|khinnena mayā tatra niraveśi nidrā|sukham.

Tad|anu paścān nigaḍita|bāhu|yugalaḥ sa bhū|suraḥ kaśā|ghāta|cihnita|gātro 'n|eka|naistriṃśik'|ânuyāto 'bhyetya mām:

‹Asau dasyur ity!›

3.12 adarśayat. parityakta|bhū|surā rāja|bhaṭā ratn'|âvāpti|prakāraṃ mad|uktam an|ākarṇya bhaya|rahitaṃ māṃ gāḍhaṃ niyamya rajjubhir ānīya kār"|âgāram;

‹Ete tava sakhāya iti!›

nigaḍitān kāṃś cin nirdiṣṭavanto mām api nigaḍita|caraṇa|yugalam akārṣuḥ. kiṃ|kartavyatā|mūḍhena nir|āśa|kleś'|ânubhaven' âvāci mayā:

3.15 ‹Nanu puruṣā vīrya|paruṣāḥ, nimittena kena nirviśatha kārā|vāsa|duḥkhaṃ dustaram? yūyaṃ vayasyā iti nirdiṣṭam etaiḥ—kim idam iti?›

En route for his country, he was eager to hunt and had the army make their encampment here in the wood. A minister of Vira·ketu, Mana·pala, was entrusted with escorting the girl. As his name "Protector of pride" implies, he is rich in pride, and has set up camp separately, together with his four-fold army of elephants, cavalry, chariots and infantry. He is racked within and turning treacherous, his spirit pained at the insult to his master.'

That brahmin with many sons was wise, penniless and 3.9
aged. My heart was filled with compassion. Thinking he should be given something, I gave him the gemstone. The best-born brahmin's face bloomed with great delight, he blessed me many times, and off he went somewhere or other. I was exhausted from the exertion on the road and enjoyed there the pleasure of sleep.

Some time later that brahmin returned, his two arms in chains, his body stamped with whip lashes, escorted by several swordsmen. He pointed me out with the words:

'Here is your devilish robber!'

The king's soldiers released the brahmin and without lis- 3.12
tening to my account of how I had acquired the gemstone they bound me up tight with rope, and conducted me undaunted to a prison house.

'Here are your friends!'

They said, pointing to some people in chains, and bound my own two feet with chains also. Undergoing hopeless torment, I had no idea what to do and inquired:

'Excuse me, men of rough valor, what brings you to suffer 3.15
the unbearable pain of prison life? They pointed me out as your associate—why is that?'

Tathā|vidhaṃ mām avekṣya bhū|surān mayā śrutaṃ Lāṭa|pati|vṛttāntaṃ vyākhyāya cora|vīrāḥ punar avocan: ‹Mahā|bhāga, Vīraketu|mantriṇo Mānapālasya kiṃkarā vayam. tad|ājñayā Lāṭ'|ēśvara|māraṇāya rātrau suruṅgā|dvāreṇa tad|agāraṃ praviśya tatra rāj'|âbhāvena viṣaṇṇā bahu|dhanam āhṛtya mah"|âṭavīṃ prāviśāma. apare|dyuś ca pad'|ânveṣiṇo rāj'|ânucarā bahavo 'bhyetya dhṛta|dhana|cayān asmān paritaḥ parivṛtya dṛḍhataraṃ baddhvā nikaṭam ānīya samasta|vastu|śodhana|velāyām ekasy' ân|arghya|ratnasy' âbhāven' âsmad|vadhāya māṇiky'|ādānāy' âsmān kil' âśṛṅkhalayann iti.›

3.18 Śruta|ratna|ratn'|âvalokana|sthāno 'ham idaṃ tad eva māṇikyam iti niścitya bhū|deva|dāna|nimittāṃ dur|avasthām ātmano janma nāmadheyaṃ yuṣmad|anveṣaṇa|paryaṭana|prakāraṃ c' ābhāṣya samay'|ôcitaiḥ saṃlāpair maitrīm akārṣam.

Tato 'rdha|rātre teṣāṃ mama ca śṛṅkhalā|bandhanaṃ nirbhidya tair anugamyamāno nidritasya dvāḥ|stha|gaṇasy' āyudha|jālam ādāya pura|rakṣān puratas abhimukh'|āgatān paṭu|parākrama|līlay" âbhidrāvya Mānapāla|śibiraṃ prāviśam. Mānapālo nija|kiṃkarebhyo mama kul'|âbhimāna|vṛtt'|ântaṃ tat|kālīnaṃ vikramaṃ ca niśamya mām ārcayat.

The brave robbers saw from the state I was in that they could trust me, told me the story about the king of the Latas which I had already heard from the brahmin and went on to say:

'Good sir, we are the servants of Mana·pala, Vira·ketu's minister. On his command we went at night to kill the lord of the Latas. We entered his dwelling by a subterranean passage. Frustrated not to find him there, we seized a lot of treasure and made off into the great jungle. The next day many of the king's servants set out following our footprints. They had us completely surrounded, weighed down by the treasure in our possession, bound us extremely tightly, and brought us back near here. When the time came for checking all the property, one priceless jewel was missing. It is clear that they have chained us in order to torture us until they can recover the gemstone.'

From what I had heard of the jewel and from where I had 3.18
found it, I was certain that it was the same one. So I told them how my present to the brahmin had got me in such a bad situation, and my birth and name, and how I had been roaming in search of you. In the course of such discussions as the occasion demanded, we became friends.

Later, at midnight, I broke the chains holding them and me. Together we took the stash of weapons from the sleeping group posted at the door. With an easy show of pointed valor I put to flight the city guards who had come from the front to face us, and we made it to the camp of Mana·pala. Mana·pala learned from his servants the details of my good family and dignity, and about my heroism in the event, so he welcomed me with respect.

Pare|dyur Mattakālena preṣitāḥ ke cana puruṣā Mānapālam upetya:

3.21 ‹Mantrin, madīya|rāja|mandire suruṅgayā bahu dhanam apahṛtya caura|vīrā bhavadīyaṃ kaṭakaṃ prāviśan. tān arpaya! no cen mahān an|arthaḥ saṃbhaviṣyat' îti!›

krūrataraṃ vākyam abruvan. tad ākarṇya roṣ'|âruṇita|netro mantrī:

‹Lāṭa|patiḥ kaḥ? tena maitrī kā? punar asya varākasya sevayā kiṃ labhyam iti?›

3.24 tān nirabhartsayat. te ca Mānapālen' ôktaṃ vipralāpaṃ Mattakālāya tath" âiv' âkathayan. kupito 'pi Lāṭa|patir do-r|vīrya|garveṇ' âlpa|sainika|sameto yoddhum abhyagāt. pūrvam eva kṛta|raṇa|niścayo mānī Mānapālaḥ saṃnaddha|yodho yuddha|kāmo bhūtvā niḥśaṅkaṃ niragāt.

Aham api sa|bahu|mānaṃ mantri|dattāni bahula|turaṃgam'|ôpetaṃ catura|sārathiṃ rathaṃ ca dṛḍhataraṃ kavacaṃ mad|anurūpaṃ cāpaṃ ca vividha|bāṇa|pūrṇaṃ tūṇīra|dvayaṃ raṇa|samucitāny āyudhāni gṛhītvā yuddha|saṃnaddho madīya|bala|viśvāsena rip'|ûddharaṇ'|ôdyuktaṃ mantriṇam anvagām.

Paras|para|matsareṇa tumula|saṃgara|karam ubhaya|sainyam atikramya samullasad|bhuj'|āṭopena bāṇa|varṣaṃ tad|aṅge vimuñcann arātiṃ prāharam. tato 'tiraya|turaṃgamaṃ

The following day some men sent by Matta·kala came to see Mana·pala. They conveyed Matta·kala's message without mincing their words:

'Minister, powerful thieves have robbed a lot of treasure 3.21
from my palace via an underground passage. Now they have entered your encampment. Hand them over! If you do not, you will regret it!'

When he heard these words the minister's eyes reddened with rage, and he threw the men out, saying:

'Who does the lord of the Latas think he is? What use is his friendship? What can we gain by serving this pathetic man?'

They faithfully reported back to Matta·kala Mana·pala's 3.24
taunt. The Latan lord was raging indeed, but his arrogance in the strength of his own arms caused him to march out for the fight with only a few soldiers. Proud Mana·pala had resolved on combat already in advance. He marched out fearlessly with his warriors in battle formation, looking for a fight.

Counting absolutely on my power, the minister was determined to defeat his enemy. With great respect he gave me the perfect weapons for war: a chariot with several horses and a skillful charioteer, extremely strong armor, and a bow my size, with a pair of quivers full of every kind of arrows. Thus equipped for the battle I accompanied Mana·pala on the charge.

In mutual enmity the two armies were locked in a tumultuous* fight. I bypassed the melee and with pride in my scintillating muscular arms let fly a rain of arrows on the flank of the battle, striking down the enemy, Matta·kala.

mad|ratham tan|nikaṭaṃ nītvā śīghra|laṅghan'|ôpeta|tadīya|ratho 'ham arāteḥ śiraḥ|kartanam akārṣam. tasmin nipatite tad|avaśiṣṭa|sainikeṣu palāyiteṣu nānā|vidha|haya|gaj'|ādi|vastu|jātam ādāya param'|ānanda|saṃnato mantrī mam' ân|eka|vidhaṃ saṃbhāvanām akārṣīt.

3.27 Mānapāla|preṣitāt tad|anucarād etad akhilam udanta|jātam ākarṇya saṃtuṣṭa|manā rāj" âbhyudgato madīya|parākrame vismayamānaḥ sa|mah"|ôtsavam amātya|bāndhav'|ânumatyā śubha|dine nija|tanayāṃ mahyam adāt.

Tato yauva|rājy'|âbhiṣikto 'ham anudinam ārādhita|mahī|pāla|citto Vāmalocanay" ânayā saha nānā|vidhaṃ saukhyam anubhavan bhavad|viraha|vedanā|śalya|sulabha|vaikalya|hṛdayaḥ siddh'|ādeśena suhṛj|jan'|âvalokana|phalaṃ pradeśaṃ Mahākāla|nivāsinaḥ param'|Ēśvarasy' ārādhanāy' âdya patnī|sametaḥ samāgato 'smi. bhakta|vatsalasya Gaurī|pateḥ kāruṇyena tvat|pad'|âravinda|saṃdarśan'|ānanda|saṃdoho mayā labdha iti.»

Tan niśamy' âbhinandita|parākramo Rājavāhanas tan|nir|aparādha|daṇḍe daivam upālabhya tasmai krameṇ' ātma|caritaṃ kathayām āsa. tasminn avasare purataḥ Puṣpodbhavaṃ vilokya sa|saṃbhramaṃ nija|niṭila|taṭa|spṛṣṭa|caraṇ'|âṅgulim udañjalim amuṃ gāḍham āliṅgy' ānanda|bāṣpa|saṃkula|saṃphulla|locanaḥ:

Then I steered my chariot with its fast horses near him, jumped on his chariot in a swift leap and cut off his head. With him fallen, what was left of his army took flight. The minister was overcome with supreme joy, seizing all manner of booty: horses, elephants and the rest; and he honored me in multiple ways.

Mana·pala sent one of his servants to tell his king this 3.27
whole account. Deeply delighted, the king did me the honor of coming out to meet me. Marvelling at my prowess, he obtained the agreement of his ministers and relatives, and one auspicious day, with great festivity, gave me his own daughter in marriage.

I was then anointed heir to the throne. Every day I pleased the king more, and with my Vama·lóchana I enjoyed every variety of bliss. But in my heart was the understandable handicap of stabbing pain at having been separated from you.* My wife and I came here today to this place to propitiate Shiva, the highest Lord, who lives in the Maha·kala temple, because a *siddha* instructed us we would thereby attain the fruit of seeing a friend. Thanks to Shiva's mercy, Gauri Párvati's husband, who feels such affection for his devotees, I have won the cream joy of beholding your lotus-feet."

After hearing Soma·datta's story, Raja·váhana applauded his valor and bemoaned destiny's punishment of an innocent man. Then he in turn told him his own adventures. That same moment Pushpódbhava appeared before them, touched the toes of the prince's feet with his own broad forehead and folded his hands before his face in greeting.

3.30 «Saumya Somadatta, ayaṃ sa Puṣpodbhava iti!» tasmai taṃ darśayam āsa. tau ca cira|viraha|duḥkhaṃ visṛjy' ânyony'|āliṅgana|sukham anvabhūtām. tatas tasy' âiva mahī|ruhasya chāyāyām upaviśya rājā s'|ādara|hāsam abhāṣata:

«Vayasya, bhū|sura|kāryaṃ kariṣṇur ahaṃ mitra|gaṇo vidit'|ârthaḥ sarvath" ântarāyaṃ kariṣyat' îti nidritān bhavataḥ parityajya niragām. tad|anu prabuddho vayasya|vargaḥ kim|iti niścitya mad|anveṣaṇāya kutra gatavān? bhavān ekākī kutra gata iti?»

3.33 So 'pi lalāṭa|taṭa|cumbad|añjali|puṭaḥ sa|vinayam alapata:

iti śrī|Daṇḍinaḥ kṛtau
Daśa|kumāra|carite
Somadatta|caritaṃ
nāma
tṛtīya ucchvāsaḥ.

Raja·váhana hastily embraced him closely, his eyes blossoming, confused with tears of joy, as he pointed out the one to the other:

"Sweet Soma·datta, here is Pushpódbhava!" 3.30

Their suffering at the long separation shed, the two of them enjoyed the pleasure of embracing each other. Then the prince sat down again in the shade of that same tree and with an eager smile said:

"Friend, I wanted to help the brahmin but I thought that if my friends knew my plan they would do everything to block it, so I left you all asleep and went away. Waking up after I had gone, what did my clutch of companions think had happened, and where did they go in search of me? Where, for example, did you go all by yourself?"

Pushpódbhava then cupped his hands together and kissed 3.33
his forehead with them, before relating modestly:

That is the end of the third chapter of
the glorious Dandin's
What Ten Young Men Did.
It is called:
What Soma·datta Did.

CHAPTER FOUR
WHAT PUSHPÓDBHAVA DID

«DEVA, MAHĪ|SUR'|ÔPAKĀRĀY' âiva devo gatavān iti niścity' âpi devena gantavyaṃ deśaṃ nirṇetum a|śaknuvāno mitra|gaṇaḥ paras|paraṃ viyujya dikṣu devam anveṣṭum agacchat. aham api devasy' ânveṣaṇāya mahīm aṭan;

kadā cid ambara|madhya|gatasy' âmbara|maṇeḥ kiraṇam a|sahiṣṇur ekasya giri|taṭa|mahī|ruhasya pracchāya|śītale tale kṣaṇam upāviśam. mama puro|bhāge dina|madhya|saṃkucita|sarv'|âvayavāṃ kūrm'|ākṛtiṃ mānuṣa|chāyāṃ nirīkṣy' ônmukho gagana|talān mahā|rayeṇa patantaṃ puruṣaṃ kiṃ cid antarāla eva day"|ôpanata|hṛdayo 'ham avalambya śanair avani|tale nikṣipya dūr'|āpāta|vīta|saṃjñaṃ taṃ śiśir'|ôpacāreṇa vibodhya śok'|âtireken' ôdgata|bāṣpa|locanaṃ taṃ bhṛgu|patana|kāraṇam apṛccham. so 'pi kara|ruhair aśru|kaṇān apanayann abhāṣata:

4.3 ‹Saumya, Magadh'|âdhināth'|âmātyasya Padmodbhavasy' ātma|saṃbhavo Ratnodbhavo nām' âham. vāṇijya|rūpeṇa Kālayavana|dvīpam upetya kām api vaṇik|kanyakāṃ pariṇīya tayā saha pratyāgacchann ambu|dhau tīrasy' ân|atidūra eva pravahaṇasya bhagnatayā sarveṣu nimagneṣu kathaṃ katham api daiv'|ānukūlyena tīra|bhūmim abhigamya nij'|âṅganā|viyoga|duḥkh'|ârṇave plavamānaḥ kasy' âpi siddha|tāpasasy' ādeś'|ādareṇa ṣoḍaśa hāyanāni kathaṃ cin nītvā duḥkhasya pāram an|avekṣamāṇo giri|patanam akārṣam iti.›

"MY LORD, EVEN THOUGH WE WERE CERTAIN that your lordship had left in order to help the brahmin, we could not deduce which way you had gone. Hence your friends separated one from the other in order to go to look for their lord in every direction. I too roamed the earth in search of your lordship.

One day, unable to bear the rays of the sky's jewel set in the middle of the heavens, I sat down for a moment on the ground in the cool shade of a certain tree growing on a mountain slope. In front of me I espied the shadow of a man, in the shape of a tortoise with all its limbs retracted at midday. Looking up I saw someone falling with great velocity down from the sky. Compassion gripped my heart and I caught him while still just in mid-descent. Laying him gently down on the ground, unconscious after his long fall, I revived him with cool remedies. His extreme suffering drew tears from his eyes as I asked him what had made him fall from the cliff. He wiped away his teardrops with his fingers and explained:

'Good sir, I am Ratnódbhava, the own child of Padmód- 4.3
bhava, minister to the overlord of Mágadha. In the course of my trading I arrived at the island of Kala·yávana. There I married a certain merchant's daughter. As I was returning home with her our vessel was smashed up in the ocean, not at all far from the shore. All were sunk, but somehow thanks to a favorable fate I made it to the shore. Yet I was drowning in an ocean of suffering at the loss of my dear lady. Only out of respect for the command of a certain accomplished ascetic could I bear somehow to keep on living, for another sixteen years. When in the end I still could see no end of

Tasminn ev' âvasare kim api nārī|kūjitam aśrāvi:

‹Na khalu samucitam idaṃ yat siddh'|ādiṣṭe pati|tanaya|milane viraham a|sahiṣṇur vaiśvānaraṃ viśas' îti!›

4.6 Tan niśamya mano|vidita|janaka|bhāvaṃ tam avādiṣam:

‹Tāta, bhavate vijñāpanīyāni bahūni santi. bhavatu. paścād akhilam ākhyātavyam. adhunā nārī|kūjitam an|upekṣaṇīyaṃ mayā. kṣaṇa|mātram atra bhavatā sthīyatām iti.›

Tad|anu so 'haṃ tvarayā kiṃ cid antaram agamam. tatra purato bhayaṃ|kara|jvāl"|ākula|huta|bhug|avagāhana|sāhasikāṃ mukulit'|âñjali|puṭāṃ vanitāṃ kāṃ cid avalokya sa|saṃbhramam analād apanīya kūjantyā vṛddhayā saha mat|pitur abhyarṇam abhigamayya sthavirām avocam:

4.9 ‹Vṛddhe, bhavatyau kutratye? kāntāre nimittena kena du-r|avasth" ânubhūyate? kathyatām iti!›

Sā sa|gadgadam avādīt:

‹Putra, Kālayavana|dvīpe Kālagupta|nāmno vaṇijaḥ kasya cid eṣā sutā Suvṛttā nāma Ratnodbhavena nija|kānten' āgacchantī jaladhau magne pravahaṇe nija|dhātryā mayā saha phalakam ekam avalambya daiva|yogena kūlam upet" āsanna|prasava|samayā kasyāṃ cid aṭavyām ātmajam asūta. mama tu manda|bhāgyatayā bāle vana|mātaṅgena gṛhīte mad|dvitīyā paribhramantī;

my grief, I chose the suicide of throwing myself from the mountain.'*

He had hardly finished when we heard a woman wailing:

'It is quite wrong for you to enter the fire that all men worship because you cannot endure the separation! The *siddha* foretold that you will be reunited with your husband and son.'

Hearing this, I realized that the man before me was my 4.6
father and said to him:

'Father, I have many things to report to you. They can wait. Later I will explain everything. For now I cannot ignore the woman's wails. Please wait here for just one moment.'

And with that I hurried on a little. There before me I saw an unknown woman, her hands pressed together to form a hollow bud of reverence, desperate to plunge into that eater of oblations, the fire, wild with ferocious flames. Rushing to pull her away from the fire, I led both her and the wailing old woman to my father, before asking the elderly lady:

'Old woman, where do you two come from? What are 4.9
you doing in such dire straits in the dreary forest? Please tell us.'

Sobbing she spoke:

'Child, this is Suvrítta, the daughter of a certain merchant called Kala·gupta, from the island of Kala·yávana. She was travelling home with her beloved husband, Ratnódbhava, when their vessel sank in the ocean. With me, her personal nurse, she clambered onto a plank, and fate carried us to shore. The time of her labour arrived, and she gave birth to a son in that strange forest. But through my bad luck a wild

4.12 «ṣoḍaśa|varṣ'|ân|antaraṃ bhartṛ|putra|saṃgamo bhaviṣyat' îti!»

siddha|vākya|viśvāsād ekasmin puṇy'|āśrame tāvantaṃ samayaṃ nītvā śokam apāraṃ soḍhum a|kṣamā samujjvalite vaiśvānare śarīram āhuti|kartum udyukt" āsīd iti.›

Tad ākarṇya nija|jananīṃ jñātvā tām ahaṃ daṇḍavat praṇamya tasyai mad|udantam akhilam ākhyāya dhātrī|bhāṣaṇa|phulla|vadanaṃ vismaya|vikasit'|âkṣaṃ janakam adarśayam. pitarau tau s'|âbhijñānam anyonyaṃ jñātvā mudit'|ântar'|ātmānau vinītaṃ mām ānand'|âśru|varṣeṇ' âbhiṣicya gāḍham āśliṣya śirasy upāghrāya kasyāṃ cin mahīruha|chāyāyām upāviśatām.

4.15 ‹Kathaṃ nivasati mahī|vallabho Rājahaṃsa iti?›

janakena pṛṣṭo 'haṃ tasya rājya|cyutiṃ tvadīya|jananaṃ sakala|kumār'|âvāptiṃ tava dig|vijay'|ārambhaṃ bhavato Mātaṅg'|ânuyānam asmākaṃ yuṣmad|anveṣaṇa|kāraṇaṃ sakalam abhyadhām. tatas tau kasya cid āśrame muner asthāpayam.

Tato devasy' ânveṣaṇa|parāyaṇo 'ham akhila|kārya|nimittaṃ vittaṃ niścitya bhavad|anugrahāl labdhasya sādhakatvasya sāhāyya|karaṇa|dakṣaṃ śiṣya|gaṇaṃ niṣpādya Vindhya|vana|madhye purātana|pattana|sthānāny upetya vividha|

elephant made off with the baby. The two of us wandered about until a *siddha* pronounced:

"After sixteen years you will be reunited with your husband and son!" 4.12

Suvrítta put her trust in this prediction and lived out that period in a holy hermitage. When the time had expired she was unable to bear her boundless grief, and hence had prepared to make an oblation of her body into the flaming fire.'

Listening to her, I realized that Suvrítta was my own mother. I prostrated myself before her, told her everything that had happened to me, and presented to her my father. The nurse's words had made his face bloom, his eyes opened wide with wonder. My parents recognized each other through private signs. Their inner beings were delighted. They anointed modest me with a rain of tears of joy, embraced me tightly, and kissed and smelled me on the head. Then they sat down in the shade of a tree and my father asked me:

'How is King Raja·hamsa, beloved of the Earth?' 4.15

I told him everything: the loss of Raja·hamsa's kingdom, your birth, how all the young men were collected together, your setting out on the conquest of the directions, that you went to accompany Matánga, and why we were searching for you. Then I settled the two of them in a sage's ashram.

My sole priority was the search for your lordship. At the outset I concluded that money is the prime means to achieve every end. Then I gathered a group of disciples who had the know-how to assist me in the magical power I had obtained by your favor. We made for the sites of ancient cities, in the

nidhi|sūcakānāṃ mahīruhāṇām adho|nikṣiptān vasu|pūrṇān kalaśān siddh'|âñjanena jñātvā rakṣiṣu paritaḥ sthiteṣu khanana|sādhanair utpādya dīnārān a|saṃkhyān rāśīkṛtya tat|kāl'|āgatam an|atidūre niveśitaṃ vaṇik|kaṭakam kaṃ cid abhyetya tatra balino balīvardān goṇīś ca krītv" ânya|dravya|miṣeṇa vasu tad|goṇī|saṃcitaṃ tair uhyamānaṃ śanaiḥ kaṭakam anayam.

4.18 Tad|adhikāriṇā Candrapālena kena cid vaṇik|putreṇa viracita|sauhṛdo 'ham amun" âiva sākam Ujjayinīm upāviśam. mat|pitarāv api tāṃ purīm abhigamayya sakala|guṇa|nilayena Bandhupāla|nāmnā Candrapāla|janakena nīyamāno Mālava|nātha|darśanaṃ vidhāya tad|anumatyā gūḍha|vasatim akaravam. tataḥ kānana|bhūmiṣu bhavantam anveṣṭum udyuktaṃ māṃ parama|mitraṃ Bandhupālo niśamy' âvadat:

‹Sakalaṃ dharaṇī|talam apāram anveṣṭum a|kaṣamo bhavān mano|glāniṃ vihāya tūṣṇīṃ tiṣṭhatu. bhavan|nāyak'|ālokana|kāraṇaṃ śubha|śakunaṃ nirīkṣya kathayiṣyām' îti.›

Tal|lapit'|âmṛt'|āśvāsita|hṛdayo 'ham anu|dinaṃ tad|upakaṇṭha|vartī kadā cid indu|mukhīṃ nava|yauvan'|âvalīḍh'|âvayavāṃ nayana|candrikāṃ Bālacandrikāṃ nāma taruṇī|ratnaṃ vaṇiṅ|mandira|Lakṣmīṃ mūrtām iv' âvalokya tadīya|lāvaṇy'|âvadhūta|dhīra|bhāvo lat"|ânta|bāṇa|bāṇa|lakṣyatām ayāsiṣam.

middle of the Vindhya forest. Magic ointment on our eyes revealed pots filled with riches, buried beneath trees that pointed to various sorts of treasure. With guards posted all around, we dug, uncovered the pots and piled up countless gold coins.* Next I approached a caravan of traders, freshly arrived and camped not far away. From them I purchased powerful oxen and loading sacks. We heaped the riches into the sacks, disguising it as some other commodity, and had the oxen carry it to the camp.

I struck up a friendship with the caravan-leader, one 4.18
Chandra·pala, a merchant's son, and together we entered Ujjáyini. I also had my parents brought to that city. Thanks to an introduction from Chandra·pala's father, Bandhu·pala, the repository of every virtue, I arranged an audience with the king of Málava. With his permission I lived there incognito. When Bandhu·pala came to know that I was all set to go in search of you in the forest region, he spoke to me as a best friend:

'It is not possible for you to search all the boundless surface of the earth. Give up the headache and be patient. As soon as I have sighted the auspicious omen* that means that you will see your leader, I will inform you.'

The ambrosia of his words filled my heart with hope. Every day I stayed very close to him, until one time I saw a jewel of a girl, like Lakshmi the goddess of Good Fortune incarnate in the merchant's house. She was Bala·chándrika, 'The young moon'; her face was a moon, her body drenched in fresh youth, and she was moonlight to the eye. My self-possession shaken by her loveliness, I had become the target of Kama the flower-arrowed one's arrows.

4.21 Cakita|bāla|kuraṅga|locanā s" âpi kusuma|sāyaka|sāyak'|ā-yamānena kaṭ'|âkṣa|vīkṣaṇena mām a|sakṛn nirīkṣya manda|mārut'|āndolitā lat" êv' âkampata. manas" âbhimukhaiś ca samākuñcitai rāga|lajj"|ântarāla|vartibhir apāṅga|vartibhir īkṣaṇa|viśeṣair nija|mano|vṛttim akathayat.

Catura|gūḍha|ceṣṭābhir asyā mano|'nurāgaṃ samyag jñātvā sukha|saṃgam'|ôpāyam acintayam.

Anyadā Bandhupālaḥ śakunair bhavad|gatiṃ prekṣiṣyamāṇaḥ pur'|ôpānta|vihāra|vanaṃ mayā sah' ôpetya kasmiṃś cin mahīruhe śakunta|vacanāni śṛṇvann atiṣṭhat. aham utkalikā|vinoda|parāyaṇo van'|ântare paribhraman sarovara|tīre cint"|ākrānta|cittāṃ dīna|vadanāṃ man|mano|rath'|âika|bhūmiṃ Bālacandrikāṃ vyalokayam. tasyāḥ sa|saṃbhrama|prema|lajjā|kautuka|manoramaṃ līlā|vilokana|sukham anubhavan su|datyā vadan'|âravinde viṣaṇṇa|bhāvaṃ madana|kadana|khed'|ânubhūtaṃ jñātvā tan|nimittaṃ jñāsyamī līlayā tad|upakaṇṭham upety' âvocisam:

4.24 ‹Su|mukhi, tava mukh'|âravindasya dainya|kāraṇaṃ kathay' êti.›

Sā rahasya|saṃjāta|viśrambhatayā vihāya lajjā|bhaye śanair abhāṣata:

‹Saumya, Mānasāro Mālav'|âdhīśvaro vārddhakasya prabalatayā nija|nandanaṃ Darpasāram Ujjayinyām abhyaṣiñcat. sa kumāraḥ sapta|sāgara|paryantaṃ mahī|maṇḍalaṃ

Her eyes timid as those of a fawn, she too gazed at me more than once with sidelong glances fatal as Kama's arrows, trembling like a creeper rocked by a gentle breeze. With meaningful glances from the outer corners of her eyes, deliberately curved in my direction and darting between passion and shame, she proclaimed her thoughts. 4.21

Thanks to her clever covert gestures I understood perfectly her mind's affection, and I pondered on a happy way to meet up.

Not long afterward Bandhu·pala was going off to divine your whereabouts by omens, so I went with him to a pleasure grove in the suburbs, where he stood listening to the bird-calls in a particular tree. Preoccupied with how to cast off my lover's longing, I was roaming through the wood when I espied, on the far shore of a lake, Bala·chándrika, the sole object of my desires, her face downcast, her mind invaded with worry. It was a pleasure to watch her lovely looks, all the more entrancing because of its confusion of love, bashfulness and desire. But seeing depression on the fair-toothed one's lotus-face, exhausted by intoxicating love's torment, I wanted to know its cause. I eagerly drew close to her and asked:

'Fair-faced lady, please tell me why your lotus-face is 4.24
dejected.'

Our seclusion gave her confidence, and putting aside embarrassment and fear she spoke softly:

'Good man, in his advancing old age, Mana·sara, the overlord of Málava, has consecrated his own dear son Darpa·sara king of Ujjáyini. That prince was determined to rule the whole sphere of the earth up to the seven seas, so appointed

pālayiṣyan nija|paitṛ|ṣvasrīyāv uddaṇḍa|karmāṇau Caṇḍavarma|Dāruvarmāṇau dharaṇī|bharaṇe niyujya tapaś|caraṇāya Rāja|rāja|girim abhyagāt.

4.27 Rājyaṃ sarvam a|sapatnaṃ śāsati Caṇḍavarmaṇi Dāruvarmā mātul'|âgra|janmanoḥ śāsanam atikramya pāradārya|para|dravy'|âpaharaṇ'|ādi duṣkarma kurvāṇo manmatha|samānasya bhavato lāvaṇy'|āyatta|cittāṃ mām ekadā vilokya kanyā|dūṣaṇa|doṣaṃ dūrīkṛtya balāt|kāreṇa rantum udyuṅkte. tac|cintayā dainyam agaccham iti.›

Tasyā manogatam mayi rāg'|ôdrekam man|mano|ratha|siddhy|antarāyaṃ ca niśamya bāṣpa|pūrṇa|locanāṃ tām āśvāsya Dāruvarmaṇo māraṇ'|ôpāyaṃ ca vicārya vallabhām avocam:

‹Taruṇi, bhavad|abhilāṣiṇaṃ duṣṭa|hṛdayam enaṃ nihantuṃ mṛdur upāyaḥ kaś cin mayā cintyate.

4.30 «Yakṣaḥ kaś cid adhiṣṭhāya Bālacandrikāṃ nivasati.

‹Tad|ākāra|saṃpad|āśā|śṛṅkhalita|hṛdayo yaḥ saṃbandha|yogyaḥ sāhasiko rati|mandire taṃ yakṣaṃ nirjitya tay" âika|sakhī|sametayā mṛg'|âkṣyā saṃlāp'|âmṛta|sukham anubhūya kuśalī nirgamiṣyati, tena cakravāka|saṃśay'|ākāra|payodharā vivāhanīy" êti› siddhen' âiken' âvād' îti.»

his paternal aunt's two despotic sons Chanda·varman and Daru·varman to take care of the land, before going off himself to do penance at Kailash, the mountain of the King of kings.*

While Chanda·varman governs the kingdom without a 4.27
single adversary, Daru·varman rebels against the command of his maternal uncle, Mana·sara, and his elder brother, and perpetrates evil acts like seizing other men's wives and other men's property. One day his eyes fell on me, my heart already lost to your loveliness, so like Kama the enchanter. Regardless of the crime it is to defile a maiden, he is resolved to enjoy me by force. It is worry about this situation which makes me depressed.'

Thus I came to know what was in her mind, about her enormous love for me, and about what stood between me and the achievement of my heart's desire. I comforted her whose eyes were filled with tears, and when I had thought out a way to kill Daru·varman, I told my beloved:

'Gentle girl, I have thought of a subtle way to kill that evil-hearted man who lusts after you. You should have your trustworthy retainers keep spreading the following story among the people of the town:

"Bala·chándrika has been possessed by some *yaksha* that 4.30
inhabits her.* A *siddha* has pronounced:

'If any man's heart is chained to the hope of enjoying her superlative beauty, and if he is bold enough to be worthy of union with her, then let him first conquer the *yaksha*, in the pleasure pavilion. Having done so he will be able to enjoy the ambrosial pleasure of conversation with this doe-eyed lady, chaperoned by a girlfriend, and will exit the pavilion a

Pura|janasya purato bhavadīyaiḥ satya|vākyair janair a|sakṛt kathanīyam. tad|anu Dāruvarmā vākyān' îtthaṃ|vidhāni śrāvaṃ śrāvaṃ tūṣṇīṃ yadi bhiyā sthāsyati tarhi varam, yadi vā daurjanyena tvayā saṅgam aṅgīkariṣyati, tadā sa bhavadīyair itthaṃ vācyaḥ:

4.33 «Saumya, Darpasāra|vasudh"|âdhip'|âmātyasya bhavato 'sman|nivāse sāhasa|karaṇam anucitam. paura|jana|sākṣikaṃ bhavan|mandiram ānītayā tayā toyaj'|âkṣyā saha krīḍann āyuṣmān yadi bhaviṣyasi tadā pariṇīya taruṇīṃ mano|rathān nirviś' êti.»

So 'py etad aṅgīkariṣyati. tvaṃ sakhī|veṣa|dhāriṇā mayā saha tasya mandiraṃ gaccha. aham ek'|ânta|niketane muṣṭi|jānu|pād'|āghātais taṃ rabhasān nihatya punar api vayasyā|miṣeṇa bhavatīm anu niḥśaṅkaṃ nirgamiṣyāmi.

Tad enam upāyam aṅgīkṛtya vigata|sādhvasa|lajjā bhavaj|janaka|jananī|sah'|ôdarāṇāṃ purata āvayoḥ prem'|âtiśayam ākhyāya sarvath" âsmat|pariṇaya|karaṇe tān anunayeḥ. te 'pi vaṃśa|saṃpal|lāvaṇy'|āḍhyāya yūne mahyaṃ tvāṃ dāsyanty eva. Dāruvarmaṇo māraṇ'|ôpāyaṃ tebhyaḥ kathayitvā teṣām uttaram ākhyeyaṃ mahyam iti.›

4.36 S" âpi kiṃ cid utphulla|sarasij'|ânanā mām abravīt:

‹Su|bhaga, krūra|karmāṇaṃ Dāruvarmāṇaṃ bhavān eva hantum arhati. tasmin hate sarvathā yuṣman|mano|rathaḥ phaliṣyati. evaṃ kriyatām. bhavad|uktaṃ sarvam aham api tathā kariṣye. iti›

happy man. Only such a one may marry this woman whose breasts are identical with a pair of *chakra·vaka* birds.'"

Now hearing such talk over and again may make Daru·varman withdraw in fear, and so much the better, but if his wicked nature drives him to want to unite with you, then your people should tell him the following:

"Good sir, it would be improper for you, a minister of 4.33
Darpa·sara, the king of the earth, to commit a violent act in our abode. Before the eyes of the townsfolk you should first lead the lotus-eyed girl to your own house. If there you manage to enjoy the game with her and live, then you can marry the young lady and attain your desires."

Of course, he will choose this option. Dressed as one of your girlfriends, I will accompany you to his house. In a quiet corner I will kill him with violent blows from my fists, knees and feet, before exiting again unharassed behind you, still disguised as your girlfriend.

Agree, then, to this plan and be free of fear and shame. Inform your father and mother and brothers of the tremendous love between us, and persuade them to do all they can to arrange our marriage. They, for their part, are bound to give you to me, a young man rich as I am in good blood, fortune and beauty. Tell them, then, about our plan to kill Daru·varman and let me know their response.'

Her lotus-face bloomed a little and she told me: 4.36

'Dear one, you are the only man who can kill the wicked Daru·varman. With him dead you will enjoy every fruit of your desires. So let it be done. I too will do everything just as you said.'

Mām a|sakṛd|vivṛtta|vadanā vilokayantī mandaṃ mandam agāram agāt. aham api Bandhupālam upetya śakuna|jñāt tasmāt ‹triṃśad|divas'|ân|antaram eva bhavat|saṅgaḥ saṃbhaviṣyat' îty› aśṛṇavam. tad|anu mad|anugamyamāno Bandhupālo nij'|āvāsaṃ praviśya mām api nilayāya visasarja.

4.39 Man|māy"|ôpāya|vāgurā|pāśa|lagnena Dāruvarmaṇā rati|mandire rantuṃ samāhūtā Bālacandrikā taṃ gamiṣyantī dūtikāṃ man|nikaṭam abhipreṣitavatī. aham api maṇi|nūpura|mekhalā|kaṅkaṇa|kaṭaka|tāṭaṅka|hāra|kṣauma|kajjalaṃ vanitā|yogyaṃ maṇḍana|jātaṃ nipuṇatayā tat|tat|sthāneṣu nikṣipya samyag|aṅgīkṛta|manojña|veṣo vallabhayā tayā saha tad|āgāra|dvār'|ôpāntam agaccham.

Dvāḥ|stha|kathit'|âsmad|āgamanena s'|ādaraṃ vihit"|âbhyudgatinā tena dvār'|ôpānta|nivārit'|â|śeṣa|parivāreṇa mad|anvitā Bālacandrikā saṃket'|āgāram anīyata. nagara|vyākulāṃ yakṣa|kathāṃ parīkṣan nāgarika|jano 'pi kutūhalena Dāruvarmaṇaḥ pratīhāra|bhūmim agamat.

Viveka|śūnya|matir asau rāg'|âtirekeṇa ratna|khacita|hema|paryaṅke haṃsa|tūla|garbha|śayanam ānīya taruṇīṃ tasyai mahyaṃ tamisrā|samyag|an|avalokita|puṃ|bhāvāya manorama|strī|veṣāya ca cāmīkara|maṇi|maya|maṇḍanāni sūkṣmāṇi citra|vastrāṇi kastūrikā|militaṃ hari|candanaṃ karpūra|sahitaṃ tāmbūlaṃ surabhīṇi kusumān' îty|ādi|vastu|jātaṃ

Turning her face frequently back to look at me, she made her way ever so slowly home. I in turn returned to Bandhu·pala. That omen expert informed me that after exactly thirty days I would meet you again. Then I accompanied Bandhu·pala to his own house, before he sent me home, too.

Daru·varman was caught, enmeshed in my deceitful plan's 4.39
snare. He invited Bala·chándrika to dally with him in his pleasure pavilion. Before setting out, she sent a confidante to get me. I skillfully deposited at their respective places about my person, all the ornaments a woman should wear: jewelled anklets, girdle, bracelets, gold bangles, earrings, pearls, silks and kohl. Perfectly adapted to my attractive guise, I escorted my beloved to the door of Daru·varman's house.

No sooner had the doorman announced our arrival than Daru·varman came to welcome us courteously in person. Dismissing every one of his servants posted about the door, he led Bala·chándrika, with me her chaperone, to the place of lovers' assignations. The townspeople, too, gathered at Daru·varman's door, curious to verify the *yaksha* story that had rumbled through town.

That man's mind was void of discretion in his overweening passion. He led the young lady to a bed stuffed with goose down, on a golden bedstead studded with jewels. In the dark night and with my costume of an attractive woman he had not noticed my masculinity. So he presented Bala·chándrika and myself with all sorts of items, such as golden and jewelled ornaments, delicate brightly colored fabrics, yellow sandalpaste blended with musk, betel* and fragrant

samarpya muhūrta|dvaya|mātraṃ hāsa|vacanaiḥ saṃlapann atiṣṭhat.

4.42 Tato rāg'|ândhatayā su|mukhī|kuca|grahaṇe matiṃ vyadhatta. roṣ'|âruṇito 'ham enaṃ paryaṅka|talān niḥśaṅko nipātya muṣṭi|jānu|pād'|āghātaiḥ prāharam. niyuddha|rabhasa|vikalam alaṃkāraṃ pūrvavan melayitvā bhaya|kaṃpitāṃ nat'|âṅgīm upalālayan mandir'|âṅgaṇam upetaḥ sādhvasa|kaṃpita iv' ôccair akūjam aham:

‹Hā! Bālacandrik"|âdhiṣṭhitena ghor'|ākāreṇa yakṣeṇa Dāruvarmā nihanyate. sahasā samāgaccha! paśyat' êmam iti!›

Tad ākarṇya militā janāḥ samudyad|bāṣpā hāhā|ninādena diśo badhirayantaḥ.

4.45 ‹Bālacandrikām adhiṣṭhitaṃ yakṣaṃ balavantaṃ śṛṇvann api Dāruvarmā mad'|ândhas tām ev' âyācata. tad asau svakīyena karmaṇā nihataḥ. kiṃ tasya vilāpen' êti?›

mitho lapantaḥ prāviśan. kolāhale tasmiṃś caṭula|locanayā saha naipuṇyena sahasā nirgato nij'|āvāsam agām.

Tato gateṣu katipaya|dineṣu paurajana|samakṣaṃ siddh'|ādeśa|prakāreṇa vivāhya tām indu|mukhīṃ pūrva|saṃkalpitān surata|viśeṣān yath"|êṣṭam anvabhūvam.

4.48 Bandhupāla|śakuna|nirdiṣṭe divase 'smin nirgatya purād bahir vartamāno netr'|ôtsava|kāri bhavad|avalokana|sukham apy anubhavām' îti.»

flowers. For nearly two hours* he went on chatting with jolly talk.

4.42 Thereupon passion blinded him, and he set his mind on seizing the pretty one's breasts. Red with rage, I hurled him at once down from the bedstead, and finished him off with blows of my fists, knees and feet. In the violence of the struggle my ornaments were messed up, so I rearranged them as they were before. Then I comforted my lovely lady, agitated with fear, before going to the courtyard of the house, where I wailed loudly, trembling as though terrified:

'Oh, woe! The dreadful *yaksha* that had possessed Bala·chándrika is killing Daru·varman. Come at once! Look at him!'

On hearing this, everyone gathered together, pouring forth tears. The roar of their howls deafened the directions. But when they were returning home they whispered in private:

4.45 'Daru·varman had heard about the powerful *yaksha* that had possessed Bala·chándrika, but even so, blind with mad desire, he wanted only her. Hence he is killed by his own action, by his own karma.* Why should we mourn him?'

In the confusion, I and she of the lively eyes cunningly and hastily exited, and went home.

A few days later I married the moon-faced one according to the *siddha*'s command, in front of the townspeople. Thereafter we were able to enjoy whenever we wished the kinds of erotic delights previously only imagined.

4.48 Today, on the day predicted by Bandhu·pala's omens, I have come out of the city. Here outside I can enjoy the additional pleasure of seeing you, a feast for my eyes."

Evaṃ mitra|vṛtt'|ântaṃ niśamy' âmlāna|mānaso Rājavāhanaḥ svasya ca Somadattasya ca vṛtt'|ântam asmai nivedya Somadattam:

«Mahākāl'|ēśvar'|ārādhan'|ân|antaraṃ bhavad|vallabhāṃ sa|parivārāṃ nija|kaṭakaṃ prāpayy' āgacch' êti!»

4.51 niyujya Puṣpodbhavena sevyamāno bhū|svargāyamānam Avantikā|puraṃ viveśa. tatra:

«Ayaṃ mama svāmi|kumāra iti.»

Bandhupāl'|ādaye bandhu|janāya kathayitvā tena Rājavāhanāya bahu|vidhāṃ saparyāṃ kārayan ‹sakala|kalā|kuśalo mahī|sura|vara iti› puri prakaṭayan Puṣpodbhavo 'muṣya rājño majjana|bhojan'|ādikam anudinaṃ sva|mandire kārayām āsa.

iti śrī|Daṇḍinaḥ kṛtau
Daśa|kumāra|carite
Puṣpodbhava|caritaṃ
nāma
caturtha ucchvāsaḥ.

On hearing his friend's story, Raja·váhana perked up, and told him his own and Soma·datta's adventures. Then he directed Soma·datta:

"As soon as you have performed your worship to the Lord Maha·kala Shiva, take your beloved wife with her entourage back to her home, and then return here."

Next, with Pushpódbhava in attendance, Raja·váhana en- 4.51
tered Avántika, the city like heaven on earth. There Pushpódbhava announced to Bandhu·pala, "Protector of his friends and relatives," and his own parents:

"Here is my master's son, the prince."

He had them honor Raja·váhana in many ways, presented him in the city as "the best of Brahmins, a god on earth, skilled in every art," and every day prepared for his sovereign a bath, feasting and so on in his own house.

That is the end of the fourth chapter of
the glorious Dandin's
What Ten Young Men Did.
It is called:
What Pushpódbhava Did.

CHAPTER FIVE
WHAT RAJA·VÁHANA DID

«Atha mīna|ketana|senā|nāyakena Malaya|giri|mahīruha|nir|antar'|āvāsi|bhujaṃgama|bhukt'|âvaśiṣṭen' êva sūkṣmatareṇa dhṛta|hari|candana|parimala|bhareṇ' êva manda|gatinā dakṣiṇ'|ânilena viyogi|hṛdaya|sthaṃ man|math'|ânalam ujjvalayan;

sahakāri|kisalaya|makarand'|āsvādana|rakta|kaṇṭhānāṃ madhukara|kala|kaṇṭhānāṃ kākalī|kala|kalena dik|cakraṃ vācālayan, māninī|mānas'|ôtkalikām upanayan, mākanda|sinduvāra|rakt'|âśoka|kiṃśuka|tilakeṣu kalikām upapādayan, Madana|mah"|ôtsavāya rasika|manāṃsi samullāsayan, vasanta|samayaḥ samājagāma.

5.3 Tasminn ati|ramaṇīye kāle 'vantisundarī nāma Mānasāra|nandinī priya|vayasyayā Bālacandrikayā saha nagar'|ôp'|ânta|ramy'|ôdyāne vihār'|ôtkaṇṭhayā paura|sundarī|samavāya|samanvitā kasya cic cūta|potakasya cchāyā|śītale saikata|tale gandha|kusuma|haridr"|âkṣata|cīn'|âmbar'|ādi|nānā|vidhena parimala|dravya|nikareṇa Manobhavam arcayantī reme.

Tatra Rati|pratikṛtim Avantisundarīṃ draṣṭu|kāmaḥ Kāma iva Vasanta|sahāyaḥ Puṣpodbhava|samanvito Rājavāhanas tad upavanaṃ praviśya, tatra tatra Malaya|mārut'|āndolita|śākhā|nirantara|samudbhinna|kisalaya|kusuma|phala|sa-

"NOW THE TIME OF SPRING ARRIVED.* In springtime the southern wind, leader of fish-bannered Kama's army, enflames the fire of desire in the heart of those lovers suffering the pangs of separation. This wind is as extremely subtle as if no more than the leftovers of the air eaten by the serpents* dwelling perpetually in the trees on the Málayan mountains, and it moves slowly as though under the burden of its yellow sandalwood perfume.

In the spring the circle of the quarters chatter with the humming and cooing of bees and cuckoos, sweet-voiced from tasting the honeydew of mango shoots.* This season produces yearning in even a proud woman's heart, and begets buds on mango trees, on *sínduka*, on the red-flowered *ashóka*, red-flowered *kímshuka* and the *tílaka* sesame bush. Spring arouses the minds of passionate men of taste for the great festival of Kama the intoxicator.

At this so delicious time, Avánti·súndari, the beloved 5.3
daughter of Mana·sara, with her dear friend Bala·chándrika, and her entourage of a bevy of town beauties, went out to play in the pleasure garden in the suburbs. On the sandy ground in the cool shade of one particular young mango tree, the princess was delighted to worship 'Mind-made' Kama with every kind of perfumed offering, with sandalwood paste, flowers, turmeric, whole grains of rice and Chinese silk.

Like Kama with Spring personified, Vasánta, as his companion, Raja·váhana entered that garden with Pushpódbhava at his side, in the hope of glimpsing Avánti·súndari there, the likeness of Rati, "Pleasure," Kama's wife. Everywhere the Málayan wind was rocking mango branches that glistened

mullasiteṣu rasāla|taruṣu kokila|kula|kīr'|āli|madhukarāṇām ālāpāñ śrāvaṃ śrāvaṃ kiṃ|cid|vikasad|indīvara|kahlāra|kairava|rājīva|rāji|keli|lola|kalahaṃsa|sārasa|kāraṇḍava|cakravāka|cakravāla|kala|rava|vyākula|vimala|śītala|salila|lalitāni sarāṃsi darśaṃ darśam, a|manda|līlayā lalanā|samīpam avāpa.

Bālacandrikayā ‹niḥśaṅkam ita āgamyatām iti› hasta|saṃjñayā samāhūto nija|tejo|nirjita|Puruhūto Rājavāhanaḥ kṛś'|ôdaryā Avantisundaryā antikaṃ samājagāma.

5.6 Yā Vasanta|sahāyena samutsukatayā Rateḥ kelī|śāla|bhañjikā|vidhitsayā kaṃ cana nārī|viśeṣaṃ viracy' ātmanaḥ krīḍā|kāsāra|śārad'|âravinda|saundaryeṇa pāda|dvayam, udyāna|vana|dīrghikā|matta|marālikā|gamana|rītyā līl"|âlasa|gati|vilāsam, tūṇīra|lāvaṇyena jaṅghe, līlā|mandira|dvāra|kadalī|lālityena manojñam ūru|yugam, jaitra|ratha|cakra|cāturyeṇa ghanaṃ jaghanam;

kiṃ|cid|vikasal|līl"|âvataṃsa|kahlāra|koraka|koṭar'|ânuvṛttyā Gaṅg"|āvarta|sa|nābhiṃ nābhim, saudh'|ārohaṇa|paripāṭyā vali|trayam, maurvī|madhukara|paṅkti|nīlima|līlayā rom'|āvalim, pūrṇa|su|varṇa|kalaśa|śobhayā kuca|dvandvam,

thickly covered with shoots, flowers and fruit. From every branch he kept on hearing* the music of flocks of cuckoos, lines of parrots and big black bees. Wherever he looked there were graceful pools, their pure cool waters resounding with the throaty cries of circles of swans, cranes, *karándava* ducks and *chakra·vaka* birds, splashing playfully among rows of slightly opened blue and sweet-smelling white lotuses, the white lotuses that open at moonrise, and night-flowering water lilies. He strode elegantly toward the woman.

Bala·chándrika invited him with a hand gesture to approach without fear. Raja·váhana's charisma was no match even for Indra, "Invoked by many,"* as he came close to slim-waisted Avánti·súndari.

She glowed with passion as though she had been created by 5.6
Kama himself. Had he whose companion is the Spring been impatient for his wife Rati, and decided to manufacture a substitute creation?* He had put together an extraordinary woman. Her two feet had the beauty of the autumn lotuses in his personal pleasure pool, and the grace of her gait was playful and languid in the manner of the motion of intoxicated swans on the long lakes in the wood in his garden. Her shanks were his lovely quivers, her thighs charming as the delightful plantain trunks at the door to his pleasure house, and her firm hips perfect as the wheels of his victory chariot.

Her navel was like an eddy in the Ganges, in the model of the hollow in the slightly opened sweet-smelling white lotus bud he wore for decoration. The three folds on her belly were arranged like the steps of his mansion, and the line of hair on her abdomen was drawn with the dark-blue

latā|maṇḍapa|saukumāryeṇa bāhū, jaya|śaṅkh'|âbhikhyayā kaṇṭham;

kamanīya|karṇa|pūra|sahakāra|pallava|rāgeṇa pratibimbī-kṛta|bimbaṃ radana|cchadam, bāṇāyamāna|puṣpa|lāvaṇyena śuci|smitam, agra|dūtikā|kala|kaṇṭhikā|kal'|ālāpa|mādhuryeṇa vacana|jātam, sakala|sainika|nāyaka|malaya|māruta|saurabhyeṇa niḥśvāsa|pavanam;

5.9 jaya|dhvaja|mīna|darpeṇa locana|yugalam, cāpa|yaṣṭi|śriyā bhrū|late, prathama|suhṛdaḥ sudh"|ākarasy' âpanīta|kalaṅkayā kāntyā vadanam, līlā|mayūra|barha|bhaṅgayā keśa|pāśaṃ ca vidhāya samasta|makaranda|kastūrikā|saṃmitena Malayaja|rasena prakṣālya karpūra|parāgeṇa saṃmṛjya nirmit" êva rarāja.

Sā mūrtimat" îva Lakṣmīr Mālav'|ēśa|kanyakā sven' âiv' ārādhyamānaṃ saṃkalpita|vara|pradānāy' āvirbhūtaṃ mūrti|mantaṃ Manmatham iva tam ālokya manda|mārut'|āndolitā lat" êva madan'|āveśavatī cakaṃpe. tad|anu krīḍā|viśrambhān nivṛttā lajjayā kāni kāny api bhāv'|ântarāṇi vyadhatta.

prettiness of the row of honeybees that form his bowstring. Her breasts had the splendor of his two golden pots full of auspicious plenty, her two arms the tenderness of his creeper bower, and her neck the famous beauty of his victory conch.

Her lips were not the subject of pale reflected comparison: they could not be likened to the red *bimba* fruit, but were that to which it is compared, the redder of the two, red as the mango bud he wears as a handsome ear ornament. Her pure smile was the beauty of the flowers that served him for arrows. Together her words were honeyed with the soft chatter of the sweet-voiced cuckoo, his leading go-between,* and the fresh air she breathed out had the fragrance of the Málayan breeze that leads all Kama's forces.

Her two eyes were the sparkle of the fish proudly displayed 5.9
on his victory banner, and her creeper-like eyebrows the glorious curve of his bow staff. Her face was formed with the luster, but without the blemishes, of his closest friend, the moon, mine of ambrosia. And it was as though he had arranged her thick tresses in the playful fan of a peacock's tail feathers. He must finally have bathed her with Málayan-grown sandalwood essence blended with musk and the honey of every flower, before dusting her with camphor talc.

This daughter of the Málavan lord was like the embodiment of the goddess Lakshmi. In Raja·váhana she saw* the mind-maddening Kama incarnate, made manifest in order to grant the unspoken wish of the princess who was even then propitiating him. Intoxicating love possessed her, and she trembled like a creeper swayed by the soft breeze. Giving

«Lalanā|janaṃ sṛjatā Vidhātrā nūnam eṣā ghuṇ'|âkṣara|nyāyena nirmitā. no ced Abja|bhūr evaṃ|vidha|nirmāṇa|nipuṇo yadi syāt tarhi tat|samāna|lāvaṇyām anyāṃ taruṇīṃ kiṃ na karot' îti?»

5.12 Sa|vismay'|ânurāgaṃ vilokayatas tasya samakṣaṃ sthātuṃ lajjitā satī kiṃ|cit|sakhī|jan'|ântarita|gātrā tan|nayan'|âbhimukhaiḥ kiṃ|cid|ākuñcitai recita|bhrū|latair apāṅga|vīkṣitair ātmanaḥ kuraṅgasy' ānāyamāna|lāvaṇyaṃ Rājavāhanaṃ vilokayanty atiṣṭhat.

So 'pi tasyās tad" ôtpādita|bhāva|rasānāṃ sāmagyrā labdha|balasy' êva viṣama|śarasya śaravyāyamāṇa|mānaso babhūva.

Sā manas' îttham acintayat:

5.15 «An|anya|sādhāraṇa|saundaryeṇ' ânena kasyāṃ puri bhāgyavatīnāṃ taruṇīnāṃ locan'|ôtsavaḥ kriyate? putra|ratnen' âmunā puraṃdhrīṇāṃ putravatīnāṃ sīmantinīnāṃ kā nāma sīmanta|mauktikī|kriyate? k" âsya devī? kim atr' āgamana|kāraṇam asya? Manmatho mām apahasita|nija|lāvaṇyam enaṃ vilokayantīm asūyay" êv' âtimātraṃ mathnan nija|nāma s'|ânvayaṃ karoti. kiṃ karomi? katham ayaṃ jñātavya iti?»

Tato Bālacandrikā tayor antar|aṅga|vṛttiṃ bhāva|vivekair jñātvā kāntā|samāja|saṃnidhau rāja|nandan'|ôdantasya sam-

up at once her playful sport, embarrassed, she displayed the gamut of conflicting emotions.

"Surely when the Creator was producing womankind it was by chance alone that he created this woman, just like the letters an insect bores by chance into wood.* If not, and if the lotus-born Brahma indeed possesses the skill to create such a one, then why has he made no other girl so lovely?"

Shy to stand exposed before the eyes of the man examining 5.12
her with such wonder and love, she tried to hide herself in the throng of her girlfriends. But Raja·váhana's loveliness held her fast like a deer in a snare, and she stood gazing into his eyes with sidelong glances and arched eyebrows slightly contracted.

His heart in turn became the target of Kama's dangerous, odd number of arrows;* Kama's potency seemingly derived from the compounding of aesthetic emotions and ambrosial sentiments she even then aroused.

She pondered as follows:

"This man is uniquely handsome. In which city are the 5.15
young women blessed with the chance to feast their eyes on him? Which mater familias wears this jewel among sons as the pearl in her headdress? What lady is queen of his heart? Why has he come here? True to his name, mind-maddening Kama torments me beyond measure. Is it because he is jealous that I gaze at this man whose beauty makes his ridiculous? What am I to do? How can I get to know him?"

Thereupon Bala·chándrika discerned the emotions of them both and realized what they felt inside. But she thought that it would be improper to communicate in full before

yag|ākhyānam an|ucitam iti loka|sādhāraṇair vākyair abhāṣata:

«Bhartṛ|dārike ayaṃ sakala|kalā|pravīṇo devatā|sāṃnidhya|karaṇa āhava|nipuṇo bhū|sura|kumāro maṇi|mantr'|âuṣadhi|jñaḥ paricary"|ârho bhavatyā pūjyatām iti.»

5.18 Tad ākarṇya nija|mano|ratham anuvadantyā Bālacandrikayā saṃtuṣṭ'|ântar|aṅgā taraṅg'|āvalī mand'|ânilen' êva Saṃkalpajen' ākulīkṛtā rāja|kanyā jita|Māraṃ kumāraṃ samucit'|āsan'|āsīnaṃ vidhāya sakhī|hastena śastena gandha|kusum'|âkṣata|ghana|sāra|tāmbūl'|ādi|nānā|jāti|vastu|nicayena pūjāṃ tasmai kārayām āsa.

Rājavāhano 'py evam acintayat:

«Nūnam eṣā pūrva|janmani me jāyā Yajñavatī. no ced etasyām evaṃ|vidho 'nurāgo man|manasi na jāyeta. śāp'|âvasāna|samaye tapo|nidhi|dattaṃ jāti|smaratvam āvayoḥ samānam eva. tath" âpi kāla|janita|viśeṣa|sūcaka|vākyair asyā jñānam utpādayiṣyāmi.»

5.21 Tasminn eva samaye ko 'pi manoramo rāja|haṃsaḥ kelī|vidhitsayā tad|upakaṇṭham agamat. samutsukayā rāja|kanyayā marāla|grahaṇe niyuktāṃ Bālacandrikām avalokya:

the assembled ladies the history of the king's dear son, and so she said in conventionally ambiguous words:

*"Princess, here is a young brahmin, a god on earth, versed in all the arts, who can conjure up the deity, skilled in sacrifices, expert in jewels, mantras and medicine. He is worthy of your worship. Please honor him." : "Princess, here is a prince, a god on earth, versed in all the arts, who can conjure up divine dignity, skilled in battles, expert in jewels, mantras and medicine. He is worthy of your attendance. Please be hospitable."**

The king's daughter was delighted at heart to hear this 5.18
echo of her own desires from Bala·chándrika. Mind-born Kama sent a frisson through her, like a row of waves rippled by a gentle breeze. She prepared a seat of honor for the young man, deadly Kama's victor, to sit on, and had her girlfriends offer him hospitality and a multitude of delicacies, such as sandal perfume, flowers, whole grains of rice, camphor and betel *pan*.

Raja·váhana, meanwhile, was wondering the following:

"This lady must have been my wife Yájñavati in a former life. If not, then my heart could not feel such spontaneous affection for her. The pious ascetic promised that as soon as his curse is completed we will both have the same ability to remember our previous lives.* Until then, I shall try to reawaken her memory with significant discourse that is nevertheless appropriate in the circumstances."

That same moment a magnificent royal swan approached 5.21
them in play. Raja·váhana saw that the princess had eagerly prompted Bala·chándrika to catch the bird. Thinking:

«Samucito vāky'|âvasara eṣa iti!»

saṃbhāṣaṇa|nipuṇo Rājavāhanaḥ sa|līlam alapat:

5.24 «Sakhi purā Śāmbo nāma kaś cin mahī|vallabho mano|vallabhayā saha vihāra|vāñchayā kamal'|ākaram avāpya tatra koka|nada|kadamba|samīpe nidr"|âdhīna|mānasaṃ rāja|haṃsaṃ śanair gṛhītvā bisa|guṇena tasya caraṇa|yugalaṃ nigaḍayitvā kāntā|mukhaṃ s'|ânurāgaṃ vilokayan manda|smita|vikasit'|âika|kapola|maṇḍalas tām abhāṣata:

‹Indu|mukhi mayā baddho marālaḥ śānto munivad āste. sv'|êcchay" ânena gamyatām iti!›

So 'pi rāja|haṃsaḥ Śāmbam aśapat:

5.27 ‹Mahī|pāla, yad asminn ambuja|khaṇḍe 'nuṣṭhāna|parāyaṇatayā param'|ānandena tiṣṭhantaṃ naiṣṭhikaṃ māṃ a|kāraṇaṃ rājya|garveṇ' âvamānitavān asi tad etat pāpmanā ramaṇī|viraha|saṃtāpam anubhav' êti!›

Viṣaṇṇa|vadanaḥ Śāmbo jīvit'|ēśvarī|viraham a|sahiṣṇur bhūmau daṇḍavat praṇamya sa|vinayam abhāṣata:

‹Mahā|bhāga yad a|jñānen' âkaravaṃ tat kṣamasv' êti!›

5.30 Sa tāpasaḥ karuṇ"|ākṛṣṭa|cetās tam avadat:

‹Rājan iha janmani bhavataḥ śāpa|phal'|â|bhāvo bhavatu. mad|vacanasy' â|moghatayā bhāvini janane śarīr'|ântaraṃ gatāyā asyāḥ sarasij'|ākṣyā rasena ramaṇo bhūtvā muhūrta|dvayaṃ mac|caraṇa|yugala|bandhana|kāritayā māsa|dvayaṃ śṛṅkhalā|nigaḍita|caraṇo ramaṇī|viyoga|viṣādam anubhūya

"Now is the perfect opportunity to speak."

With supreme eloquence he recounted amusingly:

"Friend, once upon a time, a king called Shamba went 5.24
with his beloved lady to a lake full of lotuses, in search of diversion. There near a cluster of red water lilies was a royal swan, his thoughts in the grip of sleep. The king seized it quickly, binding its feet with a string of lotus fiber. He looked lovingly at the face of his dear lady, his round cheeks blossoming in a soft smile, and said:

'Moon-faced one, the swan I have captured stands at peace like a sage. Set him free to go as he pleases.'

But the royal swan then cursed Shamba:

'O king, I am a renunciate.* I was standing in this cluster 5.27
of lotuses in utter bliss, thanks to my total focus on my austerities, when you in your royal arrogance did me wrong, quite unprovoked. To pay for this sin you shall experience the torture of separation from your lovely lady!'

Shamba's face fell. Unable to bear separation from the queen of his heart he prostrated himself full-length on the ground and humbly asked:

'Greatly blessed one, please forgive me, for I knew not what I did!'

Compassion tugged at the ascetic's heart, and he said: 5.30

'Very well, king, you will not reap the fruit of my curse in this life. But my word is infallible. Therefore, in a future birth, just when you are relishing the love of this lotus-eyed woman, then herself also in another body, because you bound my feet for two moments you will have to suffer the depression of separation from your lovely lady for two months, with your own feet bound in chains. But afterward

paścād an|eka|kālaṃ vallabhayā saha rājya|sukhaṃ labhasv' êti!›

Tad|anu jāti|smaratvam api tayor anvagṛhṇāt. tasmān marāla|bandhanaṃ na karaṇīyaṃ tvay" êti.»

5.33 S" âpi bhartṛ|dārikā tad|vacan'|ākarṇan'|âbhijñāta|sva|purātana|janana|vṛtt'|ântā:

«Nūnam ayaṃ mat|prāṇa|vallabha iti.»

Manasi jānatī rāga|pallavita|mānasā sa|manda|hāsam avocat:

5.36 «Saumya, purā Śāmbo Yajñavatī|saṃdeśa|paripālanāya tathā|vidhaṃ haṃsa|bandhanam akārṣīt. tathā hi loke paṇḍitā api dākṣiṇyen' â|kāryaṃ kurvant' îti.»

Kanyā|kumārāv evam anyonya|purātana|janana|nāmadheye paricite paras|para|jñānāya s'|âbhijñam uktvā manoja|rāga|pūrṇa|mānasau babhūvatuḥ.

Tasminn avasare Mālav'|êndra|mahiṣī parijana|parivṛtā duhitṛ|kelī|vilokanāya taṃ deśam avāpa. Bālacandrikā tu tāṃ dūrato vilokya sa|saṃbhramaṃ rahasya|nirbheda|bhiyā hasta|saṃjñayā Puṣpodbhava|sevyamānaṃ Rājavāhanaṃ vṛkṣa|vāṭik"|ântarita|gātram akarot.

5.39 Sā Mānasāra|mahiṣī sakhī|sametāyā duhitur nānā|vidhāṃ vihāra|līlām anubhavantī kṣaṇaṃ sthitvā duhitrā sametā nij'|āgāra|gamanāy' ôdyuktā babhūva. mātaram anugacchanty Avantisundarī:

you and your beloved wife, together again, will enjoy the pleasures of kingship for a long time.'

With that he also granted them both the power to remember their previous lives. And so the moral of the story is that you should not bind the swan."

Listening to his speech, the princess too recollected the 5.33
events of her former incarnation. She realized in her heart:

"This man must have been the love of my life."

Her heart blushed with budding love, and smiling sweetly she said:

"Gentle sir, Shamba of old bound the swan like that only 5.36
to grant Yájñavati's request. For thus even the world's wise men do out of gallantry what they really should not do at all."

And so the maiden and the young man had learned each other's names from the previous birth, spoken deliberately so that they might recognize each other, and their hearts overflowed with mind-born love.

At that same time the queen* of Málava was coming there with her entourage to watch her daughter at play. But Bala·chándrika saw her from a distance. Lest their secret be betrayed, she made a hasty hand gesture for Raja·váhana and, with him, Pushpódbhava to hide themselves in an avenue of trees.

Mana·sara's queen stayed a moment, partaking of the var- 5.39
ious playful diversions of her daughter and her girlfriends, and then she was ready to take her home. While Avánti·súndari followed her mother, she directed a perfect speech toward the prince, pretending to address a swan:

«Rājahaṃsa|kula|tilaka vihāra|vāñchayā kelī|vane mad|antikam āgataṃ bhavantam akāṇḍa eva visṛjya mayā samucitam iti janany|anugamanaṃ kriyate. tad anena bhavan|mano|rāgo 'nyathā mā bhūd iti!»

marālam iva kumāram uddiśya samucit'|ālāpa|kalāpaṃ vadantī punaḥ punaḥ parivṛtta|dīna|nayanā vadanaṃ vilokayantī nija|mandiram agāt.

5.42 Tatra hṛdaya|vallabha|kathā|prasaṅge Bālacandrikā|kathita|tad|anvaya|nāmadheyā Manmatha|bāṇa|patana|vyākula|mānasā viraha|vedanayā dine dine bahula|pakṣa|śaśi|kal" êva kṣāma|kṣām" āhār'|ādi|sakala|vyāpāraṃ parihṛtya rahasya|mandire Malayaja|rasa|kṣālita|pallava|kusuma|kalpita|talpa|tal'|āvarti|tanu|latā babhūva.

Tatra tathā|vidh'|âvasthām anubhavantīṃ Manmath'|ânala|saṃtaptāṃ su|kumārīṃ kumārīṃ nirīkṣya khinno vayasyā|gaṇaḥ kāñcana|kalaśa|saṃcitāni hari|candan'|ôśīra|ghana|sāra|militāni tad|abhiṣeka|kalpitāni salilāni bisa|tantu|mayāni vāsāṃsi ca nalinī|dala|mayāni tāla|vṛntāni ca saṃtāpa|haraṇāni bahūni saṃpādya tasyāḥ śarīram aśiśirayat. tad api śītal'|ôpacaraṇaṃ salilam iva tapta|taile tad|aṅge dahanam eva samantād āviścakāra.

Kiṃ|kartavyatā|mūḍhāṃ viṣaṇṇāṃ Bālacandrikām īṣad|unmīlitena kaṭ'|âkṣa|vīkṣitena bāṣpa|kaṇ'|ākulena vilokya virah'|ânal'|ôṣṇa|niḥśvāsa|glapit'|âdharayā nat'|âṅgyā śanaiḥ sa|gadgadaṃ vyalāpi:

"O most gorgeous of all Raja·hamsas, 'royal swans,' you approached me in the pleasure grove looking for entertainment. Now quite suddenly I must take my leave of you, duty-bound to accompany my mother. But please do not let this affect the way you feel!"*

And she went home, turning her sad eyes back again and again to look at his face.

At home, they talked about her heart's beloved and Bala· 5.42
chándrika told her his lineage and name. Mind-tormenting Kama's arrows fell thick and fast on her heart. Wretched at the separation, she shunned all activity, starting with eating, and each day became more and more emaciated, like the digits of the waning moon.* In her boudoir her slender frame found no rest on her bed of blossom and flowers, splashed with Málayan sandalwood juice.

Her girlfriends were desolate to see their delicate princess in such a dreadful state, burning with Kama's fire. They gathered together many remedies to stop the fever and tried to cool her body with them: water for her bath collected in golden vases mixed with green sandal, *ushíra** and camphor, and garments spun from lotus fibers, as well as fans woven from lotus leaves. But the application of even those cooling remedies only heightened the burning all over her body, like water on hot oil.

Bala·chándrika was in despair, with no idea how to help. Then the graceful Avánti·súndari opened her tear-filled eye just a little and looked at her sidelong. Her lower lip was parched from the hot sighs of the fire of separation. Sobbing softly, she spoke:

5.45 «Priya|sakhi, Kāmaḥ ‹kusum'|āyudhaḥ› ‹pañca|bāṇa› iti nūnam a|satyam ucyate. iyam aham ayo|mayair a|saṃkhyair iṣubhir anena hanye.

Sakhi, candramasaṃ vāḍav'|ânalād atitāpa|karaṃ manye. yad asminn antaḥ praviśati śuṣyati pārāvāraḥ. sati nirgate tad" âiva vardhate. doṣ'|ākarasya duṣkarma kiṃ varṇyate mayā. yad anena nija|sah'|ôdaryāḥ Padm'|ālayāyā geha|bhūtam api kamalaṃ vihanyate.

Virah'|ânala|saṃtapta|hṛdaya|sparśena nūnam uṣṇīkṛtaḥ svalpībhavati Malay'|ânilaḥ. nava|pallava|kalpitaṃ talpam idam An|aṅg'|âgni|śikhā|paṭalam iva saṃtāpaṃ tanos tanoti. hari|candanam api purā nija|yaṣṭi|saṃśleṣavad|uraga|radana|lipt'|ôlbaṇa|garala|saṃkalitam iva tāpayati śarīram.

5.48 Tasmād alam alam āyāsena śītal'|ôpacāre. lāvaṇya|jita|Māro rāja|kumāra ev' âgadaṃkāro Manmatha|jvar'|âpaharaṇe. so 'pi labdhum a|śakyo mayā. kiṃ karom' îti?»

Bālacandrikā Manoja|jvar'|âvasthā|parama|kāṣṭhāṃ gatāṃ komal'|âṅgī tāṃ Rājavāhana|lāvaṇy'|âdhīna|mānasām an|anya|śaraṇām avekṣy' ātmany acintayat:

«Kumāraḥ sa|tvaram ānetavyo mayā. no ced enāṃ smaraṇīyāṃ gatiṃ neṣyati mīna|ketanaḥ. tatr' ôdyāne kumārayor

"Dear friend. It is false to call Kama 'flower-weaponed,' or 'five-arrowed.' Here I am, under attack from innumerable arrows, and every one cast in iron. 5.45

Friend, I feel the moon burning stronger than the fire under the sea.* For the ocean evaporates only when those fires enter it, and as soon as they have left the ocean grows again. How can I describe the dreadful deeds of this maker of the night, the moon, 'a mine of faults'?* For he destroys the lotus of the day even though it is the home of his own sister, 'Lotus-dwelling' Lakshmi.*

My heart burns with the fire of separation such that the Málayan breeze cannot but be burned out of existence when it touches me. This bed made of fresh buds feeds the burning of my body as though it were spread with invisible Kama's fire. Even green sandalwood paste burns my body as if infected with virulent poison smeared from the fangs of serpents that used to cling to its tree trunk.

So please, enough, enough of these cooling remedies. 5.48
Only the royal youth, in loveliness deadly Kama's conqueror, he is the only physician who can cure me of the fever of Mind-tormenting Love. But I cannot have him. What is to become of me?"

Bala·chándrika realized that the tender-limbed one had reached the ultimate paroxysm of Love-fever, and that her heart was set on Raja·váhana's beauty, and no other would avail, so she thought to herself:

"I must hurry to bring the prince! Otherwise Kama of the fish banner will reduce her to no more than a memory. When the two young people were looking at each other there in the garden, Kama, said to be uneven with his arrows,

anyony'|âvalokana|velāyām a|sama|sāyakaḥ samaṃ mukta|sāyako 'bhūt. tasmāt kumār'|ānayanaṃ su|karam.»

5.51 Tato 'vantisundarī|rakṣaṇāya samay'|ôcita|karaṇīya|caturaṃ sakhī|gaṇaṃ niyujya rāja|kumāra|mandiram avāpa.

Puṣpa|bāṇa|bāṇa|tūṇīrāyamāna|mānaso 'n|aṅga|tapt'|âvayava|saṃparka|parimlāna|pallava|śayanam adhiṣṭhito Rājavāhanaḥ prāṇ'|ēśvarīm uddiśya saha Puṣpodbhavena saṃlapann āgatāṃ priya|vayasyām ālokya pāda|mūlam;

anveṣaṇīyā lat" êva Bālacandrik" āgat" êti saṃtuṣṭa|manā niṭila|taṭa|maṇḍanībhavad|ambuja|korak'|ākṛti|lasad|añjali|puṭām ‹ito niṣīd' êti› nirdiṣṭa|samucit'|āsan'|āsīnām Avantisundarī|preṣitaṃ sa|karpuraṃ tāmbūlaṃ vinayena dadatīṃ tāṃ kāntā|vṛtt'|ântam apṛcchat. tathā sa|vinayam abhāṇi:

5.54 «Deva krīḍā|vane bhavad|avalokana|kālam ārabhya Manmatha|mathyamānā puṣpa|talp'|ādiṣu tāpa|śamanam a|labhamānā vāmanen' êv' ônnata|taru|phalam a|labhyaṃ tvad|uraḥ|sthal'|āliṅgana|saukhyaṃ smar'|ândhatayā lipsuḥ sā svayam eva patrikām ālikhya ‹vallabhāy' âinām arpay' êti› māṃ niyuktavatī.»

Rāja|kumāraḥ patrikāṃ tām ādāya papāṭha:

«su|bhaga kusuma|su|kumāraṃ
    jagad|an|a|vadyaṃ vilokya te rūpam
mama mānasam abhilaṣati
    tvaṃ cittaṃ kuru tathā mṛdulam iti!»

fired his weapons equally at them both. Hence it will be easy to fetch the prince."

Thereupon she posted a group of girlfriends expert in the requirements of the situation to take care of Avánti·súndari, before hurrying to the royal youth's house. 5.51

Raja·váhana's heart had become a quiver for the arrows of flower-arrowed Kama. He had taken to his bed spread with buds that had withered at the touch of his limbs on fire with invisible Love. There he was talking with Push-pódbhava about the Lady mistress of his life when he saw that his beloved's friend had come.

Her hands were folded in greeting like a glistening lotus bud ornamenting her broad forehead. Overjoyed at Bala·chándrika's arrival, like a long-sought slender plant, he directed her to sit in the seat of honor, which she did. She respectfully gave him betel mixed with sandalwood sent by Avánti·súndari, while he asked her for news of his beloved girl. Demure, she told him:

"Lord, ever since she saw you in the pleasure grove she 5.54
has been tortured by mind-tormenting Kama. Not in her bed of flowers or anywhere can she find relief from the fire. Blind with love,* she longs for the pleasure of embracing your breast, as out of reach as fruit on a tall tree for a dwarf. She has written you a note, which she charged me to deliver to her beloved."

The royal youth took the note and read:

"Good sir, since seeing your blameless beauty,
which nobody can deny, tender as a flower,
my heart deeply desires that you please
make your heart equally tender."

5.57 paṭhitvā s'|ādaram abhāṣata:

«Sakhi chāyāvan mām anuvartamānasya Puṣpodbhavasya vallabhā tvam eva tasyā mṛgī|dṛśo bahiścarāḥ prāṇā iva vartase. tvac|cāturyam asyāṃ kriyā|latāyām ālavālam abhūt. tad akhilaṃ kariṣyāmi.

Nat'|âṅgyā man|manaḥ|kāṭhinyam ākhyātam. yadā kelī|vane kuraṅga|locanā locana|patham avartata tad" âiv' âpahṛta|madīya|mānasā sā sva|mandiram agāt. sā cetaso mādhurya|kāṭhinye svayam eva jānāti.

5.60 Duṣkaraḥ kany"|ântaḥ|pura|praveśaḥ. tad|anurūpam upāyam upapādya śvaḥ paraśvo vā nat'|âṅgīṃ saṃgamiṣyāmi. mad|udantam evam ākhyāya śirīṣa|kusuma|su|kumārāyā yathā śarīra|bādhā na jāyeta tathā|vidham upāyam ācar' êti!»

Bālacandrik" âpi tasya prema|garbhitaṃ vacanam ākarṇya saṃtuṣṭā kanyā|puram agacchat.

Rājavāhano 'pi yatra hṛdaya|vallabh'|âvalokana|sukham alabhata tad udyānaṃ viraha|vinodāya Puṣpodbhava|samanvito jagāma. tatra cakora|locan'|âvacita|pallava|kusuma|nikurambaṃ mahīruha|samūhaṃ, śarad|indu|mukhyā Manmatha|samārādhana|sthānaṃ ca, nat'|âṅgī|pada|paṅkti|cihnitaṃ śītala|saikata|talaṃ ca, sudatī|bhukta|muktaṃ mādhavī|latā|maṇḍap'|ântara|pallava|talpaṃ ca vilokayaṃl;

And after reading it he spoke earnestly: 5.57

"Friend, you are the beloved wife of Pushpódbhava, my companion constant as my shadow. More than that, you are like my doe-eyed lady's second soul. Your quick wit is the water trench to this business's climbing plant. Therefore I shall do exactly as she wishes.

The graceful woman referred to the hardness of my heart. But no sooner had I caught sight of her with her deer-eyes in the pleasure grove than she robbed me of my heart and took it home with her. She must decide for herself how tender or hard it is.

It is not easy to penetrate a women's harem. I must come 5.60
up with a fitting plan to do so, and then tomorrow or the day after I will call on the elegant girl. Please tell her my news and tend her so that she suffers no physical pain, for she is delicate as a *shirísha* flower."*

Delighted at his speech, pregnant with love, Bala·chándrika returned to the harem.

Hoping to shake off his pangs at their separation, Raja·váhana left with Pushpódbhava for the same garden where he had found joy in glimpsing his heart's beloved. There he saw the groves where she of *chakóra* partridge eyes had harvested a heap of buds and flowers, where she of the broad autumn-moon face had worshipped Kama, the cool sandy ground stamped with a row of her footprints, and the blossom couch within the spring creeper bower where his fair-toothed one had lain but which now was abandoned.

5.63 lalanā|tilaka|vilokana|velā|janita|śeṣāṇi smāraṃ smāraṃ manda|māruta|kaṃpitāni nava|cūta|pallavāni Madan'|âgni|śikhā iva cakito darśaṃ darśaṃ Manoja|karṇe|japānām iva kokila|kīra|madhukarāṇāṃ kvaṇitāni śrāvaṃ śrāvaṃ Māra|vikāreṇa kva cid apy avasthātum a|sahiṣṇuḥ paribabhrāma.

Tasminn avasare dharaṇī|sura ekaḥ sūkṣma|citra|nivasanaḥ sphuran|maṇi|kuṇḍala|maṇḍito muṇḍita|mastaka|mānava|sametaś catura|veṣa|manoramo yad|ṛcchayā samāgataḥ samantato 'bhyullasat|tejo|maṇḍalaṃ Rājavāhanam āśīr|vāda|pūrvakaṃ dadarśa. rājā s'|ādaram:

«Ko bhavān? kasyāṃ vidyāyāṃ nipuṇa iti?»

5.66 taṃ papraccha. sa ca:

«Vidyeśvara|nāmadheyo 'ham, aindrajālika|vidyā|kovidaḥ, vividha|deśeṣu rāja|mano|rañjanāya bhramann Ujjayinīm ady' āgato 'sm' îti»

śaśaṃsa. punar api Rājavāhanaṃ samyag ālokya:

5.69 «Asyāṃ līlā|vanau pāṇḍuratā|nimittaṃ kim iti?»

s'|âbhiprāyaṃ vihasy' âpṛcchat. Puṣpodbhavaś ca nija|kārya|karaṇaṃ tarkayann enam ādareṇa babhāṣe:

«Nanu satāṃ sakhyasy' ābhāṣaṇa|pūrvatay" â|ciraṃ rucira|bhāṣaṇo bhavān asmākaṃ priya|vayasyo jātaḥ. suhṛdām a|kathyaṃ ca kim asti?

All the time he kept remembering the tiniest irrelevant detail of meeting his perfect woman. He trembled to see everywhere the new mango sprigs being shaken by the gentle breeze, as though they were the flames of maddening Kama's fire, and he kept on hearing the hum of cuckoos, parrots and honeybees, which could have been tattlers to mind-born Kama. Unable to find peace anywhere, thanks to the metamorphosis wrought by deadly Kama, restless he roamed. 5.63

At that moment a brahmin chanced to arrive, most attractive in a handsome outfit of gorgeous fine cloth, adorned with sparkling jewel earrings, and accompanied by shaven-headed men. When he saw Raja·váhana radiating a circle of charisma in every direction, he pronounced a blessing. The prince respectfully asked him:

"Who are you, and in what science is your expertise?"

To which the brahmin declared: 5.66

"My name is Vidyéshvara, 'Master of science,' and Indra's web of magic is my forte.* Peripatetic from country to country for the entertainment of kings, I am today come to Ujjáyini."

He looked at Raja·váhana carefully again, and with a knowing laugh asked:

"Why so pale in the pleasure garden?" 5.69

Pushpódbhava, realizing that this man could assist in their project, addressed him with respect:

"In truth, a little conversation is the prelude to friendship among good men. Your pleasant words have made you instantly our dear friend. And what can one not divulge to a friend?

5.72 Kelī|vane 'smin vasanta|mah"|ôtsavāy' āgatāyā Mālav'|êndra|sutāyā rāja|nandanasy' âsya c' ākasmika|darśane 'nyony'|ânurāg'|âtirekaḥ samajāyata. satata|saṃbhoga|siddhy|upāy'|âbhāven' âsāv īdṛśīm avasthām anubhavat' îti.»

Vidyeśvaro lajj"|âbhirāmaṃ rāja|kumāra|mukham abhivīkṣya viracita|manda|hāso vyājahāra:

«Deva, bhavad|anucare mayi tiṣṭhati tava kāryam a|sādhyaṃ kim asti. aham indra|jāla|vidyayā Mālav'|êndraṃ mohayan paurajana|samakṣam eva tat|tanayā|pariṇayaṃ racayitvā kany"|ântaḥ|pura|praveśaṃ kārayiṣyām' îti vṛtt'|ânta eṣa rāja|kanyakāyai sakhī|mukhena pūrvam eva kathayitavya iti.»

5.75 Saṃtuṣṭamanā mahī|patir a|nimittaṃ mitraṃ prakaṭīkṛta|kṛtrima|kriyā|pāṭavaṃ vipralambha|kṛtrima|prema|sahaja|sauhārda|vedinaṃ taṃ Vidyeśvaraṃ sa|bahumānaṃ visasarja.

Atha Rājavāhano Vidyeśvarasya kriyā|pāṭavena phalitam iva mano|rathaṃ manyamānaḥ Puṣpodbhavena saha sva|mandiram upetya s'|ādaraṃ Bālacandrikā|mukhena nija|vallabhāyai mahī|sura|kriyamāṇaṃ saṃgam'|ôpāyaṃ vedayitvā kautuk'|ākṛṣṭa|hṛdayaḥ:

«Katham imāṃ kṣapāṃ kṣapayām' îti?»

5.78 atiṣṭhat. pare|dyuḥ prabhāte Vidyeśvaro rasa|bhāva|rīti|gati|caturas tādṛśena mahatā nija|parijanena saha rāja|bhavana|dvār'|ântikam upetya dauvārika|nivedita|nija|vṛtt'|ântaḥ

The daughter of the king of Málava came to this pleasure grove to celebrate the great spring festival. When she and this prince happened to set eyes on each other it was true love at first sight. Now, as you see, he is suffering because we cannot figure out how to win her for him to enjoy forever." 5.72

Vidyéshvara observed how the royal youth was lovely in his embarrassment, and with a gentle smile said:

"Prince, there is nothing you cannot do, if you have me as your assistant. Through my magical skills I shall confound the king of Málava, contrive your marriage with his daughter right before the eyes of the population, and arrange for you to penetrate the women's harem. But we must have one of her girlfriends let the princess know in advance what is going to happen."

The prince was overjoyed. His new friend, who had no reason to be nice to him, had revealed his genius at artifice but also knew well the difference between fake affection and spontaneous love. He took his leave of Vidyéshvara with great reverence. 5.75

Thanks to Vidyéshvara's skill at the game, Raja·váhana felt as though his dreams had already come true. After he had gone home with Pushpódbhava, they politely asked Bala·chándrika to inform his beloved about the plan that the brahmin had devised to bring them together. Impatience tugging at his heart he waited, thinking:

"How shall I get through this night?"

At dawn the following day, Vidyéshvara, that master of the modes and manipulation of taste and sentiment, approached the gate of the royal palace with his great troupe of similarly gifted performers. He gave an account of him- 5.78

sahas" ôpagamya sa|praṇāmam ‹aindrajālikaḥ samāgata' îti› dvaḥ|sthair vijñāpitena tad|darśana|kutūhal'|āviṣṭena samutsuk'|âvarodha|sahitena Mālav'|êndreṇa samāhūyamānaḥ; Vidyeśvaraḥ kakṣ"|ântaraṃ praviśya sa|vinayam āśiṣaṃ dattvā tad|anujñātaḥ parijana|tāḍyamāneṣu vādyeṣu nadatsu, gāyakīṣu mada|kala|kolikā|mañjula|dhvaniṣu samadhika|rāga|rañjita|sāmājika|mano|vṛttiṣu, picchikā|bhramaṇeṣu sa parivāraṃ parivṛtaṃ bhrāmayan mukulita|nayanaḥ kṣaṇam atiṣṭhat.

Tad|anu viṣamaṃ viṣam ulbaṇaṃ vamantaḥ phaṇ'|âlaṃkaraṇā ratna|rāji|nīrājita|rāja|mandir'|ābhogā bhogino bhayaṃ janayanto niśceruḥ. gṛdhrāś ca bahavas tuṇḍair ahi|patīn ādāya divi samacaran. tato 'gra|janmā Nara|siṃhasya Hiraṇyaka|śipor daity'|ēśvarasya vidāraṇam abhinīya mahad|āścary'|ânvitaṃ rājānam abhāṣata:

5.81 «Rājan, avasāna|samaye bhavatā śubha|sūcakaṃ draṣṭum ucitam. tataḥ kalyāṇa|paraṃpar'|âvāptaye bhavad|ātmaj"|ākārāyās taruṇyā nikhila|lakṣaṇ'|ôpetasya rāja|nandanasya ca vivāhaḥ kārya iti.»

Tad|avalokana|kutūhalena mahī|pālen' ânujñātaḥ sa saṃkalpit'|ârtha|siddhi|saṃbhāvana|saṃphulla|vadanaḥ sakala|moha|janakam añjanaṃ locanayor nikṣipya parito vyalokayat.

self to the doorkeeper, who immediately went to inform the Málavan king with a bow that a magician had arrived. The king was deeply curious to see him, and his harem was particularly keen, so the magician was invited to come in.

Entering the inner hall, Vidyéshvara humbly gave his blessing. With the king's permission the show commenced. His company began to beat their thundering drums, female singers sang sweet as the intoxicated melody of cuckoos, and, waving his peacock-feather wand to move his entourage in a ring around him, Vidyéshvara seduced the minds of all present into ever greater enthusiasm. With eyes pressed shut like buds he stood for a moment still.

Next appeared serpents dangerously spitting* virulent venom. Their hoods flared dramatically, the lines of jewels on their heads illuminated the palace, and they bred fear. Then flocks of vultures thronged the sky, seizing those king snakes in their beaks. Finally the brahmin conjured up Nara·simha, half man, half lion, tearing to pieces Hiránya·káshipu, lord of the *daitya* demons,* before announcing to the greatly amazed king:

"Your Majesty, for the finale you deserve to see something 5.81
that bodes well. And so, in order that you obtain a blessed succession, allow us to present the marriage of a young woman who has your own daughter's looks to a royal prince endowed with all the marks of distinction."

Eager for the spectacle, the king gave his permission. Vidyéshvara's face bloomed at the prospect of his wishes being fulfilled. He smeared both his eyes with a magic ointment to delude everyone and gazed all around.

Sarveṣu ‹tad aindrajālikam eva karm' êti› s'|âdbhutaṃ paśyatsu rāga|pallavita|hṛdayena Rājavāhanena pūrva|saṃketa|samāgatām an|eka|bhūṣaṇa|bhūṣit'|âṅgīm Avantisundarīṃ vaivāhika|mantra|tantra|naipuṇyen' âgniṃ sākṣīkṛtya saṃyojayām āsa. kriy"|âvasāne sati:

5.84 «Indrajāla|puruṣāḥ, sarve gacchantu bhavanta iti!» dvi|janman" ôccair ucyamāne sarve māyā|mānavā yathā|yatham antarbhāvaṃ gatāḥ. Rājavāhano 'pi pūrva|saṃkalpitena gūḍh'|ôpāya|cāturyeṇ' âindrajālika|puruṣavat kany"|ântaḥ|puraṃ viveśa. Mālav'|êndro 'pi tad|adbhutaṃ manyamānas tasmai vāḍavāya pracurataraṃ dhanaṃ dattvā, Vidyeśvaram ‹idānīṃ sādhay' êti› visṛjya svayam antar|mandiraṃ jagāma.

Tato 'vantisundarī priya|sahacarī|vara|parivārā vallabh'|ôpetā sundaraṃ mandiraṃ yayau. evaṃ daiva|mānuṣa|balena mano|ratha|sāphalyam upeto Rājavāhanaḥ sa|rasa|madhura|ceṣṭābhiḥ śanaiḥ śanair hariṇa|locanāyā lajjām apanayan surata|rāgam upanayan raho viśrambham upajanayan saṃlāpe tad|anulāpa|pīyūṣa|pāna|lolaś citra|citraṃ citta|hāriṇaṃ catur|daśa|bhuvana|vṛtt'|ântaṃ śrāvayām āsa.

iti śrī|Daṇḍinaḥ kṛtau
Daśa|kumāra|carite
'vantisundarī|pariṇayo
nāma
pañcama ucchvāsaḥ.
Samāpt" êyaṃ
Daśa|kumāra|carita|Pūrva|pīṭhikā.

In amazement everybody watched what they thought was a magic trick. Avánti·súndari had come as planned, her body adorned with every ornament. With the fire as a witness and with his skill in wedding hocus-pocus, Vidyéshvara joined her in marriage to Raja·váhana, whose heart sprouted with love. At the close of the performance the brahmin twice-born cried loudly:

"Magic creatures, may you all be gone!" 5.84

At his words every illusory person vanished, one after the other. Raja·váhana too entered the women's harem as though he were a magical man, according to the prearranged cunning secret plan. As for the Málavan king, he thought it was a wonder and bestowed on the brahmin a great abundance of wealth. Giving Vidyéshvara leave to stop now, he dismissed him, and withdrew to his private apartments.

Then Avánti·súndari went with her beloved husband to her splendid chamber, accompanied by her dear best friends. Thus, with both supernatural and human help, Raja·váhana had obtained the fruit of his desires. With honeyed gestures of affection he very gradually banished the doe-eyed one's coyness, initiated her to the erotic pleasures and in private begot her confidence. Greedy to drink the nectar of conversation with her, he narrated the simply marvelous captivating stories of the fourteen worlds.*

That is the end of the fifth chapter of
the glorious Dandin's
What Ten Young Men Did.
It is called: The Marriage of Avánti·súndari.
Part I, the Front Book of
What Ten Young Men Did, is completed.

PART II:
DANDIN'S DASHA·KUMÁRA·CHÁRITA*

CHAPTER SIX
WHAT RAJA·VÁHANA DID NEXT

Śrutvā tu bhuvana|vṛtt'|ântam uttam'|âṅganā vismaya|vikasit'|âkṣī sa|smitam idam abhāṣata:

«Dayita tvat|prasādād adya me carit'|ârthā śrotra|vṛttiḥ. adya me manasi tamo|'pahas tvayā datto jñāna|pradīpaḥ. pakvam idānīṃ tvat|pāda|padma|paricaryā|phalam. asya ca tvat|prasādasya kim upakṛtya pratyupakṛtavatī bhaveyam? a|bhavadīyaṃ hi n' âiva kiṃ cin mat|saṃbaddham.

6.3 Atha v" âsty ev' âsy' âpi janasya kva cit prabhutvam. a|śakyaṃ hi mad|icchayā vinā Sarasvatī|mukha|grahaṇ'|ôccheṣaṇīkṛto daśana|cchada eṣa cumbayitum. Ambuj'|āsanā|stana|taṭ'|ôpabhuktam uraḥ|sthalaṃ c' êdam āliṅgayitum iti.»

Priy'|ôrasi prāvṛḍ iva nabhasy *upāstīrṇa|guru|payodhara|maṇḍalā*, prauḍha|kandalī|kuḍmalam iva rūḍha|rāga|rūṣitaṃ cakṣur ullāsayantī barhi|barh'|āvalī|viḍambinā kusuma|candraka|śāreṇa madhukara|kula|vyākulena keśa|kalāpena sphurad|aruṇa|kiraṇa|kesara|karālaṃ kadamba|mukulam iva kāntasy' âdhara|maṇim adhīram ācucumba.

Tad|ārambha|sphuritayā ca rāga|vṛttyā bhūyo 'py āvartat' âtimātra|citr'|ôpacāra|śīpharo rati|prabandhaḥ.

HEARING THE STORIES OF THE FOURTEEN WORLDS,* the superlative lady's eyes were wide with wonder, and she said with a smile:

"Husband, by your grace my ears have today found their raison d'être. You have this day given my mind the light of knowledge to remove the darkness of ignorance. Now is ripe the fruit of my worship at your lotus-feet. With what kindness shall I return your favor? Everything I have is yours already.

Nevertheless even I do have some control in one respect. 6.3
For I cannot be forced against my will to kiss this lower lip, a leftover from when Sarásvati herself seized your mouth, or to embrace this broad chest already enjoyed by lotus-throned Lakshmi's cleavage."*

Like the monsoon *spreading its circles of heavy rain-bearing clouds* in the sky, she *spread the heavy spheres of her milk-bearing breasts* on her beloved's chest.* She fluttered her eyes, flushed with mounting passion like a full-blown red *kándali* flower. Her flowing hair could have been the array of a peacock's tail, spotted with flowers like the moon eyes in a peacock feather and dishevelled like a swarm of honeybees. Tentatively she kissed her beloved's ruby lower lip, awesome with an efflorescence of throbbing ruddy rays, as if she were kissing a *kadámba* bud.

From that beginning their passion mounted, and uninterrupted love-play ensued, enlivened with variations beyond measure.

6.6 Surata|kheda|suptayos tu tayoḥ svapne bisa|guṇa|nigaḍita|pādo jaraṭhaḥ kaś cij jāla|pādo 'dṛśyata. pratyabudhyetāṃ c' ôbhau. atha tasya rāja|kumārasya kamala|mūḍha|śaśi|kiraṇa|rajju|dāma|nigṛhītam iva rajata|śṛṅkhal'|ôpagūḍhaṃ caraṇa|yugalam āsīt.

Upalabhy' âiva ca ‹kim etad ity› atiparitrāsa|vihvalā mukta|kaṇṭham ācakranda rāja|kanyā. yena ca tat sakalam eva kany"|ântaḥ|puram agni|parītam iva piśāc'|ôpahatam iva vepamānam a|nirūpyamāṇa|tadātv'|āyati|vibhāgam, a|gaṇyamāna|rahasya|rakṣā|samayam, avani|tala|vipravidhyamāna|gātram, ākrānda|vidīryamāṇa|kaṇṭham, aśru|srot'|âvaguṇṭhita|kapola|talam ākulībabhūva.

Tumule c' âsmin samaye '|niyantrita|praveśāḥ ‹kiṃ kim iti› sahas" ôpasṛtya viviśur antarvaṃśikāḥ puruṣā dadṛśuś ca tad|avasthaṃ rāja|kumāram. tad|anubhāva|niruddha|nigrah'|êcchās tu sadya eva te tam arthaṃ Caṇḍavarmaṇe nivedayāṃ cakruḥ. so 'pi kopād āgatya nirdahann iva dahana|garbhayā dṛśā niśāmy' ôtpanna|pratyabhijñaḥ:

6.9 «Kathaṃ sa ev' âiṣa mad|anuja|maraṇa|nimitta|bhūtāyāḥ pāpāyā Bālacandrikāyāḥ patyur atyabhiniviṣṭa|vitta|darpasya vaideśika|vaṇik|putrasya Puṣpodbhavasya mitraṃ rūpa|mattaḥ kal"|âbhimānī n'|aikavidha|vipralambh'|ôpāya|pāṭav'|āvarjita|mūḍha|paurajana|mithy"|āropita vitatha|devat"|ânubhāvaḥ kapaṭa|dharma|kañcuko nigūḍha|pāpa|śīlaś capalo brāhmaṇa|bruvaḥ.

But when the two of them were asleep, exhausted by pleasure, then they dreamed they saw an aged web-footed swan, his feet bound with a thread of lotus fiber. They both awoke with a start, to find that our royal youth's own feet were clasped fast in a silver chain, as though slender moonrays had bound them mistaking them for lotuses. 6.6

Seeing this the royal maiden was beside herself with fright, unable to comprehend what had happened, and screamed at the top of her voice. With that the entire harem was thrown into confusion, rocked as if surrounded by fire or overrun with demons.* Blind to the future consequences of the present, and reckless of their pledge to guard the secret, the women dashed their bodies to the ground, throats torn open with screams, their cheeks veiled with torrents of tears.

In the midst of this tumult the harem guards suddenly arrived and entered, their entry unchecked, to find out what was afoot. There they saw the prince in the aforementioned predicament. Nevertheless, his majestic presence checked their desire to seize him, and so they reported the matter without delay to Chanda·varman. Then he too arrived in a fury, raging with a look of pure fire. Taking in the scene recognition struck and he began hurling abuse:

"Why, this is the same so-called brahmin upstart who is a friend of Pushpódbhava, the foreign merchant's son, overinflated with moneylust and now husband of the evil Bala·chándrika, who brought about my younger brother's death. This one is intoxicated with his own good looks and arrogant about his artistic sensibilities. By his cunning in every variety of deceptive stratagem he has the foolish citizens in his power, mistakenly attributing him with the 6.9

Katham iv' âinam anuraktā mādṛśeṣv api puruṣa|siṃheṣu s'|âvamānā pāp" êyam Avantisundarī? paśyatu patim ady' âiva śūl'|âvataṃsitam iyam an|ārya|śīlā kula|pāṃsan" îti,»

nirbhartsayan bhīṣaṇa|bhru|kuṭi|dūṣita|lalāṭaḥ Kāla iva kāla|loha|daṇḍa|karkaśena bāhu|daṇḍen' âvalambya hast'|âmbuje rekh'|âmbuja|rath'|âṅga|lāñchane rāja|putraṃ sa|rabhasam ācakarṣa.

6.12 Sa tu sva|bhāva|dhīraḥ sarva|pauruṣ'|âtibhūmiḥ sahiṣṇut"|âika|pratikriyāṃ daivīm eva tām āpadam avadhārya:

«Smara tasyā haṃsa|gāmini haṃsa|kathāyāḥ. sahasva vāsu māsa|dvayam! iti»

prāṇa|parityāga|rāgiṇīṃ prāṇa|samāṃ samāśvāsy' âri|vaśyatām ayāsīt.

6.15 Atha vidita|vārtāv ārtau mahā|devī|Mālav'|êndrau jāmātaram ākāra|pakṣa|pātināv ātma|parityāg'|ôpanyāsen' âriṇā jighāṃsyamānaṃ rarakṣatuḥ. na śekatus tu tam a|prabhutvād uttārayitum āpadaḥ.

Sa kila caṇḍa|śīlaś Caṇḍavarmā sarvam idam udanta|jātaṃ Rāja|rāja|girau tapasyate Darpasārāya sadiśya sarvam eva Puṣpodbhava|kuṭumbakaṃ sarva|svaharaṇa|pūrvakaṃ sadya eva bandhane kṣiptvā, kṛtvā ca Rājavāhanaṃ rāja|kesari|kiśorakam iva dāru|pañjara|nibaddhaṃ mūrdha|ja|jāla|

unreal power of a deity, while beneath his hypocritical cloak of religion his own sinful habits are secret.

How is it possible that wicked Avánti·súndari spurns even lions among men such as myself, but is besotted by him? This very day she will see her lord bedecking the stake, ignoble wench and blackener of her family's good name."

He could have been Yama, the god of death, Time himself, his forehead disfigured in a horrible frown. With one rod of an arm, stiff as Yama's steel staff, he seized the prince and dragged him violently by his lotus-hand that bore the auspicious lines of lotus and chariot wheel.

Instinctively brave and the apogee of all manliness, Ra- 6.12
ja·váhana realized correctly that this disaster was destined, and that the only response was resignation. The love of his life was desperate to breathe her own last. He reassured her:

"Remember that swan's words, my lady of the swan step. Be strong for two months, my soul."

And with that he gave himself up to the enemy.

The great Lady and Lord of Málava were pained to hear 6.15
of these events. They were partial to their son-in-law's good looks, and by threatening to give up their own lives saved him from being put to death by his enemy. But since they were no longer in power they were not able to rescue him completely from his misfortune.

Meanwhile, vicious by nature as by name, Chanda·varman, "Viciously protected," sent news of all that had happened to Darpa·sara, still practicing austerities on the mountain of the King of kings, Kubéra's Kailash. Then he rapidly threw every last member of Pushpódbhava's household into captivity, first confiscating all his property. He imprisoned

vilīna|cūḍā|maṇi|prabhāva|vikṣipta|kṣut|pipās"|ādi|khedaṃ ca tam avadhūta|duhitṛ|prārthanasy' Âṅga|rājasy' ôddharaṇāy' Âṅgān abhiyāsyann an|anya|viśvāsān ināya. rurodha ca bala|bhara|datta|kampaś Campām.

Camp"|ēśvaro 'pi Siṃhavarmā siṃha iv' â|sahya|vikramaḥ prākāraṃ bhedayitvā mahatā bala|samudāyena nirgatya sva|prahita|dūta|vrāt'|āhūtānāṃ sāhāyya|dān'|āyāti|sa|tvaram āpatatāṃ dharā|patīnām a|cira|kāla|bhāviny api saṃnidhāv a|datt'|âpekṣaḥ sākṣād iv' âvalepo vapuṣmān a|kṣamā|parītaḥ pratibalaṃ pratijagrāha.

6.18 Jagṛhe ca mahati saṃparāye kṣīṇa|sakala|sainya|maṇḍalaḥ pracaṇḍa|praharaṇa|śata|bhinna|varmā Siṃhavarmā kariṇaḥ kariṇam avapluty' âtimānuṣa|prāṇa|balena Caṇḍavarmaṇā. sa ca tad|duhitary Ambālikāyām abalā|ratna|samākhyātāyām atimātr'|âbhilāṣaḥ prāṇair enaṃ na vyayūyujat. api tv anīnayad apanīt'|â|śeṣa|śalyam a|kalya|saṃdho bandhanam.

Ajīgaṇac ca gaṇaka|saṃghaiḥ:

Raja·váhana like a regal lion cub in a wooden cage. But thanks to the powers of the crest-jewel hidden in his thick hair* Raja·váhana was not troubled by hunger, thirst or any affliction. Trusting no one, Chanda·varman carried his prisoner along when he marched out against the Angans* to overthrow their king, who had rejected his petition for his daughter. Laying siege to Champa, he made it shake with the burden of his forces.

The Lord of Champa, Simha·varman, "Whose armor is a lion," was like his namesake the lion, his prowess irresistible. He broke through the walls and charged forth with a great multitude of forces. He had himself already sent a fleet of messengers to summon the support of other kings, who were coming from all sides in a hurry to help. But although their presence was imminent, he paid it no heed. Full of impatience, as though arrogance incarnate and in the flesh, he attacked the opposing forces.

In the great battle which was then joined, Simha·var- 6.18
man lost the entire army of his soldiers. Hundreds of violent blows smashed his armor. With superhuman innate strength Chanda·varman leaped from his own elephant to Simha·varman's. Yet he was so madly in love with the other's daughter Ambálika, famed as the jewel of the weaker sex, that he spared his life.* Instead, inscrutable, he first extracted every arrow from Simha·varman's body, before taking him into custody.

The computations of a crowd of astrologers confirmed his intention:

«Ady' âiva kṣap'|âvasāne vivāhanīyā rāja|duhit" êti.»

6.21 Kṛta|kautuka|maṅgale ca tasminn Eka|piṅg'|â|calāt pratinivṛty' Âiṇajaṅgho nāma jaṅghā|karikaḥ prabhavato Darpasārasya pratisaṃdeśam āvedayat:

«Ayi, mūḍha! kim asti kany"|ântaḥ|pura|dūṣake 'pi kaś cit kṛp"|âvasaraḥ? sthaviraḥ sa rājā jarā|vilupta|mān'|âvamāna|citto duścarita|duhitṛ|pakṣapātī yad eva kiṃ cit pralapati tvay" âpi kiṃ tad anumatyā sthātavyam? a|vilambitam eva tasya kām'|ônmattasya citra|vadha|vārtā|preṣaṇena śravaṇ'|ôtsavo 'smākaṃ vidheyaḥ. sā ca duṣṭa|kanyā sah' ânujena Kīrtisāreṇa nigaḍita|caraṇā cārake niroddhavy" êti.»

Tac c' ākarṇya:

6.24 «Prātar eva rāja|bhavana|dvāre sa dur|ātmā kany"|ântaḥ|pura|dūṣakaḥ saṃnidhāpayitavyaḥ. Caṇḍapotaś ca mātaṅga|patir ucita|kalpan"|ôpapannas tatr' âiva samupasthāpanīyaḥ. kṛta|vivāha|kṛtyaś c' ôtthāy' âham eva tam an|ārya|śīlaṃ tasya hastinaḥ kṛtvā krīḍanakaṃ tad|adhirūḍha eva gatvā śatru|sāhāyyakāya pratyāsīdato rājanyakasya sa|kośa|vāhanasy' âvagrahaṇaṃ kariṣyām' îti.»

"I shall marry the king's daughter at the end of this very night."

The auspicious ceremony of tying the engaged-to-be-married thread was barely completed when a courier named Ena·jangha, "Black antelope shank," arrived from Kailash, Kubéra's* mountain, to announce the reigning Darpa·sara's reply: 6.21

"Idiot! Since when is the violator of the ladies' harem repaid with compassion? The king is elderly. Old age has robbed his mind of the sense of both his own self-respect and the disrespect of others, to the extent that he sides with his depraved daughter. Why, anyway, agree to abide by whatever nonsense he utters? You should rather make haste to provide a feast for my ears by sending news of that love-crazed man's gory execution. As for the corrupt girl, bind her feet, and lock her and our younger brother Kirti·sara in a cell."

Hearing this, Chanda·varman turned to his attendants and said:

"At the crack of dawn bring out before the gates of the royal palace the wicked defiler of the ladies' harem. Harness and caparison Chanda·pota, 'Fierce young bull,' lord of elephants, and station him in the same place. As soon as I have performed the marriage act, I shall myself arise and make that ignoble character the elephant's plaything.* Then I shall mount Chanda·pota and go forth to punish the troop of warrior princes coming with supplies and vehicles to help our enemy." 6.24

Pārśva|carān avekṣāṃ cakre. ninye c' âsāv ahany anyasminn unmiṣaty ev' ôṣo|rāge rāja|putro rāj'|âṅgaṇaṃ rakṣibhiḥ. upatasthe ca kṣarita|gaṇḍaś Caṇḍapotaḥ. kṣaṇe ca tasmin mumuce tad|aṅghri|yugalaṃ rajata|śṛṅkhalayā. sā c' âinaṃ candra|lekhā|cchaviḥ kācid apsaro|rūpiṇī bhūtvā pradakṣiṇīkṛtya pr'|âñjalir vyajijñapat:

«Deva dīyatām anugrah'|ārdraṃ cittam. aham asmi soma|raśmi|saṃbhavā Suratamañjarī nāma sura|sundarī.

6.27 Tasyā me nabhasi nalina|lubdha|mugdha|kala|haṃs'|ânubaddha|vaktrāyās tan|nivāraṇa|kṣobha|vicchinna|vigalitā hāra|yaṣṭir yad|ṛcchayā jātu haimavate sarasi Mandodake magn'|ônmagnasya maha|rṣer Mārkaṇḍeyasya mastake maṇi|kiraṇa|dvi|guṇita|palitam apatat. pātitaś ca kopitena ko 'pi tena mayi śāpaḥ:

‹Pāpe bhajasva loha|jātim a|jāta|caitanyā sat" îti!›

Sa punaḥ prasādyamānas tvat|pāda|padma|dvayasya māsa|dvaya|mātraṃ saṃdānatām etya nistaraṇīyām imām āpadam a|parikṣīṇa|śaktitvaṃ c' êndriyāṇām akalpayat.

6.30 An|alpena ca pāpmanā rajata|śṛṅkhalī|bhūtāṃ mām Aikṣvākasya rājño Vegavataḥ pautraḥ putro Mānasavegasya Vīraśekharo nāma vidyādharaḥ Śaṃkara|girau samadhyagamat. ātmasātkṛtā ca ten' âham āsam.

Accordingly, just as rosy dawn was breaking the following day, guards led the prince out into the palace courtyard. Chanda·pota, too, was there, his temples oozing the rut of being in heat. That same instant, the silver chain fell from Raja·váhana's ankles and turned into an *ápsaras*, a divine nymph, lustrous—slim and pale—as the new moon. She reverentially circumambulated him, and, with hands pressed together and raised in respect, explained:

"Lord, may your heart melt with kindness. I am Súrata·máñjari, 'Bouquet of erotic pleasures,' a divine woman, born from a moonbeam.*

Once upon a time a foolish goose mistook my face for 6.27
a lotus and pursued me through the sky. In the flurry of fending him off, my string of pearls snapped and fell. By chance it eventually landed in the Himalayas on the head of the great sage Markandéya just as he emerged from a plunge in the glacial Mandódaka lake. The pearls' rays made his gray hair doubly silver. In his anger he hurled an unexpected curse at me:*

'Wicked girl, you will be reborn as metal, without consciousness!'

But I was able to propitiate him, so he decided that this outrage would be expiated after a two-month period as a chain around your lotus-feet, and my senses would remain fully functional.

Having become a silver chain for my non-negligible sin, 6.30
the *vidya·dhara* Vira·shékhara, son of Mánasa·vega, grandson of Végavat, an Aikshvákan king,* discovered me on Kailash, Shiva's mountain. Thus I came into his possession.

Ath' âsau pitṛ|prayukta|vaire pravartamāne vidyādhara|cakravartini Vatsa|rāja|vaṃśa|vardhane Naravāhanadatte viras'|āśayas tad|apakāra|kṣamo 'yam iti tapasyatā Darpasāreṇa saha samasṛjyata. pratiśrutaṃ ca tena tasmai svasur Avantisundaryāḥ pradānam.

Anyadā tu viyati vyavadāyamāna|candrike mano|ratha|priyatamām Avantisundarīṃ didṛkṣur a|vaś'|êndriyas tad Indra|mandira|dyuti kumārī|puram upāsarat. antaritaś ca tiraskariṇyā vidyayā sa ca tāṃ tadā tvad|aṅk'|âpāśrayāṃ surata|kheda|supta|gātrīṃ tri|bhuvana|sarga|yātrā|saṃhāra|saṃbaddhābhiḥ kathābhir amṛta|syandinībhiḥ pratyānīyamāna|rāga|pūrāṃ nyarūpayat.

6.33 Sa tu prakupito 'pi tvad|anubhāva|pratibaddha|nigrah'|ântar'|âdhyavasāyaḥ samāliṅgy' êtaretaram atyanta|sukha|suptayor yuvayor daiva|datt'|ôtsāhaḥ pāṇḍu|loha|śṛṅkhal'|ātmanā mayā pāda|padmayor yugalaṃ tava nigaḍayitvā sa|roṣa|rabhasam apāsarat.

Avasitaś ca mam' âdya śāpaḥ. tac ca māsa|dvayaṃ tava pāratantryam. prasīd' êdānīm. kiṃ tava karaṇīyam iti?»

praṇipatantīṃ,

6.36 «Vārtay" ânayā mat|prāṇa|samāṃ samāśvāsay' êti!»

vyādiśya visasarja.

His father, Mánasa·vega, had launched a rebellion against Nara·váhana·datta, which was still in progress. Vira·shékhara was full of negative feelings toward his father's enemy, promoter of the royal line of Vatsa and Emperor of the *vidya·dhara* demigods.* Thinking that Darpa·sara's austerities would earn him the power to destroy Nara·váhana·datta, he entered into an alliance with him. Darpa·sara pledged to give Vira·shékhara his sister Avánti·súndari in marriage.

But one night when the sky was bright with moonlight Vira·shékhara lost control of his lunatic wits and longed to see Avánti·súndari, most beloved to his heart. He entered the princess's apartments, sumptuous as Indra's palace. Invisible behind a magic veil, he saw her resting her head in your lap, her limbs languid with the exhaustion of love-play. But the stories she was hearing about the creation, maintenance and reabsorption of the three world realms were ambrosial streams feeding another flood of passion in her.

Enraged, his deep determination to seize you was checked 6.33
by your majestic might. Nevertheless, once you and Avánti·súndari were asleep in overwhelming bliss in each other's arms, destiny gave him the courage to bind your lotus-feet, using me in my incarnation as a silver chain. Then he angrily rushed away.

Today my curse is ended; and likewise your two months of powerlessness.* Please, how can I be of service?"

He commanded her as she prostrated herself before him:

"Go with this news and reassure her who is as dear to me 6.36
as life!"

With which he dismissed her.

Tasminn eva kṣaṇ'|ântare:

6.39 «Hato hataś Caṇḍavarmā! Siṃhavarma|duhitur Ambālikāyāḥ pāṇi|sparśa|rāga|prasārite bāhu|daṇḍa eva balavad avalambya sa|rabhasam ākṛṣya ken' âpi duṣkara|karmaṇā taskareṇā nakha|prahāreṇa. rāja|mandir'|ôddeśaṃ ca śava|śatam ayam āpādayann a|cakita|gatir asau viharat' îti.»

vācaḥ samabhavan. śrutvā c' âitat tam eva matta|hastinam udast'|ādhoraṇo rāja|putro 'dhiruhya raṃhas'|ôttamena rāja|bhavanam abhyavartata. stambe|rama|ray'|âvadhūta|patti|datta|vartmā ca praviśya veśm'|âbhyantaram adabhr'|âbhra|nirghoṣa|gambhīreṇa svareṇ' âbhyadhāt:

«Kaḥ sa mahā|puruṣo yen' âitan mānuṣa|mātra|duṣkaraṃ mahat|karm' ânuṣṭhitam? āgacchatu! mayā sah' êmaṃ matta|hastinam ārohatu! a|bhayaṃ mad|upakaṇṭha|vartino deva|dānavair api vigṛhṇānasy' êti.»

6.42 Niśamy' âivaṃ sa pumān upoḍha|harṣo nirgatya kṛt'|âñjalir ākramya saṃjñā|saṃkucitaṃ kuñjara|gātram a|saktam adhyarukṣat. ārohantam ev' âinaṃ nirvarṇya harṣ'|ôtphulla|dṛṣṭiḥ:

«Aye! priya|sakho 'yam Apahāravarm" âiv' êti!»

Paścān niṣīdato 'sya bāhu|daṇḍa|yugalam ubhaya|bhuja|mūla|praveśitam agre 'valambya svam aṅgam āliṅgayām āsa. svayaṃ ca pṛṣṭhato valitābhyāṃ bhujābhyāṃ paryaveṣṭayat.

In the very next instant the cry went up:

"Killed, Chanda·varman is killed! Just when his rod of 6.39
an arm was stretched out in his desire to take the hand of Ambálika, Simha·varman's daughter, an unknown thief of derring-do fell upon him with force, dragged him violently off and killed him with a stroke of a claw weapon. Now that killer is amusing himself scattering hundreds of corpses around the precincts of the palace, his progress unchecked."

The moment he heard this, Prince Raja·váhana mounted that same rutting elephant and deposed the mahout. He made for the palace at top speed. Pedestrians got out of his way, shoved aside by the elephant's charge. Entering the inner court he bellowed out in a voice deep as the roar of copious clouds:

"Who is the great man who has managed this great deed, impossible for a mere mortal? Show yourself. Come mount with me on this rutting elephant! You need have no fear at my side, even in a fight against gods and demons."

Hearing this the fellow emerged, greatly delighted. With 6.42
his hands pressed together before him in salutation he approached and climbed nimbly up on the elephant, which had lowered its body at a sign. Raja·váhana looked carefully at him as he mounted. Eyes wide with delight, the prince realized:

"Wonderful! Here is my dear friend Apahára·varman."

His friend behind him had wrapped his strong arms over both his shoulders. Seizing them, Raja·váhana hugged them around himself, and then bent his own arms back to embrace Apahára·varman in turn.

6.45 Tat|kṣaṇ'|ôpasaṃhṛt'|āliṅgana|vyatikaraś c' Âpahāra|varmā cāpa|cakra|kaṇapa|karpaṇa|prāsa|paṭṭiśa|musala|tomar'|ādi|praharaṇa|jātam upayuñjānān bal'|âvaliptān pratibala|vīrān bahu|prakār'|āyodhinaḥ parikṣipataḥ kṣitau vicikṣepa. kṣaṇena c' âdrākṣīt tad api sainyam anyena samantato 'bhimukham abhidhāvatā bala|nikāyena parikṣiptam.

An|antaraṃ ca kaś cit karṇikāra|gauraḥ kuruvinda|sa|varṇa|kuntalaḥ kamala|komala|pāṇi|pādaḥ karṇa|cumbi|dugdha|dhavala|snigdha|nīla|locanaḥ kaṭi|taṭa|niviṣṭa|ratna|nakhaḥ paṭṭa|nivasanaḥ kṛś'|â|kṛś'|ôdar'|ôraḥ|sthalaḥ kṛta|hastatayā ripu|kulam iṣu|varṣeṇ' âbhivarṣan pād'|âṅguṣṭha|niṣṭhur'|âvaghṛṣṭa|karṇa|mūlena prajavinā gajena saṃnikṛṣya pūrv'|ôpadeśa|pratyayāt:

«Ayam eva sa devo Rājavāhana iti.»

6.48 Pr'|âñjaliḥ praṇamy' Âpahāravarmaṇi niviṣṭa|dṛṣṭir ācaṣṭa:

«Tvad|ādiṣṭena mārgeṇa saṃnipātitam etad Aṅga|rāja|sāhāyya|dānāy' ôpasthitaṃ rājakam. ari|balaṃ ca vihata|vidhvastaṃ strī|bāla|hārya|śastraṃ vartate. kim anyat kṛtyam iti?»

Hṛṣṭas tu vyājahār' Âpahāravarmā:

The next moment Apahára·varman had slipped out of their mutual embrace to hurl to the ground a host of warriors attacking on every side. Equipped with all manner of weapons from bow and discus, iron bar and forked javelin, to darts and sharp-edged spear, mace and club, these men were not shy to display their strength in many fighting styles. In a second he saw that same army in turn surrounded on all sides by another horde of armies rushing to attack. 6.45

Immediately a man approached on a swift elephant, which he drove on by merely grinding his big toes roughly into the roots of its ears, all the time dextrously raining a shower of arrows down on the enemy ranks. His skin shone pale as the *karni·kara* tree; his hair was black as jet. His delicate hands and feet were like lotuses; his eyes deep bright blue in whites like milk, their outer corners kissing his ears. At his hip was fixed a jewelled dagger; his clothes were of silk. Slim was his belly, and not slim his chest. Remembering the description he had earlier been given, this stranger recognized:

"This has to be Prince Raja·váhana."

Bowing down, his hands raised clasped before him in obeisance, and eyes turned to Apahára·varman, he reported: 6.48

"The princes have assembled via the routes you directed. They stand ready to give their assistance to the king of the Angas. The enemy forces are beaten and destroyed. Women and children could disarm them of their weapons now. What next?"

Delighted, Apahára·varman announced:

6.51 «Deva, dṛṣṭi|dānen' ânugṛhyatām ayam ājñā|karaḥ. so 'yam aham ev' âmunā rūpeṇa Dhanamitr'|ākhyayā c' ântarito mantavyaḥ. sa ev' âyaṃ nirgamayya bandhanād Aṅga|rājam apavarjitaṃ ca kośa|vāhanam ekīkṛty' âsmad|gṛhyeṇ' âmunā saha rājanyaken' âikānte sukh'|ôpaviṣṭam iha devam upatiṣṭhatu, yadi na doṣa iti?»

Devo 'pi:

«Yathā te rocata iti.»

6.54 tam ābhāṣya gatvā ca tan|nirdiṣṭena mārgeṇa nagarād bahir atimahato rohiṇa|drumasya kasya cit kṣaum'|âvadāta|saikate Gaṅgā|taraṅga|pavana|pāta|śītale tale dvi|radād avatatāra. prathama|samavatīrṇen' Âpahāravarmaṇā ca sva|hasta|sa|tvara|samīkṛte mātaṅga iva Bhāgīrathī|pulina|maṇḍale sukhaṃ niṣasāda.

Tathā niṣaṇṇaṃ ca tam Upahāravarm"|Ârthapāla|Pramati|Mitragupta|Mantragupta|Viśrutair Maithilena ca Prahāravarmaṇā, Kāśī|bhartrā ca Kāmapālena, Camp"|ēśvareṇa Siṃhavarmaṇā sah' ôpāgatya Dhanamitraḥ praṇipapāta.

Devo 'pi harṣ'|āviddham abhyutthitaḥ:

6.57 «Kathaṃ samasta eṣa mitra|gaṇaḥ samāgataḥ? ko nām' âyam abhyudaya iti!»

Kṛta|yath"|ôcit'|ôpacārān nirbharataraṃ parirebhe. Kāśī|pati|Maithil'|Âṅga|rājāṃś ca suhṛn|niveditān pitṛvad apa-

"My lord, please favor your obedient servant before you 6.51
with the gift of a glance. All that differentiates him from me is his physical form and his name, Dhana·mitra. Permit him to release the Angan king from captivity, and collect together the abandoned treasure and vehicles. After that, once your lordship is settled in comfort at a little distance, allow him to stand in attendance on you there, with this band of our ally warrior princes. Unless you object?"

Prince Raja·váhana responded:

"As you decide."

Thereupon he left the city by the road Apahára·varman 6.54
directed. At a cool piece of ground where a breeze blew from the Ganges' waves, a stretch of sand bright as fine linen beneath a great banyan tree, Raja·váhana dismounted from his elephant. Apahára·varman had dismounted first to hurriedly smooth the circle of Ganges sand flat with his own hands.* Raja·váhana sat down as comfortably as on an elephant's back.

Once he was seated, Dhana·mitra came forward and bowed down before him, followed by Upahára·varman, Artha·pala, Prámati, Mitra·gupta, Mantra·gupta and Víshruta, as well as the Míthilan Prahára·varman, Kama·pala, king of Kashi, and Simha·varman the Lord of Champa.

Transported with joy the prince stood up again:

"How is it possible that the entire band of my friends is 6.57
reunited here? Lucky me!"

Receiving them with due courtesy, he hugged them in close embrace. His friends presented to him the lord of Kashi and the kings of Míthila and Anga, whom he venerated

śyat. taiś ca harṣa|kampita|palitaṃ sa|rabhas'|ôpagūḍhaḥ param abhinananda.

Tataḥ pravṛttāsu prīti|saṃkathāsu priya|vayasya|gaṇ'|ânuyuktaḥ svasya ca Somadatta|Puṣpodbhavayoś caritam anuvarṇya suhṛdām api vṛtt'|ântaṃ krameṇa śrotuṃ kṛta|prastāvas tāṃś ca tad|uktāv anvayuṅkta. teṣu prathamaṃ prāha sma kil' Âpahāravarmā:

iti śrī|Daṇḍinaḥ kṛtau
Daśa|kumāra|carite
Rājavāhana|caritaṃ
nāma
prathama ucchvāsaḥ.

as fathers. He was utterly delighted when they clasped him eagerly to them, their gray hair shaking with pleasure.

Thereupon all engaged in glad conversation. At the request of his dear friends, Raja·váhana described his own adventures and those of Soma·datta and Pushpódbhava. Then it was time to hear one by one his friends' news also. He asked them to tell their stories. The first to speak was Apahára·varman:

That is the end of the first chapter of
the glorious Dandin's
What Ten Young Men Did.
It is called:
What Raja·váhana Did.

CHAPTER SEVEN
WHAT APAHÁRA·VARMAN DID

«DEVA TVAYI TAD” ÂVATĪRṆE dvij’|ôpakārāy’ âsura|vivaraṃ tvad|anveṣaṇa|prasṛte ca mitra|gaṇe ’ham api mahīm aṭann Aṅgeṣu Gaṅgā|taṭe bahiś Campāyāḥ ‹kaś cid asti tapaḥ|prabhāv’|ôtpanna|divya|cakṣur Marīcir nāma maha|rṣir iti› kutaścit saṃlapato jana|samājād upalabhy’ âmuto bubhutsus tvad|gatiṃ tam uddeśam agamam.

Nyaśāmayaṃ ca tasminn āśrame kasya cic cūta|potakasya cchāyāyāṃ kam apy udvigna|varṇaṃ tāpasam. amunā c’ âtithivad upacaritaḥ kṣaṇaṃ viśrāntaḥ:

7.3 ‹Kv’ âsau bhagavān Marīciḥ? tasmād aham upalipsuḥ prasaṅga|proṣitasya suhṛdo gatim, āścarya|jñāna|vibhavo hi sa maha|rṣir mahyā viśruta iti.›

avādiṣam. ath’ âsāv uṣṇam āyataṃ ca niḥśvasy’ âśaṃsat:

‹Āsīt tādṛśo munir asminn āśrame. tam ekadā Kāmamañjarī nām’ Âṅga|purī|vataṃsa|sthānīyā vāra|yuvatir aśru|bindu|tārakita|payodharā sa|nirvedam abhyetya kīrṇa|śikhaṇḍ’|āstīrṇa|bhūmir abhyavandiṣṭa.

7.6 Tasminn eva ca kṣaṇe mātṛ|pramukhas tad|āpta|vargaḥ s’|ânukrośam anupradhāvitas tatr’ âiv’ â|vicchinna|pātam apatat. sa kila kṛpālus taṃ janam ārdrayā gir” āśvāsy’ ārti|kāraṇaṃ tāṃ gaṇikām apṛcchat. sā tu sa|vrīḍ” êva sa|viṣād” êva sa|gaurav” êva c’ âbravīt:

"MY LORD, AFTER YOU HAD DESCENDED* into the *ásura* demon netherworld to help the brahmin, we friends dispersed in search of you. I too wandered the earth. From a gathering of people talking among themselves I learned about a great sage named Maríchi, 'Ray of light,'* endowed with the divine eye thanks to his powerful asceticism, living on the bank of the Ganges, in the land of the Angans, outside Champa. I went thither hoping to find out from him where you might be.

In that ashram I beheld, in the shade of one young mango tree, an ascetic in a sorry state. He received me as an honored guest and I rested a while, before asking:

'Where is the venerable Maríchi? I would like him to en- 7.3
lighten me as to the whereabouts of my dear friend who left us, on a mission no doubt. For Maríchi is a great sage whose fantastic mastery of superknowledge is world famous.'

Thereupon the man sighed long and hard before replying:

'There was once such a saint in this ashram. One day a young prostitute called Kama·máñjari, "Bouquet of love," the ornament of the Angan city, sought him out, in despair and disgust at the world, her bosom starred with teardrops. She saluted him respectfully, sweeping her long dishevelled tresses along the ground.

That very moment a crowd of her friends and relatives, 7.6
with her mother at their head, rushed in lamenting after her, and fell down in one packed hurry. The story goes that the compassionate ascetic calmed everyone with a soothing speech, before asking the courtesan the cause of her distress. She responded, apparently with shame, sorrow and respect in turns:

«Bhagavan, aihikasya sukhasy' â|bhājanaṃ jano 'yam āmuṣmikāya śvovasīyāy' ārt'|âbhyupapatti|vittayor bhagavat|pādayor mūlaṃ śaraṇam abhiprapanna iti.»

Tasyās tu janany udañjaliḥ palita|śāra|śikhaṇḍa|bandha|spṛṣṭa|mukta|bhūmir abhāṣata:

7.9 «Bhagavan, asyā me doṣam eṣā vo dāsī vijñāpayati. doṣaś ca mama sv'|âdhikār'|ânuṣṭhāpanam.

Eṣa hi gaṇikā|mātur adhikāro yad: duhitur janmanaḥ prabhṛty ev' âṅga|kriyā, tejo|bala|varṇa|medhā|saṃvardhanena doṣ'|âgni|dhātu|sāmyakṛtā miten' āhāreṇa śarīra|poṣaṇam; ā pañcamād varṣāt pitur apy an|atidarśanam, janma|dine puṇya|dine c' ôtsav'|ôttaro maṅgala|vidhiḥ;

adhyāpanam Anaṅga|vidyānāṃ s'|âṅgānām, nṛtya|gīta|vādya|nāṭya|citr'|āsvādya|gandha|puṣpa|kalāsu lipi|jñāna|vacana|kauśal'|ādiṣu ca samyag|vinayanam, śabda|hetu|samaya|vidyāsu vārtā|mātr'|âvabodhanam; ājīva|jñāne krīḍā|kauśale sa|jīva|nir|jīvāsu ca dyūta|kalāsv abhyantarīkaraṇam;

"Good sir, I am not worthy of happiness in the here and now. In order to find happiness in the next world I have come to take refuge at your worship's feet, famous for providing asylum to the afflicted."

Next her mother raised her folded hands before her forehead in obeisance, touched the ground with her gray-speckled plaits, then lifted herself up again to wail:

"Good sir, your humble slave* is bringing before you my 7.9
crime against her. My offense? To have seen to it that she perform the duty of her birthright.*

For it is the duty of a courtesan's mother to take care of her daughter's body, massaging it and so on, from the day she is born, nourishing it with a moderate diet to help develop its luster, vigor, clear complexion and intelligence, and to balance out the three humors, the digestive fire and all the precious bodily substances. She must ensure that from the child's fifth birthday she should not see even her own father too much, while on her birthday and auspicious days they should perform a propitious and festive ritual.

It is the duty of a courtesan's mother to instruct her daughter in the whole corpus of erotic science,* giving her the right amount of training in the arts of dance, song, music, theatre, painting, confectionery, perfumery and flower arranging, as well as calligraphy in various scripts, and how to speak eloquently and so on, with the merest smattering of grammar, logic and astrology. The mother must make her intimate with the skill of earning a living, expertise in amusements, and the art of gambling, whether on live sports or inanimate games.

7.12 abhyantara|kalāsu vaiśvāsika|janāt prayatnena prayoga|grahaṇam, yātr'|ôtsav'|ādiṣv ādara|prasādhitāyāḥ sphīta|paribarhāyāḥ prakāśanam, prasaṅgavatyāṃ saṃgīt'|ādi|kriyāyāḥ pūrva|saṃgṛhītair grāhya|vāgbhiḥ siddhi|lambhanam;

diṅ|mukheṣu tat|tac|chilpa|vittakair yaśaḥ|prakhyāpanam, kārtāntik'|ādibhiḥ kalyāṇa|lakṣaṇ'|ôdghoṣaṇam, pīṭhamarda|viṭa|vidūṣakair bhikṣuky|ādibhiś ca nāgarika|puruṣa|samavāyeṣu rūpa|śīla|śilpa|saundarya|mādhurya|prastāvanā;

yuva|jana|mano|ratha|lakṣya|bhūtāyāḥ prabhūtatamena śulken' âvasthāpanam; svato rāg'|ândhāya tad|bhāva|darśan'|ônmāditāya vā jāti|rūpa|vayo|'rtha|śakti|śauca|tyāga|dākṣya|dākṣiṇya|śilpa|śīla|mādhury'|ôpapannāya sva|tantrāya pradānam; adhika|guṇāy' â|sva|tantrāya prājñatamāy' âlpen' âpi bahu|vyapadeśen' ārpaṇam; a|sva|tantreṇa vā gāndharva|samāgamena tad|gurubhyaḥ śulk'|âpaharaṇam; a|lābhe 'rthasya kāma|svīkṛte svāminy adhikaraṇe ca sādhanam;

The daughter has to be given her practical education in the intimate arts by reliable people; she is to be publicly presented at processions, festivals and so on, carefully turned out and with a grand retinue; and her success at informal occasions for song should be ensured thanks to a claque of planted applauders. 7.12

A courtesan's mother is duty-bound to publish her daughter's fame abroad in every quarter via connoisseurs of this and that art, to have astrologers and the like proclaim her auspicious characteristics, and to ensure that parasites, catamites, comics, Buddhist nuns and other unlikely characters* praise her beauty, manners and accomplishments, charm and accomplishments, in the company of men of the world.

As soon as the girl has become the target of young men's fancy, it is her mother's duty to establish the highest possible price.* She should give her to men of independent means, whether blindly passionate by instinct or impassioned by her sentimental display. Be that as it may, they must be endowed with good birth, beauty, virility, wealth, power, honesty, generosity, dexterity, gallantry, ingenuity, courtesy and sweetness. If the candidate is inordinately gifted and absolutely brilliant, though having no independent means, she will hand her daughter over even cheap at the price, but telling everyone that it was a lot. Or if the man is still dependent she should extract the fee from his parents for what she should call a *gandhárva* elopement.* If for any reason she is not paid, then she has to get her money from a loyal patron.

7.15 raktasya duhitr" âika|cāriṇī|vrat'|ânuṣṭhāpanam, nitya|naimittika|prīti|dāyakatayā hṛta|śiṣṭānāṃ gamya|dhanānāṃ citrair upāyair apaharaṇam, a|dadatā lubdha|prāyeṇa ca vigṛhy' âsanam, pratihasti|protsāhanena lubdhasya rāgiṇas tyāga|śakti|saṃdhukṣaṇam, a|sārasya vāk|saṃtakṣaṇair lok'|ôpakrośanair duhitṛ|nirodhanair vrīḍ"|ôtpādanair any'|âbhiyogair avamānaiś c' âpavāhanam, artha|dair an|artha|pratighātibhiś c' â|nindyair ibhyair anubaddh'|ârth'|ân|artha|saṃśayān vicārya bhūyo|bhūyaḥ saṃyojanam iti.

Gaṇikāyāś ca gamyaṃ prati sajjat" âiva na saṅgaḥ. satyām api prītau na mātur mātṛkāyā vā śāsan'|âtivṛttiḥ.

Evaṃ sthite 'nayā Prajāpati|vihitaṃ sva|dharmam ullaṅghya kva cid āgantuke rūpa|mātra|dhane vipra|yūni sven' âiva dhana|vyayena ramamāṇayā māsa|mātram atyavāhi. gamya|janaś ca bhūyān artha|yogyaḥ pratyācakṣāṇay" ânayā prakopitaḥ. sva|kuṭumbakaṃ c' âvasāditam.

7.18 ‹Eṣā ku|matir! na kalyāṇ" îti.›

nivārayantyāṃ mayi vana|vāsāya kopāt prasthitā. sā ced iyam a|hārya|niścayā sarva eṣa jano 'tr' âiv' ân|anya|gatir an|aśanena saṃsthāsyata iti.»

The mother must ensure her daughter keeps her pledge to be faithful to her lover, as well as contriving in colorful ways to relieve him of what remains of his riches after they have extracted daily, occasional and spontaneous love-gifts. If the man is not a giver, or if he is better at taking, then she must get rid of him with a quarrel. A stingy lover's capacity to give can be incited with threats of the pimp. But it is her duty to drive away the impecunious man, shaming him by cutting comments, public criticism, locking up her daughter and other strategies to show her contempt. *Au contraire*, it is the professional duty of a courtesan's mother to calculate potential profit and loss before uniting her daughter only with unobjectionable rich men, the sort who provide wealth and ward off poverty. 7.15

As for the harlot, she has only to be fond of her lover, without getting attached. Even if it is true love, she must never disobey her mother or her mother's mother.*

Such was the arrangement, but my daughter violated her professional code ordained by the Creator, Praja·pati.* She has been enjoying herself for an entire month with some random brahmin boy whose only resource is his beauty, thus frittering away her own money. Not only that but her rejections angered other lovers who were good for greater riches. She has brought ruin on her household. I tried to stop her, warning:

'You are out of your mind! This is indecent.' 7.18

At which she stormed off in a huff to live in the forest. If her decision is final then we all have no choice but to stay right here and wait for death by starvation."

Arodīt.

7.21 Atha sā vāra|yuvatis tena

«Bhadre, nanu duḥkh'|ākaro 'yaṃ vana|vāsaḥ. tasya phalam apavargaḥ svargo vā. prathamas tu tayoḥ prakṛṣṭa|jñāna|sādhyaḥ prāyo duḥsaṃpāda eva, dvitīyas tu sarvasy' âiva su|labhaḥ kula|dharm'|ânuṣṭhāyinaḥ. tad a|śaky'|ārambhād uparamya mātur mate vartasv' êti!»

s'|ânukaṃpam abhihitā,

7.24 «Yad' îha bhagavat|pāda|mūlam a|śaraṇam, śaraṇam astu mama kṛpaṇāyā hiraṇya|retā deva ev' êti!»

udamanāyata. sa tu munir anuvimṛśya gaṇikā|mātaram avadat:

«Saṃprati gaccha gṛhān. pratīkṣasva kānicid dināni yāvad iyaṃ su|kumārā sukh'|ôpabhoga|samucitā saty araṇya|vāsa|vyasanen' ôdvejitā bhūyo|bhūyaś c' âsmābhir vibodhyamānā prakṛtāv eva sthāsyat' îti.»

7.27 «Tath" êti» tasyāḥ pratiyāte sva|jane sā gaṇikā tam ṛṣim a|laghu|bhaktir dhaut'|ôdgamanīya|vāsinī n' âty|ādṛta|śarīra|saṃskārā vana|taru|pot'|ālavāla|pūraṇair devat"|ârcana|kusum'|ôccay'|âvacaya|prayāsair n' âika|vikalp'|ôpahāra|karmabhiḥ Kāma|śāsan'|ârthe ca gandha|mālya|dhūpa|dīpa|nṛtya|gīta|vādyābhiḥ kriyābhir ekānte ca tri|varga|saṃbandhinībhiḥ kathābhir adhyātma|vādaiś c' ânurūpair alpīyas" âiva kālen' ânvarañjayat.

And she burst out crying.

Thereupon the holy man, all sympathetic, addressed the 7.21
young woman of the multitude:

"Good lady. This forest life is a mine of trouble, you know. Its fruit is either final liberation or heaven. But the first of these two can be attained only with superlative insight; for most people it is out of reach. While the second is easy for anyone to win by simply fulfilling the duties of your birth. Therefore stop attempting the impossible and do what your mother thinks best!"

Kama·máñjari's hackles rose:

"If there is no asylum for me here at your worship's feet, 7.24
then I will take refuge in fire, the god with the golden semen. Woe is me!"

The sage reflected a moment before telling the harlot's mother:

"Go home now. Wait a few days. The delicate girl was born for the good life and will tire of tiresome jungle life. I shall not cease to admonish her. She will soon return to normal."

Her people agreed and left, and the courtesan attached 7.27
herself to the sage, with no light devotion. She wore a uniform of plain washed clothes, and paid physical refinements little notice. She watered the trenches around forest saplings, diligently plucked bouquets of wildflowers to offer the deity, performed offerings of many kinds and was ready with perfume, garlands, incense, lamps, dance, song and music, all for Shiva, Love's punisher.* Thereby, and by intimate conversations on the three goals of life, namely piety, profit

Ekadā ca rahasi raktaṃ tam upalakṣya:

«Mūḍhaḥ khalu loko yat saha dharmeṇ' ârtha|kāmāv api gaṇayat' îti.»

7.30 kiṃ cid asmayata.

«Kathaya, vāsu, ken' âṃśen' ârtha|kām'|âtiśāyī dharma|stav'|âbhipreta iti?»

preritā Marīcinā lajjā|mantharam ārabhat" âbhidhātum:

7.33 «Itaḥ kila janād bhagavatas tri|varga|bal'|â|bala|jñānam. atha v" âitad api prakār'|ântaraṃ dāsa|jan'|ânugrahasya. bhavatu. śrūyatām.

Nanu dharmād ṛte 'rtha|kāmayor an|utpattir eva. tad|an|apekṣa eva dharmo nivṛtti|sukha|prasūti|hetur ātma|samādhāna|mātra|sādhyaś ca. so 'rtha|kāmavad bāhya|sādhaneṣu n' âtyāyatate.

Tattva|darśan'|ôpabṛṃhitaś ca yathā kathaṃ cid apy anuṣṭhīyamānābhyāṃ n' ârtha|kāmābhyāṃ bādhyate. bādhito 'pi c' âlp'|āyāsa|pratisamāhitas tam api doṣaṃ nirhṛtya śreyase 'n|alpāya kalpate.

7.36 Tathā hi: Pitāmahasya Tilottam"|âbhilāṣaḥ, Bhavānī|pater mauni|patnī|sahasra|saṃdūṣaṇam, Padma|nābhasya ṣoḍaśa|sahasr'|ântaḥ|pura|vihāraḥ, Prajāpateḥ sva|duhitary api

and pleasure,* and model discussions on the nature of God, she had soon won his heart.

When Kama·máñjari was sure of his secret love, she remarked one day with a little laugh:

"People are really foolish who equate profit and pleasure with piety."

Maríchi prompted her to elaborate with the question: 7.30

"Tell me, maid, how far above profit and pleasure do you propose to rank piety?"

Hesitant with modesty she began her declamation:

"What could your worship possibly learn from someone 7.33
like me about the relative strength or frailty of the three goals of life! But maybe this is yet another way for you to be too kind to your devoted servant. Be that as it may, I shall indeed tell you what I think.

Without piety, I ask, where would profit and pleasure come from? Piety, on the other hand, can beget the bliss of liberation completely independent of those two, produced simply by mental concentration on one's self. Unlike profit and pleasure, piety relies on no external means.

Moreover, when piety is supplemented with insight into reality, it becomes immune to the effects of profit and pleasure, howsoever those two are being pursued. If piety is ever blemished, with a minimal effort it can be restored. What is more, the removal of that additional fault creates tremendous blessings.

Take the examples* of the grandfather god Brahma's lust 7.36
for the *ápsaras* Tilóttama; Párvati's lord Shiva's corruption of a thousand sages' wives; lotus-navelled Krishna's dalliance with his harem of sixteen thousand; Praja·pati's move to

praṇaya|pravṛttiḥ, Śacī|pater Ahalyā|jāratā, Śaś'|âṅkasya guru|talpa|gamanam, Aṃśu|mālino Vaḍavā|laṅghanam, Anilasya Kesari|kalatra|samāgamaḥ, Bṛhaspater Utathya|bhāry"|âbhisaraṇam, Parāśarasya dāśa|kanyā|dūṣaṇam, Pārāśaryasya bhrātu|dāra|saṃgatiḥ, Atrer mṛgī|samāgama iti.

A|marāṇāṃ ca teṣu teṣu kāryeṣv āsura|vipralambhanāni jñāna|balān na dharma|pīḍām āvahanti. dharma|pūte ca manasi nabhas' îva na jātu rajo 'nuṣajyate. tan manye n' ârtha|kāmau dharmasya śatatamīm api kalāṃ spṛśata iti.»

Śrutv" âitad ṛṣir udīrṇa|rāga|vṛttir abhyadhāt:

7.39 «Ayi vilāsini sādhu paśyasi. na dharmas tattva|darśināṃ viṣay'|ôpabhogen' ôparudhyata iti. kiṃ tu janmanaḥ prabhṛty artha|kāma|vārtt'|ân|abhijñā vayam. jñeyau c' êmau kiṃ|rūpau kiṃ|parivārau kiṃ|phalau c' êti.»

Sā tv āvādīt:

«Arthas tāvad arjana|vardhana|rakṣaṇ'|ātmakaḥ, kṛṣi|pāśupālya|vāṇijya|saṃdhi|vigrah'|ādi|parivāraḥ tīrtha|pratipādana|phalaś ca.

take in marriage even his own daughter Sandhya; Shachi's lord, Indra, becoming Ahályá's lover; the moon with the hare mark, Soma, violating his teacher Brihas·pati's bed; the sun wreathed in rays, Surya, mounting Áshvini as a mare; the wind Vayu uniting with the wife of Késari the monkey, to beget Hanumán; Brihas·pati's seduction of his elder brother Utáthya's wife; Paráshara's defilement of the fisherman's daughter Sátyavati; their own son Vyasa's union with his brother's wives; and Atri's conjunction with the doe woman.

But these immortals' ungodly tricks, in their respective carryings-on, harm their piety not a bit, thanks to their insight. For, like dust in the sky, filthy passion* never sticks to the mind purified by virtue. Thus, in my opinion, profit and pleasure cannot touch even a hundredth part of piety."

Listening to her speech only aroused the sage's passion. He responded:

"Oh, coquette, how cleverly you see that the enjoyment 7.39
of sensual objects cannot interfere with the piety of those who understand the truth. However, I have been innocent of the ways of profit and passion from the day I was born. The time has come for me to become acquainted with them both, their substance, their contexts and their rewards."

She then explained:

"To begin with profit, it is acquisition, and the growth and security of what one has acquired; its context might be agriculture, animal husbandry, trade, peace or war; and its fruit is the endowment of worthy causes.

7.42 Kāmas tu viṣay'|âtisakta|cetasoḥ strī|puṃsayor niratiśaya|sukha|sparśa|viśeṣaḥ. parivāras tv asya yāvad iha ramyam ujjvalaṃ ca. phalaṃ punaḥ param'|āhlādanam, paras|para|vimarda|janma, smaryamāṇa|madhuram, udīrit'|âbhimānam, an|uttamaṃ sukham aparokṣaṃ svasaṃvedyam eva. tasy' âiva kṛte viśiṣṭa|sthāna|vartinaḥ kaṣṭāni tapāṃsi mahānti dānāni dāruṇāni yuddhāni bhīmāni samudra|laṅghan'|ādīni ca narāḥ samācarant' îti.»

Niśamy' âitan niyati|balān nu tat|pāṭavān nu sva|buddhi|māndyān nu sva|niyamam anādṛtya tasyām asau prāsajat. sā su|dūraṃ mūḍh'|ātmānaṃ ca taṃ pravahaṇena nītvā puram udāra|śobhayā rāja|vīthyā sva|bhavanam anaiṣīt. abhūc ca ghoṣaṇā «śvaḥ Kām'|ôtsava iti!»

Uttaredyuḥ snāt'|ânuliptam āracita|mañju|mālam ārabdha|kāmi|jana|vṛttaṃ nivṛtta|sva|vṛtt'|âbhilāṣaṃ kṣaṇa|mātra|gate 'pi tayā vinā dūyamānaṃ tam ṛṣim ṛddhimatā rāja|mārgeṇ' ôtsava|samājaṃ nītvā kva cid upavan'|ôddeśe yuvati|jana|śata|parivṛtasya rājñaḥ saṃnidhau smita|mukhena tena:

7.45 «Bhadre, bhagavatā saha niṣīd' êti.»

As for pleasure, it is the particular sensation of supreme bliss between a man and a woman focussed entirely on sense objects. Its context is everything that is gorgeous and splendiferous in the world. And its reward: the highest joy, born from mutual friction, sweet to remember, increasing one's self-respect, perfect manifest bliss, and only experienced in and by oneself.* It is for the sake of this pleasure alone that distinguished men perform gruesome mortifications, give enormous gifts, fight horrific battles, make terrifying sea voyages, and so on and on." 7.42

Whether at the mercy of fate, or because of her skill, or indeed the infirmity of his own mind, hearing her argument made him forget his vows and fall for her completely. So far gone was he in his infatuation that she was able to carry him in a carriage to the city, taking the splendidly decorated royal road right to her house. Along the way there were public announcements that the following day would be the festival of Love.

The next morning the holy man was bathed, anointed and decorated with a charming garland. He had begun to act like a man in love, renouncing all desire for independent action, and disconsolate if without her for even a moment. She led him along the splendid royal road to a festival gathering somewhere in a park. There they approached the king, with his entourage of hundreds of young ladies. With a smile on his face he invited her:

"My dear, please take a seat with the holy man." 7.45

ādiṣṭā sa|vibhramaṃ kṛta|praṇāmā sa|smitaṃ nyaṣīdat. tatra kācid utthāya baddh'|âñjalir uttam'|âṅganā:

«Deva jit" ânay" âham. asyai dāsyam adya|prabhṛty abhyupetaṃ may" êti.»

7.48 prabhuṃ prāṇaṃsīt. vismaya|harṣa|mūlaś ca kolāhalo lokasy' ôdajihīta. hṛṣṭena ca rājñā mah"|ârhai ratn'|ālaṃkārair mahatā ca paribarheṇ' ânugṛhya visṛṣṭā vāra|mukhyābhiḥ paura|mukhyaiś ca gaṇaśaḥ praśasyamānā sva|bhavanam a|gatv" âiva tam ṛṣim abhāṣata:

«Bhagavan, ayam añjaliḥ. ciram anugṛhīto 'yaṃ dāsa|janaḥ. sv'|ârtha idānīm anuṣṭheya iti!»

Sa tu rāgād aśani|hata iv' ôdbhrāmy' âbravīt:

7.51 «Priye, kim etat? kuta idam audāsīnyam? kva gatas tava mayya|sādhāraṇo 'nurāga iti?»

Atha sā sa|smitam idam avādīt:

«Bhagavan yay" âdya rāja|kule mattaḥ parājayo 'bhyupetas tasyāś ca mama ca kasmiṃś cit saṃgharṣe:

7.54 ‹Marīcim āvarjitavat" îva ślāghasa iti!›

tay" âsmy aham adhikṣiptā. dāsya|paṇa|bandhena c' âsminn arthe prāvartiṣi. siddh'|ârthā c' âsmi tvat|prasādād iti.»

Sa tayā tath" âvadhūto durmatiḥ kṛt'|ânuśayaḥ śūnyavan nyavartiṣṭa. yas tay" âivaṃ kṛtas tapasvī tam eva māṃ mahā|bhāga manyasva. sva|śakti|niṣiktaṃ rāgam uddhṛtya tay" âiva bandhakyā mahad|vairāgyam arpitam. a|cirād eva śakya

Kama·máñjari made a pretty curtsey and sat down smiling. Next a second perfection of womanhood stood up, her hands pressed together before her forehead in respect. She bowed down to the king, with the words:

"My lord, she has defeated me. From today onward I am her slave."

The company burst out in a hullabaloo of amazement and 7.48
delight. The king, too, was amused. He favored the courtesan with very valuable jewel ornaments and a large retinue before letting her go. Crowds of prominent courtesans and gentlemen applauded her. Even before going home, she told the sage:

"Reverend sir, farewell. You have been too kind to your servant for too long. Now go back to your own business!"

He was utterly bewildered with love, as though struck by Indra's thunderbolt, and asked:

"Darling, what do you mean? Why so indifferent now? 7.51
Where has your extraordinary love for me gone?"

Then she laughed and told him:

"Reverend sir. The woman who conceded defeat at my hands in the royal group today had once sneered at me in a quarrel:

'You are as proud as if you had conquered Maríchi!' 7.54

So for a bet with servitude as the stake I set about the task. And by your grace I have won."

She had rejected the stupid man. Full of remorse and utterly deflated, he went home. You should know, good sir, that I am the one she beggared.* That seductress managed to impregnate me with passion, then she killed it, and her final gift was absolute dispassion. Very soon I will be myself

ātmā tvad|artha|sādhana|kṣamaḥ kartum. asyām eva tāvad vas' Âṅga|puryāṃ Caṃpāyām iti.›

7.57 Atha tan|manaś|cyuta|tamaḥ|sparśa|bhiy" êv' âstaṃ ravir agāt. ṛṣi|muktaś ca rāgaḥ saṃdhyātven' âsphurat. tat|kathā| datta|vairāgyāṇ' îva kamala|vanāni samakucan.

Anumata|muni|śāsanas tv aham amun" âiva sah' ôpāsya saṃdhyām anurūpābhiḥ kathābhis tam anuśayya nīta|rātriḥ.

Pratyunmiṣaty udaya|prastha|dāva|kalpe kalpa|druma|kisalay'|âvadhīriṇy aruṇ'|ârciṣi taṃ namaskṛtya nagarāy' ôdacalam.

7.60 Adarśāṃ ca mārg'|âbhyāsa|vartinaḥ kasy' âpi kṣapaṇaka| vihārasya bahir vivikte rakt'|âśoka|khaṇḍe niṣaṇṇam a|spṛṣṭa| samādhim ādhi|kṣīṇam agra|gaṇyam an|abhirūpāṇāṃ kṛpaṇa|varṇaṃ kam api kṣapaṇakam. urasi c' âsya śithilita|mala| nicayān mukhān nipatato 'śru|bindūn alakṣayam. aprākṣaṃ c' ântik'|ôpaviṣṭaḥ:

‹Kva tapaḥ kva ca ruditam? na ced rahasyam icchāmi śrotuṃ śoka|hetum iti.›

So 'brūta:

7.63 ‹Saumya, śrūyatām. aham asyām eva Caṃpāyāṃ Nidhipālita|nāmnaḥ śreṣṭhino jyeṣṭha|sūnur Vasupālito nāma. vairūpyāt tu mama Virūpaka iti prasiddhir āsīt. anyaś c' âtra

again, and ready and able to perform the service you ask of me. Until then, you should take up residence in Champa, the Angan city of my story.'

At that point the sun went down, apparently afraid of the touch of the blind darkness that had fallen away from the sage's spirit. The sunset glimmered with the fiery passion* from which he had been liberated. Forests of lotuses closed up, colorless, as though his tale had made them, too, lose interest in the world. 7.57

Obeying the holy man's instructions, we performed the twilight rites together.* As I lay down beside him we passed the night in such talk as seemed appropriate.

When the rosy-rayed sun rose again it was like a wildfire on the peaks of its eastern rising-mountain, far more crimson than the flaming shoots of the wish-fulfilling tree. I took my respectful leave and set out for the city.

On the way I saw a mendicant sitting looking wretched in a lonely clump of *ashóka** trees, outside a monastery for practitioners of the Jain Path.* Meditation had not helped this paragon of the unblessed, but he was wasted with anxiety. I could see too that teardrops falling to his chest from his face had dissolved the accumulation of dirt thereon. I sat down nearby and asked: 7.60

'What do tears have to do with the ascetic life? If it is no secret, I would like to hear what caused this anguish.'

He told me:

'Gentle sir, you will hear. I am Vasu·pálita, the eldest son of Nidhi·pálita, a prominent merchant in the city Champa over there. But because I was so unattractive I was dubbed Virúpaka, "Ugly." There was another in town who was Sun- 7.63

Sundaraka iti yath"|ârtha|nāmā kalā|guṇaiḥ samṛddho vasunā n' âtipuṣṭo 'bhavat.

Tasya ca mama ca vapur|vasunī nimittīkṛtya vairaṃ vai-r'|ôpajīvibhiḥ paura|dhūrtair udapādyata. ta eva kadā cid āvayor utsava|samāje svayam utpāditam anyony'|âvamāna|mūlam adhikṣepa|vacana|vyatikaram upaśamayya:

«Na vapur vasu vā puṃstva|mūlam, api tu prakṛṣṭa|gaṇikā|prārthya|yauvano hi yaḥ sa pumān. ato yuvati|lalāma|bhūtā Kāmamañjarī yaṃ sā kāmayate sa haratu su|bhaga|patākām! iti»

7.66 vyavāsthāpayan. abhyupety' âvāṃ prāhiṇuva tasyai dūtān. aham eva kil' âmuṣyāḥ smar'|ônmāda|hetur āsam. āsīnayoś c' âvayor mām ev' ôpagamya sā nīl'|ôtpala|mayam iv' âpāṅga|dām'|âṅge mama muñcantī taṃ janam apatrapay" âdhomukhaṃ vyadhatta.

Su|bhagaṃ|manyena ca mayā sva|dhanasya sva|gṛhasya sva|gaṇasya sva|dehasya sva|jīvitasya ca s" âiv' ēśvarīkṛtā. kṛtaś c' âham anayā mala|mallaka|śeṣaḥ.

Hṛta|sarva|svastayā c' âpavāhitaḥ prapadya lok'|ôpahāsa|lakṣyatām a|kṣamaś ca soḍhuṃ dhik|kṛtāni paura|vṛddhānām iha jain'|āyatane munin" âiken' ôpadiṣṭa|mokṣa|vartmā su|kara eṣa veṣo veśa|nirgatānām ity udīrṇa|vairāgyas tad api kaupīnam ajahām.

dáraka, "Handsome" by name and handsome by nature. He was rich in all artistic qualities, but a cash pauper.

Tricky townspeople who live off disputes made us hate each other, just because of his looks and my money. It was they who had started it, but one day at a festival gathering when we were exchanging insults born out of mutual contempt they took it upon themselves to pacify the situation, ruling that:

"Neither looks nor lucre make the man. Only if the most superior courtesan desires your youth, then you can call yourself a man. Everyone knows that Kama·máñjari is the jewel in the crown among such ladies hereabout. The man she chooses for her love will wave the flag of his good fortune."

Together we accepted the challenge and dispatched mes- 7.66
sengers to invite her. Believe it or not, it seemed that it was I who made her mad with love. For I was the one she approached, as we two men sat there, casting me sidelong glances like a lasso of blue-black lotuses. And the other man was forced to look away, humiliated.

Imagining myself lucky, I made her mistress of my wealth, my home, my people, my body and my very life. In return she reduced me to a rag around my pudenda.*

First she robbed me of all my well-being,* then she threw me out. I became the universal laughingstock. The tut-tutting of the city elders was unbearable. Finally, here in this Jain establishment, a holy man rerouted me toward spiritual release. Thinking their rule of nudity only fitting for one who has come from a whorehouse, I renounced all attachment and gave up that loincloth, too.

7.69 Atha punaḥ prakīrṇa|mala|paṅkaḥ prabala|keśa|luñcana|vyathaḥ prakṛṣṭatama|kṣut|pipās'|ādi|duḥkhaḥ sthān'|āsana|śayana|bhojaneṣv api dvipa iva nava|graho balavatībhir yantraṇābhir udvejitaḥ pratyavāmṛśam:

«Aham asmi dvi|jātiḥ. a|sva|dharmo mam' âiṣa pākhaṇḍa|path'|âvatāraḥ. śruti|smṛti|vihiten' âiva vartmanā mama pūrva|jāḥ prāvartanta. mama tu manda|bhāgyasya nindya|veṣam a|manda|duḥkh'|āyatanaṃ Hari|Hara|Hiraṇya|garbh'|ādi|devat"|âpavāda|śravaṇa|nairantaryāt prety' âpi niraya|phalam a|phalaṃ vipralambha|prāyam īdṛśam idam a|dharma|vartma dharmavat samācaraṇīyam āsīd iti!»

pratyākalita|sva|durnayaḥ piṇḍī|khaṇḍaṃ viviktam etad āsādya paryāptam aśru muñcām' îti.›

7.72 Śrutvā c' âitad anukaṃpamāno 'bravam:

‹Bhadra, kṣamasva! kaṃ cit kālam atr' âiva nivasa. nijena dyumnen' âsāv eva veśyā yathā tvāṃ yojayiṣyati tathā yatiṣye. santy upāyās tādṛśā iti!›

āśvāsya tam anūtthito 'ham.

7.75 Nagaram āviśann eva c' ôpalabhya loka|vādāl lubdha|samṛddha|pūrṇāṃ puram ity arthānāṃ naśvaratvaṃ ca pradarśya prakṛti|sthānam ūnvidhāsyan Karṇī|suta|prahite pathi matim akaravam.

But the next thing I knew I was caked in a layer of filth, 7.69
in agony at the violent tearing out of my hair, and suffering the most excruciating hunger, thirst, you name it. Whether standing, sitting, lying down or feeding, I was like a newly caught elephant not yet broken in, straining against harsh restraints. And so I began to reflect:

"I am a twice-born Hindu. It is against my religion to convert to this heretic path. My forefathers followed only the road laid down in *Shruti*—the Vedic scriptures—and *Smriti*—the lawbooks and so forth.* Nevertheless it was my wicked fate to be driven to practice this irreligious way as though it were a religion. Its nakedness is disgusting. It is a temple to excruciating agony. Even when I am dead my reward will be hell, because I have listened to non-stop blasphemy against the gods, all of them: Hari Vishnu, Hara Shiva and Brahma, born from the golden egg. The reward is no reward. It is a big con!"

In this way I condemned my own offenses, and came to sit here in the lonely *ashóka* grove, where now I abandon myself to tears.'

I was full of sympathy for his story, and said: 7.72

'My good man, bear up! Wait right here for a little while. I will make your courtesan give you back all your wealth. There are ways and means!'

With these words of assurance I took my leave.

No sooner had I entered the city but the general conversa- 7.75
tion showed me that the city was full of rich misers. I made up my mind to demonstrate to them the transient vanity of material objects, and restore them to their natural status, by following the path laid out in Karni·suta's thief's manual.*

Anupraviśya ca dyūta|sabhām akṣa|dhūrtaiḥ samagaṃsi. teṣāṃ ca pañcaviṃśati|prakārāsu sarvāsu dyūt'|âśrayāsu kalāsu kauśalam, akṣa|bhūmi|hast'|ādiṣu c' âtyanta|dur|upalakṣyāṇi kūṭa|karmāṇi, tan|mūlāni s'|âvalepāny adhikṣepa|vacanāni, jīvita|nirapekṣāṇi saṃrambha|viceṣṭitāni;

sabhika|pratyaya|vyavahārān nyāya|bala|pratāpa|prāyān aṅgīkṛt'|ârtha|sādhana|kṣamān, baliṣu sāntvanāni durbaleṣu bhartsitāni, pakṣa|racanā|naipuṇam, ucc'|âvacāni pralobhanāni glaha|prabheda|varṇanāni, dravya|saṃvibhāg'|âudāryam antar" ântar" âślīla|prāyān kalakalān ity etāni c' ânyāni c' ânubhavan na tṛptim adhyagaccham.

7.78 Ahasaṃ ca kiṃ cit pramāda|datta|śāre kva cit kitave. pratikitavas tu nirdahann iva krodha|tāmrayā dṛśā mām abhivīkṣya:

‹Śikṣayasi re dyūta|vartma hāsa|vyājena? āstām ayam a|śikṣito varākaḥ. tvay" âiva tāvad vicakṣaṇena deviṣyām' îti.›

Dyūt'|âdhyakṣ'|ânumatyā vyatyaṣajat. mayā jitaś c' âsau ṣoḍaśa|sahasrāṇi dīnārāṇām. tad|ardhaṃ sabhikāya sabhyebhyaś ca dattv" ârdhaṃ svīkṛty' ôdatiṣṭham. udatiṣṭhaṃś ca tatra|gatānāṃ harṣa|garbhāḥ praśaṃs'|ālāpāḥ. prārthayamāna|sabhik'|ânurodhāc ca tad|agāre 'tyudāram abhyavahāra|vidhim akaravam.

I entered a gambling house to mix with the dodgy gamblers. Their expertise in every aspect of the gambling art was obvious, in all twenty-five of its varieties. Their tricks were incredibly difficult to spot, what they could do with their hands on the diceboard, for example, tricks that provoked aggressive abusive language. They acted on impulse, reckless of their survival.

The keeper of the gaming house permitted transactions that required reasoning, force and fierce threats to recover what one was owed. Strongmen were sweet-talked, weaklings intimidated. They were brilliant at taking sides. I saw them set the whole gamut of traps and elaborate vividly every kind of wager. In sharing their winnings they were generous. And everywhere there was the roar of obscene language. Noting all this and much besides gave me no confidence.

Just then one of the gamblers lost his attention and with 7.78
it a piece, and I gave a little smile. But his opponent turned on me with a look of flaming fury as though actually on fire and roared:

'Hey! Is your smile supposed to teach us the game? Enough of this pathetic know-nothing. If you are so clever, then I will play you now.'

With the dice master's assent, the game commenced. I beat him to the tune of sixteen thousand pieces of gold. Half of my winnings I gave to the proprietor of the gaming establishment and his staff, and stood up with my half.* With me rose thrilled applause and congratulations from everyone there. Accepting our host's invitation I dined most sumptuously at his home.

7.81 Yan|mūlaś ca me durodar'|âvatāraḥ sa me Vimardako nāma viśvāsyataraṃ dvitīyaṃ hṛdayam āsīt. tan|mukhena ca sārataḥ karmataḥ śīlataś ca sakalam eva nagaram avadhārya;

dhūrjaṭi|kaṇṭha|kalmāṣa|kālatame tamasi nīla|nivasan'|ârdhoruka|parihito baddha|tīkṣṇa|kaukṣeyakaḥ phaṇi|mukha|kākalī|saṃdaṃśaka|puruṣa|śīrṣaka|yoga|cūrṇa|yoga|vartikā|māna|sūtra|karkaṭaka|rajju|dīpa|bhājana|bhramara|karaṇḍaka|prabhṛty an|ek'|ôpakaraṇa|yuktaḥ;

gatvā kasya cil lubdh'|ēśvarasya gṛhe saṃdhiṃ chittvā paṭa|bhāsa|sūkṣma|cchidr'|ālakṣit'|ântargṛha|pravṛttir a|vyatho nija|gṛham iv' ânupraviśya nīvīṃ sāra|mahatīm ādāya niragām.

7.84 Nīla|nīrada|nikara|pīvara|timira|nibiḍitāyāṃ rāja|vīthyāṃ jhaṭiti śata|hradā|saṃpātam iva kṣaṇam ālokam alakṣayam. ath' âsau nagara|devat" êva nagara|moṣa|roṣitā niḥsaṃbādha|velāyāṃ niḥsṛtā saṃnikṛṣṭā kācid unmiṣad|bhūṣaṇā yuvatir āvir āsīt.

‹K" âsi vāsu? kva yās' îti?›

sa|dayam uktā trāsa|gadgadam agādīt:

7.87 ‹Ārya, pury asyām arya|varyaḥ Kuberadatta|nāmā vasati. asmy ahaṃ tasya kanyā. māṃ jāta|mātrāṃ Dhanamitra|nāmne 'tratyāy' âiva kasmaicid ibhya|kumārāy' ânvajānād bhāryāṃ me pitā. sa punar asminn atyudāratayā pitror ante vittair nijaiḥ krītv" êv' ârthi|vargād dāridryaṃ daridrati saty

Meanwhile, Vimárdaka, 'Crusher,' on whose account I had entered the game, became like my second and more reliable heart. He taught me about the entire city, its riches, its business and its habits. 7.81

One dark night, blue-black as dark as the dark-blue neck of Shiva after he had drunk the poison, I dressed in a dark-blue cloak, fitted a sharp sword at my arm, and took up my load of tools: a spade in the shape of a cobra's hood, a sounding whistle, pliers, a head-shaped hole plug, magic powder, a magical wick, measuring cord, a wrench and a rope, a lamp, and a box of bees to snuff out lights.*

Off I went to the house of one of the miser masters, where I cut an opening in the wall. Through a tiny peephole in the shutters I reconnoitered the interior before entering, unmolested as though it were my own home, and made off with his moneybag full of treasure.

The main road was swallowed up in the fleshy gloom of 7.84
a bank of dark-blue storm clouds. Suddenly I saw a light, for an instant only, like a hundred light rays colliding in a flash of lightning. It revealed a young woman with glittering jewelry just nearby. She looked like the city's patron goddess, abroad at this lonely hour in her fury at the theft in her town.

'Who are you, my girl? Where are you going?'

I asked her gently. Between sobs of fear, she told me:

'Sir, there lives in this town a noble merchant, called Ku- 7.87
béra·datta. I am his daughter. The day I was born my father promised me in marriage to a local rich man's son called Dhana·mitra. But after his parents had passed away Dhana·mitra was so generous that he used his riches to more or less buy poverty from a crowd of beggars. He may have been

ath' Ôdāraka iti ca prīta|lok'|âdhiropit'|âpara|ślāghya|nāmani;

varayaty eva tasmin māṃ taruṇībhūtām adhana ity adattv" Ârthapati|nāmne kasmaicid itarasmai yath"|ârtha|nāmne sārthavāhāya ditsati me pitā. tad a|maṅgalam adya kila prabhāte bhāv' îti jñātvā prāg eva priyatama|datta|saṃketā vañcita|sva|janā nirgatya bāly'|âbhyastena vartmanā Manmath'|âbhisarā tad|agāram abhisarāmi. tan māṃ muñca! gṛhāṇ' âitad bhāṇḍam iti›

unmucya mahyam arpitavatī. dayamānaś c' âham abravam:

7.90 ‹Ehi sādhvi. tvāṃ nayeyaṃ tvat|priy'|āvasatham iti.›

Tri|caturāṇi padāny udacalam. āpatac ca dīpik'|āloka|parilupyamāna|timira|bhāraṃ yaṣṭi|kṛpāṇa|pāṇi nāgarika|balam an|alpam. dṛṣṭv" âiva pravepamānāṃ kanyakām avadam:

‹Bhadre mā bhaiṣīḥ. asty ayam asi|dvitīyo me bāhuḥ. api tu mṛdur ayam upāyas tvad|apekṣayā cintitaḥ. śaye 'haṃ bhāvita|viṣa|vega|vikriyaḥ. tvay" âpy amī vācyāḥ:

7.93 «Niśi vayam imāṃ purīṃ praviṣṭāḥ. daṣṭaś ca mam' âiṣa nāyako darvī|kareṇ' âmuṣmin sabhā|gṛha|koṇe. yadi vaḥ

penniless, but the people were so delighted with him that they gave him a new epithet in praise, Udáraka, "Generous."

Now that I am a young woman he still wants to marry me. But because he is penniless my father will not give me to him. Instead he intends to give me to another man, some big caravan merchant called Artha·pati, "Lord of commodities," by name and by nature. I discovered that this disastrous event was due to happen today at dawn. Having already arranged a rendezvous with my beloved, I gave my people the slip, and set out on the road I have so often walked since I was a child. With the god of love as my companion I am on my way to my beloved's house. So please let me go! Here, you can take this jewelry.'

And she unfastened her ornaments and handed them over. Full of compassion, I said:

'Come, good maid, I shall escort you to your love's house.' 7.90

We had gone just three or four steps when we came across a force of no few city police. The light of their torches drove the night away; and in their hands were truncheon and sword. As soon as we saw them the girl started to tremble. I told her:

'Do not be afraid, miss. Look, here is my arm and its friend a sword. For your sake I have thought of a way to deal with them gently. I am going to lie down and pretend to have a fit from the effect of spreading poison. You must tell them:

"It was night when we reached this city. My husband 7.93
here was bitten by a hooded serpent at the corner of that assembly house. If one of you gentlemen knows a magic

kaś cin mantravit kṛpāluḥ sa enam ujjīvayan mama prāṇān āhared a|nāthāyā iti.» iti.›

S" âpi bālā gaty|antar'|â|bhāvād bhaya|gadgada|svarā bāṣpa|durdin'|âkṣī baddha|vepathuḥ kathaṃ katham api gatvā mad|uktam anvatiṣṭhat. aśayiṣi c' âhaṃ bhāvita|viṣa|vikriyaḥ teṣu kaś cin nar'|êndr'|âbhimānī māṃ nirvarṇya mudrā|tantra|mantra|dhyān'|ādibhiś c' ôpakramy' â|kṛt'|ârthaḥ.

‹Gata ev' âyaṃ kāla|daṣṭaḥ. tathā hi stabdha|śyāvam aṅgam, ruddhā dṛṣṭiḥ, śānta ev' ôṣmā. śuc" âlaṃ vāsu, śvo 'gni|sātkariṣyāmaḥ. ko 'tivartate daivam iti?›

7.96 sah' êtaraiḥ prāyāt. utthitaś c' âham Udārakāya tāṃ nītv" âbravam:

‹Aham asmi ko 'pi taskaraḥ. tvad|gaten' âiva cetasā sahāya|bhūtena tvām imām abhisarantīm antar" ôpalabhya kṛpayā tvat|samīpam anaiṣam. bhūṣaṇam idam asyā iti›

aṃśu|paṭala|pāṭita|dhvānta|jālaṃ tad apy arpitavān. Udārakas tu tad ādāya sa|lajjaṃ ca sa|harṣaṃ ca sa|saṃbhramaṃ ca mām abhāṣata:

7.99 ‹Ārya, tvay" âiv' êyam asyāṃ niśi priyā me dattā. vāk punar mam' âpahṛtā. tathā hi na jāne vaktum.

remedy, please take pity, resuscitate him and save my life, I am at your mercy." '

It was true that the girl had no other recourse, so with sobs of fear in her voice, her eyes raining tears, overcome with trembling, and with a great effort, she went and did as she had been told. Meanwhile, I lay down and started to mimic the agonies of venom. One of them did indeed fancy himself a powerful healer. First he examined me and then treated me with every possible talisman, potion, spells and thought magic, but without the least result.

'This one is a goner, bitten by a black serpent and in the jaws of death.* You can tell by his stiff, gray body, his glassy gaze and his lost warmth. Stop grieving, my girl, tomorrow we will perform the cremation rites. No one escapes their destiny.'

And with those words he and the others left. Then I got 7.96
up, escorted the woman to her 'Generous' Udáraka, and explained to him:

'I am no more than a thief. I found this lady en route for you with only her heart set on you as companion. Feeling sorry for her, I escorted her to your presence. Here is her jewelry.'

When I handed them over as well, the veil of darkness was torn apart by their radiating light rays. Udáraka took what I had given him and then addressed me, bashfully, with both delight and confusion:

'Noble sir, you and you alone have this night given me 7.99
my beloved. But in so doing you have robbed me of my speech. For I know not what to say.

Tvat|karm' âitad adbhutam iti. idaṃ na te sva|śīlam adbhutavat pratibhāti. n' âivam anyen' âpi kṛta|pūrvam iti pratiniyat" âiva vastu|śaktiḥ. na hi tvayy anyadīyā lobh'|ādayaḥ. tvay" âdya sādhut" ônmīlit" êti tat|prāyas tvat|pūrv'|âvadānebhyo na rocate. dṛṣṭam idānīm audāryasya sva|rūpam iti tvad|āśayam an|anumānya na yukto niścayaḥ.

Tvay" âmunā su|kṛtena krīto 'yaṃ dāsa|jana ity a|sāram atigarīyasā krīṇās' îti sa te prajñ"|âdhikṣepaḥ. priyā|dānasya pratidānam idaṃ śarīram iti tad|alābhe nidhan'|ônmukham idam api tvay" âiva dattam. atha v" âitāvad atra prāpta|rūpam. adya|prabhṛti bhartavyo 'yaṃ dāsa|jana iti!›

7.102 Mama pādayor apatat. utthāpya c' âinam uras" ôpaśliṣy' âbhāṣiṣi:

‹Bhadra, k" âdya te pratipattir iti?›

So 'bhyadhatta:

7.105 ‹Na śaknomi c' âinām atra pitror an|abhyanujñay" ôpayamya jīvitum. ato 'syām eva yāminyāṃ deśam imaṃ jihāsāmi. ko v" âham? yathā tvam ājñāpayas' îti.›

Atha may" ôktam:

I could say that what you have done is absolutely marvelous—but how could behavior that for you is instinctive seem absolutely marvelous? If I were to say that no one has ever done such a good deed before, one could object that the potential of everything is preordained by fate. For you have none of the greed and other faults of other people. Shall I say that today you have displayed real goodness—but that would not be fair to your earlier acts of heroism, pure real goodness every one. Perhaps I have seen the true nature of magnanimity—but without taking into account your intentions, how can I be sure?

If I were to say that with your good deed you had purchased me as a slave, that would be to insult your intelligence, to suggest that you would pay so dearly for something worthless. I could say that in return for your gift of my beloved I give you my life—but it is you who have given me my life, for without her I would have gone headlong to my destruction. Whatever—this much is right and proper: from today onward, you must keep me as your slave!'

With which he fell at my feet. I raised him up, clasped 7.102
him to my breast and asked:

'Good man, what are your plans now?'

He replied:

'Because I cannot marry her and live in this city without 7.105
her father's permission, I want to leave this place this very night. But who am I? I shall do as you command.'

Then I said:

‹Asty etat. sva|deśo deś'|ântaram iti n' êyaṃ gaṇanā vidagdhasya puruṣasya. kiṃ tu bāl" êyam an|alpa|saukumāryā, kaṣṭāḥ pratyavāya|bhūyiṣṭhāś ca kāntāra|pathāḥ. śaithilyam iva kiṃ cit prajñā|sattvayor an|arthen' ēdṛśena deśa|tyāgena saṃbhāvyate. tat sah' ânayā sukham ih' âiva vastavyam. ehi. nayāv' âināṃ svam ev' āvāsam iti.›

7.108 A|vicār'|ânumatena tena sadya ev' âināṃ tad|gṛham upanīya tay" âiv' âpasarpa|bhūtayā tatra mṛd|bhāṇḍ'|âvaśeṣam acorayāva. tato niṣpatya kva cin muṣitakaṃ nidhāya samuccalantau nāgarika|saṃpāte mārga|pārśva|śāyinaṃ kva cin matta|vāraṇam upari|puruṣam ākṛṣy' âdhyārohāva.

Graiveya|prota|pāda|yugalena ca may" ôtthāpyamāna eva pātit'|âdhoraṇa|pṛthul'|ôraḥ|sthala|pariṇataḥ purītal|latā|parīta|danta|kāṇḍaḥ sa rakṣika|balam akṣiṇot. adhvaṃsayāva c' âmun" âiv' Ârthapati|bhavanam. apavāhya ca kvacana jīrṇ'|ôdyāne śākhā|grāhikay" âvātarāva. sva|gṛha|gatau ca snātau śayanam adhyaśiśriyāva.

Tāvad ev' ôdagād udadher uday'|âcal'|êndra|padma|rāga|śṛṅga|kalpaṃ kalpa|druma|hema|pallav'|āpīḍa|pāṭalaṃ pataṅga|maṇḍalam.

'It is true that wise men do not distinguish between home and away. On the other hand, your maiden is exceedingly delicate, and jungle roads are rough and rather dangerous. In such circumstances it would be judged something like a lapse of wisdom and strength to leave without good reason. All things considered, you should stay quietly here with her. Come, we will take her back to her home.'

Without hesitation, he agreed. Straightaway we escorted 7.108
her home. There, while she kept a lookout, we stole everything but the clay pots. Then we left, stashed the stolen goods somewhere, and as we were hurrying along we ran into the city police. A rutting elephant was lying down there beside the road. We dragged off his mahout and climbed on.

Just as I had my two feet pushed inside the chain around the elephant's neck, prodding him to stand up, he bent his head and struck a slanting blow with his tusks on the broad chest of the mahout who had been thrown down. With the man's intestines twisted like a creeper around his branch-like tusks, he then smashed through the band of guards. Still on the same elephant, we demolished Artha·pati's house. After that we rode off to an overgrown garden where we were able to dismount by grabbing hold of a tree branch. Once home, we bathed, and lay down on our beds.

The same moment, the sun's sphere rose from the ocean, like the ruby horn of the lordly eastern sunrise mountain, rosy as the cluster of golden buds on heaven's wish-fulfilling tree.

7.111 Utthāya ca dhauta|vaktrau pragetanāni maṅgalāny anuṣṭhāy' âsmat|karma|tumulaṃ puram anuvicarantāv aśṛṇuva vara|vadhū|gṛheṣu kolāhalam. ath' ârthair Arthapatiḥ Kuberadattam āśvāsya Kulapālikā|vivāhaṃ māsāv adhikam akalpayat. upahvare punar ity aśikṣayaṃ Dhanamitram:

‹Upatiṣṭha sakhe ek'|ânta eva carma|ratna|bhastrikām imāṃ puraskṛty' Âṅga|rājam. ācakṣva ca:

«Jānāty eva devo n' âika|koṭi|sārasya Vasu|mitrasya māṃ Dhanamitraṃ nām' âika|putram. so 'haṃ mūla|haratvam ety' ârthi|vargād asmy avajñātaḥ. mad|artham eva saṃvardhitāyāṃ Kulapālikāyāṃ mad|dāridrya|doṣāt punaḥ Kuberadattena duhitary Arthapataye ditsitāyām udvegād ujjhitum asūn upanagara|bhavaṃ jarad|vanam avagāhya kaṇṭha|nyasta|śastrikaḥ ken' âpi jaṭ"|ādhareṇa nivāry' âivam uktaḥ:

7.114 ‹Kiṃ te sāhasasya mūlam iti?›

May" ôktam:

‹Avajñā|sodaryaṃ dāridryam. iti›

7.117 Sa punar evaṃ kṛpālur anvagrahīt:

‹Tāta, mūḍho 'si. n' ânyat pāpiṣṭhatamam ātma|tyāgāt. ātmānam ātman" ân|avasādy' âiv' ôddharanti santaḥ. santy upāyā dhan'|ârjanasya bahavaḥ, na ko 'pi cchinna|kaṇṭha|pratisaṃdhāna|pūrvasya prāṇa|lābhasya.

We both got up, washed our faces, and performed the early 7.111
morning auspicious rituals. As we strolled around the town, tumultuous with talk of what we had been up to, we heard the hullabaloo in the houses of the bridegroom and bride. Artha·pati had reassured Kubéra·datta with commodities, and was now arranging that his marriage with Kula·pálika, 'Her family's protector,' should be postponed by one month. Alone together again, I instructed Dhana·mitra as follows:

'Go to the king of the Angas, my friend, and present him with this precious little leather pouch, but in private. Inform him:

"My lord, surely you know who I am: Dhana·mitra, the only son of Vasu·mitra the billionaire. But I stand before you in disgrace, bereft of my birthright at the hands of a crowd of beggars. Kula·pálika was promised to me all her life, but because of my offensive poverty Kubéra·datta decided to give his daughter to Artha·pati. I was so distraught that I planned to end my life. To do so I hid myself away in an ancient wood in the suburbs.* The knife was at my throat when a dreadlocked ascetic interrupted me, asking:

'What ground for your violent act of desparation?' 7.114

To which I replied:

'Poverty, the brother of disgrace.'

The compassionate man then took pity on me, saying: 7.117

'My child, you are deluded. Nothing is so utterly heinous as suicide. Good men rescue themselves all by themselves, and never despair. Many are the ways to acquire wealth, but there is no earthly way to procure life if one must first reunite a severed throat.

Kim anena? so 'smy ahaṃ mantra|siddhaḥ. sādhit" êyaṃ lakṣa|grāhiṇī carma|ratna|bhastrikā. ciram aham asyāḥ prasādāt kāma|rūpeṣu kāma|pradaḥ prajānām avātsam. matsariṇyāṃ jarasi bhūmi|svargam atr' ôddeśe pravekṣyann āgataḥ.

7.120 Tām imāṃ pratigṛhāṇa. mad|anyatra c' êyaṃ vaṇigbhyo vāra|mukhyābhyo vā dugdhe iti hi tad|gatā pratītiḥ. kiṃ tu yat sakāśād anyāy' âpahṛtaṃ tat tasmai pratyarpaṇīyam. nyāy'|ârjitaṃ tu deva|brāhmaṇebhyas tyājyam. ath' êyaṃ devat" êva śucau deśe niveśy' ârcyamānā prātaḥ prātaḥ su|varṇa|pūrṇ" âiva dṛśyate. sa eṣa kalpa iti.›

Baddh'|âñjalaye mahyam enāṃ dattvā kim api grāva|cchidraṃ prāviśat.

Iyaṃ ca ratna|bhūtā carma|bhastrikā devāy' â|nivedya n' ôpajīvy" êty ānītā. paraṃ tu devaḥ pramāṇam iti.»

7.123 Rājā ca niyatam eva vakṣyati:

«Bhadra, prīto 'smi. gaccha. yath"|êṣṭam imām upabhuṅkṣv' êti!»

Bhūyaś ca brūhi:

7.126 «Yathā na kaś cid enāṃ muṣṇāti tath" ânugṛhyatām iti!»

Tad apy avaśyam asāv abhyupeṣyati.

Never mind! I am an expert in magic mantra spells and conjured up myself this precious little pouch filled with hundreds of thousands of gold pieces. I have lived a long time in Kama·rupa, Assam,* fufilling people's desires with its help. Now, in my jealous old age, I have come here in search of heaven on earth.

Here, you take the pouch. My experience is that, apart 7.120
from myself, only merchants and eminent courtesans can milk it.* But on this condition, that whatever one has blatantly taken from another must first be restored unto him. Not only that, but whatever one has earned honestly must be donated to the gods and brahmins. Thereupon this pouch must be installed in a pure place, and worshipped like a god. Then every daybreak it will be found to be full of gold. That is the procedure.'

I folded my hands together respectfully and he gave me the bag, before disappearing into a rocky cave.

I have brought it here because it seemed wrong to get my living from this little leather pouch, a precious jewel in itself, without first reporting it to your Lordship. It is for your Lordship to decide."

To which the king is sure to respond: 7.123

"Good man, I am pleased with you. Go forth and make the most of this bag however you like."

You should in turn ask again:

"If you would only guarantee that no one will be permitted 7.126
to steal it!"

That, too, he will certainly promise.

Tataḥ sva|gṛham etya yath"|ôktam artha|tyāgaṃ kṛtvā dine dine varivasyamānāṃ steya|labdhair arthair naktam āpūrya prāhṇe lokāya darśayiṣyasi. tataḥ Kuberadattas tṛṇāya matv" Ârthapatim artha|lubdhaḥ kanyakayā svayam eva tvām upasthāsyati. atha kupito 'rthapatir vyavahartum artha|garvād abhiyokṣyate. taṃ ca bhūyaś citrair upāyaiḥ kaupīn'|âvaśeṣaṃ kariṣyāvaḥ. svakaṃ cauryam anen' âiv' âbhyupāyena su|pracchannaṃ bhaviṣyat' îti.›

7.129 Hṛṣṭaś ca Dhanamitro yath"|ôktam anvatiṣṭhat. tad ahar eva man|niyogād Vimardako 'rthapati|sev"|âbhiyuktas tasy' Ôdārake vairam abhyavardhayat. artha|lubdhaś ca Kuberadatto nivṛty' Ârthapater Dhanamitrāy' âiva tanayāṃ s'|ânunayaṃ prāditsata. pratyabadhnāc c' Ârthapatiḥ.

Eṣv eva divaseṣu Kāmamañjaryāḥ svasā yavīyasī Rāgamañjarī nāma pañca|vīra|goṣṭhe saṃgītakam anuṣṭhāsyat' îti sāndr'|ādaraḥ samāgaman nāgara|janaḥ. sa c' âhaṃ saha sakhyā Dhanamitreṇa tatra saṃnyadhiṣi.

Pravṛtta|nṛtyāyāṃ ca tasyāṃ dvitīyaṃ raṅga|pīṭhaṃ mam' âbhūn manaḥ. tad|dṛṣṭi|vibhram'|ôtpala|vana|satr'|âpaśrayaś ca Pañca|śaro bhāva|rasānāṃ sāmagryāt samudita|bala iva mām atimātram avyathayat.

Thereupon you should go home and give away your property as prescribed. Every day you should worship the bag, and at night fill it with stolen goods, which in the morning you can show the world. As a result, the greedy miser Kubéra·datta will no longer give a straw for Artha·pati. He will automatically unite you with his daughter. This will infuriate Artha·pati. His rich man's arrogance will drive him to sue for compensation. Whereupon we two will devise plentiful colorful ways to reduce him in his turn to nothing but a rag to cover his privates. The same ruse will also ensure that our own thievery remains well concealed.'

Dhana·mitra was delighted, and did as I had instructed. 7.129
That same day Vimárdaka got himself employed in the service of Artha·pati, on my direction, and started feeding that man's hatred for Udáraka, the 'Generous' Dhana·mitra. Meanwhile, Kubéra·datta, the greedy miser, rejected Artha·pati and humbly sought to bestow his daughter on Dhana·mitra. But Artha·pati tried to block him with legal proceedings.

In the same period the news went about that Kama·máñjari's younger sister Raga·máñjari, 'Bouquet of love and melodies,'* was to do a musical show in the public assembly hall. The townsfolk gathered with eager curiosity. I too went along, accompanied by my friend Dhana·mitra.

The moment she began, my mind was transformed into a second stage for her performance, such was the impression she made upon me. Love with his five arrows took cover in the lotus cluster of her twinkling glances. He tormented me excruciatingly, his own might reinforced by the completeness of the emotions and sentiments she portrayed.*

7.132 Ath' âsau nagara|devat" êva nagara|moṣa|roṣitā līlā|kaṭ'|âkṣa|mālā|śṛṅkhalābhir nīl'|ôtpala|palāśa|śyāmalābhir mām abadhnāt. nṛty'|ôtthitā ca sā siddhi|lābha|śobhinī—kiṃ vilāsāt, kim abhilāṣāt, kim a|kasmād eva vā, na jāne—asakṛn māṃ sakhībhir apy an|upalakṣiten' Âpāṅga|prokṣitena sa|vibhram'|ārecita|bhrūlatam abhivīkṣya, s'|âpadeśaṃ ca kiṃ cid āviṣkṛta|daśana|candrikaṃ smitvā, loka|locana|mānas'|ânuyātā prātiṣṭhata.

So 'haṃ sva|gṛham etya dur|nivāray'|ôtkaṇṭhayā dūrī-kṛt'|āhāra|spṛhaḥ śiraḥ|śūla|sparśanam apadiśan vivikte talpe muktair avayavair aśayiṣi. atiniṣṇātaś ca madana|tantre mām abhyupetya Dhanamitro rahasy akathayat:

‹Sakhe, s" âiva dhanyā gaṇikā|dārikā, yām evaṃ bhava-n|mano 'bhiniviśate. tasyāś ca mayā sulakṣitā bhāva|vṛttiḥ. tām apy a|cirād a|yugma|śaraḥ śara|śayane śāyayiṣyati. sthā-n'|âbhiniveśinoś ca Vāma|yatna|sādhyaḥ samāgamaḥ. kiṃ tu sā kila vāra|kanyakā gaṇikā|sva|dharma|pratīpa|gāminā bhadr'|ôdāreṇ' āśayena samagirata:

7.135 «Guṇa|śulk" âham na dhana|śulkā. na ca pāṇi|grahaṇād ṛte 'nya|bhogyaṃ yauvanam iti.»

She bound me then in chains, as though she were the city's patron goddess enraged at the robbery in her city, but the chains were the garlands of her playful side glances from eyes like the nearly black petals of blue lotuses. And when she had risen radiant with success from her dance,* she kept looking toward me—whether coquettishly, out of desire, or just because, I know not. Even her friends did not notice her looking at me, consecrated as she was by Kama, arching charmingly her creeper-like eyebrows. She smiled to herself to reveal the moonlight of her teeth, before she left, followed by the eyes and minds of the population. 7.132

I went home. Irresistible longing banished all desire for food, and, pleading a stabbing headache as an excuse, I lay down, limbs sprawled, on my lonely bed. Dhana·mitra, already a veritable expert in the science of intoxicating love, came to confide in me:

'My friend, she is a lucky girl, the harlot's daughter on whom your heart is so set. And I observed carefully how her own emotions developed. Love, he of the odd number of arrows, will soon have her too lying on a bed of arrows. Since you two have fixed your attentions on such worthy objects, crooked Love could make an effort and bring about your union. However, rumor has it that your harlot maiden has taken a vow manifesting a goodness of character quite the opposite of what one expects from a prostitute. She has announced:

"My bride-price will be counted in virtues, not riches. Nor shall anyone but me enjoy my youth without first taking my hand in marriage." 7.135

Tac ca muhuḥ pratiṣidhy' âkṛt'|ârthā tad|bhaginī Kāmamañjarī mātā ca Mādhavasenā rājānam aśru|kaṇṭhyau vyajijñapatām:

«Deva yuṣmad|dāsī Rāgamañjarī rūp'|ânurūpa|śīla|śilpa|kauśalā pūrayiṣyati mano|rathān ity āsīd asmākam atimahaty āśā. s" âdya mūla|cchinnā. yad iyam atikramya sva|kula|dharmam artha|nirapekṣā guṇebhya eva svaṃ yauvanaṃ vicikrīṣate. kula|strī|vṛttam ev' â|cyutam anutiṣṭhāsati. sā ced iyaṃ deva|pād'|ājñay" âpi tāvat prakṛtim āpadyeta tadā peśalaṃ bhaved iti.»

7.138 Rājñā ca tad|anurodhāt tath" ânuśiṣṭā saty apy an|āśrav" âiva sā yad" āsīt tad" âsyāḥ svasā mātā ca rudita|nirbandhena rājñe samagiretām:

«Yadi kaś cid bhujaṅgo 'smad|icchayā vin" âināṃ bālāṃ vipralabhya nāśayiṣyati sa taskaravad vadhya iti.»

Tad evaṃ sthite dhanād ṛte na tat|sva|jano 'numanyate. na tu dhana|dāy' âsāv abhyupagacchat' îti vicintyo 'tr' âbhyupāya iti.›

7.141 Atha may" ôktam:

‹Kim atra cintyam? guṇais tām āvarjya gūḍhaṃ dhanais tat|sva|janaṃ toṣayāva iti.›

Although her sister Kama·máñjari and her mother Mádhava·sena have repeatedly tried to dissuade her, they have done so in vain. With tears in their throats they went to inform the king:

"Your Majesty, it was our greatest hope that your humble servant Raga·máñjari would fulfill everyone's aspirations, her loveliness of form matched by her loveliness of character and accomplishments. But today that hope has been cut off at the root. She has so transgressed her kind's duties and lifestyle that she proposes to sell her own youth only in exchange for virtues, and without giving a thought to profit. Absolutely inflexible, she wants only to copy the upright customs of housewives. If the command of Your Majesty's person at least could bring her to her senses, that would be simply marvelous."

Even when the king himself commanded as they had peti- 7.138
tioned she paid no heed. Next her sister and mother vowed to the king with weeping persistence:

"If any charming creep* should take advantage of this child and violate her without our approval, he must be executed like a thief."

All this being so, her relations will never consent without payment, nor will she on the other hand ever agree to one who pays. This is the problem to which we must think up a solution.'

My response was: 7.141

'What is there to think about? I shall win her over with my virtues, and in secret you and I shall compensate her family with money.'

Tataś ca kāṃ cit Kāmamañjaryāḥ pradhāna|dūtīṃ Dharmarakṣitāṃ nāma Śākya|bhikṣukīṃ cīvara|piṇḍa|dān'|ādin" ôpasaṃgṛhya tan|mukhena tayā bandhakyā paṇa|bandham akaravam:

7.144 ‹Ajina|ratnam Udārakān muṣitvā mayā tubhyaṃ deyaṃ, yadi pratidānaṃ Rāgamañjar" îti.›

So 'haṃ saṃpratipannāyāṃ ca tasyāṃ tathā tam arthaṃ saṃpādya mad|guṇ'|ônmāditāyā Rāgamañjaryāḥ kara|kisalayam agrahīṣam.

Yasyāṃ ca niśi carma|ratna|steya|vādas tasyāḥ prārambhe kāry'|ântar'|âpadeśen' āhūteṣu śṛṇvatsv eva nāgara|mukhyeṣu mat|praṇidhir Vimardako 'rthapati|gṛhyo nāma bhūtvā Dhanamitram ullaṅghya bahv atarjayat. uktaṃ ca Dhanamitreṇa:

7.147 ‹Bhadra kas tav' ârtho yat parasya hetor māṃ ākrośasi? na smarāmi svalpam api tav' âpakāraṃ mat|kṛtam iti.›

So bhūyo 'pi tarjayann iv' âbravīt:

‹Sa eṣa dhana|garvo nāma yat parasya bhāryāṃ śulka|krītāṃ punas tat|pitarau dravyeṇa vilomya svīcikīrṣasi. bravīṣi ca:

7.150 «Kas tav' âpakāro mat|kṛta iti?»

Nanu pratītam ev' âitat «sārthavāhasy' Ârthapater Vimardako bahiścarāḥ prāṇā iti.» so 'haṃ tat|kṛte prāṇān api parityajāmi. brahma|hatyām api na pariharāmi. mam' âika|rātra|jāgara|pratīkāras tav' âiṣa carma|ratn'|âhaṃkāra|dāha|jvara iti.›

Next, with a donation that included a religious robe and almsfood, I procured the collusion of one Buddhist nun called Dharma·rákshita, Kama·máñjari's chief confidante. With her mediation I struck a deal with that harlot:

'I shall steal Udáraka's precious purse for you, if you give 7.144
me in exchange Raga·máñjari.'

Once she had agreed I handed over the goods, and received in return Raga·máñjari's hand, a tender shoot, having already seduced her with my qualities.

That night the rumor spread that the precious pouch had been stolen. Earlier in the evening the prominent townsfolk had been called together on the pretext of some other business, to be the audience for my plant Vimárdaka, to all appearances a crony of Artha·pati, when he insulted Dhana·mitra and threatened him repeatedly. Dhana·mitra asked:

'Good man, why are you hurling abuse at me on someone 7.147
else's behalf? I cannot remember doing you even the slightest harm.'

Still pretending to threaten him, Vimárdaka responded:

'You and your rich man's arrogance. You try to take possession of another man's wife, already paid for, turning her parents' heads with money. And you dare ask:

"What harm have I done you?" 7.150

Everyone knows that I, Vimárdaka, am the caravan-leader Artha·pati's alter ego. They are not wrong. I would give up even my own life for his sake. More than that, I would not shrink even from killing a brahmin. This burning fever of yours, your selfishness caught from the precious pouch, I will cure you of it simply by staying awake for one night.'

Tathā bruvāṇaś ca paura|mukhyaiḥ s'|âmarṣaṃ niṣidhy' âpavāhito 'bhūt. iyaṃ ca vārtā kṛtrim'|ārtinā Dhanamitreṇa carma|ratna|nāśam ādāv ev' ôpakṣipya pārthivāya niveditā. sa c' Ârthapatim āhūy' ôpahvare pṛṣṭavān:

7.153 ‹Aṅga kim asti kaś cid Vimardako nām' âtrabhavata iti?›

Tena ca mūḍh'|ātmanā:

‹Asti, deva, paraṃ mitram. kaś ca ten' ârtha iti?›

7.156 kathite rājñ" ôktam:

‹Api śaknoṣi tam āhvātum iti?›

‹Bāḍham asmi śakta iti.›

7.159 Nirgatya sva|gṛhe veśa|vāṭe dyūta|sabhāyām āpaṇe ca nipuṇam anviṣyan n' ôpalabdhavān. kathaṃ v" ôpalabhyeta sa varākaḥ? sa khalu Vimardako mad|grāhita|tvad|abhijñāna|cihno man|niyogāt tvad|anveṣaṇāy' Ôjjayinīṃ tad|ahar eva prātiṣṭhata.

Arthapatis tu tam a|dṛṣṭvā tat|kṛtam aparādham ātma|saṃbaddhaṃ matvā mohād bhayād vā pratyākhyāya punar Dhanamitreṇa vibhāvite kupitena rājñā nigṛhya nigaḍa|bandhanam anīyata.

Teṣv eva divaseṣu vidhinā kalp'|ôktena carma|ratnaṃ dogdhu|kāmā Kāmamañjarī pūrva|dugdhaṃ kṣapaṇībhūtaṃ Virūpakaṃ rahasy upasṛtya tato 'pahṛtaṃ sarvam artha|jā-

But while Vimárdaka was carrying on like this the leading citizens indignantly intervened to chase him right away. With counterfeit distress, Dhana·mitra reported the whole story to the king, beginning with the disappearance of his precious pouch. The king then summoned Artha·pati and asked him in private:

'Good sir, is a certain Vimárdaka an associate of yours?' 7.153

The deluded man replied:

'My lord, he is my closest friend. What do you wish of him?'

The king asked: 7.156

'Could you call him here?'

'Assuredly I can.'

And he exited. But hunting meticulously in his own 7.159 house, the brothel quarter, the gambling hall and the market, he could not find him. How indeed could the poor chap have found him? For that same day Vimárdaka had set out for Ujjáyini. I had sent him to look for you, Prince Raja·váhana, and had taught him the signs by which he could recognize you.

When Artha·pati failed to find him, he feared that the crime Vimárdaka had committed would be ascribed to him. In a panic, he lost his head and denied responsibility. But after Dhana·mitra had again pressed his case the angry king seized Artha·pati and had him bound in chains.

Meanwhile, Kama·máñjari had her heart set on milking the precious purse, according to the prescribed procedure. She slipped off in secret to 'Ugly' Virúpaka, the one she had milked dry in the past, when she had reduced him to a Jain mendicant. She restored to him everything she had stolen,

naṃ tasmai pratyarpya sa|praśrayaṃ ca bahv anunīya pratyāgamat.

7.162 So 'pi kathaṃ cin nirgranthika|grahān mocit'|ātmā mad|anuśiṣṭo hṛṣṭatamaḥ sva|dharmam eva pratyapadyata. Kāmamañjary api katipayair ev' âhobhir aśmantaka|śeṣam ajina|ratna|doh'|āśayā svam abhyudayam akarot. atha mat|prayukto Dhanamitraḥ pārthivaṃ mitho vyajñāpayat:

‹Deva, y" êyaṃ gaṇikā Kāmamañjarī lobh'|ôtkarṣāl Lobhamañjar" îti lok'|ôpakrośa|pātram āsīt s" âdya muśal'|ôlūkhalāny api nirapekṣaṃ tyajati. tan manye mac|carma|ratna|lābha|hetuḥ. tasya khalu kalpas tādṛśaḥ. vaṇigbhyo vāra|mukhyābhyaś ca dugdhe n' ânyebhya iti hi tad|gatā pratītiḥ. ato 'muṣyām asti me śaṅk" êti!›

Sā sadya eva rājñā saha jananyā samāhūyata. vyathita|varṇen' êva may" ôpahvare kathitam:

7.165 ‹Nūnam, ārye, sarva|sva|tyāgād atiprakāśād āśaṅkanīya|carma|ratna|lābhā tad|anuyogāy' Âṅga|rājena samāhūyase. bhūyo|bhūyaś ca nirbaddhayā tvayā niyatam asmi tad|āgatitven' âham apadeśyaḥ. tataś ca me bhāvī citra|vadhaḥ. mṛte ca mayi na jīviṣyaty eva te bhaginī. tvaṃ ca niḥsvībhūtā. carma|ratnaṃ ca Dhanamitram eva pratibhajiṣyati.

property and personnel, and humbly ingratiated herself to him in many ways, before returning home.

For his part, on my advice Virúpaka did in the end manage to liberate himself from the clutches of those attachmentless* Jains and was absolutely thrilled to return to his own religion. As for Kama·máñjari, within just a few days she had reduced her own prosperity to nothing but the ashes of the hearth, in anticipation of milking the precious pouch. At that point I sent Dhana·mitra to privately inform the king: 7.162

'Your Majesty, the well-known courtesan Kama·máñjari, "Bouquet of love," used to be the butt of everybody's abuse, nicknamed Lobha·máñjari, "Bouquet of greed," because of her overweening greed. Well, today she is giving everything away to charity without a second thought, right down to her pestles and mortars. I believe that this must be prompted by her acquisition of my precious purse. For such is indeed its due procedure. My experience with it is that only merchants or leading courtesans can milk it, and no one else. Hence I accuse that woman!'

The king immediately summoned Kama·máñjari and her mother. I put on an agitated expression and spoke to them in private first:

'Noble ladies, in so publicly giving away everything you have to charity you were bound be under suspicion of having the precious purse. That is why the king of the Angas has summoned you. You will be repeatedly pressed until forced to betray me as your source for coming by it. Next thing you know they will put me to a gory death. But with me dead your sister will not be able to live on. Not only will you have nothing left, but the precious pouch will fall again 7.165

tadiyam āpat samantato 'n|arth'|ânubandhinī. tat kim atra pratividheyam iti?›

Tayā taj|jananyā c' âśrūṇi visṛjy' ôktam:

‹Asty ev' âitad asmad|bāliśyān nirbhinna|prāyaṃ rahasyam. rājñaś ca nirbandhād dvis triś catur nihnuty' âpi niyatam āgatir apadeśy" âiva coritasya tvayi. tvayi tv apadiṣṭe sarvam asmat|kuṭumbam avasīdet.

7.168 Arthapatau ca tad|apayaśo rūḍham. Aṅga|pura|prasiddhaṃ ca tasya kīnāśasy' âsmābhiḥ saṃgatam. amun" âiva tad asmabhyaṃ dattam ity apadiśya varam ātmā gopāyitum iti›

Mām abhyupagamayya rāja|kulam agamatām. rājñ" ânuyukte ca:

‹N' âiṣa nyāyo veśa|kulasya yad dātur apadeśaḥ. na hy arthair nyāy'|ârjitair eva puruṣā veśam upatiṣṭhant' îti.›

7.171 a|sakṛd atipraṇudya karṇa|nāsā|cched'|ôpakṣepa|bhīṣitābhyāṃ dagdha|bandhakībhyāṃ sa eva tapasvī taskaratven' Ârthapatir agrāhyata. kupitena ca rājñā tasya prāṇeṣ' ûdyato daṇḍaḥ. pr'|âñjalinā Dhanamitreṇ' âiva pratyaṣidhyata:

‹Ārya, Maurya|datta eṣa varo vaṇijām. īdṛśeṣv aparādheṣv asubhir a|viyogaḥ. yadi kupito 'si hṛta|sarvasvo nirvāsanīyaḥ pāpa eṣa iti.›

into Dhana·mitra's clutches. The present emergency will be disastrous all around. How can we now prevent it?'

Kama·máñjari and her mother burst into tears, saying:

'We are the fools to have all but given our secret away. Under pressure from the king we may be able to deny it twice, thrice or even four times, but inevitably we will be compelled to name you as the source of the stolen property. But if you are named then our whole family is doomed.

Artha·pati is anyway already saddled with the disgrace of 7.168
the affair, and all of Anga·pura knows of our close connection with that brute. So the best way to protect ourselves will be to confess that he was the one who gave us the thing.'

They got me to agree, and then went off to the royal court, where the king questioned them both. They kept parrying his interrogation, saying:

'It is improper for prostitutes to name their patrons. After all, not every man who frequents prostitutes does so with honestly earned funds.'

But when they were intimidated with the suggestion of 7.171
having ears and nose cut off, those wily whores betrayed poor old Artha·pati himself as the thief. The king was furious and condemned him to death.* At which point Dhana·mitra raised his hands before him in supplication and intervened:

'My Lord, the Mauryan king granted merchants the privilege of exemption from execution for such crimes.* If you are angry, first confiscate all this crook's chattels and then send him into exile.'

Tan|mūlā ca Dhanamitrasya kīrtir aprathata. aprīyata ca bhartā. paṭaccara|ccheda|śeṣo 'rthapatir artha|mattaḥ sarva| paura|jana|samakṣaṃ niravāsyata.

7.174 Tasy' âiva dravyāṇāṃ tu kena cid avayavena sā varākī Kāmamañjarī carma|ratna|mṛga|tṛṣṇik'|âpaviddha|sarvasvā s'| ânukaṃpaṃ Dhanamitr'|âbhinoditena bhū|pen' ânvagṛhyata. Dhanamitraś c' âhani guṇini Kulapālikām upāyaṃsta.

Tad evaṃ siddha|saṃkalpo Rāgamañjarī|gṛhaṃ hema|ratna|pūrṇam akaravam. asmiṃś ca pure lubdha|samṛddha| vargas tathā muṣito yathā kapāla|pāṇiḥ svair eva dhanair mad|viśrāṇitaiḥ samṛddhīkṛtasy' ârthi|vargasya gṛheṣu bhikṣ'|ârtham abhramat. na hy alam atinipuṇo 'pi puruṣo niyati|likhitāṃ lekhām atikramitum.

Yato 'ham ekadā Rāgamañjaryāḥ praṇaya|kopa|praśamanāya sānunayaṃ pāyitāyāḥ punaḥ punaḥ praṇaya|samarpita|mukha|madhu|gaṇḍūṣam āsvādam āsvādaṃ maden' âspṛśye. śīlaṃ hi mad'|ônmādayor a|mārgeṇ' âpy ucita|karmasv eva pravartanam. yad aham upoḍha|madaḥ:

7.177 ‹Nagaram idam ekay" âiva śarvaryā nirdhanīkṛtya tvad| bhavanaṃ pūrayeyam iti!›

Born of this intervention, Dhana·mitra's fame spread all around. The ruler too was pleased. Artha·pati was once mad for commodities, now he was sent into exile before the eyes of all the citizens with nothing but a piece of old rag to preserve his modesty.

Unlucky Kama·máñjari had given up all she owned for the 7.174
mirage* of the precious pouch. But the king took pity on her and, prompted by Dhana·mitra, granted her a portion of Artha·pati's property. As for Dhana·mitra, on an auspicious day he married Kula·pálika.

Then, with my wishes thus achieved, I filled the house of Raga·máñjari with gold and jewels. The city's miserly rich class was so despoiled that they wandered from house to house of the beggar class with a broken bowl in their hands begging for alms. For I had made the beggars rich, by bestowing on them the riches of the wealthy. But still there is no man so fantastically cunning that he can step outside the lines drawn up by inevitable destiny.

And so it came to pass. One day, when I was tenderly giving Raga·máñjari little drinks to pacify her love piques, I continued drinking in sips of liquor delivered up in love from her mouth, one after another. Intoxication had me in its grasp. It is traditional that drunkenness and overexcitement make one lose the plot even in one's habitual actions. Which is why, as my madness mounted, I announced:

'In just one night I am going to reduce this city to poverty 7.177
and fill your house with riches!'

Pravyathita|priyatamā|praṇām'|âñjali|śapatha|śat'|âtivartī matta|vāraṇa iva rabhasa|cchinna|śṛṅkhalaḥ kay" âpi dhātryā Śṛgālik"|ākhyay" ânugamyamāno n' âtiparikaro 'si|dvitīyo raṃhasā pareṇ' ôdacalam.

Abhipatato 'pi nāgarika|puruṣān a|śaṅkam eva vigṛhya taskara iti tair abhihanyamāno 'pi n' âtiprakupitaḥ krīḍann iva mad'|âvasanna|hasta|patitena nistriṃśena dvitrān eva hatv" âvaghūrṇamāna|tāmra|dṛṣṭir apatam.

7.180 An|antaram ārta|ravān visṛjantī Śṛgālikā mam' âbhyāsam agamat. abadhye c' âham aribhiḥ. āpadā tu mad'|âpahāriṇyā sadya eva bodhitas tat|kṣaṇ'|ôpajātayā pratibhayā vyacīcaram:

‹Aho! mam' êyaṃ moha|mūlā mahaty āpad āpatitā. prasṛtataraṃ ca sakhyaṃ mayā saha Dhanamitrasya mat|parigrahatvaṃ ca Rāgamañjaryāḥ. mad|enasā ca tau prorṇutau śvo niyataṃ nigrahīṣyete. tad iyam iha pratipattir yay" ânuṣṭhīyamānayā man|niyogatas tau paritrāsyete. māṃ ca kadā cid an|arthād itas tārayiṣyata iti.›

Kam apy upāyam ātman" âiva nirṇīya Śṛgālikām agādiṣam:

7.183 ‹Apehi jaratike! yā tām artha|lubdhāṃ dagdha|gaṇikāṃ Rāgamañjarikām ajina|ratna|mattena śatruṇā me mitra|cchadmanā Dhanamitreṇa saṃgamitavatī sā hat" âsi. tasya pāpa-

My darling was deeply distressed, but I paid no heed to her prostrations, protestations and imprecations. I was like a rutting elephant breaking free of my chains. Rather ill-equipped, I charged forth at top speed with a sword as my companion, and followed by Raga·máñjari's nurse Shrigálika.

Without thinking I fought off the city police who happened to cross my path. Crying thief, they began to beat me, but I did not lose my temper completely. I only struck down two or three playfully with my sword before it fell from my hand, feeble with drunkenness, and I fell myself, my vision a crimson whirlpool.

Immediately Shrigálika started pouring forth shrieks of 7.180
distress, and rushed to my side. But my enemies had already bound me. My crisis banished my intoxication. All at once I was wide awake. With the wisdom born of the moment, I calculated:

'Oh, no! My foolish intoxication has brought this great calamity on my head. It is very public knowledge that Dhana·mitra is my friend, and Raga·máñjari my betrothed. They will both be implicated in my guilt, and are bound to be arrested tomorrow. But I have a plan of action. If they follow it to the letter they will be saved. In the end it may even rescue me too from this disastrous situation.'

First I worked out the details within myself, and then shouted out loud to Shrigálika:

'Go away, you old bag! You are the one who fixed up Raga· 7.183
máñjari's union with Dhana·mitra. She is no more than a filthy prostitute, greedy for gain. He is my enemy who pretended to be my friend, out of his mind on account of

sya carma|ratna|moṣād duhituś ca te sār'|ābharaṇ'|âpahārād aham adya niḥśalyam utsṛjeyaṃ jīvitam iti!›

Sā punar uddhaṭita|jñā parama|dhūrtā s'|âśru|gadgam udañjalis tān puruṣān sa|praṇāmam āsāditavatī sāmapūrvaṃ mama purastād ayācata:

‹Bhadrakāḥ, pratīkṣadhvaṃ kaṃ cit kālaṃ yāvad asmād asmadīyaṃ sarvaṃ muṣitam artha|jātam avagaccheyam iti.›

7.186 Tath" êti taiḥ pratipanne punar mat|samīpam āsādya:

‹Saumya, kṣamasv' âsya dāsī|janasy' âikam aparādham. astu sa kāmaṃ tvat|kalatr'|âbhimarśī vair'|āspadaṃ Dhanamitraḥ. smaraṃs tu cira|kṛtāṃ te paricaryām anugrahītum arhasi dāsīṃ Rāgamañjarīm. ākalpa|sāro hi rūpājīvā|janaḥ. tad brūhi kva nihitaṃ tasyā bhūṣaṇam iti.›

Pādayor apatat. tato dayamāna iv' âham abravam:

7.189 ‹Bhavatu, mṛtyu|hasta|vartinaḥ kiṃ mam' âmuṣyā vair'|ânubandhen' êti?›

Tad bruvann iva karṇa ev' âinām aśikṣayam:

‹Evam evaṃ pratipattavyam iti.›

7.192 Sā tu pratipann'|ârth" êva:

‹Jīva ciram! prasīdantu te devatāḥ! devo 'py Aṅga|rājaḥ pauruṣa|prīto mocayatu tvām! ete 'pi bhadra|mukhās tava dayantām iti!›

the precious purse. But now you have lost. I have robbed that criminal of his precious pouch and stolen your daughter's treasured ornaments. At least I can now give up my life without a twinge of regret!'

She knew how to take a hint, and was brilliant at deceit. Sobbing with tears, she approached those men, prostrating herself, her hands raised in supplication. As I watched, she implored:

'Good sirs, please hold back for a little while until I can find out what has become of all the property this man has stolen from us.'

Once they had agreed, she again came close and fell at my 7.186
feet with the words:

'Gentle sir, forgive your devoted wife's one and only offense. By all means, you are free to hate Dhana·mitra for ravishing your wife. But you should not forget how long your slave Raga·máñjari has served you faithfully. Forgive her. A courtesan who lives off her looks is nothing without her trappings. So please tell me where you have stashed her ornaments.'

I pretended to be sympathetic, saying:

'It is true, now that I am in the hands of death, why should 7.189
I keep hating her?'

And as though I were telling what she had asked I whispered precise instructions into her ear:

'Do this, and then that, and then the other.'

She acted as though she had got what she wanted, saying: 7.192

'Live long! May the gods have mercy on you! May the Angan king too be pleased with your valor and release you! And may these fine fellows also take pity on you!'

kṣaṇād apāsarat. ānīye c' âham ārakṣika|nāyakasya śāsanāc cārakam.

7.195 Ath' ôttaredyur āgatya dṛptataraḥ su|bhaga|mānī sundaraṃ|manyaḥ pitur atyayād a|cir'|âdhiṣṭhit'|âdhikāras tāruṇya|madād an|atipakvaḥ Kāntako nāma nāgarikaḥ kiṃ cid iva bhartsayitvā māṃ samabhyadhatta:

‹Na ced Dhanamitrasy' âjina|ratnaṃ pratiprayacchasi na ced vā nāgarikebhyaś coritakāni pratyaparyasi drakṣyasi pāram aṣṭādaśānāṃ kāraṇānām, ante ca mṛtyu|mukham iti.›

Mayā tu smayamānen' âbhihitam:

7.198 ‹Saumya, yady api dadyāmā janmano muṣitaṃ dhanaṃ na tv Arthapati|dār"|âpahāriṇaḥ śatror me mitra|mukhasya Dhanamitrasya carma|ratna|pratyāśāṃ pūrayeyam. adattv" âiva tad ayutam api yātanānām anubhaveyam. iyaṃ me sādhīyasī saṃdh" êti!›

Ten' âiva krameṇa vartamāne sāntvana|tarjana|prāye pratidinam anuyoga|vyatikare 'nuguṇ'|ânna|pāna|lābhāt katipayair ev' âhobhir viropita|vraṇaḥ prakṛti|stho 'ham āsam.

Atha kadā cid A|cyut'|âmbara|pīt'|ātapa|tviṣi kṣayiṇi vāsare hṛṣṭa|varṇā Śṛgālik" ôjjvalena veṣeṇ' ôpasṛtya dūra|sth'|ânucarā mām upaśliṣy' âbravīt:

In a moment she was gone, and on the order of the commander of the guard I had been taken off to jail.

The following day the chief of the city police, called Kántaka, 'Lovely,' came to see me. He was highly conceited, fancying himself blessed and beautiful, and was just recently appointed to his post, on the death of his father. With the cockiness of his tender age he was quite immature. To start with, he threatened me a bit, then pronounced: 7.195

'Unless you hand back Dhana·mitra's precious pouch and also render unto the citizens their stolen property, you will become acquainted with every one of the eighteen kinds of torture and will in the end look death himself in the face.'

Smiling, I replied:

'Good man, even if I were to give up the fortune I have robbed since my birth, I shall never satisfy Dhana·mitra's wish for the return of the precious purse. That rapist of Artha·pati's wife is my enemy, though he puts on the face of a friend. I shall never give him the pouch, but would rather suffer even ten thousand tortures. You have my very firm pledge!' 7.198

The protracted interrogation, mostly cajoling or threats, continued in this way on a daily basis. Meanwhile, within just a few days of eating and drinking wholesome things my wounds were healed and I was back to health.

Then one evening, as the day was dying, the sun's luster saffron as the robes of Vishnu the immovable, Shrigálika approached, splendidly attired and with a pleased expression. Leaving her attendants standing at a distance, she embraced me and said:

7.201 ‹Ārya, diṣṭyā vardhase. phalitā tava sunītiḥ. yathā tvay" ādiśye tathā Dhanamitram ety' âbravam:

«Ārya tav' âivam āpannaḥ suhṛd ity uvāca:

‹Aham adya veśa|saṃsarga|su|labhāt pāna|doṣād baddhaḥ. tvayā punar a|viśaṅkam ady' âiva rājā vijñāpanīyaḥ:

7.204 «Deva, deva|prasādād eva pur" âpi tad ajina|ratnam Artha-pati|muṣitam āsāditam. atha tu bhartā Rāgamañjaryāḥ kaś cid akṣa|dhūrtaḥ kalāsu kavitveṣu loka|vārtāsu c' âtivaicakṣaṇyān mayā samasṛjyata.

Tat|saṃbandhāc ca vastr'|ābharaṇa|preṣaṇ'|ādinā tad|bhāryāṃ pratidinam anvavarte. tad asāv aśaṅkiṣṭa nikṛṣṭ'|āśayaḥ kitavaḥ. tena ca kupitena hṛtaṃ tac carma|ratnam ābharaṇa|samudgakaś ca tasyāḥ.

Sa tu bhūyaḥ steyāya bhramann agṛhyata nāgarika|puruṣaiḥ. āpannena c' âmun" ânusṛtya rudatyai Rāgamañjarī|paricārikāyai pūrva|praṇay'|ânuvartinā tad|bhāṇḍa|nidhān'|ôddeśaḥ kathitaḥ. mam' âpi carma|ratnam upāy'|ôpakrānto yadi prayacched iha deva|pādaiḥ prasādaḥ kārya iti!»

7.207 Tathā niveditaś ca Nara|patir asubhir mām a|viyojy' ôpacchandanair eva svaṃ te dāpayituṃ prayatiṣyate. tan naḥ pathyam iti!›»

'Noble sir, you are to be congratulated. Your perfect plan has borne fruit. I went to Dhana·mitra just as you instructed and informed him: 7.201

"Noble sir, your friend is in such-and-such trouble. He tells you:

'I caught the curse of the drink, so easy to contract in the company of a courtesan, and hence am today under arrest. You must go at once without delay and explain to the king:

"My Lord, by Your Majesty's grace I was able to recover the precious pouch stolen by Artha·pati. This time, however, the trouble started when I struck up a friendship with the husband of Raga·máñjari, a rogue with the dice, a friendship founded on his phenomenal brilliance in the arts, letters and society ways. 7.204

As his friend I used to attend to his wife on a daily basis, rendering such services as sending garments and ornaments. But that base-minded crook became suspicious of my behavior. In his anger he took my precious pouch as well as her jewelry casket.

Then, when he was on the prowl for something else to steal, the city police apprehended him. Raga·máñjari's womanservant had followed him in tears, and now that he was in trouble he reverted to his old feelings of love, telling her where he had stashed Raga·máñjari's box. If he can be persuaded to return my precious pouch as well, then perhaps Your Majesty could have mercy on him!"

Once you have told all this to the king, that Lord of men, he will not have me cut to pieces with swords, but will try to coax me into giving back what is yours. That would be a healthy turn of events for us!'" 7.207

Śrutv" âiva ca tvad|anubhāva|pratyayād an|atitrasnunā tena tat tath" âiva saṃpāditam. ath' âhaṃ tvad|abhijñāna|pratyāyitāyā Rāgamañjaryāḥ sakāśād yath"|êpsitāni vastūni labhamānā rāja|duhitur Ambālikāyā dhātrīṃ Māṅgalikāṃ tvad|ādiṣṭena mārgeṇ' ânvarañjayam. tām eva ca saṃkramīkṛtya Rāgamañjaryāś c' Âmbālikāyāḥ sakhyaṃ param avīvṛdham.

Ahar ahaś ca nava|navāni prābhṛtāny upaharantī kathāś citrāś citta|hāriṇīḥ kathayantī tasyāḥ paraṃ prasāda|pātram āsam.

7.210 Ekadā ca harmya|gatāyās tasyāḥ sthāna|sthitam api karṇa|kuvalayaṃ srastam iti samādadhatī pramatt" êva pracyāvya punar utkṣipya bhūmes ten' ôpa|kanyāpuraṃ kāraṇena ken'|âpi bhavan'|âṅgaṇaṃ praviṣṭasya Kāntakasy' ôpari pravṛtta|kuhara|pārāvata|trāsan"|âpadeśāt prahasantī prāhārṣam.

So 'pi tena dhanyaṃ|manyaḥ kiṃ cid unmukhaḥ smayamāno mat|karma|prahāsitāyā rāja|duhitur vilāsa|prāyam ākāram ātm'|âbhilāṣa|mūlam iva yathā saṃkalpeyat tathā may" âpi saṃjñay" âiva kim api caturam āceṣṭitam. ākṛṣṭa|dhanvanā ca Manasijena viddhaḥ sa digdha|phalena patriṇ" âtimugdhaḥ kathaṃ katham apy apāsarat.

No sooner had he heard your instructions than Dhana·mitra did exactly as he was told, hardly afraid at all because of his confidence in your authority. Next I got the confidence of Raga·máñjari with your token of recognition, and could borrow all that I wanted from her to win over Mangálika, Princess Ambálika's nurse, just as you had instructed. Once Mangálika had promised her assistance, I was able to nurture the best of friendships between Raga·máñjari and Ambálika.

Every day I presented Ambálika with new gifts, and told her wonderful captivating stories. And so I became the dearest object of her favor.

One day when the princess was in the summerhouse, I was 7.210
rearranging a blue water lily at her ear as if it had slipped, even though it had not moved from its place. Pretending to be careless, I let it fall and then picked it up again from the ground. Kántaka, the police superintendent, had just then entered the palace courtyard next to the harem for some reason. Laughing aloud I tossed the flower on the pretext of startling the doves who were engaged in acts of love but deliberately hit him on the head.

At this the man thought he was in luck and raised his head a bit with a smile. The princess was laughing at my antics, but I managed something really very clever, to gesticulate so that he should imagine that the sheer coquetry of her countenance was inspired by desire for him. Mind-born Love had drawn full his bow and his feathered arrow with its poisoned tip had struck home, depriving Kántaka of his senses. With a great deal of trouble he somehow managed to leave the place.

S" âyaṃ ca rāja|kany"|âṅgulīyaka|mudritāṃ vāsa|tāmbūla|paṭṭ'|âṃśuka|yugala|bhūṣaṇ'|âvayava|garbhāṃ ca vaṅgerikāṃ kayā cid bālikayā grāhayitvā Rāgamañjary" îti nītvā Kāntakasy' āgāram agām. agādhe ca rāga|sāgare magno nāvam iva mām upalabhya param ahṛṣyat.

7.213 Avasth"|ântarāṇi ca rāja|duhituḥ su|dāruṇāni vyāvarṇayantyā mayā sa durmatiḥ sudūram udamādyata. tat|prārthitā c' âhaṃ tvat|priyā|prahitam iti mam' âiva mukha|tāmbūl'|ôcchiṣṭ'|ânulepanaṃ nirmālyaṃ malin'|âṃśukaṃ c' ânyedyur upāharam. tadīyāni ca rāja|kany"|ârtham ity upādāya cchannam ev' âpoḍhāni.

Itthaṃ ca saṃdhukṣita|manmath'|âgniḥ sa ev' âikānte may" ôpamantrito 'bhūt:

«Ārya, lakṣaṇāny eva tav' â|visaṃvādīni. tathā hi mat|prātiveśyaḥ kaś cit kārtāntikaḥ:

7.216 ‹Kāntakasya haste rājyam idaṃ patiṣyati. tādṛśāni tasya lakṣaṇān' îti.›

ādikṣat. tad|anurūpam eva ca tvām iyaṃ rāja|kanyakā kāmayate. tad ek'|āpatyaś ca rājā tayā tvāṃ samāgatam upalabhya kupito 'pi duhitur maraṇa|bhayān n' ôcchetsyati. pratyuta prāpayiṣyaty eva yauva|rājyam. itthaṃ c' âyam artho 'rth'|ânubandhī. kim iti tāta n' ārādhyate?

Later I went to Kántaka's house with one of the young women to carry a small cane basket intended for Raga·máñjari and sealed with the princess's signet ring. Within it were perfumes, betel nut, a silk outfit and some ornaments. Sunk as he was in the bottomless ocean of desire, he was as ecstatic to see me as though I were the lifeboat for a drowning man.

I described in detail the dreadful emotional torments that 7.213
had meanwhile plagued the princess, so driving the evil-hearted man out of his mind. At his entreaty I brought the following day some supposed gifts from his darling, in fact betel from my own mouth, my leftover ointment, the remains of a garland, and a dirty garment. The things he wanted to go to the king's daughter I took away, but only to throw them in the rubbish.

After I had inflamed the fire of his maddening love in this way, I took him aside and counselled:

"My Lord, the auspicious marks you bear cannot tell a lie. You see, one of my neighbors is a fortune-teller who has foretold:

'This kingdom will fall into Kántaka's hands. Such are the 7.216
omens.'

It all fits with the fact that our king's daughter is in love with you. The king has only one child. So when he finds out that you have had intercourse with her, however angry he may be he will not come between you, lest that kill his daughter. Quite the reverse, he is sure to bestow on you the rank of crown prince. Thus one prize will follow another. Why, then, my dear, do you not help things along?

Yadi kumārī|pura|praveś'|âbhyupāyaṃ n' âvabudhyase nanu bandhan'|āgāra|bhitter vyāma|trayam antarālam ārāma|prākārasya? kena cit tu hastavat" âikāgārikeṇa tāvatīṃ suraṅgāṃ kārayitvā praviṣṭasy' ôpavanaṃ tav' ôpariṣṭād asmad|āyatt" âiva rakṣā. raktataro hi tasyāḥ parijano na rahasyaṃ bhetsyat' îti.»

7.219 So 'bravīt:

«Sādhu, bhadre, darśitam! asti kaś cit taskaraḥ khanana|karmaṇi Sagara|sutānām iv' ânyatamaḥ. sa cel labdhaḥ kṣaṇen' âitat karma sādhayiṣyat' îti.»

«Katamo 'sau? kim iti na labhyata iti?» may" ôkte «yena tad Dhanamitrasya carma|ratnaṃ muṣitam iti» tvām eva sa niradikṣat.

7.222 «Yady evam ehi! ‹tvay" âsmin karmaṇi sādhite citrair upāyais tvām ahaṃ mocayiṣyām' îti› śapatha|pūrvaṃ ten' âbhisaṃdhāya siddhe 'rthe bhūyo 'pi nigaḍayitvā;

‹Yo 'sau cauraḥ sa sarvath" ôpakrāntaḥ, na tu dhārṣṭya|bhūmiḥ prakṛṣṭa|vairas tad ajina|ratnaṃ darśayiṣyat' îti!›

rājñe vijñāpya citram enaṃ haniṣyasi. tathā ca saty arthaḥ sidhyati, rahasyaṃ ca na sravat' îti.»

7.225 May" ôkte so 'tihṛṣṭaḥ pratipadya mām eva tvad|upapralobhane niyujya bahir avasthitaḥ. prāptam itaḥ paraṃ cintyatām iti.›

If you are having trouble figuring out a way to enter the princess's apartment, has it occurred to you that the prison compound and the wall of the pleasure garden are only eighteen feet apart? You could arrange for some handy thief who breaks into lonely houses to dig a tunnel that far, and thereby enter the garden. From there we will take care of your protection. For Ambálika's attendants are very devoted and will not give away her secret."

To which he replied: 7.219

"Good lady, an excellent tip! I do know a burglar as good as the sixty thousand tunnelling sons of Ságara when it comes to a digging job.* If I can get him then the job will be finished in the blink of an eye."

I asked who this man could be, and why he should not be got. In response Kántaka specified none other than you: 'the one who stole Dhana·mitra's precious pouch.'

"If that is so, then go for it! Get him to agree by swearing 7.222
that you will come up with some good trick to release him as soon as he has pulled off this job. Once you have got what you want, chain him up again. Inform the king:

'I have tried everything with this thief, but he is stolidly insolent, overweeningly hostile, and will not say where that precious pouch is.'

After which you can put him to a gory death. In this way you will have got what you want, and your secret cannot escape."

He was delighted at my suggestion, agreed, has appointed 7.225
none other than me to win you over, and is waiting outside. So far so good. What next?'

Prītena ca may" ôktam:

‹Mad|uktam alpam, tvan|naya ev' âtra bhūyān. ānay' âinam iti!›

7.228 Ath' ānīten' âmunā man|mocanāya śapathaḥ kṛtaḥ, mayā ca rahasy'|ânirbhedāya. vinigaḍīkṛtaś ca snāna|bhojana|vilepanāny anubhūya nity'|ândhakārāt kārā|bhitti|koṇād ārabhy' ôrag'|āsyena suraṅgām akaravam. acintayaṃ c' âivam:

‹Hantu|manas" âiv' âmunā man|mocanāya śapathaḥ kṛtaḥ. tad enaṃ hatv" âpi n' â|satya|vāda|doṣeṇa spṛśya iti.›

Niṣpatataś ca me nigaḍanāya prasāryamāṇa|pāṇes tasya pāden' ôrasi nihatya patitasya tasy' âiv' âsi|dhenvā śiro nyakṛntam. akathamaṃ ca Śṛgālikām:

7.231 ‹Bhaṇa, bhadre, kathaṃ|bhūtaḥ kanyā|pura|saṃniveśo mahān ayaṃ prayāso vṛth" âiva mā bhūt. amutra kiṃ cic corayitvā nivartiṣya iti.›

Tad|upadarśita|vibhāgaṃ c' âvagāhya kany"|ântaḥ|puraṃ prajvalatsu maṇi|pradīpeṣu:

n'|âika|krīḍā|kheda|suptasya parijanasya madhye mahita|mah"|ârgha|ratna|pratyupta|siṃh'|ākāra|danta|pāde haṃsa|tūla|garbha|śayy"|ôpadhāna|śālini kusuma|lava|cchurita|paryante paryaṅka|tale;

Pleased, I said:

'The instructions I had given you were nothing; you have taken things much further forward. Bring him in.'

Once she had led Kántaka in, he made the oath to release 7.228
me, and I to not divulge his secret. Freed from my chains, I was able to bathe, dine and generally freshen up. Then, starting from the perpetually dark corner of the jail wall, I dug the tunnel with a serpent-shaped spade. As I did so I pondered:

'With his mind set on killing me, that man has sworn to set me free. In this case, even if I kill him I will not be contaminated with the sin of breaking a promise.'

Indeed, as I was coming out of the tunnel he had already stretched forth his hand to chain me anew, but I kicked him in the chest, he fell down, and with a dagger* I slit his throat. Then I asked Shrigálika:

'Tell me, dear lady, how lies the suite of the princess's 7.231
apartments? I would not want this great effort to have been in vain, so I plan to steal something thence before I escape.'

She explained the arrangement of the women's harem, and in I plunged. In the flickering light of jewelled lamps I saw the king's daughter:

In the midst of her sleeping attendants, themselves tired out after not a few entertainments, she was sound asleep on her bed. The bed's feet were carved ivory lions, studded with gorgeous precious jewels. It was resplendent with goose-down-stuffed mattress and cushions and bestrewn with little flowers.

7.234 dakṣiṇa|pāda|pārṣṇy|adhobhāg'|ânuvalit'|êtara|caraṇ'|âgra|pṛṣṭham, īṣad|vivṛtta|madhura|gulpha|saṃdhi, paras|par'|ā-śliṣṭa|jaṅghā|kāṇḍam, ākuñcita|komal'|ôbhaya|jānu, kiṃ|ci-d|vellit'|ôru|daṇḍa|yugalam;

adhi|nitamba|srasta|mukt'|âika|bhuja|lat"|âgra|peśalam, apāśray'|ânta|nihit'|ākuñcit'|êtara|bhuja|lat"|ôttāna|tala|kara|kisalayam, ā|bhugna|śroṇi|maṇḍalam, ati|śliṣṭa|Cīn'|âṃśuk'|ântarīyam, an|ativalita|tanutar'|ôdaram;

a|tanutara|niḥśvās'|ārambha|kampamāna|kaṭhora|kuca|kuḍmalam, ā|tiraścīna|bandhura|śirodhar'|ôddeśa|dṛśyamā-na|niṣṭapta|tapanīya|sūtra|paryasta|padma|rāga|rucakam, ar-dha|lakṣy'|âdhara|karṇa|pāśa|nibhṛta|kuṇḍalam;

7.237 upari|parāvṛtta|śravaṇa|pāśa|ratna|karṇikā|kiraṇa|mañja-rī|piñjarita|viṣama|vyāviddh'|ā|śithila|śikhaṇḍa|bandhanam, ātma|prabhā|paṭala|durlakṣya|pāṭal'|ôttar'|âdhara|vivaram, gaṇḍasthalī|saṃkrānta|hasta|pallava|darśita|karṇ'|âvataṃsa|kṛtyam;

upari|kapol'|ādarśa|tala|niṣikta|citra|vitāna|patra|jāti|janita|viśeṣaka|kriyam, āmīlita|locan'|êndīvaram, a|vibhrānta|bhrū|patākam, udbhidyamāna|śrama|jala|pulaka|bhinna|śithila|candana|tilakam, ānan'|êndu|saṃmukh'|âlaka|lataṃ ca;

The princess lay with her left foot curled under her right heel, her sweet ankle joints slightly flexed, smooth calves pressed close one against the other. Both tender knees were a little bent, the pair of her broad thighs somewhat asplay. 7.234

Her hand at the tip of one of her long slender arms fell delicately slack over her hip. The creeper-sprout-like hand of the other bent arm held the side of her helpless head in its outstretched palm. Her round haunches slightly curved, she was closely embraced by a slip of Chinese silk,* and her so slender belly had just the right amount of folds.

With the effort of breathing deeply her ripe blossoming breasts trembled. I could see a ruby-and-gold pendant set in chains of burnished gold, a little crooked at her beautifully sloping neck, and could half discern her earring out of sight behind her entrancing ear.

In an uneven disarray, her braids were not tightly bound, 7.237
but they were tawny red with the cluster of rays coming from the jewel ear ornament facing upward at her captivating ear. It was difficult to be certain of the gap between her begonia-pink lips—her own glow was so dense and distracting. Her cheek was entrusted to her bud-like hand, which simultanously modelled the job of ear ornament.

Above hung a splendid embroidered canopy, its reflection on her upturned mirror-like cheek playing the part of painted beauty marks. The blue day-lotuses of her eyes were closed. The banners of her eyebrows were unmoving. As drops of perspiration appeared, they mixed with and dissolved the saffron mark on her forehead, and creeper-like curls framed her moon-like face.

viśrabdha|prasuptām atidhaval'|ôttara|cchada|nimagna|prāy'|âikapārśvatayā cira|*vilasana*|kheda|niścalāṃ śarad|ambhodhar'|ôtsaṅga|śāyinīm iva saudāmanīṃ rāja|kanyām apaśyam.

7.240 Dṛṣṭv" âiva sphurad|Anaṅga|rāgaś cakitaś corayitavya|niḥspṛhas tay" âiva tāvac coryamāṇa|hṛdayaḥ kiṃ|kartavyatā|mūḍhaḥ kṣaṇam atiṣṭham. atarkayaṃ ca:

‹Na ced imāṃ vāma|locanām āpnuyāṃ na mṛṣyati māṃ jīvituṃ Vasanta|bandhuḥ. a|saṃketita|parāmṛṣṭā c' êyam atibālā vyaktam ārta|svareṇa nihanyān me mano|ratham. tato 'ham ev' āghnīya. tad iyam atra pratipattir iti.›

Nāga|danta|lagna|niryāsa|kalka|varṇitaṃ phalakam ādāya maṇi|samudgakād varṇa|vartikām uddhṛtya tāṃ tathā śayānāṃ tasyāś ca māṃ ābaddh'|âñjaliṃ caraṇa|lagnam ālikham āryāṃ c' âitām:

7.243 ‹Tvām ayam ābaddh'|âñjali
dāsa|janas tam imam artham arthayate:
svapihi mayā saha surata|
vyatikara|khinn" âiva mā m" âivam!›

Hema|karaṇḍakāc ca vāsa|tāmbūla|vīṭikāṃ karpūra|sphuṭikāṃ pārijātakaṃ c' ôpayujy' âlaktaka|pāṭalena tad|rasena

Her one side was all but submerged under an exceedingly bright white bedcover, making her look like a flash of lightning lying in the embrace of an autumn cloud, motionless with the exhaustion of long *flashing*, or, in the princess's case, *frolicking*.*

No sooner had I seen her than I was rooted to the spot, throbbing with invisible Love's passion. Not only had I lost my desire to rob but she was robbing me of my heart. At an imbecilic loss, I stood there a moment, speculating: 7.240

'Unless I can have this lovely-eyed lady, Love, Spring's companion, will not suffer me to keep on living. Yet if I should lay a hand on such an innocent girl without prior sign from her she will for sure cry out in distress, crushing my desire. And I would have destroyed myself. This, then, is my plan.'

I took down a writing tablet smeared with resin paste from the peg where it hung, picked up a paintbrush from a jewel case, and made a sketch of her lying as I have described, with myself at her feet, hands folded together in adoration. I inscribed it with this verse in *arya* meter:*

'Here I am—your slave, 7.243
hands folded in subservience.
I beg of you this one thing:
that you should sleep with me beside you,
and only exhausted after erotic union, and not,
not tired in the way you are now.'

From a golden casket I then took a perfumed betel *pan* preparation, a pinch of camphor and some *pari·játaka* gum. Chewing this all up I spat out the juice, pink as lac, spraying the image of a pair of devoted *chakra·vaka* birds on the

sudhā|bhittau cakravāka|mithunaṃ niraṣṭhīvam. aṅgulīya-ka|vinimayaṃ ca kṛtvā kathaṃ|katham api niragām.

Suraṅgayā ca pratyetya bandhan'|âgāraṃ tatra baddhasya nāgarika|varasya Siṃhaghoṣa|nāmnas teṣv eva dineṣu mitratven' ôpacaritasya:

7.246 ‹Evaṃ mayā hatas tapasvī Kāntakaḥ, tat tvayā pratibhidya rahasyaṃ labdhavyo mokṣa ity.›

upadiśya saha Śṛgālikayā nirakrāmiṣam. nṛ|pati|pathe ca samāgatya rakṣika|puruṣair agṛhye. acintayaṃ ca:

‹Alam asmi javen' âpasartum anāmṛṣṭa ev' âibhiḥ. eṣā punar varākī gṛhyeta. tad idam atra prāpta|rūpam iti.›

7.249 Tān eva capalam abhipatya sva|pṛṣṭha|samārpita|kūrparaḥ parāṅ|mukhaḥ sthitvā:

‹Yady aham asmi taskaraḥ, bhadrā badhnīta mām. yuṣmākam ayam adhikāraḥ, na punar asyā varṣīyasyā iti.›

avādiṣam. sā tu tāvat" âiv' ônnīta|mad|abhiprāyā tān sa|praṇāmam abhyetya:

7.252 ‹Bhadra|mukhāḥ, mam' âiṣa putro vāyu|grastaś ciraṃ cikitsitaḥ. pūrvedyuḥ prasanna|kalpaḥ prakṛti|stha eva jātaḥ. jāt'|āsthayā mayā bandhanān niṣkramayya snāpito 'nulepitaś ca paridhāpya niṣpravāṇi|yugalam abhyavahārya param'|ânnam auśīre 'dya kāma|cāraḥ kṛto 'bhūt. atha niśīthe bhūya eva vāyu|nighnaḥ:

whitewashed wall.* Having swapped our rings, I tore myself away with difficulty.

I returned via the tunnel to the prison, where I advised Simha·ghosha, a prominent citizen imprisoned there whom I had befriended during those days of captivity:

'Right, now that I have killed the dastardly Kántaka, if 7.246
I were you I would win my freedom by informing on his secret plot.'

After which I walked out with Shrigálika. Once we were on the royal highway I was spotted by the men of the guard. I considered a moment:

'I could run away at top speed without their being able to touch me. But they would catch this poor old woman I am with. Okay, I know exactly what will work.'

Quick as a flash I rushed at them, and then stood there 7.249
facing away, holding my elbows out behind my back, saying:

'If I am a thief, then arrest me, good sirs. You are the men for the job, not this old hag.'

She needed to hear no more to guess the gist of my plan, so she approached them with a respectful bow:

'Gentlemen, this is my son. He has been long possessed 7.252
by some mysterious vapor, and was being treated for it. Yesterday my dear boy seemed normal again, more or less calm. Naïvely I had him released from the restraints, made him bathe, anoint himself and dress in an outfit fresh from the loom. He had rice pudding to eat, and was free to sit up or lie down as he wished. But when midnight came he was once again overcome with his demons, whereupon he charged headlong out onto the royal highway, ranting:

«Nihatya Kāntakaṃ nṛpati|duhitrā rameyam iti!»

raṃhasā pareṇa rāja|patham abhyapatat. nirūpya c' âhaṃ putram evaṃgatam asyāṃ velāyām anudhāvāmi. tat prasīdata. baddhv" âinaṃ mahyam arpayat' êti!›

7.255 Yāvad asau krandati tāvad ahaṃ:

‹Sthavire, kena devo mātariśvā baddha|pūrvaḥ? kim ete kākāḥ śauṅgeyasya me nigrahītāraḥ? śāntaṃ pāpam iti!›

adhāvam. asāv apy amībhiḥ:

7.258 ‹Tvam ev' ônmattay" ân|unmatta ity unmattaṃ muktavatī. kas tam idānīṃ badhnāt' îti?›

kadarthitā rudaty eva mām anvadhāvat.

Gatvā ca Rāgamañjarī|gṛhaṃ cira|viraha|kheda|vihvalām imāṃ bahu|vidhaṃ samāśvāsya taṃ niśā|śeṣam anayam. pratyūṣe c' Ôdārakeṇa samagacche.

7.261 Atha bhagavantaṃ Marīciṃ veśa|kṛcchrād utthāya punaḥ pratitapta|tapaḥ|prabhāva|pratyāpanna|divya|cakṣuṣam upasaṃgamya ten' âsmy evaṃbhūtaṃ tvad|darśanam avagamitaḥ.

Siṃhaghoṣaś ca Kāntak'|âpacāraṃ nirbhidya tat|pade prasannena rājñā pratiṣṭhāpitas ten' âiva cāraka|suraṅgā|pathena kanyā|pura|praveśaṃ bhūyo 'pi me samapādayat. samagaṃsi c' âhaṃ Śṛgālikā|mukha|visṛta|vārt'|ânuraktayā rāja|duhitrā.

"First I am going to kill Kántaka, and then I am going to enjoy myself with the princess!"

Realizing the state my son was in, I was chasing after him at this hour of the night. So please, I beg you, put him in chains, and hand him back to me.'

She was still wailing when I interposed: 7.255

'Old woman, no one chains the wind god. Do these crows think they can catch me, an eagle? Goodness gracious me! Heavens above!'

And away I ran. Those men scolded Shrigálika:

'You must have been crazy to set loose a crazy man think- 7.258
ing that he was sane. Who will catch him now?'

At which she ran off after me in tears.

I made for Raga·máñjari's house. She was in a state, agitated and exhausted because of our long separation, so I spent the rest of the night there consoling her in many ways. Then at daybreak I rejoined Udáraka, the 'Generous' Dhana·mitra.

Next I sought out the venerable Maríchi. He had got over 7.261
his torments with the courtesan and was again cultivating the torments of religious penance, potent enough that he had regained his divine sight. He revealed that I would set eyes on you, just as it has come to pass.

Elsewhere, Simha·ghosha had won over the king by disclosing Kántaka's misdeeds and was appointed in his place. He then could arrange for me to reenter the ladies' harem by the familiar tunnel route from the prison. There I was united with the princess. Shrigálika's stories had already made her fall in love with me.

Teṣv eva divaseṣu Caṇḍavarmā Siṃhavarm"|âvadhūta|duhitṛ|prārthanaḥ kupito 'bhiyujya puram avāruṇat. a|marṣaṇaś c' Âṅga|rājo yāvad ariḥ pārigrāmikaṃ vidhim ācikīrṣati tāvat svayam eva prākāraṃ nirbhidya pratyāsannān api sahāyān a|pratīkṣamāṇo nirgaty' âbhyadhika|balena vidviṣā mahati saṃparāye bhinna|varmā Siṃhavarmā balād agṛhyata.

7.264 Ambālikā ca balavad abhigṛhya Caṇḍavarmaṇā haṭhāt pariṇetum ātma|bhavanam anīyata. kautukaṃ ca sa kila kṣap'|âvasāne vivāha ity abadhnāt. ahaṃ ca Dhanamitra|gṛhe tad|vivāhāy' âiva pinaddha|maṅgala|pratisaras tam evam avocam:

‹Sakhe, samāpatitam ev' Âṅga|rāj'|âbhisaraṃ rāja|maṇḍalam. su|gūḍham eva saṃbhūya paura|vṛddhais tad upāvartaya. upāvṛttaś ca kṛtta|śirasam eva śatruṃ drakṣyas' îti.›

‹Tath" êti› ten' âbhyupagate gat'|âyuṣo 'muṣya bhavanam utsav'|ākulam upasamādhīyamāna|pariṇay'|ôpakaraṇam itas|tataḥ|praveśa|nirgama|pravṛtta|loka|saṃbādham a|lakṣya|śastrikaḥ saha praviśya maṅgala|pāṭhakair Ambālikā|pāṇi|pallavam agnau sākṣiṇy ātharvaṇena vidhin" ârpyamāṇam āditsamānasy' āyāminaṃ bāhu|daṇḍam ākṛṣya cchurikay" ôrasi prāhārṣam. sphurataś ca katipayān anyān api Yama|viṣayam agamayam.

Those were the days when Simha·varman had rejected Chanda·varman's request for his daughter, infuriating Chanda·varman, who attacked and set siege to the city. The Angan king Simha·varman had lost his patience and broken through his very own walls even as the enemy was all set to carry out their siege strategy to enter the town.* He sallied forth without waiting for his allies, although they were not far off. In the great battle with his far more numerous enemy Simha·varman's armor was smashed, and he was captured.

Chanda·varman also abducted Ambálika, taking her off 7.264
to his private residence to marry her under duress. They say that he had already tied the engaged-to-be-married thread, because the wedding was planned for at the end of the night. Meanwhile, at Dhana·mitra's house, I too had fastened on the auspicious marriage-string, so that I could wed the princess. I told Dhana·mitra:

'My friend, the Angan king's circle of ally kings are very nearby. Take the city elders and lead the allies close in complete secrecy. When you return you will see that the enemy will have been decapitated.'

After he agreed, I went, with my dagger concealed, to Chanda·varman's residence. His life was already over. The place was all aflurry with festivities, wedding accoutrements were being gathered together, and there was a throng of people busy coming and going hither and thither. I entered among the auspicious brahmin officiants. With the fire as witness, the Athárvan domestic priest was ceremonially holding out Ambálika's bud-like hand for that man. He was about to take it when I dragged him toward me by the long strong arm he was even then stretching forth,

7.267 Hata|vidhvastaṃ ca tad|gṛham anuvicaran vepamāna|madhura|gātrīṃ viśāla|locanām abhiniśāmya tad|āliṅgana|sukham anububhūṣus tām ādāya garbha|gṛham avikṣam.

Asminn eva kṣaṇe tav' âsmi nav'|âmbu|vāha|stanita|gambhīreṇa svareṇ' ânugṛhīta iti!»

Śrutvā ca smitvā ca devo 'pi Rājavāhanaḥ

7.270 «Katham asi kārkaśyena Karṇīsutam apy atikrānta iti.»

abhidhāya punar avekṣy' Ôpahāra|varmāṇam:

«Ācakṣva! tav' êdānīm avasara iti.»

7.273 abhāṣata. so 'pi sa|smitaṃ praṇamy' ārabhat' âbhidhātum:

iti śrī|Daṇḍinaḥ kṛtau

Daśa|kumāra|carite

'pahāravarma|caritaṃ

nāma

dvitīya ucchvāsaḥ.

and stabbed him in the chest with my knife. Several others jumped on me, but I sent them all packing to the land of Yama, god of death.

As I hunted through his house, destroyed and deserted, 7.267
I espied her of the tapering eyes, her sweet body atremble. Longing to enjoy the pleasure of her embrace, I carried her off into the inner chamber.

But just at that moment I was blessed with the sound of your voice, deep as the boom of newly gathered stormclouds!"

Prince Raja·váhana listened and smiled.

"Extraordinary! Your ruthlessness surpasses even that of 7.270
wily Karni·suta, patron of thieves."

And with that he looked toward Upahára·varman, saying:

"Speak! It is your turn now."

Upahára·varman then bowed down with a smile, and be- 7.273
gan to tell:

That is the end of the second chapter of
the glorious Dandin's
What Ten Young Men Did.
It is called:
What Apahára·varman Did.

CHAPTER EIGHT
WHAT UPAHÁRA·VARMAN DID

«Eṣo 'smi paryaṭann ekadā gato Videheṣu. Mithilām apraviśy' âiva bahiḥ kva cin maṭhikāyāṃ viśramitum etya kay" âpi vṛddha|tāpasyā datta|pādyaḥ kṣaṇam alinda|bhūmāv avāsthiṣi. tasyās tu mad|darśanād eva kim apy ābaddha|dhāram aśru prāvartata.

‹Kim etad amba? kathaya kāraṇam iti!›

8.3 pṛṣṭā sa|karuṇam ācaṣṭa:

‹Jaivātṛka! nanu śrūyate patir asyā Mithilāyāḥ Prahāravarmā nām' āsīt. tasya khalu Magadha|rājo Rājahaṃsaḥ paraṃ mitram āsīt. tayoś ca vallabhe Bala|Śambalayor iva Vasumatī|Priyaṃvade sakhyam a|pratimam adhattām.

Atha prathama|garbh'|âbhinanditāṃ tāṃ ca priya|sakhīṃ didṛkṣuḥ Priyaṃvadā Vasumatīṃ saha bhartrā Puṣpa|puram agamat. tasminn eva ca samaye Mālavena Magadha|rājasya mahaj|janyam ajani. tatra leśato 'pi durlakṣāṃ gatim agaman Magadha|rājaḥ.

8.6 Maithil'|êndras tu Mālav'|êndra|prayatna|prāṇitaḥ sva|viṣayaṃ pratinivṛtto jyeṣṭhasya Saṃhāravarmaṇaḥ sutair Vikaṭavarma|prabhṛtibhir vyāptaṃ rājyam ākarṇya svasrīyāt Suhma|pater daṇḍ'|âvayavam āditsur aṭavī|patham avagāhya lubdhaka|lupta|sarvasvo 'bhūt.

"THERE I WAS, WANDERING ABOUT until one day I reached Vidéha. Without actually entering Míthila* I went to take rest in a small hermitage outside the city. I stopped awhile on the veranda and some ancient woman ascetic gave me water for washing my feet. But no sooner had she set eyes on me than she poured forth a stream of tears for some reason.

'What is this, mother? Tell me why you weep!'

I asked. She told me, sorrowfully: 8.3

'May you live long! You must have heard that the Lord of this city of Míthila was Prahára·varman, and that Raja·hamsa, the king of Mágadha, was his closest friend. Like the wives of the *ásuras* Bala and Shámbala, the kings' wives, Priyam·vada and Vásumati, formed a friendship without compare.

One day, Priyam·vada conceived the desire to visit her dear friend Vásumati, who had then been blessed with her first pregnancy. Together with her husband Prahára·varman, they set out for Pushpa·pura. That was exactly the time when an enormous war broke out between the king of Mágadha and the Málavan king. In that war every last trace of the Mágadhan king was erased from view.

The lord of Málava intervened to save the life of Prahá- 8.6
ra·varman, the king of Míthila, who departed to return to his own country. But he heard that his kingdom had been usurped by Víkata·varman, 'Hideous,' and the other sons of his eldest brother, Saṃhára·varman. In the hope of obtaining military reinforcements from the Lord of Suhma,* his sister's son, he took a road leading deep into the jungle, where bandits robbed him of all he had.

Tat|sutena ca kanīyasā hasta|vartinā sah' âikākinī vana|cara|śara|varṣa|bhaya|palāyitā vanam agāhiṣi. tatra ca me śārdūla|nakh'|âvalīḍha|nipatitāyāḥ pāṇi|bhraṣṭaḥ sa bālakaḥ kasy' âpi kapilā|śavasya kroḍam abhyalīyata. tac|chav'|ākarṣiṇaś ca vyāghrasy' âsūn iṣur iṣv|asana|yantra|muktaḥ kṣaṇād alikṣat. bhilla|dārakaiḥ sa bālo 'pāhāri.

Sā tv ahaṃ moha|suptā ken' âpi vṛṣṇi|pālen' ôpanīya svaṃ kuṭīram āveśya kṛpay" ôpakrānta|vraṇā svasthībhūya sva|bhartur antikam upatiṣṭhāsur a|sahāyatayā yāvad vyākulībhavāmi tāvan mam' âiva duhitā saha yūnā ken' âpi tam ev' ôddeśam āgamat.

8.9 Sā bhṛśaṃ ruroda. rudit'|ânte ca sā sārtha|ghāte sva|hasta|gatasya rāja|putrasya Kirāta|bhartṛ|hasta|gamanam, ātmanaś ca ken' âpi vana|careṇa vraṇa|viropaṇam svasthāyāś ca punas ten' ôpayantuṃ cintitāyā nikṛṣṭa|jāti|saṃsarga|vaiklavyāt pratyākhyāna|pāruṣyam, tad|a|kṣameṇa c' âmunā vivikte vipine sva|śiraḥ|kartan'|ôdyamam, anena yūnā yadṛcchayā dṛṣṭena tasya dur|ātmano hananam, ātmanaś c' ôpayamanam ity akathayat.

In fright at the woodsmen's rain of arrows I took flight with the younger of his sons in my arms, and plunged all alone into the forest. There a tiger struck me down with a pat of the paw, and the baby tumbled from my hands. He clung cowering to the belly of a tawny cow's corpse. The tiger was dragging that carcass away when suddenly he was struck by an arrow discharged from a bow contraption. The child was carried off by the wild *bhilla* boys.

Fallen senseless in a swoon, a woodsman carried me off and into his hut. Thanks to his kind tending of my wounds, I recovered my health. I wanted to return to my master's side, but without assistance I could not. I was in great distress when my own daughter arrived there with a young man whom I did not know.

She was weeping desperately. Only after she had stopped 8.9
her crying did she tell me everything: how after the slaughter of the convoy the child prince who was in her hands had fallen into the hands of the leader of the savage *kirátas*; and how her own wounds had been healed by one forest-dweller; but that once she was well again he had got the idea of marrying her, forcing her to refuse him roughly, so disgusted was she at the proposition of uniting with an outcaste. She told how, unable to bear the insult, he was about to behead her in a secluded thicket. The young man she was then with had chanced to see what was happening. He killed the wicked other man and married her himself. All this story she narrated.

Sa tu pṛṣṭo Maithil'|êndrasy' âiva ko 'pi sevakaḥ kāraṇa|vilambī tan|mārg'|ânusārī jātaḥ. saha tena bhartur antikam upasṛtya putra|vṛtt'|ântena śrotram asya devyāḥ Priyaṃvadāyāś c' âdahāva.

Sa ca rājā diṣṭa|doṣāj jyeṣṭha|putraiś ciraṃ vigṛhya punar a|sahiṣṇutay" âtimātraṃ ciraṃ prayudhya baddhaḥ. devī ca bandhanaṃ gamitā.

8.12 Dagdhā punar aham asminn api vārddhake hata|jīvitam apārayantī hātuṃ pravrajyāṃ kil' âgrahīṣam. duhitā tu mama hata|jīvit'|ākṛṣṭā Vikaṭavarma|mahā|devīṃ Kalpasundarīṃ kil' âśiśriyat.

Tau ced rāja|putrau nirupadravāv ev' âvardhiṣyetām, iyatā kālena tav' êmāṃ vayo|'vasthām asprakṣyetām. tayoś ca sator na dāyādā nar'|êndrasya prasahya|kāriṇo bhaveyur iti.›

pramanyur abhiruroda. śrutvā ca tāpasī|giram aham api pravṛddha|bāṣpo nigūḍham abhyadhām:

8.15 ‹Yady evam amba samāśvasihi. nanv asti kaś cin munis tvayā tad|avasthayā putr'|âbhyupapādan'|ârthaṃ yācitas tena sa labdho vardhitaś ca. vārt" êyam atimahatī. kim anayā? so 'ham asmi.

On being asked, he turned out to be one of our Maithilan Lord's attendants who had been delayed on some business, and was now following his master's road. In his company my daughter and I caught up with our master, only to burn painfully his and Queen Priyam·vada's ears with the news of what had become of their two sons.

Fate was against King Prahára·varman. For a long time he fought against the sons of his eldest brother, but when he could resist no longer he battled on long and hard until captured. His queen was also taken into captivity.

I too am cursed that even in this my old age I was too weak 8.12
to give up my worthless life. Instead I renounced everything to become a *sannyási*. My daughter was still attached to her accursed life. She managed to find employment with Kalpa·súndari, the great queen of Víkata·varman.

If only those two princes had been able to grow up, without such unhappy accidents, then they would by now have reached the same age and stage as you. And if they had lived, then the king's kinsmen could not have treated him so violently.'

She was so upset that she started crying again. On hearing the mendicant woman's account I too burst into tears. I addressed her confidentially:

'In that case, mother, you can take heart now. When you 8.15
were in that predicament, did you not ask a hermit if he could rescue the boy? Well, he found the child and brought him up. It is a very long story. Never mind. The point is that I am that boy.

Śakyaś ca may" âsau Vikaṭavarmā yathā|kathaṃ cid upaśliṣya vyāpādayitum. anujāḥ punar atibahavaḥ, tair api ghaṭante paura|jānapadāḥ. māṃ tu na kaś cid ihatya īdṛktayā jano jānāti. pitarāv api tāvan māṃ na saṃvidāte, kim ut' êtare. tad enam artham upāyena sādhayiṣyām' îti!›

agādiṣam. sā tu vṛddhā sa|ruditaṃ pariṣvajya muhuḥ śirasy upāghrāya prasnuta|stanī sa|gadgadam agadat:

8.18 ‹Vatsa, ciraṃ jīva! bhadraṃ tava! prasanno 'dya bhagavān vidhiḥ. ady' âiva Prahāravarmaṇy adhi Videhā jātāḥ, yataḥ pralambamāna|pīna|bāhur bhavān apāram etac choka|sāgaram ady' ôttārayituṃ sthitaḥ. aho! mahad bhāga|dheyaṃ devyāḥ Priyaṃvadāyā iti!›

Harṣa|nirbharā snāna|bhojan'|ādinā mām upācarat. aśiśriyaṃ c' âsmin maṭh'|âikadeśe niśi kaṭa|śayyām. acintayaṃ ca:

‹Vin" ôpadhin" âyam artho na sādhyaḥ. striyaś c' ôpadhīnām udbhava|kṣetram. ato 'ntaḥ|pura|vṛtt'|ântam asyā avagamya tad|dvāreṇa kiñcij jālam ācareyam iti.›

8.21 Cintayaty eva mayi mah"|ârṇav'|ônmagna|mārtaṇḍa|turaṅgama|śvāsa|ray'|âvadhūt" êva vyāvartata triyāmā. samud-

I am quite capable of slaying that Víkata·varman, if I can somehow get close to him. But he has too many younger brothers. Citizens and country people alike are on their side. Moreover, there is no one in this place who knows me for who I am. Even my parents would not recognize me, how much less anyone else. Be that as it may, I shall come up with a good plan to resolve the situation!'

Those were my words. The old women embraced me in tears. She kept smelling at and kissing my head. Her breasts could have been oozing milk, so warm was her motherly love. She sobbed and stammered:

'Child, long may you live! God bless you! Almighty fate 8.18
has been kind today. Today is the day the Vidéhans will have Prahára·varman as their ruler again, now that you with your far-reaching brawny arms have come to rescue us from our limitless ocean of suffering. Ah! Queen Priyam·vada is enormously fortunate!'

Beside herself with delight, my old nurse took courteous care of me with a bath, dinner and everything else. That night I lay down on a straw sleeping mat at one side of the cell, and I pondered:

'Cunning deception is the only way ahead in this situation. And it is women who are the fertile begetters of deceptions. This being so, I must discover from this woman some intelligence about the harem, and then with her help I shall lay a snare.'

Even while I was mulling things over, the night with its 8.21
three watches was sent packing. It seemed to have been shaken off by the vehemence of the snorts of the sun's horses emerging from the great ocean. Maker of the day, the sun

ra|garbha|vāsa|jaḍīkṛta iva manda|pratāpo divasa|karaḥ prādur āsīt.

Utthāy' âvasāyita|dina|mukha|niyama|vidhis tāṃ me mātaram avādiṣam:

‹Amba, jālmasya Vikaṭavarmaṇaḥ kaccid antaḥ|pura|vṛtt'|ântam abhijānās' îti?›

8.24 An|avasita|vacana eva mayi kācid aṅganā pratyadṛśyata. tāṃ c' âvekṣya sā me dhātrī harṣ'|âśru|kuṇṭhita|kaṇṭham ācaṣṭa:

‹Putri Puṣkarike, paśya bhartṛ|dārakam! ayam asāv a|kṛpayā mayā vane parityaktaḥ punar apy evam āgata iti.›

Sā tu harṣa|nirbhara|nipīḍitā ciraṃ prarudya, bahu vilapya, śāntā punaḥ, sva|mātrā rāj'|ântaḥ|pura|vṛtt'|ânt'|ākhyāne nyayujyata. uktaṃ ca tayā:

8.27 ‹Kumāra, Kāmarūp'|ēśvarasya Kalindavarma|nāmnaḥ kanyā Kalpasundarī kalāsu rūpe c' âpsaraso 'py atikrāntā, patim abhibhūya vartate. tad|eka|vallabhaḥ sa tu bahv|avarodho 'pi Vikaṭavarm" êti.›

Tām avocam:

‹Upasarp' âināṃ mat|prayuktair gandha|mālyaiḥ. upajanaya c' â|samāna|doṣa|nind"|ādinā sva|bhartari dveṣam. anurūpa|bhartṛ|gāminīnāṃ ca Vāsavadatt"|ādīnāṃ varṇanena grāhay' ânuśayam. avarodh'|ântareṣu ca rājño vilasitāni su|gūḍhāny api prayatnen' ânviṣya prakāśayantī mānam asyā vardhay' êti!›

appeared with faint radiance as if it were numbed by its sojourn in the ocean's belly.

I got up, completed the regular daybreak rituals and then addressed my foster mother:

'Mother, you must have some information about the harem of the villain Víkata·varman?'

The words were not quite out of my mouth when another 8.24
woman appeared. On seeing her, my nurse cried out, her throat choked with tears of joy:

'Púshkarika, my daughter, look, this is our master's boy! I abandoned him heartlessly in the forest, but now he has come back by himself.'

In the grip of overwhelming joy, Púshkarika wept long and moaned much. When she had calmed down again her mother urged her to tell what she knew about the royal harem. She said:

'Prince, Kalpa·súndari is the daughter of Kalínda·varman, 8.27
the Lord of Kama·rupa. In beauty and talents the heavenly *ápsaras*es are no match for her. But she does not respect her lord husband. Víkata·varman, on the other hand, regardless of the many concubines in his collection, is in love only with her.'

I instructed her:

'Bring your queen the perfumes and garlands I will give you. Find fault with the union of non-equals and do whatever else it takes to make her hate her husband. Describe the ideal husbands of Vásava·datta* and other famous ladies, so that she will resent her marriage. Make also every effort to discover even the king's most secret dalliances with others

8.30 Punar idam ambām avocam:

‹Ittham eva tvay” âpy an|anya|vyāpārayā nṛp’|âṅgan” âsāv upasthātavyā. praty|ahaṃ ca yad yat tatra vṛttaṃ tad asmi tvay” âiva bodhyaḥ. mad|uktā punar iyam udarka|svāduno ’smat|karmaṇaḥ prasādhanāya cchāy” êv’ ân|apāyinī Kalpasundarīm anuvartatām. iti›

Te ca tam arthaṃ tath” âiv’ ânvatiṣṭhatām.

8.33 Keṣucid dineṣu gateṣv ācaṣṭa māṃ mad|ambā:

‹Vatsa, mādhav” îva picu|mand’|āśleṣiṇī yath” âsau śocyam ātmānaṃ manyeta tath” ôpapādya sthāpitā. kiṃ bhūyaḥ kṛtyam iti?›

Punar aham abhilikhy’ ātmanaḥ pratikṛtim:

8.36 ‹Iyam amuṣmai neyā. nītāṃ c’ âināṃ nirvarṇya sā niyatam evaṃ vakṣyati:

«Nanv asti kaś cid īdṛś’|ākāraḥ pumān iti?»

Pratibrūhy enām:

8.39 «Yadi syāt tataḥ kim iti?»

Tasya yad uttaraṃ sā dāsyati tad aham asmi pratibodhanīya iti.›

Sā ‹tath” êti› rāja|kulam upasaṅkramya, pratinivṛttā mām ek’|ânte nyavedayat:

8.42 ‹Vatsa, darśito ’sau citra|paṭas tasyai matta|kāśinyai. citrīyamāṇā c’ âsau:

«Bhuvanam idaṃ sa|nāthīkṛtaṃ yad deve ’pi Kusuma|dhanvani n’ ēdṛśī vapuḥ|śrīḥ samnidhatte. citram etac citrataram. na ca tam avaimi ya īdṛśam ihatyo nirmimīte. ken’ êdam ālikhitam iti?»

in his harem. Then divulge them to feed Kalpa·súndari's jealous anger.'

Next I turned again to my foster mother: 8.30

'You too should make it your exclusive business to attend on the king's wife. Report to me daily in person everything that takes place in the harem. I have instructed your daughter here to stay like a shadow unswervingly at Kalpa·súndari's side, so that we can carry out my plan and enjoy its sweet rewards.'

The two of them performed their tasks exactly as instructed.

Several days had gone by when my old nurse reported: 8.33

'My dear boy, she has been reduced to considering herself wretched as the fragrant jasmine when it has to embrace the bitter-barked *nimba* tree.* What should I do next?'

I then made a drawing in my likeness, saying:

'Take this to her. Once she has it, and has studied it, she 8.36
is bound to ask:

"Can there exist a man who looks like this?"

Respond to her:

"What if there were?" 8.39

Then bring me her answer to this question.'

My nurse promised to do so, left for the royal palace, and, when she had returned again, took me aside to tell:

'Dear child, I showed her the picture, fabulous fascinating 8.42
woman that she is. She studied it, and was amazed:

"This Earth has met its Lord, for even Kama the god of the flower-bow does not possess such physical glory. This work of art is most wonderful. I know no one in the land who could depict such a man. Who created this image?"

ādṛtavatī vyāhṛtavatī ca. mayā ca smeray" ôdīritam:

8.45 «Devi, sadṛśam ājñāpayasi. bhagavān makara|ketur apy evaṃ sundara iti na śakyam eva sambhāvayitum. atha ca vistīrṇ" êyam arṇava|nemiḥ. kva cid īdṛśam api rūpaṃ daiva|śaktyā sambhavet. atha tu yady evaṃ|rūpo rūp'|ânurūpa|śilpa|śīla|vidyā|jñāna|kauśalo yuvā mahā|kulīnaś ca kaś cit saṃnihitaḥ syāt sa kiṃ lapsyata iti?»

Tay" ôktam:

«Amba, kiṃ bravīmi? śarīraṃ hṛdayaṃ jīvitam iti sarvam idam alpam an|arhaṃ ca. tato na kiñcil lapsyate. na ced ayaṃ vipralambhas tasy' âmuṣya darśan'|ânubhavena yath" êdaṃ cakṣuś carit'|ârthaṃ bhavet tath" ânugrahaḥ kārya iti!»

8.48 Bhūyo 'pi mayā dṛḍhatarīkartum upanyastam:

«Asti ko 'pi rāja|sūnur nigūḍhaṃ caran. amuṣya Vasant'|ôtsave saha sakhībhir nagar'|ôpavana|vihāriṇī Ratir iva vigrahiṇī yadṛcchayā darśana|pathaṃ gat" âsi. gataś c' âsau Kāma|śar'|âika|lakṣyatāṃ mām anvavartiṣṭa.

Mayā ca vām anyony'|ânurūpair durlabhair ākār'|ādibhir guṇ'|âtiśayaiś ca preryamāṇayā tad|racitair eva kusuma|śekhara|srag|anulepan'|ādibhiś ciram upāsit" âsi. sādṛśyaṃ ca svam anena svayam ev' âbhilikhya tvat|samādhi|gāḍhatva|darśanāya preṣitam.

She spoke in earnest. With a smile I told her:

"My lady, your pronouncement is only proper. One could not imagine even Love himself, the Lord with the *mákara* on his banner, to be so handsome. Nevertheless, this earth encircled by the ocean is vast. It is possible that the power of destiny could produce such a beautiful man, somewhere. If, then, such a one did exist—a young man, nobly born, handsome as his picture, and as talented, well mannered, learned and intelligent as he is beautiful—what may he hope for?" 8.45

She replied:

"Good woman, what shall I say? My body, my heart, my life: all these are worthless trifles. Hence there is nothing for him to hope for. If this is no trick, then grant my eyes the favor of fulfillment by actually seing this person."

In order to consolidate her desire yet more, I then said: 8.48

"He does exist, a royal prince living incognito. During the spring festival of Love when you were amusing yourself in the city park with your girlfriends, like Love's wife Rati the goddess of desire herself incarnate, his eyes chanced to fall on you. Become the single target of Love's arrows he turned to me for guidance.

You two are made for each other, both uncommonly beautiful, for example, and with superlative virtues. This realization drove me to wait on you all this time, with the crowns of flowers, garlands and perfumes that he himself prepared. It was he himself who drew his self-portrait, sent to show you the intensity of his single-minded devotion.

8.51 Eṣa ced artho niścitas tasy' âmuṣy' âtimānuṣa|prāṇa|sattva|prajñā|prakarṣasya na kiñcid duṣkaraṃ nāma. tam ady' âiva darśayeyam. saṅketo deya iti.»

Tayā tu kiñcid iva dhyātvā punar abhihitam:

«Amba, tava n' âitad idānīṃ gopyatamam. ataḥ kathayāmi. mama tātasya rājñā Prahāravarmaṇā saha mahatī prītir āsīt. mātuś ca me Mānavatyāḥ priya|vayasyā devī Priyaṃvad" āsīt. tābhyāṃ punar ajāt'|âpatyābhyām eva kṛtaḥ samayo 'bhūt:

8.54 ‹Āvayoḥ putravatyāḥ putrāya duhitṛmatyā duhitā dey" êti.›

Tātas tu māṃ jātāṃ pranaṣṭ'|âpatyā Priyaṃvad" êti prārthayamānāya Vikaṭavarmaṇe daivād dattavān. ayaṃ ca niṣṭhuraḥ pitṛ|drohī n' âtyupapanna|saṃsthānaḥ kām'|ôpacāreṣv a|labdha|vaicakṣaṇyaḥ kalāsu kāvya|nāṭak'|ādiṣu mand'|âbhiniveśaḥ śaury'|ônmādī dur|vikatthano 'n|ṛta|vādī c' â|sthāna|varṣī.

N' âtirocate ma eṣa bhartā viśeṣataś c' âiṣu vāsareṣu. yad ayam udyāne mad|antaraṅga|bhūtāṃ Puṣkarikām apy upānta|vartinīm an|ādṛtya mayi baddha|sāpatnya|matsarām an|ātmajñām ātma|nāṭakīyāṃ Ramayantikāṃ nām' âpatya|nirviśeṣaṃ mat|saṃvardhitāyāś campaka|latāyāḥ svayam avacitābhiḥ sumanobhir alam akārṣīt. mad|upabhukta|mukte citra|kūṭa|garbha|vedikā|gate ratna|talpe tayā saha vyahārṣīt.

Once you are committed, he will be able to overcome every obstacle with his superhuman and outstanding vigor, character and intelligence. I could introduce you this very day. All you need do is give the signal." 8.51

The queen seemed to meditate a moment before replying: "My mother, I can no longer hide from you my story. So I will tell you all. My dear father's best friend was King Prahára·varman, and his queen, Priyam·vada, was my mother Mánavati's dearest companion. Even before these two had had any offspring they made a pledge:

'If one of us has a daughter and the other a son, then we will give them to each other in marriage.'* 8.54

But, as fate would have it, when I was born and Víkata·varman was asking for my hand my father gave me to him, thinking that Priyam·vada's sons were lost. He is a brute who plots against his own uncle. Physically poorly endowed, he has no skill in love affairs, and his interest in such cultivations as poetry and the performing arts is pathetic. He is crazy about his own bravery, a terrible braggard, a speaker of untruths, and he bestows his favors on the unworthy.

I do not like my husband much, and least of all these days. For recently he personally picked the lovely fragrant yellow flowers from a climbing *chámpaka* that I had hand-reared precisely as though it were my child. Next, then and there in the garden and quite disregarding my intimate confidante Púshkarika, who was just nearby, he decorated Ramayántika with the flowers. She is one of his dancing girls, who knows not her place and even harbors jealousy toward me as if she were a rival wife. Thereupon he took his pleasure with her on the very jewelled couch where I had just been relaxing,

8.57 A|yogyaś ca pumān avajñātuṃ ca pravṛttaḥ. tat kim ity apekṣyate? para|loka|bhayaṃ c' âihikena duḥkhen'ântaritam. a|viṣahyaṃ hi yoṣitām Anaṅga|śara|niṣaṅgībhūta|cetasām an|iṣṭa|jana|saṃvāsa|yantraṇā|duḥkham.

Ato 'munā puruṣeṇa mām ady' ôdyāna|mādhavī|gṛhe samāgamaya. tad|vārtā|śravaṇa|mātreṇ' âiva hi mam' âtimātraṃ mano 'nuraktam.

Asti c' âyam artha|rāśiḥ. anen' âmuṣya pade pratiṣṭhāpya tam ev' âtyantam upacarya jīviṣyām' îti.»

8.60 May" âpi tad abhyupetya pratyāgatam. ataḥ paraṃ bhartṛ|dārakaḥ pramāṇam iti.›

Tatas tasyā eva sakāśād antaḥ|pura|niveśam antarvaṃśika|puruṣa|sthānāni pramada|vana|pradeśān api vibhāgen' âvagamya;

asta|giri|kūṭa|pāta|kṣubhita|śoṇita iva śoṇībhavati bhānu|bimbe, paścim'|âmbudhi|payaḥ|pāta|nirvāpita|pataṅg'|âṅgāra|dhūma|saṃbhāra iva bharita|nabhasi tamasi vijṛmbhite, para|dāra|parāmarś'|ônmukhasya mam' ācāryakam iva kartum utthite guru|parigraha|ślāghini grah'|âgresare kṣapākare;

before I had left, there on the platform in the grotto of the pleasure mountain.

That this worthless man has the nerve to insult me! Why 8.57
should I then respect him? My fears about the next world are remote compared with the suffering of here and now. The moment a woman's mind has become the quiver for invisible Love's arrows how shall she bear the torture of being forced to share her life with someone she detests?

For all these reasons, do arrange for me to meet with the man you talk of, today in the *mádhavi* spring jasmine pavilion in the garden. Just hearing about him is enough to make my mind mightily besotted.

I have a mountain of wealth. With it I will set him up in the place of that Víkata·varman, and I shall live attending to him only, to his every need."

I have come straight from agreeing to the plan. Young 8.60
prince, you must be the measure of the next move.'

Next I had the old woman explain to me section by section the lie of the ladies' apartments, where the harem guards were stationed, as well as the different areas of the pleasure garden.

Then the sun's sphere turned crimson, as though its blood had been shaken and stirred up during its fall onto the peak of the mountain where it sets. Darkness gaped, filling the sky like a mass of smoke from the hot coal that was the sun when it was quenched by falling into the waters of the western ocean. The moon, nightmaker and leader of the planets, passionate admirer of the wife of Brihas·pati, preceptor of the gods,* arose, as if in order to be my guide, now that I too was intent on violating another man's wife.

8.63 Kalpasundarī|vadana|puṇḍarīkeṇ' êva mad|darśan'|âtirāga|pratham'|ôpanatena smayamānena candra|maṇḍalena sandhukṣamāṇa|tejasi bhuvana|vijigīṣ"|ôdyate deve Kusuma|dhanvani, yath" ôcitaṃ śayanīyam abhaje. vyacītaraṃ ca:

‹Siddha|prāya ev' âyam arthaḥ. kiṃ tu para|kalatra|laṅghanād dharma|pīḍā bhavet. s" âpy artha|kāmayor dvayor upalambhe śāstra|kārair anumat" âiv' êti.

Guru|jana|bandha|mokṣ'|ôpāya|sandhinā mayā c' âiṣa vyatikramaḥ kṛtas, tad api pāpaṃ nirhṛtya kiyaty" âpi dharma|kalayā māṃ samagrayed iti.

8.66 Api tv etad ākarṇya devo Rājavāhanaḥ suhṛdo vā kiṃ nu vakṣyant' îti?›

Cintā|parādhīna eva nidrayā parāmṛśye. adṛśyata ca svapne Hasti|vaktro bhagavān. āha sma ca:

‹Saumya Upahāravarman, mā sma te durvikalpo bhūt. yatas tvam asi mad|aṃśaḥ. Śaṅkara|jaṭ'|ābhāra|lālan'|ôcitā Sura|sarid asau vara|varṇinī. sā ca kadā cin mad|viloḍan"|â|sahiṣṇur mām aśapat:

8.69 «Ehi martyatvam! iti»

Aśapyata mayā ca:

«Yath" êha bahu|bhogyā tathā prāpy' âpi mānuṣyakam an|eka|sādhāraṇī bhav' êti!»

Love with his flower-bow was all eager, full of desire to conquer the world, his own bright energy inflamed by the moon's circle, smiling brightly as though it were Kalpa·sún-dari's lotus-face first presenting itself in its intense passion to see me. That was the time when as usual I sought my bed. I brooded: 8.63

'The deed is all but done. Nevertheless the violation of another man's wife could be an offense against dharma, the religious law. Still, the authors of the lawbooks permit even such an offense if one will win thereby both material profit and love.

Moreover, I shall perform this transgression with the ulterior motive of bringing about my parents' liberation from bondage. Thus my action will not only be sin-free but may even gain me a certain modicum of religious merit.

But when Prince Raja·váhana or my friends hear of it, I 8.66
know not what they will say.'

Lost in such musings, sleep overcame me. In my dream I saw the elephant-headed god, Ganesh, who told me:

'Good Upahára·varman, be free of your misgivings. For you are a part of me, and your beautiful woman is none other than the divine river, the Ganges, fit to be fondled by the Lord Shiva Shánkara, the ornament of his dreadlocks. Once upon a time she was unable to bear my splashing her about, and cursed me:

"May you be reborn as a mortal subject to death!" 8.69

I cursed her in turn:

"May you become a human, too, and common to more than one man, just as here you are enjoyed by many!"

8.72 Abhyarthitaś c' ânayā:

«Eka|pūrvāṃ punas tvām ev' ôpacarya yāvaj|jīvaṃ rameyam iti.»

Tad ayam artho bhavya eva bhavatā nirāśaṅkya iti.›

8.75 Pratibudhya ca prīti|yuktas tad ahar api priyā|saṅketa|vyatikar'|ādi|smaraṇen' âham anaiṣam.

Anye|dyur an|anyathā|vṛttir An|aṅgo mayy ev' êṣu|varṣam avarṣat. aśuṣyac ca jyotiṣmataḥ prabhā|mayaṃ saraḥ. prāsarac ca timira|mayaḥ kardamaḥ.

Kārdamika|nivasanaś ca dṛḍhatara|parikaraḥ khaḍga|pāṇir upahṛt'|ôpaskaraḥ smaran mātṛ|dattāny abhijñānāni rāja|mandira|parikhām udambhasam upātiṣṭham.

8.78 Ath' ôpa|khātaṃ mātṛ|gṛha|dvāre Puṣkarikayā prathama|saṃnidhāpitāṃ veṇu|yaṣṭim ādāya tayā śāyitayā ca parikhāṃ, sthāpitayā ca prākāra|bhittim alaṅghayam. adhiruhya pakv'|êṣṭaka|citena gopur'|ôpari|tal'|âdhirohiṇā sopāna|pathena bhuvam avātaram.

Avatīrṇaś ca vakula|vīthīm atikramya campak'|āvali|vartmanā manāg iv' ôpasṛty' ôttarāhi karuṇaṃ cakravāka|mithuna|ravam aśṛṇavam. punar udīcā pāṭali|pathena sparśa|labhya|viśāla|saudha|kuḍy'|ôdareṇa śara|kṣepam iva gatvā punaḥ prācā piṇḍī|bhāṇḍīra|khaṇḍa|maṇḍit'|ôbhaya|pārśvena saikata|pathena kiñcid uttaram atikramya punar avācīṃ cūta|vīthīm agāhiṣi.

She then pleaded: 8.72

"Let me have only one previous husband before then enjoying the rest of my life serving only you."

Thus all this is bound to come to pass, and you should have no apprehensions.'

I awoke joyful and passed that day, too, daydreaming 8.75
about every aspect of my appointment with my beloved.

The following day, invisible Love had nothing else to do but showered his rain of arrows on me, just me. Then the lake of the luminous sun's radiance dried up. And the mire of darkness spread forth.

I dressed in a mud-black cloak, girded tightly my loins, and gathered together what I needed, sword in hand. Bearing in mind the directions given by my dear old nurse, I made for the water-filled moat around the royal palace.

Púshkarika had already stashed a bamboo pole there near 8.78
the ditch by the door of her mother's house. I took the pole, laid it down to cross the moat, and stood it up to scale the rampart wall. A flight of steps built from piled baked bricks led to the upper floor of the principal gate. Climbing up and over, I reached the ground on the other side.

Once I had descended, I passed a row of *bákula* trees. Advancing just a little farther along an avenue of yellow-flowered *chámpaka* trees, I heard the plaintive calls of a pair of separated *chakra·vaka* birds away to the north. Next I took a northbound way lined with begonia trumpet-flowers for about as far as an arrow flies, feeling the bulging wall of the enormous palace. Then I turned east on a gravel path adorned on both sides with groves of banyan and *ashóka* trees. Heading south I plunged into an alley of mangoes.*

Tataś ca gahanataram udar'|ôparacita|ratna|vedikaṃ mādhavī|latā|maṇḍapam īṣad|vivṛta|samudgak'|ônmiṣita|bhāsā dīpavartyā nyarūpayam.

8.81 Praviśya c' âika|pārśve phulla|puṣpa|nirantara|kuraṇṭa|pota|paṅkti|bhitti|parigataṃ garbha|gṛham, avanipatit'|âruṇ'|âśoka|latā|mayam abhinava|kusuma|koraka|pulaka|lāñchitaṃ pratyagra|pravāla|paṭala|pāṭalaṃ kapāṭam udghāṭya prāvikṣam.

Tatra c' āsīt sv|āstīrṇaṃ kusuma|śayanam, surat'|ôpakaraṇa|vastu|garbhāś ca kamalinī|palāśa|saṃpuṭāḥ, danta|mayas tāla|vṛntaḥ, surabhi|salila|bharitaś ca bhṛṅgārakaḥ. samupaviśya muhūrtaṃ viśrāntaḥ parimalam atiśayavantam āghrāsiṣam.

Aśrauṣaṃ ca manda|mandaṃ pada|śabdam. śrutv" âiva saṅketa|gṛhān nirgatya rakt'|âśoka|skandha|pārśva|vyavahit'|âṅga|yaṣṭiḥ sthito 'smi.

8.84 Sā ca su|bhrūr a|suṣīma|kāmā śanair upetya tatra mām adṛṣṭvā balavad avyathiṣṭa. vyasṛjac ca matta|rāja|haṃs" îva kaṇṭha|rāga|valgu|gadgadāṃ giram:

‹Vyaktam asmi vipralabdhā! n' âsty upāyaḥ prāṇitum. ayi hṛdaya kim idam akāryaṃ kāryavad adhyasya tad|asambhavena kim evam uttāmyasi? Bhagavan Pañca|bāṇa kas tav' âparādhaḥ kṛto mayā yad evaṃ dahasi na ca bhasmīkaroṣ' îti?›

There by the twinkling lamplight of a covered lantern slightly ajar I made out a bower of thickly entwined climbing jasmine framing a jewelled platform.

First I went in at one side, only to find within a further 8.81
door, made from bent-over red *ashóka* branches aquiver with a fine down of newborn buds, the whole begonia-pink with the thatch of fresh shoots. Opening this door, I entered the inner chamber, its walls lined with uninterrupted rows of young yellow amaranths in full flower.

Inside there was a beautifully bestrewn bed of flowers, and lotus-leaf caskets containing accessories for love-play, as well as an ivory fan, and a golden pitcher full of fragrant water. I sat down for a moment's repose, breathing in the superlative scents.

Soon I heard the sound of footsteps, soft and slow. Without delay I exited the assignation chamber and stood with my slim frame screened by the lower trunk of a red-flowering *ashóka* tree.

The beautiful-browed one, hotly in love, drew quietly 8.84
near. Not finding me there, she became violently agitated. Like an intoxicated royal swan she cried out in a lovely impassioned choked cry:

'It is obvious that I have been deceived! There is no way for me to go on living. Oh, my heart, you were the one to suppose this impossibility possible. How can you be so distraught that it is impossible after all? O god of Love with your five arrows, how have I sinned against you that you should keep me burning in this way but not reduce me to ashes?'

Ath' âham āvirbhūya vivṛta|dīpa|bhājanaḥ:

8.87 ‹Bhāmini nanu bahv aparāddhaṃ bhavatyā Citta|janmano yad amuṣya jīvita|bhūtā Ratir ākṛtyā kadarthitā; dhanur yaṣṭir bhrū|latābhyām, bhramara|mālā|mayī jyā nīl'|âlaka|dyutibhiḥ, astrāṇy apāṅga|vīkṣita|vṛṣṭibhiḥ, mahā|rajana|dhvaja|paṭ'|âmśukaṃ danta|cchada|mayūkha|jālaiḥ;

prathama|suhṛn Malaya|mārutaḥ parimala|paṭīyasā niḥśvāsa|pavanena, para|bhṛta|rutam atimañjulaiḥ pralāpaiḥ, puṣpa|mayī patākā bhuja|yaṣṭibhyām, dig|vijay'|ārambha|pūrṇa|kumbha|mithunam uroja|kumbha|yugalena, krīḍā|saro nābhi|maṇḍalena, saṃnāhya|rathaḥ śroṇi|maṇḍalena, bhava|ratna|toraṇa|stambha|yugalam ūru|yugalena, līlā|karṇa|kisalayaṃ caraṇa|tala|prabhābhiḥ.

Ataḥ sthāna eva tvāṃ dunoti Mīna|ketuḥ. māṃ punar an|aparādham adhikam āyāsayat' îty eṣa eva tasya doṣaḥ.

8.90 Tat prasīda sundari! jīvaya māṃ jīvan'|âuṣadhibhir iv' âpāṅgair Anaṅga|bhujaṅga|daṣṭam iti!›

At this point I opened my lamp cover to reveal my presence:

'How wonderfully passionate you are! Of course, you have 8.87
offended mind-born Love in many ways, for, to begin with, has your beauty not shamed his wife Passion, his very life? Moreover, his own bow cannot compare to your eyebrow creepers, and his bowstring made of a garland of bees is nothing compared with your lustrous blue-black locks. Similarly, your sidelong glances trump his missiles, and the light beams radiating from your lips outshine the spangled cloth of his great radiant banner.

How can one compare his accomplice the Málayan sandal breeze with the intensely scented pure air of your breath? What of his cuckoo's* cooing compared with your melodious burble? Your two long slender arms outdo his flowered flagstaff. Your pair of pot-like breasts outdo the couple of vases filled auspiciously when he sets out on his conquest of the world. The circle of your navel outdoes his pleasure pool. The circles of your hips outdo the wheels of his armored chariot. And your twin thighs outdo the god's twin jewelled gate pillars. Even the tender sprout ornamenting his ear is no match for the radiance from the soles of your feet.

Hence you see it is only fair for fish-bannered Love to set you on fire. But I, I am completely innocent, and yet he is torturing me yet more cruelly. That is his real crime.

Cheer up, then, pretty one! I am bitten by the serpent 8.90
invisible Love. Resuscitate me with the life-giving medicine of your side glances!'

āśliṣṭavān. arīramaṃ c' Ânaṅga|rāga|peśala|viśāla|locanām. avasit'|ârthāṃ c' ā|rakta|valit'|ēkṣaṇām, īṣat|sveda|rekh'|ôdbheda|jarjarita|kapola|mūlām, an|argala|kala|pralāpinīm, aruṇa|daśana|kararuh'|ârpaṇa|vyatikarām, atyartha|pariśla-th'|âṅgīm ārtām iva lakṣayitvā mānasīṃ śārīrīṃ ca dhāraṇāṃ śithilayann ātmānam api tayā samān'|ârtham āpādayam.

Tat|kṣaṇa|vimukta|saṅgatau rat'|âvasānikaṃ vidhim anubhavantau cira|paricitāv iv' âtigūḍha|viśrambhau kṣaṇam avātiṣṭhāvahi. punar aham uṣṇam āyataṃ ca niḥśvasya kiñcid dīna|dṛṣṭiḥ sa|cakita|prasāritābhyāṃ bhujābhyām enām an|atipīḍaṃ pariṣvajya n' âtiviśadam acumbiṣam. aśru|mukhī tu sā:

8.93 ‹Yadi prayāsi nātha prayātam eva me jīvitaṃ gaṇaya! naya mām api! na ced asau dāsa|jano niṣprayojana iti.›

añjalim avataṃsatām anaiṣīt. avādiṣaṃ ca tām:

‹Ayi mugdhe, kaḥ sa|cetanaḥ striyam abhikāmayamānāṃ n' âbhinandati? yadi mad|anugraha|niścalas tav' âbhisandhir ācar' âvicāraṃ mad|upadiṣṭam. ādarśaya rahasi rājñe mat|sādṛśya|garbhaṃ citra|paṭam. ācakṣva ca:

8.96 «Kim iyam ākṛtiḥ puruṣa|saundaryasya pāram ārūḍhā na v" êti?».

«Bāḍham ārūḍh" êti!»

nūnam asau vakṣyati. brūhi bhūyaḥ:

I embraced and then sported with her, decorated with Love's passion and eyes wide. She rolled her slightly red eyes in surrender. Little lines of sweat broke forth, speckling the lower edges of her cheeks, and she murmured unrestrained moans. We exchanged ruddy puncturing from teeth and nail. When her limbs went completely limp as if in a dead faint I could tell that she was gratified. Accordingly I relaxed my firmness of mind and body to reach the same stage.

Separated, we two had reunited the same second, lying there a while enjoying the postcoital rites, utterly intimate, as though we had known one another a long time. Then I heaved a deep and feverish sigh, embraced her feebly in my outstretched trembling arms and kissed her anxiously with a mournful look. With tears on her face she folded her hands at her forehead in decorative supplication and said:

'If you leave and end this, lord, then be sure you will be 8.93
ending my life, too. Take me with you! If you do not, your slave will have no reason to live.'

I told her:

'Oh, sweet girl, what feeling man would not welcome a woman who is in love with him? If your heart is truly set on me, then do what I say without delay. Secretly show the king, your husband, the picture bearing my likeness. And ask him:

"Has this figure not attained the peak of manly beauty?" 8.96

"Indeed it has!"

He is bound to respond. Tell him then:

8.99 «Yady evam, asti k" âpi tāpasī deś'|ântara|bhramaṇa|labdha|prāgalbhyā mama ca mātṛbhūtā. tay" êdam ālekhya|rūpaṃ puraskṛty' âham uktā:

‹So 'sti tādṛśo mantro yena tvam upoṣitā parvaṇi viviktāyāṃ bhūmau puro|hitair huta|mukte sapt'|ârciṣi naktam ekākinī śataṃ candana|samidhaḥ, śatam aguru|samidhaḥ, karpūra|muṣṭīḥ, paṭṭa|vastrāṇi ca prabhūtāni hutvā bhaviṣyasy evam|ākṛtiḥ.

Atha cālayiṣyasi ghaṇṭām. ghaṇṭā|puṭa|kvaṇit'|āhūtaś ca bhartā bhavatyai sarva|rahasyam ākhyāya nimīlit'|âkṣo yadi tvām āliṅget, iyam ākṛtir amum upasaṅkrāmet. tvaṃ tu bhaviṣyasi yathā pur"|ākār" âiva.

8.102 Yadi bhavatyai bhavat|priyāya c' âivaṃ roceta, na c' âsmin vidhau visaṃvādaḥ kārya iti.›

Vapuś ced idaṃ tav' âbhimataṃ saha suhṛn|mantribhir anujaiḥ paura|jānapadaiś ca saṃpradhārya teṣām apy anumate karmaṇy abhimukhena stheyam iti.»

Sa niyatam abhyupaiṣyati. punar asyām eva pramada|vana|vāṭī|śṛṅgāṭikāyām ātharvaṇikena vidhinā saṃjñapita|paśun" âbhihutya mukte hiraṇya|retasi tad|dhūma|śamanena saṃpraviṣṭena may" âsminn eva latā|maṇḍape sthātavyam.

"In that case—I met an ascetic woman who has travelled in foreign lands and so knows what she is talking about. She has become like a mother to me. She was the one to place this painted form before my eyes, saying: 8.99

'I have a mantra with the following effect: First you must fast. Then, on the night of the new moon, all alone at a lonely spot where the priests have finished making their oblations, you should sacrifice into that seven-tongued fire: one hundred sandalwood sticks, one hundred sticks of light aloe, a handful of camphor and numerous luxury garments. Doing so, you will metamorphose into the image of this picture.

Next, you should sound the bell whose hollow tinkling will summon your husband thither. He must tell you all his secrets. If he then closes his eyes and embraces you, these looks will be transferred to him, and you will regain your original appearance just as you were.

If your beloved and you like the idea, do not alter any 8.102
part of the ritual.'

Would you not like to become this handsome? Talk it over with your friends and ministers, your relations and your subjects, urban and rustic. If they too approve of the plan, then put it into action forthwith."

He is bound to go for it. Next, let the Athárvan priest ritually slaughter the sacrificial beast and offer it into the golden-seeded fire, here in this very pleasure garden, at the grove where the four roads meet. When the fire has gone out, its quelled smoke will be the signal for me to enter this same arbor and wait.

8.105 Tvaṃ punaḥ pragāḍhāyāṃ pradoṣa|velāyām ālapiṣyasi karṇe kṛta|narma|smitā Vikaṭavarmāṇam:

«Dhūrto 'si tvam a|kṛtajñaś ca. mad|anugraha|labdhen' âpi rūpeṇa loka|locan'|ôtsav'|āyamānena mat|sapatnīr abhiramayiṣyasi. n' âham ātma|vināśāya vetāl'|ôtthāpanam ācareyam iti.»

Śrutv" êdaṃ tvad|vacaḥ sa yad vadiṣyati tan mahyam ekākiny upāgatya nivedayiṣyasi. tataḥ param aham eva jñāsyāmi.

8.108 Mat|pada|cihnāni c' ôpavane Puṣkarikayā pramārjay' êti.›

Sā ‹tath" êti› śāstr'|ôpadeśam iva mad|uktam ādṛty' â|tṛpta|surata|rāg" âiva kathaṃ katham apy agād antaḥ|puram. aham api yathā|praveśaṃ nirgatya svam ev' āvāsam ayāsiṣam.

Atha sā matta|kāśinī tathā tam artham anvatiṣṭhat. atiṣṭhac ca tan|mate sa durmatiḥ. abhramac ca paura|jānapadeṣv iyam adbhutāyamānā vārtā:

8.111 ‹Rājā kila Vikaṭavarmā devī|mantra|balena deva|yogyaṃ vapur āsādayiṣyati. nūnam eṣa vipralambho n' âtikalyāṇaḥ. k" âiva kathā pramādasya. svasminn ev' ântaḥ|pur'|ôpavane sv'|âgra|mahiṣy" âiva saṃpādyaḥ kil' âyam arthaḥ. tathā hi Bṛhaspati|pratima|buddhibhir mantribhir apy abhyūhy' ânumataḥ. yady evaṃ bhāvi n' ânyad ataḥ param asti kiñcid adbhutam. acintyo hi maṇi|mantr'|âuṣadhīnāṃ prabhāva iti.›

Once the dark night is far advanced, speak into Víkata·varman's ear with a simulated playful laugh: 8.105

"You are an ungrateful brute. Even though it is thanks to me that you will become beautiful, a carnival for the eyes of all the world, my co-wives will be the one you will give the pleasure of enjoying you. Well, I am not going to raise a ghost for my own destruction."

Afterward come alone to tell me how the king responds on hearing your words. I shall know what to do next.

Please have Púshkarika sweep away my footprints in the 8.108
grove.'

She agreed, honoring my words as though they were a scriptural injunction. With her erotic passion unquenched she reluctantly withdrew to the harem. I too left the way I had entered and went to my own lodging.

Soon the fabulous fascinating woman had carried out her part just so. The wicked fool did exactly as she advised. The fantastic story spread through the population of town and country:

'They say King Víkata·varman is going to acquire a body 8.111
worthy of the gods, thanks to his lady wife's magical mantra power. Surely this cannot be a trick, but must be a great blessing. How can one even mention deception? Apparently his principal queen will perform the transformation herself in the harem garden. After all, even the ministers, clever as Brihas·pati himself, have debated the matter and approve. If this does indeed come to pass it would be the most amazing thing. Is not the magical might of gemstones, mantras and herbs far beyond our understanding?'

Prasṛteṣu loka|pravādeṣu prāpte parva|divase pragāḍhāyāṃ prauḍha|tamasi pradoṣa|velāyām antaḥ|pur'|ôdyānād udairayad Dhūrjaṭi|kaṇṭha|dhūmro dhūm'|ôdgamaḥ. kṣīr'|ājya|dadhi|tila|gaura|sarṣapa|vasā|māṃsa|rudhir'|āhutīnāṃ ca parimalaḥ pavan'|ânusārī diśi diśi prāvātsīt.

Praśānte ca sahasā dhūm'|ôdgame tasminn aham aviśam. niś'|ânt'|ôdyānam āgamac ca gaja|gāminī. āliṅgya ca māṃ sa|smitaṃ samabhyadhatta:

8.114 ‹Dhūrta, siddhaṃ te samīhitam. avasitaś ca paśur asau. amuṣya pralobhanāya tvad|ādiṣṭayā diśā may" ôktam:

«Kitava! na sādhayāmi te saundaryam. evaṃ sundaro hi tvam apsarasām api spṛhaṇīyo bhaviṣyasi kim uta mānuṣīṇām. madhukara iva nisarga|capalo yatra kva cid āsajjati bhav'|ādṛśo nṛśaṃsa iti.»

Tena tu me pādayor nipaty' âbhihitam:

8.117 «Rambh"|ūru, sahasva mat|kṛtāni duścaritāni! manas" âpi na cintayeyam itaḥ param itara|nārīm. tvarasva prastute karmaṇ' îti!»

Tad aham īdṛśena vaivāhikena nepathyena tvām abhisṛtavatī. prāg api rāg'|âgni|sākṣikam An|aṅgena guruṇā datt" âiva tubhyam eṣā jāyā. punar ap' îmaṃ jāta|vedasaṃ sākṣīkṛtya sva|hṛdayena datt" êti.›

The people's talk spread far and wide. The new-moon day arrived. Night had fallen and the darkness was total when from the harem garden there rose a column of smoke, blue-purple as the poisoned throat of Shiva. The fragrance of burnt offerings—milk, ghee, curds, sesame and white mustard seeds, animal fat, meat and blood—was borne on the breeze, filling the directions.

As soon as the rising smoke had disappeared, I entered. She of the graceful elephant gait came too into the palace garden. Embracing me, she said with a smile:

'Dear deceiver, your wish is come true. That beast is up 8.114
for it. He has had it.* I spoke to him in the way you said would trick him:

"You rogue! I am not going to make you handsome. For if you become handsome even the *ápsaras*es, celestial nymphs, will desire you, let alone mortal women. Cruel men like you are naturally fickle, honeybees attaching yourselves here and there as you feel like it."

At which he threw himself at my feet, saying:

"My beauty with thighs smooth as the plantain tree, for- 8.117
give my offenses! From now on I will not even think a thought about other women. Please hurry up, get on with the matter at hand!"

Thus I am come out to you, dressed in this wedding costume. I became your wife already, given to you by my guardian invisible Love, with the fire of passion as our witness. Now this sacrificial fire witnesses my own heart giving me to you once again.'

Prapadena caraṇa|pṛṣṭhe niṣpīḍy' ôtkṣipta|pāda|pārṣṇir i-tar'|êtara|vyatiṣakta|komal'|âṅguli|dalena bhuja|latā|dvayena kandharāṃ mam' āveṣṭya sa|līlam ānanam ānamayya svayam unnamita|mukha|kamalā vibhrānta|viśāla|dṛṣṭir asakṛd abhyacumbat.

8.120 Ath' âinām:

‹Ih' âiva kuraṇṭaka|gulma|garbhe tiṣṭha yāvad ahaṃ nirgatya sādhayeyaṃ sādhyaṃ samyag iti.›

Visṛjya tām upasṛtya hom'|ânala|pradeśam aśoka|śākh'|âvalambinīṃ ghaṇṭām acālayam. akūjac ca sā taṃ janaṃ Kṛt'|ânta|dūt" îv' āhvayantī. prāvartiṣi c' âham a|guru|candana|pramukhāni hotum. āyāsīc ca rājā yath"|ôktam deśam. śaṅk"|āpannam iva kiñcit sa|vismayaṃ vicārya tiṣṭhantam abravam:

8.123 ‹Brūhi satyaṃ bhūyo 'pi me bhagavantaṃ citra|bhānum eva sākṣīkṛtya! na ced anena rūpeṇa mat|sapatnīr abhiramayiṣyasi tatas tvay' îdaṃ rūpaṃ saṅkrāmayeyam iti.›

Sa tad" âiva ‹devy ev' êyam, n' ôpadhir iti› sphuṭ'|ôpajāta|saṃpratyayaḥ prāvartata śapathāya. smitvā punar may" ôktam:

‹Kiṃ vā śapathena? k" âiva hi mānuṣī māṃ paribhaviṣyati? yady apsarobhiḥ saṅgacchase, saṅgacchasva kāmam!

8.126 Kathaya kāni te rahasyāni! tat|kathan'|ânte hi tvat|svarūpa|bhraṃśa iti.›

So 'bravīt:

She stood on tiptoes on my feet, lifting her heels in the air, and embraced my neck with her two long, slender creeper-like arms, interlacing her delicate petal fingers. Bending my face playfully down toward her, she raised up the lotus of her own face, her long eyes rolling, and kissed me again and again.

When I let her go, I told her: 8.120

'Just stay here in the bosom of the yellow *kurántaka* amaranth thicket while I go forth to pull off our perfect plan.'

Off I went to where the *homa* sacrificial fire had been. There I rang the bell hanging from an *ashóka* branch. It tolled as though it were the terminator Death's harbinger who summoned the man. Meanwhile I started offering into the fire a pile of flimsy aloe and sandalwood. The king approached the arranged spot. He hesitated in surprise, standing there in some doubt. I addressed him, in his wife's words:

'Make an oath on the truth to me again, with the fire, 8.123
Lord of light, as your witness! If you swear not to take your pleasure with my co-wives once these good looks are yours, then I will transfer this body to you now.'

Instantly totally convinced that here was his queen and no trick, he prepared to make his pledge. I smiled then, saying:

'What need of an oath? For which woman on earth would dare disrespect me. If you are able to enjoy intercourse with *ápsaras*es, celestial ladies, then go ahead at your pleasure.

Tell me now your secrets. At the end of their telling will 8.126
be the end of your present body.'

He began his confession:

‹Asti baddho mat|pituḥ kanīyān bhrātā Prahāravarmā. taṃ viṣ'|ânnena vyāpādy' âjīrṇa|doṣaṃ khyāpayeyam iti mantribhiḥ sah' âdhyavasitam.

8.129 Anujāya Viśālavarmaṇe daṇḍa|cakraṃ Puṇḍra|deś'|âbhikramaṇāya ditsitam.

Paura|vṛddhaś ca Pāñcālikaḥ Paritrātaś ca sārthavāhaḥ Khanati|nāmno Yavanād vajram ekaṃ vasundharā|mūlyaṃ laghīyas" ârgheṇa labhyam iti mam' âik'|ânte 'mantrayetām.

Gṛha|patiś ca mam' ântaraṅga|bhūto jana|pada|mahattaraḥ Śatahalir alīka|vāda|śīlam avalepavantaṃ duṣṭa|grāmaṇyam An|anta|sīraṃ janapada|kopena ghātayeyam iti daṇḍa|dharān uddhāra|karmaṇi mat|prayogān niyoktum abhyupāgamat.

8.132 Ittham idam a|cira|prastutaṃ rahasyam iti.›

ākarṇya tam:

‹iyat tav' āyuḥ. upapadyasva svakarm'|ôcitāṃ gatim! iti›

8.135 cchurikayā dvidhākṛtya kṛtta|mātraṃ tasminn eva pravṛtta|sphīta|sarpiṣi hiraṇya|retasy ajuhavam. abhūc c' âsau bhasmasāt.

Atha strī|svabhāvād īṣad|vihvalāṃ hṛdaya|vallabhāṃ samāśvāsya hasta|kisalaye 'valambya gatvā tad|gṛham anujñay" âsyāḥ sarvāṇy antaḥ|purāṇy āhūya sadya eva sevāṃ dattavān.

'My father's younger brother, Prahára·varman, is my prisoner. My ministers and I have resolved to assassinate him with poisoned food, and then give out that it was an attack of dysentery.

I intend to give my younger brother Vishála·varman an army division with which to attack the land of the Pundras.* 8.129

The city elder Pañchálika and Paritráta the caravan-leader have advised me privately that the Greek Khánati has a diamond costing the earth for sale at a negligible price.

And Shata·hali, "One hundred plows," head of my household, trusty as my heart, sheriff of the country, has already undertaken on my behalf to command the wielders of power not to interfere in our plot to stir up the population to destroy Anánta·sira, a wicked arrogant landlord and a habitual liar.

Such are my most recent secret enterprises.' 8.132

Having heard him out I announced:

'Your life is over. Prepare to meet the destiny your deeds deserve!'

And I cut him in two with my sword. No sooner was he chopped into pieces than I offered him as an oblation into the aforementioned golden-seeded sacrificial fire, feeding its flames with a mountain of ghee. The man was reduced to ashes. 8.135

Afterward the love of my heart was a little upset, as is a woman's wont. I comforted her, then led her home by her tender shoot of a hand. With her consent I summoned all the members of the harem, and gave them spontaneous audience.

Sa|vismita|vilāsinī|sārtha|madhye kañcid vihṛtya kālaṃ visṛṣṭ'|âvarodha|maṇḍalas tām eva saṃhat'|ūrūm ūr'|ûpapīḍaṃ bhuj'|ôpapīḍaṃ c' ôpagūhya talpe 'bhiramayann alpām iva tāṃ niśām atyanaiṣam.

8.138 Alabhe ca tan|mukhāt tad|rāja|kulasya śīlam. uṣasi snātvā kṛta|maṅgalo mantribhiḥ saha samagacche. tāṃś c' âbravam:

‹Āryāḥ, rūpeṇ' âiva saha parivṛtto mama svabhāvaḥ. ya eṣa viṣ'|ânnena hantuṃ cintitaḥ pitā me sa muktvā svam etad rājyaṃ bhūya eva grāhayitavyaḥ. pitṛvad amuṣmin vayaṃ śuśrūṣay" âiva vartāmahe. na hy asti pitṛ|vadhāt paraṃ pātakam iti.›

Bhrātaraṃ ca Viśālavarmāṇam āhūy' ôktavān:

8.141 ‹Vatsa, na su|bhikṣāḥ sāṃprataṃ Puṇḍrāḥ. te duḥkha|moh'|ôpahatās tyakt'|ātmāno rāṣṭraṃ naḥ samṛddham abhidraveyuḥ. ato muṣṭi|vadhaḥ sasya|vadho vā yad" ôtpadyate tad" âbhiyāsyasi. n' âdya yātrā yukt" êti.›

Nagara|vṛddhāv apy alāpiṣam:

‹Alpīyasā mūlyena mah"|ârhaṃ vajra|vastu m" âstu me labhyaṃ dharma|rakṣāyai, tad|anuguṇen' âiva mūlyen' âdaḥ krīyatām iti.›

8.144 Śatahaliṃ ca rāṣṭra|mukhyam āhūy' ākhyātavān:

‹Yo 'sāv An|anta|sīraḥ Prahāravarmaṇaḥ pakṣa iti ināśayiṣitaḥ, so 'pi pitari me prakṛti|sthe kim iti nāśyeta, tat tvay" âpi tasmin saṃrambho na kārya iti.›

I sported a short while among the bevy of astonished ladies before sending the circle of concubines away. Then I embraced only her of the solid thighs, squeezing her with my own thighs and arms. We spent the night frolicking on the bed. It seemed all too brief.

My queen also taught me the customs of the royal house- 8.138
hold. At daybreak I bathed, and after I had performed my ritual duties held a meeting with my ministers. I told them:

'Gentlemen! Along with my looks my character has also changed. The uncle of mine we had planned to kill with poisoned food is to be released. He should be reinstated once more to this his kingdom. We will do nothing but obey him like a father. No crime is worse than parricide.'

Next, I called in my new brother Vishála·varman, and said:

'My dear, the people of Pundra are not well provisioned 8.141
these days. In their suffering, stupidity might overwhelm them, making them reckless of their lives, and they could launch an attack on our prosperous kingdom. Therefore you should only attack them when they have stocks of corn or a harvest to ruin. Now is not the time to invade.'

I also addressed the two city elders:

'I do not want to obtain a very valuable diamond for a negligible price, because I wish to preserve righteousness, *dharma*. I shall buy it at its proper value.'

Then I summoned the governor Shata·hali and declared: 8.144

'Anánta·sira was asking to be killed for being an ally of Prahára·varman. But now that my father has been restored to his position, why should we kill his friend? Make no attempt against him.'

Ta ime sarvam ābhijñānikam upalabhya ‹sa ev' âyam iti› niścinvānā vismayamānāś ca tāṃ mahā|devīṃ ca praśaṃsanto mantra|balāni c' ôdghoṣayanto bandhanāt pitarau niṣkrāmayya svaṃ rājyaṃ pratyapādayan.

8.147 Ahaṃ ca tayā me dhātryā sarvam idaṃ mama ceṣṭitaṃ rahasi pitror avagamayya praharṣa|kāṣṭh'|âdhirūḍhayos tayoḥ pāda|mūlam abhaje. abhajye ca yauva|rājya|lakṣmyā tad|anujñātayā.

Prasādhit'|ātmā deva|pāda|viraha|duḥkha|durbhagān bhogān nirviśan, bhūyo 'sya pitṛ|sakhasya Siṃhavarmaṇo lekhyāc Caṇḍavarmaṇaś Camp"|âbhiyogam avagamya;

‹Śatru|vadho mitra|rakṣā c' ôbhayam api karaṇīyam ev' êti›

8.150 a|laghunā laghu|samutthānena sainya|cakreṇ' âbhyasaram. abhūvaṃ ca bhūmis tvat|pāda|lakṣmī|sākṣātkriyā|mah"|ôtsav'|ānanda|rāśer iti.»

Śrutv" âitad devo Rājavāhanaḥ sa|smitam avādīt:

«Paśyata pāratalpikam upadhi|yuktam api guru|jana|bandha|vyasana|mukti|hetutayā duṣṭ'|âmitra|pramāpaṇ'|âbhyupāyatayā rājy'|ôpalabdhi|mūlatayā ca puṣkalāv artha|dharmāv apy arīradhat. kiṃ hi buddhimat|prayuktaṃ n' âbhyupaiti śobhām iti.»

8.153 Arthapāla|mukhe nidhāya snigdha|dīrghāṃ dṛṣṭim

My ministers took note of all these tokens of recognition, and were convinced that I was their old king. Amazed, they congratulated me and my queen, proclaiming aloud the power of magic charms. They had my parents released from imprisonment and reinstated them to their throne.

Through that nurse of mine I told you about, I had se- 8.147
cretly informed my mother and father that I had arranged everything. When I paid my respects at their feet they were quite beside themselves with delight. On their command I was honored with the fortune of becoming crown prince.

My spirit was at peace, but nevertheless the pleasures I enjoyed were tainted by the grief of my separation from Your Highness's presence. At that point I learned through a letter from this friend of my father's, Simha·varman, that Chanda·varman had attacked Champa. Thinking:

'To kill the enemy and protect a friend is my double duty!'

I marched out with an army great in weight but light on 8.150
its feet. Thus I found myself under a mountain of delight, the great festival occasioned by seeing again the glory of your feet."

At the end of the story Prince Raja·váhana smiled, saying:

"Take note how seducing another man's wife twinned with fraud has reinforced in abundance both material profit and religious merit. For thanks to these crimes you could procure your parents' release from the oppression of captivity, slay the wicked enemy and win back a kingdom. Whatever an intelligent man does becomes a noble act."

He fixed a long loving look on the face of Artha·pala and 8.153
commanded him:

«Ācaṣṭāṃ bhavān ātmīya|caritam. iti» ādideśa. so 'pi baddh'|âñjalir abhidadhe:

iti śrī|Daṇḍinaḥ kṛtau
Daśa|kumāra|carite
Upahāravarma|caritaṃ
nāma
tṛtīya ucchvāsaḥ.

"Now you tell what you have been up to."
With his hands folded respectfully Artha·pala then related:

That is the end of the third chapter of
the glorious Dandin's
What Ten Young Men Did.
It is called:
What Upahára·varman Did.

CHAPTER NINE
WHAT ARTHA·PALA DID

«Deva so 'ham apy ebhir eva suhṛdbhir eka|karm' ūrmi|māli|nemi|bhūmi|valayaṃ paribhramann upāsaraṃ kadā cit Kāśī|purīṃ Vārāṇasīm.

Upaspṛśya maṇi|bhaṅga|nirmal'|âmbhasi Maṇikarṇikāyām Avimukteśvaraṃ Bhagavantam Andhaka|mathanam abhipraṇamya pradakṣiṇaṃ paribhraman puruṣam ekam āyāmavantam āyasa|parigha|pīvarābhyāṃ bhujābhyām ābadhyamāna|parikaram a|virata|rudit'|ôcchūna|tāmra|dṛṣṭim adrākṣam. atarkayaṃ ca:

9.3 ‹Karkaśo 'yaṃ puruṣaḥ, kārpaṇyam iva varṣati kṣīṇa|tāraṃ cakṣuḥ, ārambhaś ca sāhas'|ânuvādī. nūnam asau prāṇa|niḥspṛhaḥ kim api kṛcchraṃ priya|jana|vyasana|mūlaṃ prapitsate. tat pṛcchayam enam asti cen mam' âpi ko 'pi sāhāyya|dān'|âvakāśaḥ.›

Tam enam abhyupety' êty apṛccham:

‹Bhadra, saṃnāho 'yaṃ sāhasam avagamayati. na ced gopyam icchāmi śrotuṃ śoka|hetum iti.›

9.6 Sa māṃ sa|bahu|mānaṃ nirvarṇya:

‹Ko doṣaḥ? śrūyatām iti.›

Kva cit karavīra|tale mayā saha niṣaṇṇaḥ kathām akārṣīt:

"My Lord, I was on the same mission as these friends here. Thus I wandered the circle of the earth ringed by the wave-garlanded ocean until one day I arrived in Varánasi, the city of Kashi.*

First I performed my ritual ablutions in the sacred water of Mani·kárnika, flawless as a fragment of a jewel. Next I bowed down before the Lord Avimúktéshvara, slayer of Ándhaka. As I was making my clockwise circumambulation I saw an exceedingly tall man girding up his loins with two arms stout as iron bars. His eyes were copper-red and swollen from incessant crying. That made me wonder to myself:

'This fellow is tough, but his eyes seem to be raining 9.3
wretchedness, their pupils shrunk away. What he is about bespeaks a desperate act of violence. I am sure he is indifferent to his own survival, and is set on perpetrating some dreadful deed on account of the suffering of his loved ones. In which case I should inquire if there is any way I could be of assistance.'

I approached him and asked:

'My good sir, you seem to be arming yourself for some violent deed. If it is not a secret, please tell me why you are grieving.'

He looked me over with a great deal of respect, before 9.6
saying:

'What harm can it do? You will hear.'

We sat down together at the foot of a *kara·vira* tree, and he told his story:

9.9 ‹Mahā|bhāga, so 'ham asmi pūrveṣu kāma|caraḥ Pūrṇabhadro nāma gṛha|pati|putraḥ. prayatna|saṃvardhito 'pi pitrā daiva|cchand'|ânuvartī caurya|vṛttir āsam.

Ath' âsyāṃ Kāśī|puryām arya|varyasya kasya cid gṛhe corayitvā rūp'|âbhigrāhito baddhaḥ. vadhye ca mayi matta|hastī Mṛtyuvijayo nāma hiṃsā|vihārī rāja|gopur'|ôpari|tal'|âdhirūḍhasya paśyataḥ Kāmapāla|nāmna uttam'|âmātyasya śāsanāj jana|kaṇṭha|rava|dviguṇita|ghaṇṭā|ravo maṇḍalita|hasta|kāṇḍaṃ samabhyadhāvat.

Abhipatya ca mayā nirbhayena nirbhartsitaḥ pariṇaman dāru|khaṇḍa|suṣir'|ânupraviṣṭ'|ôbhaya|bhuja|daṇḍa|caṇḍa|ghaṭṭita|pratimāno bhītavan nyavartiṣṭa. bhūyaś ca netrā jāta|saṃrambheṇa nikāma|dāruṇair vāg|aṅkuśa|pāda|pātair abhimukhīkṛtaḥ. may" âpi dviguṇ'|ābaddha|manyunā nirbhartsy' âbhihato nivṛty' âpādravat.

9.12 Atha may" ôpetya sa|rabhasam ākruṣṭo ruṣṭaś ca yantā; «Hanta! mṛto 'si kuñjar'|âpasad' êti.»

niśitena vāraṇena vāraṇaṃ muhur muhur abhighnan niryāṇa|bhāge katham api mad|abhimukham akarot. ath' âvocam:

9.15 «Apasaratu dvipa|kīṭa eṣaḥ! anyaḥ kaś cin mātaṅga|patir ānīyatām, yen' âhaṃ muhūrtaṃ vihṛtya gacchāmi gantavyāṃ gatim iti.»

'Illustrious sir, I am Purna·bhadra, the son of a headman, 9.9
a traveller at large in eastern lands. My father brought me up with discipline, but I obeyed the will of destiny and became a professional thief.

One day when I was robbing an eminent merchant's house here in Kashi I was caught in the act and jailed. On the order of the chief minister, Kama·pala, I was sentenced to be killed by the bloodthirsty rutting elephant Mrityu·víjaya, "Conqueror of death." Kama·pala sat watching from his position on the upper floor of the royal gate. The clamor from the people's throats doubled the clamor of the elephant's bells as he rushed at me, massive trunk curled.

I challenged him fearlessly in his charge. Slipping both my arms through a hollow log of wood, when the elephant bent down to strike I jabbed him savagely between his tusks with my reinforced arms. Taking fright, he took flight. Enraged, his mahout forced him to turn back, raining fierce blows with his feet, goad and voice. My own rage was redoubled. I again challenged and then attacked, at which he changed direction and ran away.

Next I aggressively charged at his rider, yelling and infu- 9.12
riating him. He cried out:

"Damn you, accursed elephant! You are dead."

Beating with his sharpened goad at the sensitive outer corner of the elephant's eye again and again, he somehow managed to drive him back around to face me. Then I shouted:

"This worm of an elephant should slink off home! Bring 9.15
on another, an elephant king with whom I can dally a moment before I reach my inevitable destination."

Dṛṣṭv" âiva sa māṃ ruṣṭam udgarjantam utkrānta|yantṛ|niṣṭhur'|ājñaḥ palāyiṣṭa. mantriṇā punar aham āhūy' âbhyadhāyiṣi:

«Bhadra, mṛtyur ev' âiṣa Mṛtyuvijayo nāma hiṃsā|vihārī. so 'yam api tāvat tvay" âivaṃ|bhūtaḥ kṛtaḥ. tad viramya karmaṇo 'smān malīmasāt. kim alam asi pratipady' âsmān ārya|vṛttyā vartitum? iti»

9.18 «Yath" ājñāpito 'sm' îti.»

vijñāpito 'yaṃ mayā mitravan mayy avartiṣṭa.

Pṛṣṭaś ca may" âikadā rahasi jāta|viśrambheṇ' âbhāṣata sva|caritam:

9.21 «Āsīt Kusumapure rājño ripuṃ|jayasya mantrī Dharmapālo nāma viśruta|dhīḥ śruta|ṛṣiḥ. amuṣya putraḥ Sumitro nāma pitr" âiva samaḥ prajñā|guṇeṣu. tasy' âsmi dvaimāturaḥ kanīyān bhrāt" âham.

Veśeṣu vilasantaṃ mām asau vinaya|rucir avārayat. avārya|durnayaś c' âham apasṛtya diṅ|mukheṣu bhraman yadṛcchay" âsyāṃ Vārāṇasyāṃ pramada|vane Madana|daman'|ārādhanāya nirgatya saha sakhībhiḥ kanduken' ânukrīḍamānāṃ Kāśī|bhartuś Caṇḍasiṃhasya kanyāṃ Kāntimatīṃ nāma cakame. katham api samagacche ca.

Atha cchannaṃ viharatā kumārī|pure sā may" āsīd āpanna|sattvā. kaṃ cit sutaṃ ca prasūtavatī. mṛta|jāta iti so 'paviddho rahasya|nirbheda|bhayāt parijanena krīḍā|śaile. śabaryā ca śmaśān'|âbhyāsaṃ nītaḥ. tay" âiva nivartamāna-

The elephant saw me roaring furiously, and ignoring his driver's harsh commands he fled.* At this the minister called me over to pronounce:

"Good man, this bloodthirsty Mrityu·víjaya is death incarnate. Yet you have reduced him to this state. Renounce now your former foul employment. Are you prepared to agree to follow an honorable profession under me?"

"I am at your service!" 9.18

I replied respectfully. And we became friends.

One day, when we were alone together, I asked him to share his story. Trusting me by then, he did so:

"There was in Kúsuma·pura (Pátali·putra) a king, Raja· 9.21
hamsa, victor over his enemies. He had a minister called Dharma·pala, famed for his intelligence and known as a religious sage. He in turn had a son Sumítra, his father's equal in wisdom and all good qualities. I am that son's younger brother, but by a different mother.

My brother, who loved to be good, tried to hold me back from sporting with prostitutes. But I was irrepressibly dissolute and left home to start my wanderings all over the place. One day I came by chance here to Varánasi, where I fell in love with Kántimati, the daughter of Chanda·simha, Lord of Kashi. She was playing at ball with her girlfriends in the pleasure garden where they had gone to honor Shiva, Love's tamer. I even managed to have intercourse with her.

From then on I lived in hiding with her in the ladies' apartments. She fell pregnant, and gave birth to a son. Her attendants were scared that the secret would come out, so they told her it was stillborn and abandoned the baby on the landscaped hill in the park. Thence a *shábari* mountain

yā niśīthe rāja|vīthyām ārakṣika|puruṣair abhigṛhya tarjitayā daṇḍa|pāruṣya|bhītayā nirbhinna|prāyaṃ rahasyam.

9.24 Rāj'|ājñayā niśīthe 'ham ākrīḍana|giri|darī|gṛhe viśrabdha|prasuptas tay" ôpadarśito yath"|ôpapanna|rajju|baddhaḥ śmaśānam upanīya mātaṅg'|ôdyatena kṛpāṇena prājihīrṣye. niyati|balāl lūna|bandhas tam asim ācchidy' āntyajaṃ tam anyāṃś ca kāṃś cit prahṛty' âpāsaram.

A|śaraṇaś ca bhramann aṭavyām ekad" âśru|mukhyā kay" âpi divy'|ākārayā sa|paricārayā kanyay" ôpāsthāyiṣi. sā mām añjali|kisalay'|ôttaṃsitena mukha|vilola|kuntalena mūrdhnā praṇamya mayā saha vana|vaṭa|drumasya kasy' âpi mahataḥ pracchāya|śītale tale niṣaṇṇā.

‹K" âsi, vāsu? kuto 'sy āgatā? kasya hetor asya me prasīdas' îti?›

9.27 S'|âbhilāṣam ābhāṣitā mayā vāṅ|mayaṃ madhu|varṣam avarṣat:

‹Ārya, nāthasya yakṣāṇāṃ Maṇibhadrasy' âsmi duhitā Tārāvalī nāma. s" âhaṃ kadā cid Agastya|patnīṃ Lopāmudrāṃ namaskṛty' âpāvartamānā Malaya|gireḥ paret'|āvāse Vārāṇasyāḥ kam api dārakaṃ rudantam adrākṣam. ādāya c' âinaṃ tīvra|snehān mama pitroḥ saṃnidhim anaiṣam. anaiṣīc ca

woman carried it off to the charnel-ground area. Just when she was returning at midnight, the city watch apprehended her on the royal road. They made threats, frightening her with the severity of the punishment. In the end, she gave away almost the whole secret story.

On the order of the king, in the middle of the night she 9.24
showed them where I was, sleeping peacefully in a grotto of the pleasure mountain. They bound me with whatever cords were at hand and led me off to the cremation ground. There an outcaste* was to slay me with a sword. Thanks to good luck, only my bonds were cut, I was able to snatch away the sword, and struck the outcaste and some others with it, before making my escape.

With nowhere to take refuge, I wandered through the wilderness until I met a maiden accompanied by an entourage. She looked divine, but with tears on her face. Her locks tumbling about her face, she bowed down before me, adorning her head with her sprout-like hands folded in obeisance. Together we sat down on the ground in the cool shade of a great wild banyan. Ardently I asked:

'Who are you, my girl? Whence have you come? And to what do I owe the pleasure?'

In reply she showered me with a rain of honey-sweet 9.27
words:

'Noble sir, I am Tarávali, the daughter of Mani·bhadra, lord of the *yakshas*.* One day I went to pay my respects to Agástya's* wife Lopa·mudra. On my way back from the Málayan mountain, I saw a baby boy bawling in the house of the dead at Varánasi. Acute affection compelled me to pick him up and carry him to my parents. My father took

me pitā devasy' Âlak"|ēśvarasy' āsthānīm. ath' âham āhūy' ājñaptā Hara|sakhena:

«Bāle, bāle 'smin kīdṛśas te bhāva iti?»

9.30 «Aurasa iv' âsmin vatse vatsalat" êti.» mayā vijñāpitaḥ.

«Satyam āha varāk" îti.»

Tan|mūlām atimahatīṃ kathām akarot. tatr' âitāvan may" âvagatam:

9.33 Tvaṃ kila Śaunakaḥ Śūdrakaḥ Kāmapālaś c' âbhinnaḥ. Bandhumatī Vinayavatī Kāntimatī c' âbhinnā. Vedimaty Āryadāsī Somadevī c' âik" âiva. Haṃsāvalī Śūrasenā Sulocanā c' ân|anyā. Nandinī Raṅgapatāk" Êndrasenā c' â|pṛthagbhūtā.

Yā kila Śaunak'|âvasthāyām agni|sākṣikam ātma|sātkṛtā gopa|kanyā s" âiva kil' Āryadāsī punaś c' âdya Tārāval" îty abhūvam. bālaś ca kila Śūdrak'|âvasthe tvayy Āryadāsy|avasthāyāṃ mayy udabhūt. avardhyata ca Vinayavatyā sneha|vāsanayā. sa tu tasyāṃ Kāntimaty|avasthāyām ady' ôdabhūt.

Evam an|eka|mṛtyu|mukha|paribhraṣṭaṃ daivān may" ôpalabdhaṃ tam Eka|piṅg'|ādeśād vane tapasyato Rājahaṃsasya devyai Vasumatyai tat|sutasya bhāvi|cakra|vartino Rājavāhanasya paricary"|ârthaṃ samarpya, gurubhir abhyanujñātā kṛt'|ânta|yogāt kṛt'|ânta|mukha|bhraṣṭasya te pāda|padma|śuśrūṣ"|ârtham āgat" âsm' îti.›

him to the audience hall of the god Kubéra, Lord of Álaka.* Shiva's friend Kubéra then summoned me and inquired:

"Child, what are your feelings to this other child?"

"I feel maternal love toward him as though he were my 9.30
own son." I replied.

"The poor girl speaks the truth."

Kubéra said, and told the baby's long, long story. This is the gist that I gathered:*

You, according to what Kubéra said, are Sháunaka, Shúd- 9.33
raka, and now Kama·pala, all in one.* Bándhumati, Vináyavati and Kántimati are apparently one and the same. Védimati, Arya·dasi and Soma·devi are likewise one. Hamsávali, Shura·sena and Sulóchana are no different from each other, it seems. And Nándini, Ranga·patáka and Indra·sena are not in fact separate people.

What is more, it turns out that I who am Tarávali in this life am the same milkmaid Arya·dasi whom you, when you were Sháunaka, did the honor of marrying with the sacred fire as witness. Moreover, Kubéra told me that when you were Shúdraka and I was Arya·dasi we had a baby boy. But he was brought up by Vináyavati, whose affection perfumed her next birth.* Thus now that she is Kántimati he has been born to her.

The baby had already tumbled from the jaws of death more than once when I chanced to find him. Kubéra, with his yellow mark in the place of one eye, commanded me to hand him over to Vásumati, the queen of Raja·hamsa, then retired to the forest to practice austerities. The boy was to be the attendant of their son Raja·váhana, destined to become a wheel-turning emperor. Now that destiny's

9.36 Tac chrutvā tām an|eka|janma|ramaṇīm a|sakṛd āśliṣya harṣ'|âśru|mukho muhur muhuḥ sāntvayitvā tat|prabhāva|darśite mahati mandire 'har|niśaṃ bhūmi|durlabhān bhogān anvabhūvam. dvi|trāṇi dināny atikramya matta|kāśinīṃ tām avādiṣam:

‹Priye, pratyapakṛtya mat|prāṇa|drohiṇaś Caṇḍasiṃhasya vaira|niryātana|sukham anububhūṣām' îti.›

Tayā sa|smitam abhihitam:

9.39 ‹Ehi, kānta, Kāntimatī|darśanāya nayāmi tvām iti.›

Sthite 'rdha|rātre rājño vāsa|gṛham anīye. tatas tac|chiro|bhāga|vartinīm ādāy' âsi|yaṣṭiṃ prabodhy' âinaṃ prasphurantam abravam:

‹Aham asmi bhavaj|jāmātā bhavad|anumatyā vinā tava kany"|âbhimarṣī. tam aparādham anuvṛtyā pramārṣṭum āgata iti.›

9.42 So 'tibhīto mām abhipraṇamy' āha:

‹Aham eva mūḍho 'parāddhaḥ, yas tava duhitṛ|saṃsarg'|ânugrāhiṇo graha|grasta iv' ôtkrānta|sīmā samādiṣṭavān vadham. tad" āstā Kāntimatī, rājyam idaṃ mama ca jīvitam apy adya|prabhṛti bhavad|adhīnam! iti›

avādīt. ath' âpare|dyuḥ prakṛti|maṇḍalaṃ saṃnipātya vidhivad ātmajāyāḥ pāṇim agrāhayat. aśrāvayac ca tanaya|

power has snatched you from the teeth of fateful death, my parents have sent me here to serve at your lotus-feet.'

She had been my lovely wife in many previous births. As 9.36
soon as she had finished speaking, I embraced her many times. Again and again I consoled her, with tears of joy on my face. With her magical power she conjured up a great palace where day and night I enjoyed pleasures impossible to find on earth. When two or three days had passed I told my intoxicating beauty:

'Beloved, I want to enjoy the pleasure of taking revenge by getting back at Chanda·simha for threatening my life.'

She said with a smile:

'Come, my love, I will take you to see Kántimati.' 9.39

At midnight she transported me to the king's bedchamber. He kept a sword by his head. Picking it up by the handle, I woke him. While he quaked I spoke these words:

'I am the son-in-law who violated your maiden daughter without your permission, come to erase that offense as it and you deserve.'*

Terrified, he prostrated himself before me, pleading: 9.42

'I am a fool. The offense is all mine. You were gracious enough to unite with my daughter, and yet like one possessed by an evil star I overstepped the boundaries of decency to the extent of condemning you to death. Let alone Kántimati, from today onward this my kingdom and my very life are in your hands.'

So he spoke. Then on the following day he convened his circle of ministers so that I could formally receive his daughter's hand. Tarávali revealed to Kántimati what had

vārtā Tārāvalī Kāntimatyai, Somadevī|Sulocan"|Êndrasenā-bhyaś ca pūrva|jāti|vṛtt'|ântam.

9.45 Ittham ahaṃ mantri|pad'|âpadeśaṃ yauva|rājyam anubhavan viharāmi vilāsinībhir iti.»

Sa evaṃ mādṛśe 'pi jantau paricary"|ânubandhī bandhur ekaḥ sarva|bhūtānām alasakena svar|gate śvaśure, jyāyasi ca śyāle Caṇḍaghoṣa|nāmni strīṣv atiprasaṅgāt prāg eva kṣaya|kṣīṇ'|āyuṣi, pañca|varṣa|deśīyaṃ Siṃhaghoṣa|nāmānaṃ kumāram abhyaṣecayat. avardhayac ca vidhin" âinaṃ sa sādhuḥ.

Tasy' âdya yauvan'|ônmādinaḥ paiśunya|vādino durmantriṇaḥ katicid āsann antaraṅgabhūtāḥ. taiḥ kil' âsāv ittham agrāhyata:

9.48 «Prasahy' âiva svasā tav' âmunā bhujaṅgena saṃgṛhītā. punaḥ prasupte rājani prahartum udyat'|âsir āsīt. ten' âsmai tat|kṣaṇa|prabuddhena bhīty" ânunīya dattā kanyā. taṃ ca deva|jyeṣṭhaṃ Caṇḍaghoṣaṃ viṣeṇa hatvā, bālo 'yam a|samartha iti tvam ady' âpi prakṛti|viśrambhaṇāy' ôpekṣitaḥ. kṣiṇoti ca purā sa kṛtaghno bhavantam. tam ev' Ântaka|puram abhigamayituṃ yatasv' êti.»

become of her son, and to Soma·devi, Sulóchana and Indra·sena the accounts of their previous incarnations.*

And that is the story of how I came to live with many ravishing ladies, ostensibly a minister but enjoying the life of a crown prince." 9.45

This Kama·pala was a brother to all living beings without distinction. He even honored humble me that I could attend on him. Meanwhile, an attack of flatulence carried his father-in-law off to heaven. His older brother-in-law Chanda·ghosha had been addicted to women. Hence he had already used up his life span in dissolution. Thus he anointed Prince Simha·ghosha king, then about five years old. That virtuous Kama·pala brought the child up properly.

Today this King Simha·ghosha is flushed with the pride of youth. Some of his evil ministers have become his slanderous confidants. He seems to have been persuaded by them as follows:

"That snake of a husband took your sister in marriage 9.48
by sheer force. Not only that, he was all set to slay the sleeping king with a sword had he not that instant awoken and been intimidated into handing over his daughter to appease Kama·pala. But he did murder your elder brother Chanda·ghosha with poison. He only keeps you alive to keep the confidence of his subjects, reasoning that you are an impotent child. Before long the ingrate is bound to kill you, too. You should endeavor to dispatch him first to the city of Death."

Sa tathā dūṣito 'pi yakṣiṇī|bhayān n' âmuṣmin pāpam ācaritum aśakat. eṣu kila divaseṣv a|yathā|pūrvam ākṛtau Kāntimatyāḥ samupalakṣya rāja|mahiṣī Sulakṣaṇā nāma sa|praṇayam apṛcchat:

«Devi, n' âham ayathātathyena vipralambhanīyā. kathaya tathyaṃ ken' êdam a|yathā|pūrvam ānan'|âravinde tav' âiṣu vāsareṣv iti.»

9.51 Sā tv avādīta:

«Bhadre, smarasi kim ady' âpy ayathātathyena kiṃ cin may" ôkta|pūrvam? sakhī me Tārāvalī sa|patnī ca kim api kaluṣit'|āśayā rahasi bhartrā mad|gotr'|âpadiṣṭā praṇayam apy upekṣya praṇamyamān" âpy asmābhir upoḍha|matsarā prāvasat. avasīdati ca naḥ patiḥ. ato me daurmanasyam iti.»

Tat prāyeṇ' âik'|ânte Sulakṣaṇayā kāntāya kathitam.

9.54 Ath' âsau nir|bhayo 'dya priyatamā|viraha|pāṇḍubhir avayavair, dhairya|stambhit'|âśru|paryākulena cakṣuṣā, uṣma|śvāsa|śoṣitābhir iv' ân|atipeśalābhir vāgbhir viyogaṃ darśayantaṃ katham api rāja|kule kāryāṇi kārayantaṃ, pūrva|saṃketitaiḥ puruṣair abhigrāhy' âbandhayat.

Tasya kila sthāne sthāne doṣān udghoṣya tath" ôddharaṇīye cakṣuṣī yathā tan|mūlam ev' âsya maraṇaṃ bhaved iti.

Although the boy had been corrupted in this way, fear of the *yakshi* Tarávali prevented him from doing Kama·pala harm. I was told that those same days his principal queen, Sulákshana, noticed a change in Kántimati's appearance. She asked her courteously:

"Queen, do not deceive me with falsehood. Please tell me the truth about why your lotus-face is so changed these days."

So Kántimati told her: 9.51

"Good lady, can you remember me ever before today saying anything untrue? My friend and co-wife Tarávali somehow had her feelings offended because our husband called her by my name when they were alone together.* She would not hear his entreaties even when we all begged her, and finally her inflated pride made her move out. Now our lord and master is dispirited. All of which has made me quite depressed."

Once they were in private, Sulákshana told her dear husband the king the full story.

Freed from his fear, Simha·ghosha has now had Kama·pa- 9.54
la seized by men previously engaged for such an eventuality, and is holding him captivity. Kama·pala's loss had been manifest, his limbs colorless through separation from his beloved, his eyes agitated with the effort of holding back his tears, and his words no longer very tender, apparently desiccated by his heated sighs. Only with difficulty had he been managing to delegate the affairs of the royal household.

It is reported that his crimes are to be promulgated far and wide before both his eyes will be gouged out in a manner bound to kill him.

Ato 'tr' âik'|ânte yath"|êṣṭam aśru muktvā tasya sādhoḥ puraḥ prāṇān moktu|kāmo badhnāmi parikaram iti.›

9.57 May" âpi tat pitṛ|vyasanam ākarṇya paryaśruṇā so 'bhihitaḥ:

‹Saumya, kiṃ tava gopāyitvā? yas tasya suto yakṣa|kanyayā devasya Rājavāhanasya pāda|śuśrūṣ"|ârthaṃ devyā Vasumatyā hasta|nyāsaḥ kṛtaḥ so 'ham asmi. śakṣyāmi sahasram api su|bhaṭānām ud|āyudhānāṃ hatvā pitaraṃ mocayitum. api tu saṃkule yadi kaś cit pātayet tad|aṅge śastrikāṃ sarva eva me yatno bhasmani hutam iva bhaved iti.›

An|avasita|vacana eva mayi mahā|nāśī|viṣaḥ prākāra|randhreṇ' ôdairayac chiraḥ. tam ahaṃ mantr'|âuṣadhi|balen' âbhigṛhya Pūrṇabhadram abravam:

9.60 ‹Bhadra, siddhaṃ naḥ samīhitam. anena tātam a|lakṣyamāṇaḥ saṃkule yadṛcchayā patitena nāma daṃśayitvā tathā viṣaṃ stambhayeyaṃ yathā ‹mṛta ity› udāsyeta. tvayā tu mukta|sādhvasena mātā me bodhayitavyā:

«Yo yakṣyā vane devyā Vasumatyā hast'|ârpito yuṣmat|sūnuḥ, so 'nuprāptaḥ pitur avasthāṃ mad|upalabhya buddhi|balād ittham ācariṣyati. tvayā tu mukta|trāsayā rājñe preṣaṇīyam:

Now you know why I am weeping to my heart's content here away from everybody, and why I am girding my loins because I want to give up my life before this virtuous man does.'

I, too, wept to hear of this peril my father was in, and 9.57
recounted:

'Good sir, why should I hide it from you? Kama·pala's son whom the *yaksha* maiden placed in the hands of Queen Vásumati so that he should attend on the prince Raja·vá-hana, that is I. I, Artha·pala, am ready to slay thousands of great warriors with weapons upraised in order to liberate my father. But the problem is that in the melee someone might strike his person with a sword and then my entire effort would be as fruitless as an oblation into ashes.'

Before I had finished speaking, an enormous deadly poisonous snake raised its head from a hole in the wall. Through the power of mantras and herbs I captured him and then informed Purna·bhadra:

'Friend, our wishes are fulfilled. Unseen in the throng, I 9.60
shall contrive to let this serpent fall onto my dear father as if it were an accident. The snake will bite him, but I will stay the working of the poison in such a way that everyone nevertheless gives him up for dead. You must not worry, and go to inform my mother Kántimati:

"Your son whom the *yakshi* entrusted to Queen Vásumati's care in the forest has just arrived. I have told him the situation his father is in. Thanks to his intelligence he plans to do such-and-such. Be free of fear but send word to the king:

‹Eṣa khalu kṣatra|dharmo yad bandhur abandhur vā duṣṭaḥ sa nirapekṣaṃ nigrāhya iti. strī|dharmaś c' âiṣa yad aduṣṭasya duṣṭasya vā bhartur gatir gantavy" êti. tad aham amun" âiva saha cit'|âgnim ārokṣyāmi. yuvati|jan'|ânukūlaḥ paścimo vidhir anujñātavya iti.›

9.63 Sa evaṃ nivedito niyatam anujñāsyati. tataḥ svam ev' āgāram ānīya kāṇḍa|paṭī|parikṣipte vivikt'|ôddeśe darbha|saṃstaraṇam adhiśāyya svayaṃ kṛt'|ânumaraṇa|maṇḍanayā tvayā ca tatra saṃnidheyam. ahaṃ ca bāhya|kakṣ"|āgatas vayā praveśayiṣye. tataḥ pitaram ujjīvya tad|abhiruciten' âbhyupāyena ceṣṭiṣyāmaha iti.»›

Sa ‹tath" êti› hṛṣṭataras tūrṇam agamat.

Ahaṃ tu ghoṣaṇā|sthāne ciñcā|vṛkṣaṃ ghanatara|vipula|śākham āruhya gūḍha|tanur atiṣṭham. āruḍhaś ca loko yathā|yatham uccaiḥ sthānāni. uccā|vaca|pralāpāḥ prastutāḥ. tāvan me pitaraṃ taskaram iva paścād baddha|bhujam uddhura|dhvani|mahā|jan'|ânuyātam ānīya mad|abhyāsa eva sthāpayitvā mātaṅgas trir aghoṣayat:

9.66 ‹Eṣa mantrī Kāmapālo rājya|lobhād bhartāraṃ Caṇḍasiṃhaṃ, yuva|rājaṃ Caṇḍaghoṣaṃ ca viṣ'|ânnen' ôpāṃśu hatvā, punar devo 'pi Siṃhaghoṣaḥ pūrṇa|yauvana ity amuṣmin pāpam ācariṣyan, viśvāsād rahasya|bhūmau punar amātyaṃ Śiva|nāgam āhūya, Sthūṇam Aṅgāravarṣaṃ

'It is indeed the duty of a kshatriya to punish an evildoer, regardless of whether he is a relation or not. Equally it is the duty of a wife to share the destiny of her husband, whether he is an evildoer or not. Therefore I shall mount the funeral pyre beside my husband.* You must give your permission for this last rite, the last of the rites befitting a young woman.'

Asked in these terms he is bound to assent. You then 9.63
should take the body home. There, in a private space screened off with curtains, you should have him laid on a bed of *darbha* grass. Adorn yourself with the ornaments of a woman who is about to follow closely her husband to death,* and wait there. When I reach the courtyard, let me in. I will bring my father back to life and then we can all act according to what he thinks best." '

Delighted, he agreed and hurried off.

For my part, I went to the site of the proclamation, climbed a tamarind tree thick-grown with abundant branches, and stayed there out of sight. Gradually everyone had climbed up to high positions, wherever they could. Loud-voiced discussions commenced. Soon my father was led forth, arms bound behind as though he were a thief, and followed by a mob and unrestrained uproar. The executioner* stood him just below me, before declaring three times:

'Here stands the minister Kama·pala. His greed for the 9.66
kingdom drove him to secretly murder his master Chanda·simha, as well as the heir to the throne Chanda·ghosha, with poisoned food. Next he plotted to harm King Simha·ghosha, for he in turn had meanwhile come of age. He summoned the minister Shiva·naga, whom he trusted, to a

ca rāja|vadhāy' ôpajapya, taiḥ svāmi|bhaktyā vivṛta|guhyo rājya|kāmukasya brāhmaṇasy' ândha|tamasa|praveśo nyāyya iti prāḍvivāka|vākyād akṣy|uddharaṇāya nīyate.

Punar anyo 'pi yadi syād a|nyāya|vṛttis tam apy evam eva yath"|ârheṇa daṇḍena yojayiṣyati deva iti.›

Śrutv" âitad baddha|kalakale mahā|jane pitur aṅge pradīpta|śirasam āśī|viṣaṃ nyakṣipam. ahaṃ ca bhīto nām' âvaplutya tatr' âiva jan'|ânulīnaḥ kruddha|vyāla|daṣṭasya tātasya vihita|jīva|rakṣo viṣaṃ kṣaṇād astambhayam. apatac ca sa bhūmau mṛta|kalpaḥ. prālapaṃ ca:

9.69 ‹Satyam idaṃ rāj'|âvamāninaṃ daivo daṇḍa eva spṛśat' îti. yad ayam akṣibhyām avanipena vin" âcikīrṣitaḥ prāṇair eva viyojito vidhin" êti.›

Mad|uktaṃ ca kecid anvamanyanta, apare punar ninin-duḥ. darvī|karas tu tam api caṇḍālaṃ daṣṭv" ārūḍha|trāsa|druta|loka|datta|mārgaḥ prādravat.

Atha mad|ambā Pūrṇabhadra|bodhit'|ârthā tādṛśe 'pi vyasane n' âtivihvalā kula|parijan'|ânuyātā padbhyām eva dhīram āgatya mat|pitur uttam'|âṅgam utsaṅge dhārayanty āsitvā rājñe samādiśat:

secluded location, and conspired with Sthuna and Angára·varsha to kill the king. But, devoted to their master, these men revealed the secret plot. Now a judge has ruled that justice for a brahmin who lusts after royal power is to enter into blind darkness. Accordingly, he has been brought here to have both eyes put out.*

If anyone else breaks the law, then the king will condemn them, too, to the punishment they deserve, just like this man.'

The great crowd buzzed at his words. I dropped the venomous serpent, its gleaming hood expanded, onto my father's body. Then I jumped down after it, pretending to be terrified. The furious snake had bitten my dear father. To save his life I slipped through the crowd right there, and at once halted the effects of the poison. He fell to the ground exactly as though dead. I cried out:

'It is true what they say. Fate punishes anyone who does 9.69
not respect the king. For it is destiny that has deprived this man of his life, while the king only intended to deprive him of both eyes.'

Some people applauded my words, while others reproached me. But then the hooded serpent bit the executioner as well, before slipping away down the road, clear since the crowd had scattered in the grip of panic.

In the meantime, Purna·bhadra had informed my mother about what was really going on. Even at such a difficult time she did not become delirious. Followed by her household attendants, she came steady on her own two feet. She sat holding my father's head in her lap, and sent word to the king:

9.72 ‹Eṣa me patis tav' âpakartā na v" êti daivam eva jānāti. na me 'nay" âsti cintayā phalam. asya tu pāṇi|grāhakasya gatim an|anuprapadyamānā bhavat|kulaṃ kalaṅkayeyam. ato 'numantum arhasi bhartrā saha cit'|âdhirohaṇāya mām iti.›

Śrutvā c' âitat prīti|yuktaḥ samādikṣat kṣit'|īśvaraḥ:

‹Kriyatāṃ kul'|ôcitaḥ saṃskāraḥ. utsav'|ôttaraṃ ca paścimaṃ vidhi|saṃskāram anubhavatu me bhaginī|patir iti.›

9.75 Caṇḍāle tu mat|pratiṣiddha|sakala|mantra|vādi|prayāse saṃsthite:

‹Kāmapālo 'pi kāla|daṣṭa ev' êti.›

Sva|bhavan'|ôpanayanam amuṣya sva|māhātmya|prakāśanāya mahī|patir anvamaṃsta. ānītaś ca pitā me viviktāyāṃ bhūmau darbha|śayyām adhiśāyya sthito 'bhūt. atha ma-d|ambā maraṇa|maṇḍanam anuṣṭhāya, sa|karuṇaṃ sakhīr āmantrya, muhur abhipraṇamya bhavana|devatāṃ yatna|nivārita|parijan'|ākranditā pitur me śayana|sthānam ekākinī prāvikṣat.

9.78 Tatra ca pūrvam eva Pūrṇabhadr'|ôpasthāpitena ca mayā Vainateyatāṃ gatena nirviṣīkṛtaṃ bhartāram aikṣata. hṛṣṭatamā patyuḥ pādayoḥ paryaśru|mukhī praṇipatya māṃ ca muhur muhuḥ prastuta|stanī pariṣvajya saharṣa|bāṣpa|gadgadam agadat:

'The gods only know whether this my husband sinned 9.72
against you or not. It is fruitless for me to worry about the question. But I should be a stain on your house if I did not share the fate of this man who took my hand in marriage. Therefore you must grant me leave to mount the pyre beside my husband.'

The king was full of joy to hear this and ordained:

'Let the proper family life-cycle rituals be carried out. My sister's husband should have the ceremony of the last rites, complete with a festival.'

The executioner had died, thanks to my blocking all the 9.75
efforts of the snake charmers to counteract the poison. This convinced the king that:

'Kama·pala, too, must be in the jaws of death.'

In order to make a public show of his own magnanimity, he gave permission for my father to be carried to his own house. Once brought there, he was laid down on a bed of *darbha* grass in a private area, where he remained. Then my mother dressed herself in the ornaments of her impending death, tenderly bid farewell to her lady friends, bowed down many times before the domestic deities, and, managing to halt her household's wails, she entered all alone the place where my father lay.

There she saw her master completely freed by me from the 9.78
poison's grip. For Purna·bhadra had already let me in, I a veritable Gáruda, natural enemy of snakes.* Overjoyed, she threw herself at her husband's feet, her face covered in tears. She could not embrace me enough, oozing maternal love like breast milk. Sobbing tears of delight, she stammered:

‹Putra, yo 'si jāta|mātraḥ pāpayā mayā parityaktaḥ sa kim artham evaṃ mām atinirghṛṇām anugṛhṇāsi? atha v" âiṣa nir|aparādha eva te janayitā. yuktam asya pratyānayanam antak'|ânanāt.

Krūrā khalu Tārāvalī yā tvām upalabhy' âpi tattvataḥ Kuberād a|samarpya mahyam arpitavatī devyai Vasumatyai. s" âiva vā sadṛśa|kāriṇī. na hi tādṛśād bhāgya|rāśer vinā mādṛśo jano 'lpa|puṇyas tav' ârhati kala|pralāp'|âmṛtāni karṇābhyāṃ pātum.

9.81 Ehi pariṣvajasv' êti!›

Bhūyo|bhūyaḥ śirasi jighranty aṅkam āropayantī Tārāvalīṃ garhayantī āliṅgayanty aśrubhir abhiṣiñcantī c' ôtkampit'|âṅga|yaṣṭir anyādṛśy" êva kṣaṇam ajaniṣṭa.

Janayit" âpi me narakād iva svargam, tādṛśād vyasanāt tathā|bhūtam abhyudayam āruḍhaḥ, Pūrṇabhadreṇa vistareṇa yathā|vṛtt'|ântam āvedito bhagavato Maghavato 'pi bhāgyavantam ātmānam ajīgaṇat. manāg iva ca mat|sambandham ākhyāya harṣa|vismit'|ātmanoḥ pitror akathayam:

9.84 ‹Ājñāpayataṃ k" âdya naḥ pratipattiḥ.'

Pitā me prābravīt:

'My son, I was wicked to abandon you as soon as you were born. How, then, do you treat me so kindly when I was pitiless to you? But perhaps it is because of the complete innocence of your father. It was only proper for you to rescue him from the jaws of death the destroyer.

Tarávali was undeniably cruel.* For, after learning from Kubéra the truth about your identity, she did not return you to me but handed you over to Queen Vásumati. On the other hand, perhaps she did the right thing. After all, someone like me, so poor in merit, does not deserve to have her ears drink in the ambrosial nectar of your sweet chatter, without having such a mountain of good fortune as the queen.

Come and embrace me!' 9.81

She smelled and kissed me on the head again and again, and sat me on her lap, blaming Tarávali, embracing me, and anointing me with her tears. Her delicate frame trembled and in a moment she looked transformed.

My father, too, might as well have ascended to heaven from hell, risen from such danger to the present superlative success. Purna·bhadra had filled him in on all the details of what had happened. He reckoned himself more blessed than even the bountiful Lord Indra. I more or less hinted at my part in the story to my parents' amazed delight, before asking them:

'You two must decide what course of action we follow 9.84
today.'

At which my father addressed me:

‹Vatsa, gṛham ev' êdam asmadīyam ativiśāla|prākāra|valayam a|kṣayy|āyudha|sthānam. alaṅghyatamā ca guptiḥ. upakṛtāś ca may" âtibahavaḥ santi sāmantāḥ. prakṛtayaś ca bhūyas yo na me vyasanam anurudhyante. subhaṭānāṃ c' ân|eka|sahasram asty eva sa|suhṛt|putra|dāram.

9.87 Ato 'tr' âiva katipayāny ahāni sthitvā bāhy'|âbhyantar aṅgān kopān utpādayiṣyāmaḥ. kupitāṃś ca saṃgṛhya protsāhy' âsya prakṛty|amitrān utthāpya sahajāṃś ca dviṣaḥ durdāntam enam ucchetsyāma iti.›

‹Ko doṣaḥ? tath" âstv iti.›

Tātasya matam anvamaṃsi.

9.90 Tath" âsmāsu pratividhāya tiṣṭhatsu rāj" âpi vijñāpit'|ôdanto jāt'|ânutāpaḥ pāragrāmikān prayogān prāyaḥ prāyuṅkta. te c' âsmābhiḥ praty|aham ahanyanta.

Asminn ev' âvakāśe Pūrṇabhadra|mukhāc ca rājñaḥ śayyā|sthānam avagamya tad" âiva sv'|ôdavasita|bhitti|koṇād ārabhy' ôrag'|āsyena suraṅgām akārṣam. gatā ca sā bhūmi|svarga|kalpam an|alpa|kanyakā|janaṃ kam apy uddeśam. avyathiṣṭa ca dṛṣṭv" âiva sa māṃ nārī|janaḥ.

Tatra kācid indu|kal" êva sva|lāvaṇyena Rasātal'|ândhakāraṃ nirdhunānā, vigrahiṇ" îva Devī Viśvaṃbharā, Hara|gṛhiṇī Vāsura|vijayāy' âvatīrṇā, Pātālam āgatā gṛhiṇ" îva bhagavataḥ Kusuma|dhanvanaḥ, rāja|Lakṣmīr iv' ân|eka|du-

'My dear son, our home here is enclosed by a massive rampart, and its armory is inexhaustible. The fortification is totally impregnable. Very many of the neighboring vassal kings are under obligation to me. Nor is much of the population enamored of how I have been abused. What is more, there are thousands of warriors on my side together with their friends, sons and kinsmen.

Let us therefore stay here for some days, stirring up the 9.87
fury of the king's intimates and outsiders. Once we have won over the disaffected, incited his natural enemies and instigated his enemies by blood, then we shall eradicate the untamed man.'*

'What harm in trying? Let it be as you prescribe.'

I agreed with my dear father's plan.

Thus we took defensive steps to stand our ground. While 9.90
we were doing so, the king too was given a report on events. He was stung thereby and set about launching multiple hostile measures. These we repelled day after day.

At the same time, Purna·bhadra had explained to me where the king's bedchamber was. Without delay I dug a tunnel with a serpent-headed shovel, starting from the corner of the wall of our own house. The tunnel came out in a place the image of heaven on earth, filled with not a few ladies. As soon as they had seen me, this female assembly became agitated.

Among them was one maiden of such pure brightness that she looked like a doll made of burnished gold. She could have been a digit of the moon, the way her loveliness banished darkness from the Rasa·tala netherworld. At the same time, she was the image of the mighty goddess Earth;

r|nṛpa|darśana|parihārāya mahī|vivaraṃ praviṣṭā, niṣṭhapta| kanaka|putrik" êv' âvadāta|kāntiḥ kanyakā candana|lat" êva Malaya|mārutena mad|darśanen' ôdakampata.

9.93 Tathā|bhūte ca tasminn aṅganā|samāje kusumit" êva kā-śa|yaṣṭiḥ pāṇḍu|śirasijā sthavirā kācic caraṇayor me nipatya trāsa|dīnam abrūta:

‹Dīyatām abhaya|dānam asmay an|anya|śaraṇāya strī|janāya. kim asi deva|kumāro Danuja|yuddha|tṛṣṇayā Rasātalaṃ vivikṣuḥ. ājñāpaya ko 'si kasya hetor āgato 's' îti.›

Sā tu mayā pratyavādi:

9.96 ‹Su|datyaḥ, mā sma bhavatyo bhaiṣuḥ! aham asmi dvijāti| vṛṣāt Kāmapālād devyāṃ Kāntimatyām utpanno 'rthapālo nāma. saty arthe nija|gṛhān nṛpa|gṛhaṃ suraṅgay" ôpasarann ih' ântare vo dṛṣṭavān. kathayata kāḥ stha yūyaṃ, katham iha nivasath' êti.›

S" ôdañjalir udīritavatī:

‹Bhartṛ|dāraka! bhāgyavatyo vayaṃ yās tvām ebhir eva cakṣurbhir an|agham adrākṣma. śrūyatām:

and Durga, Shiva's wife descended to earth in order to defeat Vásura;* or Rati the wife of the flower-bowed god of Love come down to Patála the lowest underworld; and Lakshmi the goddess of royal Glory who had penetrated the earth's cavity to hide from the sight of more than one bad king. Seeing me made her tremble like a sandalwood branch made to tremble by the Málayan breeze.

One of the company of women, agitated as I said, was an 9.93
old woman, the white hair on her head making her look like *kasha* grass in dense white bloom. She fell at my feet to beg, wretched with terror:

'Please grant the women before you the gift of freedom from fear. We are at your mercy. Are you a divine prince who has decided to visit the underworld because you were thirsty to battle with Danu's demon sons?* Tell us who you are, and why you have come.'

I replied to her:

'Fair maids, you need have no fear of me. I am Artha·pa- 9.96
la, born to Kama·pala, bull among Brahmins, and his Lady Kántimati. On a mission, I was tunnelling from our house to the king's palace when I found you here in my path. Now you tell me who you all are, and how you come to live in this place.'

With her hands raised in respectful greeting to her forehead, she narrated:

'Royal prince! Fortunate indeed are we to see you unharmed with our own eyes. Hear our story:

9.99 Yas tava mātāmahaś Caṇḍasiṃhaḥ ten' âsyāṃ devyāṃ Līlāvatyāṃ Caṇḍaghoṣaḥ Kāntimat" îty apatya|dvayam udapādi. Caṇḍaghoṣas tu yuvarājo 'tyāsaṅgād aṅganāsu rāja|yakṣmaṇā sura|kṣayam agād antarvatnyāṃ devyām Ācāravatyām. amuyā c' êyaṃ Maṇikarṇikā nāma kanyā prasūtā. atha prasava|vedanayā mukta|jīvit" Ācāravatī patyur antikam agamat. atha devaś Caṇḍasiṃho mām āhūy' ôpahvare samājñāpayat:

«Ṛddhimati, kanyak" êyaṃ kalyāṇa|lakṣaṇā. tām imāṃ Mālav'|êndra|nandanāya Darpasārāya vidhivad vardhayitvā ditsāma. bibhemi ca Kāntimatī|vṛtt'|ântād ārabhya kanyakānāṃ prakāś'|âvasthāpanāt. ata iyam arāti|vyasanāya kārite mahati bhūmi|gṛhe kṛtrima|śaila|garbh'|ôtkīrṇa|nānā|maṇḍapa|prekṣā|gṛhe pracura|paribarhayā bhavatyā saṃvardhyatām. asty atra bhogya|vastu varṣa|śat'|ôpabhogen' âpy a|kṣayyam iti.»

Sa tath" ôktvā nija|vāsa|gṛhasya dvy|aṅgula|bhittāv ardha|pādaṃ kiṣku|viṣkambham uddhṛtya ten' âiva dvāreṇa sthānam idam asmān avīviśat. iha ca no vasantīnā dvādaśa samāḥ samatyayuḥ. iyaṃ ca vatsā taruṇībhūtā. na c' âdy' âpi smarati rājā.

Your maternal grandfather Chanda·simha begat two children by his queen, Lilávati. They were Chanda·ghosha and Kántimati. But Chanda·ghosha the crown prince was overfond of women and so consumption carried him off to the abode of the gods, even while his wife Achásravati was great with child. She gave birth to a daughter Mani·kárnika, whom you see before you. Next, Achásravati lost her life in the agony of childbirth, going to join her husband. Afterward King Chanda·simha summoned me and instructed me in secret: 9.99

"Ríddhimati, 'Prospera', this maiden, bears auspicious marks. Once she has been brought up, I would like to give her in lawful marriage to Darpa·sara, the Málavan lord's dear son. But since what happened to Kántimati I am afraid to rear girls in public view. Therefore, you and a plentiful retinue should bring her up in the vast subterranean palace that I have had built in the event that we are beset by the enemy. It contains a variety of pavilions and entertainment halls, all carved out of the hollow of a man-made hill. There is a store of luxury items there, inexhaustible even within a hundred years."

After he had said this, he lifted up a hatch a cubit long in the two-fingers-deep wall of his own bedchamber. That was the very door through which he had us enter this place. Here we have passed a full twelve years. And meanwhile this dear girl has become a young woman. But still today the king does not remember her.*

9.102 Kāmam iyaṃ pitāmahena Darpasārāya saṃkalpitā. tvad|ambayā Kāntimatyā c' êyaṃ garbhasth" âiva dyūta|jitā sva|mātrā tav' âiva jāyātvena samakalpyata. tad atra prāpta|rūpaṃ cintyatāṃ kumāreṇ' âiv' êti.›

Tāṃ punar avocam:

‹Ady' âiva rāja|gṛhe kim api kāryaṃ sādhayitvā pratinivṛtto yuṣmāsu yath"|ârhaṃ pratipatsya iti.›

9.105 Ten' âiva dīpa|darśita|bila|pathena gatvā sthite 'rdha|rātre tad ardha|pādaṃ pratyuddhṛtya vāsa|gṛhaṃ praviṣṭo viśrabdha|suptaṃ Siṃhaghoṣaṃ jīva|grāham agrahīṣam. ākṛṣya ca tam ahim iv' âhi|śatruḥ sphurantam amun" âiva bhitti|randhra|pathena straiṇa|saṃnidhim anaiṣam. ānīya ca sva|bhavanam āyasa|nigaḍa|saṃdita|caraṇa|yugalam, avanamita|malina|vadanam, aśru|bahala|rakta|cakṣuṣam ek'|ânte janayitror mam' âdarśayam. akathayaṃ ca bila|kathām.

Atha pitarau prahṛṣṭatarau taṃ nikṛṣṭ'|āśayaṃ niśāmya, bandhane niyamya, tasyā dārikāyā yath"|ârheṇa karmaṇā māṃ pāṇim agrāhayetām. a|nāthakaṃ ca tad|rājyam asmad|āyattam eva jātam. prakṛti|kopa|bhayāt tu man|mātrā mumukṣito 'pi na mukta eva Siṃhaghoṣaḥ.

It is true that her paternal grandfather intended her for Darpa·sara. But her own mother pledged her as wife to none other than you, since your mother Kántimati had won her in a game of dice even while she was still in the womb. Therefore you, prince, should think out what is best to do about this situation.' 9.102

I replied to her:

'First, there is something I must do in the palace. With my mission accomplished I will return among you and do the necessaries.'

It was midnight. They showed me with lamps the mouth of the passage. I followed it, raised the half-foot trapdoor from the inside and entered the bedchamber. Simha·ghosha was sound asleep, so I was able to catch him alive. He squirmed like a snake caught by his enemy the Gáruda, as I dragged him by the same passage through the opening in the wall, and brought him before the womenfolk. From there I led him to our house, where I privately presented him to my parents, both feet bound with an iron chain, his dirty face bowed down, eyes reddened with floods of tears. I also related to them the story of the subterranean cavern. 9.105

My father and mother were more than delighted. They looked at the man of despicable character, placed him under confinement, and arranged for me to receive the hand of that young lady in marriage with the appropriate rites. Rulerless, his kingdom fell under our control. Although my mother wished to release Simha·ghosha, this was not done, for fear of the people's anger.

Tathā|sthitāś ca vayam Aṅga|rājaḥ Siṃhavarmāṃ deva|pādānāṃ bhaktimān kṛta|karmāṃ c' êty amitr'|âbhiyuktam enam abhyasarāma. abhūvaṃ ca bhavat|pāda|paṅkaja|rajo|'nugrāhyaḥ. sa c' êdānīṃ bhavac|caraṇa|praṇāma|prāyaś|cittam anutiṣṭhatu sarva|duścarita|kṣālanam an|āryaḥ Siṃhaghoṣa iti!»

9.108 Arthapālaḥ pr'|âñjaliḥ praṇanāma. devo 'pi Rājavāhanaḥ:

«Bahu parākrāntam! bah'|ûpayuktā ca buddhiḥ! mukta|bandhas te śvaśuraḥ paśyatu mām! iti»

Abhidhāya bhūyaḥ Pramatim eva paśyan prīti|smeraḥ:

9.111 «Prastūyatāṃ tāvad ātmīyaṃ caritam» ity ajñāpayat.

iti śrī|Daṇḍinaḥ kṛtau
Daśa|kumāra|carite
'rthapāla|caritaṃ
nāma
caturtha ucchvāsaḥ.

That is the position we were in when we charged out to assist Simha·varman, king of the Angas, who was under attack from the enemy, because he was devoted to your own person and had acted for your benefit. This is how I was able to be favored by the lotus pollen that is the dust from your feet.* May the unworthy Simha·ghosha prostrate himself many times at your feet, and perform the atonement that will efface all his offenses!"

Artha·pala raised his hands in obeisance and bowed down. 9.108
Prince Raja·váhana then remarked:

"You have been really heroic! And you have really applied your intelligence! Release your father-in-law from his confinement and let him present himself before me."

Next he looked at Prámati, and commanded with a delighted smile:

"Now it is your turn to tell us about your adventures!" 9.111

That is the end of the fourth chapter of
the glorious Dandin's
What Ten Young Men Did.
It is called:
What Artha·pala Did.

CHAPTER TEN
WHAT PRÁMATI DID

So 'pi praṇamya vijñāpayām āsa:

«Deva, devasy' ânveṣaṇāya dikṣu bhramann abhraṃ|kaṣasy' âpi Vindhya|pārśva|rūḍhasya vanas|pater adhaḥ, pariṇata|pataṅga|bāla|pallav'|âvataṃsite paścima|dig|aṅganā|mukhe palval'|âmbhasy upaspṛśy' ôpāsya sandhyāṃ tamaḥ|samīkṛteṣu nimn'|ônnateṣu gantum a|kṣamaḥ, kṣamā|tale kisalayair uparacayya śayyāṃ śiśayiṣamāṇaḥ, śirasi kurvann añjalim:

10.3 ‹Yā asmin vanas|patau vasati devatā s" âiva me śaraṇam astu śarāru|cakra|cāra|bhīṣaṇāyāṃ Śarva|gala|śyāma|śārvar'|ândhakāra|pūr'|ādhmāta|gaṃbhīra|gahvarāyām asyāṃ ma-h"|âṭavyām ekakasya me prasuptasy' êti!›

upadhāya vāma|bhujam aśayiṣi. tataḥ kṣaṇād ev' âvani|durlabhena sparśen' âsukhāyiṣata kim api gātrāṇi, āhlādayiṣat' êndriyāṇi, abhyamanāyiṣṭa c' ântar'|ātmā, viśeṣataś ca hṛṣitās tanūruhāḥ, paryasphuran me dakṣiṇa|bhujaḥ.

‹Kathaṃ nv idam? iti›

10.6 Manda|mandam unmiṣann upary accha|candrāt apacche-da|kalpaṃ śukl'|âṃśuka|vitānam aikṣiṣi. vāmato valita|dṛṣṭiḥ samayā saudha|bhittiṃ citr'|āstaraṇa|śāyinam ativiśrabdha|prasuptam aṅganā|janam alakṣayam.

HE IN TURN BOWED DOWN, and related:

"My Lord, I was roaming the quarters in search of you, my Lord. When I could go no further I halted underneath a great tree, lord of the forest, a skyscraper* growing on the slope of the Vindhya mountains.* When the face of the Goddess of the West was crowned with young pink shoots from the setting sun, I bathed in a small pond and performed my evening ritual. The night had levelled out hill and valley around. I prepared a bed of young leaves on the ground. Before lying down I raised my hands to my head in prayer to ask:

'May the god who lives in this great tree protect me while 10.3
I sleep all alone in this vast forest, terrifying with gangs of wild animals on the prowl and its dense depths swollen full with the blinding night, horridly black as the throat of horrid Shiva.'

After which I went to sleep on my left arm. A moment later a sensation rare on earth strangely delighted my limbs, my senses rejoiced, my inner being was ecstatic and the hair on my body was thrilled with goose bumps, while my right arm throbbed.*

'What in heaven is this?'

I thought, slowly and carefully opening my eyes to see 10.6
above me a canopy of bright white cloth, like a slice of the crystal-clear moon. Turning my gaze to my left, I spied a bevy of ladies sound asleep, lying on gorgeous spreads beside the wall of a mansion.

Dakṣiṇato datta|cakṣur āgalita|stan'|âmśukām, amṛta|phena|paṭala|pāṇḍura|śayana|śāyinīm, ādi|varāha|damṣṭr'|âmśu|jāla|lagnām aṃsa|srasta|dugdha|sāgara|dukūl'|ôttarīyāṃ bhaya|sādhva|samūrchitām iva dharaṇīm;

aruṇ'|âdhara|kiraṇa|bāla|kisalaya|lāsya|hetubhir ānan'|âravinda|parimal'|ôdvāhibhir niḥśvāsa|mātariśvabhir Īśvar'|ēkṣaṇa|dahana|dagdhaṃ sphuliṅga|śeṣam Anaṅgam iva sandhukṣayantīm;

10.9 antaḥ|supta|ṣaṭpadam ambujam iva jāta|nidraṃ sarasam āmīlita|locan'|êndīvaram ānanaṃ dadhānām, Airāvata|mad'|âvalepa|lūn"|âpaviddhām iva nandana|vana|kalpa|vṛkṣa|ratna|vallarīm, kām api taruṇīm ālokayam.

Atarkayaṃ ca:

‹Kva gatā sā mah"|âṭavī? kuta idam ūrdhv'|âṇḍa|kapāla|saṃpuṭ'|ôdar'|ôllekhi Śakti|dhvaja|śikhara|śūl'|ôtsedhaṃ saudham āgatam? kva ca tad|araṇya|sthalī|samāstīrṇaṃ pallava|śayanam? kutastyaṃ c' êdam indu|gabhasti|sambhāra|bhāsuraṃ haṃsa|tūla|dukūla|śayanam?

10.12 Eṣa ca ko nu śīta|raśmi|kiraṇa|rajju|dolā|paribhraṣṭa|mūrchita iv' âpsarogaṇaḥ svaira|suptaḥ sundarī|janaḥ? kā c' êyaṃ

Directing my eyes to my right, I made out a young woman. Lying in her bed pale as a heap of ambrosial froth, her bodice slipped down slightly, she looked like the Earth swooning in fear, clinging to the halo of rays on the Primordial Boar's tusks, her upper silk slip being the milky ocean flowing from the Earth's shoulders.*

The gusts of her breath bore upward the fragrance from her lotus-face, making the young shoots that were the luster of her red lips dance. With those gusts she seemed to rekindle bodiless Love, reduced to a spark since incinerated by Lord Shiva's burning stare.

I thought I was looking at a jewelled creeper from the 10.9
wish-fulfilling tree in Indra's Elysian grove of Delight, cut down and discarded by Indra's white elephant Airávata, intoxicated with rut. Her face was a pool in which its blue lotus-eyes were closed. Now that she was asleep, her face had become a single lotus with two six-legged bees asleep within.

I mused:

'Where has the great forest gone? Whence has this mansion come? From bottom to top it is tall as spear-bannered Karttikéya's temple's crest, so tall it scratches the belly of the upper cosmic eggshell's vault.* Where too is my bed of leaves spread out on that forest's floor? And whence this bed of silk stuffed with goose down, bright as a bundle of moonbeams?

Who is this company of heavenly *ápsaras*es? They sleep at 10.12
perfect ease, as if unconscious after a fall from a swing spun of cool-beamed moon rays. And who is this image of the

dev" îv' Âravinda|hastā śārada|śaśāṅka|maṇḍal'|âmala|dukūl'|ôttara|cchadam adhiśete śayana|talam?

Na tāvad eṣā deva|yoṣā yato manda|mandam indu|kiraṇaiḥ saṃvāhyamānā kamalin" îva saṅkucati. bhagna|vṛnta|cyuta|rasa|bindu|śabalitaṃ pāka|pāṇḍu|cūta|phalam iv' ôdbhinna|sveda|rekham ālakṣyate gaṇḍa|sthalam. abhinava|yauvana|vidāha|nirbhar'|ōṣmaṇi kuca|taṭe vaivarṇyam upaiti varṇakam. vāsasī ca paribhog'|ânurūpaṃ dhūsarimāṇam ādarśayataḥ. tad eṣā mānuṣy eva.

Diṣṭyā c' ân|ucchiṣṭa|yauvanā yataḥ saukumāryam āgatāḥ saṃhatā iv' âvayavāḥ, prasnigdhatamā api pāṇḍut"|ânuviddh" êva deha|cchaviḥ, danta|pīḍ"|ânabhijñatayā n' âtiviśada|rāgo mukhe, vidruma|dyutir adhara|maṇiḥ, an|atyāpūrṇam ārakta|mūlaṃ campaka|kuḍmala|dalam iva kaṭhoraṃ kapola|talam, Anaṅga|bāṇa|pāta|mukt'|āśaṅkaṃ ca viśrabdha|madhuraṃ supyate, na c' âitad|vakṣaḥ|sthalaṃ nirdaya|vimarda|vistārita|mukha|stana|yugalam, asti c' ân|atikrānta|śiṣṭa|maryāda|cetaso mam' âsyām āsaktiḥ.

10.15 Āsakty|anurūpaṃ punar āśliṣṭā yadi spaṣṭam ārta|raveṇ' âiva saha nidrāṃ mokṣyati. ath' âhaṃ na śakṣyāmi c' ân|upaśliṣya śayitum. ato yad bhāvi tad bhavatu! bhāgyam atra parīkṣiṣya iti.›

Spṛṣṭ'|âspṛṣṭam eva kim apy āviddha|rāga|sādhvasaṃ lakṣya|suptaḥ sthito 'smi.

royal goddess Lakshmi, bearer of the lotus, lying on her bed spread with silk spotless as the orb of the autumn moon?*

At least I can infer that she is not a divine woman, because she has closed her eyes like a lotus closed under the slow and gentle massage of moonbeams. Marked by a line of sweat drops, her cheek is like a mango fruit, pale-yellow ripe, dotted with drops of sap dripping from the broken stalk. Her bosom burns with the fierce fire of tender youth, blanching the bright makeup thereon. And her two garments appear dusty-gray, bearing witness to their use. Hence I can deduce that she is definitely a mortal being.*

To my good fortune, her maidenhead looks unsullied, because her lovely tender limbs seem firm, because however deeply gorgeous, her bodily complexion is yet suffused with pallor, and because there is no loud passionate red on her face, which has yet to experience the bite of tooth marks. Because her ruby lip is splendid as coral, her round cheeks like the petals of a *chámpaka* bud, reddish at the base and not fully expanded, and because she sleeps the sweet sleep of carelessness, free from the fear of invisible Love's arrows falling. Nor has pitiless pressing squashed the breasts on her chest. And because I, who could never transgress a civilized man's bounds of propriety, have fallen in love with her.

But if I embrace as my love demands she will of course 10.15
awake with a cry of distress. Nevertheless, I cannot lie down again without embracing her. So, come what may, I shall now test my good fortune.'

I touched her lightly, hardly touching her, and lay there pretending to be asleep, pulled between passion and terror.

S" âpi, kim apy utkaṃpinā rom'|ôdbhedavatā vāma|pārśvena sukhāyamānena, manda|manda|jṛmbhik'|ārambha|manthar'|âṅgī, tvaṅgad|agra|pakṣmaṇoś cakṣuṣoḥ, alasa|tānta|tārakeṇ' ân|atipakva|nidrā|kaṣāyit'|âpāṅga|parabhāgeṇa yugalen' ēṣad unmiṣantī, trāsa|vismaya|harṣa|rāga|śaṅkā|vilāsa|vibhrama|vyavahitāni vrīḍ"|ântarāṇi kāni kāny api Kāmen' âdbhut'|ânubhāven' âvasth"|ântarāṇi kāryamāṇā;

10.18 parijana|prabodhan'|ôdyatā giraṃ Kām'|āvega|para|vaśaṃ hṛdayam aṅgāni ca sādhvas'|āyāsa|sambadhyamāna|sveda|pulakāni kathaṃ katham api nigṛhya, sa|spṛheṇa madhura|kūṇita|tribhāgeṇa manda|manda|pracāritena cakṣuṣā mad|aṅgāni nirvarṇya, dūr'|ôtsarpita|pūrva|kāy" âpi tasminn eva śayane sa|cakitam aśayiṣṭa.

Ajaniṣṭa me rāg'|āviṣṭa|cetaso 'pi kim api nidrā. punar an|anukūla|sparśa|duḥkh'|āyatta|gātraḥ prābudhye. prabuddhasya ca me s" âiva mah"|âṭavī tad eva taru|talaṃ sa eva patr'|āstaro 'bhūt. vibhāvarī ca vyabhāsīt. abhūc ca me manasi:

‹Kim ayaṃ svapnaḥ? kiṃ vipralambho vā? kim iyam āsurī daivī vā? k" âpi māyā? yad bhāvi tad bhavatu! n' âham idaṃ tattvato n' âvabudhya mokṣyāmi bhūmi|śayyām. yāvad|āyur atratyāyai devatāyai pratiśayito bhavām' îti›

For her part, my lady's left side responded pleasurably with a little tremble, breaking out in a thrill of hairs standing on end. Her inactive body began to yawn ever so delicately. She opened both eyes a fraction, the tips of their eyelids aflutter, pupils languid with fatigue, unfinished sleep reddening their superlative outer corners. Love whose mastery is awesome made her experience altered states, the mix of fear, surprise, amusement, passion, doubt, coquetry and lovely confusion, modestly restrained.

On the point of rousing her attendants, she struggled 10.18
to control her voice, her heart, hostage to Love's invasion, and her limbs, dotted with the perspiration that breaks out under the stress of fear. With eyes meandering slowly and carefully, their outer corners sweetly crinkled up, she studied my body longingly. And although she slipped her top half away she continued to lie, tremulous, in the same bed with me.

Despite passion invading my mind, I felt somewhat sleepy. Next thing, the touch of an unpleasant sensation on my body woke me. I awoke to see that same great forest, the same tree trunk and the same bed of strewn leaves. Night turned to dawn. I thought it over:

'Was this a dream, or was it a trick? Was she a demoness, or a divinity? Or some illusion? Whatever happens, I shall not leave my bed on the ground until I have understood what this experience really was. Until my questions are answered, I shall lie here fasting before the goddess of this place, for as long as I live.'*

10.21 Niścita|matir atiṣṭham.

Ath' āvirbhūya k" âpi, ravi|kar'|âbhitapta|kuvalaya|dāma|tānt'|âṅga|yaṣṭiḥ, kliṣṭa|nivasan'|ôttarīyā, nir|alaktaka|rūkṣa|pāṭalena niḥśvās'|ōṣma|jarjarita|tviṣā danta|cchadena vamant" îva virah'|ânalam, an|avarata|salila|dhārā|visarjanād rudhir'|âvaśeṣam iva lohitataraṃ dvitayam akṣṇor udvahantī, kula|cāritra|bandhana|pāśa|vibhrameṇ' âika|veṇībhūtena keśa|pāśena nīl'|âṃśuka|cīra|cūḍikā|parivṛtā pati|vratā|patāk" êva sañcarantī;

kṣāma|kṣām" âpi devat"|ânubhāvād an|atikṣīṇa|varṇ'|âvakāśā sīmantinī, praṇipatantaṃ māṃ praharṣ'|ôtkaṃpitena bhuja|latā|dvayen' ôtthāpya, putravat pariṣvajya, śirasy upāghrāya, vātsalyam iva stana|yugalena stanya|cchalāt prakṣarantī, śiśireṇ' âśruṇā niruddha|kaṇṭhī, sneha|gadgadaṃ vyāhārṣīt:

10.24 ‹Vatsa, yadi vaḥ kathitavatī Magadha|rāja|mahiṣī Vasumatī mama haste bālam Arthapālaṃ nidhāya, kathāṃ ca kāñcid ātma|bhartṛ|putra|sakhī|jan'|ânubaddhāṃ Rāja|rāja|pravartitāṃ kṛtv" ântardhānam agād ātmajā Maṇibhadrasy' êti s" âham asmi vo jananī.

My mind made up, I held my ground. 10.21

Thereupon a woman appeared before me. Her slim frame was limp as a string of blue water lilies withered in the sun's rays. Under and outer clothes were worn out. Her lips seemed to spew forth the fire of separation from one's beloved, their luster scorched in the furnace of her out-breaths, pale pink, chapped and unpainted. Both her eyes were totally red, as though the flow of rivers of ceaseless tears had left nothing but blood. Her hair was bound into a single braid, captivating as if it were the bond binding her whole family's good character. Dressed in a blue cloth now, a rag she moved like the banner of chaste and virtuous wives.*

However emaciated the lady was, her divine essence had not allowed all manifest color to fade away completely. I bowed down before her, but with two slender arms wavering with joy she lifted me and embraced me like a son, smelling and kissing my head, oozing forth motherly love in the form of mother's milk from her two breasts. Her throat choked on cold tears, stammering with love, her words faltered:

'My child, did Vásumati, the queen of the Mágadhan king, tell you how Mani·bhadra's daughter Tarávali entrusted the baby Artha·pala to her hands, then transmitted everything that Kubéra, King of kings, had related concerning her own husband, son and girlfriends, before finally disappearing? If she did, know now that I am that Tarávali, your mother. 10.24

Pitur vo Dharmapāla|sūnoḥ Sumitr'|ânujasya Kāmapālasya pāda|mūlān niṣkāraṇa|kopa|kaluṣit'|āśayā proṣy' ânuśaya|vidhurā svapne ken' âpi rakṣorūpeṇ' ôpetya śapt" âsmi:

«Caṇḍikāyāṃ tvayi varṣa|mātraṃ vasāmi pravāsa|duḥkhāy' êti!»

10.27 bruvat" âiv' âham āviṣṭā prābudhye. gataṃ ca tad varṣaṃ varṣa|sahasra|dīrgham. atītāyāṃ tu yāminyāṃ deva|devasya Try|ambakasya Śrāvastyām utsava|samājam anubhūya bandhu|janaṃ ca sthāna|sthānebhyaḥ samnipatitam abhisamīkṣya, mukta|śāpā patyuḥ pārśvam abhisarām' îti prasthitāyām eva mayi tvam atr' âbhyupetya,

«Prapanno 'smi śaraṇam ihatyāṃ devatām! iti»

prasupto 'si. evaṃ śāpa|duḥkh'|āviṣṭayā tu mayā tadā na tattvataḥ paricchinno bhavān. api tu śaraṇ'|āgatam a|viralapramādāyām asyāṃ mah"|âṭavyām a|yuktaṃ parityajya gantum iti mayā tvam api svapann ev' âsi nītaḥ. pratyāsanne ca tasmin deva|gṛhe punar acintayam:

10.30 «Katham iha taruṇen' ânena saha samājaṃ gamiṣyām' îti?»

Atha rājñaḥ Śrāvast"|īśvarasya yath"|ârtha|nāmno Dharmavardhanasya kanyāṃ Navamālikāṃ gharma|kāla|su|bhage kanyā|pura|vimāna|harmya|tale viśāla|komalaṃ śayyā|talam adhiśayānāṃ yadṛcchay" ôpalabhya,

My mind muddied with baseless anger, I walked out on your respected father, Kama·pala, Dharma·pala's son, and Sumítra's younger brother.* Miserable with remorse, a *rák-shasa* demon visited me in a dream and cursed me:

"Untamed woman,* I am going to possess you for a whole year to make you feel the suffering of separation from your home."

When I woke up, I had been possessed. That year is now 10.27
over, long as a thousand years. Last night there was a gathering in Shravásti for the festival of Try·ámbaka Shiva, god of gods. I knew about it and could see my relatives gathering there from all over. Thinking that since now I was released from the curse I was free to go to the side of my lord and husband, I was just setting out when you arrived here, and announced:

"I claim the protection of the deity of this place!"

With which you went to sleep. So worn out was I with the suffering of the curse that I did not then recognize you. Nevertheless, I was sure that it would be wrong to abandon someone who has sought refuge here in the great forest with its not infrequent dangers, and so I took you with me, even as you slept. But once I came close to that temple I had second thoughts:

"How shall I join the present gathering with this young 10.30
man?"

Thereupon I chanced upon the maiden Nava·málika, daughter of the Lord of Shravásti, King Dharma·várdhana, "Increaser of Goodness" by name and by nature. She was asleep on her broad and beautiful couch, on the roof

«Diṣṭy" êyaṃ suptā parijanaś ca gāḍha|nidraḥ. śetām ayam atra muhūrta|mātraṃ brāhmaṇa|kumāro yāvat kṛta|kṛtyā nivartey' êti.»

10.33 Tvāṃ tatra śāyayitvā tam uddeśam agamam. dṛṣṭvā c' ôtsava|śriyam, nirviśya ca sva|jana|darśana|sukham, abhivādya ca Tri|bhuvan'|ēśvaram, ātm'|âlīka|pratyākalan'|ôpārūḍha|sādhvasaṃ ca namaskṛtya bhakti|praṇata|hṛdayā bhagavatīm Ambikāṃ tayā Giri|duhitrā devyā sa|smitam:

«Ayi, bhadre, mā bhaiṣīḥ! bhav' êdānīṃ bhartṛ|pārśva|gāminī! gatas te śāpa iti.»

Anugṛhītā sadya eva pratyāpanna|mahimā pratinivṛtya dṛṣṭv" âiva tvāṃ yathāvad abhyajānām:

10.36 «Kathaṃ mat|suta ev' âyaṃ vatsasy' Ârthapālasya prāṇa|bhūtaḥ sakhā Pramatir iti. pāpayā may" âsminn a|jñānād audāsīnyam ācaritam. api c' âyam asyām āsakta|bhāvaḥ. kanyā c' âinaṃ kāmayate yuvānam. ubhau c' êmau lakṣya|suptau trapayā sādhvasena v" ânyonyam ātmānaṃ na vivṛṇvāte.

Gantavyaṃ ca mayā. kām'|āghrātay" âpy anayā kanyayā rahasya|rakṣaṇāya na samābhāṣitaḥ sakhī|janaḥ parijano vā. nayāmi tāvat kumāram. punar ap' îmam arthaṃ labdha|lakṣo yath" ôpapannair upāyaiḥ sādhayiṣyat' îti.»

of her mansion in the harem palace, so pleasant in the hot summertime.*

"What luck! She sleeps and her attendants are in a deep sleep. This brahmin boy can lie here for just a moment until I return with my obligations accomplished."

I laid you down there and went to the place of the festival. I 10.33
looked on its majesty, delighted in seeing my people, saluted the Lord of the Three Worlds and paid my respects to the Goddess Ámbika, my heart prostrate with devotion, but highly fearful that she would enumerate my misdemeanors. That divine daughter of the Himalayan mountains smiled at me and spoke:*

"Come, dear lady. Do not be afraid! You should go now to the side of your husband. Your curse is over."

Thus favored, I at once regained my magical power, so, when I returned, as soon as I saw you I recognized:

"Why, this is none other than my son Prámati, the dearer- 10.36
than-life companion of my child Artha·pala. It was wicked of me not to recognize him and to treat him indifferently. Moreover, now he is in love with this maiden, and she loves the young man back. The two of them are pretending to be asleep, and out of bashfulness or fear they do not open their hearts to each other.

But I must go. Love devours this girl, and she still has not said anything to her girlfriends and attendants, wanting to keep her secret safe. For now I will remove the young man. It will be up to him to succeed in this affair, by whatever means may present themselves once he receives the sign."

Mat|prabhāva|prasvāpitaṃ bhavantam etad eva patra|śayanam pratyanaiṣam. evam idaṃ vṛttam. eṣā c' âhaṃ pitus te pāda|mūlaṃ pratyupasarpeyam iti.›

10.39 Pr'|âñjaliṃ māṃ bhūyo|bhūyaḥ pariṣvajya śirasy upāghrāya kapolayoś cumbitvā sneha|vihvalā gat" āsīt.

Ahaṃ ca Pañca|bāṇa|vaśyaḥ Śrāvastīm abhyavartiṣi. mārge ca mahati nigame naigamānāṃ tāmra|cūḍa|yuddha|kolāhalo mahān āsīt. ahaṃ ca tatra saṃnihitaḥ kiñcid asmeṣi. saṃnidhi|niṣaṇṇas tu me vṛddha|viṭaḥ ko 'pi brāhmaṇaḥ śanaiḥ smita|hetum apṛcchat. abravaṃ ca:

‹Katham iva nārikela|jāteḥ prācya|vāṭa|kukkuṭasya pratīcya|vāṭaḥ puruṣair a|samīkṣya balākā|jātis tāmra|cūḍo bala|pramāṇ'|âdhikasy' âiva prativisṛṣṭa iti?›

10.42 So 'pi taj|jñaḥ:

‹Kim a|jñair ebhir vyutpāditaiḥ? tūṣṇīm āssv' êti!›

Upahastikāyās tāmbūlaṃ karpūra|sahitam uddhṛtya mahyaṃ dattvā, citrāḥ kathāḥ kathayan kṣaṇam atiṣṭhat. prāyudhyata c' âtisaṃrabdham anu|prahāra|pravṛtta|sva|pakṣa|mukta|kaṇṭhī|rava|ravaṃ vihaṅgama|dvayam. jitaś c' âsau pratīcya|vāṭa|kukkuṭaḥ.

10.45 So 'pi viṭa|brāhmaṇaḥ sva|vāṭa|kukkuṭa|vijaya|hṛṣṭo mayi vayo|viruddhaṃ sakhyam upetya tad|ahaḥ svagṛha eva snāna|bhojan'|ādi kārayitv" ôttaredyuḥ Śrāvastīṃ prati yāntaṃ mām anugamya,

By my magic power I put you into a deep sleep and carried you back to this same bed of leaves. That is the whole story. Now I must go to your father's presence.'

I raised my hands pressed together in obeisance, she em- 10.39
braced me many times, kissed and smelled my head, kissed me on both cheeks, and, agitated with emotion, she was gone.

Slave to five-arrowed Love, I then returned to Shravásti. In a great market on the road, the marketers were in an enormous uproar around a red-crested cockfight. I drew near, with a little smile. One old brahmin rogue sitting near asked quietly why I was smiling. I told him:

'I am wondering how it is possible that these gentlemen have not stopped to think. They have set a red-crested *baláka* cock of the crane variety from the western district against a *nárikéla* cock of the coconut breed from the eastern district, when the *nárikéla* is far superior in strength and size!'*

He was also one of the cognoscenti: 10.42

'What use to coach these ignoramuses? Better to hold one's peace.'

From his pouch he drew out betel mixed with camphor to give me, and then tarried awhile, regaling me with colorful anecdotes. The two birds were locked in close combat, each strike accompanied by their supporters' lion roars.* In the end the cock from the western district was defeated.

The wily brahmin was delighted with the victory* of the 10.45
cock from his region. Despite the incongruity of our ages, he befriended me. That day he had me bathe, eat and rest at his own home, and the following day accompanied me

‹Smartavyo 'smi saty artha iti.›
mitravad visṛjya pratyayāsīt.

10.48 Ahaṃ ca gatvā Śrāvastīm adhva|śrānto bāhy'|ôdyāne latā|maṇḍape śayito 'smi. haṃsaka|rava|prabodhitaś c' ôtthāya kām api kvaṇita|nūpura|mukharābhyāṃ caraṇābhyāṃ mad|antikam upasarantīṃ yuvatīm adrākṣam. sā tv āgatya sva|hasta|vartini citra|paṭe likhitaṃ mat|sadṛśaṃ kim api puṃ|rūpaṃ māṃ ca paryāyeṇa nirvarṇayantī sa|vismayaṃ sa|vitarkaṃ sa|harṣaṃ ca kṣaṇam avātiṣṭhata. may" âpi tatra citra|paṭe mat|sādṛśyaṃ paśyatā tad|dṛṣṭi|ceṣṭitam an|ākasmikaṃ manyamānena:

‹Nanu sarva|sādhāraṇo 'yaṃ ramaṇīyaḥ puṇy'|ārāma|bhūmi|bhāgaḥ. kim iti cira|sthiti|kleśo 'nubhūyate? nan' ûpaveṣṭavyam! iti›

abhihitā sā sa|smitam ‹anugṛhīt" âsm' îti› nyaṣīdat. saṅkathā ca deśa|vārt'|ânubaddhā kācan' āvayor abhūt. kathā|samśritā ca sā:

10.51 ‹Deś'|âtithir asi. dṛśyante ca te 'dhva|śrāntān' îva gātrāṇi. yadi na doṣo mad|gṛhe 'dya viśramitum anugrahaḥ kriyatām! iti›

aśaṃsat. ahaṃ ca

‹Ayi, mugdhe, n' âiṣaḥ doṣo guṇa ev' êti.›

10.54 Tad|anumārga|gāmī tad|gṛha|gato rāj'|ârheṇa snāna|bhojan'|ādin" ôpacaritaḥ sukhaṃ niṣaṇṇo rahasi paryapṛcchye:

‹Mahā|bhāga, dig|antarāṇi bhramatā kaccid asti kiñcid adbhutaṃ bhavat" ôpalabdham? iti›

as I set out for Shravásti. Bidding farewell like a friend he said:

'Remember me if the need arises.'

Then he turned back homeward.

Upon reaching Shravásti, I lay down exhausted from the road in a creeper bower in a park on the outskirts. Awoken by the tinkle of anklets, I got up to see a young woman coming toward me, both feet noisy with jangling anklets. When she reached me she stopped a moment and looked intently with amazement, questioning and delight, back and forth from me to the image of a man who looked just like me, drawn on a picture that she held in her hand.* Seeing my likeness on that picture, I realized that her eye movements were no coincidence, so I asked: 10.48

'Please, this charming spot with its auspicious grove is of course open to everyone. Why suffer to stand for long? Should you not be seated?'

With a smile, she thanked me and sat down. We two conversed awhile on local news. In the course of the conversation, she declared:

'You are a guest in my country. And your limbs seem weary from the road. If you are not offended, please rest for the day at my home.' 10.51

I replied:

'Dear girl, I am not at all offended, but honored, rather.'

Following where she led, I came to her house, where I was waited on with a bath, a feast and a rest, fit for a king. While I sat relaxing, she asked me, when we were alone: 10.54

'Good sir, on your travels in other lands, did you ever witness any extraordinary happening?'

Mam' âbhavan manasi:

10.57 ‹Mahad idam āś"|āspadam. eṣā khalu nikhila|parijana|sambādha|samlakṣitāyāḥ sakhī rāja|dārikāyāḥ, citra|paṭe c' âsminn api tad|upari|viracita|sita|vitānaṃ harmya|talam, tad|gataṃ ca prakāma|vistīrṇaṃ śarad|abhra|paṭala|pāṇḍuraṃ śayanam, tad|adhiśāyinī ca nidr"|ālīḍha|locanā mam' âiv' êyaṃ pratikṛtiḥ.

Ato nūnam An|aṅgena s" âpi rāja|kanyā tāvatīṃ bhūmim āropitā yasyām a|sahya|madana|jvara|vyathit'|ônmāditā satī sakhī|nirbandha|pṛṣṭa|vikriyā|nimittā cāturyeṇ' âitad|rūpa|nirmāṇen' âiva samartham uttaraṃ dattavatī. rūpa|samvādāc ca samśayānay" ânayā pṛṣṭo bhindyām asyāḥ samśayaṃ yath"|ânubhava|kathanen' êti.›

Jāta|niścayo 'bravam:

10.60 ‹Bhadre dehi citra|paṭam! iti›

Sā tv arpitavatī madd|haste. punas tam ādāya tām api vyāja|suptām ullasan|madana|rāga|vihvalāṃ vallabhām ekatr' âiv' âbhilikhya,

‹Kācid evaṃbhūtā yuvatir īdṛśasya puṃsaḥ pārśva|śāyiny araṇyānī|prasuptena may" ôpalabdhā. kil' âiṣa svapna iti.›

10.63 ālapaṃ ca. hṛṣṭayā tu tayā vistarataḥ pṛṣṭaḥ sarvam eva vṛtt'|ântam akathayam. asau ca sakhyā man|nimittāny avasth"|ântarāṇy avarṇayat. tad ākarṇya ca:

It then occurred to me:

'What a great occasion for hope. This woman must be a companion of the princess I first saw surrounded by all her attendants. Indeed, on this picture is the terrace with the white canopy constructed above it, as well as the bed, pale as a multitude of autumn clouds,* deliciously vast. And lying thereon, eyes closed tight in sleep, is my own double. 10.57

Hence there is no doubt that invisible Love has pushed the royal maiden so far that she was losing her mind,* tormented by the unbearable fever of intoxicating love. When her friends persistently asked the cause of this transformation, her only adequate reply was to skillfully create this image. Now this suspicious girl is full of questions because my looks and the painting are so similar. Let me answer her doubts by decribing what happened.'

With new confidence, I asked:

'Good lady, hand me the painting.' 10.60

She placed it in my hands. Taking it, I sketched my beloved on the same couch, pretending to sleep, but in fact delirious with the passion of intoxicating Love coursing through her. Then I explained:

'Fast asleep in the great forest I saw a young woman like this lying beside the man in the picture. But was this really a dream?'

She was thrilled, and asked me to explain in detail the whole sequence of events, which I did. She then described her friend's altered states for which I was responsible. I heard her out, before contriving to persuade her: 10.63

‹Yadi tava sakhyā mad|anugrah'|ônmukhaṃ mānasam, gamaya kānicid ahāni. kam api kanyā|pure nirāśaṅka|nivāsa|karaṇam upāyam āracayy' āgamiṣyām' îti.›

kathañcid enām abhyupagamayya, gatvā tad eva kharvaṭaṃ vṛddha|viṭena samagaṃsi.

10.66 So 'pi sa|sambhramaṃ viśramayya tath" âiva snāna|bhojan'|ādi kārayitvā rahasy apṛcchat:

‹Ārya, kasya hetor acireṇ' âiva pratyāgato 'si?›

Pratyavādiṣam enam:

10.69 ‹Sthāna ev' âham āryeṇ' âsmi pṛṣṭaḥ. śrūyatām. asti hi Śrāvastī nāma nagarī. tasyāḥ patir apara iva dharma|putro Dharmavardhano nāma rājā. tasya duhitā pratyādeśa iva Śriyaḥ, prāṇā iva Kusuma|dhanvanaḥ, saukumārya|viḍambita|nava|mālikā Navamālikā nāma kanyā.

Sā mayā samāpatti|dṛṣṭā Kāma|nārāca|paṅktim iva kaṭākṣa|mālāṃ mama marmaṇi vyakirat. tac|chaly'|ôddharaṇa|kṣamaś ca Dhanvantari|sadṛśas tvad|ṛte n' êtaro 'sti vaidya iti pratyāgato 'smi. tat prasīda kañcid upāyam ācaritum!

Ayam ahaṃ parivartita|strī|veṣas te kanyā nāma bhaveyam. anugataś ca mayā tvam upagamya dharm'|āsana|gataṃ Dharmavardhanaṃ vakṣyasi:

10.72 «Mam' êyam ek" âiva duhitā. jāta|mātrāyāṃ tv asyāṃ janany asyāḥ saṃsthitā. mātā ca pitā ca bhūtv" âham eva vyavardhayam. etad|artham eva vidyā|mayaṃ śulkam arjituṃ

'If your girlfriend's heart is really set on favoring me, then let a few days pass. I shall return as soon as I have figured out a strategem to abide unmolested in the harem.'

Then I went back to the last market town to rejoin the old rogue.

He hurried to make me take rest, and waited on me as 10.66
before with bath, food and so on. Then, when we were alone together, he asked:

'Good sir, why have you returned so quickly?'

I explained to him:

'Good sir, good question. I shall tell you why. There is, as 10.69
you know, a city named Shravásti, whose Lord is King Dharma·várdhana. He is like another son of Dharma, another Yudhi·shthira.* His daughter is the maiden Nava·málika. She puts glorious Shri Lakshmi to shame, and is the very life and soul of Love with his flower-bow. Her tenderness humiliates her namesake, the *nava·málika* jasmine.

When I chanced to see her she wounded me at my vulnerable points with a garland of glances that were more like a fivefold volley of Love's arrows. Knowing that there was no doctor who could extract her weapons but you, the image of Dhanvántari doctor of the gods, I returned here.* Please be so kind as to apply some remedy.

I am here to dress in women's clothing and pretend to be your daughter. You should lead me then before Dharma·várdhana on his judgment throne, and inform him:

"This is my only daughter. No sooner was she born but 10.72
her mother was dead. I alone have been both mother and father in bringing her up. A certain brahmin son was born to a family with which we are permitted to marry. In order

gato 'bhūd Avanti|nagarīm Ujjayinīm asmad|vaivāhya|kula|jaḥ ko 'pi vipra|dārakaḥ. tasmai c' êyam anumatā dātum itarasmai na yogyā. taruṇī bhūtā c' êyam. sa ca vilambitaḥ. tena tam ānīya pāṇim asyā grāhayitvā tasmin nyasta|bhāraḥ samnyasiṣye.

Dur|abhirakṣatayā tu duhitīṇāṃ mukta|śaiśavānāṃ viśeṣataś c' â|mātṛkāṇām iha devaṃ mātṛ|pitṛ|sthānīyaṃ prajānām āpanna|śaraṇam āgato 'smi. yadi vṛddhaṃ brāhmaṇam adhītinam a|gatim atithiṃ ca mām anugrāhya|pakṣe gaṇayaty ādirāja|carita|dhuryo devaḥ s" âiṣā bhavad|bhuja|cchāyām akhaṇḍita|cāritrā tāvad adhyāstāṃ yāvad asyāḥ pāṇi|grāhakam ānayeyam iti.»

Sa evam ukto niyatam abhimanāyamānaḥ sva|duhitṛ|samnidhau māṃ vāsayiṣyati. gatas tu bhavān āgāmini māsi Phālgune phalgunīṣ' ûttarāsu bhāvini rāj'|ântaḥ|pura|janasya tīrtha|yātr'|ôtsave, tīrtha|snānāt prācyāṃ diśi go|rut'|ântaram atikramya, vānīra|valaya|madhya|vartini Kārttikeya|gṛhe, kara|tala|gatena śukl'|âmbara|yugalena sthāsyasi.

10.75 Sa khalv aham an|abhiśaṅka ev' âitāvantaṃ kālaṃ sah' âbhivihṛtya rāja|kanyayā bhūyas tasminn utsave Gaṅg"|âmbhasi viharan vihāra|vyākule kanyakā|samāje magn'|ôpasṛtas tvad|abhyāsa ev' ônmaṅkṣyāmi. punas tvad|upahṛte vāsasī paridhāy' âpanīta|dārikā|veṣo jāmātā nāma bhūtvā tvām ev'

to gain the wealth of knowledge that will win her hand, he went to Ujjáyini, city of Avánti. She is betrothed to him, and can be given to no other. But she is a young woman now, and he is slow to return. I need to go myself to fetch him. Then I can give him her hand, settle the household burden on him and renounce domestic life to become a *sannyási*.

Knowing how difficult it is to control daughters who are past childhood, and especially a motherless one, I am come here to Your Majesty. You are mother and father for your subjects, and refuge of the fallen. Your Majesty is a leader whose exploits equal those of the first king, Manu.* I am an old brahmin, well read but helpless, and your guest. If you should count me among those to be favored, then let her stay within the shelter of your arms, her reputation unbroken, until I return with her fiancé."

He is bound to be pleased to hear this, and will install me to live near his own daughter. You should then leave. At full moon the following month of Phalgun* it will be time for the women of the king's harem to celebrate the festival of pilgrimage to the *tirtha* fords. Then proceed the distance of a bull's bellow east of the bathing ghat, and wait for me at the temple of Skanda Karttikéya, situated in the middle of a cane enclosure, bearing a suit of white clothes.

In the meanwhile, have no fear, I shall not worry a bit but 10.75
will amuse myself with the princess. During the festival I will be having fun in the Ganges' waters. While all the girls are absorbed in their games, I will dive out of sight and swim up to where you are. Then I will change out of your daughter's clothes into those you will have brought. Thus transformed

ânugaccheyam. nṛp'|ātmajā tu mām itas tato 'nviṣy' ân|āsādayantī,

«Tayā vinā na bhokṣya iti.»

rudaty ev' âvarodhane sthāsyati. tan|mūle ca mahati kolāhale krandatsu parijaneṣu rudatsu sakhī|janeṣu śocatsu paurajaneṣu kiṅkartavyatā|mūḍhe sāmātye pārthive tvam āsthānīm etya māṃ sthāpayitvā vakṣyasi:

10.78 «Deva, sa eṣa me jāmātā tav' ârhati śrī|bhuj'|ārādhanam.

Adhītī caturṣv āmnāyeṣu, gṛhītī ṣaṭsv aṅgeṣu, ānvīkṣikī|vicakṣaṇaḥ, catuḥ|ṣaṣṭi|kal"|āgama|prayoga|caturaḥ, viśeṣeṇa gaja|ratha|turaṅga|tantra|vit, iṣv|asan'|âstra|karmaṇi gad"|āyuddhe ca nirupamaḥ, purāṇ'|êtihāsa|kuśalaḥ, kartā kāvya|nāṭak'|ākhyāyikānām, vettā s'|Ôpaniṣado 'rtha|śāstrasya, nir|matsaro guṇeṣu, viśrambhī suhṛtsu, śakyaḥ samvibhāga|śīlaḥ śruta|dharo gata|smayaś ca.

N' âsya doṣam aṇīyāṃsam apy upalabhe, na ca guṇeṣv avidyamānam. tan mādṛśasya brāhmaṇa|mātrasya na labhya eṣa sambandhī. duhitaram asmai samarpya, vārddhak'|ôcitam antyam āśramaṃ saṅkrameyam, yadi devaḥ sādhu manyata iti.»

into your so-called son-in-law, I will accompany you. The princess will search for me everywhere. When she does not find me she will stay in the palace, crying:

"I cannot eat without her."

This will cause a great commotion, with her attendants weeping, her girlfriends crying, the townsfolk grieving. The king and his ministers will be at a loss as to how to proceed. That will be the moment for you to enter the assembly room, bring me before the king and announce:

"My Lord. Here is my son-in-law, worthy to pay his re- 10.78
spects to your majestic arms.

He is well read in the four sacred traditions—the Vedas—and has grasped the six auxiliary sciences. He is brilliant at logical philosophy and a skillful practitioner of every theoretical detail of the sixty-four practical arts. Particularly expert in driving elephants, chariots and horses, he is without competition in the use of arrow-shooting bows and missiles, and in fighting with a mace. He is well versed in the Puránas and history, a composer of poetry, drama and stories, and an expert in the *Artha/śāstra* and the Upánishads. He is without envy in the appreciation of others' qualities, a reliable friend, of sweet address, a habitual sharer, bearer of learning and free of pride.

I have been unable to find even the least atom of vice in him, nor any virtue he does not possess. So you see, a simple brahmin like myself can hardly claim this man as relative. I will give him my daughter and then retire to the last *áshrama* stage of life, as is proper for old age, if your Lordship thinks it good."

10.81 Sa idam ākarṇya vaivarṇy'|ākrānta|vaktraḥ param upeto vailakṣyam ārapsyate 'nunetum a|nityat"|ādi|saṅkīrtanen' âtra|bhavantaṃ mantribhiḥ saha. tvaṃ tu teṣām adatta|śrotro mukta|kaṇṭhaṃ ruditvā cirasya bāṣpa|kuṇṭha|kaṇṭhaḥ kāṣṭhāny āhṛty' âgniṃ sandhukṣya rāja|mandira|dvāre cit'|âdhirohaṇāy' ôpakramiṣyase.

Sa tāvad eva tvat|pādayor nipatya s'|āmātyo nara|patir a|nūnair arthais tvām upacchandya duhitaraṃ mahyaṃ dattvā mad|yogyatā|samārādhitaḥ samastam eva rājya|bhāraṃ mayi samarpayiṣyati.

So 'yam abhyupāyo 'nuṣṭheyaḥ yadi tubhyaṃ rocata iti.›

10.84 So 'pi paṭu|viṭānām agraṇīr a|sakṛd|abhyasta|kapaṭa|prapañcaḥ Pāñcāla|śarmā yath"|ôktam abhyadhikaṃ ca nipuṇam upakrāntavān. āsīc ca mama samīhitānām a|hīna|kāla|siddhiḥ. anvabhavaṃ ca madhukara iva Navamālikām ārdra|sumanasam.

Asya rājñaḥ Siṃhavarmaṇaḥ sāhāyya|dānaṃ suhṛt|saṅketa|bhūmi|gamanam ity ubhayam apekṣya, sarva|bala|sandohena Campām imām upagato daivād deva|darśana|sukham anubhavām' îti.»

Śrutv" âitat Pramati|caritaṃ smita|mukulita|mukha|nalinaḥ:

When he hears this, all color will leave the king's face and he will be terribly embarrassed. Together with his ministers, he will strive to console your honorable self with discourses on impermanence and suchlike. But you must refuse to listen to them, crying out with open throat for a long time, until, throat choked with tears, you fetch logs, kindle the fire and prepare to ascend the funeral pyre right in the palace gateway. 10.81

At that moment the king and his ministers will throw themselves at your feet. First they will win you over with no mean amount of wealth, and then he will bestow on me his daughter. Indeed, totally convinced of my suitability for the position, he will hand over to me the burden of the kingdom.

Such is the plan we should adopt, if it pleases you.'

Foremost among the cunning and wily, Pañchála·sharman had more than once performed the full array of trickery. He then skillfully set about my scheme and even more. In no time at all my desires were fulfilled. Like a honeybee at a succulent *nava·málika* young jasmine, I enjoyed Nava·málika the woman. 10.84

Intending both to be of assistance to King Simha·varman and to reach the place of rendezvous with my friends, I advanced here to Champa with the whole multitude of my forces, where fate granted me the delight of seeing Your Majesty."

The king's son's lotus-face blossomed in a smile when he heard what Prámati had done:

10.87 «Vilāsa|prāyam ūrjitam mṛdu|prāyaṃ ceṣṭitam, iṣṭa eṣa mārgaḥ prajñāvatām. ath' êdānīm atra|bhavān praviśatu! iti»

Mitraguptam aikṣata kṣit'|īśa|putraḥ.

iti śrī|Daṇḍinaḥ kṛtau
Daśa|kumāra|carite
Pramati|caritaṃ
nāma
pañcama ucchvāsaḥ.

"A strong story distinguished by lightness of touch, deeds tempered by gentility. Such is the path beloved of the wise. Now it is for you, sir, to enter the narrative." 10.87

With which words he looked at Mitra·gupta.

That is the end of the fifth chapter of
the glorious Dandin's
What Ten Young Men Did.
It is called:
What Prámati Did.

CHAPTER ELEVEN
WHAT MITRA·GUPTA DID

So 'py ācacakṣe:

«Deva, so 'ham api suhṛt|sādhāraṇa|bhramaṇa|kāraṇaḥ Suhmeṣu Dāmalipt'|āhvayasya nagarasya bāhy'|ôdyāne mah"|ântam utsava|samājam ālokayam. tatra kva cid atimukta| latā|maṇḍape kam api vīṇā|vāden' ātmānaṃ vinodayantam utkaṇṭhitaṃ yuvānam adrākṣam. aprākṣaṃ ca:

11.3 ‹Bhadra, ko nām' âyam utsavaḥ? kim arthaṃ vā samārabdhaḥ? kena vā nimitten' ôtsavam an|ādṛty' âik'|ânte bhavān utkaṇṭhita iva parivādinī|dvitīyas tiṣṭhat' îti?›

So 'bhyadhatta:

‹Saumya, Suhma|patis Tuṅgadhanvā nām' ân|apatyaḥ prārthitavān amuṣminn āyatane vismṛta|Vindhya|vāsa|rāgaṃ vasantyā Vindhya|vāsinyāḥ pāda|mūlād apatya|dvayam. anayā ca kil' âsmai pratiśayitāya svapne samādiṣṭam:

11.6 «Samutpatsyate tav' âikaḥ putraḥ, janiṣyate c' âikā duhitā. sa tu tasyāḥ pāṇi|grāhakam anujīviṣyati. sā tu saptamād varṣād ārabhy' ā|pariṇayanāt prati|māsaṃ Kṛttikāsu kanduka|nṛtyena guṇavad|bhartṛ|lābhāya māṃ samārādhayatu. yaṃ ca abhilaṣet s" âmuṣmai deyā. sa c' ôtsavaḥ Kanduk'| ôtsava|nām" âstv iti!»

Tato 'lpīyasā kālena rājñaḥ priya|mahiṣī Medinī nām' âikaṃ putram asūta. samutpannā c' âikā duhitā. s" âdya kanyā Kandukāvatī nāma Somāpīḍāṃ devīṃ kanduka|vihāreṇ' ārādhayitum āgamiṣyati.

HE IN TURN began his story:

"My Lord, I too was roaming with the same purpose as our friends. In a suburban park of the city of Dama·lipta in the Suhman country, I came across a vast festival gathering. In an *atimúkta* creeper bower there I saw a melancholic young man distracting himself playing a *vina* lute. I asked him:

'Good sir, what is the name of this festival? Or, rather, 11.3
why is it being held? And for what reason do you ignore it, staying in seclusion like someone pining, with only your seven-stringed lute as company?'

He explained:

'Kind gentleman, the Lord of Suhma, Tunga·dhanvan, was childless. He prayed at the feet of Durga Vindhya·vá-sini for two children. "She who dwells in the Vindhyas" was dwelling here, forgetting her passion for her Vindhyan home. According to the tradition, he lay fasting before her to secure his prayer when she foretold in a dream:

"You shall have one son, and one daughter will be born. 11.6
But your son will be subordinate to the man who takes her hand in marriage. As for the girl, from her seventh year until her wedding, she is to worship me with a ball dance every month on the Pleiades, so that she may have a virtuous husband. When she falls in love with someone, to him she is to be given. And let the festival be known as the Festival of the Ball."

A short time thereafter, the king's dear queen, Médini, "Earth," bore a son, and a daughter was born. She, the maiden Kandukávati, "Bearer of the ball," will come today to worship Devi Soma·pidá with a ball-game.

Tasyās tu sakhī Candrasenā nāma dhātreyikā mama priy" āsīt. sā c' âiṣu divaseṣu rāja|putreṇa Bhīmadhanvanā balavad anuruddhā. tad aham utkaṇṭhito Manmatha|śara|śalya|duḥkh'|ôdvigna|cetāḥ kalena vīṇā|raveṇ' ātmānaṃ kiñcid āśvāsayan viviktam adhyāsa iti.›

11.9 Asminn eva kṣaṇe kim api nūpura|kvaṇitam upātiṣṭhat. āgatā ca kācid aṅganā. dṛṣṭv" âiva sa enām utphulla|dṛṣṭir utthāy' ôpagūhya gāḍham upagūḍha|kaṇṭhaś ca tayā tatr' âiv' ôpāviśat. aśaṃsac ca:

‹S" âiṣā me prāṇa|samā yad|viraho dahana iva dahati mām. idaṃ ca me jīvitam apaharatā rāja|putreṇa mṛtyun" êva niruṣmatāṃ nītaḥ. na ca śakṣyāmi rāja|sūnur ity amuṣmin pāpam ācaritum. ato 'nay" ātmānaṃ su|dṛṣṭaṃ kārayitvā tyakṣyāmi niṣpratikriyān prāṇān iti.›

Sā tu paryaśru|mukhī samabhyadhāt:

11.12 ‹Mā sma, nātha, mat|kṛte 'dhyavasyaḥ sāhasam! yas tvam uttamāt sārthavāhād Arthadāsād utpadya Kośadāsa iti gurubhir abhihita|nāmadheyaḥ punar mad|atyāsaṅgād Veśadāsa iti dviṣadbhiḥ prakhyāpito 'si, tasmiṃs tvayy uparate yady ahaṃ jīveyaṃ nṛ|śaṃso veśa iti samarthayeyaṃ loka|vādam. ato 'dy' âiva naya māṃ īpsitaṃ deśam iti.›

Sa tu māṃ abhyadhatta:

‹Bhadra, bhavad|dṛṣṭeṣu rāṣṭreṣu katamat samṛddhaṃ sampanna|sasyaṃ sat|puruṣa|bhūyiṣṭhaṃ c' êti?›

But it is her girlfriend and foster sister* Chandra·sena with whom I have fallen in love. She, however, is these days being forcibly held by the king's son Bhima·dhanvan. That is why I am pining, my heart afflicted with the piercing grief of maddening Love's arrows, sitting all alone trying to cheer myself up a little with the lute's sweet voice.'

Just then the jangle of anklets drew near, and a woman 11.9
arrived. The moment he saw her his eyes bloomed. He jumped up and embraced her deeply. With her clasping his neck, they sat down again on the same spot. He exclaimed:

'Here is she, dearer to me than the air that I breathe, separation from whom burns me like fire. Since the prince took her, my life, away from me, like death he took away my body heat. Yet because he is the king's son I dare do him no harm. Therefore I only wanted her to take a good look at me before I abandon my desperate life.'

Her face covered in tears, she pleaded:

'My Lord, do not commit this dreadful deed on my ac- 11.12
count. Born to Artha·dasa, "Slave to profit," best of caravan-leaders, your parents named you Kosha·dasa, "Slave to treasure." But because of your overfondness of me your enemies renamed you Vesha·dasa, "Slave of the courtesan." With you dead I would be living proof of the popular saying that a courtesan is wicked and a man's downfall.* Therefore lead me this very day away to any country you choose.'

At this he turned to me:

'Good man, of the kingdoms you have visited, which is really prosperous, with a fine harvest, and with the greatest number of good inhabitants?'

11.15 Tam aham īṣad vihasy' âbravam:

‹Bhadra, vistīrṇ" êyam arṇav'|âmbarā. na paryanto 'sti sthāna|sthāneṣu ramyāṇām jana|padānām. api tu na ced iha yuvayoḥ sukha|nivāsa|kāraṇaṃ kam apy upāyam utpādayituṃ śaknuyāṃ tato 'ham eva bhaveyam adhva|darś" îti.›

Tāvat" ôdairata raṇitāni maṇi|nūpurāṇām. ath' âsau jāta|sambhramā:

11.18 ‹Prāpt" âiv' êyaṃ bhartṛ|dārikā Kandukāvatī kanduka|krīḍitena devīṃ Vindhya|vāsinīm ārādhayitum. a|niṣiddha|darśanā c' êyam asmin Kanduk'|ôtsave. sa|phalam astu yuṣmac|cakṣuḥ. āgacchataṃ draṣṭum. aham asyāḥ sakāśa|vartinī bhaveyam. iti›

ayāsīt. tām anvayāva c' āvām. mahati ratna|raṅga|pīṭhe sthitāṃ prathamaṃ tāmr'|âuṣṭhīm apaśyam. atiṣṭhac ca sā sadya eva mama hṛdaye. na may" ânyena v" ântarāle dṛṣṭā. citrīy'|āviṣṭa|cittaś c' âcintayam:

‹Kim iyaṃ Lakṣmīḥ? na hi na hi. tasyāḥ kila haste vinyastaṃ kamalam, asyās tu hasta eva kamalam. bhukta|pūrvā tu sā purātanena puṃsā pūrva|rājaiś c' âsyāḥ punar an|a|vadyam ayātayāmaṃ ca yauvanam. iti›

11.21 cintayaty eva mayi s" ân|agha|sarva|gātrī vyatyasta|hasta|pallav'|âgra|spṛṣṭa|bhūmir ālola|nīla|kuṭil'|âlakā sa|vibhramaṃ bhagavatīm abhivandya kandukam *a|manda|rāga*|rūṣit'|*âkṣam* Anaṅgam iv' ālambata.

Laughing a little, I replied: 11.15

'Good sir, this earth girdled by the oceans is very vast. There is no end to its charming countries all over the place. Nevertheless, only if I cannot first come up with some ruse to ensure that you two live happily here, only then will I personally be your guide.'

The tinkling of jewelled anklets rang out that moment. The maiden made haste to leave, saying:

'My master's daughter Kandukávati has just arrived to 11.18
worship the goddess Vindhya·vásini with ball games. It is not forbidden to see her on this Kánduka festival. May your eyes find their raison d'être. Come, you two, and watch. I shall be at her side.'

And we both followed after her. First I saw the red-lipped one on the great jewelled dancing stage. Yet all of a sudden she had literally occupied my heart, without me or anyone else seeing her move between the two. My mind filled with wonder, I thought:

'Can this be Lakshmi herself? It cannot be, she is not. For they say that Lakshmi has a lotus in her hand, but this one's hand is itself a lotus. And while Vishnu Naráyana, the primeval man, and kings of old have all already enjoyed union with Lakshmi, this one's maidenhead is blameless and fresh.'

I had yet to complete my thought when she whose every 11.21
limb was impeccable touched the tips of her crossed bud-like hands to the ground, gracefully saluted the feet of the goddess with a toss of her blue-black curled locks and then picked up the ball, painted with *deep red spots*, as though it were Love himself, his *eyes* red with *quick passion*.*

Līlā|śithilaṃ ca bhūmau muktavatī. mand'|ôtthitaṃ ca kiñcit|kuñcit'|âṅguṣṭhena prasṛta|komal'|âṅgulinā pāṇi|pallavena samāhatya, hasta|pṛṣṭhena c' ônnīya, caṭula|dṛṣṭi|lāñchitaṃ stabakam iva bhramara|māl"|ânuviddham avapatantam ākāśa ev' âgrahīt. amuñcac ca. madhya|vilambita|laye druta|laye mṛdu|mṛdu ca praharantī tat|kṣaṇaṃ cūrṇa|padam adarśayat.

Praśāntaṃ ca taṃ nirdaya|prahārair udapādayat. viparyayeṇa ca prāśamayat. pakṣam ṛjv|āgataṃ ca vāma|dakṣiṇābhyāṃ karābhyāṃ paryāyeṇ' âbhighnatī śakuntam iv' ôdasthāpayat. dūr'|ôtthitaṃ ca prapatantam āhatya gīta|mārgam āracayat. pratidiśaṃ ca gamayitvā pratyāgamayat.

11.24 Evam an|eka|karaṇa|madhuraṃ viharantī, raṅga|gatasya rakta|cetaso janasya prati|kṣaṇam ucc'|âvacāḥ praśaṃsā|vācaḥ pratigṛhṇatī, tat|kṣaṇ'|ārūḍha|viśrambhaṃ Kośadāsam aṃse 'valambya;

kaṇṭakita|gaṇḍam utphull'|ēkṣaṇaṃ ca mayy abhimukhībhūya tiṣṭhati tat|pratham'|âvatīrṇa|Kandarpa|kārita|kaṭ'|âkṣa|dṛṣṭis tad|anumārga|vilasita|līl"|āñcita|bhrū|latā, śvās'|ânila|veg'|ândolitair danta|chada|raśmi|jālair līlā|pallavair iva mukha|kamala|parimala|grahaṇa|lolān ālinas tāḍayantī;

With languid playfulness she let it fall to the ground. When it bounced slowly back upward she hit it down with her bud-like hand, thumb slightly crooked in and delicate fingers outstretched. Then she threw it up from the back of her hand. As it fell down through the air she fired tremulous glances at it, so that it became like a posy studded with a garland of bees. She caught it and let it go again. In that moment, she gave a display of footwork and rhythm, moderate, slow and then rapid, striking the ball ever so gently.

Every time the ball's tempo slowed she made it go faster with merciless blows, alternating with slowing it down again. When the ball fell obliquely or straight down she would strike it with her left and right hand in turn so that it stayed aloft like a bird. As it fell headlong after rising high in the sky she would strike it so that she could leap ten steps forward to catch it. After making it go in every direction, she made it come back to its starting point.

Playing like this so sweetly with such variety, she received 11.24
every instant loud and quiet cries of praise from the people gathered around the stage, their minds entranced.* I leaned on Kosha·dasa's shoulder, my trust in him growing by the moment.

Standing facing her, the down on my cheeks stood on end and my eyes widened in wonder. Love revealed himself before her for the first time then, making her cast a sidelong look at me, her eyebrows playfully arched, sportively following the ball's lead. Bees hovered to catch the fragrance from her lotus-mouth. But the force of her out-breaths rocked the mass of light rays from her lips, slapping the bees as if with playful sprigs.

maṇḍala|bhramaṇeṣu kandukasy' âtiśīghra|pracāritayā viśant" îva mad|darśana|lajjayā puṣpa|mayaṃ pañjaram, pañca|bindu|prasṛteṣu pañc' âpi pañca|bāṇa|bāṇān yugapad iv' âbhipatatas trāsen' âvaghaṭṭayantī, go|mūtrikā|pracāreṣu *ghana|darśita|rāga|vibhramā* vidyul|latām iva viḍambayantī;

11.27 bhūṣaṇa|maṇi|raṇita|datta|laya|saṃvādi|pāda|cāram, apadeśa|smita|prabhā|niṣikta|bimb'|âdharam, apasraṃsita|pratisamāhita|śikhaṇḍa|bhāram, samāghaṭṭita|kvaṇita|ratna|mekhalā|guṇam, añcit'|ôtthita|pṛthu|nitamba|lambi|vicalad|aṃśuk'|ôjjvalam;

ākuñcita|prasṛta|vellita|bhuja|lat"|âbhihata|lalita|kandukam, āvarjita|bāhu|pāśam, parivartita|trika|vilagna|lola|kuntalam, avagalita|karṇa|pūra|kanaka|patra|pratisamādhāna|śīghrat"|ân|atikramita|prakṛta krīḍam, a|sakṛd|utkṣipyamāṇa|hasta|pāda|bāhy'|âbhyantara|bhrānta|kandukam;

avanaman'|ônnamana|nairantarya|naṣṭa|dṛṣṭa|madhya|yaṣṭikam, avapatan'|ôtpatana|viparyasta|mukt'|āhāram, aṅkurita|gharma|salila|dūṣita|kapola|patra|bhaṅga|śoṣaṇ'|âdhikṛta|śravaṇa|pallav'|ânilam, āgalita|stana|taṭ'|âṃśuka|niyamana|vyāpṛt'|âika|pāṇi|pallavaṃ ca;

Spinning in circles, she made the ball move so incredibly quickly that she appeared to have entered a cage made of flowers, in modesty under my gaze. It seemed that in fear she repelled five-arrowed Love's arrows, which fell all at the same time, striking the ball five times so that it looked like five spots. As she moved about in a zigzag *expressing dense flutters of passion*, she was just like a streak of lightning *highlighting a violent flash against a cloud*.*

The princess played on most wonderfully, sitting and 11.27
standing, closing up and opening out again like a flower, and stopping and starting.

The jewels in her ornaments jingled in unison, and in time with the movement of her feet. The radiance of an artless smile anointed her cherry-red lip. The weight of her locks was tossed aside and then fell back in place. The strings of her jewelled girdle tinkled as they brushed up against each other. Luminous with her dancing, a silk garment fluttered from her broad, splendidly curved hips.

She struck the ball gracefully with her long slender arms, drawing them in, throwing them out, and moving them all about, and she hooked her arms together, leaning forward. Her waving tresses clung between her rotating shoulder blades. The game, once commenced, was not allowed to cease as she speedily put back in place the gold ear ornament that had fallen down from her ear. The ball was whirled outside and within her hands and feet, tossed up again and again.

11.30 niṣady' ôtthāya nimīly' ônmīlya sthitvā gatvā c' âiv' âticitraṃ paryakrīḍata rāja|kanyā.

Abhihatya bhū|tal'|ākāśayor api krīḍ"|ântarāṇi darśanīyāny eken' âiv' ân|eken' êva kanduken' âdarśayat.

Candrasen"|ādibhiś ca priya|sakhībhiḥ saha vihṛtya vihṛt'|ânte c' âbhivandya devīṃ manasā me s'|ânurāgeṇ' êva parijanena c' ânugamyamānā, kuvalaya|śaram iva Kusuma|śarasya mayy apāṅgaṃ samarpayantī, s'|âpadeśam a|sakṛd|āvartyamāna|vadana|candra|maṇḍalatayā sva|hṛdayam iva mat|samīpe preritaṃ pratinivṛttaṃ na v" êty ālokayantī, saha sakhībhiḥ kumārī|puram agamat.

11.33 Ahaṃ c' Ânaṅga|vihvalaḥ sva|veśma gatvā Kośadāsena yatnavad atyudāraṃ snāna|bhojan'|ādikam anubhāvito 'smi. s" âyaṃ c' ôpasṛtya Candrasenā rahasi māṃ praṇipatya patyur aṃsam aṃsena praṇaya|peśalam āghaṭṭayanty upādiśat. ācaṣṭa ca hṛṣṭaḥ Kośadāsaḥ:

‹Bhūyāsam evam yāvad|āyur āyat'|âkṣi tvat|prasādasya pātram iti.›

Bending up and down without interruption, her slender 11.30
midriff vanished and reappeared. Her pearl necklace was tossed about by her swooping up and down. The breeze from the sprig decorating her ear was duty-bound to dry the pretty paintings on her cheeks, spoiled by the sprouting of perspiration. And all the time one of her bud-like hands was occupied in restraining the silken garment from slipping down her bosom.

Then she put on a show of different spectacular games, striking the ball to the ground and into space, juggling what looked like many balls but was in fact just one.

Thereafter she played with Chandra·sena and her other dear girlfriends. When their game was over, she bowed down before the goddess and went away to her royal quarters with her girlfriends. Full of love, my heart accompanied her like a servant. As she was leaving she struck me with a sidelong glance like the blue lily arrow of flower-arrowed Love.* On one pretense or another she kept turning back the circle of her moon-face, as though looking back to see if her own heart, which she had sent in my direction, would return or not.

Delirious with invisible Love I went home with Kosha·da- 11.33
sa. He took extra-special care of me, with the most splendid bath, feasting and the rest. In the evening Chandra·sena furtively sought us out. After prostrating herself before me she sat down beside Kosha·dasa, touching shoulder to shoulder in love's sweet way. Kosha·dasa was thrilled and said:

'O long-eyed one, may you favor me like this for as long as I live.'

Mayā tu sa|smitam abhihitam:

11.36 ‹Sakhe, kim etad āśāsyam? asti kiñcid añjanam. anayā tad|akta|netrayā rāja|sūnur upasthito vānarīm iv' âināṃ drakṣyati viraktaś c' âināṃ punas tyakṣyat' îti.›

Tayā tu smeray" âsmi kathitaḥ:

‹So 'yam āryeṇ' ājñākaro jano 'ty|artham anugṛhītaḥ yad asminn eva janmani mānuṣaṃ vapur apanīya vānarīkariṣyate. tad āstām idam. anyath" âpi siddhaṃ naḥ samīhitam.

11.39 Adya khalu Kanduk'|ôtsave bhavantam avahasita|Manobhav'|ākāram abhilaṣantī roṣād iva Śambara|dviṣ" âti|mātram āyāsyate rāja|putrī. so 'yam artho vidita|bhāvayā mayā sva|mātre tayā ca tan|mātre mahiṣyā ca manuj'|êndrāya nivedayiṣyate.

Vidit'|ârthas tu pārthivas tvayā duhituḥ pāṇiṃ grāhayiṣyati. tataś ca tvad|anujīvinā rāja|putreṇa bhavitavyam. eṣa hi devatā|samādiṣṭo vidhiḥ. tvad|āyatte ca rājye n' âlam eva tvām atikramya mām avaroddhum Bhīmadhanvā. tat sahatām ayaṃ tri|caturāṇi dinān' îti.›

Mām āmantrya priyaṃ c' ôpagūhya pratyayāsīt. mama Kośadāsasya ca tad|ukt'|ânusāreṇa bahu vikalpayatoḥ kathañcid akṣīyata kṣapā.

Then I asked with a smile:

'Do you think this is no more than a hope, my friend? I know a magical ointment. If we smear it on Chandra·sena's eyes, then when the prince will see her as a monkey he will fall out of love and spurn her instead.' 11.36

With a laugh, she told me:

'I am your obedient servant, and would be more than grateful if you could remove my human form and turn me into a monkey, in this very life.* But, this plan aside, there is an alternative route to make our wishes come true.

For the princess is terribly afflicted by an apparently furious Love, Shámbara's foe.* Today at the Ball Festival you made a mockery of mind-made Love's good looks, and she longs for you. I am a connoisseur of her emotional state. I will report this state of affairs to my mother, and she will pass it on to Médini, the princess's mother, who will finally inform the king. 11.39

Once the king has been informed of how things stand, he is sure to make you accept his daughter's hand. From then on the prince will become your subordinate. After all, such is the rule and regulation imposed by the goddess. With the kingdom in your power, Bhima·dhanvan will not dare defy you in holding me captive. Therefore Kosha·dasa here need be patient for just another three or four days.'

After bidding me farewell, she embraced her beloved and left. Somehow Kosha·dasa and I got through the night, with myriad questions leading on from what she had told us.

11.42 Kṣap"|ânte ca kṛta|yath"|ôcita|niyamas tam eva priyā|darśana|su|bhagam udyān'|ôddeśam upagato 'smi. tatr' âiva c' ôpasṛtya rāja|putro nir|abhimānam anukūlābhiḥ kathābhir mām anuvartamāno muhūrtam āsta.

Nītvā c' ôpakāryām ātma|samena snāna|bhojana|śayan'|ādi|vyatikareṇ' ôpācarat. talpa|gataṃ ca svapnen' ânubhūyamāna|priyā|darśan'|āliṅgana|sukham āyasena nigaḍena atibalavad|bahu|puruṣaiḥ pīvara|bhuja|daṇḍ'|ôparuddham abandhayan mām. pratibuddhaṃ ca sahasā samabhyadhāt:

‹Ayi, durmate, śrutam ālapitaṃ hatāyāś Candrasenāyā jāla|randhra|niḥsṛtaṃ tad|ek'|âvabodha|prayuktay" ânayā kubjayā. tvaṃ kil' âbhilaṣito varākyā Kandukavatyā, tava kil' ânujīvinā mayā stheyam, tvad|vacaḥ kil' ân|atikramatā mayā Candrasenā Kośadāsāya dāsyata iti.›

11.45 uktvā pārśvacaraṃ puruṣam ekam āloky' âkathayat:

‹Prakṣip' âinaṃ sāgara iti!›

Sa tu labdha|rājya iv' âtihṛṣṭaḥ:

11.48 ‹Deva, yad ājñāpayas' îti.›

yath"|ādiṣṭam akarot.

Ahaṃ tu nir|ālambano bhujābhyām itas tataḥ spandamānaḥ kim api kāṣṭhaṃ daiva|dattam uras" ôpaśliṣya tāvad aploṣi yāvad apāsarad vāsaraḥ śarvarī ca sarvā. pratyuṣasy

At the end of the night, I first performed the appropriate rituals, before going to that very blessed part of the park where I had beheld my beloved. The king's son also made his way to the same place, and stayed awhile, attending on me courteously with winning conversation. 11.42

He invited me to his pavilion, where he hosted me as his equal with a surfeit of bathing, dining and reclining. On my couch I was enjoying in a dream the bliss of seeing my beloved and embracing her, when he had a gang of super-strong men restrain my long brawny arms and bind me up in an iron chain. As soon as I had awoken he announced:

'You fool, I had appointed a hunchback woman exclusively to inform on the despicable Chandra·sena.* She heard everything her charge said through a hole in the window. She tells me that you are the object of pathetic Kandukávati's affections, and that you are the one I am supposed to be subordinate to, and that you thought that I would not dare disobey you but be obliged to cede Chandra·sena to Kosha·dasa.'

After his speech he turned and told one of the men attending at his side: 11.45

'Throw him in the ocean!'

Terribly thrilled, as though he had acquired a kingdom, the man responded:

'My lord, your command will be done.' 11.48

And he did as he had been told.

Adrift, my arms spun me this way and that before I could clasp to my chest a plank, destiny's gift. I floated until a whole day and a night had slipped away. As the next dawn broke I spotted a vessel with Greeks on board. They pulled

adṛśyata kim api vahitram. amutr' āsan Yavanāḥ. te mām uddhṛtya Rāmeṣu|nāmne nāvika|nāyakāya kathitavantaḥ:

11.51 ‹Ko 'py ayam āyasa|nigaḍa|baddha eva jale labdhaḥ puruṣaḥ. so 'yam api siñcet sahasraṃ drākṣāṇāṃ kṣaṇen' âiken' êti.›

Asminn eva kṣaṇe n' âika|naukā|parivṛtaḥ ko 'pi madgur abhyadhāvat. abibhayur Yavanāḥ. tāvad atijavā naukāḥ śvāna iva varāham asmat|potaṃ paryarutsata. prāvartata ca saṃprahāraḥ. parājāyiṣata Yavanāḥ. tān aham a|gatīn avasīdataḥ samāśvāsy' âlapiṣam:

‹Apanayata me nigaḍa|bandhanam! ayam aham avasādayāmi vaḥ sapatnān iti.›

11.54 Amī tath" âkurvan. sarvāṃś ca tān pratibhaṭān bhalla|varṣiṇā bhīma|ṭaṅkṛtena śārṅgeṇa lava|lavīkṛt'|âṅgān akārṣam. avaplutya hata|vidhvasta|yodham asmat|pota|saṃsakta|potam amutra nāvika|nāyakam an|abhisaram abhipatya jīva|grāham agrahīṣam. asau c' āsīt sa eva Bhīmadhanvā. taṃ c' âham avabudhya jāta|vrīḍam abravam:

‹Tāta, kiṃ dṛṣṭāni kṛt'|ânta|vilasitān' îti?›

Te tu sāmyātrikā madīyen' âiva śṛṅkhalena tam atigāḍhaṃ baddhvā, harṣa|kilakilā|ravam akurvan, māṃ c' âpy apūjayan.

11.57 Durvārā tu sā naur an|anukūla|vāta|nunnā dūram abhipatya kam api dvīpaṃ nibiḍam āśliṣṭavatī. tatra ca svādu pānīyam edhāṃsi kanda|mūla|phalāni ca sañjighṛkṣavo gāḍha|pātita|śilā|valayam avātarāma. tatra c' āsīn mahā|śailaḥ. so 'ham:

me up out of the water and informed their captain, Ramé-shu:*

'We found this man in the water bound in an iron chain. 11.51
He could water a thousand vines in one second.'

Just then a Cormorant war galley in the middle of a large flotilla attacked, terrifying the Greeks. Like dogs against a boar, the fast-moving boats blocked us in. Hand-to-hand battle ensued. The Greeks were overpowered. When they had no way out and were losing hope I urged them on, crying:

'Release me from my chains. I am here to defeat your enemies.'

They did as I asked. With a dreadful twang of my bow 11.54
and a rain of crescent-bladed arrows I made mincemeat of all those opponents. I jumped across onto their ship, which was lashed to ours. Every warrior had been slain and destroyed. Their captain was without protection. I charged and caught him alive. He was, it turned out, the very same Bhima·dhanvan. Recognizing him, I told the shamefaced prince:

'My dear, are you not a spectator of the plays of fate?'

Then the sailors bound him tightly with the chain that had bound me. They roared with whoops of delight and honored me with their worship.

Meanwhile, propelled by unfavorable winds, our unsteer- 11.57
able ship was driven far until it found harbor by an impenetrable island. We let drop deep a stone bracelet anchor before alighting there, hoping to collect sweet water, fuel, and bulbs, roots and fruit. There was a great mountain on the island. I thought to myself:

‹Aho! ramaṇīyo 'yaṃ parvata|nitamba|bhāgaḥ, kāntatar" êyaṃ gandha|pāṣāṇavaty upatyakā, śiśiram idam indīvar'|âravinda|makaranda|bindu|candrak'|ôttaraṃ gotra|vāri, ramyo 'yam an|eka|varṇa|kusuma|mañjarī|mañjulataras taru|van'|ābhoga iti!›

a|tṛptatarayā dṛśā bahu|bahu paśyann a|lakṣit'|âdhyārūḍha|kṣoṇī|dhara|śikharaḥ śoṇībhūtam utprabhābhiḥ padma|rāga|sopāna|śilābhiḥ kim api nālīka|parāga|dhūsaraṃ saraḥ samadhyagamam. tatra snātaś ca kāṃś cid amṛta|svādūn bisa|bhaṅgān āsvādya, aṃsa|lagna|kalhāras tāra|vartinā ken' âpi bhīma|rūpeṇa brahma|rākṣasen' âbhipatya:

11.60 ‹Ko 'si? kutastyo 's' îti?›

nirbhartsayat" âbhyadhīye. nirbhayena ca mayā so 'bhyadhīyata:

‹Saumya so 'ham asmi dvi|janmā. śatru|hastād arṇavam, arṇavād Yavana|nāvam, Yavana|nāvaś citra|grāvāṇam enaṃ parvata|pravaraṃ gato yadṛcchay" âsmin sarasi viśrāntaḥ. bhadraṃ tav' êti.›

11.63 So 'brūta:

‹Na ced bravīṣi praśnān aśnāmi tvām iti.›

May" ôktam:

11.66 ‹Pṛcchā tāvad bhavatu! iti›

Ath' āvayor ekay" āryay" āsīt samlāpaḥ:

‹Kiṃ krūraṃ?›

‹strī|hṛdayaṃ.›

11.69 ‹Kiṃ gṛhiṇaḥ priya|hitāya?›

‹dāra|guṇāḥ.›

'Ah, how delightful is this mountain flank! How very charming this lowland with its sulfurous green and yellow stones! This mountain brook has cool water, moonlets of blue lotus nectar drops on its surface. And this forest expanse is particularly attractive, with clusters of multi-colored flowers.'

My sight was not in the least satiated, but I kept on looking all around, without noticing that I had ascended to the peak of the earth-bearing mountain. There I discovered a pool, dusky-gray with lotus pollen, and ruddy with reflections from the ruby rocks forming its steps. I bathed, tasted some lotus fibers sweet as ambrosia, and had draped some white water lilies about my shoulders when a hideous-looking brahmin demon who lived on its bank fell upon me.*

'Who are you? Where have you come from?' 11.60

I was interrogated with menace. Fearless, I answered him:

'Gentle sir, I am a twice-born brahmin. Chance took me from the hand of my enemy into the ocean, from the ocean onto a Greek ship, and from the Greek ship to this superlative mountain of fabulous colored rocks, where I was resting beside this pool. Blessings be upon you.'

He said: 11.63

'If you cannot answer my questions, I will eat you up.'

I replied:

'Go ahead, ask!' 11.66

Our interchange fitted into a single *arya* verse:*

'What is cruel?'

'The heart of a woman.'

'What is dear and beneficial for a householder?' 11.69

'The virtues of a housewife.'

‹Kaḥ kāmaḥ?›

‹saṅkalpaḥ.›

‹Kiṃ duṣkara|sādhanaṃ?›

‹prajñā.›

11.72 Tatra Dhūminī|Gominī|Nimbavatī|Nitambavatyaḥ pramāṇam ity›

Upadiṣṭo mayā so 'brūta:

‹Kathaya kīdṛśyas tā iti!›

11.75 Atr' ôdāharam:

‹Asti Trigarto nāma jana|padaḥ. tatr' āsan gṛhiṇas trayaḥ sphīta|sāra|dhanāḥ s'|ôdaryā Dhanaka|Dhānyaka|Dhanyak'|ākhyāḥ. teṣu jīvatsu na vavarṣa varṣāṇi dvādaśa Daśa|śat'|âkṣaḥ.

Kṣīṇa|sāraṃ sasyam, oṣadhyo vandhyāḥ, na phalavanto vanaspatayaḥ, klībā meghāḥ, kṣīṇa|srotasaḥ sravantyaḥ, paṅka|śeṣāṇi palvalāni, nir|nisyandāny utsa|maṇḍalāni, viralībhūtaṃ kanda|mūla|phalam, avahīnāḥ kathāḥ, galitāḥ kalyāṇ'|ôtsava|kriyāḥ, bahulībhūtāni taskara|kulāni,

11.78 anyonyam abhakṣayan prajāḥ, paryaluṭhann itas|tato balākā|pāṇḍurāṇi nara|śiraḥ|kapālāni, paryahiṇḍanta śuṣkāḥ kāka|maṇḍalyaḥ, śūnyībhūtāni nagara|grāma|kharvaṭa|puṭa|bhedan'|ādīni.

Ta ete gṛha|patayaḥ sarva|dhānya|nicayam upayujy' âj'|âvikaṃ gavala|gaṇaṃ gavāṃ yūthaṃ dāsī|dāsa|janam apatyāni jyeṣṭha|madhyama|bhārye ca krameṇa bhakṣayitvā:

'What is desire?'

'Imagination.'

'What is the means to achieve the difficult?'

'Wisdom.

And of these responses the respective proofs are: Dhúmini, Gómini, Nímbavati and Nitámbavati.' 11.72

When I had added that, he asked:

'Tell me, what sort of women are these?'*

Thus I related:* 11.75

'There was a land called Tri·garta.* In that land there were three householders, full brothers, of swollen wealth and property. Their names were Dhánaka, Dhányaka and Dhanyaka—"Richard," "Ritchie," and "Rick."* During their lifetime it came to pass that Indra of the thousand eyes withheld rain for twelve years.*

The grain lost its kernel, plants became sterile, trees bore no fruit, the clouds were barren, streams lost their current, pools were no more than mud, springs all around ceased to flow, bulbs, roots and fruit were scarce, communication dried up, auspicious festivals and rituals melted away, and the community of thieves multiplied.

The population fed on one another, human skulls pale as cranes rolled about hither and thither, rookeries of parched crows roamed about, and cities, villages, market towns, towns and everywhere became desolate. 11.78

The aforementioned householders first used up all their stores of grain, before consuming in turn goats and sheep, their stock of buffaloes, their herd of cows, their female and male slaves, their children, and then the wives of the eldest and the middle brother. In the end they decided:

«Kaniṣṭha|bhāryā Dhūminī śvo bhakṣaṇīy" êti.»

11.81 samakalpayan. ayaṃ kaniṣṭho Dhanyakaḥ priyāṃ svām attum a|kṣamas tayā saha tasyām eva niśy apāsarat. mārga|klāntāṃ c' ôdvahan vanaṃ jagāhe.

Sva|māṃs'|âsṛg|apanīta|kṣut|pipāsāṃ tāṃ nayann antare kam api nikṛtta|pāṇi|pāda|karṇa|nāsikam avani|pṛṣṭhe viceṣṭamānaṃ puruṣam adrākṣīt. tam apy ārdr'|āśayaḥ skandhen' ôdvahan kanda|mūla|mṛga|bahule gahan'|ôddeśe yatna|racita|parṇa|śālaś ciram avasat. amuṃ ca ropita|vraṇam iṅgudī|tail'|ādibhir āmiṣeṇa śāken' ātma|nirviśeṣaṃ pupoṣa.

Puṣṭaṃ ca tam udrikta|dhātum ekadā mṛg'|ânveṣaṇāya ca prayāte Dhanyake sā Dhūminī riraṃsay" ôpātiṣṭhat. bhartsit" âpi tena balāt|kāram arīramat. nivṛttaṃ ca patim udak'|âbhyarthinam:

11.84 «Uddhṛtya kūpāt piba! rujati me śiraḥ śiro|roga iti.»

udañcanaṃ sarajjuṃ puraś cikṣepa. udañcantaṃ ca taṃ kūpād apaḥ kṣaṇāt pṛṣṭhato gatvā praṇunoda.

Taṃ ca vikalaṃ skandhen' ôduhya deśād deś'|ântaraṃ paribhramantī pativratā|pratītiṃ lebhe bahu|vidhāś ca pūjāḥ. punar Avanti|rāj'|ânugrahād atimahatyā bhūtyā nyavasat.

"Tomorrow we will eat Dhúmini, our youngest brother's wife."

This youngest brother, Dhanyaka, could not bear to eat 11.81
his beloved. So that very night he fled, taking her with him. She became exhausted by the journey. With her on his shoulders they entered the forest.

He warded off her hunger and thirst with his own flesh and blood and carried her on into the jungle. There on the way he saw a man writhing on his back, his hands, feet, ears and nose all amputated.* Dhanyaka's heart melted and he bore him too on his shoulders until they came to a place deep in the wood where there were many bulbs, roots and deer. Here he labored to construct a leaf-shelter, where they lived for a long while. Dhanyaka healed the other man's wounds with such treatments as *íngudi* oil, and he nourished him the same as himself with meat and vegetables.

One day, when Dhanyaka had gone off to hunt for deer, Dhúmini wanted to enjoy herself and attended on the other man, now well fed and abounding in precious bodily fluids. Although he rebuffed her, she forcefully had her way. When her husband returned he asked for water, but she said:

"Draw some from the well to drink. My head is splitting 11.84
with a headache."

With which she tossed before him bucket and rope. Then, when he was drawing water from the well, she was behind him in a moment, and pushed him in.

Dhúmini took the cripple on her shoulders and roamed from country to country. Acquiring a reputation as a *pa-ti·vrata*, a "faithful wife," she also received every kind of

11.87 Atha pānīy'|ârthi|sārtha|jana|samāpatti|dṛṣṭ'|ôddhṛtam Avantiṣu bhramantam āhār'|ârthinaṃ bhartāram upalabhya sā Dhūminī:

«Yena me patir vikalīkṛtaḥ sa durātm" âyam iti!»

Tasya sādhoś citra|vadham ajñena rājñā samādeśayāṃ cakāra. Dhanyakas tu datta|paścād|bandho vadhya|bhūmiṃ nīyamānaḥ sa|śeṣatvād āyuṣaḥ:

11.90 «Yo mayā vikalīkṛto 'bhimato bhikṣuḥ sa cen me pāpam ācakṣīta yukto me daṇḍa iti.»

a|dīnam adhikṛtaṃ jagāda.

«Ko doṣa iti?»

11.93 upanīya darśite 'muṣmin sa vikalaḥ paryaśruḥ pāda|patitas tasya sādhos tat|sukṛtam a|satyāś ca tasyās tathā|bhūtaṃ duścaritam ārya|buddhir ācacakṣe. kupitena rājñā virūpita|mukhī sā duṣkṛta|kāriṇī kṛtā śvabhyaḥ pācikā. kṛtaś ca Dhanyakaḥ prasāda|bhūmiḥ. tad bravīmi:

«Strī|hṛdayaṃ krūram iti.» ›

Punar anuyukto Gominī|vṛtt'|ântam ākhyātavān:

11.96 ‹Asti Draviḍeṣu Kāñcī nāma nagarī. tasyām an|eka|koṭi|sāraḥ śreṣṭhi|putraḥ Śakti|kumāro nām' āsīt. so 'ṣṭā|daśa|varṣa|deśīyaś cintām āpede:

worship. Eventually the king of Avánti Ujjáyini granted her his favor, so that she came to live in enormous prosperity.

One day our Dhúmini caught sight of her erstwhile hus- 11.87
band wandering through Avánti, begging for food. By chance he had been spotted and pulled out of the well by caravan traders looking for water. She accused:

"This brute is the man who disfigured my husband!"

Thereby she had the unknowing king sentence the good man to a violent death. But when Dhanyaka was being led to the execution ground, his hands bound behind his back, he boldly called to the one in charge of him, his life not over yet:

"If the beggar I am charged with having mutilated con- 11.90
demns me himself, then I deserve the punishment."

The officer thought:

"What harm in checking?"

He took Dhanyaka and showed him to the cripple, who 11.93
threw himself at the good man's feet in floods of tears. Noble-minded himself, he proclaimed the good deeds the accused had done, and all the evil actions of that wicked wife. The furious king had the evildoer's face disfigured and made her a dog-eater, an outcaste.* Dhanyaka, on the other hand, he made the object of his generosity. This is the story that prompts me to conclude:

"A woman's heart is cruel." '

Questioned again, I told Gómini's story:*

'There was in the Dravidian country a city called Kan- 11.96
chi.* There lived a merchant's son named Shakti·kumára, a multimillionaire in wealth. When he was about to turn eighteen the thought struck him:

«N' âsty a|dārāṇām an|anuguṇa|dārāṇāṃ vā sukhaṃ nāma. tat kathaṃ nu guṇavad vindeyaṃ kalatram? iti»

Atha para|pratyay'|āhṛteṣu dāreṣu yādṛcchikīṃ saṃpattim an|abhisamīkṣya kārt'|ântiko nāma bhūtvā vastr'|ânta|pinaddha|śāli|prastho bhuvaṃ babhrāma.

11.99 «Lakṣaṇa|jño 'yam iti.»

amuṣmai kanyāḥ kanyāvantaḥ pradarśayāṃ babhūvuḥ. yāṃ kāñcil lakṣaṇavatīṃ sa|varṇāṃ kanyāṃ dṛṣṭvā sa kila sma bravīti:

«Bhadre, śaknoṣi kim anena śāli|prasthena guṇavad annam asmān abhyavahārayitum? iti»

11.102 So hasit'|âvadhūto gṛhād gṛhaṃ praviśy' âbhramat.

Ekadā tu Śibiṣu Kāverī|tīra|pattane saha pitṛbhyām avasita|maha"|rddhim avaśīrṇa|bhavana|sārāṃ dhātryā pradarśyamānāṃ kāñcana virala|bhūṣaṇāṃ kumārīṃ dadarśa. asyāṃ saṃsakta|cakṣuś c' âtarkayat:

«Asyāḥ khalu kanyakāyāḥ sarva ev' âvayavā n' âti|sthūlā n' âti|kṛśā n' âti|hrasvā n' âti|dīrghā na vikaṭā mṛjāvantaś ca.

11.105 Rakta|tal'|âṅgulī yava|matsya|kamala|kalaś'|ādy|an|eka|puṇya|lekhā|lāñchitau karau, sama|gulpha|sandhī māṃsalāv a|śirālau c' âṅghrī, jaṅghe c' ânu|pūrva|vṛtte, pīvar'|ûru|graste iva dur|upalakṣye jānunī, sakṛd|vibhaktaś catur|asraḥ

"There is no happiness for those who have no wife, nor for those who have the wrong sort of wife. But how am I to find a wife with qualities?"

Not expecting chance success with a wife chosen on the advice of others, he disguised himself as a fortune-teller, and with a package of rice tied up in the hem of his clothes he travelled the earth. When they saw him, all those with daughters thought:

"He has the auspicious marks." II.99

Hence they brought their daughters to show him. But every time he was presented with a maiden with the auspicious marks and of his caste,* he asked her, the story goes:

"Good lady, are you able to prepare for us some good food with this kilo of rice?"

Laughed at and rejected, he roamed in this fashion from II.102
house to house.

Then one day among the Shibis, in a town on the bank of the Kavéri River,* he saw a maiden with hardly any ornaments, presented to him by her nurse. She had lost not only her parents but also her great wealth, and her house and property had been dispersed. His eyes riveted on her, he considered:

"Not one of this girl's limbs is too thick or too thin, too short or too long. They are none of them deformed but are all splendid.

Her two hands with their red, hennaed fingers and palms II.105
are bedecked with many auspicious marks such as barley-corn, fish, lotus, vase and the rest.* Her strong calves have even ankles and are free of prominent veins, her legs taper regularly, and her two knees are scarcely visible but, as it

kakundara|vibhāga|śobhī rath'|âṅg'|ākāra|saṃsthitaś ca nitamba|bhāgaḥ, tanutaram īṣan|nimnaṃ gambhīraṃ nābhi|maṇḍalaṃ, vali|trayeṇa c' âlaṃkṛtam udaram;

urobhāga|vyāpināv unmagna|cūcukau viśāl'|ārambha|śobhinau payodharau, dhana|dhānya|putra|bhūyastva|cihna|lekhā|lāñchita|tale snigdh'|ôdagra|komala|nakha|maṇī ṛjv|anupūrva|vṛtta|tāmr'|âṅgulī saṃnat'|âṃsa|deśe saukumāryavatyau nimagna|parva|sandhī ca bāhu|late;

tanvī kambu|vṛtta|bandhurā ca kandharā, vṛtta|madhya|vibhakta|rāg'|âdharam a|saṅkṣipta|cāru|cibukam āpūrṇa|kaṭhina|gaṇḍa|maṇḍalam a|saṅga|tānu|vakra|nīla|snigdha|bhrū|latam an|atipraudha|tila|kusuma|sadṛśa|nāsikam a|sita|dhavala|rakta|tri|bhāga|bhāsura|madhur'|âdhīra|sañcāra|manthar'|āyat'|ēkṣaṇam indu|śakala|sundara|lalāṭam indra|nīla|śil''|ākāra|ramy'|âlaka|paṅkti dvi|guṇa|kuṇḍalita|mlāna|nālīka|nāla|lalita|lamba|śravaṇa|pāśa|yugalam ānana|kamalam;

II.108 an|atibhaṅguro bahulaḥ paryante 'py a|kapila|rucir āyāmavān ek'|âika|nisarga|sama|snigdha|nīlo gandha|grāhī ca mūrdhaja|kalāpaḥ.

S'' êyam ākṛtir na vyabhicarati śīlam. āsajjati ca me hṛdayam asyām eva. tat parīkṣy' âinām udvaheyam. a|vimṛ-

were, are swallowed up by her plump thighs. The radiant region of her hips is perfectly symmetrical and all square, and her buttocks curved like chariot wheels. The very graceful circle of her navel is deep and slightly indented, and her belly is decorated with the ideal three folds.

Her breasts are lovely, with broad beginnings, covering her whole bosom, and pert nipples. Her long slim arms with their discreet joints flow ever so softly from her sloping shoulders. Their surface is decorated with marks signifying an abundance of wealth, grain and sons. Her nails are like red jewels, glossy, long and delicate, and her fingers straight, regularly rounded and reddish.

Her slender neck is curved and undulating like a conch shell. Her face is a lotus. Her red lips pout in the middle, and her dear chin is strong and present. The globes of her cheeks are full and firm, her blue-black glistening gracefully arched eyebrows do not join, her nose is like a sesame flower in first bloom. Her eyes, deep and long, are black and white, and red in the outer corners, shining, rolling and sweetly tremulous. Her brow is lovely as the crescent moon. Her fringe of delightful locks is like sapphire gems. And the lobes of her twin beautiful ears are adorned with twice-coiled wilting lotus stalks.

Her whole head of hair was not too curled, and plentiful, 11.108
and even at the very tips not tawny in color, long, blue-black and glossy, each strand growing evenly, and sweet-smelling.

This body before me must represent also her character.* My heart is set on this girl already. But I shall put her to the test before taking her in marriage. For it is a fact that regret

śya|kāriṇā hi niyatam anekāḥ patanty anuśaya|paramparā iti.»

Snigdha|dṛṣṭir ācaṣṭa:

11.111 «Bhadre, kaccid asti kauśalaṃ śāli|prasthen' ânena saṃpannam āhāram asmān abhyavahārayitum? iti»

Tatas tayā vṛddha|dāsī s'|ākūtam ālokitā. tasya hastāt prastha|mātraṃ dhānyam ādāya kva cid alind'|ôddeśe su|sikta|saṃmṛṣṭe datta|pāda|śaucam upāveśayat. sā kanyā tān gandha|śālīn saṅkṣudya mātrayā viśoṣy' ātape muhur muhuḥ parivartya sthira|samāyāṃ bhūmau nālī|pṛṣṭhena mṛdu|mṛdu ghaṭṭayantī tuṣair a|khaṇḍais taṇḍulān pṛthak cakāra. jagāda ca dhātrīm:

«Mātaḥ, ebhis tuṣair arthino bhūṣaṇa|mṛjā|kriyā|kṣamaiḥ svarṇa|kārāḥ. tebhya imān dattvā labdhābhiḥ kākiṇībhiḥ sthiratarāṇy an|aty|ārdrāṇi n' âti|śuṣkāṇi kāṣṭhāni, mitaṃ|pacāṃ sthālīm ubhe śarāve c' āhar' êti!»

11.114 Tathā|kṛte tayā tāṃs taṇḍulān an|ati|nimn'|ôttāna|vistīrṇa|kukṣau kakubh'|ôlūkhale loha|patra|veṣṭita|mukhena sama|śarīreṇa vibhāvyamāna|madhya|tānavena vyāyatena guruṇā khādireṇa musalena catura|lalit'|ôtkṣepaṇ'|âvakṣepaṇ'|āyāsita|bhujam a|sakṛd aṅgulībhir uddhṛty' ôddhṛty' âvahatya śūrpa|śodhita|kaṇa|kiṃśārukāṃs taṇḍulān a|sakṛd adbhiḥ prakṣālya, kvathita|pañca|guṇe jale datta|cullī|pūjā prākṣipat.

succeeds regret in succession for the man who acts without deliberation."

With an affectionate look he asked:

"Good lady, do you have the skill to prepare for us a wonderful meal from this kilo of rice?" II.111

In response she gave the old servant woman a meaningful look. Taking the kilo of rice grain from the man's hand, the old lady gave him water to clean his feet before inviting him to sit down on the terrace before the door, well sprinkled and swept. The girl pounded the fragrant rice a little,* and dried it in the sun, turning it over many times. Then, rubbing it ever so delicately with the back of a stalk on some firm and even ground, she separated the grains from the unbroken husks. She directed her nurse:

"Mother, the goldsmiths need these husks to polish their jewelry. Give them these and with the small change you get in return* bring some solid firewood, not too sappy and not too dry, a small clay cooking pot, and a pair of platters."

When the old woman had done all that, the girl took a II.114
long, heavy *khádira* wood pestle of solid body with slender middle, its face dressed in a sheet of iron, and a *kákubha* wood mortar whose belly was not too deep, but shallow and broad.* Placing those grains in the mortar, she fatigued her arms tossing the pestle up and throwing it down with graceful skill. All the time she kept separating, lifting and threshing the rice with her fingers. With a winnowing basket she sieved off dust and the noxious awn. Then she washed the grains many times with water, and, offering a small amount in sacrifice to the hearth, she threw the rice into boiling water five times its quantity.

Praślath'|âvayaveṣu prasphuratsu taṇḍuleṣu mukul'|âvasthām ativartamāneṣu saṅkṣipy' ânalam upahita|mukha|pidhānayā sthāly" ânna|maṇḍam agālayat. darvyā c' âvaghaṭṭya mātrayā parivartya sama|pakveṣu siktheṣu tāṃ sthālīm adho|mukhīm avātiṣṭhipat.

Indhanāny antaḥ|sārāṇy ambhasā samabhyukṣya praśamit'|âgnīni kṛṣṇ'|âṅgārīkṛtya tad|arthibhyaḥ prāhiṇot:

11.117 «Ebhir labdhāḥ kākiṇīr dattvā śākaṃ ghṛtaṃ dadhi tailam āmalakaṃ ciñcā|phalaṃ ca yathā|lābham ānay' êti!»

Tath" ânuṣṭhite ca tayā dvitrān upadaṃśān upapādya tad|anna|maṇḍam ārdra|vāluk"|ôpahita|nava|śar'|âvagatam atimṛdunā tāla|vṛnt'|ânilena śītalīkṛtya sa|lavaṇa|sambhāraṃ datt'|âṅgāra|dhūpa|vāsaṃ ca saṃpādya, tad apy āmalakaṃ ślakṣṇa|piṣṭam utpala|gandhi kṛtvā dhātrī|mukhena snānāya tam acodayat.

Tayā ca snāna|śuddhayā datta|tail'|āmalakaḥ krameṇa sasnau. snātaḥ sikta|mṛṣṭe kuṭṭime phalakam āruhya pāṇḍu|haritasya tri|bhāga|śeṣa|lūnasya aṅgaṇa|kadalī|palāśasy' ôpari śarāva|dvayaṃ dattam ārdram abhimṛśann atiṣṭhat.

When the grains of rice were quite flaccid all over and swelling, like closed buds no longer, she reduced the fire. She strained the scum from the boiled rice by covering the mouth of the pot with its lid.* Then, with a ladle, she knocked and stirred the rice carefully around. Once the boiled rice was evenly cooked she tipped the pot over, face downward.

The firewood that was still strong inside she sprinkled with water to extinguish its fire, thus creating black charcoal. This she dispatched to those who wanted it, telling her nurse:

"With the small change you receive for these pieces of II.117
charcoal, bring whatever vegetables, ghee, curd, oil, myrobalan and tamarind fruit you can purchase."

After the old woman had done as she was asked, the girl prepared two or three vegetable relishes. She had poured the boiled rice scum down into a new grass cup placed on wet sand. Now she cooled it by fanning an extremely soft breeze with a palm leaf. She finished this preparation by adding salt and the fragrance from frankincense that she had placed on the coals. As for the myrobalan, she ground it finely to release the lotus perfume, and had her nurse press their guest to bathe.

The girl was clean, having already bathed. She handed Shakti·kumára oil and astringent myrobalan so he could bathe and freshen up in turn. Once he had bathed, he took his place on a wooden seat on the sprinkled and swept paved floor. He sat touching the two damp platters he had been given, placed on a quarter cut from a pale-green leaf from the plantain in the courtyard.

II.120 Sā tu tāṃ peyām ev' âgre samupāharat. pītvā c' âpanīt'|âdhva|klamaḥ prahṛṣṭaḥ praklinna|sakala|gātraḥ sthito 'bhūt. tatas tasya śāly|odanasya darvī|dvayaṃ dattvā sarpir|mātrāṃ sūpam upadamśaṃ c' ôpajahāra. imaṃ ca dadhnā ca tri|jātak'|âvacūrṇitena surabhi|śītalābhyāṃ ca kālaśeya|kāñjikābhyāṃ śeṣam annam abhojayat. sa|śeṣa ev' ândhasy asāv atṛpyat.

Ayācata ca pānīyam. atha nava|bhṛṅgāra|sambhṛtam a|guru|dhūpa|dhūpitam abhinava|pāṭalī|kusuma|vāsitam utphull'|ôtpala|grathita|saurabhaṃ vāri nālī|dhār'|ātmanā pātayāṃ babhūva.

So 'pi mukh'|ôpahita|śarāveṇa hima|śiśira|kaṇa|karālit'|âruṇāyamān'|âkṣi|pakṣmā dhāra|rav'|âbhinandita|śravaṇaḥ sparśa|sukh'|ôdbhinna|rom'|āñca|karkaśa|kapolaḥ parimala|pravāl'|ôtpīḍa|phulla|ghrāṇa|randhro mādhurya|prakarṣ'|āvarjita|rasan"|êndriyas tad acchaṃ pānīyam ākaṇṭhaṃ papau.

II.123 Śiraḥ|kaṃpa|saṃjñā|vāritā ca punar apara|karakeṇ' ācamanam adatta kanyā. vṛddhayā tu tad|ucchiṣṭam apohya harita|gomay'|ôpalipte kuṭṭime svam ev' ôttarīya|karpaṭaṃ vyavadhāya kṣaṇam aśeta.

First, she served him the aforementioned rice-gruel. When he had drunk it he sat there refreshed, the road's fatigue banished and his every limb rehydrated. Next, she gave him two ladles full of the good boiled rice and offered him a sauce of pure clarified butter and a relish.* Finally, she offered him the rest of the rice to eat, with curd sprinkled with the three spices (mace, cardamon and cinnamon) and with both buttermilk and sour gruel, fragrant and cool. Once he had eaten his fill there was still some food left over. II.120

He requested water. Accordingly she poured a stream of water through a tube, water that had been collected in a new pitcher and fumigated with aloe, perfumed with newly opened *pátali* red begonia flowers and infused with the scent of full-blown lotuses.

He then raised the dish to his mouth and from it drank his throat full of that clear water.* As he did so his eyelashes* looked reddish and magnified by drops cold as snow. His ears rejoiced in the singsong of the flowing water, his cheeks were rugged with horripilating down from the blissful sensation, his nostrils flared with the gushing flow of a stream of scent, and his tongue was prostrate with the heights of sweetness.

Signalled to stop by a nod of the head, the maiden then presented him with water from another small water pot to ritually rinse his mouth.* The old lady removed the leftovers, and when the pavement had been smeared with fresh green cow dung, Shakti·kumára spread out his ragged cloak and lay down for a while. II.123

Parituṣṭaś ca vidhivad upayamya kanyāṃ ninye. nītv” âi-
tad|an|apekṣaḥ kām api gaṇikām avarodham akarot. tām apy
asau priya|sakhīm iv’ ôpācarat. patiṃ ca daivatam iva muk-
ta|tandrā paryacarat. gṛha|kāryāṇi c’ â|hīnam anvatiṣṭhat.
parijanaṃ ca dākṣiṇya|nidhir ātm’|âdhīnam akarot.

Tad|guṇa|vaśīkṛtaś ca bhartā sarvam eva kuṭumbaṃ ta-
d|āyattam eva kṛtvā tad|ek’|âdhīna|jīvita|śarīras tri|vargaṃ
nirviveśa. tad bravīmi:

11.126   «Gṛhiṇaḥ priya|hitāya dāra|guṇā iti.» ›

Tatas ten’ ânuyukto Nimbavatī|vṛttam ākhyātavān:

‹Asti Saurāṣṭreṣu Valabhī nāma nagarī. tasyāṃ Gṛhagupta|
nāmno Guhyak’|êndra|tulya|vibhavasya nāvika|pater duhitā
Ratnavatī nāma. tāṃ kila Madhumatyāḥ samupāgamya Ba-
labhadro nāma sārthavāha|putraḥ paryaṇaiṣīt.

11.129   Tay” âpi nava|vadhvā rahasi rabhasa|vighnita|surata|sukho
jhaṭiti dveṣam alp’|êtaraṃ babandha. na tāṃ punar draṣ-
ṭum iṣṭavān. tad|gṛh’|āgamanam api suhṛd|vākya|śat’|âtivartī
lajjayā parijahāra. tāṃ ca durbhagāṃ tadā|prabhṛty eva:

Afterward, altogether delighted, he married the girl with due ceremony and took her away with him. But once he had brought her home he neglected her, starting a dalliance with one or another courtesan. The girl even treated this woman as a dear friend. She unflaggingly served her husband and master as though he were a god, and performed her household duties without fail. A treasure of beautiful manners, she won the devotion of all her servants.

Entranced by her virtues, her husband transferred the whole household entirely into her charge. Himself devoted to her exclusively body and soul, he enjoyed the three ends of man: love, wealth and religion. This is the story that prompts me to conclude:

"What is dear and beneficial for a householder? The virtues 11.126
of a housewife." '

The *brahma·rákshasa* pressed me on to tell Nímbavati's story:*

'In Sauráshtra* there is a town called Válabhi, where lived Griha·gupta, a sea lord wealthy as Kubéra, Lord of the *gúhyaka*s. He had a daughter, Rátnavati. The son of a caravan-leader, Bala·bhadra, came from Mádhumati and married her, the story goes.

But when they were alone together the new bride rashly 11.129
obstructed his erotic bliss and so he spontaneously developed no small hatred for her. He did not want to even see her anymore. In shame he renounced coming to her house, disregarding a hundred requests from friends. From then on her family and other people insulted the unlucky wretched girl, saying:

«N' êyaṃ Ratnavatī Nimbavatī c' êyam! iti»

sva|janaḥ para|janaś ca paribabhūva. gate ca kasmiṃś cit kāle sā tv anutapyamānā:

11.132 «Kā me gatir? iti»

vimṛśantī kām api vṛddha|pravrājikāṃ mātṛ|sthānīyāṃ deva|śeṣa|kusumair upasthitām apaśyat. tasyāḥ puro rahasi sa|karuṇaṃ ruroda. tay" âpy udaśru|mukhyā bahu|prakāram anunīya rudita|kāraṇaṃ pṛṣṭā trapamāṇ" âpi kārya|gauravāt kathañcid abravīt:

«Amba, kiṃ bravīmi? daurbhāgyaṃ nāma jīvan|maraṇam ev' âṅganānām viśeṣataś ca kula|vadhūnām. tasy' âham asmy udāharaṇa|bhūtā. mātṛ|pramukho 'pi jñāti|vargo mām avajñay" âiva paśyati. tena su|dṛṣṭāṃ māṃ kuru. na cet tyajeyam ady' âiva niṣprayojanān prāṇān. ā virāmāc ca me rahasyaṃ n' āśrāvyam! iti»

11.135 Pādayoḥ papāta. s" âinām utthāpy' ôdbāṣp" ôvāca:

«Vatse, m" âdhyavasyaḥ sāhasam. iyam asmi tvan|nideśa|vartinī. yāvati mam' ôpayogas tava tāvati bhavāmy an|any'|ādhīnā. yady ev' âsi nirviṇṇā tapaś cara tvaṃ mad|adhiṣṭhitā pāralaukikāya kalyāṇāya. nanv ayam udarkaḥ prāktanasya duṣkṛtasya yad anen' ākāreṇ' ēdṛśena śīlena jātyā c' âivaṃbhūtayā samanugatā saty a|kasmād eva bhartṛ|dveṣyatāṃ

"She is no Rátnavati, 'Jewelled one,' but she is Nímbavati, 'Tree of bitter fruits.'"

With the passing of time, she was filled with remorse, worrying:

"What will become of me?" II.132

Then she saw the old woman mendicant who was a mother figure to her draw near, with flowers left over from an offering to a god.* Before her but only her she wept piteously. The old woman's face was also drenched in tears as she tried to soothe her every way she could, and asked why she was crying. Despite her embarrassment, the severity of the situation drove the girl to speak:

"How can I tell you, mother? The wretchedness of being forsaken by one's husband is sheer living death for any woman, but how much more so for a noblewoman? Of this I have now become an example. Led by my mother, of all people, my whole family utterly despises me. You have to help me regain their respect. If you cannot, then this very day I shall give up my useless life. But you must not divulge my secret until it is too late."

And the young woman fell at the old woman's feet. In II.135
tears she pulled her up and said:

"My child, do not do anything drastic and violent. I am at your command. As long as you need me I am dedicated to you. If you really are dissatisfied, then you should follow my example and embark on the ascetic path so that you may find happiness in the next world. This crisis must be the result of earlier misdeeds, for how else could you, endowed as you are with this beauty, such good character, and such high birth, become hated by your husband, without reason?

gat" âsi. yadi kaś cid asty upāyaḥ pati|droha|pratikriyāyai, darśay' âmum. matir hi te paṭīyas" îti.»

Ath' âsau kathañcit kṣaṇam adho|mukhī dhyātvā dīrgh'|ôṣṇa|śvāsa|pūrvam avocat:

11.138 «Bhagavati, patir eva daivataṃ vanitānām, viśeṣataś ca kulajānām. atas tac|chuśrūṣaṇ"|âbhyupāya|hetu|bhūtaṃ kiñcid ācaraṇīyam.

Asty asmat|prātiveśyo vaṇik. abhijanena vibhavena rāj'|ântaraṅga|bhāvena ca sarva|paurān atītya vartate. tasya kanyā Kanakavatī nāma mat|samāna|rūp'|âvayavā mam' âtisnigdhā sakhī.

Tayā saha tad|vimāna|harmya|tale tato 'pi dvi|guṇa|maṇḍitā vihariṣyāmi. tvayā tu tan|mātṛ|prārthanaṃ sa|karuṇam abhidhāya mat|patir etad|gṛhaṃ kathañcan' āneyaḥ. samīpa|gateṣu ca yuṣmāsu krīḍā|mattā nāma kandukaṃ bhraṃśayeyam. atha tam ādāya tasya haste dattvā vakṣyasi:

11.141 ‹Putra, tav' êyaṃ bhāryā|sakhī Nidhi|pati|dattasya sarva|śreṣṭhi|mukhyasya kanyā Kanakavatī nāma. tvām iyam an|avastho niṣkaruṇaś c' êti Ratnavatī|nimittam atyarthaṃ nindati. tad eṣa kanduko vipakṣa|dhanaṃ pratyarpaṇīyam iti.›

Sa tath" ôkto niyatam unmukhībhūya tām eva priya|sakhīṃ manyamāno mām baddh'|âñjali yācamānāyai mahyaṃ bhūyas tvat|prārthitaḥ s'|âbhilāṣam arpayiṣyati. tena randhreṇ' ôpaśliṣya rāgam ujjvalīkṛtya yath" âsau kṛta|saṅketo deś'|ântaram ādāya māṃ gamiṣyati tath" ôpapādanīyam iti.»

If you can think of a way to reverse your lord and master's betrayal, then reveal it. For your mind is sharper."

Head down, the girl thought deeply a moment before heaving a deep fevered sigh and saying:

"My lady, a woman's husband is her deity, and how much 11.138
more so for wellborn ladies. Hence it is imperative that we find a way for me to serve him anew.

We have a merchant neighbor who towers above the whole population in his noble descent, wealth and being the king's closest confidant. His daughter Kánakavati, 'Golden one,' looks just like me, and is my dearest friend.

I shall go now and dally with her on the palace roof terrace, twice as finely adorned as she. In the meantime, you should somehow contrive to bring my husband to her house, convincing him of her mother's gracious invitation. When you are close I shall let fall a ball, as though in the flurry of the game. Pick it up and place it in his hand, saying:

'My son, she is your wife's friend Kánakavati, daughter of 11.141
Nidhi·pati·datta, foremost of all merchants. She is hypercritical of you on Rátnavati's account, thinking you inconstant and heartless. Hence you should hand the ball back as enemy property.'

He is certain to comply, and, looking up, will take me for my best friend. Hands folded in respectful salutation, I will beg him and, urged on by you, he will gallantly return the ball. Exploit that opening to ignite his passion to the extent that you can persuade him to arrange a rendezvous to elope with me to another country."

Harṣ'|âbhyupetayā c' ânayā tath" âiva saṃpāditam. ath' âitām Kanakavat" îti vṛddha|tāpasī|pralabdho Balabhadraḥ sa|ratna|sār'|ābharaṇām ādāya niśi nīrandhre tamasi prāvasat. sā tu tāpasī vārtām āpādayat:

11.144 «Mandena mayā nir|nimittam upekṣitā Ratnavatī śvaśurau ca paribhūtau suhṛdaś c' âtivartitāḥ. tad atr' âiva saṃsṛṣṭo jīvituṃ jihrem' îti Balabhadraḥ pūrvedyur mām akathayat. nūnam asau tena nītā vyaktiś c' â|cirād bhaviṣyat' îti.»

Tac chrutvā tad|bāndhavās tad|anveṣaṇaṃ prati śithila|yatnās tasthuḥ. Ratnavatī tu mārge kāñcit paṇya|dāsīṃ saṅgṛhya tay" ôhyamāna|pāthey'|ādy|upaskarā Kheṭaka|puram agamat.

Amutra ca vyavahāra|kuśalo Balabhadraḥ svalpen' âiva mūlena mahad|dhanam upārjayat. paur'|âgra|gaṇyaś c' āsīt. parijanaś ca bhūyān artha|vaśāt samājagāma. tatas tāṃ prathama|dāsīṃ:

11.147 «Na karma karoṣi, dṛṣṭaṃ muṣṇāsi, a|priyaṃ bravīṣ" îti!» paruṣam uktvā bahv atāḍayat. ceṭī tu prasāda|kāl'|ôpakhyāta|rahasyasya vṛtt'|ânt'|âika|deśam ātta|roṣā nirbibheda. tac chrutvā tu lubdhena daṇḍa|vāhinā paura|vṛddha|samnidhau:

«Nidhipatidattasya kanyāṃ Kanakavatīṃ moṣeṇa apahṛty' âsmat|pure nivasaty eṣa durmatir Balabhadraḥ. tasya sarvasva|haraṇaṃ bhavadbhir na pratibandhanīyam. iti»

Thrilled with delight, the old renunciate woman pulled everything off just so. She tricked Bala·bhadra into thinking that he was looking at Kánakavati. One pitch-black night he carried her off with her jewelry and personal property. The ascetic woman meanwhile spread the following story:

"Bala·bhadra told me yesterday that he had been a fool 11.144
to reject Rátnavati without reason, and to have insulted his parents-in-law and offended his friends. Therefore, he said, he was too ashamed to live with her here. It is obvious that he has taken her away. All will be clear before long."

When they heard this, Rátnavati's relations relaxed their efforts to search for her. She, meanwhile, had purchased on the road a slave to carry their luggage, provisions and so on, until they reached Khétaka.

There Bala·bhadra, with his business acumen, built a great fortune out of almost no capital. He became first among the citizens, assembling with his wealth a vast household. One day he spoke harshly to that first womanservant:

"You do no work! You steal whatever you see! Your words 11.147
are insolent!"

And he beat her hard. The servant was beside herself with rage. To pay him back she disclosed part of the story, confided to her in times of good favor. When the jealous magistrate heard it he denounced the man roundly before the city elders:

"Bala·bhadra is evil. Before settling in our town he had stolen away Kánakavati, daughter of Nidhi·pati·datta. Your good selves should not stand in the way of the confiscation of his estate."

11.150 nitarām abhartsayata. bhītaṃ ca Balabhadram adhijagāda Ratnavatī:

«Na bhetavyam. brūhi:

‹N' êyaṃ Nidhipatidatta|kanyā Kanakavatī. Valabhyām eva Gṛhagupta|duhitā Ratnavatī nām' êyaṃ dattā pitṛbhyāṃ mayā ca nyāy'|ôḍhā. na cet pratītha praṇidhiṃ prahiṇut' âsyā bandhu|pārśvam iti.›»

11.153 Balabhadras tu tath" ôktvā śreṇī|prātibhāvyena tāvad ev' âtiṣṭhad yāvat tat|pura|lekhya|labdha|vṛtt'|ânto Gṛhaguptaḥ Kheṭaka|puram āgatya saha jāmātrā duhitaram atiprītaḥ pratyanaiṣīt. tathā dṛṣṭvā Ratnavatī Kanakavat" îti bhāvayatas tasy' âiva Balabhadrasy' âtivallabhā jātā.

Tad bravīmi:

«Kāmo nāma saṅkalpa iti.»›

11.156 Tad|an|antaram asau Nitambavatī|vṛtt'|ântam aprākṣīt. so 'ham abravam:

‹Asti Śūra|seneṣu Mathurā nāma nagarī. tatra kaś cit kula|putraḥ kalāsu gaṇikāsu c' âtirakto mitr'|ârthaṃ sva|bhuja|mātra|nirvyūḍh'|ân|eka|kalahaḥ Kalahakaṇṭaka iti karkaśair abhikhyāpit'|ākhyaḥ pratyavātsīt.

Sa c' âikadā kasya cid āgantoś citrakarasya haste citra|paṭaṃ dadarśa. tatra kācid ālekhyagatā yuvatir āloka|mātreṇ' âiva Kalahakaṇṭakasya kām'|āturaṃ cetaś cakāra. sa ca tam abravīt:

11.159 «Bhadra, viruddham iv' âitat pratibhāti. yataḥ kulajā|durlabhaṃ vapuḥ, ābhijātya|śaṃsinī ca namratā, pāṇḍurā ca mukha|cchaviḥ, an|ati|paribhukta|subhagā ca tanuḥ prau-

Bala·bhadra was terrified, but Rátnavati explained to him: II.150
"Do not fear. Tell them:

'She is not Kánakavati, Nidhi·pati·datta's daughter. In fact her name is Rátnavati, and she is the daughter of Griha·gupta, also of Válabhi. We are legally married, with her parents' blessing. If you do not believe me, send an envoy to her family.'"

Bala·bhadra said as he had been told. He remained un- II.153
der bail of the guild until Griha·gupta reached Khétaka town, informed of events by letter. Overjoyed, he took his daughter and son-in-law home. Seeing what had transpired, Bala·bhadra, who had thought she was Kánakavati, loved Rátnavati all the more.

This is the story that prompts me to conclude:

"What is desire? Imagination." '

Immediately the *brahma·rákshasa* asked for Nitámbavati's II.156
story.* I told him:

'In Shura·sena is the city of Máthura.* There lived a son of good family addicted to the arts and to courtesans. On his friends' account he fought and won many a fight, bare-handed. Ruffians renamed him, accordingly, Kálaha·kántaka, "A thorn in a fight."

One day he saw a painting in the hand of a recently arrived painter. A young woman was depicted there. At first sight of her likeness, Kálaha·kántaka's mind was tormented by desire. He asked the artist:

"Good man, this seems to be a contradiction. For her II.159
physical beauty is rare among those of good family, but her humility proclaims nobility of birth. Her complexion is pale, her body's bounty not over-consumed, and her gaze of

ḍhat"|ânuviddhā ca dṛṣṭiḥ. na c' âiṣā proṣita|bhartṛkā pravāsa|cihnasy' âika|veṇy|āder adarśanāt. lakṣma c' âitad|dakṣiṇa|pārśvavarti.

Tad iyaṃ vṛddhasya kasya cid vaṇijo n' âtipuṃstvasya yath"|ârha|sambhog'|â|lābha|pīḍitā gṛhiṇī tvay" âtikauśalād yathā|dṛṣṭam ālikhitā bhavitum arhat' îti.»

Sa tam abhipraśasy' âśaṃsat:

II.162 «Satyam idam. Avantipuryām Ujjayinyām Anantakīrti|nāmnaḥ sārthavāhasya bhāryā yath"|ârtha|nāmā Nitambavatī nām' âiṣā saundarya|vismitena may" âivam ālikhit" êti.»

Sa tad" âiv' ônmanāyamānas tad|darśanāya parivavrāj' Ôjjayinīm. bhārgavo nāma bhūtvā bhikṣā|nibhena tad|gṛhaṃ praviśya tāṃ dadarśa. dṛṣṭvā c' âtyārūḍha|manmatho nirgatya paura|mukhyebhyaḥ śmaśāna|rakṣām ayācata. alabhata ca. tatra labdhaiś ca śav'|âvaguṇṭhana|paṭ'|ādibhiḥ kām apy Arhantikāṃ nāma śramaṇikām upāsāṃ cakre.

Tan|mukhena ca Nitambavatīm upāṃśu mantrayām āsa. sā c' âināṃ nirbhartsayantī pratyācacakṣe. śramaṇikā|mukhāc ca duṣkara|śīla|bhraṃśāṃ kula|striyam upalabhya rahasi dūtikām aśikṣayat:

II.165 «Bhūyo 'py upatiṣṭha sārthavāha|bhāryām! brūhi c' ôpahvare:

piercing confidence. Yet her husband is not absent abroad, because one does not see the signs of separation such as wearing her hair in a single plait. And the mark is on her right side.

Thus I can deduce that she whom you have so skillfully depicted true to life must be a married woman, housewife to some aged merchant past his most virile, causing her to suffer the deprivation of the physical pleasures she deserves."

The painter congratulated him and elaborated:

"You are right. She is the wife of the caravan-leader Anán- 11.162
ta·kirti in Avánti·puri in Ujjáyini. Her name is Nitámbavati, 'Great hips,' and she deserves it. Amazed at her beauty, I painted her just as you see."

Out of his mind to see her, Kálaha·kántaka set off that same moment for Ujjáyini. In the guise of an astrologer fortune-teller he entered her house ostensibly for alms, and saw her. The vision only aggravated his intoxicating love. He exited and went to apply to the leading citizens for employment as caretaker of the charnel-ground. They appointed him. There he collected the cloths used to wrap corpses. With them he won over a wandering Buddhist nun called Arhántika, "Deserving."*

She acted as go-between for him to Nitámbavati. But the housewife rebuked and rebutted her. The nun explained that it is nearly impossible to corrupt the morals of a woman of good breeding, so he gave his messenger fresh secret instructions:

"Go one more time to the caravan-leader's wife. When 11.165
you are alone together, tell her:

‹Saṃsāra|doṣa|darśanāt samādhim āsthāya mumukṣamāṇo mādṛśo janaḥ kula|vadhūnāṃ śīla|pātane ghaṭata iti kva ghaṭate. etad api tvam atyudārayā samṛddhyā rūpeṇ' âti|mānuṣeṇa prathamena vayas" ôpapannāṃ kim itara|nārī|su|labhaṃ cāpalaṃ spṛṣṭaṃ na v" êti parīkṣā kṛtā. tuṣṭā asmi tav' âivam a|duṣṭa|bhāvatayā.

Tvām idānīm utpann'|âpatyāṃ draṣṭum icchāmi. bhartā tu bhavatyāḥ kena cid graheṇ' âdhiṣṭhitaḥ pāṇḍu|roga|durbalo bhoge c' â|samarthaḥ sthito 'bhūt. na ca śakyaṃ tasya vighnam a|pratikṛty' âpatyam asmāl labdhum. ataḥ prasīda!

11.168 Vṛkṣa|vāṭikām ekākinī praviśya mad|upanītasya kasya cin mantra|vādinaś channam eva haste caraṇam arpayitvā tad|abhimantritena praṇaya|kupitā nāma bhūtvā bhartāram urasi prahartum arhasi. upary asāv uttama|dhātu|puṣṭim ūrjit'|âpaty'|ôtpādana|kṣamām āsādayiṣyati. anuvartiṣyate devīm iv' âtrabhavatīm. n' âtra śaṅkā kāry" êti.›

Sā tath" ôktā vyaktam abhyupaiṣyati. naktaṃ māṃ vṛkṣa|vāṭikāṃ praveśya tām api praveśayiṣyasi. tāvat" âiva tvay" âham anugṛhīto bhaveyam iti.»

Sā tath" âiv' ôpapāditavatī. so 'tiprītas tasyām eva kṣapāyāṃ vṛkṣa|vāṭikāṃ gato Nitambavatīṃ nirgranthikā|prayatnen' ôpanītāṃ pāde parāmṛśann iva hema|nūpuram ekam

'I have seen for what they are the evils of *samsára*, the cycle of birth, death and rebirth. Ever since, I practice meditation in the hope of attaining liberation. Why on earth would someone like me wish to corrupt a noblewoman's morals? You are endowed with such a vast fortune, otherworldly beauty and the beginnings of youth. I was in fact testing you to find out whether or not you too are touched by the fickleness so common among other women. I am delighted that no aspersions have been cast on your character.

Now I would like to see you beget offspring. But my lady's husband is under the influence of a malignant star, feeble with jaundice and clearly incapable of consummating the union. Until we have remedied that obstacle of his, you will be unable to have children by him. Therefore, please do as I say.

Go unaccompanied to the garden grove. I will lead there a 11.168
magician. Discreetly place your foot in his hand. He will put a charm on it. Then you only have to strike your husband on the chest with it in a fit of simulated lover's pique. Thereupon his precious bodily fluids will be so replenished that he will be fit to procreate mighty offspring. He will worship your ladyship like a goddess. Do not have any doubt in this matter.'

Obviously she will say yes and agree. Lead me tonight to the garden grove and then bring her there also. If you would just do me this one favor."

The nun performed exactly as instructed. Beside himself with joy, Kálaha·kántaka went that same night to the garden grove. The passionless nun had with great difficulty managed to bring Nitámbavati there. He pretended to stroke

ākṣipya cchurikay" ūru|mūle kiñcid ālikhya drutataram apāsarat.

II.171 Sā tu sāndra|trāsā svam eva durnayaṃ garhamāṇā jighāṃsant" îva śramaṇikāṃ tad vraṇaṃ bhavana|dīrghikāyāṃ prakṣālya dattvā paṭa|bandhanaṃ sāmay'|âpadeśād aparaṃ c' âpanīya nūpuraṃ śayana|parā tri|caturāṇi dināny ek'|ânte ninye.

Sa dhūrtaḥ ‹vikreṣya iti› tena nūpureṇa tam Anantakīrtim upāsasāda. sa dṛṣṭvā:

«Mama gṛhiṇyā ev' âiṣa nūpuraḥ, katham ayam upalabdhas tvay" êti?»

II.174 tam a|bruvāṇaṃ nirbandhena papraccha. sa tu:

«Vaṇig|grāmasy' âgre vakṣyām' îti.»

sthito 'bhūt. punar asau gṛhiṇyai:

II.177 «Sva|nūpura|yugalaṃ preṣay' êti!»

sandideśa. sā ca sa|lajjaṃ sa|sādhvasaṃ ca:

«Adya rātrau viśrāma|praviṣṭāyāṃ vṛkṣa|vāṭikāyāṃ prabhraṣṭo mam' âikaḥ praśithila|bandho nūpuraḥ. so 'dy' âpy anviṣṭo na dṛṣṭaḥ. sa punar ayaṃ dvitīya iti.»

II.180 aparaṃ prāhiṇot. anayā ca vārtay" âmuṃ puraskṛtya sa vaṇig vaṇig|jana|samājam ājagāma. sa c' ânuyukto dhūrtaḥ sa|vinayam āvedayat:

her foot but snatched off one gold anklet, and then cut a small mark with his dagger at the root of her thigh, before fleeing at a run.

Nitámbavati was absolutely terrified. Blaming her own 11.171
bad judgment, she would have liked to murder the nun. She cleaned the wound at the long lake by her house, bound it with a cloth bandage, and, pretending to be ill, she removed the other anklet before taking to her bed, where she spent three or four days in isolation.

Meanwhile, the rogue approached Anánta·kirti with the offer to sell the anklet. On seeing it, he asked forcefully:

"This anklet belongs to none other than my wife. How did you get hold of this?"

But Kálaha·kántaka stood his ground, refusing to answer, 11.174
insisting:

"I will only explain before the guild of merchants."

Then Anánta·kirti sent word to his wife:

"Send your pair of anklets." 11.177

With shame and fear she submitted only one of the two, with the excuse:

"Just last night I lost one anklet when I had gone to the garden grove to relax. The fastening was loose. Although we searched for it today we could not find it. Here though is the other one."

At this news the merchant followed the young man to 11.180
the assembly of merchants. There the scoundrel responded demurely to the questioning:

«Viditam eva khalu vo yath" âhaṃ yuṣmad|ājñayā pitṛ|vanam abhirakṣya tad|upajīvī prativasāmi. lubdhāś ca kadā cin mad|darśana|bhīravo niśi daheyur api śavān' îti niśāsv api śmaśānam adhiśaye.

Apare|dyur dagdh'|â|dagdhaṃ mṛtakaṃ citāyāḥ prasabham ākarṣantīṃ śyām'|ākārāṃ nārīm apaśyam. artha|lobhāt tu nigṛhya bhayaṃ sā saṅgṛhītā. śastrikay" ūru|mūle yadṛcchayā kiñcid ullikhitam. eṣa ca nūpuraś caraṇād ākṣiptaḥ. tāvaty eva druta|gatiḥ sā palāyiṣṭa. so 'yam asy' āgamaḥ. paraṃ bhavantaḥ pramāṇam iti.»

11.183 Vimarśe ca tasyāḥ śākinītvam aikamatyena paurāṇām abhimatam āsīt. bhartrā ca parityaktā tasminn eva śmaśāne bahu vilapya pāśen' ôdbadhya martu|kāmā tena dhūrtena naktam agṛhyata. anunītā ca:

«Sundari, tvad|ākār'|ônmāditena mayā tvad|āvarjane bahūn upāyān bhikṣukī|mukhen' ôpanyasya teṣv a|siddheṣu punar ayam upāyo yāvaj|jīvam a|sādhāraṇīkṛtya rantum ācaritaḥ. tat prasīd' ân|anya|śaraṇāy' âsmai dāsa|janāy' êti!»

Muhur muhuś caraṇayor nipatya prayujya sāntva|śatāni tām a|gaty|antarām ātma|vaśyām akarot. tad idam uktam:

11.186 «Duṣkara|sādhanaṃ prajñ" êti.»›

"You all know, of course, how I have been earning my living while I live here by protecting the grove of the ancestors on your command. Even at night I sleep in the charnel-ground, because sometimes misers actually burn their corpses by night lest I should notice and make them pay.

The other day I spotted a dusky lady roughly dragging half-burned human remains from a funeral pyre. Suppressing my fear, hunger for profit prompted me to seize her. I accidentally cut a small mark with my dagger at the root of her thigh, and pulled this anklet from her foot. That was all I could do before she fled at a run. That is how I acquired the anklet. But it is for you sirs to be the final judge."

Upon deliberation the citizens agreed unanimously that 11.183
Nitámbavati was one of Durga's witches.* Repudiated by her husband, she went that night to the same charnel-ground. With a great deal of weeping she fixed up a noose with which to hang herself, when our scoundrel took hold of her. He dissuaded her, saying:

"My beauty, I was maddened by your looks. In order to win you over, I tried everything with the nun as go-between. But when all failed I put this unparalleled plan into action so that I could enjoy you for the rest of my life. Please forgive me, your humble slave without any other salvation."

Prostrating himself again and again at her feet, he employed hundreds of conciliatory words. What choice did she have but to finally succumb. This is the story that prompts me to conclude:

"What is the means to achieve the difficult? Wisdom."' 11.186

Sa c' êdam ākarṇya brahma|rākṣaso mām apūpujat.

Asminn eva kṣaṇe n' âtiprauḍha|puṃnāga|mukula|sthūlāni muktā|phalāni saha salila|bindubhir ambara|talād apatan. ahaṃ tu:

11.189 ‹Kiṃ nv idam? iti›

uccakṣur ālokayan kam api rākṣasaṃ kāñcid aṅganāṃ viceṣṭamāna|gātrām ākarṣantam apaśyam.

‹Katham apaharaty a|kāmām api striyam an|ācāro nairṛta iti?›

11.192 Gagana|gamana|manda|śaktir a|śastraś c' âtapye. sa tu mat|sambandhī brahma|rākṣasaḥ:

‹Tiṣṭha! tiṣṭha pāpa! kv' âpaharas' îti?›

bhartsayann utthāya rākṣasena samasṛjyata. tāṃ tu roṣād an|apekṣ"|âpaviddhām a|mara|vṛkṣa|mañjarīm iv' ântarikṣād āpatantīm unmukha|prasārit'|ôbhaya|karaḥ karābhyām agrahīṣam. upagṛhya ca vepamānāṃ saṃmīlit'|âkṣīṃ mad|aṅga|sparśa|sukhen' ôdbhinna|rom'|âñcāṃ tādṛśīm eva tām an|avatārayann atiṣṭham.

11.195 Tāvat tāv ubhāv api śaila|śṛṅga|bhaṅgaiḥ pādapaiś ca rabhas" ônmūlitair muṣṭi|pāda|prahāraiś ca paras|param akṣapayetām.

Punar aham atimṛduni pulinavati kusuma|lava|lāñchite saras|tīre 'varopya sa|spṛhaṃ nirvarṇayaṃs tāṃ mat|prāṇ'|âika|vallabhāṃ rāja|kanyāṃ Kandukavatīm alakṣyam. sā hi

After the *brahma·rákshasa* had heard my tales he treated me with respect.

Just then, pearls fat as closed white lotus buds fell with drops of water from the sky.* Thinking:

'What is this?' 11.189

I lifted my eyes to look and saw a *rákshasa* dragging a woman, her limbs flailing.

'How dare the wicked demon steal the woman against her wishes?'*

I was mortified to have neither the power to go into the 11.192
sky, nor my sword. But my companion the *brahma·rákshasa* threatened the *rákshasa*:

'Stop! Stop right there, criminal! Where are you taking her?'

And he flew up and started grappling with him. In his rage the other paid not the slightest regard to the woman's safety. She fell from the heavens like a sprig from the celestial tree of the immortals. Facing upward with both arms outstretched, I caught her in my arms. After catching her I stood without putting her down, while she trembled, eyes pressed closed, thrilling with goose bumps all over at the blissful touch of my body.

In the meantime, those two were attacking each other 11.195
with broken-off mountain peaks and violently uprooted trees, and with blows from their fists and feet.

Then I laid the woman down on the extremely soft sandy bank beside the pool, adorned with plucked flowers. Studying her with desire I realized that she was none other than the one true love of my life, Princess Kandukávati. While I

mayā samāśvāsyamānā tiryaṅ mām abhinirūpya jāta|pratyabhijñā sa|karuṇam arodīt. avādīc ca:

‹Nātha, tvad|darśanād upoḍha|rāgā tasmin Kanduk'|ôtsave punaḥ sakhyā Candrasenayā tvat|kathābhir eva samāśvāsit" âsmi. tvaṃ kila samudra|madhye majjitaḥ pāpena mad|bhrātrā Bhīmadhanvanā iti śrutvā sakhī|janaṃ parijanaṃ ca vañcayitvā jīvitaṃ jihāsur ekākinī krīḍā|vanam upāgamam.

11.198 Tatra ca mām acakamata kāma|rūpa eṣa rākṣas'|âdhamaḥ. so 'yaṃ mayā bhītayā avadhūta|prārthanaḥ sphurantīṃ māṃ nigṛhy' âbhyadhāvat. atr' âivam avasito 'bhūt. ahaṃ ca daivāt tav' âiva jīvit'|ēśasya haste patitā. bhadraṃ tav' êti!›

Śrutvā ca tayā sah' âvaruhya nāvam adhyāroham. muktā ca nauḥ prativāta|preritā tām eva Dāmaliptāṃ pratyupātiṣṭhat. avarūḍhāś ca vayam a|śrameṇa.

‹Tanayasya ca tanayāyāś ca nāśād an|any'|âpatyas Tuṅgadhanvā Suhma|patir niṣkalaḥ svayaṃ sa|kalatra eva niṣkalaṅka|Gaṅgā|rodhasy an|aśanen' ôparantuṃ pratiṣṭhate. saha tena martum icchaty an|anya|nātho 'nuraktaḥ paura|vṛddha|loka iti.›

11.201 aśru|mukhīnāṃ prajānām ākrandam aśṛṇuma. ath' âham asmai rājñe yathā|vṛttam ākhyāya tad|apatya|dvayaṃ pratyarpitavān. prītena tena jāmātā kṛto 'smi Dāmalipt'|ēśva-

consoled her she looked at me askance, then with recognition born started lamenting piteously. She explained:

'My lord, as soon as I had seen you at that Festival of the Ball I conceived a passion for you. Later my girlfriend Chandra·sena inspired me further with stories of your exploits. But then I heard that my wicked brother Bhima·dhanvan had drowned you in the middle of the sea. I gave my girlfriends and attendants the slip, and went all alone to the pleasure garden, determined to end my life.

There this shape-shifting vilest of *rákshasas* fell in love 11.198
with me. Terrified, I rejected his petition. He seized me, I struggled, and off we flew. Now here he has lived his last. And destiny arranged for me to fall into your hands, of all people, the lord of my life. Blessings upon you!'

After hearing this, I descended the mountain with her, and we boarded ship. Once set sail, the ship was driven by contrary winds until it neared our own Dama·lipta, where we landed without any trouble. There we heard the population lamenting with tears on their faces:

'The lord of Suhma Tunga·dhanvan is desolate at the loss of both his son and daughter. Nor does he have any other offspring. He and his wife have resolved to starve themselves to death on the bank of the blemishless Ganges.* The senior citizens love him and would have no other lord. They want to die at his side.'

Then I related to this king all that had happened and 11.201
restored to him his two children. Delighted, the Lord of Dama·lipta made me his son-in-law, and his son became my subordinate. I commanded him to give up Chandra·se-

reṇa. tat|putro mad|anujīvī jātaḥ. mad|ājñaptena c' âmunā prāṇavad ujjhitā Candrasenā Kośadāsam abhajat.

Tataś ca Siṃhavarma|sāhāyy'|ârtham atr' āgatya bhartus tava darśan'|ôtsava|sukham anubhavām' îti.»

Śrutvā:

II.204 «Citr" êyaṃ daiva|gatiḥ. avasareṣu puṣkalaḥ puruṣakāra iti!»

abhidhāya bhūyaḥ smit'|âbhiṣikta|danta|cchado Mantragupte harṣ'|ôtphullaṃ cakṣuḥ pātayām āsa devo Rājavāhanaḥ. sa kila kara|kamalena kiñcit saṃvṛt'|ānano lalita|vallabhā|rabhasa|datta|danta|kṣata|vyasana|vihval'|âdhara|maṇir nir|oṣṭhya|varṇam ātma|caritam ācacakṣe:

iti śrī|Daṇḍinaḥ kṛtau
Daśa|kumāra|carite
Mitragupta|caritaṃ
nāma
ṣaṣṭh'|ôcchvāsaḥ.

na, whom he loved like his life. She became Kosha·dasa's wife.

After all that, I had come here to the aid of Simha·varman and now I can enjoy the pleasure of feasting my eyes on you, master."

When Prince Raja·váhana had heard Mitra·gupta's story, he remarked:

"The ways of fate are fantastic! Abundant prowess only 11.204
when it is called for!"

Then, with a smile anointing his lips, the prince let his eyes fall, wide open with pleasure, on Mantra·gupta. That man half covered his face with his lotus-like hands before beginning his own story. For his ruby lips were in an agony of agitation, perforated with bite marks that his beloved had bestowed in her forceful love-play. Hence he was compelled to speak without using the labial lip sounds: *p*, *b* and *m*:*

That is the end of the sixth chapter of
the glorious Dandin's
What Ten Young Men Did.
It is called:
What Mitra·gupta Did.

CHAPTER TWELVE
WHAT MANTRA·GUPTA DID

«RĀJ'|ÂDHIRĀJA|NANDANA, naga|randhra|gatasya te gatiñ jñāsyann ahañ ca gataḥ kadā cit Kaliṅgān. Kaliṅga|nagarasya n' âtyāsanna|saṅsthita|jana|dāha|sthāna|saṅsaktasya kasya cit kāntāra|dharaṇijasy' āstīrṇa|sarasa|kisalaya|saṅstare tale niṣadya nidr"|ālīḍha|dṛṣṭir aśayiṣi.

Galati ca Kālarātri|śikhaṇḍa|jālak'|ândhakāre calita|rakṣasi kṣarita|nīhāre nija|nilaya|nilīna|niḥśeṣa|jane nitānta|śīte niśīthe ghanatara|sāla|śākh'|ântarāla|nirhrādi netra|niṅsinīn nidrān nigṛhvat karṇa|deśaṅ gataṅ:

12.3 ‹Kathaṅ khalen' ânena dagdha|siddhena riraṅsā|kāle nideśan ditsatā jana eṣa rāgeṇ' ân|argalen' ârdita itthaṅ khilīkṛtaḥ? kriyet' âsy' âṇaka|nar'|êndrasya kena cid an|anta|śaktinā siddhy|antarāya iti!›

kiṅkarasya kiṅ|karyāś c' âtikātaraṅ raṭitan. tad ākarṇya:

‹Ka eṣa siddhaḥ? kā ca siddhiḥ? kiñ c' ânena kiṅkareṇa kariṣyata iti?›

12.6 didṛkṣ"|ākrānta|hṛdayaḥ kiṅkara|gatayā diśā kiñ cid antaraṅ gatas taralatara|nar'|âsthi|śakala|racit'|âlaṅkār'|ākrānta|kāyan dahana|dagdha|kāṣṭha|niṣṭh'|âṅgāra|rajaḥ|kṛt'|âṅga|rāgan taḍil|lat"|ākāra|jaṭā|dharaṅ hiraṇya|retasy araṇya|cakr'|ândhakāra|rākṣase kṣaṇa|kṣaṇa|gṛhīta|nān"|êndhana|grāsa|cañcad|arciṣi dakṣiṇ'|êtareṇa kareṇa tila|siddh'|ârthak'|ā-

"O DEAR SON OF THE KING OF KINGS, I wanted to learn where you had gone after vanishing into the cave in the solid rock.* Eventually, I reached the Kalíngan country. Not very close to the Kalíngan city was a forest adjacent to the funeral-ground. At the foot of a large tree I took a seat on a covering of scattered succulent shoots. I lay down, eyes sealed, no longer awake.

In the intensely cold dead of the night, darkness oozed a thick net like Kala·ratri's hairlocks,* fiends were stalking, fog had started to flow and every last soul was safely settled down in their own residences. Then through the dense interior of sal foliage I heard a sound that woke rest-kissed eyes. It was the dreadfully distressed cry of a servant and his wife:

'Why does this accursed villainous sorcerer want to give 12.3
us an order at the very instant we want to enjoy with one another? He thwarts us exactly when we are afflicted with unrestrained lust. If only one with infinite skill could end this worthless quack's tricks!'

Hearing this, I was filled with a heartfelt desire to discover:

'Who is this sorcerer? What are his tricks? And what is it that this servant has to do?'

Following a short distance in the direction the servant 12.6
had taken, I saw the sorcerer. He was totally covered with extraordinarily shiny decorations constructed of slivers of skeleton. Anointed with ash, ground to dust out of the wood incinerated in funeral fires, he wore dreadlocks that looked like flashes of lightning. With his sinister hand, not his right, he was scattering into the golden-seeded fire tiny efficacious oil-seeds,* which crackled incessantly. The fire

dīn nirantara|caṭacaṭāyitān ākirantaṅ kañ cid adrākṣan. tasy' âgre sa kṛt'|âñjaliḥ kiṅkaraḥ»

‹Kiṅ karaṇīyan, dīyatān nideśa iti!›

atiṣṭhat. ādiṣṭaś c' âyan ten' âti|nikṛṣṭ'|āśayena:

12.9 ‹Gaccha Kaliṅga|rājasya Kardanasya kanyāṅ Kanakalekhāṅ kanyā|gṛhād ih' ānay' êti!›

Sa ca tath" âkārṣīt. tataś ca tān trāsen' â|laghīyas" âsra|jarjareṇa ca kaṇṭhena raṇa|raṇik"|āgṛhītena ca hṛdayena:

‹Hā tāta! hā janan' îti!›

12.12 krandantīṅ kīrṇa|glāna|śekhara|sraji śīrṇa|nahane śirasijānāṅ sañcaye nigṛhy' âsinā śilā|śitena śiraś cikartiṣay" âceṣṭata. jhaṭiti c' ācchidya tasya hastāt tāṅ śastrikān tayā nikṛtya tac|chiraḥ sa|jaṭā|jālan nikaṭasthasya kasya cij jīrṇa|sālasya skandha|randhre nyadhiṣi. tan nidhyāya hṛṣṭataraḥ sa rākṣasaḥ kṣīṇ'|âdhir akathayat:

‹Ārya, kadaryasy' âsya kadarthanān na kadā cin nidr" āyāti netre. tarjayati trāsayati c' âkṛtye c' ājñān dadāti. tad atra kalyāṇa|rāśinā sādhīyaḥ kṛtaṅ yad eṣa nara|kākaḥ kāraṇānān nārakīṇāṅ rasa|jñānāya nītaḥ śīt'|êtara|dīdhiti|dehajasya nagaran. tad atra dayā|nidher an|anta|tejasas te 'yañ janaḥ kāñ cid ājñāñ cikīrṣati. ādiśa! alaṅ kāla|haraṇen' êti!›

Anaṅsīt. ādiśañ ca taṅ:

was the fiend of the jungle zone's darkness. Receiving various fuels as food, it ceaselessly licked its tongues of fire. In front of the scorcerer stood the servant, his hands folded in salutation:

'What would you like done? Give the order!'

To which that overly vile character ordered:

'Go forth and fetch Kánaka·lekha, the daughter of Kár- 12.9
dana, king of Kalínga, out of her ladies' quarters.'

The servant did exactly that. Not a little afraid, tears shattering her voice and anxiety invading her heart, the girl cried out:

'Oh, Daddy! Oh, Lady, source of your daughter's life!'*

The sorcerer seized her stack of hair, its tie torn and the 12.12
garland decoration scattered and wilted. With his sword whetted on a stone he lunged to cut off her head. Instantly I snatched the sword out of his hand and with it severed his own head, and the tangled dreadlocks attached. I stashed it in the hollow of an adjacent ancient sal tree trunk.* The *rákshasa* gazed on the event with great delight, his anguish extinguished, and announced:

'Good sir, this nasty tyrant's harassing denied our eyes any rest ever. He harried and terrified and ordered us to do dreadful deeds. In your vast goodness you have done a truly great thing here in sending this crow of a guy to taste the flavors of infernal agonies in the city of Death, the hot-rayed sun's son. Henceforward I would like to carry out what you order, treasury of kindness, of infinite glory. Give your orders! Enough delay!'

He genuflected. I gave the instructions he had requested:

12.15 ‹Sakhe, s" âiṣā saj|jan'|ācaritā saraṇir yad aṇīyasi kāraṇe 'n|aṇīyān ādaraḥ sandṛśyate. na ced idan n' êcchasi s" êyaṅ sannat'|âṅga|yaṣṭir a|kleś'|ârhā saty anen' â|kṛtya|kāriṇ" âtyarthaṅ kleśitā tan nay' âinān nija|nilayan n' ânyad itaḥ kiñ cid asti citt'|ārādhanan na iti.›

Atha tad ākarṇya karṇa|śekhara|nīla|nīraj'|āyitān dhīra-tara|tārakān dṛśan tiryak kiñ cid añcitāṅ sañcārayantī, sali-la|cara|ketana|śar'|āsan'|ānatāñ cillikā|latāl̄ lalāṭa|raṅga|stha-lī|nartakīl̄ līl"|âlasāl̄ lāsayantī, kaṇṭakita|rakta|gaṇḍa|lekhā rāga|lajj"|ântarāla|cāriṇī caraṇ'|âgreṇa tiraścīna|nakh'|ârciś| candrikeṇa dharaṇī|talaṅ sācīkṛt'|ānana|sarasijal̄ likhantī; danta|cchada|kisalaya|laṅghinā harṣ'|âsra|salila|dhārā|śīka-ra|kaṇa|jāla|kleditasya stana|taṭa|candanasy' ârdratān nira-syat" āsy'|ântarāla|niḥsṛtena tanīyas" ânilena hṛdaya|lakṣya| dalana|dakṣa|Rati|sahacara|śara|syadāyitena taraṅgita|daśana| candrikāṇi kānicid etāny akṣarāṇi kala|kaṇṭhī|kalāny asṛjat:

12.18 ‹Ārya, kena kāraṇen' âinan dāsa|janaṅ kāla|hastād ācchidy' ân|antaraṅ rāg'|ânila|cālita|raṇa|raṇikā|taraṅgiṇy Anaṅga|sā-gare kirasi? yathā te caraṇa|sarasija|rajaḥ|kaṇikā tath" âhañ cintanīyā. yady asti dayā te 'tra jane an|anya|sādhāraṇaḥ karaṇīyaḥ sa eṣa caraṇ'|ārādhana|kriyāyāṅ.

'Friend, this is the traditional conduct of the good, to return a tiny favor with such significant honor. Unless you do not wish it, would you return this virtuous lady, slender and curvaceous, to her own house. She who does not in the least deserve to suffer has suffered inordinately at the hands of this doer of dreadful deeds. Nothing would satisfy our heart further.'* 12.15

When she heard this, Kánaka·lekha rolled her slightly contracted eyes sideways, their central stars ever so steady, lovely as the dusky indigo lotuses adorning her ears.* With wanton grace she caused the cricket lines of hair over her eyes* to dance on her forehead's high stage, arched like the arrow-shooter of fish-flagged Love. The down thrilled on her reddened cheeks and she felt alternating lust and shyness. She turned her lotus-face away, and with her toes she drew signs on the surface of the earth, lunar rays glancing off her toenails.

She uttered the following few words, sweet as the croak of the sweet-voiced cuckoo. Doing so, the faint gentle gusts released within her throat caused her teeth to radiate floods of lunar light. The wind also dried the sandal on her heaving chest, wetted under the fine drizzling flow of her tears of joy. The gusts were winged with the swiftness of the shafts of Delight's lover, Love, skilled at shattering hearts.

'Gentle sir, why did you snatch your slave girl out of 12.18
death's clutches only to cast her at once into invisible Love's ocean, where the wind of lust drives waves of dreadful desire? I would like to count for less to you than the dust on your lotus-feet. If you feel anything for the one in front of you, then grant her the exclusive favor of dedication to your feet.

Yadi ca kany"|āgār'|âdhyāsane rahasya|kṣaraṇād an|artha āśaṅkyeta, n' âitad asti. raktatarā hi nas tatra sakhyaś ceṭyaś ca. yathā na kaścid etaj jñāsyati, tathā yatiṣyanta iti.›

Sa c' âhan Dehajen' ā|karṇ'|ākṛṣṭa|sāyak'|āsanena cetasy ati|nirdayan tāḍitas tat|kaṭ'|âkṣa|kāl'|āyasa|nigaḍa|gāḍha|saṅyataḥ kiṅkar'|ānana|nihita|dṛṣṭir agādiṣaṅ:

12.21 ‹Yath" êyaṅ ratha|caraṇa|jaghanā kathayati tathā cen n' ācareyan nayeta nakra|ketanaḥ kṣaṇen' âiken' â|kīrtanīyān daśāñ. janañ c' âinaṅ saha nay' ânayā kanyayā kanyā|gṛhaṅ hariṇa|nayanay" êti.›

Nītaś c' âhan niśā|careṇa śārada|jaladhara|jāla|kānti kanyakā|niketanan. tatra ca kāñ cit kāla|kalāñ candr'|ānanā|nideśāc candra|śāl'|âika|deśe tad|darśana|calita|dhṛtir atiṣṭhaṅ.

Sā ca sva|cchandaṅ śayānāḥ kara|tal'|ālasa|saṅghaṭṭan'|âpanīta|nidrāḥ kāścid adhigat'|ârthāḥ sakhīr akārṣīt. ath' āgatya tāś caraṇa|nihita|śirasaḥ kṣarad|asra|karālit'|ēkṣaṇā nija|śekhara|kesar'|âgra|sal̄lagna|ṣaṭ|caraṇa|gaṇa|raṇita|saṅśayita|kala|giraḥ śanair akathayan:

12.24 ‹Ārya, yad aty|āditya|tejasas ta eṣā nayana|lakṣyatāṅ gatā tataḥ kṛt'|ântena na gṛhītā. dattā c' êyañ Cittajena garīyasā sākṣīkṛtya rāg'|ânalan. tad anen' āścarya|ratnena nalin'|âkṣa-

In case you fear disaster lest the secret that you dwell in the ladies' quarters should trickle out, know that this cannot occur. For there I have girlfriends and servants who are totally faithful. They will ensure that no one shall discover our secret.'

So there I was, with a heart that was a sitting target for cruel Love's arrow-shooter that he had drawn all the way to his ears, as well as caught fast in the iron chains of her dark slanting eyes. Staring fixedly at the servant's face I said:

'If I do not act just as this gorgeous one with thighs like 12.21
chariot wheels wants, then alligator-flagged Love will in a second take her where no word can ever reach.* Therefore I shall go with this deer-eyed girl when you lead her to her ladies' quarters.'

I followed the night-stalker to the king's daughter's residence. It was as glorious as a range of white clouds after the rainy season. On the lunar-faced girl's order I stayed a short while in roof-terrace quarters, all steadiness lost since the sight of her.

She, however, roused several of her soundly drowsing girlfriends with a lazy shake of her hand, and they learned our situation. They then drew close, touching their heads at your narrator's feet,* eyes wide with flowing tears. Their soft sweet voices were at risk of confusion with the soft noise of flocks of six-footed honey-creators* clinging to the flowers' crests on their garland crowns, when they said:

'Gentle sir, your glory is greater than that of the sun. 12.24
Thanks to you laying your eyes on our friend, death could not take her. In his role as guardian, Love, whose nativity is in fancy, has given her to you with the fire of desire as

sya te ratna|śaila|śilā|tala|sthiraṁ rāga|taralen' ālaṅkriyatāṁ hṛdayan. tad asyāś carit'|ârthaṁ stana|taṭaṁ gāḍh'|āliṅganaiḥ sadṛśatarasya sahacarasy' êti.›

Tataḥ sakhī|janen' âti|dakṣiṇena dṛḍhatarīkṛta|sneha|nigalas tayā sannat'|âṅgyā saṅgaty' âraṁsi.

Atha kadā cid āyāsita|jāyā|rahita|cetasi lālas'|âli|laṅghana|glāna|ghana|kesare rājad|araṇya|sthalī|lalāṭa|līlāyita|tilake lalit'|Ânaṅga|rāj'|âṅgīkṛta|nirnidra|karṇikāra|kāñcana|cchatre dakṣiṇa|dahana|sārathi|ray'|āhṛta|sahakāra|cañcarīka|kalike kāl'|âṇḍaja|kaṇṭha|rāga|rakta|rakt'|âdharā|rati|raṇ'|âgra|sannāha|śālini śālīna|kanyak"|ântaḥkaraṇa|saṅkrānta|rāga|laṅghita|lajje Dardura|giri|taṭa|candan'|āśleṣa|śītal'|ânil'|ācārya|datta|nānā|latā|nṛtta|līle kāle;

12.27 Kaliṅga|rājaḥ sah' âṅganā|janena saha ca tanayayā sakalena ca nagara|janena daśa trīṇi ca dināni dinakara|kiraṇa|jāl'|â|laṅghanīye raṇad|ali|saṅgha|laṅghita|nata|lat"|âgra|kisalay'|ālīḍha|saikata|taṭe tarala|taraṅga|śīkar'|āsāra|saṅga|śītale sāgara|tīra|kānane krīḍā|rasa|jāt'|āsaktir āsīt.

witness. Your eyes are lotus flowers, yet your heart is as hard as the rock-face of the rocky jewel at the center of the world.* Let it wear now the decoration that is this wonderful jewel glittering with red desire.* Thus her heaving chest will have found its raison d'être in close clinches with a really worthy other half.'

Exceedingly courtly, her girlfriends had tightened the chains of our love. Thereafter I delighted in togetherness with that curvaceous lady.

Then arrived the season that tortures travelers' hearts, their wives far away. The dense *késara* flower sinks under the assault of hungry honey-creators. The *tílaka* graces the forehead of glowing forestland. The lovely Love king uses the wide-awake *karni·kara* as his golden sunshade. Then the southern wind, charioteer of fire, fetches large dark honey-creators to the still closed flowers on the tree of that favorite golden-skinned juicy Indian fruit.* The calls of dark-egged cuckoos engender lust in gorgeous red-kissered* ladies, thus excellently fitted out for the joust of erotic delight. Desire transcends shyness as the instinct of retiring girls. Cool with the touch of sandal since it was in the skirts of the Dárdura crag, the wind teaches various dangling greenery to dance with grace.*

The king of Kalínga had acquired a fondness for the flavor 12.27
of recreation, hence in that season he went to stay thirteen days in a seashore grove, together with his ladies and his daughter and all the townsfolk. Radiating sun rays could not violate the forest. The sandy shore was licked with foliage shoots weighed down with noisy honey-creators on

Atha santata|gīta|saṅgīta|saṅgat'|âṅganā|sahasra|śṛṅgāra|helā|nir|argal'|Ânaṅga saṅgharṣa|harṣitaś ca rāga|tṛṣṇ'|âika|tantras tatra randhre Āndhra|nāthena Jayasiṅhena salila|taraṇa|sādhan'|ānīten' ân|eka|saṅkhyen' ânīkena drāg āgaty' âgṛhyata sa|kalatraḥ.

Sā c' ânīyata trāsa|taral'|âkṣī dayitā naḥ saha sakhī|janena Kanakalekhā. tad" âhan dāhen' Ânaṅga|dahana|janiten' ântarit'|āhāra|cintaś cintayan dayitāṅ galita|gātra|kāntir ity atarkayaṅ:

12.30 ‹Gatā sā Kaliṅga|rāja|tanayā janitrā janayitryā ca sah' âri|hastan. nirasta|dhair yaś ca tāṅ sa rājā niyataṅ sañjighṛkṣet. tad|a|sahā ca sā satī gara|ras'|ādinā sadyaḥ santiṣṭheta. tasyāñ ca tādṛśīn daśāṅ gatāyāñ janasy' âsy' Ân|anyajena hanyeta śarīra|dhāraṇā. sā kā syād gatir iti.›

Atr' ântara Āndhra|nagarād āgacchann agra|jaḥ kaś cid aikṣyata. tena c' êyaṅ kathā kathitā:

‹Yathā kila Jayasiṅhen' ân|eka|nikāra|datta|saṅgharṣeṇa jighāṅsitaḥ sa Kardanaḥ Kanakalekhā|darśan'|âidhitena rāgeṇ' ârakṣyata. sā ca dārikā yakṣeṇa kena cid adhiṣṭhitā na tiṣṭhaty agre nar'|ântarasya nar'|êndrasya ca. āyasyati ca nar'|êndra|sārtha|saṅgrahaṇena tan nirākariṣyan nar'|êndro na c' âsti siddhir iti.›

the attack. Crashing waves granted drenching drizzle and the sensation of cool.

The king's sole concern was his thirst for desire. He delighted in the rivalry of his thousand ladies for wanton erotic delights, united in continuous song and concert. At this hour of weakness, Jaya·singha,* Lord of Andhra, suddenly attacked with a vast force of soldiers, conveyed in seafaring vessels. The king and his household were seized.

Eyes aquiver in fear, our darling Kánaka·lekha was also taken, together with her girlfriends. Thenceforward I lost all interest in food. Thinking only of her, on fire with hot Love—the god long ago incinerated in Shiva's glare—and utterly lusterless to look at, I reflected:

'Together with her father and his wife, the Kalíngan king's 12.30
daughter has fallen into the hands of his foe. That king is sure to lose his head and want to lay his hands on her. She will not tolerate that, and in her virtue would at once kill herself, with a deadly drink or otherwise. With her lost, Love will not allow that I should live on. How will it all end?'

At that very juncture I caught sight of a high-caste fellow who had left the Andhran city. He told the following tale:

'Jaya·singha was furious at all the insults he had received. He was all set to kill Kárdana. However, seeing Kánaka·lekha kindled his desire, and so Kárdana is saved. The daughter, on the other hand, is under the influence of a *yaksha*, and will stand in front of no one, not even the king. A host of savants are assisting the king in his efforts to exorcise the *yaksha*, so far without success.'*

12.33 Tena c' âhan darśit'|āśaḥ Śaṅkara|nṛtta|deśa|jātasya jarat|sālasya skandha|randhr'|ântar|jaṭā|jālan niṣkṛṣya tena jaṭilatāṅ gataḥ kanthā|cīra|sañcay'|ântarita|sakala|gātraḥ kāṅś cic chiṣyān agrahīṣan. tāṅś ca nān"|āścarya|kriy"|âtisaṅhitāj janād ākṛṣṭ'|ânna|cel'|ādi|tyāgān nitya|hṛṣṭān akārṣaṅ. ayāsiṣañ ca dinaiḥ kaiścid Āndhra|nagaran.

Tasya n' âtyāsanne salila|rāśi|sadṛśasya kala|haṅsa|gaṇa|dalita|nalina|dala|saṅhati|galita|kiñjalka|śakala|śārasya sārasa|śreṇi|śekharasya sarasas tīra|kānane kṛta|niketanaḥ sthitaḥ. śiṣya|jana|kathita|citra|ceṣṭ"|ākṛṣṭa|sakala|nāgara|jan'|âbhisandhāna|dakṣaḥ san diśi diś' îty akīrtye janena:

‹Ya eṣa jarad|araṇya|sthalī|saras|tīre sthaṇḍila|śāyī yatis tasya kila sakalāni sa|rahasyāni sa|ṣaḍ|aṅgāni ca cchandāṅsi rasan'|âgre sannihitāni, anyāni ca śāstrāṇi. yena yāni na jñāyante sa teṣān tat|sakāśād artha|nirṇayaṅ kariṣyati. a|satyen' âsya n' āsyaṅ saṅsṛjyate. sa|śarīraś c' âiṣa dayā|rāśiḥ. etat|saṅgraheṇ' âdya cirañ carit'|ârthā dīkṣā.

12.36 Tac|caraṇa|rajaḥ|kaṇaiḥ kaiś|cana śirasi kīrṇair an|ekasy' ân|eka ātaṅkaś cirañ cikitsakair a|saṅhāryaḥ saṅhṛtaḥ. tad|aṅghri|kṣālana|salila|sekair niṣkalaṅka|śirasān naśyanti

In his words I was shown a new chance. I retrieved the tangled dreadlocks I had stashed within the old sal tree trunk growing in the charnel-ground, the site of Shánkara Shiva's dance, and therewith turned into a dreadlocked ascetic sadhu. Dressed in a hoard of rags and a tattered cloth, I was thoroughly disguised. Next I recruited a circle of devoted students. I ensured their constant contentedness with the offerings of food, clothes and so on that I extorted locally, having taken everyone in through a variety of wonderful tricks. After a few days I set out for the Andhran city. 12.33

Neither too close nor too far away, I halted and settled into residence in a lakeside grove. The lake held an ocean of water, dotted with fallen lotus-leaf offcuts, left over after flocks of royal swans have shredded thousands of lotus shoots, and crowned with flocks of cranes. The students I had gathered attracted all the townsfolk with talk of the wonders I had done. Their clever cheat, I was the talk of every quarter:

'This renunciant who lies down on the altar in the ancient lakeside forest ground, he is said to know inside out* all the Vedas with their secrets and the six accessory works, as well as the other sciences. So if there is anything you do not understand, he can deliver clarity. Never has an untruth sullied his tongue. He is infinite kindness incarnate. Religious consecration, *diksha*, is fulfilled at last thanks to his favor.

Countless sicknesses of countless sufferers that doctors have long failed to cure are cured. You need only scatter a few grains of the dust of his feet on the head. If you anoint stainless heads with his used foot-water it will destroy 12.36

kṣaṇen' âiken' âkhila|nar'|êndra|yantra|laṅghinaś caṇḍa|tā-rā|grahāḥ. na tasya śakyaṅ śakter iyattā|jñānan. na c' âsy' âhaṅkāra|kaṇik" êti.›

Sā c' êyaṅ kath" ân|eka|jan'|āsya|sañcāriṇī tasya Kanakalekh"|âdhiṣṭhāna|dhanad'|ājñākara|nirākriyā|sakta|cetasaḥ kṣatriyasy' ākarṣaṇāy' âśakat. sa c' âhar ahar āgaty' ādareṇ' âtigarīyas" ârcayann arthaiś ca śiṣyān saṅgṛhṇann adhigata|kṣaṇaḥ kadā cit kāṅkṣit'|ârtha|sādhanāya śanair ayāciṣṭa.

Dhyāna|dhīraḥ sthāna|darśita|jñāna|sannidhiś c' âinan nirīkṣya nicāyy' âkathayan:

12.39 ‹Tāta, sthāna eṣa hi yatnaḥ. tasya hi kanyā|ratnasya sakala|kalyāṇa|lakṣaṇ'|âika|rāśer adhigatiḥ kṣīra|sāgara|raśan"|âlaṅkṛtāyāḥ Gaṅg"|ādi|nadī|sahasra|hāra|yaṣṭi|rājitāyā Dhar"|âṅganāyā ev' āsādanāya sādhanan.

Na ca sa yakṣas tad|adhiṣṭhāyī kena cin nar'|êndreṇa tasyā līl"|âñcita|nīla|nīraja|darśanāyā darśanaṅ sahate. tad atra sahyatān trīṇy ahāni yair ahaṅ yatiṣye 'ryasy' âsya sādhanāy' êti.›

Yath"|ādiṣṭe ca hṛṣṭe kṣit'|īśe gate niśi nir|niśākar'|ârciṣi nīrandhr'|ândhakāra|kaṇa|nikara|nigīrṇa|daśa|diśi nidrā|nigaḍita|nikhila|jana|dṛśi nirgatya jala|tala|nilīna|gāhanīyan

in an instant the dread influence of disastrous stars* and constellations that have defeated doctors' every conjuring contrivance. His faculties defy definition. Nor is he in the least egotistical.'

This story travelled the tongues of no few citizens until it could finally attract the kshatriya king whose heart was set on exorcising the god of wealth's* *yaksha* servant who had taken control of Kánaka·lekha. Every day he visited, and I was treated with ever so serious honor. He also won the students over with gifts. When he felt the occasion had arrived, he quietly entreated for the realization of his heart's desire.

Lost in religious reflection that revealed how close was the relevant knowledge, I stared at his face until I was sure, and then said:

'Child, your effort is right and good. For in winning this 12.39
jewel of a girl, unique collocation of all lucky features, you will in fact also win the fair Lady Earth herself, adorned with the white sea of stars in the sky as her girdle,* and radiant with a necklace of a thousand rivers, starting with the Ganges.

Nevertheless, the *yaksha* who controls her will allow no king to see her whose gracefully contracted eyes are indigo as dusky lotuses. You should therefore wait for three days, within which I shall endeavor to get your good self what you want.'

The Lord of the Earth was delighted. Off he went as ordered. That night the night's sun shed no light, the ten directions were swallowed in unending grains of dense darkness and everyone's eyes were sealed in rest when I went out.

nīrandhraṁ kṛcchrā|cchidrīkṛt'|ântarālan tad ekataḥ saras|taṭan tīrtha|sannikṛṣṭaṁ kena cit khanana|sādhanen' âkārṣaṁ. ghana|śil"|êṣṭik"|ācchanna|chidr'|ānanan tat|saras|tīra|deśaṁ janair a|śaṅkanīyan niścitya;

12.42 din'|ādi|snāna|nirṇikta|gātraś ca nakṣatra|santāna|hāra|yaṣṭy|agra|grathita|ratnaṁ kṣaṇad'|ândhakāra|gandha|hasti|dāraṇ'|âika|kesariṇaṁ kanaka|śaila|śṛṅga|raṅga|lāsya|līlā|naṭaṁ gagana|sāgara|*ghana*|taraṅga|rāji|laṅghan'|âika|nakraṁ kāry'|â|kārya|sākṣiṇaṁ sahasr'|ârciṣaṁ Sahasr'|âkṣa|dig|aṅgan"|âṅga|rāga|rāgāyita|kiraṇa|jālaṁ rakta|nīraj'|âñjalin" ārādhya nija|niketanan nyaśiśriyaṁ.

Yāte ca dina|traye, asta|giri|śikhara|gairika|taṭa|sādhāraṇa|cchāya|tejasy a|cala|rāja|kanyakā|kadarthanay" ântarikṣ"|ākhyena Śaṅkara|śarīreṇa saṁsṛṣṭāyāḥ Sandhy"|âṅganāyā rakta|candana|carcit'|âika|stana|kalaśa|darśanīye din'|âdhināthe jan'|âdhināthaḥ sa āgatya janasy' âsya dharaṇi|nyasta|caraṇa|nakha|kiraṇa|chādita|kirīṭaḥ kṛt'|âñjalir atiṣṭhat. ādiṣṭaś ca:

Digging with great difficulty, I at last excavated a cavity near the lakeside ford. It was hard to discern, hidden under water where you would have to dive to access it. Afterward I checked that no one could guess at anything untoward around the lakeshore, concealing the hole entrance with a thick cover of stones and rushes.

Then I cleansed thoroughly with the wash that starts the 12.42
day. With handfuls of red lotuses I honored the thousand-rayed sun god, whose radiating rays redden with rouge the lady of the thousand-eyed Indra's East. The sun is the jewel fastened at the center of the necklace of constellations set all in a row.* He is the one and only lion who can tear at the rutting trunked* darkness of the night, the actor dancing gracefully on the stage of the axial rocky elevation's* golden horn, the one and only crocodile that can cross the *dense* range of waves *which are the clouds* in the heavens' ocean, and the witness to all that is done, good and evil. After that I returned to our house.

The three days were over. The overlord of the day was as striking as a golden vase, or as one half of the Dusk lady's attractive chest anointed with red sandal when she was united with Shánkara, incarnate as that called Sky,* in order to torture his wife, the daughter of the king of the high still hills.* Then the overlord of the citizens arrived, and stood with hands folded in salutation, resting his crown on the ground, where it was veiled in the rays of your servant's toenails. He received his instructions:

‹Diṣṭyā! dṛṣṭ" êṣṭa|siddhiḥ. iha jagati hi na nirīhan dehinaṅ śriyaḥ saṅśrayante. śreyāṅsi ca sakalāny analasānāṅ haste nitya|sānnidhyāni. yatas te sādhīyasā sac|cariten' ân|ākalita|kalaṅken' ârciten' âty|ādara|niciten' ākṛṣṭa|cetasā janen' ânena sara idan tathā saṅskṛtaṅ yath" êha te 'dya siddhiḥ syāt.

12.45 Tad etasyān niśi galad|ardhāyāṅ gāhanīyaṅ. gāhan'|ân|antarañ ca salila|tale satata|gatīn antaḥ|sañcāriṇaḥ sannigṛhya yathā|śakti śayyā kāryā. tataś ca taṭa|skhalita|jala|sthagita|jalaja|khaṇḍa|calita|daṇḍa|kaṇṭak'|âgra|dalita|deha|rāja|haṅsa|trāsa|jarjara|rasita|sandatta|karṇasya janasya kṣaṇād ākarṇanīyañ janiṣyate jala|saṅghātasya kiñ cid āraṭitaṅ.

Śānte ca tatra salila|raṭite klinna|gātraḥ kiñ cid ārakta|dṛṣṭir yen' ākāreṇa niryāsyasi nicāyya tan nikhila|jana|netr'|ānanda|kāriṇan na sa yakṣaḥ śakṣyaty agrataḥ sthitaye. sthiratara|nihita|sneha|śṛṅkhalā|nigaḍitañ ca kanyakā|hṛdayaṅ kṣaṇen' âiken' â|sahanīya|darśan'|ântarāyaṅ syāt. asyāś ca Dhar"|âṅganāyā n' âty|ādara|nirākṛt'|âri|cakrañ cakraṅ kara|tala|gatañ cintanīyan. na tatra saṅśayaḥ.

Tac ced icchasy an|eka|śāstra|jñāna|dhīra|dhiṣaṇair adhikṛtair itaraiś ca hit'|aiṣi|gaṇair ākalayya jālika|śatañ c' ānāyya, antaraṅga|nara|śatair yath"|êṣṭa|dṛṣṭ'|ântarālaṅ saraḥ kriyeta.

'Congratulations! I have the vision to achieve what you desire. After all, here in the real world fortune does not favor those who do not strive to achieve her. And every felicity is always within reach of energetic hands. Your excellent good deeds, untainted with stain, honored and filled with great reverence, have attracted this individual's soul. Hence I have consecrated this lake so that here, today, you will find success.

Now, when this very night is half trickled away you are 12.45
to dive into the lake. As soon as you have dived in you should lie as long as you can on the floor underwater, your ever-active inhalation and exhalation held within you. Next, when water rolls crashing against and off the shore, shaking lotus clusters, their stalks' thorns will thrust into the flesh of the royal *hansa.** Terrified, they will utter a wounded cry to catch the ear of anyone listening. Then one will also hear at once the frightening roar of rushing ruffled water.

Once that roar of water has quieted down, you will arise, wet all over, eyes slightly reddened, a joy for everyone to see. Confronted with your new looks, the *yaksha* will not know how to resist you. Instantly locked in chains of love, fixedly set on you, the lady's heart will allow no hindrance to looking at you. You will certainly see the circle of this lady Earth too safe in your hands, the circle of all your foes annihilated without the least effort. These results are guaranteed.

If this is what you want, then consult with your officers, astute indeed, thanks to their learning in various sciences, and with crowds of other well-wishers. Call out one hundred fishers with nets. Together with another hundred servants

rakṣā ca tīrāt triṅśad|daṇḍ'|ântarāle sainika|janena s'|ādaraṅ racanīyā. kas tatra taj jānāti yac chidreṇ' ârayaś cikīrṣant' îti.›

12.48 Tat tasya hṛdayahāri jātan. tad|adhikṛtaiś ca tatra kṛtye randhra|darśan'|â|sahair icchāñ ca rājñaḥ kanyak"|âtirāga|janitān nitānta|niścalān niścity' ârya eṣa na niṣiddhaḥ. tathā|sthitaś ca tad|āsādana|dṛḍhatar'|āśayaś ca sa ākhyāyata:

‹Rājann, atra te jan'|ânte ciraṅ sthitan na c' âikatra cira|sthānan naḥ śastaṅ. kṛta|kṛtyaś ca na iha draṣṭāsi. ‹yasya te rāṣṭre grās'|ādy|āsāditan tasya te kiñ cid an|ācarya kāryāṅ gatir ārya|garhy" êti.› atr' âitac cira|sthānasya kāraṇan. tac c' âdya siddhaṅ.

Gaccha gṛhān! yath"|ârha|jalena hṛdya|gandhena snātaḥ sita|srag|aṅga|rāgaḥ śakti|sadṛśena dānen' ārādhita|dharaṇi|tala|taitila|gaṇas tila|sneha|sikta|yaṣṭy|agra|grathita|vartik"|âgni|śikhā|sahasra|grasta|naiś'|ândhakāra|rāśir āgaty' ârtha|siddhaye yatethā iti.›

12.51 Sa kila kṛtajñatān darśayan:

‹A|siddhir eṣā siddhiḥ, yad a|sannidhir ih' āryāṇāṅ. kaṣṭā c' êyan niḥsaṅgatā yā nir|āgasan dāsa|janan tyājayati. na ca niṣedhanīyā garīyasāṅ gira iti.›

loyal to the death they will dredge the lake interior. Have your forces stay carefully on guard thirty yards* away on shore. For who knows what your foes would not wish to try there, given the chance.'

These words touched his heart. His officers could see no 12.48
holes in the undertaking. Further, they were under no illusions as to how strongly set was the king's wish, founded in his lust for the girl. Hence they did not contradict their lord. Thus he was ready, and resolutely resolved on winning her, when I announced:

'O king, we have stayed long in this region of yours, although it is contraindicated for such as us to stay anywhere long. As soon as your goal is won you will see us here no longer. Honored Aryans* would criticize anyone who has received food and the like in your country yet leaves without having done you any service. That was why we stayed here this long, and today that is achieved.

Go to your house. Wash in sweetly fragrant water fit for a king, wear scented oil and a white garland, and honor all those who are gods on the face of the earth, the highest caste, with offerings that suit your dignity. Tonight you should let a thousand fire-crested torches feed on the dense darkness, their twisted wicks doused in the oil of the tiny oil-rich seed.* And then draw near to win your goal.'

He certainly showed his gratitude: 12.51

'Such success is a failure if your reverence does not stay in the vicinity. Your unselfishness is cursed if it drives you to forsake your innocent servant. Yet who dares contradict the words of the weighty ones?'

Snānāya gṛhān ayāsīt. ahañ ca nirgatya nirjane niśīthe saras|tīra|randhra|nilīnaḥ san|nīṣac|chidra|datta|karṇaḥ sthitaḥ. sthite c' ârdha|rātre kṛta|yath"|ādiṣṭa|kriyaḥ sthāna|sthāna|racita|rakṣaḥ sa rājā jālika|janān ānīya nirākṛt'|ântaḥ|śalyaṅ śaṅkā|hīnaḥ saraḥ|salilaṅ sa|līla|gatir agāhata.

12.54 Gatañ ca kīrṇa|keśaṅ saṅhata|karṇa|nāsaṅ sarasas talaṅ hāstinan nakra|līlayā nīr'|âti|nilīna|yāyī tan tathā|śayānaṅ kandharāyāṅ kanthayā nyagrahīṣaṅ. kharatara|Kāla|daṇḍa|ghaṭṭan'|âticaṇḍaiś ca kara|caraṇa|tal'|āghātair nirdaya|datta|nigrahaḥ kṣaṇen' âiken' âjahāt sa ceṣṭān. tataś c' ākṛṣya tac|charīrañ chidre nidhāya nīrān nirayāsiṣaṅ.

Sadyaḥ|saṅgatānāñ ca sainikānān tad atyacitrīyat' ākār'|ântara|grahaṇaṅ. gaja|skandha|gataḥ sita|cchatr'|ādi|sakala|rāja|cihna|rājitaś caṇḍatara|daṇḍi|daṇḍa|tāḍana|trasta|jana|datt'|ântarālayā rāja|vīthyā yātas tān niśāṅ rasa|nayana|nirasta|nidrā|ratir anaiṣan.

Nīte ca jan'|âkṣi|lakṣyatāl lākṣā|rasa|digdha|dig|gaja|śiraḥ|sadṛkṣe Śakra|dig|aṅganā|ratn'|ādarśe 'rka|cakre kṛta|karaṇīyaḥ kiraṇa|jāla|karāla|ratna|rāji|rājita|rāj'|ârh'|āsan'|ādhyāsī

And off he went to his house to wash. I set out in the deserted night and hid in the hole on the lakeshore, listening through a chink. The king had done everything as instructed, setting guards here and there, and calling fishers with nets. Once they had dredged out anything that ran the risk of introducing danger into the equation, he was free of fear. When half the night was over, the king dived into the lake water with a jaunty gesture.

He reached the ground under the lake, as far down as 12.54
a tusker, his floating hair strewn all around, ears and nose tightly corked. With the stealth of a crocodile I slid totally concealed in the water. Even as he lay there, I lassoed his neck with the ragged cloak I wore.* Then I heartlessly attacked the king with kicks and fists, wild as the rough harsh lashes of the rod of the lord of the Underworld.* In an instant his struggle was over. Dragging his carcass, I stashed it in the hollow, after which I arose out of the water.

At once the soldiers crowded around, filled with wonder that he was externally so very different to look at. Set on the shoulders of the greatest creature in the jungle, I was decorated with all the insignia of royalty, starting with the white sunshade. I travelled the royal highway, cleared of all the citizens frightened of getting a thrashing with the rods of ferocious staff-holders. That entire night, delight allowed the new king's* eyes none of the joy of rest.

The circle of the sun revealed itself to everyone's view like the jewelled looking glass of the Lady of the lordly Indra's eastern direction, and like the head of one of the eight directional tuskers anointed with red lac-juice. Then I undertook the royal dawn duties. Next I ascended the regal

yathā|sadṛś'|ācāra|darśinaḥ śaṅkā|yantrit'|âṅgān sannidhi|niṣādinaḥ sahāyān agādiṣan:

12.57 ‹Dṛśyatāṅ śaktir ārṣī yat tasya yater ajeyasy' êndriyāṇāṅ saṅskāreṇa nīrajasā nīraja|sānnidhya|śālini saharṣ'|ālini sarasi sarasija|dala|sannikāśa|cchāyasy' âdhikatara|darśanīyasy' ākār'|ântarasya siddhir āsīt.

Adya sakala|nāstikānāñ jāyeta lajjā|nataṅ śiraḥ. tad idānīñ Candra|śekhara|Naraka|śāsana|Sarasij'|āsan'|ādīnān tridaś'|ēśānāṅ sthānāny aty|ādara|racita|nṛtya|gīt'|ādy|ārādhanāni kriyantāṅ. hriyantāñ ca gṛhād itaḥ kleśa|nirasana|sahāny arthi|sārthair dhanān' îti.›

Āścarya|ras'|âtireka|hṛṣṭa|dṛṣṭayas te:

12.60 ‹Jaya, jagad|īśa! jayena s'|âtiśayan daśa diśaḥ sthagayan nijena yaśas" ādirāja|yaśāṅs' îti.›

a|sakṛd āśāsy' āracayan yath"|ādiṣṭāḥ kriyāḥ. sa c' âhan dayitāyāḥ sakhīṅ hṛdaya|sthānīyāṅ Śaśāṅkasenāṅ kanyakāṅ kadā cit kāry'|ântarāgatā rahasy ācakṣiṣi:

‹Kaccid ayañ janaḥ kadā cid āsīd dṛṣṭa iti?›

12.63 Atha sā harṣa|kāṣṭhāṅ gatena hṛdayen' ēṣad ālakṣya daśana|dīdhiti|latāḿ līl"|âlasaḿ lāsayantī lalit'|āñcita|kara|śākh'|ân-

throne, glittering with rows of jewels, radiating shocking rays. Hovering in the vicinity, torsos twisted in terror, friends waited on their lord, each carrying out their allotted tasks. I announced:

'See the religious force of the *rishi* saints! The sensual 12.57
world never defeated this renunciate. Thanks to his sin-free* consecration of the lake full of lotuses where the honey-workers are glad, in it I could attain a new look far far lovelier than the old one, with a lotus flower luster.

Today all heretics will have to let their heads fall in disgrace. For with carefully constructed services of song and dance and so on, you are this day to adore in the residences of the thirteen Lords: Shiva with the lunar crescent as his crest; Vishnu Krishna conqueror of Náraka; the Creator who sits on a lotus; and the rest. And hordes of those with nothing should leave this house with the riches that can efface their worries.'

Looking delighted, and feeling overflowing wonder, they cried out again and again:

'Victory to the Lord of the World! Through your victory 12.60
you will fill all the ten directions and with your glory outdo the glory of the first king.'*

And they did as ordered. At a certain juncture I noticed that the lady Shashánka·sena, dearest friend of our wife, had drawn near on a task. Taking her aside I asked:

'Do you recognize your king's current incarnation?'

She cast a little glance toward her interrogator, and her 12.63
heart elevated to the highest ecstasy. Her teeth flashed long elegant rays with languid allure, until she hid her tender soft red shoot-like toothcovers* with gracefully curved fingers.

tarita|danta|chada|kisalayā harṣa|jala|kleda|jarjara|nir|añjan'|ēkṣaṇā racit'|âñjāliḥ:

‹Nitarāñ jāne yadi na syād aindrajālikasya jālaṅ kiñ cid etādṛśaṅ. kathañ c' âitat? kathay' êti!›

sneha|niryantraṇaṅ śanair agādīt. ahañ c' âsyai kārtsnyen' ākhyāya tad|ānana|saṅkrāntena sandeśena sañjanayya saha|caryā nir|atiśayaṅ hṛday'|āhlādan, tataś c' âitayaḥ dayitayā nir|argalīkṛt'|âti|satkṛta|Kaliṅga|nātha|nyāya|dattayā saṅgaty'

12.66 Āndhra|Kaliṅga|rājya|śāsī tasy' âsy' âriṇā lilaṅghayiṣitasy' Âṅga|rājasya sāhāyyakāy' âlaghīyasā sādhanen' āgaty' âtra te sakhi|jana|saṅgatasya yādṛcchika|darśan'|ānanda|rāśi|laṅghita|cetā jāta iti.›

Tasya tat|kauśalaṅ smita|jyotsn'|âbhiṣikta|danta|chadaḥ saha suhṛdbhir abhinandya:

«Citram idaṃ mahā|muner vṛttam. atr' âiva khalu phalitam atikaṣṭaṃ tapaḥ. tiṣṭhatu tāvan narma. harṣa|prakarṣa|spṛśoḥ prajñā|sattvayor dṛṣṭam iha svarūpam. ity» abhidhāya punaḥ:

12.69 «Avataratu bhavān iti.»

bahu|śrute Viśrute vikaca|rājīva|sadṛśaṃ dṛśaṃ cikṣepa devo Rājavāhanaḥ.

iti śrī|Daṇḍinaḥ kṛtau
Daśa|kumāra|carite
Mantragupta|caritaṃ
nāma
saptam'|ôcchvāsaḥ.

Tears of joy cracked her eyes rinsed free of kohl, as she folded her hands and said softly with the directness of affection:

'Of course I know you, if this is no conjuror's illusion that only contrives to look like what I know. Yet you have to tell how this could occur!'

I told her everything, and the news travelled with her to enlighten her girlfriend, whose heart was delighted to the highest degree. Next, the Kalíngan king was freed of his chains, and treated with great honor. He officially handed darling Kánaka·lekha over so that I could unite with her.

Thus it was as ruler of the Andhra and Kalínga countries 12.66
that I went with no insignificant forces to the aid of the Angan king, since his foe was getting ready to attack. And here I fell under the attack of vast delight to have chanced to find you and all our friends."

His lips bathed in a brilliant smile, the prince Raja·váhana and all their friends applauded Mantra·gupta's skill:*

"How marvelous the part the great spiritual hero played. His dreadful penance has borne fruit already in this very life, it seems. But, joking apart, one sees here the nature of the union of wisdom and courage, with the attainment of the highest delight as their offspring!"

And turning his gaze like two fully opened blue lotuses 12.69
on Víshruta, greatly learned by name and by nature, he exhorted him:

"It is your turn now."

That is the end of the seventh chapter of
the glorious Dandin's
What Ten Young Men Did.
It is called: What Mantra·gupta Did.

CHAPTER THIRTEEN
WHAT VÍSHRUTA DID

ATHA SO 'PY ācacakṣe:

«Deva, may" âpi paribhramatā Vindhy'|âṭavyā ko 'pi kumāraḥ kṣudhā tṛṣā ca kliśyann a|kleś'|ârhaḥ kva cit kūp'|âbhyāśe 'ṣṭa|varṣa|deśīyo dṛṣṭaḥ. sa ca trāsa|gadgadam agadat:

13.3 ‹Mahā|bhāga, kliṣṭasya me kriyatām ārya sāhāyyakam. asya me prāṇ'|âpahāriṇīṃ pipāsāṃ pratikartum udakam udañcann iha kūpe ko 'pi niṣkalo mam' âika|śaraṇa|bhūtaḥ patitaḥ. tam alam asmi n' âham uddhartum iti.›

Ath' âham abhyetya vratatyā kay" âpi vṛddham uttārya taṃ ca bālaṃ vaṃśa|nālī|mukh'|ôddhṛtābhir adbhiḥ phalaiś ca pañca|ṣaiḥ śara|kṣep'|ôcchritasya lakuca|vṛkṣasya śikharāt pāṣāṇa|pātitaiḥ pratyānīta|prāṇa|vṛttim āpādya, taru|tala|niṣaṇṇas taṃ jarantam abravam:

‹Tāta, ka eṣa bālaḥ? ko vā bhavān? kathaṃ c' êyam āpad āpann" êti?›

13.6 So 'śru|gadgadam agadat:

‹Śrūyatāṃ mahā|bhāga. Vidarbho nāma janapadaḥ. tasmin Bhoja|vaṃśa|bhūṣaṇam, aṃś'|âvatāra iva Dharmasya, ati|sattvaḥ, satyavādī, vadānyaḥ, vinītaḥ, vinetā prajānām, rañjita|bhṛtyaḥ; kīrtimān, udagro buddhi|mūrtibhyām, utthāna|śīlaḥ, śāstra|pramāṇaḥ, śakya|bhavya|kalp'|ārambhī; saṃbhāvayitā budhān, prabhāvayitā sevakān, udbhāvayitā bandhūn, nyagbhāvayitā śatrūn;

AND SO VÍSHRUTA TOO began his tale:

"My Lord, like the others, I was wandering around in the Vindhyan forest when I spotted a young boy about eight years old beside a well. Such a child does not deserve to suffer, but he was suffering, from hunger and thirst. Between sobs of fear he stammered:

'Good sir, I am in distress. You must help me, noble sir. A 13.3
decrepit old man who was my only recourse, he was drawing water to quench my killer thirst when he fell into this well. I am not strong enough to pull him out.'

I hurried to the well and rescued the old man with a long strong creeper I found. Then I threw stones as high as an arrow's flight to knock five or six fruits down from the top of a *lákucha* tree. With these and with water drawn up via a bamboo pipe I restored the vital functions of them both. Taking my seat beneath the tree, I asked the elderly gentleman:

'Father, who is this boy? And who indeed are you? How did this trouble come about?'

Choking back his tears, he sobbed: 13.6

'I will tell you, good sir. There is a kingdom called Vidárbha.* In that kingdom there lived one Punya·varman, auspicious by name and auspicious to name. He was an ornament to Bhoja's line, like a piece of Dharma come to earth.* Mightily heroic, speaker of the truth, munificent and courteous, he educated his subjects, and won the devotion of his staff. He was famous, exalted in both intellect and beauty, always striving, a textbook ruler and the patron of projects feasible, favorable all around, and sound.* The

a|saṃbaddha|pralāpeṣv a|datta|karṇaḥ, kadā cid apy a|vi|tṛṣṇo guṇeṣu, ati|nadīṣṇaḥ kalāsu, nediṣṭho dharm'|ârtha|saṃhitāsu; svalpe 'pi sukṛte sutarāṃ pratyupakartā, pratyavekṣitā kośa|vāhanayoḥ, yatnena parīkṣitā sarv'|âdhyakṣaṇām, utsāhayitā kṛta|karmaṇām anurūpair dāna|mānaiḥ; sadyaḥ pratikartā daiva|mānuṣīṇām āpadām, ṣāḍguṇy'|ôpayoga|nipuṇaḥ, manu|mārgeṇa praṇetā cāturvarṇyasya, puṇya|ślokaḥ, Puṇyavarmā nām' āsīt.

13.9 Sa puṇyaiḥ karmabhiḥ prāṇya puruṣ'|āyuṣam, punar a|puṇyena prajānām agaṇyat' âmareṣu. tad|an|antaram Anantavarmā nāma tad|āyatir avanim adhyatiṣṭhat. sa sarva|guṇaiḥ samṛddho 'pi daivād daṇḍa|nītyāṃ n' âty|ādṛto 'bhūt.

Tam ekadā rahasi Vasurakṣito nāma mantri|vṛddhaḥ, pitur asya bahumataḥ, pragalbha|vāg abhāṣata:

«Tāta, sarvair v" ātma|saṃpad abhijanāt prabhṛty a|nyūn" âiv' âtrabhavati lakṣyate. buddhiś ca nisarga|paṭvī kalāsu nṛtya|gīt'|ādiṣu citreṣu ca kāvya|vistareṣu prāpta|vistārā tav' êtarebhyaḥ prativiśiṣyate. tath" âpy asāv a|pratipady' ātma|

wise he honored, his dependents he promoted, his kin he elevated and his enemies he humiliated.

Never did he pay any attention to inconsequential chatter, while his thirst for good qualities was never sated, and he was thoroughly skilled in all the arts and intimate with the religious (*dharma*) and political (*artha*) codes. Even a trifling good deed he would repay with interest. He took personal care of his treasury and vehicles, going to particular trouble to supervise all his managers, and encouraging those who carried out their duties with financial reward and praise as merited. If any misfortune occurred, divine or human, he could remedy it at once, thoroughly expert in the application of the six expedients of royal foreign policy, and the guide of the four castes along the path laid down by Manu.*

Thanks to his meritorious deeds, he breathed the full 13.9
human life span, before his subjects' lack of merit drove him to join the immortals. Without interruption his son Anánta·varman succeeded him to power over the earth. Although blessed with every other good quality, fate had not made him overly diligent in statecraft.

One day the old minister Vasu·rákshita, "Protector of wealth," highly respected by the new king's father and eloquent in speech, addressed Anánta·varman in private:

"My child, my lord clearly does not lack even the least of the personal blessings, starting with your noble birth.* Moreover, your naturally sharp intellect distinguishes itself from that of others by your breadth of knowledge of all the performing arts, dance and music, as well as painting and even the finer points of poetry. Nevertheless your intellect

saṃskāram artha|śāstreṣu, an|agni|saṃśodhit" êva hema|jātir n' âtibhāti buddhiḥ.

13.12 Buddhi|śūnyo hi bhū|bhṛd aty|ucchrito 'pi parair adhyāruhyamāṇam ātmānaṃ na cetayate. na ca śaktaḥ sādhyaṃ sādhanaṃ vā vibhajya vartitum. a|yathā|vṛttaś ca karmasu pratihanyamānaḥ svaiḥ paraiś ca paribhūyate. na c' âvajñātasy' ājñā prabhavati prajānāṃ yoga|kṣem'|ārādhanāya. atikrānta|śāsanāś ca prajā yat|kiṃcana|vādinyo yathā|kathaṃ|cid|vartinyaḥ sarvāḥ sthitīḥ saṃkireyuḥ. nir|maryādaś ca loko lokād ito 'mutaś ca svāminam ātmānaṃ ca bhraṃśayate.

Āgama|dīpa|dṛṣṭena khalv adhvanā sukhena vartate loka|yātrā. divyaṃ hi cakṣur bhūta|bhavad|bhaviṣyatsu vyavahita|viprakṛṣṭ'|ādiṣu ca viṣayeṣu śāstraṃ nām' â|pratihata|vṛtti. tena hīnaḥ sator apy āyata|viśālayor locanayor andha eva jantur artha|darśaneṣv a|sāmarthyāt.

Ato vihāya bāhya|vidyāsv abhiṣaṅgam āgamaya daṇḍa|nītiṃ kula|vidyām. tad|arth'|ânuṣṭhānena c' āvarjita|śakti|siddhir a|skhalita|śāsanaḥ śādhi ciram udadhi|mekhalām urvīm iti.»

13.15 Etad ākarṇya:

«Sthāna eva gurubhir anuśiṣṭam. tathā kriyata iti.»

has not observed its proper cultivation, namely in the study of affairs of state, and hence it does not shine to its fullest, just like gold that has not been burnished in fire.

Now, a master of the earth, however highly exalted, if his 13.12
intellect is barren, cannot notice when he is being dominated by others. Nor is he able to act making the necessary discrimination between ends and means. Acting inappropriately and thwarted in his activities, his own staff will despise him, as will others. Lacking respect, his command cannot ensure his subjects' well-being. Once his people overstep his orders, saying whatever they feel like and doing likewise, they will confuse the status quo. A population without limits on its behavior will bring disaster on its master and itself in both this world and the next.

Worldly affairs will proceed smoothly, provided only that their road is lit by the light of learning. For political science is none other than the divine eye, its activity unrestricted in every matter that has been, is, and will come to pass, as well as in matters hidden or distant, for example. The man without that insight, although his eyes be long and wide, is nothing but a blind creature,* since he has not the capacity to see his way through politics.

Give up now therefore your addiction to the superficial arts, and study political science, the art of your bloodline. By employing its methods and deploying the three royal powers, might, counsel and vigor,* your authority will be inviolate and you shall rule long over the sea-girt earth."

When the king heard this, he thought: 13.15

"The wise man gives me good advice. I shall do as he says."

antaḥ|puram aviśat. tāṃ ca vārtāṃ pārthivena pramadā| saṃnidhau prasaṅgen' ôdīritām upaniśamya samīp'|ôpaviṣṭaś citt'|ânuvṛtti|kuśalaḥ prasāda|vitto gīta|nṛtya|vādy'|ādiṣv a|bāhyo bāhya|nārī|parāyaṇaḥ paṭur a|yantrita|mukho bahu|bhaṅgi|viśāradaḥ para|marm'|ânveṣaṇa|paraḥ parihāsayitā parivāda|ruciḥ paiśunya|paṇḍitaḥ saciva|maṇḍalād apy utkoca|hārī sakala|durnay'|ôpādhyāyaḥ kāma|tantra|karṇa| dhāraḥ kumāra|sevako Vihārabhadro nāma smita|pūrve vyajñāpayat:

13.18 «Deva, daiv'|ânugraheṇa yadi kaś cid bhājanaṃ bhavati vibhūtes tam a|kasmād ucc'|âvacair upa|pralobhanaiḥ kadarthayantaḥ svārthe sādhayanti dhūrtāḥ.

Tathā hi: kecit pretya kila labhyair abhyuday'|âtiśayair āśām utpādya muṇḍayitvā śiro baddhvā darbha|rajjubhir ajinen' ācchādya nava|nīten' ôpalipy' ân|aśanaṃ ca śāyayitvā sarvasvaṃ svīkariṣyanti. tebhyo 'pi ghoratarāḥ pāṣaṇḍinaḥ putra|dāra|śarīra|jīvitāny api mocayanti.

Yadi kaś cit paṭu|jātīyo n' âsyai mṛga|tṛṣṇikāyai hasta|gataṃ tyaktum icchet, tam anye parivāry' āhuḥ:

With which he withdrew to his private apartment. There Vihára·bhadra, his courtier since childhood, was sitting closeby and all ears when the Lord of the Earth mentioned in passing before his harem what had taken place. Vihára·bhadra was skilled at gratifying his wishes, known to be the favorite, no stranger to song, dance, music and the rest, and obsessed with other men's women. Sharp and of untrammelled tongue, he was clever at paronomasia and double entendre, and loved to spy out other people's weak points. He was amusing, brilliant at spreading scandal and a pundit in backbiting. Able to extract bribes even from the circle of ministers, he was the professor of every iniquity and at the helm of licentiousness. With a smile on his face, Vihára·bhadra told the king:

"My Lord, if fate is kind enough to make someone a ves- 13.18
sel for greatness, then wily rogues will torment him unprovoked with allurements great and small, in order to achieve their own ends.

For example: some will plant hopes about the supreme felicity to be had in the hereafter, persuading their victim to have his head shaved, gird his loins with holy *darbha* grass, wear the skin of a black antelope, smear himself with fresh butter and go to sleep without having eaten;* and all this so they can get their hands on everything he owns. Heretics more horrendous than these will go so far as to relieve him of his sons, his wife, his body and his very life.

If someone has enough native wit not to wish to renounce all his holdings for this mirage, then there are others who will encircle him, claiming:

13.21 ‹Ekām api kākiṇīṃ kārṣāpaṇa|lakṣam āpādayema, śastrād ṛte sarva|śatrūn ghātayema, eka|śarīra|mātram api martyaṃ cakra|vartinaṃ vidadhīmahi, yad yasmad|uddiṣṭena mārgeṇ' ācaryata iti.›

Sa punar imān pratyāha:

‹Ko 'sau mārga iti?›

13.24 Punar ime bruvate:

‹Nanu catasro rāja|vidyāḥ, trayī vārt" ānvīkṣikī daṇḍa|nītir iti. tāsu tisras trayī|vārt'|ānvīkṣikyo mahatyo manda|phalāś ca. tās tāvad āsatām.

Adhīṣva tāvad daṇḍa|nītim! iyam idānīm ācārya|Viṣṇuguptena Maury'|ârthe ṣaḍbhiḥ śloka|sahasraiḥ saṃkṣiptā. s" âiv' êyam adhītya samyag anuṣṭhīyamānā yath"|ôkta|karma|kṣam" êti.›

13.27 Sa ‹tath" êty› adhīte śṛṇoti ca. tatr' âiva jarāṃ gacchati. tat tu kila śāstraṃ śāstr'|ântar'|ânubandhi. sarvam eva vāṅ|mayam a|viditvā na tattvato 'dhigamyate. bhavatu kālena bahun" âlpena vā tad|arth'|âdhigatiḥ.

Adhigata|śāstreṇa c' ādāv eva putra|dāram api na viśvāsyam. ātma|kukṣer api kṛte ‹taṇḍulair iyadbhir iyān odanaḥ saṃpadyate, iyata odanasya pākāy' âitāvad indhanaṃ paryāptam iti› mān'|ônmāna|pūrvakaṃ deyam.

'We can produce a lakh, a hundred thousand pieces, of silver from a single cowrie-shell penny, and we can slay all enemies without using a weapon. We can transform a mortal in just one life into a wheel-turning emperor. But one must follow the path we prescribe.' 13.21

He will respond to them:

'What is this path?'

They will then explain: 13.24

'Royal statecraft has, as you know, four branches: the three Vedas, commerce and agriculture, philosophy and political science.* The first three of these, namely the three Vedas, commerce and agriculture, and philosophy, are vast and slow to bear fruit. So do not bother with them.

Dedicate yourself to the study of political science. Indeed, this has now been collected into a compendium by the master Vishnu·gupta for the use of the Mauryan king, in six thousand verses.* Only master this science, and apply it properly, and you will achieve the aforementioned powers.'

He will agree, and study, and listen. And he will grow old 13.27
doing so. For that single text, it turns out, is connected to other texts. Unless one knows all this chain of discourses, then none of it will be truly understood. But at least it is actually possible to grasp the gist of it, whether it takes forever, or no time at all.

No sooner have you mastered the science than you can trust no one, not even your son or wife. Even with respect to one's belly, everything has first to be weighed up and measured: 'x amount of rice grains will produce y amount of cooked rice; and in order to cook y amount of cooked rice, z amount of firewood is sufficient.'

Utthitena ca rājñā kṣālit'|âkṣālite mukhe muṣṭim ardha|muṣṭiṃ v" âbhyantarī|kṛtya kṛtsnam āya|vyaya|jātam ahnaḥ prathame 'ṣṭame bhāge śrotavyam. śṛṇvata ev' âsya dvi|guṇam apaharanti te 'dhyakṣa|dhūrtāḥ. catvāriṃśataṃ Cāṇaky'|ôpadiṣṭān āharaṇ'|ôpāyān sahasradh" ātma|buddhy" âiva te vikalpayitāraḥ.

13.30 Dvitīye 'nyonyaṃ vivadamānānāṃ prajānām ākrośād dahyamāna|karṇaḥ kaṣṭaṃ jīvati. tatr' âpi prāḍvivāk'|ādayaḥ sv'|êcchayā jaya|parājayau vidadhānāḥ pāpen' âkīrtyā ca bhartāram ātmānaṃ c' ârthair yojayanti.

Tṛtīye snātuṃ bhoktuṃ ca labhate. bhuktasya yāvad andhaḥ|pariṇāmas tāvad asya viṣa|bhayaṃ na śāmyaty eva.

Caturthe hiraṇya|pratigrahāya hastaṃ prasārayann ev' ôttiṣṭhati.

13.33 Pañcame mantra|cintayā mahāntam āyāsam anubhavati. tatr' âpi mantriṇo madhyasthā iv' ânyonyaṃ mithaḥ saṃbhūya, doṣa|guṇau dūta|cāra|vākyāni śaky'|â|śakyatāṃ deśa|kāla|kāry'|âvasthāś ca sv'|êcchayā viparivartayantaḥ sva|para|mitra|maṇḍalāny upajīvanti. bāhy'|âbhyantarāṃś ca kopān gūḍham utpādya prakāśaṃ praśamayanta iva svāminam a|vaśam avagṛhṇanti.

When the king wakes up,* whether or not he has yet had a chance to rinse his mouth, and after getting down him a handful or half of nourishment, he must spend the first eighth of the day hearing the account of income and outgoings. But even while he is listening these wily roguish superintendents will rob him of twice as much again. Chánakya taught forty ways to steal.* These men's own cunning multiplies those forty thousandfold.

In the second watch the king endures a dreadful time, 13.30
getting his ears burned with the abusive shouting of his subjects, quarrelling with one another. Then, too, the judges and the rest assign victory or loss according to whim, thereby winning for their master guilt and ill repute, and for themselves profit.

With the third watch he is free to bathe and eat. But until the food he eats is digested he cannot be free from the fear that it was posioned.

The fourth watch he has to stand holding his hands out to receive gold without pause.

For the fifth watch he is under the great stress of policy 13.33
worries. Here again his ministers collude with one another pretending to be neutral. Exactly as they feel like they pervert faults and merits, the reports of envoys and spies, what is realistic and what not, and place, time, task and situation. Thus they feed off the circles of their own and others' allies. In secret they stir up local and foreign hostilities and then in public behave as though pacifying them. All of which to perpetuate their master's impotence.

Ṣaṣṭhe svaira|vihāro mantro vā sevyaḥ. so 'sy' âitāvān svaira|vihāra|kālā yasya tisras tripād'|ôttarā nāḍikāḥ.

Saptame catur|aṅga|bala|pratyavekṣaṇa|prayāsaḥ.

13.36 Aṣṭame 'sya senā|pati|sakhasya vikrama|cintā|kleśaḥ.

Punar upāsy' âiva saṃdhyāṃ prathame rātri|bhāge gūḍha|puruṣā draṣṭavyāḥ. tan|mukhena c' âti|nṛśaṃsāḥ śastr'|âgni|rasa|praṇidhayo 'nuṣṭheyāḥ.

Dvitīye bhojan'|ân|antaraṃ śrotriya iva sv'|âdhyāyam ārabhate.

13.39 Tṛtīye tūrya|ghoṣeṇa saṃviṣṭaś caturtha|pañcamau śayīta kila. katham iv' âsy' âjasra|cint"|āyāsa|vihvala|manaso varākasya nidrā|sukham upanamet?

Punaḥ ṣaṣṭhe śāstr'|âcintā|kārya|cint"|ārambhaḥ.

Saptame tu mantra|graho dūt'|âbhipreṣaṇāni ca. dūtāś ca nām' ôbhayatra priy'|ākhyāna|labdhān arthān vīta|śulka|bādha|vartmani vaṇijyayā vardhayantaḥ kāryam a|vidyamānam api leśen' ôtpādy' ân|avarataṃ bhramanti.

The sixth watch he can dedicate to whatever recreation he chooses, provided he is not instead receiving advice. His free time adds up to just three gongs.*

The seventh is for the strain of reviewing the four wings of his forces.

In the eighth watch comes the hassle of planning con- 13.36
quests in company with his generals.

Then again he has to perform the evening ritual, before spending the first watch of the night interviewing his secret agents. They in turn carry instructions to bloodthirsty spies who employ steel, fire and poison.*

In the second he may eat, but must then turn immediately, like a conscientious brahmin, to his private Vedic readings.

At the third watch he goes to bed, to the tumult of trum- 13.39
pets, and he is supposed to be able to lie down for the fourth and fifth watches. But how indeed can this wretch find the pleasure of sleep, his mind feverish with the pricks of perpetual worry?

Then at the sixth watch he has to begin again, struggling with the political treatises and fretting about their application.

And in the seventh watch of the night he must take advice and send out his emissaries. As for those ambassadors, everyone knows that they augment the reward that sweet-talking earns them from both sides by trading on the road, free of the annoyance of taxes. They conjure up some excuse for work when there is not even a speck of it to be found, in order that they can continue roaming around incessantly.

13.42 Aṣṭame puro|hit'|ādayo 'bhyety' âinam āhuḥ:

‹Adya dṛṣṭo duḥsvapnaḥ. duḥsthā grahāḥ. śakunāni c' âśubhāni. śāntayaḥ kriyantām. sarvam astu sauvarṇam eva homa|sādhanam. evaṃ sati karma guṇavad bhavati. Brahma|kalpā ime brāhmaṇāḥ. kṛtam ebhiḥ svasty|ayanaṃ kalyāṇataraṃ bhavati. te c' âmī kaṣṭa|dāridryā bahv|apatyā yajvāno vīryavantaś c' âdy' âpy a|prāpta|pratigrahāḥ. dattaṃ c' âibhyaḥ svargyam āyuṣyam ariṣṭa|nāśanaṃ ca bhavat' îti.›

Bahu bahu dāpayitvā tan|mukhena svayam upāṃśu bhakṣayanti.

13.45 Tad evam ahar|niśam a|vihita|sukha|leśam āyāsa|bahulam a|virala|kadarthanaṃ ca nayato nayajñasy' âstāṃ cakra|vartitā sva|maṇḍala|mātram api dur|ārakṣyaṃ bhavet. śāstrajña|samājñāto hi yad dadāti, yan mānayati, yat priyaṃ bravīti, tat sarvam atisaṃdhātum ity a|viśvāsaḥ. a|viśvāsyatā hi janma|bhūmir a|lakṣmyāḥ.

Yāvatā ca nayena vinā yāti loka|yātrā sa lokata eva siddhaḥ. n' âtra śāstreṇ' ârthaḥ. stanaṃ|dhayo 'pi hi tais tair upāyaiḥ stana|pānaṃ jananyā lipsate. tad apāsy' âti|yantraṇām anubhūyantāṃ yath"|êṣṭam indriya|sukhāni. ye 'py upadiśanti:

In the eighth and last watch of the night the royal priests and their ilk enter to announce to the king: 13.42

'We have seen inauspicious dreams this night. The planets are not favorable. Nor are the bird omens good. We must perform rites of appeasement. Let a full set of *homa* sacrifice implements be made, out of solid gold. That way the ritual will be meritorious. These brahmins before you are the equals of Brahma himself. When they make the prayers to bring good fortune, everything turns out particularly well. But they are terribly poverty-stricken and overrun with offspring, these powerful performers of sacrifices. Yet until today they have received no donations. Give them gifts, and you shall have heaven, long life and the obliteration of evil omens.'

They make him make more and more offerings, all the while sneakily gobbling them up themselves.

Thus you must realize that the prudent king spends his 13.45
time day and night in a plethora of labors, in incessant torment, without the least pleasure. Just his own sphere of power will be difficult to preserve, let alone becoming a wheel-turning emperor. When you allow yourself to be guided by political men, then whatever you give, or praise, or call dear will be mistrusted as Machiavellian. Mistrust, moreover, is the breeding ground of a king's misfortune.

The world itself is proof enough how far its affairs can proceed without policy. Treatises have no place in this business. After all, even a tiny suckling manages to drink from his mother's breast by one way or another. Say farewell to over-the-top restraint and enjoy sensual pleasures fully. Some may teach:

‹Evam indriyāṇi jetavyāni, evam ari|ṣaḍ|vārgas tyājyaḥ, sām'|ādir upāya|vargaḥ sveṣu pareṣu c' âjasraṃ prayojyaḥ, saṃdhi|vigraha|cintay" âiva neyaḥ kālaḥ, svalpo 'pi sukhasy' âvakāśo na deya iti.›

13.48 Tair apy ebhir mantri|bakair yuṣmattaś caury'|ârjitaṃ dhanaṃ dāsī|gṛheṣv eva bhujyate. ke c' âite varākāḥ? ye 'pi mantra|karkaśāḥ śāstra|tantra|kārāḥ Śukr'|Āṅgirasa|Viśālakṣa|Bāhudantiputra|Parāśara|prabhṛtayas taiḥ kim ari|ṣaḍ|vargo jitaḥ kṛtaṃ vā taiḥ śāstr'|ânuṣṭhānam? tair api hi prārabdheṣu kāryeṣu dṛṣṭe siddhy|asiddhī. paṭhantaś c' â|paṭhadbhir atisaṃdhīyamānā bahavaḥ.

Nanv idam upapannaṃ devasya yad uta sarva|lokasya vandyā jātir a|yāta|yāmaṃ vayo darśanīyaṃ vapur a|parimāṇā vibhūtiḥ. tat sarvaṃ sarv'|â|viśvāsa|hetunā sukh'|ôpabhoga|pratibandhinā bahu|mārga|vikalpanāt sarva|kāryeṣv a|mukta|saṃśayena tantr'|āvāpen' âiva mā kṛthā vṛthā.

Santi hi te dantināṃ daśa sahasrāṇi hayānāṃ lakṣa|trayam an|antaṃ ca pādātam. api ca pūrṇāny eva hema|ratnaiḥ kośa|gṛhāṇi. sarvaś c' âiṣa jīva|lokaḥ samagram api yuga|sahasraṃ bhuñjāno na te koṣṭh'|âgārāṇi recayiṣyati. kim idam a|paryāptaṃ yad any'|ârjitāy' āyāsaḥ kriyate. jīvitaṃ hi nāma janmavatāṃ catuḥ|pañc' âpy ahāni. tatr' âpi bhoga|yogyam

'The senses must be conquered like this... This is the way to give up the six enemies, the passions, ... Both allies and enemies should always be handled with appeasement and the other three tactics.* You should devote your time to the negotiation of peace treaties and to hostilities. There must not be the slightest opportunity for pleasure.'

Yet where else do these same hypocritical crane counsel- 13.48
lors spend the fortunes they have cheated you out of but in brothels? And what of these poor wretches, the strict politicians who wrote the treatises and fixed the rules, from Shukra, Angírasa, Vishaláksha Bahu·danti·putra and Paráshara onward* —do you think they conquered the collection of six enemies, the passions, or put their own preachings into practice? They too met failure as often as success in the projects they undertook. Many indeed are those learned in the texts who have been taken in by illiterates.

Is Your Majesty not blessed with a pedigree praised by the whole population, fresh youth, a beautiful body and boundless riches? Do not fritter away all your birthright wasting yourself on domestic and foreign policy, which only causes total mistrust, thwarts the enjoyment of pleasures and means one can never be certain about any move since there is the option of so many routes.

You have ten thousand elephants, three hundred thousand —three lakhs—of horses, and endless foot soldiers. Besides, your treasuries are filled to the top with gold and jewels. Nor will your granaries ever be emptied, even if the population of this whole entire world feeds off them for a thousand aeons. Is this not enough, that you must trouble yourself in order to acquire more? Are we not born to live but four or five

alp'|âlpaṃ vayaḥ|khaṇḍam. a|paṇḍitāḥ punar arjayanta eva dhvaṃsante. n' ârjitasya vastuno lavam apy āsvādayitum īhante.

13.51 Kiṃ bahunā? rājya|bhāraṃ bhāra|kṣameṣv antaraṅgeṣu bhaktimatsu samarpya, apsaraḥ|pratirūpābhir antaḥ|purikābhī ramamāṇo gīta|saṃgīta|pāna|goṣṭhīś ca yatha"|rtu bandhan yath"|ârhaṃ kuru śarīra|lābham! iti»

Pañc'|âṅga|spṛṣṭa|bhūmir añjali|cumbita|cūḍaś ciram aśeta. prāhasīc ca pratiphulla|locano 'ntaḥ|pura|pramadā|janaḥ. jana|nāthaś ca sa|smitam:

«Uttiṣṭha! nanu hit'|ôpadeśād guravo bhavantaḥ. kim iti gurutva|viparītam anuṣṭhitam? iti»

13.54 tam utthāpya krīḍā|nirbharam atiṣṭhat.

Ath' âiṣu dineṣu bhūyo|bhūyaḥ prastute 'rthe preryamāṇo mantri|vṛddhena vacas" âbhyupetya manas" âiv' â|cittajña ity avajñātavān. ath' âivaṃ mantriṇo manasy abhūt:

‹Aho! me mohād bāliśyam. a|rucite 'rthe codayann arth' îv' âkṣi|gato 'ham asya hāsyo jātaḥ. spaṣṭam asya ceṣṭānām āyathāpūrvyam.

days? Even then the time for pleasure is only a minuscule fraction of our life. Idiots return to dust even while they are busy acquiring more. They would not dream of tasting even a soupçon of the goods they have amassed.

Must I go on? Leave the burden of running the kingdom to 13.51
those who are qualified to bear it, devoted servants in whom you have confidence. You should enjoy yourself with the ladies of your harem, who rival the *ápsaras*es in their beauty, and arrange parties of song, music and drinking, according to the season. Do justice to your physical existence!"

With that, Vihára·bhadra threw himself to the ground, touching it with the five parts of his body, and lay there still, his folded hands kissing his headdress. The ladies of the harem laughed out loud, eyes blossoming. The lord of his people smiled and said, raising him up:

"Arise! Your good advice* makes you, my lord, my guru. So why do you behave in this far from venerable manner?"

After which the king committed himself to boundless 13.54
entertainment.

In the days that followed, the old minister kept on at the king, urging him again and again to implement what they had discussed. With his mouth the king agreed, but with his mind he paid no notice, thinking that the old man could not read his thoughts. Thereupon the minister realized:

'Alas! I have been a deluded fool. By pressing him to unappealing business, I am become like a beggar, laughable and a thorn in his eye. How blatantly his behavior is totally transformed.

13.57 Tathā hi: na māṃ snigdhaṃ paśyati, na smitapūrvaṃ bhāṣate, na rahasyāni vivṛṇoti, na haste spṛśati, na vyasaneṣv anukampate, n' ôtsaveṣv anugṛhṇāti, na vilomana|vastūni preṣayati, na mat|sukṛtāni pragaṇayati, na me gṛha|vārtāṃ pṛcchati, na mat|pakṣyān pratyavekṣate, na māṃ āsanna|kāryeṣv abhyantarīkaroti, na māṃ antaḥ|puraṃ praveśayati.

Api ca: māṃ an|arheṣu karmasu niyuṅkte, mad|āsanam anyair avaṣṭabhyamānam anujānāti, mad|vairiṣu viśrambhaṃ darśayati, mad|uktasy' ôttaraṃ na dadāti, mat|samāna|doṣān vigarhayati, marmaṇi māṃ upahasati, sva|matam api mayā varṇyamānaṃ pratikṣipati, mah"|ârhāṇi vastūni mat|prahitāni n' âbhinandati, naya|jñānāṃ skhalitāni mat|samakṣaṃ mūrkhair udghoṣayati.

Satyam āha Cāṇakyaḥ:

13.60 «citta|jñān'|ânuvartino 'n|arthyā api priyāḥ syuḥ.
dakṣiṇā api tad|bhāva|bahiṣkṛtā dveṣyā bhaveyur iti.»

Tath" âpi kā gatiḥ? a|vinīto 'pi na parityājyaḥ pitṛ|paitāmahair asmādṛśair ayam adhipatiḥ. a|parityajanto 'pi kam upakāram a|śrūyamāṇa|vācaḥ kurmaḥ. sarvathā nayajñasya Vasantabhānor Aśmak'|êndrasya haste rājyam idaṃ patitam. api nām' āpado bhāvinyaḥ prakṛtistham enam āpādayeyuḥ. an|artheṣu sulabha|vyalīkeṣu kva cid utpanno 'pi dveṣaḥ sad|vṛttam asmai na rocayet. bhavatu. bhavitā tāvad

No longer does he look at me with affection, or speak to me with a smile. He does not tell me his secrets, or touch my hand. He neither sympathises with my troubles nor favors me at festivals. I am sent no persuasive gifts, nor are my good services noticed. He asks not how my family fares, nor looks out for my allies. He does not confide in me his intimate projects, nor does he invite me into his inner apartments, the harem. 13.57

Quite the contrary, he employs me on menial tasks and permits others to occupy my seat. He displays absolute trust in my enemies, and does not reply to my questions. General faults he criticizes in me, and he mocks me where it hurts. Even if I describe exactly what he is thinking, he rejects it. He shows no pleasure in extremely valuable gifts that I send, and has fools proclaim the blunders of political minds in front of me.

Chánakya was right to proclaim:

"Even the unworthy will be beloved, 13.60
If they accommodate to his every inclination.
But even the skilled will become hated,
If they do not take his state of mind into account."*

Still, what is to be done? However uncouth this overlord, we, who were with his father and his father's father, cannot abandon him. Yet even if we do not forsake him, what service can we render when our words are not heard. One thing is certain, this kingdom is for the taking and already in the hands of Vasánta·bhanu, the politically astute Lord of Áshmaka.* If only the impending disasters could bring Anánta·varman back to his senses. But even if he learns to

anarthaḥ. stambhita|piśuna|jihvo yathā|kathaṃ|cid a|bhraṣṭa|padas tiṣṭheyam iti.›

Evaṃ|gate mantriṇi rājani ca kāma|vṛtte Candrapālito nām' Âśmak'|êndr'|âmātyasya' Êndrapālitasya sūnur a|sad|vṛttaḥ pitṛ|nirvāsito nāma bhūtvā bahubhiś cāraṇa|gaṇair bahvībhir an|alpa|kauśalābhiḥ śilpa|kāriṇībhir an|eka|channa|kiṃkaraiś ca gūḍha|puruṣaiḥ parivṛto 'bhyetya vividhābhiḥ krīḍābhir Vihārabhadram ātmasād akarot. amunā c' âiva saṃkrameṇa rājany āspadam alabhata.

13.63 Labdha|randhraś ca sa yad yad vyasanam ārabhate tat tath" êty avarṇayat:

«Deva, yathā mṛgayā hy aupakārikī na tath" ânyat! atra hi vyāyām'|ôtkarṣād āpats' ûpakartā dīrgh'|âdhva|laṅghana|kṣamo jaṅghājavaḥ, kaph'|âpacayād ārogy'|âika|mūlam āśay'|âgni|dīptiḥ, medo|'pakarṣād aṅgānāṃ sthairya|kārkaśy'|âti|lāghav'|ādīni, śīt'|ôṣṇa|vāta|varṣa|kṣut|pipāsā|sahatvaṃ, sattvānām avasth"|ântareṣu citta|ceṣṭita|jñānaṃ, hariṇa|gavala|gavay'|ādi|vadhena sasya|lopa|pratikriyā, vṛka|vyāghr'|ādi|ghātena sthala|patha|śalya|śodhanaṃ, śail'|âṭavī|pradeśānāṃ vividha|karma|kṣamāṇām ālocanam, āṭavika|varga|viśrambhaṇam, utsāha|śakti|saṃdhukṣaṇena pratyanīka|vitrāsanam iti bahutamā guṇāḥ.

hate bad behavior that facilitates such suffering, that hate cannot make him love the path of goodness. Be that as it may. Adversity is on its way. I will have to manage somehow to keep my footing and curb my treacherous tongue.'

The minister had decided, and the king was occupied with indulging his desires, when Chandra·pálita, the son of Indra·pálita, the Áshmakan lord's minister, arrived, claiming to have been banished by his father for bad behavior. With an entourage of troupes of performers, many highly talented dancing girls, and spies disguised as servants, he first won Vihára·bhadra over with a variety of entertainments. The same techniques enabled him to get a firm hold on the king.

Whatever vice the king was engaged in, Chandra·pálita 13.63
exploited the opportunity to describe it as perfect:*

"My Lord, there is nothing as healthy as hunting! It has too many good qualities. For example, it makes one swift of shank, able to bound over long distances, and its preeminent athleticism is very useful in an emergency. Hunting reduces phlegm, hence sparking up the belly's fire, the one thing to keep illness away. By reducing fat the limbs gain strength, hardness and extreme agility, among other advantages. It teaches one to endure cold, heat, wind, rain, hunger and thirst; and it teaches insight into the thoughts and actions of animals in various situations. Killing deer, wild buffalo and wild oxen, to name but a few, protects the harvest from destruction;* while slaying wolves, tigers and other ferocious beasts clears the roads and tracks of those threats. On the hunt one inspects mountainous and forested districts, where anything could happen, and wins the trust of their

Dyūte 'pi dravya|rāśes tṛṇavat tyāgād an|upamānam āśay'|âudāryaṃ, jaya|parājay'|ân|avasthānād dharṣa|viṣādayor avidheyatvaṃ, pauruṣ'|âika|nimittasy' āmarṣasya vṛddhiḥ, akṣa|hasta|bhūmy|ādi|gocarāṇām atyanta|dur|upalakṣyāṇāṃ kūṭa|karmaṇām upalakṣaṇād an|anta|buddhi|naipuṇyam, eka|viṣay'|ôpasaṃhārāc cittasy' âticitram aikāgyram, adhyavasāya|sahacareṣu sāhaseṣv atiratiḥ, ati|karkaśa|puruṣa|pratisaṃsargād an|anya|dharṣaṇīyatā, mān'|âvadhāraṇam, a|kṛpaṇaṃ ca śarīra|yāpanam iti.

13.66 Uttam'|âṅgan"|ôpabhoge 'py artha|dharmayoḥ sa|phalīkaraṇaṃ, puṣkalaḥ puruṣ'|âbhimānaḥ, bhāva|jñāna|kauśalam, a|lobha|kliṣṭam āceṣṭitam, akhilāsu kalāsu vaicakṣaṇyam, a|labdh'|ôpalabdhi|labdh'|ânurakṣaṇa|rakṣit'|ôpabhoga|bhukt'|ânusaṃdhāna ruṣṭ'|ânunay'|ādiṣv ajasram abhyupāya|racanayā buddhi|vācoḥ pāṭavam, utkṛṣṭa|śarīra|saṃskārāt su|bhaga|veṣatayā loka|saṃbhāvanīyatā, paraṃ suhṛt|priyatvam, garīyasī parijana|vyapekṣā, smita|pūrv'|âbhibhāṣitvam, udrikta|sattvatā, dākṣiṇy'|ânuvartanam, apaty'|ôtpādanen' ôbhaya|loka|śreyaskaratvam iti.

jungly inhabitants. By thus kindling your aggressive power you put fear in the hearts of your enemies.

It is the same with gambling: to give up a mountain of money as though it were straw requires an incomparable generosity of character. Since winning and losing are so uncertain, neither arrogance or despair can hold sway. Gambling increases that ferocity which is the only mark of manliness. One's intelligence is sharpened to the extreme, through having to catch the crooked dealings, so very tricky to spot, that are par for the course with skill at dice, board games and so on. Because one has to concentrate on a single object, gambling produces a marvelous single-pointedness of mind. It also gives one a true passion for risky undertakings with which perseverance goes hand in hand. Through coming up against extremely hard men, no one else can intimidate. Further, one learns certain self-confidence, and to hold oneself with dignity.

The enjoyment of lovely ladies is no different: is it not 13.66
the fruition of the twin aims of man, profit and religion? Masculine pride is the order of the day, as is skill at divining people's inner feelings, selfless acts untainted by greed, and brilliance at every single art. One acquires eloquence and ingenuity in the process of perpetually devising strategies, first to win the woman who is not yet won and then keep hold of her once she is won, to enjoy her once she is kept hold of, to keep charming her once she has been enjoyed, and to win her back again when she is in a rage. Because one has elegantly to decorate one's person, handsome dress makes one the object of everyone's respect. Enjoying lovely ladies teaches great affection for friends, a weightier regard

Pāne 'pi nānā|vidha|roga|bhaṅga|paṭīyasām āsavānām āsevanāt spṛhaṇīya|vayo|'vasthāpanam, ahaṃkāra|prakarṣād a|śeṣa|duḥkha|tiraskaraṇam, aṅgaja|rāga|dīpanād aṅgan"|ôpabhoga|śakti|saṃdhukṣaṇam, aparādha|pramārjanān manaḥ|śaly'|ônmārjanam, a|śāṭhya|śaṃsibhir an|argala|pralāpair viśvās'|ôpabṛṃhaṇaṃ, matsar'|ân|anubandhād ānand'|âikatānatā, śabd'|ādīnām indriy'|ârthānāṃ sātatyen' ânubhavaḥ, saṃvibhāga|śīlatayā suhṛd|varga|saṃvargaṇam, an|upamānam aṅga|lāvaṇyam, an|uttarāṇi vilasitāni, bhay'|ârti|haraṇāc ca sāṃgrāmikatvam iti.

Vāk|pāruṣyaṃ daṇḍo dāruṇo dūṣaṇāni c' ârthānām eva yath" âvakāśam aupakārikāṇi. na hi munir iva nara|patir upaśama|ratir abhibhavitum ari|kulam alam, avalambituṃ ca loka|tantram iti.»

13.69 Asāv api gur'|ûpadeśam iv' âtyādareṇa tasya matam anvavartata. tac|chīl'|ânusāriṇyaś ca prakṛtayo vi|śṛṅkhalam asevanta vyasanāni. sarvaś ca samāna|doṣatayā na kasya cic chidr'|ânveṣaṇāy' âyatiṣṭa.

for attendants, speaking with a smile, increased vitality and courteous behavior. Finally, the fulfillment of profit and religion is that in begetting offspring one creates blessings in both this world and the hereafter.

Drinking is equally beneficial. The assiduous partaking of liquors perfectly designed to destroy all sorts of disease keeps one forever enviably young. The inflation of one's ego banishes every last trouble. Moreover, by inflaming lust for women, drinking kindles the power to enjoy the ladies. Effacing the memory of crimes committed, it extracts the thorns of remorse from one's mind. Through free talk that shouts guilelessness, drinking feeds trust, and because it is the opposite of selfishness it brings unadulterated joy. It grants uninterrupted enjoyment of all the objects of the senses, music and the rest. Sharing is the drinker's habit; through it one wins a bevy of friends. Limbs become incomparably lovely, and gestures the last word. In the end, because it removes the pain that is fear, drinking makes one heroic.

Unkind words, cruel punishment and the confiscation of property, too, can all on occasion be good for the health. For, after all, when a lord of men, a king, adores tranquility like a holy man, how will he ever defeat his enemies or hold on to secular power?"

As for King Anánta·varman, well, he followed Chandra· 13.69
pálita's advice as earnestly as if it were the prescriptions of a guru. His subjects followed his lead, dedicating themselves to unfettered vice. Since everyone was equally guilty, no one dared to denounce anyone else's defects.

Samāna|bhartṛ|prakṛtayas tantr'|âdhyakṣāḥ svāni karma|phalāny abhakṣayan. tataḥ kramād āya|dvārāṇi vyaśīryanta. vyaya|mukhāni viṭa|vidheyatayā vibhor ahar ahar vyavardhanta.

Sāmanta|paura|jānapada|mukhyāś ca samāna|śīlatay" ôpārūḍha|viśrambheṇa rājñā sa|jānayaḥ pāna|goṣṭhīṣv abhyantarīkṛtāḥ svaṃ svam ācāram atyacāriṣuḥ. tad|aṅganāsu c' ân|ek'|âpadeśa|pūrvam apācaran nar'|êndraḥ. tad|antaḥ|pureṣu c' âmī bhinna|vṛtteṣu manda|trāsā bahu|sukhair avartanta. sarvaś ca kul'|âṅganā|janaḥ pāṃsula|jana|bhaṅgi|bhāṣaṇa|rato bhagna|cāritra|yantraṇas tṛṇāy' âpi na gaṇayitvā bhartṝn dhātṛ|gaṇa|mantraṇāny aśṛṇot.

13.72 Tan|mūlāś ca kalahāḥ sāmarṣāṇām udabhavan. ahanyanta durbalā balibhiḥ. apahṛtāni dhanavatāṃ dhanāni taskar'|ādibhiḥ. apahṛta|paribhūtayaḥ prahatāś ca pātaka|pathāḥ. hata|bāndhavā hṛta|vittā vadha|bandh'|āturāś ca mukta|kaṇṭham ākrośann aśru|kaṇṭhyaḥ prajāḥ. daṇḍaś c' â|yathā|praṇīto bhaya|krodhāv ajanayat. kṛśa|kuṭumbeṣu lobhaḥ padam adhatta. vimānitāś ca tejasvino mānen' âdahyanta. teṣu teṣu c' âkṛtyeṣu prāsaran par'|ôpajāpāḥ.

In imitation of their master and his subjects, the administration's superintendents gobbled up themselves the fruits of their office. Thereupon the channels of revenue gradually crumbled, while the mouths of expenditure grew larger every day, with the sovereign under the influence of scoundrels.

Neighboring kings, eminent townsmen and country folk, too, practiced the same morality. With exaggerated trust the king initiated them with their wives into his drinking parties, where they violated their habitual good behavior. With more than one excuse, the Lord of men, the king himself, misbehaved with their women. After that those men had little fear to enjoy many pleasures with his harem, its virtue shattered. All the well-bred ladies revelled in the witty talk of libertines, any restraint banished from their behavior. They did not give a straw for their husbands and instead gave their attentions to the intrigues of their scores of paramours.

Such carryings-on provoked quarrels between indignant 13.72
parties. The strong slew the weak. Thieves led the plunder of the riches of the wealthy. Fear of reproof removed, people trod the paths of sin. With their relations slain, their wealth taken, and threatened with murder and imprisonment, the population gave full vent to their cries, with tears in their throats. The random administering of punishment begot fear and anger. In families reduced to poverty, avarice took hold. The disaffected illustrious burned with humiliation. Among so many evils, the enemies' overtures to rebellion insinuated themselves without difficulty.

Tadā ca mṛga|yuv'|ēṣa|mṛga|bāhulya|varṇanen' âdri|droṇīr an|apasāra|mārgāḥ śuṣka|tṛṇa|vaṃśa|gulmāḥ praveśya dvārato 'gni|visargaiḥ, vyāghr'|ādi|vadhe protsāhya tan|mukha|pātanaiḥ, iṣṭa|kūpa|tṛṣṇ'|ôtpādanen' âtidūra|hāritānāṃ prāṇa|hāribhiḥ kṣut|pipās"|âbhivardhanaiḥ, tṛṇa|gulma|gūḍha|channa|taṭa|pradara|pāta|hetubhir viṣama|mārga|pradhāvanaiḥ;

viṣa|mukhībhiḥ kṣurikābhiś caraṇa|kaṇṭak'|ôddharaṇaiḥ, viṣvag|visara|vicchann'|ânuyātṛtay" âikākīkṛtānāṃ yath"|êṣṭa|ghātanaiḥ, mṛga|deh'|âparāddhair nām' êṣu|mokṣaṇaiḥ, sa|paṇa|bandham adhiruhy' âdri|śṛṅgāṇi dur|adhirohāṇy an|anya|lakṣyaiḥ prabhraṃśanaiḥ, āṭavika|chadmanā vipineṣu virala|sainikānāṃ pratirodhanaiḥ;

13.75 akṣa|dyūta|pakṣi|yuddha|yātr'|ôtsav'|ādi|saṃkuleṣu balavad|anupraveśanair itareṣāṃ hiṃs"|ôtpādanaiḥ, gūḍh'|ôtpādita|vyalīkebhyo '|priyāṇi prakāśaṃ labdhvā sākṣiṣu tad vikhyāpy' â|kīrti|gupti|hetubhiḥ parākramaiḥ, para|kalatreṣu suhṛttven' âbhiyojya jārān bhartṝn ubhayaṃ vā prahṛtya

Then Anánta·varman's army was reduced to smithereens, its warriors completely wiped out, in a great variety of devious plots perpetrated by poisoners and others in the employ of the Lord of Áshmaka. For example, by describing an abundance of deer and fawns, they lured men to enter mountain valleys where there was no way out filled with dry grass and bamboo thickets, which they then set on fire from the entrance. They incited people to kill tigers and other dangerous animals, only to throw them into the tiger's jaws. They increased some men's hunger and thirst until it was fatal, by inspiring desire for a particular well and making them go very far in search of it. Some were persuaded to run along rugged tracks that terminated in a fall from a precipice or into a chasm concealed by thick clumps of grass.

Others had thorns extracted from their feet with daggers with poisoned tips. Some they could kill at their leisure, once they had isolated them, separating them from their companions scattered in every direction. They fired arrows directly at others, with the excuse of having mistaken them for the flank of a deer. With others they made a wager to climb mountain peaks difficult to ascend, from where they hurled them down without anyone seeing. Disguised as forest-dwellers they ambushed some lonely groups of soldiers in thickets.

Some were pushed to enter the brawls at dice gambling, 13.75
cockfights, festivals, fairs and so on, where they were provoked to violence against one another. Secretly they harassed some into resentment, but accepted the comebacks in public, denouncing them before witnesses, so that their victims were forced to take flight to conceal the dishonor.

tat|sāhas'|ôpanyāsaiḥ, yoga|nārī|hāritānāṃ saṃketeṣu prāg upa|nilīya paścād abhidruty' â|kīrtanīyaiḥ pramāpaṇaiḥ;

upapralobhya bila|praveśeṣu nidhāna|khananeṣu mantra|sādhaneṣu ca vighna|vyāja|sādhyair vyāpādanaiḥ, matta|gaj'|âdhirohaṇāya prerya pratyapāya|nivartanaiḥ, vyāla|hastinaṃ kopayitvā lakṣyīkṛta|mukhya|maṇḍaleṣv apakramaṇaiḥ, dāy'|ādy|arthe vivadamānān upāṃśu hatvā pratipakṣeṣv a|yaśaḥ|pātanaiḥ;

sāmanta|pura|jana|padeṣv a|yathā|vṛttān a|prakāśam abhiprahṛtya tad|vairināṃ aghoṣaṇaiḥ, yog'|âṅganābhir ahar|niśam abhiramayya rāja|yakṣm'|ôtpādanaiḥ, vastr'|ābharaṇa|māly'|âṅga|rāg'|ādiṣu rasa|vidhāna|kauśalaiḥ, cikitsā|mukhen' āmay'|ôpabṛṃhaṇair anyaiś c' âbhyupāyair Aśmak'|êndra|prayuktās tīkṣṇa|rasad'|ādayaḥ prakṣapita|pravīram Anantavarma|kaṭakaṃ jarjaram akurvan.

13.78 Atha Vasantabhānur Bhānuvarmāṇaṃ nāma Vānavāsyaṃ protsāhy' Ânantavarmaṇā vyagrāhayat. tat|parāmṛṣṭa|rāṣṭra|paryantaś c' Ânantavarmā tam abhiyoktuṃ bala|samutthānam akarot. sarva|sāmantebhyaś c' Âśmak'|êndraḥ prāg upety' âsya priyataro 'bhūt. apare 'pi sāmantāḥ samagaṃsata. gatvā c' âbhyarṇe Narmadā|rodhasi nyaviśan.

They pressed some on other men's wives as if they were being friendly, only to murder the lovers, the husbands, or both, letting it be known that the violence was between the parties. Others they would first lure to a rendezvous offered with attractive treacherous women, before then falling upon them ignominiously.

They lured some into caves to dig up treasure or perform mantra magic, before destroying them in faked accidents. Others they urged to mount rutting elephants and then refrained from rescuing them, or they infuriated a vicious elephant only to drive it into the midst of the leaders, making them a target. They secretly assassinated people who were quarrelling about inheritance and so forth, and pinned the blame on their adversaries.

In the cities and countries of feudatory princes they murdered troublemakers in private, but accused their enemies of the deed. Some men they compelled to delight day and night with tricky ladies, until they sickened with consumption. Others they professed to treat, but in fact aggravated their diseases thanks to expertly impregnating their clothes, ornaments, garlands, ointments and so on with poison. All these and more were the devious ways the Áshmakan lord obliterated Anánta·varman's army.

Next, Vasánta·bhanu incited Bhanu·varman, of Vana·va- 13.78
si,* to march against Anánta·varman. When the borders of Anánta·varman's kingdom were breached, he mobilized forces to resist the attack. First to arrive of all the feudatory princes was the Lord of Áshmaka, Vasánta·bhanu, ingratiating himself with Anánta·varman. The other vassal

Tasmiṃś c' âvasare mahā|sāmantasya Kuntala|pater Avantidevasy' ātma|nāṭakīyāṃ Kṣmātalorvaśīṃ nāma Candrapālit'|ādibhir atipraśasta|nṛtya|kauśalām āhūy' Ânantavarmā nṛtyam adrākṣīt. ati|raktaś ca bhuktavān imāṃ madhu|mattām. Aśmak'|êndras tu Kuntala|patim ekānte samabhyadhatta:

«Pramatta eṣa rājā kalatrāṇi naḥ parāmṛśati. kiyaty avajñā soḍhavyā. mama śatam asti hastināṃ pañcaśatāni ca te. tad āvāṃ saṃbhūya Mural"|ēśaṃ Vīrasenam Ṛṣīk'|ēśam Ekavīraṃ Koṅkaṇa|patiṃ Kumāraguptaṃ Nāsikya|nāthaṃ ca Nāgapālam upajapāva. te c' âvaśyam asy' â|vinayam a|sahamānā asman|maten' âiv' ôpāvarteran. ayaṃ ca Vānavāsyaḥ paraṃ me mitram. amun" âinaṃ dur|vinītam agrato vyatiṣaktaṃ pṛṣṭhataḥ prāharema. kośa|vāhanaṃ ca vibhajya gṛhṇīma iti.»

13.81 Hṛṣṭena c' âmun" âbhyupete viṃśatiṃ var'|âṃśukānāṃ pañca|viṃśatiṃ kāñcana|kuṅkuma|kambalānāṃ prābhṛtīkṛty' āpta|mukhena taiḥ sāmantaiḥ saṃmantrya tān api sva|matāv asthāpayat. uttaredyus teṣāṃ sāmantānāṃ Vānavāsyasya c' Ânantavarmā naya|dveṣād āmiṣatvam agamat. Va-

rulers gathered, too. They marched out a short distance and pitched camp on the bank of the Nármada River.

Anánta·varman used this occasion to ask for Kshma·talórvashi, "The nymph Úrvashi on Earth." She was the personal dancing girl of the greatest feudatory prince, Avánti·deva, king of Kúntala, whose performing skills Chandra·pálita and the others had particularly lauded. She danced before Anánta·varman. He became infatuated with her and took advantage of her while she was under the influence of alcohol.* The Lord of Áshmaka took the king of Kúntala aside and said:

"This king is out of control. Now he violates our women. How much humiliation must we bear? I have one hundred elephants and you have five hundred. Let us join forces together. We can persuade Vira·sena, ruler of Múrala, and the ruler of Rishíka, Eka·vira, as well as Kumára·gupta, Lord of Kónkana, and Naga·pala, Lord of Nasíkya, to join us in our plot.* I am sure that they cannot bear his insolence, either, and will agree to our plan. Besides, this king of Vana·vasi who attacks Anánta·varman is my closest friend. With him engaging the reprobate from the front, we can strike from behind. We shall seize his treasury and vehicles and share them out between us."

Delighted, Avánti·deva agreed. With gifts of twenty best- 13.81
quality silk garments and twenty-five gold-trimmed saffron-dyed blankets, Vasánta·bhanu's trusties negotiated with those feudatory princes on his behalf, and brought them around to his way of thinking. On the following day Anánta·varman became the victim of his allies and the Vana·vasyan

santabhānuś ca tat|kośa|vāhanam avaśīrṇam ātm'|âdhiṣṭitam eva kṛtvā:

«Yathā|balaṃ ca vibhajya gṛhṇīta. yuṣmad|anujñayā yena kena cid aṃśen' âhaṃ tuṣyām' îti.»

śāṭhyāt sarv'|ânuvartī ten' âiv' āmiṣeṇa nimittīkṛten' ôtpādita|kalahaḥ sarva|sāmantān adhvaṃsayat. tadīyaṃ ca sarvasvaṃ svayam ev' âgrasat. Vānavāsyaṃ kena cid aṃśen' ânugṛhya pratyāvṛtya sarvam Anantavarma|rājyam ātmasād akarot.

13.84 Asmiṃś c' ântare mantri|vṛddho Vasurakṣitaḥ kaiścin maulaiḥ saṃbhūya bālam enaṃ Bhāskaravarmāṇam asy' âiva jyāyasīṃ bhaginīṃ trayodaśa|varṣāṃ Mañjuvādinīm anayoś ca mātaraṃ mahā|devīṃ Vasuṃdharām ādāy' âpasarpann āpado 'syā bhāvitayā dāha|jvareṇa deham ajahāt.

Asmādṛśair mitrais tu nītvā Māhiṣmatīṃ bhartṛ|dvaimāturāya bhrātre Mitravarmaṇe s'|âpatyā devī darśit" âbhūt. tāṃ c' āryām anāryo 'sāv anyath" âbhyamanyata. nirbhartsitaś ca tayā:

«Sutam iyam a|khaṇḍa|cāritrā rājy'|ârhaṃ cikīrṣat' îti.»

13.87 nairghṛṇyāt tam enaṃ bālam ajighāṃsīt. idaṃ tu jñātvā devy" âham ājñaptaḥ:

king, and all because he did not like politics. Vasánta·bhanu, meanwhile, took control of his abandoned treasury and vehicles, proposing:

"Divide and claim the spoils according to each one's forces. I shall be more than happy with whatever portion you all grant me."

This gambit met with everyone's approval. But he went on to use the same bait as a means to spawn quarrels among all the allies, culminating in them destroying one another. Thus in the end he swallowed for himself the entirety of Anánta·varman's possessions. Rewarding the Vana·vasyan king with a small share, Vasánta·bhanu appropriated Anánta·varman's entire kingdom.

Meanwhile, the old minister Vasu·rákshita took this child 13.84
you rescued, Bháskara·varman, his elder sister, the thirteen-year-old Manju·vádini, and the mother of them both, the great queen Vasun·dhara, "Wealthy Earth," and they escaped, together with some ministers who had been with the family for generations. But inevitable disaster threw the old man into a burning fever, and he gave up his body.

After that, loyal friends including myself took the queen and her children to Mahíshmati,* and presented them to Mitra·varman, her husband's brother by a different mother. He, however, ignoble being, had different ideas toward the noble lady. When she spurned him, he thought:

"She plans only to prepare her son for kingship, with her virtue intact."

Cruelly he planned to kill this her child you see before you. 13.87
As soon as the queen realized his intentions she instructed me:

«Tāta Nālījaṅgha, jīvat" ânen' ârbhakeṇa yatra kva cid avadhārya jīva. jīveyaṃ ced aham apy enam anusariṣyāmi. jñāpaya māṃ kṣema|pravṛttaḥ sva|vārtām iti.»

Ahaṃ tu saṃkule rāja|kule kathaṃ cid enaṃ nirgamayya Vindhy"|âṭavīṃ vyagāhiṣi. pāda|cāra|duḥkhitaṃ c' âinam āśvāsayituṃ ghoṣe kva cid ahāni kānicid viśramayya tatr' âpi rāja|puruṣa|saṃpāta|bhīto dūr'|âdhvam apāsaram.

13.90 Tatr' âsya dāruṇa|pipāsā|pīḍitasya vāri dātu|kāmaḥ kūpe 'sminn apabhraṃśya patitas tvay" âivam anugṛhītaḥ. tvam ev' âsy' âtaḥ śaraṇam edhi vi|śaraṇasya rāja|sūnor! iti›

Añjalim abadhnāt.

‹Kim īyā jāty" âsya māt" êti?›

13.93 anuyukte may" âmun" ôktam:

‹Pāṭaliputrasya vaṇijo Vaiśravaṇasya duhitari Sāgaradattāyāṃ Kosal'|êndrāt Kusumadhanvano 'sya mātā jāt" êti.›

‹Yady evam etan|mātur mat|pituś c' âiko mātāmaha iti.›

13.96 sa|snehaṃ tam ahaṃ sasvaje. vṛddhen' ôktam:

‹Sindhu|dattā|putrāṇāṃ katamas te pit" êti?›

‹Suśruta iti,›

13.99 ukte so 'tyahṛṣyat. ahaṃ tu:

"My dear Nali·jangha, 'Reed shank,' while this boy still lives, find a refuge where he can survive. If I too survive, then I will follow him. Once you have found safety, inform me of your situation."

I somehow managed to get him out of that chaotic royal household, and we plunged into the Vindhyan forest. Going on foot pained the child, so to let him recover we took a rest for several days in some cowherds' station. But I was terrified of an attack by the king's men even there, and we travelled on far along the road.

When, on the journey, he was afflicted with a dreadful 13.90
thirst, I wanted to give him water, but slipped and fell into this well, from where you have rescued me. Hence you are the one who should now protect the unprotected prince!'

He pressed his hands together in supplication. I asked:

'Whose line is his mother from?'

He told me: 13.93

'His mother was born to Kúsuma·dhanvan the Lord of Kósala, and his wife Ságara·datta, daughter of the merchant Vaishrávana of Pátali·putra.'

'In that case his mother and my father have the same paternal grandfather.'

With which I embraced the child affectionately. The old 13.96
man asked:

'Which of the sons of Sindhu·datta was your father's father?'

'Súshruta'

I replied, to his great delight. Then I solemnly declared: 13.99

‹Taṃ nay'|âvaliptam Aśmak'|êndraṃ nayen' âiv' ônmūlya bālam enaṃ pitrye pade pratiṣṭhāpayeyam. iti›

pratijñāya:

13.102 ‹Katham asy' âināṃ kṣudhaṃ kṣapayeyam iti?›

acitanyam. tāvad āpatitau ca kasy' âpi vyādhasya trīn iṣūn atītya dvau mṛgau sa ca vyādhaḥ. tasya hastād avaśiṣṭam iṣu|dvayaṃ kodaṇḍaṃ c' ākṣipy' âvidhyam. ekaḥ sa|patrākṛto 'nyaś ca niṣpatrākṛto 'patat. taṃ c' âikaṃ mṛgaṃ dattvā mṛgayave, anyasy' âpaloma|tvacaḥ klom' âpohya niṣkulākṛtya vikṛty' ôrv|asthi|grīv'|ādīni śūlākṛtya dāvāṅgāreṣu taptena' āmiṣeṇa tayor ātmanaś ca kṣudham atyatārṣam. etasmin karmaṇi mat|sauṣṭhaven' âtihṛṣṭaṃ Kirātam asmi pṛṣṭavān:

‹Api jānāsi Māhiṣmatī|vṛtt'|ântam iti?›

13.105 Asāv ācaṣṭa:

‹Tatra vyāghra|tvaco dṛtīś ca vikrīy' âdy' âiv' āgataḥ. kiṃ na jānāmi. Pracaṇḍavarmā nāma Caṇḍavarm"|ânujo Mitravarma|duhitaraṃ Mañjuvādinīṃ vilipsur abhyet' îti ten' ôtsav'|ôttarā pur" îti.›

Atha karṇe jīrṇam abravam:

13.108 ‹Dhūrto Mitravarmā duhitari samyak pratipattyā mātaraṃ viśvāsya tan|mukhena pratyākṛṣya bālakaṃ jighāṃsati. tat pratigatya kuśalam asya mad|vārtāṃ ca devyai raho ni-

'By pure statecraft I shall extirpate that Lord of Áshmaka who drips with such arrogance about his statecraft, and I shall establish this boy in the position that is his patrimony.'

Then I fretted:

'How shall I assuage his hunger?' 13.102

Just then two deer rushed onto the scene. They had outstripped three arrows of some hunter, who then arrived himself. I snatched the bow and the two remaining arrows from his hand, and fired them. Both deer fell, one pierced all the way to the arrow's feathers, the other so that even the feathers passed through and out the other side. I gave one to the deerhunter, and the other I skinned completely and cleaned, gutted its lungs and entrails, then butchered the thighbones, neck and so on, and skewered it. Finally I cooked the meat on forest coals, before it banished the hunger of the boy, the old man and myself. The woodsman was most impressed with my elegant performance of the job. I asked him:

'Do you have any news from Mahíshmati?'

He replied: 13.105

'I am come from there only today. I had been selling tiger skins and leather bags. Of course I know the news. Prachánda·varman, the younger brother of Chanda·varman, is coming to marry Mañju·vádini, Mitra·varman's daughter. Hence the city is full of festivities.'

At this I whispered into the old man's ear:

'That knave Mitra·varman plans to reassure the mother 13.108
by treating her daughter well. He hopes to persuade her to call back her little boy so that he can kill him. You should go now therefore and secretly inform the queen that the boy

vedya punaḥ kumāraḥ śārdūla|bhakṣita iti prakāśam ākrośanaṃ kāryam. sa durmatir antaḥ|prīto bahir duḥkhaṃ darśayan devīm anuneṣyati. punas tvayā tan|mukhena sa vācyaḥ:

«Yad|apekṣayā tvan|matam atyakramiṣaṃ so 'pi bālaḥ pāpena me para|lokam agāt. adya tu tvad|ādeśa|kāriṇy ev' âham iti.»

Sa tath"|ôktaḥ prītiṃ pratipady' âbhipatsyati. punar anena vatsa|nābha|nāmnā mahā|viṣeṇa saṃnīya toyaṃ tatra mālāṃ majjayitvā tayā sa vakṣasi mukhe ca hantavyaḥ.

13.111 «Sa ev' âyam asi|prahāraḥ pāpīyasas tava bhavatu yady asmi pati|vrat" êti.»

Punar anen' âgadena saṃgamite 'mbhasi tāṃ mālāṃ majjayitvā sva|duhitre deyā. mṛte tu tasmiṃs tasyāṃ ca nir|vikārāyāṃ satyāṃ sat" îty ev' âināṃ prakṛtayo 'nuvartiṣyante. punaḥ Pracaṇḍavarmaṇe saṃdeśyam:

«A|nāyakam idaṃ rājyam. anen' âiva saha bālik" êyaṃ svīkartavy" êti.»

13.114 Tāvad āvāṃ kāpālika|veṣa|channau devy" âiva dīyamāna|bhikṣau puro bahir upaśmaśānaṃ vartsyāvaḥ. punar ārya|prāyān paura|vṛddhān āptāṃś ca mantri|vṛddhān ek'|ânte bravītu devī:

is safe, and about my involvement. Then bewail in public that the prince was eaten up by a tiger. That wicked man will be delighted within but externally will display grief to attract the queen. Next have her say to him:

"For the boy's sake I rejected your wishes. Now, to pay for my sin, he is the one who has gone to the next world. Today I am ready to do as you command."

He will be delighted to hear this, and will throw himself at her. For her part, the queen should have mixed previously this strong poison I am giving you called *vatsa·nabha** into water and have dunked a garland in it, with which she should thereupon strike him on the chest and face.

"You are sinful, and if I am a faithful wife then this harm- 13.111
less object will cut you like a sword."*

Afterward she should mix this antidote I give you into the water, plunge the garland again, and pass it on to her own daughter. When he dies, and the young woman remains unaffected, the population will honor her as a true and virtuous wife. Next, the queen should send word to Prachánda·varman:

"This kingdom is without a ruler. It is yours for the taking, and with it my daughter here."

By then, the young prince and I will have disguised our- 13.114
selves in the bone-and-ashes mortuary costume of *kapálika* ascetics,* and will be haunting the subsidiary charnel-ground outside the city, unwilling to accept alms from any other than the queen herself. Thereupon the queen is to address the mostly noble elder citizens and trusted old ministers, in private:

«Svapne 'dya me devyā Vindhyavāsinyā kṛtaḥ prasādaḥ:

‹Adya caturthe 'hani Pracaṇḍavarmā mariṣyati. pañcame 'hani Revā|taṭa|vartini mad|bhavane parīkṣya vaijanyaṃ janeṣu nirgateṣu kapāṭam udghāṭya tvat|sutena saha ko 'pi dvija|kumāro niryāsyati.

13.117 Sa rājyam idam anupālya bālaṃ te pratiṣṭhāpayiṣyati. sa khalu bālo mayā vyāghrī|rūpayā tiraskṛtya sthāpitaḥ. sā c' êyaṃ vatsā Mañjuvādinī tasya dvijāti|dārakasya dāratven' âiva kalpit" êti.›

Tad etad ati|rahasyaṃ yuṣmāsv eva guptaṃ tiṣṭhatu yāvad etad upapatsyata iti.» ›

Sa sāṃpratam atiprītaḥ prayāto 'rthaś c' âyaṃ yathā|cintitam anuṣṭhito 'bhūt. prati|diśaṃ ca loka|vādaḥ prāsarpat:

13.120 ‹Aho, māhātmyaṃ pati|vratānām! asi|prahāra eva hi sa mālā|prahāras tasmin jātaḥ. na śakyam upadhi|yuktam etat|karm' êti vaktuṃ yatas tad eva dattaṃ dāma duhitre stana|maṇḍanam eva tasyai jātaṃ, na mṛtyuḥ. yo 'syāḥ pati|vratāyāḥ śāsanam ativartate sa bhasm' âiva bhaved iti.›

Atha mahā|vrati|veṣeṇa māṃ ca putraṃ ca bhikṣāyai praviṣṭau dṛṣṭvā prasnuta|stanī pratyutthāya harṣ'|ākulam abravīt:

"This night the goddess Vindhya·vásini, 'Who dwells in the Vindhyas,' favored me by revealing herself in a dream, saying:

'On the fourth day from today Prachánda·varman will die. On the fifth day when the people have left you should inspect my house, my temple on the bank of the Reva, the "roaring" Nármada River, to verify that it is completely deserted. Subsequently, from within, a young brahmin will open the door and emerge with your son.

The brahmin youth will save and preserve the kingdom, 13.117
and install your boy on the throne. In the form of a tigress, it was I who made that child disappear, in order to preserve him. As for your daughter Mañju·vádini, she is fated to become the wife of that same young brahmin.'

You should keep this whole plan very secret, hidden only among you, until it has come to pass."'

Rightly overjoyed with the arrangement, the old man set off, and everything transpired just as planned. Thus in every quarter the rumor of the population spread:

'Amazing, the charismatic power of a chaste and virtuous 13.120
wife! For the strike of her garland proved indeed to be the cut of a sword for the king. Nor can it be claimed that there was anything suspicious about the business, because when she passed the same object on to her daughter it proved to be no more than an ornament for her breast, not death. Whoever transgresses the command of this chaste and virtuous wife will be reduced to ashes.'

Next, the son and I in our ascetic outfits entered the palace to get alms. Seeing us, the milk flowed from her breasts with maternal affection as she rose and in a flurry of delight spoke:

‹Bhagavan, ayam añjaliḥ. a|nātho 'yaṃ jano 'nugṛhyatām. asti mam' âikaḥ svapnaḥ sa kiṃ satyo na v" êti?›

13.123 May" ôktam:

‹Phalam asy' âdy' âiva drakṣyas' îti.›

‹Yady evaṃ bahu bhāga|dheyam asyā vo dāsyāḥ. sa khalv asyāḥ sānāthya|śaṃsī svapna iti.›

13.126 Mad|darśana|rāga|baddha|sādhvasāṃ Mañjuvādinīṃ pragamayya, bhūyo 'pi sā harṣa|garbham abrūta:

‹Tac cen mithyā so 'yaṃ yuṣmadīyo bālaka|pālī śvo mayā niroddhavya iti.›

May" âpi sa|smitaṃ Mañju|vādinī|rāga|līna|dṛṣṭi|līḍha|dhairyeṇ' âbhihitaṃ,

13.129 ‹Evam astv iti.›

Labdha|bhaikṣo Nālījaṅgham ākārya nirgamya tataś ca taṃ c' ânuyāntaṃ śanair apṛccham:

‹Kv' âsāv alp'|āyuḥ prathitaḥ Pracaṇḍavarm" êti?›

13.132 So 'brūta:

‹Rājyam idaṃ mam' êty apāsta|śaṅko rājā|sthāna|maṇḍapa eva tiṣṭhaty upāsyamānaḥ kuśīlavair iti.›

‹Yady evam udyāne tiṣṭh' êti!›

13.135 Taṃ jarantam ādiśya tat|prākār'|âika|pārśve kva cic chūnya|maṭhikāyāṃ mātrāḥ samavatārya tad|rakṣaṇa|niyukta|rāja|putraḥ kṛta|kuśīlava|veṣa|līlaḥ Pracaṇḍavarmāṇam ety' ânvarañjayam.

'My lord, here are my hands pressed together in supplication. Please favor me who am at your mercy. The dream I had, was it true or not?'

I announced: 13.123

'You shall see the fruit of it this very day.'

'If that is so then your slave is greatly blessed. For my dream seemed to predict that my daughter would gain her protector.'

Mañju·vádini was flustered by the love that had possessed 13.126
her the moment she saw me, but her mother made her step forward. Then, swallowing her delight, she spoke again:

'If the predictions turn out to be false, tomorrow I shall imprison this boy student of yours.'

My composure, too, had been melted by Mañju·vádini's look of completely absorbed love, as I agreed with a smile,

'Yes, it shall be as you say.' 13.129

Our alms received, we went out, with a sign to Nali·jangha, whereupon he followed us and I could quietly ask:

'Where is that famous short-lived Prachánda·varman?'

He replied: 13.132

'All doubt discarded that this kingdom is his, he remains right within the palace pavilion, being waited upon by entertainers.'

'In that case, wait for me in the garden.'

Having instructed the old man, I then dropped our paltry 13.135
possessions into an empty hut on the other side of the wall, gave the young prince the job of guarding them, and, dressed in the gay costume of an acrobat, I went to entertain Prachánda·varman.

Anurañjit'|ātape tu samaye jana|samāja|jñān'|ôpayogīni saṃhṛtya nṛtya|gīta|nānā|rutāni hasta|caṅkramaṇam ūrdhva|pād'|âlāta|pād'|āpīḍa|vṛścika|makara|laṅghan'|ādīni matsy'|ôdvartan'|ādīni ca karaṇāni punar ādāy' ādāya, āsanna|vartināṃ kṣurikās tābhir upahita|varṣmā citra|duṣkarāṇi karaṇāni śyena|pāt'|ôtkrośa|pāt'|ādīni darśayan, viṃśati|cāp'|ântarāl'|âvasthitasya Pracaṇḍavarmaṇaś churikay" âikayā praty|urasaṃ prahṛtya:

‹Jīvyād varṣa|sahasraṃ Vasantabhānur iti!›

13.138 abhigarjan mad|gātram utkartum udyat'|âseḥ kasy' âpi cāra|bhaṭasya pīvar'|âṃsa|bāhu|śikharam ākramya tāvat" âiva taṃ vicetīkurvann ākulaṃ ca lokam uccakṣūkurvan dvi|puruṣ'|ôcchritaṃ prākāram atyalaṅghayam. avaplutya c' ôpavane:

‹Mad|anupātinām eṣa panthā dṛśyata iti.›

bruvāṇa eva Nālījaṅgha|samīkṛta|saikat'|âspaṣṭa|pāda|nyāsayā tamāla|vīthyā c' ânu|prākāraṃ prācā prati|pradhāvitaḥ punar avāc" ôccit'|êṣṭaka|citatvād a|lakṣya|pātena pradrutya laṅghita|prākāra|vapra|khāta|valayas tasyāṃ śūnya|maṭhikāyāṃ tūrṇam eva praviśya pratimukta|pūrva|veṣaḥ saha kumāreṇa mat|karma|tumula|rāja|dvāri duḥkha|labdha|vartmā śmaśān'|ôddeśam abhyagām.

When the evening sun reddened, I caught the attention of the assembled crowd with an entrancing display of dance and song, and mimicry of the cries of all kinds of birds and animals. Seamlessly, I waved my hands about, with my feet in the air, repeatedly rolling my head around, extending one foot and bending the other. I mimed the poised scorpion leap and the crocodile jump and so on, and flipped from side to side like a fish. Then I plucked daggers here and there from those seated at the front. With these deposited about my person, I performed amazing impossible feats such as the flight of a falcon and the flight of an osprey. Prachánda·varman was sitting twenty bow lengths away when I struck him full on the chest with one of the daggers, roaring:

'May Vasánta·bhanu live a thousand years!'*

One valiant warrior actor raised his sword to slash my 13.138
body, but I sprang onto his high stout shoulders, which was enough to confound him, and with the eyes of the confused crowd on me I jumped over the wall, two men tall. Landing in the garden, I only exclaimed:

'My pursuers will be able to see these tracks,"

Before I rushed headlong eastward along the wall beside a row of *tamála* trees, while Nali·jangha levelled my faint footprints in the sand. Next I raced southward, the direction of my flight invisible thanks to the brick-covered path. Jumping over the wall, the rampart, the moat and the fence, I raced into the aforementioned empy hut. There I put on my previous costume, and the prince and I set out for the charnel-ground. We only found a way through with difficulty at the royal gate, which was in tumult at my deed.

13.141 Prāg eva tasmin Durgā|gṛhe pratim"|âdhiṣṭhāna eva mayā kṛtaṃ bhagna|pārśva|sthairya|sthūla|prastara|sthagita|bāhya|dvāraṃ bilam.

Atha galati madhya|rātre varṣa|var'|ôpanīta|mah"|ârha|ratna|bhūṣaṇa|paṭṭa|nivasanau tad bilam āvāṃ praviśya tūṣṇīm atiṣṭhāva. devī tu pūrvedyur eva yath"|ârham agni|saṃskāraṃ Mālavāya dattvā Pracaṇḍavarmaṇe, Caṇḍavarmaṇe ca tām avasthām Aśmak'|êndr'|ôpadhikṛtām eva saṃdiśya;

uttaredyuḥ praty|uṣasy eva pūrva|saṃketita|paur'|āmātya|sāmanta|vṛddhaiḥ sah' âbhyetya Bhagavatīm arcayitvā sarva|jana|pratyakṣaṃ parīkṣita|kukṣi|vaijanyaṃ tad|bhavanaṃ vidhāya datta|dṛṣṭiḥ saha janena sthitvā paṭīyāṃsaṃ paṭaha|śabdam akārayat.

13.144 Aṇutara|randhra|praviṣṭena tena nāden' âhaṃ datta|saṃjñaḥ śiras" âiv' ôtkṣipya sa|pratimaṃ loha|pāda|pīṭham aṃsala|puruṣa|prayatna|duścalam ubhaya|kara|vidhṛt'|âika|pārśvam ekato niveśya niragamam. niragamayaṃ ca kumāram. atha yathā|pūrvam arpayitvā Durgām udghāṭita|kapāṭaḥ pratyakṣībhūya pratyaya|hṛṣṭa|dṛṣṭi spaṣṭa|rom'|âñcam udyat'|âñjali rūḍha|vismayaṃ ca praṇipatantīḥ prakṛtīr abhyadhām:

I had already burrowed in advance a tunnel right at the base of the idol in that house and temple of Durga, and had concealed its exterior entrance behind a solid slab, prised loose from the setting of its edges. 13.141

Later, as the midnight hour was passing, the two of us entered the tunnel, and stayed there in silence, dressed in the silk and greatly valuable jewelled ornaments brought to us by a eunuch from the harem. The queen, meanwhile, had given Prachánda·varman the Málavan his due cremation rites just the day before, and sent word to Chanda·varman that it was the Lord of Áshmaka who had arranged the assassination.

The next day at dawn she set out with her elder citizens, ministers and feudatory princes to worship the Goddess, as previously arranged. Before the eyes of everyone, she inspected the shrine and verified that the goddess's house was deserted. Then she stood watching with her people while the kettledrums rolled a deep roar on her command.

That roar penetrated through a microscopic aperture to give me the signal. With my head I pushed up the copper pedestal carrying the idol, which even a muscleman would have had a task to move, and taking hold of one edge with both hands I pushed it to one side, and emerged, before bringing the prince out, too. Having reinstalled the Durga as before, I opened the door panels and we were revealed before the eyes of everyone. Suddenly amazed, the population prostrated themselves on the ground, eyes delighted with the revelation, visibly thrilled to the hair on their bodies, and hands raised, palms together. I addressed them: 13.144

‹Ittham Devī Vindhyavāsinī man|mukhena yuṣmān ājñāpayati:

«Sa eṣa rāja|sūnur āpanno mayā sa|kṛpayā śārdūla|rūpeṇa tiraskṛty' âdya vo dattaḥ. tam enam adya|pabhṛti mat|puttratay" â|manda|mātṛ|pakṣa iti parigṛhṇantu bhavantaḥ.»

13.147 Api ca dur|ghaṭa|kūṭa|koṭi|ghaṭanā|pāṭava|prakaṭa|śāṭhya|niṣṭhur' Âśmaka|ghaṭa|ghaṭṭan'|ātmānaṃ māṃ manyadhvam asya rakṣitāram. rakṣā|nirveśaś c' âsya svas" êyaṃ su|bhrūr abhyanujñātā mahyam Āryay" êti.›

Śrutv" âitat:

‹Aho! bhāgyavān Bhoja|vaṃśo yasya tvam Āryā|datto nātha iti!›

13.150 aprīyanta prakṛtayaḥ. sā tu vācām a|gocarāṃ harṣ'|âvasthām aspṛśan me śvaśrūḥ. tad ahar eva ca yathāvad agrāhayan Mañjuvādinī|pāṇi|pallavam. prapannāyāṃ ca yāminyāṃ samyag eva bilaṃ pratyapūrayam. a|labdha|randhraś ca loko naṣṭa|muṣṭi|cint"|ādi|kathanair abhyupāy'|ântara|prayuktair divy'|âṃśatām eva mama samarthayamāno mad|ājñāṃ n' âtyavartata.

Rāja|putrasy' Āryā|putra iti prabhāva|hetuḥ prasiddhir āsīt. taṃ ca guṇavaty ahani bhadrākṛtam upanāyya puro|hi-

'The goddess Vindhya·vásini commands you through me as follows:

"The royal prince you see before you was in trouble, when I took pity and in the form of a tiger whisked him out of view. Today I render him to you. From this day forward you good people should embrace him, knowing that he does not lack power on his maternal side, since he is like my son."

Moreover, the Goddess orders you to consider me the 13.147
prince's guardian. For my one ambition is to smash cruel Áshmaka's frame. His treachery and cruelty are now public in his cunning hatching of many dastardly plots. In return for my protection the noble Goddess has granted me the boy's fair-browed sister.'

The populace were delighted at my words:

'Wonderful! The line of Bhoja is blessed that the noble Goddess has bestowed you as Lord and Protector!'

My mother-in-law was speechless with joy. That very same 13.150
day she gave me in formal marriage the tender sprout-like hand of Mañju·vádini. Once night had fallen I carefully filled the tunnel in, so that people would never find the opening. Because no one had found it, and because I could, for example, divine what someone had lost, or held in a closed fist, and what someone was thinking, as well as by alternative expedients I employed, everyone was convinced that I must be a divine emanation. None dared disobey my command.

Celebrated as the son of the noble Goddess, the prince's power was assured. On the auspicious day, I had him shaved according to the ritual, and the royal family priest initiated him with the sacred thread. All the while instructing him in

tena pāṭhayan nītiṃ rāja|kāryāṇy anvatiṣṭham. acintayaṃ ca:

‹Rājyaṃ nāma śakti|tray'|āyattam. śaktayaś ca mantra|prabhāv'|ôtsāhāḥ paras|par'|ânugṛhītāḥ kṛtyeṣu kramante. mantreṇa hi viniścayo 'rthānāṃ, prabhāveṇa prārambhaḥ, utsāhena nirvahaṇam.

13.153 Ataḥ pañc'|âṅga|mantra|mūlo dvi|rūpa|prabhāva|skandhaś catur|guṇ'|ôtsāha|viṭapo dvi|saptati|prakṛti|patraḥ ṣaḍ|guṇa|kisalayaḥ śakti|siddhi|puṣpa|phalaś ca naya|vanaspatir netur upakaroti.

Sa c' âyam an|ek'|âdhikaraṇatvād a|sahāyena dur|upajīvyaḥ. yas tv ayam Āryaketur nāma Mitravarma|mantrī sa Kosal'|âbhijanatvāt kumāra|mātṛ|pakṣo mantri|guṇaiś ca yuktaḥ tan|matim avamaty' âiva dhvasto Mitravarmā, sa cel labdhaḥ peśalam iti.›

Atha Nālījaṅghaṃ rahasy aśikṣayam:

13.156 ‹Tāta, āryam Āryaketum ek'|ânte brūhi:

«Ko nv eṣa māyā|puruṣo ya imāṃ Rājya|lakṣmīm anubhavati? sa c' âyam asmad|bālo bhujaṅgen' âmunā parigṛhītaḥ. kim udgīryeta grasyeta v" êti?»

Sa yad vadiṣyati tad asmi bodhya iti.›

13.159 So 'nyad" âivaṃ māṃ āvedayat:

political science, I administered the royal duties. One day, I reflected:

'A kingdom, it is true, depends on the three powers: good counsel, majesty and energy. When those powers are in mutual harmony they advance deeds and duties. Good counsel decides what projects to engage in, majesty gives them impetus, and energy brings them to completion.

Hence the ruler's friend is the tree of policy. Its roots 13.153
are the five parts of advice, the two forms of majesty its trunk, the four kinds of energy its branches, the seventy-two *prákritis* (constituents) its leaves, the six qualities its buds,* and power its flowers and success its fruit.

But this tree of policy has so many ramifications that it is impossible to exploit it without a political partner. If we could obtain Mitra·varman's minister, Arya·ketu, that would be simply marvelous. He is the prince's mother's natural ally, since both are from Kósala, and is endowed with an adviser's good qualifications. After all, it was precisely through disregarding his counsel that Mitra·varman came to ruin.'

Then I secretly instructed Nali·jangha:

'Dear father, take the noble Arya·ketu aside and mutter 13.156
to him:

"Who does he think he is, this impostor who is taking advantage of Lakshmi, this kingdom's glory? Our boy the prince is totally in that charming snake's clutches. Will he swallow him up, or spit him out?"

Let me know how he responds.'

Later he brought me the following report: 13.159

‹Muhur upāsya prābhṛtaiḥ pravartya citrāḥ kathāḥ saṃvāhya pāṇi|pādam ati|visrambha|datta|kṣaṇaṃ tam aprākṣaṃ tvad|upadiṣṭena nayena. so 'py evam akathayat:

«Bhadra, m" âivaṃ vādīḥ! abhijanasya śuddhi|darśanam a|sādhāraṇaṃ buddhi|naipuṇam atimānuṣaṃ prāṇa|balam a|parimāṇam audāryam aty|āścaryam astra|kauśalam an|alpaṃ śilpa|jñānam anugrah'|ārdraṃ cetas tejaś c' âpy a|viṣahyam abhyamitrīṇam ity asminn eva saṃnipātino guṇāḥ, ye 'nyatr' âik'|âikaśo 'pi durlabhāḥ.

13.162 Dviṣatām eṣa cira|bilva|drumaḥ prahvānāṃ tu candana|tarus tam uddhṛtya nītijñaṃ|manyam Aśmakam imaṃ ca rāja|putram anena pitrye pade pratiṣṭhitam eva viddhi. n' âtra saṃśayaḥ kārya iti.» ›

Tac c' âpi śrutvā bhūyo|bhūyaś c' ôpadhābhir viśodhya taṃ me mati|sahāyam akaravam. tat|sakhaś ca satya|śauca|yuktān amātyān vividha|vyañjanāṃś ca gūḍha|puruṣān udapādayam. tebhyaś c' ôpalabhya lubdha|samṛddham aty|utsiktam a|vidheya|prāyaṃ ca prakṛti|maṇḍalam;

a|lubdhatām abhikhyāpayan, dhārmikatvam udbhāvayan nāstikān kadarthayan kaṇṭakān viśodhayan a|mitr'|ôpadhīr apaghnan cāturvarṇyaṃ ca sva|dharma|karmasu sthāpayan abhisamāhareyam arthān. artha|mūlā hi daṇḍa|viśiṣṭa|kar-

'I courted the minister persistently with presents, engaged him in lively conversation, massaged his hands and feet, and when the moment of total confidence arrived, then I asked him just as you had instructed. He responded as follows:

"Good man, you should not talk like this. The regent glows with the luster of good birth, and has uncommonly sharp intelligence. His physical strength is superhuman, his loftiness of mind immeasurable, his skill in missiles exceedingly marvelous, his knowledge of the arts not inconsiderable, his heart oozes kindness, and his valor too is irresistible and channelled straight against the enemy. Thus in him all good qualities coincide, while they are rare to find even individually in others.

For his enemies he is a poisonous *chira·bilva*, a woodapple 13.162
tree, while to his allies he is a soothing sandal. Know that he will extirpate that Áshmaka who thought himself expert in politics and install this king's son in his hereditary place. Of this I am certain." '

After I heard that I subjected Arya·ketu to several more tests of his character,* before making him my partner in planning. With his agreement I appointed ministers committed to truth and integrity, and spies in various disguises. Through these both I learned about my subjects, who were greedy and wealthy, self-inflated, and all but uncontrollable.

Then I publicized my own lack of greed, promoted religiosity, harassed atheists,* purged criminal thorns to the state, repelled enemy plots, and established the four castes in the business of their respective religious duties, and all in order that I should amass material wealth. For any undertaking that involves politics has to be founded on wealth.

m'|ārambhāḥ. na c' ânyad asti pāpiṣṭhaṃ tatra daurbalyāt. Ity ākalayya yogān anvatiṣṭham.

iti śrī|Daṇḍinaḥ kṛtau
Daśa|kumāra|carite
Viśruta|caritaṃ
nāma
aṣṭam'|ôcchvāsaḥ.

Nor is there anything worse in politics than weakness in that respect. With these thoughts in mind I pursued our projects with determination.

That is the end of the eighth chapter of
the glorious Dandin's
What Ten Young Men Did.
It is called:
What Víshruta Did.*

PART III:
POSTSCRIPT CONCLUSION

CHAPTER FOURTEEN
WHAT VÍSHRUTA DID NEXT

VYACINTAYAM ca:

Sarvo 'py atiśūraḥ sevaka|vargo mayi tath" ânurakto yath" ājñayā jīvitam api tṛṇāya manyate. rājya|dvitaya|sainya|sāmagyrā ca n' âham Aśmak'|ēśād Vasantabhānor nyūno nīty|āviṣṭaś ca. ato Vasantabhānuṃ parājitya Vidarbh'|âdhipater Anantavarmaṇas tanayaṃ Bhāskaravarmāṇaṃ pitrye pade sthāpayitum alam asmi.

14.3 Ayaṃ ca rāja|sūnur Bhavānyā putratvena parikalpitaḥ. ahaṃ c' âsya sāhāyye niyukta iti sarvatra kiṃvadantī saṃjāt" âsti. ady' âpi c' âitan mat|kapaṭa|kṛtyaṃ na ken' âpi viditam, atra|sthāś ca asmin Bhāskaravarmaṇi rāja|tanaye:

‹Ayam asmat|svāmino 'nantavarmaṇaḥ putro Bhavānyāḥ prasādād etad rājyam avāpsyat' îti.›

baddh'|āśā vartante. Aśmak'|ēśa|sainyaṃ ca rāja|sūnor Bhavānī|sāhāyyaṃ viditvā:

14.6 ‹Daivyāḥ śakteḥ puro na balavatī mānavī śaktir iti.›

Asmābhir vigrahe cala|cittam iv' ôpalakṣyate. atratyāś ca maulāḥ prakṛtayaḥ prathamam eva rāja|sut'|âbhyuday'|âbhilāṣiṇya idānīṃ ca punar mayā dāna|mān'|ādy|āvārjanena viśvāsitā viśeṣeṇa rāja|putram ev' âbhikāṅkṣanti. Aśmak'|êndr'|ântaraṅgāś ca bhṛtyā madīyair viśvāsyatamaiḥ puruṣaiḥ prabhūtāṃ prītim utpādya mad|ājñayā rahas' îty upajaptāḥ:

I REFLECTED:

The whole terribly brave body of staff here are so devoted to me that if I commanded it they would think their lives worth no more than a blade of grass. Nor am I inferior to Vasánta·bhanu, Lord of Áshmaka, with the combined military apparatus of both kingdoms, and being steeped in political know-how. I am strong enough therefore to first defeat Vasánta·bhanu and then install Bháskara·varman, Anánta·varman's son, overlord of Vidárbha, in his inherited position.

The report that the goddess Bhaváni has deemed this 14.3
prince to be her son and enjoined me to be his guardian has spread everywhere. Until this day no one has discovered that I perpetrated this deceit. The people here have placed their hopes on our prince Bháskara·varman:

'Through the favor of the Goddess, our master Anánta·varman's son is sure to regain his kingdom.'

Even the army of the Áshmakan king knows that the prince is under the Goddess's protection. They reason:

'In the face of divine power, mortal power is impotent.' 14.6

The army's mind seems to waver with regard to engaging us in battle. The hereditary subjects of this place desired from the first the prince's success, but now that I have inspired their confidence by bestowing gifts and honors and so forth, they want the king's son above all else. My most trusted men have won the powerful affection of the Áshmakan lord's personal staff, making secret overtures on my command:

‹Yūyam asman|mitrāṇi, ato 'smākaṃ śubh'|ôdarkaṃ vaco vācyam eva. atra Bhavānyā rāja|sūnoḥ sāhāyyakāya viśrutaṃ Viśrutaṃ niyujya tadd|hasten' Âśmak'|êndrasya Vasantabhānos tat|pakṣe sthitvā ye c' ânena saha yotsyante teṣām apy Antak'|âtithi|bhavanam.

14.9 Yāvad Aśmak'|êndreṇa sa janya|vṛttir na jātas tāvad enam Anantavarma|tanayaṃ Bhāskaravarmāṇam anusariṣyatha. sa vīta|bhayo bhūyasīṃ pravṛttim āsādya sa|parijanaḥ sukhena nivatsyati na ced Bhavānī|tri|śūla|vaśyo bhaviṣyati.

Bhavānyā ca mam' êty ājñaptam asti yad eka|vāraṃ sarveṣāṃ kathaya. ato 'smākaṃ yuṣmābhiḥ saha maitrīm avabudhy' âsman|mukhena sarvebhyo vārtam. iti›

ākarṇya te 'śmak'|êndr'|ântaraṅga|bhṛtyā rāja|sūnor Bhavānī|varaṃ viditvā pūrvam eva bhinna|manasa āsan. viśeṣataś ca madīyam iti vacanaṃ śrutvā te sarve 'pi mad|vaśe samabhavan. etaṃ sarvam api vṛtt'|ântam avabudhy' Âśmak'|ēśena vyacinti:

14.12 ‹Yad rāja|sūnor maulāḥ prajās tāḥ sarvā apy enam eva prabhum abhilaṣanti. madīyaś ca bāhya ābhyantaro bhṛtya|vargo bhinna|manā iva lakṣyate. evaṃ yady ahaṃ kṣamām avalambya gṛha eva sthāsyāmi tata utpann'|ôpajāpaṃ sva|rājyam api paritrātuṃ na śakṣyāmi.

'You are our friends. Hence we are obliged to tell you what will bring you a happy ending. Everyone knows that Bhaváni has appointed Víshruta as the prince's guardian, to make with his own hand Vasánta·bhanu the Áshmakan Lord a guest in Death's house. Any man who stands and fights with Vasánta·bhanu will meet the same fate.

You should change sides to Bháskara·varman, Anánta·var- 14.9
man's son, before he engages the Áshmakan Lord in battle. Freed from fear, whoever thus ensures his continued favorable existence will live on in happiness with all his entourage, instead of being conquered by the goddess Bhaváni's trident.

Moreover, Bhaváni herself had commanded Víshruta to inform everyone of this, once and for all. It is because she recognizes our loving friendship with you that she is telling this to every one of you in person, through us.'

The Áshmakan Lord's personal staff listened, their minds already divided since they had learned of Bhaváni's boon to the prince. Now that they had heard what was presented as my personal message, they came over to my side, to a man. As soon as the Áshmakan Lord discovered what had happened, he thought to himself:

'Every last one of this prince's hereditary subjects yearn for 14.12
him as their Lord. And my personal staff appear, from what I can see, to have split loyalties. This being so, if I should give way to complacency and abide only in my house, then I would be incapable of preserving even my own kingdom, now that mutterings of revolt have begun.

Ato yāvatā bhinna|cittena mad|avabodhakaṃ prakaṭayatā mad|balena saha mitho|vacanaṃ na saṃjātaṃ tāvat" âiva tena sākaṃ vigrahaṃ racayāmi. ity evaṃ vihite sa vaśyaṃ mad|agre kṣaṇam avasthāsyat' îti.›

niścity' â|nyāyena para|rājya|kramaṇa|pātaka|preritaḥ sa|sainyo mṛtyu|mukham iv' âsmat|sainyam abhyayāt. tam abhyāyāntaṃ viditvā rāja|putraḥ puro 'bhavat. ato 'śmak'|êndram eva turag'|âdhirūḍho yāntam abhyasaram. tāvat sarvā eva tat|senā:

14.15 ‹Yad ayam etāvato '|parimitasy' âsmat|sainyasy' ôpary eka ev' âbhyāgacchati tatra Bhavānī|vara ev' â|sādhāraṇaṃ kāraṇaṃ, n' ânyad. iti›

niścity' ālekhya|likhit" êv' âvasthitā. tato may" âbhigamya saṃgarāya samāhūto Vasantabhānuḥ sametya mām asi|prahāreṇa dṛḍham abhyahan. ahaṃ ca śikṣā|viśeṣa|viphalita|tad|asi|prahāraḥ pratiprahāreṇa taṃ prahaty' âvakṛttam Aśmak'|êndra|śiro 'vanau vinipātya tat|sainikān avadam:

‹Ataḥ param api ye yuyutsavo bhavanti te sametya mayā yudhyantām. na ced rāja|tanaya|caraṇa|praṇāmaṃ vidhāya tadīyāḥ santaḥ sva|sva|vṛtty|upabhoga|pūrvakaṃ nijān nijān adhikārān niḥśaṅkaṃ paripālayantaḥ sukhen' âvatiṣṭhantv iti.›

Therefore I should contrive to go into battle against him now, before he can speak in secret with my wavering army, and they betray my purpose. If I can arrange this, then he will be able to resist me no longer than an instant.'

Thus he resolved. Driven by the sin of the unfounded preemptive strike against another's kingdom, he and his army charged at our army as though into the jaws of death. When our prince learned that he was on the battle-charge he sortied out to meet him. Then I too sallied forth mounted on a horse to the advancing Áshmakan Lord. At this his entire army were convinced:

'The one and only reason that this man would ride out all 14.15
alone against our so limitless forces must be the Bhaváni's pledge. Otherwise he would not dare.'

And with that they stopped where they were, motionless as though drawn in a picture. Next I advanced and challenged Vasánta·bhanu to single combat. He charged and struck me hard with a blow of his sword. But I was able to parry that swordstroke with my superior swordsmanship and strike him with a return cut, decapitating the Áshmakan Lord and hurling his head to the ground, before I addressed his troops:

'Whoever wishes to keep on fighting after this should ride out and fight with me. If anyone does not wish to fight, you should offer obeisance to the prince's feet. Becoming his men, you will each be able to fearlessly maintain your own positions of authority in such a way that you each can enjoy your own livelihood as before, and so live here happily.'

14.18 Mad|vacana|śravaṇ'|ân|antaraṃ sarve 'py Aśmak'|êndra|sevakāḥ sva|sva|vāhanāt sahas" âvatīrya rāja|sūnum ānamya tad|vaśa|vartinaḥ samabhavan.

Tato 'haṃ tad Aśmak'|êndra|rājyaṃ rāja|sūnusād vidhāya tad|rakṣaṇ'|ârthaṃ maulān svān adhikāriṇo niyujy' ātmī-bhūten' Âśmak'|êndra|sainyena ca sākaṃ Vidarbhān abhyetya rāja|dhānyāṃ taṃ rāja|tanayaṃ Bhāskaravarmāṇam abhiṣicya pitre pade nyaveśayam.

Ekadā ca mātrā Vasuṃdharayā sah' âvasthitaṃ taṃ rājānaṃ vyajijñapam:

14.21 ‹May" âikasya kāryasy' ārambhaś cikīrṣito 'sti. sa yāvan na sidhyati tāvan mayā na kutr' âpy ekatr' âvasthātuṃ śakyam. ata iyaṃ mad|bhāryā tvad|bhaginī Mañjuvādinī kiyanty ahāni yuṣmad|antikam eva tiṣṭhatu. ahaṃ ca yāvad iṣṭa|jan'|ôpalambhaṃ kiyantam apy anehasaṃ bhuvaṃ vibhramya tam āsādya punar atra sameṣyām' îti›

ākarṇya mātr" ânumatena rājñ" âham agādi:

‹Yad etad asmākam etad|rājy'|ôpalambha|lakṣaṇasy' âitāvato 'bhyudayasy' â|sādhāraṇo hetur bhavān eva. bhavantaṃ vinā kṣaṇam apy asmābhir iyaṃ rājya|dhurā na nirvāhyā. ataḥ kim evaṃ vakti bhavān? iti›

14.24 ākarṇya mayā pratyavādi:

Immediately upon hearing my speech, every single one of the Áshmakan Lord's staff rapidly dismounted from their own mounts or vehicles, bowed down before the prince and became his obedient servants. 14.18

Thereupon I arranged for the Áshmakan Lord's kingdom to become the prince's property, and assigned his hereditary men to govern and guard over it. Appropriating the Áshmakan Lord's army we marched to the country of Vidárbha, where in the capital I anointed Prince Bháskara·varman king, and installed him in his ancestral position.

One day, when that king was in the company of his mother, Vasun·dhara, I requested:

'There remains one task that I would like to undertake. 14.21
As long as it is unachieved I will be unable to stay quietly in any one place. Therefore Mañju·vádini, my wife and your sister, should live with you for some days. Meanwhile, I shall journey across the earth for as long as imperishable time until I find the person I am looking for. Once I have found him I shall return here without ado.'

The king heard me out, confirmed his mother's agreement, and announced:

'You are the single reason for our very great fortune in recovering this kingdom. Without you we could not bear to carry this kingdom's yoke for even one moment. Why, then, do you say these things?'

I listened and replied: 14.24

‹Yuṣmābhir ayaṃ cintā|lavo 'pi na citte cintanīyaḥ. yuṣmad|gṛhe yaḥ saciva|ratnam Ārya|ketur asti sa īdṛg|vidhānām an|ekeṣāṃ rājyānāṃ dhuram udvoḍhuṃ śaktaḥ. tatas taṃ tatra niyujy' âhaṃ gamiṣyāmi.›

ity|ādi|vacana|saṃdohaiḥ pralobhito 'pi sa|jananīko nṛpo 'n|ekair āgrahair māṃ kiyantam api kālaṃ prayāṇ'|ôpakramān nyavartayat.

14.27 Utkal'|âdhipateḥ Pra|caṇḍa|varmaṇo rājyaṃ mahyaṃ prādāt. ahaṃ ca tad rājyam ātmasāt kṛtvā rājānam āmantrya yāvat tvad|anveṣaṇāya prayāṇ'|ôpakramaṃ karomi tāvad ev' Âṅga|nāthena Siṃhavarmaṇā sva|sāhāyyāy' ākārito 'tra samāgataḥ pūrva|puṇya|vipākāt svāminā samagaṃsi.»

'Do not give this concern even the slightest thought. You have in your household Arya·ketu, a jewel among ministers, who would be capable of carrying forward the yokes of a plurality of kingdoms like this. That is why I shall appoint him to the task before I take my leave.'

But however much I tried to persuade the king and his mother with this and other accumulated arguments, they most insistently postponed the day of my departure for a while longer.

They gave me the kingdom of Prachánda·varman, king 14.27
of Útkala. Having taken possession of that kingdom and taken leave of the king, I was just making preparations to set out in search of you, my Lord, when Simha·varman, king of the Angas, summoned me to his aid. Thus I rushed to this place, and my previous good deeds were rewarded in my being reunited with you, my Lord."

CHAPTER FIFTEEN: FINALE

Tatas te tatra saṃgatā Apahāravarm'|Ôpahāravarm'|Ârthapāla|Pramati|Mitragupta|Mantragupta|Viśrutāḥ kumārāḥ Pāṭalipure yauvarājyam upabhuñjānaṃ samākāraṇe pūrva|kṛta|saṃketaṃ Vāmalocanayā bhāryayā saha kumāraṃ Somadattaṃ sevakair ānāyya;

sa|Rājavāhanāḥ saṃbhūy' âvasthitā mithaḥ sa|pramoda|saṃvalitāḥ kathā yāvad vidadhati tāvat Puṣpapurād rājño Rājahaṃsasy' ājñā|patram ādāya samāgatā rāja|puruṣāḥ praṇamya Rājavāhanaṃ vyajijñapan:

15.3 «Svāmin, etaj janakasya Rājahaṃsasy' ājñā|patraṃ gṛhyatām. iti»

ākarṇya samutthāya bhūyo|bhūyaḥ s'|ādaraṃ praṇamya sadasi tad ājñā|patram agrahīt. śirasi c' ādhāya tata uttāry' ôtkīlya rājā Rājavāhanaḥ sarveṣāṃ śṛṇvatām ev' âvācayat:

«Svasti! śrīḥ! Puṣpapura|rāja|dhānyāḥ śrī|Rājahaṃsa|bhū|patiś Campā|nagarīm adhivasato Rājavāhana|pramukhān kumārān āśāsy' ājñā|patraṃ preṣayati.

15.6 Yathā yūyam ito māṃ āmantrya praṇamya prasthitāḥ pathi kasmiṃś cid van'|ôddeśa upa|Śiv'|ālayaṃ skandh'|āvāram avasthāpya sthitāḥ. tatra Rājavāhanaṃ Śiva|pūj"|ârthaṃ niśi Śiv'|ālaye sthitaṃ prātar anupalabhy' âvaśiṣṭāḥ sarve 'pi kumārāḥ:

‹Sah' âiva Rājavāhanena Rājahaṃsaṃ praṇaṃsyāmo na cet prāṇāṃs tyakṣyāma iti.›

AND SO THE YOUNG MEN were assembled there: Apahára·varman, Upahára·varman, Artha·pala, Prámati, Mitra·gupta, Mantra·gupta and Víshruta. They sent servants to collect and bring Prince Soma·datta together with his wife Vama·lóchana. He had been enjoying the position of crown prince in Pátali·pura, and had been awaiting the rendezvous.

All together, including Raja·váhana, they were exchanging stories with one another, full of delight, when some of the king's men arrived from Pushpa·pura, bearing an official letter from Raja·hamsa. They bowed before Raja·váhana, and proclaimed:

"Master, please accept this missive from your father, Ra- 15.3
ja·hamsa."

On hearing this he rose, bowed repeatedly and respectfully to the assembly, and received the official letter. The royal Raja·váhana raised the letter to his forehead in respect, then lowered and opened it, before reading it out for all to hear:

"Hail! Good fortune! From the royal capital of Pushpa·pura the glorious Lord of the Earth Raja·hamsa salutes the young men with Raja·váhana at their head, currently residing in the city of Champa, and sends them this missive.

After you took leave of me, paid your respects and went 15.6
forth from here, you set up camp and stayed somewhere in the forest near a Shiva temple. There in the night Raja·váhana got up in order to do worship to Shiva in Shiva's abode, but in the morning the remaining young men were none of them able to find him. They pledged:

'Only with Raja·váhana beside us shall we bow down again before Raja·hamsa. If we cannot find him, then we shall give up our lives.'

pratijñāya sainyaṃ parāvartya Rājavāhanam anveṣṭuṃ pṛthak prasthitāḥ. etaṃ bhavad|vṛtt'|ântaṃ tataḥ pratyāvṛttānāṃ sainikānāṃ mukhād ākarṇy' â|sahya|duḥkh'|ôdanvati magna|manasāv ubhāv ahaṃ yuṣmaj|jananī ca:

15.9 ‹Vāmadev'|āśramaṃ gatv" âitad vṛtt'|ântaṃ tad|viditaṃ vidhāya prāṇa|parityāgaṃ kurva iti.›

niścitya tad|āśramam upagatau taṃ muniṃ praṇamya yāvat sthitau tāvad eva tena tri|kāla|vedinā muninā viditam ev' âsman|manīṣitam. niścayam avabuddhya prāvāci:

‹Rājan, prathamam ev' âitat sarvaṃ yuṣman|manīṣitaṃ vijñāna|balād ajñāyi. yad ete tvat|kumārā Rājavāhana|nimitte kiyantam an|ehasam āpadam āsādya bhāgy'|ôdayād a|sādhāraṇena vikrameṇa vihita|dig|vijayāḥ prabhūtāni rājyāny upalabhya ṣoḍaś'|âbd'|ânte vijayinaṃ Rājavāhanaṃ puraskṛtya pratyetya tava Vasumatyāś ca pādān abhivādya bhavad|ājñā|vidhāyino bhaviṣyanti. atas tan|nimittaṃ kim api sāhasaṃ na vidheyam iti.›

15.12 Tad ākarṇya tat|pratyayād dhairyam avalamby' âdya|prabhṛty ahaṃ devī ca prāṇān adhārayāva. idānīm āsanna|vartiny avadhau Vāmadev'|āśramaṃ gatvā vijñaptiḥ kṛtā:

Then they sent their army home and set out separately one by one in search of Raja·váhana. When we heard this news of what had happened to you from the soldiers who had returned home from there, I and your mother were both plunged into an ocean of unbearable grief. Together we resolved:

'We shall go to the hermitage of Vama·deva, tell him what 15.9
has happened, and then together give up our lives.'

So we went to his hermitage and bowed down before the holy man. But, even while we were standing there, that holy man who knows everything in the three times—the past, the present and the future—understood perfectly our intentions. Realizing our resolve, he addressed us:

'King, I knew from the first all this that you desire, thanks to my special insight. For a certain length of indestructible time these young men of yours will undergo hardship on Raja·váhana's account. Then their good fortune will return and with their uncommon prowess they will go on their *Dig·víjaya* and conquer the quarters as had they set out to do, winning numerous kingdoms. When sixteen years will have passed they will return, led by the victorious Raja·váhana, to salute the feet of yourself and Vásumati, ready to do as you command. Therefore you should not commit anything rash on their account.'

On hearing this, the queen and I plucked up courage and 15.12
from that day forward we kept ourselves alive. Now, with the period of time near its end, we proceeded to Vama·deva's hermitage, and requested:

‹Svāmin, tvad|ukt'|âvadhiḥ pūrṇa|prāyo bhavati. tat|pravṛttis tvay" âdy' âpi vijñāyata iti.›

Śrutvā munir avadat:

15.15 ‹Rājan, Rājavāhana|pramukhāḥ sarve 'pi kumārā an|ekān durjayāṇ śatrūn vijitya dig|vijayaṃ vidhāya bhū|valayaṃ vaśīkṛtya Campāyām ekatra sthitāḥ. tav' ājñā|patram ādāya tad|ānayanāya preṣyantāṃ śīghram eva sevakā iti.›

Muni|vacanam ākarṇya bhavad|ākāraṇāy' ājñā|patraṃ preṣitam asti. ataḥ paraṃ cet kṣaṇam api yūyaṃ vilambaṃ vidhāsyatha tato māṃ Vasumatīṃ ca mātaraṃ kath"|âvaśeṣāv eva śroṣyath' êti jñātvā pānīyam api pathi bhūtv" âpeyam. iti»

Evaṃ pitur ājñā|patraṃ mūrdhni vidhṛtya gacchem' êti niścayaṃ cakruḥ. atha vaśīkṛta|rājya|rakṣā|paryāptāni sainyāni samarthatarān puruṣān āptān sthāne sthāne niyujya kiyatā sainyena mārga|rakṣāṃ vidhāya;

15.18 pūrva|vairiṇaṃ Mālav'|ēśaṃ Mānasāraṃ parājitya tad api rājyaṃ vaśīkṛtya Puṣpapure rājño Rājahaṃsasya devyā Vasumatyāś ca pādān namasyāmaḥ. evaṃ niścitya sva|sva|bhāryā|saṃyutāḥ parimitena sainyena Mālav'|ēśaṃ prati prasthitāḥ.

Prāpya c' Ôjjayinīṃ tad" âiva sahāya|bhūtais taiḥ kumāraiḥ parivṛtena Rājavāhanen' âtibalavān api Mālav'|ēśo Mānasāraḥ kṣaṇena parājigye nihataś ca. tatas tad|duhita-

'Master, the period of time you named is more or less over. Do you know today how he is, our son?'

The holy man listened and replied:

'King, all the young men, with Raja·váhana foremost 15.15
among them, have conquered more than one recalcitrant enemy, they have carried out their conquest of the quarters and overpowered the circumference of the earth, and now they are staying somewhere in Champa. You should very quickly send servants bearing your official letter to bring them home.'

When we heard the sage's words we sent this missive to call you home. If you delay even a moment more, then you will only be able to hear about me and your mother Vásumati, because we will exist no longer. Bear this in mind and do not even stop to drink water once you are on the road."

At this they touched the father's missive obediently to their heads, took heed, and resolved to depart. Next they appointed good men, more than capable, in the positions required, and forces sufficient to guard the overpowered kingdoms, and took military force to ensure their safety on the road.

Then they decided to first conquer their old enemy Ma- 15.18
na·sara, Lord of Málava, and subjugate his kingdom, before paying obeisance to King Raja·hamsa and his queen, Vásumati, in Pushpa·pura. Accompanied by their wives and with a modest army, they travelled toward the Málavan lord.

When they reached Ujjáyini, Raja·váhana, with the young men in attendance and as allies, defeated Mana·sara the Málavan lord, although he was extremely powerful, there and then in but a moment, and killed him. They took with

ram Avantisundarīṃ samādāya Caṇḍavarmaṇā tan|mantriṇā pūrvaṃ kārā|gṛhe rakṣitaṃ Puṣpodbhavaṃ kumāraṃ sa|kuṭumbaṃ tata unmocitaṃ saha nītvā;

Mālav'|êndra|rājyaṃ vaśīkṛtya tad|rakṣaṇāya kāṃś cit sainya|sahitān mantriṇo niyujy' âvaśiṣṭa|parimita|sainya|sahitās te kumārāḥ Puṣpapuraṃ sametya Rājavāhanaṃ puraskṛtya tasya Rājahaṃsasya mātur Vasumatyāś ca caraṇān abhivanditavantaḥ.

15.21 Tau ca putra|samāgamaṃ prāpya param'|ānandam adhigatau. tato rājño Vasumatyāś ca devyāḥ samakṣaṃ Vāmadevo Rājavāhana|pramukhānāṃ daśānām api kumārāṇām abhilāṣaṃ vijñāya tān ājñāpayat:

«Bhavantaḥ, sarve 'py eka|vāraṃ gatvā svāni rājyāni nyāyena paripālayantu. punar yad" êcchā bhavati tadā pitroś caraṇ'|âbhivandanāy' āgantavyam iti.»

Tatas te sarve 'pi kumārās tan|muni|vacanaṃ śirasy ādhāya taṃ praṇamya pitarau ca, gatvā dig|vijayaṃ vidhāya, pratyāgaman'|ântaṃ sva|sva|vṛttaṃ pṛthak|pṛthaṅ muni|samakṣaṃ nyavedayan. pitarau ca kumārāṇāṃ nija|parākram'|âvabodhakāny ati|durghaṭāni caritāny ākarṇya param'|ānandam āpnutām. tato rājā muniṃ sa|vinayaṃ vyajijñapat:

them Avánti·súndari, his daughter, released the prince Pushpódbhava from the prison where Mana·sara's minister had previously incarcerated him and his family, and took him with them, too.

Once the young men had subjugated the Málavan Lord's kingdom, and appointed some ministers equipped with an army to guard it, they continued with what was left of their modest army to Pushpa·pura, where with Raja·váhana at their head they saluted the feet of Raja·hamsa and Raja·váhana's mother, Vásumati.

Those two had attained the heights of bliss as soon as 15.21
their son had returned. Next Vama·deva, who understood the shared desire of all ten young men led by Raja·váhana, commanded them, in the presence of the king and his queen, Vásumati:

"Sirs, you should all go now at the same time, and govern your own kingdoms according to the law. Whenever the wish arises again, then come and pay your respects to the feet of Raja·váhana's father."

At this, every one of the young men took heed of the sage's words, and bowed down to him and the parents. In the holy man's presence they related each individually their own respective adventures from when they had left and set out on their conquest of the quarters until their homecoming. The parents, too, derived the highest bliss when they heard about the young men's dreadfully difficult deeds that revealed their personal heroism. Afterward the king humbly requested the holy man:

15.24 «Bhagavan, tava prasādād asmābhir manuja|mano|rath'|âdhikam a|vāṅ|manasa|gocaraṃ sukham adhigatam. ataḥ paraṃ mama svāmi|caraṇa|saṃnidhau vānaprasth'|āśramam adhigaty' ātma|sādhanam eva vidhātum ucitam.

Ataḥ Puṣpapura|rājye Mānasāra|rājye ca Rājavāhanam abhiṣicy' âvaśiṣṭāni rājyāni navabhyaḥ kumārebhyo yath"|ôditaṃ saṃpradāya te kumārā Rājavāhan'|ājñā|vidhāyinas tad|eka|matyā vartamānāś catur|udadhi|mekhalāṃ Vasuṃdharāṃ samuddhṛtya kaṇṭakān upabhuñjanti tathā vidheyaṃ svāmin" êti.»

Teṣāṃ tat|pitur vānaprasth'|āśrama|grahaṇ'|ôpakrama|niṣedhe bhūyāṃ samāgrahaṃ vilokya munis tān avadat:

15.27 «Bhoḥ, kumārakāḥ, ayaṃ yuṣmaj|janaka etad|vayaḥ|samucite pathi vartamānaḥ kāya|kleśaṃ vin" âiva mad|āśramastho vānaprasth'|āśram'|āśrayaṇaṃ sarvathā bhavadbhir na nivāraṇīyaḥ. atra sthitas tv ayaṃ bhagavad|bhaktim upalapsyate. bhavantaś ca pitṛ|saṃnidhau na sukham avāpsyant' îti.»

Maha|rṣer ājñām adhigamya te pitur vānaprasth'|āśram'|âdhigama|pratiṣedh'|āgraham atyajan. Rājavāhanaṃ Puṣpapure 'vasthāpya tad|anujñayā sarve 'pi parijanāḥ svāni svāni rājyāni pratipālya sv'|êcchayā pitroḥ samīpe gat'|āgatam akurvan. evam avasthitās te Rājavāhana|pramukhāḥ sarve 'pi kumārā Rājavāhan'|ājñayā sarvam api vasudhā|valayaṃ nyāyena paripālayantaḥ paras|param aikamatyena vartamānāḥ

"Good sir, by your gracious favor we have been able to attain an indescribable and unimaginable happiness that exceeds the desires of men. Now it is only proper for me to enter the stage of life called 'the forest-dweller,' living close to the master's feet, working to liberate my soul. 15.24

Hence, master, it is for you to anoint Raja·váhana to the kingdoms of both Pushpa·pura and Mana·sara, and hand the remaining kingdoms over to the other nine young men according to the accounts they have just given. Arrange things so that these young men will carry out Raja·váhana's commands, and act with one mind with him, and please extirpate any thorns so that they can fully enjoy the Lady Earth, engirdled by the four oceans."

When the sage perceived that the young men remained determined to oppose Raja·váhana's parents' plan to enter the forest-dwelling stage of life, he explained to them:

"Come, young men, by no means should you prevent your 15.27
father from progressing to the forest-dwelling stage of life, now that he is at the right age for renunciation. Dwelling in my ashram, he will be completely free of physical hardship. Abiding here he will be absorbed in devotion to the god. Nor would you find happiness while your parents are present."

Having understood the great sage's command, they abandoned their persistent opposition to the father's departure to be a forest-dweller. Raja·váhana was installed in Pushpa·pura and every one of his followers governed each their own kingdoms by his consent. Whenever they wanted to they went back and forth to his father. When all the young men without exception had been thus established with Raja·váhana at their head, they governed the entire circumference

Puraṃdara|prabhṛtibhir apy ati|durlabhāni rājya|sukhāny anvabhūvan.

iti śrī|Daṇḍinaḥ kṛtau
Daśa|kumāra|carite
Uttara|pīṭhikā.
Samāptaṃ
Daśa|kumāra|caritam.

of the earth justly and following Raja·váhana's command, acting as of one mind with one another. They enjoyed kingly pleasures out of reach for even the gods and even for the king of the gods Indra himself.

That is the end of the End Book of
the glorious Dandin's
What Ten Young Men Did.
What Ten Young Men Did
is completed.

NOTES

0.2 There is no reason to think that these verses belong to the oldest layer of the text, Dandin's original. Here Vishnu is invoked with a multiple repetition of the word *daṇḍa*, lit. stick, or: pole, stem, mast, rod, axle, pillar, staff. This word is used because it is in the original author's name, *Daṇḍin*, "the bearer of the stick." The identification of Tri·víkrama's massive leg is first with the parasol pole supporting the cosmic egg's upper shell, then with the lotus that sprang from Vishnu's navel and on which Brahma was born, and so on. Tri·víkrama's effortless yet total conquest was the chosen model for medieval Indian kings, as is witnessed by its repeated depiction in monumental art, where Tri·víkrama is the incarnation of Vishnu with which a ruler can most naturally identify.

1.1 Pushpa·puri (Pátali·putra), was the Emperor Ashóka's capital, identified with modern Patna, in Bihar, North India.

1.2 *Daṇḍa* again.

1.2 Raja·hamsa is literally "Swan among kings." The "swan of kings" is the best because of the connotations of whiteness which in turn implies bright fame, etc., and beautiful grace and elegance.

1.3 In Sanskrit literature, fame or glory is visualized as white. The autumn, or harvest, moon is particularly large and bright. Shiva's laughter is white because it is all teeth, and Kailash is white with snow.

1.4 The king's dominion over his lands or the Earth, in Sanskrit a feminine noun, is like that of a lover over his beautiful beloved.

1.5 Kama's danger derives from his invisibility. Once upon a time he disturbed the god Shiva when he was performing a fire-ritual. Enraged, Shiva incinerated Kama with the flame from his third eye, and since that conflagration Kama has been "Bodiless" (*An/aṅga*) and, with the further level of psychological interpretation, "Mind-made" (*Mano/ja*). Cf. KuSam. III.72. Here his implements reason, surely Shiva would not turn his fury on a lady?

1.7 These birds that live as devoted couples, red like ruddy geese, are in India the epitome of constant romantic faithful love, comparable to the colloquial English "lovey-dovey." Cf. Ragh. III.24.

1.8 The italics represent a Sanskrit pun or double entendre, wordplay or paronomasia (*śleṣa*), an extremely common feature of some forms of literature, although not much used in the present book. Thus, "caressed in endless enjoyments" can also be translated as "caressed in the hoods of Anánta." Anánta is another name for Shesha, the primordial serpent that wears the Earth as a diadem on its head.

1.11 Málava was a kingdom in northwest India whose capital was Ujjáyini or Avánti. From the end of the fourth century CE, under the Guptas, Ujjáyini was known as a particularly prestigious artistic center.

1.16 This *sīmanta* life-cycle ritual (*saṃskāra*) takes place in the fourth (or sixth or eighth) month of pregnancy. The husband parts his pregnant wife's hair with a branch bearing green fruit. Cf. Manu, Yaj I.11.

1.23 One of the twelve *jyotir·linga*s, the dozen luminous "phalluses of light" of Shiva distributed across the Indian continent. The shrine at Ujjain was immortalized in Kali·dasa's *Megha/dūta*.

1.27 At the time of the churning of the primordial ocean, Shiva swallowed *haláhala* poison from the demons, which turned his throat blue for all times. Blue-throat is hence one of his regular epithets, particularly in the alternative form, Nila·kantha.

1.28 The Sanskrit term for the kings' wives, *avarodha*, literally means "restraint," and so is very close to the Arabic "harem" for a "prohibited" place, where the women must remain, unmolested.

1.35 The sweet-throated bird is either a dove or a cuckoo. Its first meaning in Sanskrit is cuckoo, while for Anglophone sensibilities the dove has a sweeter call.

1.42 Harish·chandra was a king of the lunar dynasty, and a remote ancestor of Rama, famed for his generosity and sense of duty. Rama·chandra is the hero of the "Ramáyana."

1.43 An ashram (*āśrama*) is literally "a place of exertion," i.e., religious spiritual striving. Now it has come to signify also a spiritual holiday camp for tourists.

1.58 Not politically correct, but terms like *shábara*, *kiráta*, *pulínda* and *bhilla*—interchangeable in classical Sanskrit literature and in the present book—refer to tribes of hunters regarded as outcastes living in the forests of central India. They are depicted as terrifying meat-eaters and wine-drinkers, who carry off women and carry out human sacrifices. *Shábaras* may be the same as the Suars of modern India.

1.64 Chándika Durga is the Goddess in her terrible form, especially as the slayer of Máhisha, the buffalo demon. Hers is the favorite cult of the *shábara* tribals, who offer her human sacrifice. Cf. for such a ritual the lengthy description in Bana's *Kādambarī*.

1.71 An auspicious day is a juncture of the lunar cycle, at the full or new moon, or the eighth or fourteenth of either half-cycle.

1.71 Lit. *a/balā*, "no-strength."

1.75 Persuasive words (*sāma*) and gifts (*dāna*) are two of the four political means (*upāya*), the others being dividing (*bheda*) and punishment (*daṇḍa*).

1.80 The land of the "black greeks" (*kāla/yavana*), probably Zanzibar, off the coast of Arabia.

1.93 The god of love is considered deadly, and given the same epithet as the god of death, Mara.

1.97 This is what happened historically. Donations of villages or land, even to deities installed in icons in temples, are recorded in many copper-plate inscriptions.

1.102 Kamándaki composed a celebrated nineteen-chapter epitome of his master Kautílya's *Artha/śāstra*, the *Nīti/sāra*.

2.1 Son of Shiva and Párvati, Skanda Karttikéya is the prince par excellence, the ideal of the chaste young warrior. He was born of Shiva's seed after it had fallen into the fire, Agni, who was unable to bear its intensity and cast it off into the Ganges. He has six heads and is called Karttikéya because of his intimate relationship with his nurses, if not surrogate mothers, the six Kríttika (seven Pleiades, minus the least visible).

2.9 Matánga, lit. "Elephant," is also the name of a tribal group, one of the lowest castes, responsible, like the *kirátas* and so on, for carrying off ladies.

2.13 Yama, the god of death, is here called Shámana, euphemistically the "Pacifier" or the "Destroyer." Chitra·gupta is the infernal recorder or clerk who keeps the register of good and evil deeds. The complex of seven hells is described in the *Purāṇas*.

2.17 Letters in Sanskrit are "imperishable" (*a/kṣara*), because they and the whole hieratic language are held to have a beginningless relationship to the phenomenal reality they describe.

2.22 In South India, in the Sahyadri mountains, near Nasik. In the "Ramáyana" (III), it was here that Rama confronted ascetic-devouring *rákshasa*s. It is named after Dándaka, whose kingdom was transformed into a forest as a result of a curse.

2.31 The *ásura*s are ancient deities, anti-gods, whose Indo-European origins they share with, for example, Ahura, in the Zoroastrian Avesta. In mythology, it is often only an avatar of Vishnu who can defeat them, such as when Nara·simha destroys Hiránya·káshipu (cf. also below p. 163).

2.33 Love is intoxicating and maddening; both of which are *madana / mada* in Sanskrit, with Indo-European cognates in "mead" (the intoxicating alcohol), and "mad" and "madness."

2.33 Lakshmi, the goddess who incarnates Majesty, is considered the king's wife, hence Kalíndi would become his second wife.

2.34 In Sanskrit, the same metaphor of horripilation or hairs standing on end expresses the biological manifestation of thrilling with a frisson of delight.

2.35 Gems are believed to be able to have magical powers, such as counteracting thirst and hunger.

2.36 Vishála Ujjáyini is Ujjain the Vast. Here and below (p. 133), the author is alluding to the famous verse of Kali·dasa's *Megha/dūta*

(I.30) in which Ujjain is lauded as an enormous (*viśālā*) piece of heaven, brought down to earth by its inhabitants when their merit that keeps them in heaven runs out.

3.1 Brahmins are "highest born" (*agra/janma*) because they were said, in the Rig Veda's creation hymn (X.90), to have been created from the head of Púrusha (Man), and/or because they were created first.

3.5 In northwest India, west of the Nármada River, southern Gujerat including Bharuch (Broach), Vadodara (Baroda) and Ahmedabad. The other kingdom is Pariyátra, with its capital at Pátali (Patna).

3.26 *Tumula*, the Sanskrit word for "tumultuous," is a clear example of close Proto-Indo-European ancestry.

3.28 *Víraha·/víyoga·bhakti*, the pain of separation from a beloved, is a particularly important trope in Indian literature. Kali·dasa's Meghadūta, *The Cloud Messenger*, reports the communication of separated lovers via their cloud go-between.

4.3 Tradition condoned this form of suicide, throwing oneself from a cliff (*bhṛgu/pāta*, aka *Bháirava·stava*, "praise for Bháirava Shiva"), for elderly persons who feel their natural time has come. In ancient India, there were four classifications of sanctioned suicide, according to the element used: by earth, as here; by fire; by water; and by air, which entails fasting to death.

4.17 The Sanskrit *dīnāra* is a loanword derived from the Latin *denarius*.

4.19 Lit. "bird."

4.26 Because of his megalomaniac aspirations, Darpa·sara went off to do penance, to gain the supernatural power to actually take over the whole inhabited world. He is following in his father's footsteps, for Mana·sara had extracted an invincible weapon from Shiva by his penance. Both men's names emphasize their overweening pride (*māna, darpa*), one of the six risky passions that threaten a king, second only to desire. But it is not for a young kshatriya to renounce his manly duties and act like a religious brahmin, and so Darpa·sara's withdrawal to the Himalayas is an act of hubris.

4.30 Here and in "What Mantra·gupta Did" (p. 469), possession by a *yaksha* is a fraudulent device designed to get rid of an unwanted suitor.

4.41 The English "sandal[wood]" is a loanword from the Sanskrit *chándana* (via the medieval Latin "sandalum").

4.41 Lit. two *muhúrta*, each forty-eight minutes.

4.45 Double sense of *karma*: "action" and "karma."

5.1 We return to our hero, Prince Raja·váhana, with the particular romance that Khoroche, for example, claims defines this book and gives it its real name, as the latter portion of another surviving work, the *Avanti/sundarī* (cf. above p. 23). Despite the transmission of the colophon to this chapter, which gives the title as "The Marriage of Avánti·súndari" *(Avanti/sundarī/pariṇaya)*—and is faithfully reproduced at the chapter's conclusion—we title it here "What Raja·váhana Did," to be continued when the chapter is interrupted by the beginning of Dandin's original text.

5.1 This passage, a conventional description of spring, the season that constantly arouses love (cf. KuSam IV.24), is full of the *ka*s and *ma*s that make up the Sanskrit word for love, *kama*. In a highly atmospheric conceit, serpents are commonly believed to feed on air (cf. their epithets *śvasana|bhuk, pavan'|âśana*).

5.2 The Sanskrit for "mango" here means, literally, "co-operative" (*sahakārī*), because the tree was used as a lovers' hideout.

5.4 That he hears repeatedly, implies that he was pacing up and down.

5.5 Indra's epithet is well earned, for he has the greatest number of hymns addressed to him in the Rig Veda.

5.6 The substitute creation could also be taken as a doll manufactured for Rati when she is lonely, missing Kama.

5.8 The *dūtikā|dūti* is a stock character in Sanskrit literature. Cf. for the cuckoo as Kama's go-between: Ragh IX.47.

5.10 *Cakṣuḥ|prīti*, "eye-affection," is the first stage of love (KaSu v.1.5).

5.11 Or monkeys on typewriters producing Shakespeare, in our analogy. *Ghuṇ'|ākṣara*, "letters bored by an insect," stands for any fortuitous event.

5.13 Kama's arrows are both uneven (*viṣama*), since they are five, and rough (*viṣama*), since they cause injury. The five arrows, each of different flowers, are uneven in number because, so often, A loves B but B loves C and so on.

5.17 This double meaning depends on the ambiguity of, e.g., *kumāra*, simply "a young man," or "a prince." The key to the double entendre is whether he is a "brahmin, skilled in sacrifices," or in fact not really a "brahmin" at all but a kshatriya "skilled in battles," and an eligible suitor for Avánti·súndari.

5.20 The memory of marriage in a previous life is a favorite device of this author, who uses it to legitimate love marriages.

5.27 Lit. a lifelong student, who lives in perfect abstinence and chastity, though he looks like a regular bird. I.e., he is a special bird, the ascetic type.

5.38 Lit. in Sanskrit: "she-buffalo" (*mahiṣī*).

5.40 In the literature separation, "erotic disjunction" *(vipralambha/śṛṅgāra)* is thought to be intrinsic to the development of love.

5.42 This Sanskrit word for "moon" *(śasin)* means lit. "that which has a hare in it."

5.43 This fragrant root is Andropogon muricatus, today known as vetiver, a sedative tea.

5.46 The Aurva submarine fire consumes seawater each day, keeping the sea within bounds. Born from a hiding place in one of his female relatives' thighs *(ūru)*, Aurva, furious at the massacre of his family, undertook terrible pyromaniac austerities. The alarmed gods requested him to plunge his fire into the ocean, where it remains in the form of a horse's head vomiting flames, manifest as marine volcanoes.

5.46 Depending on how one analyzes the compound, there are two simultaneous translations: *doṣā/kara*, "maker of the night" and *doṣ'/ākara* "a mine of faults."

5.46 Both the moon and Lakshmi were born from the churning of the milk ocean. The moon makes the day-lotus close at night, notionally locking Lakshmi out of her home.

5.54 Lit. "memory." *Smara* is another name for love.

5.60 *Shirísha* flowers are a frequent standard of delicacy. They are also edible—like nasturtiums.

5.67 Conjuring, like every technique including thievery, was in India codified. It often appears in literature, cf. *Ratnāvalī* IV. Peacock feathers are integral to a magician's get-up, and are supposed to create an illusion when wielded, as will be seen below.

5.80 The Sanskrit root *vam* is cognate with the English "vomit."

5.80 Nara·simha was an avatar of Vishnu. Hiránya·káshipu had been granted invulnerability by Brahman, to be killed neither by man nor animal, neither by day nor by night. He lorded it over the three worlds and was going to kill his own son Prahláda for persisting in his worship of Vishnu. So at twilight—between day and night—Vishnu became half man, half lion, took the demon over his thigh and tore his guts out—an image that became a favorite in temple iconography. As with the vultures and serpents, this story anticipates the coming conquests of our young men.

5.86 In the famous *Kāma/sūtra*, one is advised to entertain a lover with stories of heroes and heroines, such as are found in the *Purāṇas*, and in the "Maha·bhárata" especially (KaSu III.3.17). According to Pauránic cosmogony, the cosmic egg divides into seven heavenly levels (*bhúvana*) and seven lower worlds, hence the fourteen worlds that Raja·váhana tells about. These tales are told as exemplary justifications of the *gandhárva* marriage, i.e., unceremonial unsupervised union, that is taking place.

6.1 *In medias res*, in the middle of the telling of Avánti·súndari and Raja·váhana's love affair, we reach the point where Dandin's surviving original text begins. The language changes abruptly, with a far more sophisticated style from here on. The Sanskrit text begins numbering anew here, calling this Chapter One, but we number it Chapter Six, as a continuation of the preceding five chapters. The chapter colophons here printed faithfully preserve the independent numbering of the Parts.

6.3 She is paying her beloved the compliment of implying that he is a king with the two best possible wives, Sarásvati and Lakshmi. But it is Lakshmi who represents kingship and prosperity as well as beauty, while Sarásvati is the ancient goddess of eloquence, the goddess of speech and the alphabet as well as of music (and therefore the emblem of the CLAY SANSKRIT LIBRARY, depicted in the center of the series' dust jacket). Indeed, the two are rarely co-wives, and are more likely to be rivals. Cf. Ragh VI.29.

6.4 With skillful wordplay on *payodhara* to compare the fullness of her breasts to the swelling of rain clouds, the whole compound is construed with two different objects of the spreading, mentioned separately, "on his chest" and "in the sky."

6.7 *Piśācas* are demons who feed on raw human flesh, often a subdivision of *rákshasa* demons.

6.16 The gift of Matánga from the underworld, which we learned about above, p. 95.

6.16 The Angan kingdom is in the east of Mágadha (east of Bihar), on the right bank of the Ganges. The capital Champa/Chandan/Anga·puri is at the confluence of the Ganges and the Champa River, very near to modern Bhagalpur. Anga refers both to the country and to its inhabitants.

6.18 Ambálika shares her name (a diminutive of "mother") with the principal queen at her pivotal moment in the *Áśva/medha*. An *Ashva·medha* is the Vedic "Horse sacrifice," the culmination of a yearlong wandering by a horse from kingdom to kingdom, performed initially for offspring, and then for royal domination.

6.21 Kubéra's epithet here is Eka·pinga, "Having a single yellow mark in place of an eye." He had offended Párvati by looking at her with his left eye. She cursed him, burning that eye out, and turning the right eye yellow ("Ramáyana" *Uttara* VII.13.24ff). His mention here reminds one that his offense was unintentional, so that Darpa·sara is that much more liable to fail, given his conscious megalomania.

6.24 Cf. Manu VIII.34, in which a certain type of thief to whom one had entrusted something is to be trampled by an elephant. The stake—mentioned earlier—is for thieves who enter in the night; Manu IX.276.

6.26 The divine ladies, *ápsaras*es, are in fourteen families, one of which was born from moonbeams.

6.27 Cf. the famous episode in which Indra tried to shake Markandéya from his devotions, but despite *gandhárva*n songs, springtime and a breeze undressing beautiful *ápsaras*es, the sage remained unmoved.

6.30 *Vidya·dharas* are demigods who inhabit the Himalayas, flying through the air and changing shape at will. With their own cities, and kings, they were very important in Buddhism. The Aikshvákan king is from the family of Ikshváku, although neither Végavat nor Mánasa·vega are in the list of kings of Ikshváku. The Shakyan clan, in which Siddhártha, the man who would become the Buddha, was born, belongs to the Aikshvákan line.

6.31 Nara·váhana·datta, son of Udáyana, king of Vatsa, is the principal hero of *Kathā/sarit/sāgara* XIV.1 and of Gunádhya's *Bṛhat/kathā*. He killed the *vidya·dhara* Mánasa·vega for having seduced his wife and so became king of the *vidya·dharas* (VIII.14-16).

6.34 Their fates were bound together by two apparently unrelated curses.

6.54 The Ganges is here Bhagi·rathi, the daughter of Bhagi·ratha. Bhagi·ratha was a pious ascetic king who brought down the celestial Ganges to purify his ancestors' ashes. They were the sixty thousand sons of Sagara who had been obliterated by Vishnu during their father's *Ashva·medha*, for which please see the note above ad §6.18.

7.1 In addition to translations of the whole book, this chapter has also been elegantly translated separately by VAN BUITENEN, together with the following chapter, as well as the brief later "Tale of Gomini" excerpted from "What Mitra·gupta Did," in *Tales of Ancient India* (Chicago 1959).

7.1 Maríchi is a mythical and prestigious figure who, tradition holds, was born of the spirit of Brahma himself.

7.9 Just as the English word "slave" is derived from the ethnonym "Slav," the Sanskrit word *dāsa* (fem. *dāsī*) is cognate with *dāsyu*, the people described as displaced and enslaved by the incoming Indo-Aryans in the Vedic hymns.

7.9 *Sv'|âdhikāra* is what one's station demands, the rights and duties of each individual in ancient Indian society, so that someone born a harlot is duty-bound to be a good harlot, with prostitution as her proper profession, while having no right to any other employment or pastime.

7.11 The following is closely derived from the *Kāma|sūtra*, especially the third chapter—the sixty-four arts that a woman must master.

7.13 The *Kāma|sūtra* adds garland-sellers, perfumers and tavern-keepers—all are essential intermediaries. Buddhist nuns are famous for that role, as here below p. 241 and p. 443; cf. above all the Tamil *Manimekhalai*. The same function is reportedly performed to this day by, for example, Thera·vada nuns in Kathmandu.

7.14 The word for price, *śulka*, is ambiguous; it could refer to a dowry or bride-price, or to earthier, hourly rates. In the treatises about love, all this is treated: the required qualities of men to whom a courtesan should attach herself; the many ways of extorting money from a lover, including claiming to have been robbed by bandits, or to have been the victim of fire; and how to get rid of penniless suitors.

7.14 One of the eight legitimate forms of marriage in the legal textbooks, the *Dharma Shastras*, the *gandhárva* marriage is a love marriage, based on mutual love and without ceremonies, or, rather, an elopement. Cf. Manu III.32.

7.16 A courtesan's mother and grandmother are known to often be cruel and avaricious, cf. KaSu VI.2.3.

7.17 It is not blasphemy, as it would be in, for example, the monotheistic religions, to say that God created prostitution. Praja·pati is the same as Brahma, the creator of all, including their individual respective duties and rights, their *sva/dharma*.

7.27 Or: all for the teaching of love.

7.27 These three human preoccupations, archetypal in India, will be the subject of the following discourse.

7.36 Although the courtesan's knowledge of mythology is good, she makes a few mistakes in her innocence. Thus, for example, Tilóttama is known to have seduced Indra, Shiva and everyone, but not Brahma.

7.37 With paronomasia, the same word *rajas* refers to both "dust" and "[filthy] passion."

7.42 In philosophy, *sva/saṃvedya*, "to be experienced only in and by itself," is said of consciousness, not of the blissful fruit of pleasure.

7.56 Compare VAN BUITENEN's nice translation: "I am the saint she made a martyr out of."

7.57 *Rāga* refers here to both "color" and "passion," while in the next sentence its opposite, *vairāgyam*, is both "dispassion" and "lack of color."

7.58 Ablutions at dawn and dusk, the junctures (*saṃdhi*) of day and night, are and were compulsory for twice-born brahmins, kshatriyas and *vaishyas*.

7.60 Lit. *sans souci*, "without grief" (*a/śoka*), where *souci* and *śoka* are closely etymologically related.

7.60 Jainism was an ascetic heterodoxy founded by the Jina Maha·vira in the sixth century BCE. Maha·vira was a close contemporary of the Buddha, though his senior in age and more radical in his asceticism. Jains have long been considered as two groups, one naked, the Dig·ámbaras (lit. "clothed in sky"), the other "dressed in white" simple robes, the Shvetámbaras. On initiation, their hair is not just shaved but pulled out painfully, strand by strand.

7.67 VAN BUITENEN: "All she left me was my loincloth."

7.68 From the Sanskrit for well-being, *sv/asti* give us the word for well-being's symbol, the *svastika*.

7.70 Never mind that "Hinduism" is here an anachronism, if not a misnomer. *Shruti* is "revelation" (lit. "that which is heard"), received by the *rishis* from Brahma. *Shruti* is the four branches of the Veda: *Saṃhitā, Brāhamaṇa, Āraṇyaka* and *Upánishad*s. *Smriti* (lit. "that which is remembered") is the human transmissions of exegesis, *Dharma/śāstra*, epics and *Purāṇa*s.

7.75 Karni·suta, with all the aliases one would expect of an operator in the criminal underworld (aka Mula·deva, aka Kalánkura, aka Mula·bhadra), wrote the thieves' annals of theft.

7.80 By law, the *sabhika* is entitled to 5% of wins over one hundred, and 10% of wins under one hundred (Yaj II.199). With his generosity, Apahára·varman is making an investment.

7.82 There is a comic exaggeration of the number of implements the burglar could carry. Many are also enumerated in the *Mṛc/chakaṭika* III. The whistle has a low tone and is blown to ascertain whether inhabitants are asleep. The magic powder could be sleeping powder.

7.95 The word for "black" and "serpent" and "death" is the same, *kāla*. He has been bitten both by a deadly black snake and by death.

7.113 Here the Sanskrit word *upa/nagara* has the same etymology as the English "suburb."

7.119 Kama·rupa corresponds to modern-day east Bengal and west Assam, east of the banks of the Karatóya River, with its ancient capital at Prag·jyótisha.

7.120 The Sanskrit employs the same metaphor of "milking."

7.130 *Rāga* can mean both "love" and "melody," this latter the name of the Indian musical modes with which many outside India are now familiar.

7.131 Human feelings are classified by Sanskrit aesthetic theory into eight or nine sentiments (*rasas*), each of which has its own primary emotion (*sthāyi/bhāva*).

7.132 Sanskrit differentiates between the *nṛtya* that we have here, a dance with the mime of feelings, and *nṛtta*, a dance to music and hand beats.

7.139 *Bhujaṅga* can be both a "slimy lover," literally "a serpent," and a "gallant" and a "husband."

7.162 "Without attachment," lit. "without knots," Jains (and Buddhists) are supposed to care nothing for material comforts, and Jains have to further ensure that no impurity sticks to them and keeps them in the clutches of *samsára*.

7.171 In Sanskrit, literally "raised the rod (*daṇḍa*) over his life."

7.172 Chandra·gupta, who ruled in the late fourth century BCE, was the patron of Chánakya/Kautílya's *Artha/śāstra*—a text that will be central especially to Víshruta's story below—but this exemption seems not to be mentioned there.

7.174 The Sanskrit for "mirage" has the picturesque etymology "deer's thirst."

7.220 Ságara received his name because he was born "with the poison" (*sa/gara*) given to his mother by his father's other wife. When performing his hundredth *Ashva·medha* sacrifice, the culminating Horse Sacrifice, which in theory entitles one to Indra's kingdom, Indra defensively stole the crucial horse, and carried it off down to the underworld. Ságara's myriad sons searched all over the earth before they started digging downward—thus increasing the boundaries of the ocean—hence called in Sanskrit *sāgara*.

7.230 "Dagger" here, *asi/dhenu*, means in Sanskrit "that to which the sword stands as a cow," i.e., a sword's baby calf.

7.235 There are numerous references to Chinese silk in Sanskrit literature (Shak I.33, KuSam VII.3 etc. ASh III).

7.239 At this end of the long sentence, *vilasana* is to be translated twice, as both "flashing" and "frolicking."

7.242 Sanskrit meter is extremeley elaborate in its classification. *Āryā* meter is different from the majority of Sanskrit meters—which are analyzed by the variety of feet—in being merely based on the number of measures (one in a light syllable, two in a heavy syllable) in each quarter verse. In quarters a and c there should be twelve measures, in quarter b eighteen, and in d fifteen.

7.244 In the *Kāma/sūtra*, Vatsyáyana describes four ways for a man to court his lover: i) paint his own likeness, ii) compose an amorous poem, iii) give a love present, and iv) exchange rings.

7.263 Strategic interventions include severing supply links, breaking water tanks, etc. (Manu VII.195-196).

8.1 Janak·pur, in modern-day Nepal, north of Madhu·vani.

8.6 This is the country to the west of Vanga, or eastern Bengal, named after Suhma, the fourth son of Bali. The capital was Tamra·lipta/Dama·lipta.

8.29 Vásava·datta is the eponymous heroine of Subándhu's work. Betrothed to Pushpa·ketu, she was carried off by Kandárpa·ketu. She is also the heroine of the *Kathā/sarit/sāgara* cycle, according to which her father planted a wooden elephant containing soldiers—a Trojan horse—to capture his desired son-in-law, an Orpheus figure who spent his time charming animals with his lute in the forest. Udáyana was then ordered to teach Vásava·datta music. He also seduced her. Their history inspired many stories and plays. Holding up the same ideal example, in the *Mālatī/mādhava* (II) Kamándaki similarly gets Málati to love Mádhava and hate all others. Cf. KaSu V.2.1, V.4.2.3, V.4.14, 63-64.

8.34 Normally, the *mádhavi* jasmine chooses to climb only around sweet-smelling trees, such as the mango.

8.54 Prenatal betrothal of close friends' children accords with Vatsyáyana's precept (KaSu V.4.30).

8.62 Brihas·pati is the planet Jupiter, whose wife Tara was abducted by the moon, Soma (Chandra). Refusing to give her back, Soma, the ruler of planets and plants since Vedic times, caused a war between the gods and demons.

8.79 Tradition has it that *bákula* trees blossom when young women sprinkle them with mouthfuls of wine. Begonia is the *pāṭali* of Pátali·putra/Pushpa·pura. *Ashóka* trees are traditionally said to blossom in spring when ladies strike them with feet wearing jingling anklets and painted with lac. They are one of the five arrows of Love. The mango is another of Love's five arrows.

8.88 The word here for cuckoo means literally "nourished by another" (*para/bhṛta*).

8.114 Both verbal phrases—"up for it" and "had it"—translate the same Sanskrit participle, *avasita*.

8.129 Pundra is a district of eastern Bengal, the neighbor of Vidéha, in the north of present-day Bengal.

9.1 The most famous sacred city in India, situated on one bank of the Ganges, has many names. It is dedicated to Shiva. The foremost *tīrtha*, or bathing ghat, is the Mani·kárnika, whose elaborate mythology is detailed in the *Purānas*. The Mani·kárnika ("Ear-jewel") is named for its mythical origins. Part of Shiva's earring is said to have fallen into the water there. To this day vast numbers of pilgrims gather to perform their ablutions in the river—rinsing the mouth, taking a sip and spitting the water out again as a religious act—washing away their spiritual impurities. Death in Varánasi is a blessing that guarantees instant *mokṣa*, release from the endless cycle of rebirths. Avimúktéshvara is the celebrated Shiva·linga at Benares. In the ancient texts, Benares is sometimes called Avimúkta, "Never forsaken," the city that Shiva has never abandoned.

9.16 The Sanskrit for "flee" (root *palāy*) is etymologically related to the English.

9.24 *Matánga* refers to both an "outcaste" and an "elephant," making this an allusion to the elephant who was supposed to have killed Purna·bhadra previously.

9.28 Like many supernaturals in this story, Mani·bhadra is a character borrowed from the *Kathā/sarit/sāgara*, where he is mentioned as Kubéra's younger brother (XVIII,121). That is why she brings Kubéra the baby.

9.28 Agástya, the pitcher-born sage, was the guardian of South India; according to the "Ramáyana," he liberated it from the *rákshasas* when Rama, his wife and his brother took refuge in his hermitage. He bestowed Vishnu's bow on Rama, and returned with him to Ayódhya at the end of their exile.

9.28 Álaka is above Meru on the peaks of the Himalayas, and is inhabited also by Shiva (*Megha/dūta* vv.63ff).

9.32 The following network of reincarnations, a gist indeed, requires a meta-generational family tree to be understood.

9.33 Thus our hero Kama·pala is identified with two earlier men, whose reincarnation he is, just as they are the same as one another in different lives across the stream of reincarnation. Tarávali had been married to Kama·pala also before as Arya·dasi to Sháunaka, but had had a child with him when he was

Shúdraka. That child is the same boy now reborn from Kántimati putting Kama·pala in trouble—through his maternal grandfather he is thus entitled to the kingdom of Kashi. The boy is reborn to the same father, by a different mother. Tarávali fostered it instinctively because she had previously been his mother. He is Artha·pala (another of whose previous mothers was Arya·dasi when he was nursed by Vináyavati, who became Kántimati), who is telling Raja·váhana his story. Kama·pala reincarnates as a total of three named men, each of whom had five wives.

9.34 Such perfuming is also the language of Buddhism and the "latent impressions" (lit. "perfumings," *vāsanā*) that are the mechanism for the working out of karma.

9.41 Note the two verbs distinguished only by their preverbs: *abhi/mṛś* (to violate) and *pra/mṛś* (to erase); and the pun on *anuvṛti*, both "acting according to your wishes" and "by repetition of the same act of daring."

9.44 Who are these ladies? Is there something missing, perhaps that would have been explained in the original beginning of the book, or in the missing section of the *Avanti/sundarī*? Even Dandin himself forgets to mention them as Kántimati's attendants. But, what is worse, Soma·devi was supposed to be Arya·dasi, i.e., also Tarávali; when two incarnations of the same meet, does the world explode? Thus three more ladies were married to Kama·pala in previous lives. In which case all nine of the women mentioned above had been his wives. With the addition of Tarávali, that makes a total of ten.

9.52 The accidental addressing of one girlfriend by the name of another is alluded to by Sanskrit poets as a constant source of trouble. Cf. Vik 29, Shak VI.5, KuSam IV.8.

9.62 This practice is of course the infamous suttee, literally "good woman" (*satī*), i.e., a wife who is faithful up to and including the end.

9.63 Since the idea is to enact the denial of the wife being left a widow, what she puts on is the dress of a *suvāsinī*, a woman whose husband is still alive: a saffron robe and bodice, and ornaments including the *maṅgala/sūtra*, the auspicious thread she wears around her neck as long as her husband lives; she should also untie her hair and smear her forehead with rubbed turmeric, which is symbolic of married life.

9.65 *Matánga*, the outcaste again. According to Manu (X.56), an outcaste (*caṇḍāla*) is responsible for executions of criminals condemned to death by the king.

9.66 It is doubly criminal to condemn an innocent man and a brahmin. After all, the murder of a brahmin is strictly prohibited in the Dharma treatises, even if he has committed the worst of crimes. A brahmin is to be banished without being harmed (Manu VIII.380).

9.78 The mythical bird Gáruda was the king of birds and Vishnu's mount. After his mother was enslaved by the mother of the serpents, Gáruda had to provide *ámrita*, Indra's ambrosia of immortality (with all three words, *á/mrita*, ambrosia, and immortality, sharing a single etymology—Sanskrit, Greek and Latin, respectively), to get her back. He placed it on a bed of *kusha* grass, but Indra recovered it before the serpents could enjoy, so instead they licked the grass, thus acquiring forked tongues. Throughout this work serpents symbolize bad kings.

9.80 The Sanskrit for "cruel" is *krūra*, the two words being Indo-European cognates.

9.87 One has three classes of enemies: those "by birth" (*sahaja-śatru*)—relatives, such as, here, Kama·pala and Artha·pala; "ordinary foes" (*prakṛti-śatru*)—whose property is nearby, such as neighbors; and "the enemy by act" (*kṛtrima-śatru*)—who have done great harm or been wronged (cf. *Artha/śāstra* VI.2.19).

9.92 Rasa·tala is the fourth and hence the middle of the seven underworlds. Durga is an intriguing comparison, since she is the ferocious form of Shiva's wife, and the destroyer of demons.

9.94 In Sanskrit, the metaphor for desire is "thirst" (*tṛṣṇa*), where in English it is more common to be "hungry"—the desires of a hot and dry climate versus a cold and damp one. The 'thirst for power' incorporates the imputation that power intoxicates.

9.101 He had died without having informed anyone of the ladies' hiding place.

9.107 We have already had a double entendre with the same word as here (*rajas*, cf. above p. 592), but with different senses. Here *rajas* refers to both "dust" and "pollen."

10.2 Literally: *abhraṃ*—"the sky"—*kaṣ*—"to rub, scratch, scrape"; an epithet more normally applied to mountains. Cf. the nearly obsolete original English reference of skyscraper to a sail on a ship.

10.2 The chain stretching from the east to the west of central India. In literature, the Vindhyans contain the hostile forest where *kirátas* and suchlike live.

10.4 In males, this throbbing indicates impending good fortune (cf. Shak I or II.15 and Ragh VI.68).

10.7 The cosmogonic Puránic myth of Varáha, the Primordial Boar, is that he is the form that the creator god Praja·pati took to personify sacrifice and to lift the Earth out of immersion in the original wave on his snout and tusks.

10.11 Following the original undifferentiated first principle of creation, an egg formed, within which Brahma proceeded to emit different creatures. The palace is like a skyscraper, as tall as the spire of the war god with the tallest spear.

10.13 Deities wear clothes that are perpetually dust-free, and fresh garlands; they do not blink or leave a shadow, and they float just above the ground.

10.20 Literally "to lie down," the verb here(*pratiśi*) refers to lying down and fasting in front of a deity until one gets what one wants. Elsewhere this lying down is called a *prāy'/ôpaveśa* ("sitting down [to fast] unto death"). It is traditional for a brahmin petitioner to seek satisfaction at the door of the court, since a king cannot risk being party to the crime of brahminicide. In the chronicle of medieval Kashmir, the *Rāja/taraṅgiṇī*, unscrupulous brahmins are so abusing this cleft stick, that the state goes to pot. Gandhi nationalized the ancient Indian practice of hunger-striking.

10.22 The ultimate comparison of a chaste wife without her husband is Sita, who was stolen from Rama by Rávana ("Ramáyana" IV.15). Such women whose husbands are absent wear dark, threadbare clothes and plait their hair (Shak VII).

10.25 Instead of Sumítra, this should be Sumántra. In the *Pūrva/pīṭhikā*, Prámati is the son of Súmati. Here he is the son of Tarávali and Kama·pala, and the half brother of Artha·pala.

10.26 A *caṇḍikā* is a virago as well as a name of the Goddess, when she is the warrior protectress of young women.

10.31 The Indian seasons are six. The hot summertime precedes the rejuvenating summer rainy season.

10.33 Ámbika, "Mother," is one of most common names of the Goddess. Quick to anger, hence Tarávali's fear, here she is gentle and attentive, and identified—as Shiva's devoted wife—with Párvati, daughter of the mountains.

10.41 *Baláka*, the "crane" breed, is thin, pale and long-necked, while the *nárikéla*, "coconut," variety is round, brown and robust.

10.44 The Sanskrit word for bird here, *vihaṅ/gama*, literally "moving in the sky," is a fine example of the polyvalency of Sanskrit vocabulary, since it can refer equally also to "cloud," "arrow," "sun" or "moon." *Rava*, the Sanskrit for "roar," is etymologically related to the English "rave."

10.45 "Victory" and the Sanskrit *vijaya* are etymologically cognate, and both are frequent as personal names, also in their feminine forms.

10.48 For the second time, a picture is a crucial plot device, cf. above p. 291 and p. 307. It is not the last time that art plays such a pivotal part, cf. below p. 441.

10.57 After the summer rainy season, when the full clouds are black, autumn clouds are empty of rain, and hence white.

10.58 "Losing one's mind" (*unmāda*) is only the first of the ten stages of lovesickness.

10.69 Yudhi·shthira, son of the god Dharma, and a model king, was the eldest of the five Pándava brothers, heroes of the "Maha·bhárata."

10.70 *Paṅkti* means both "volley" and "five." Doctor of the gods, Dhanvántari was one of the fourteen jewels born from the primordial churning of the ocean of milk, with a cup of medicinal nectar in his hands.

10.73 Or: "of the first kings." Manu was the mythical ancestor of humanity (*manuṣya*, "Man"), to whom is ascribed the eponymous law code.

10.74 February-March, Phalgun is the month of the spring season and Holi, the great spring festival.

11.8 Literally "sister in milk," i.e., fed by the same wet nurse.

11.12 *Nṛ/śaṃsa* is translated twice, as "wicked" and, literally, as "a man's downfall."

11.21 For a discussion of the virginal and geopolitical connotations of this intriguing ballgame, and its relatives in Sanskrit literature, please see SIEGFRIED LIENHARD's 1999 article.

11.24 It is a venerable Indian tradition to cry out one's appreciation at the appropriate points during a performance. In Europe this is done only at sporting events; in India, in the middle of classical-music recitals.

11.26 Both Kandukávati and the lightning are described by the same words at the same time, but differently.

11.32 The blue-lily is one of Kama's five flower arrows.

11.38 Chandra·sena's wit contrasts a helpful immediate transformation into a monkey, with a karmic reincarnation as a monkey at her next rebirth.

11.39 Kama was also born as Pradyúmna, Krishna's son, and then kidnapped by the demon Shámbara, who threw him into the sea. Fishermen found him inside a big fish. When mature, he challenged Shámbara, and defeated and decapitated him. This epithet is particularly apposite here, considering Mitra·gupta's fate: he too will be thrown by a villain into the sea, only to defeat him in the end.

11.44 Hunchbacks are listed in the *Artha/śāstra* as suitable spies to watch and destroy an enemy (XIV.1.2).

11.50 Raméshu could be an Indian name, although during this period Arabs were the chief traders and navigators in the Indian Ocean and the China Sea. Nevertheless, the crew might have been Persians, or indeed literally Greeks, trading wine, and perhaps settled on the coast near Suhma.

11.59 Brahmin demons (*brahma/rākṣasa*) appear in the "Ramáyana," where they guard the sacrifice, interfering only when the rites have not been performed correctly (I.8). In general, *rákshasa* demons can be good or bad, although on the whole they tend to be monsters. In the "Ramáyana" they are the enemies of Rama, the incarnation of Vishnu, disturbing sacrifices, changing form at will, and feeding on human flesh.

11.67 Cf. above p. 596.

11.74 Our hero sees a way of postponing his consumption by the demon, charming him with storytelling, à la *The 1001 Nights*.

II.75 Dhúmini's story: What is cruel? The heart of a woman. This and the following story are also found in the Pali Játakas (*Cullapaduma* and *Mahāummagga jātaka*s, respectively). Cf. for a comparison of the two versions, CHAKRAVARTY, N. 1922.

II.76 An arid country in ancient times, the desert east of Shatádru, between the Sutlej and Sarásvati rivers, including Ludhiána and Patiála to the north and the desert to the south. The frame of this story is borrowed from the *Kathā/sarit/sāgara* (x.65), with variants that emphasize the woman's cruelty.

II.76 Although strictly speaking *dhānya* is grain, while *dhana* is wealth, both are etymologically related, and hence we can directly translate the trio of names. Please note the exceptional accentuation to differentiate Dhányaka *(Dhānyaka)* and Dhanyaka *(Dhanyaka)*.

II.76 "Rain" and "year" are the same word, *varṣa*, in Sanskrit. Indra is the god of rain.

II.82 Such punishment was common in ancient India, especially in battle, where score was kept by counting the numbers of fallen by the piles of their severed ears or noses. The injuries were matched with corresponding plastic-surgery skills, e.g., rhinoplasty, to replace the severed noses.

II.93 The lowest of the low in the caste hierarchy, only "a cooker of dogs" *(śva/pāk)* is reduced to eating dog meat.

II.95 What is dear and beneficial for a householder? The virtues of a housewife.

II.96 The Pállava capital, west of present-day Chennai (Madras).

II.100 This is one of only two occurrences in this book of the Sanskrit *varṇa*, "caste," literally "color."

II.103 This Shibi is in South India. It is Chola country, crossed by the Kavéri, and not the famous country of Shibi, near Gandhára, in present-day Pakistan.

II.105 The precise location of these auspicious marks is important. Thus, depending on the position of outlines of barleycorns on the fingers, they indicate wealth, progeny, good fortune, etc.

II.109 It is a regular trope, not only in Sanskrit literature, that you can judge a book by its cover. How much more so in a world of reincarnation and being born to what one deserves? Cf. Śāk IV.p. 86, etc.

II.112 It is in order to preserve the fragrance of rice that traditionally one should not wash it, a convention often disregarded today.

II.113 The small change here referred to is not coins but cowrie shells (fr. Hindi *kaurī*), *kākiṇī*, long used as currency in South Asia and Africa.

II.114 *Khádira* wood, used for the pestle, is cashew, the wood recommended for a Vedic sacrificial stake. *Kákubha* wood, used for the mortar, is from the *árjuna* tree, and is still used today to make the mast from which devotees suspend themselves for mortification at festivals. These woods bear witness that even for vegetarian preparations an evocation of the violence of sacrificial killing is required.

II.115 As with the apocryphal plethora of words for snow in the Inuit language, there are in Sanskrit a number of words for the different stages of the processing of rice: *anna*, "food," is "boiled rice," and is a different word from the uncooked grains, while *siktha* is another word for "boiled rice," but without the generalization to food.

II.120 The sauce is *sūpa*, etymologically close to "soup," said by Sanskrit etymologists to be so called because "it is drunk with pleasure" (*su*khena *pī*yate). Pure clarified butter here is *sarpis*, distinguished from ghee in being runny and not solid.

II.122 The word for "clear, pellucid, pure," *acchā*, is extremely frequent in modern Hindi, with multiple functions, including an affirmative "good," and a rhetorical "really?"

II.122 Literally: "eyewings," *akṣi/pakṣman*.

II.123 At the beginning and conclusion of any religious rite, as well as after a bath, drinking, sneezing, sleep, meals, walking through a street, and changing clothes, a twice-born man should rinse his mouth three times with a little water taken from the palm of his hand, cf. Manu V.145.

II.127 What is desire? Imagination.

II.128 Modern Kathiawar, in west India.

II.133 Not only are flowers and other delicacies offered to a god, but the "leftovers" are received back again, as a blessed gift from the deity, *prasāda*.

II.156 What is the means to achieve the difficult? Wisdom.

II.157 On the banks of the Yámuna, the birthplace of Krishna. This story is borrowed from the *Kathā/sarit/sāgara*.

11.163 The go-between nun could equally be a Jain.

11.183 This is what happens in the *Vetāla/pañca/viṃśati* in the *Bṛhat/kathā*; cf. *Kathā/sarit/sāgara* XII.8.

11.188 Four complex stories have come between the original story, interrupted at p. 417 above, and this is its continuation.

11.191 This is a reference to the *rákshasa* marriage, one of the eight legitimate forms in the *Dharma/śāstras*, in which a girl is forcibly seized and carried away after the defeat or destruction of her relatives in battle.

11.200 Suicide as a form of blackmail is well attested in Sanskrit literature and the *Artha/śāstra*, and has been seen already above, p. 602 and p. 391. For example, a creditor will go and sit at the door of his debtor and threaten to starve himself to death until he is repaid. Here the king wants to make the goddess responsible for his death, since she gave him children only to take them away.

11.205 Mantra·gupta's wounded lips prevent him from uttering labial phonemes, as great a disadvantage when communicating in Sanskrit as it is when using English. Strictly speaking, the Sanskrit labials comprise: *p*, *ph*, *b*, *bh*, *m*, *v*, *u*, *ū*, *o* and *au*. However, in English the vowels are not labial, and *v*—and *f* and *w*, which do not occur in Sanskrit—are semi-bi-labials, and hence not excluded here. Despite the prohibition on saying *m*, the chapter as printed elsewhere includes countless *anusvāras* (*ṃ*), which should serve as a reminder that *anusvāra* is always the homorganic nasal—and is faithfully represented as such in the following labial-free pages—and not *m*, unless preceding *p*, *b* or *m*, which could not happen in the following chapter. A minor example of the difficulties entailed is the exclusion of even our hero's name, Mantra·gupta. Such linguistic feats are not rare in Sanskrit literature, nor are they unknown in European literature, the best-known case being the French novelist PEREC's *La Disparition*, an entire novel written without using the letter *e*.

12.1 The first forced circumlocution, because one cannot say "mountain." Dandin himself selected the vivid epithet *na/ga*, "no-go," "does not go," also expressible as *a/cala* with the same meaning.

12.2 Kala·ratri is the dark night of destruction at the end of world, as well its personification in the goddess Durga.

12.6 Such as the two we cannot mention: sesame and white mustard.

12.11 "Mother" is one of the most difficult words to paraphrase—although "father's wife" was one option—since it is perhaps *the* universal labial, from Indo-European to Chinese, to Semitic languages, to Swahili. "Genetrix" would be a direct translation of the slightly less awkward Sanskrit *jananī*, "begetter."

12.12 A sorcerer sacrificing an innocent at the charnel-ground is an extraordinarily common trope in Sanskrit literature. Cf. Mal Madh V, where Aghóra·ghanta tries to kill Málati when Mádhava rescues her.

12.15 Mantra·gupta uses "our" uncharacteristically, to avoid "my" (*me/mama*).

12.16 The word "indigo" came to English from sixteenth-century Portuguese, from the Greek *indikon*, "Indian [dye]," used here as a substitute for the illicit word "blue."

12.16 Dandin could not say *bhrū/latā*. We cannot say "brows."

12.21 If Mantra·gupta does not comply, Love will make Kánaka·lekha no more than a memory, which is to say that she will die of a broken heart. In Sanskrit polite discourse and drama, the death of the main character is taboo, like a hopeless ending in Hollywood movies. Hence even the mention of the possibility of a hero's or heroine's demise must be euphemistic.

12.23 One of the difficulties in this chapter is the prohibition on "me" and "mine," hence here the self-referential "your narrator's feet."

12.23 "Honey-creators" is coined by analogy with the usual Sanskrit for bumblebee, *madhu/kara*, "honey-maker."

12.24 The unmentionable "Mount Meru."

12.24 *Rāga* is again both "red" and "desire."

12.26 The here forbidden fruit, the mango.

12.26 While "red-lipped/mouthed" are out of bounds, "red-orificed" would be a bit too much.

12.26 The Dárdura crag is that portion of the Ghats which forms the southern boundary of Mysore. The wind is often referred to by Sanskrit poets as a dancing master.

12.28 The conventional transliteration of this Sanskrit name would be Jaya·simha, but since labials are outlawed here, we revert to the phonetically more faithful Jaya·singha, with *ng* representing the class nasal *(ṅ)* otherwise obscured by the literalistic transliteration of the *anusvára* by *m/ṃ*. Cf. for example, the country name Singapore, Singha·pura, "Lion city."

12.32 Both "king" and "savant doctor" are *nar'|êndra*, "lords of men."

12.35 The Sanskrit idiom is actually "has on the tip of his tongue," but, "tip" is a forbidden word.

12.36 Cf. the etymology of "dis aster," "bad star," here in Sanskrit "fierce star," *caṇḍa|tārā*.

12.37 Kubéra.

12.39 "The white sea of stars in the sky" is a circumlocution for the Milky Way, called "milk ocean" (*kṣīra|sāgara*) in Sanskrit.

12.42 The constellations are twenty-seven. Hence the image is of a necklace with twenty-seven pearls.

12.42 "Trunked" is a paraphrase for the forbidden "elephant, pachyderm"; in Sanskrit, literally, "having a hand/trunk," *hastin*. A *gandha|hastin* is an elephant whose ichor smells particularly pungent.

12.42 The unmentionable Meru, again.

12.43 One of the eight forms of Shiva, cf. Shak I.1.

12.43 Her names, which cannot be pronounced here, are Uma and Párvati.

12.45 Transcribed here *hansa*, representing the way the nasal is in fact pronounced, instead of the conventional *ham|ṃsa*. Note also how much closer this brings the word's orthography to its Indo-European cognates, "gander" and the German *Gans*.

12.47 *Daṇḍa*—the root of our author's name—a "rod," i.e., a measure of four "hands," *hasta*.

12.49 Literally, "nobles," precluded by its forbidden labial.

12.50 The highest caste are Brahmins; and the tiny oil-rich seeds are sesame.

12.54 While *mákara*, the water creature borne on Kama's banner, is a forbidden word in this chapter, Mantra·gupta's comparison with a crocodile, *nakra*, indirectly identifies him with the Love God's attribute.

12.54 *Kāla*, literally "Time," or Yama.

12.55 A paraphrase for "my."

12.57 *Rajas*, "passionate pollution," is supposed to predominate in men, as opposed to *sattva*, "pure goodness," in gods, and *tamas*, "dark ignorance," in demons.

12.60 Manu or simply earlier kings, cf. above p. 604.

12.63 "Lips," onomatopoeically labial, are next to impossible to paraphrase, although "toothcovers" is one of their regular epithets in Sanskrit.

12.67 All these labials, at last! And a hint of self-congratulation on the part of our author?

13.7 Vidárbha stretched from the banks of the Krishna to near the banks of the Nármada. It was such a great kingdom that it was also called Maha·rashtra, the name of one of the biggest states in India to this day. Its capital was Kúndina·pura.

13.7 Cf. Ragh VIII.16. The famous race of the Bhojas branch of the Yádavas.

13.7 The first manifestation of an elaborate satire and representation of the *Artha/śāstra* in this chapter. In Kautílya, a king can judge his ally's worth according to whether his undertakings are feasible (*śakya*), sound (*kalya*, here *kalpa*) or favorable all around, of public utility (*bhavya*) (VII.8.11, or: 114,115).

13.8 The six expedients are (*Artha/śāstra* VII.1.2): peace or alliance (*saṃdhi*), war (*vigraha*), march or expedition against the enemy (*yāna*), halt or ceasefire, abstention (*āsana*), duplicity (*dvaidhībhāva*) and seeking shelter (*saṃśraya*). The rules for the four castes are given in the *Mānava/dharma/śāstra*, and at the beginning of the *Artha/śāstra* (I.3.5ff).

13.11 High birth is similarly the first qualification for a king in the *Artha/śāstra* (VI.i.3.). Given the choice between a powerful or a highborn monarch, subjects prefer the latter (VIII.2.22).

13.13 Cf. ASh VIII.2.9: without the "eye of science" a king is blind.

13.14 Cf. in the text below, p. 543 and p. 511: the treasury and army (*prabhu/śakti*), discernment through ministers' counsel (*mantra/śakti*), and personal energy (*utsāha/śakti*).

13.19 This description fits the initiatory rite of the sacrificer *(yajamāna)* at the *Agni·shtoma*, the pressing of *soma*, a most prestigious Vedic sacrifice.

13.25 Not all of a monarch's training is practical: philosophy or meditation are also important (ASh I.2; cf. the young Alexander and his tutor Aristotle).

13.26 The Mauryan king is Chandra·gupta, king of Pátali·putra and hero of the *Mudrā/rákshasa*, who ruled at the end of the fourth century BCE. His minister is credited with the composition of the famous *Artha/śāstra*, which apparently enabled the sound foundation—once Chandra·gupta had won the Nandan throne—of the whole Mauryan dynasty, of which the Emperor Ashóka is the most prominent scion. Vishnu·gupta is also known as Kautílya, and also Chánakya. But the historicity of the authorship is dubious. Throughout the work, Vishnu·gupta (alias Chánakya), the author, refers to the authority of his master Kautílya.

13.29 The following description of twenty-four hours in the life of the king is a veritable pastiche of the *Artha/śāstra* (I.19).

13.29 Listed, with their respective sanctions and punishments, at ASh II.8.20.

13.34 A gong (*nāḍikā*) is equivalent to a water pot (*ghaṭika*), used to measure twenty-four minutes of time, or a third of a watch; the watch thus amounts to precisely seventy-two minutes, or a little under an hour and a quarter.

13.37 Such spies disguise themselves as ascetics, the deaf or mute, or brigands, and go out to poison enemy troops, for example. ASh XIV.1 gives a detailed list of the most efficacious poisons for polluting water reservoirs.

13.47 The six enemies, the six passions, are: sexual desire (*kāma*), anger (*krodha*), greed (*lobha*), pride (*māna*), arrogance (*mada*) and wanton delight (*harṣa*). The four tactics are to: negotiate, offer gifts, foment dissension and turn to weapons only as the last resort (Manu VII.107).

13.48 These five are Kautílya's predecessors. Shukra is also called Úshanas, the preceptor of the *ásuras*. Angírasa is otherwise known as Brihas·pati, the preceptor of gods. Both are mythical founders of political science, and both are also ascribed authorship of canonical lawbooks (*smṛtis*). Vishaláksha is a name of Shiva as the author of a treatise, and Bahu·danti·putra, the son of Indra (Bahu·danti), is Jaya·datta. Both are referred to by Kautílya. Paráshara is the famous chief *smṛti* authority of the present Kali age.

13.53 "Good advice" is the name of the well-known book of fables, the *Hit'/ôpadeśa*.

13.61 Áshmaka is the old name of Travancore.

13.63 In the *Artha/śāstra*, the following four vices born from desire are enumerated, and their respective gravity is debated (VIII.3).

13.64 The theorists permitted hunting primarily on this ground.

13.78 Vana·vasi, in South India, was the seat of the Kadámba kings in the sixth and seventh centuries.

13.79 Compare the beginning of the *Iliad*, when the Greek armies are camped along the seashore and Achilles is furious that Agamemnon has taken away Briseis, his concubine.

13.80 The Múrala is the principal river of Kérala, the strip of land between the Western Ghats and the sea, north of Kavéri, probably including Malabar. All the kingdoms named here are neighbors of Vidárbha. Together they comprise the whole of South India: Áshmaka, Kúntala, Múrala, Rishíka, Kónkana, Nasíkya and Vana·vasi.

13.85 The capital of the Háihayas or Kalachuris, to the north of the Nármada.

13.110 *Vatsa·nabha*, "child's/calf's navel (musk)" is a tree whose toxicity is taught in the *Artha/śāstra* (XIV.1.29) in order to destroy enemy forces in secret.

13.111 Her words are double-edged, for at the same time that she makes the vow that depends on her virtue, the *asi/dhārā/vratam*, the "standing on a sword edge vow," she pledges in code to execute him.

13.114 *Kapálika*s are Shaivites who bear a skull (*kapála*), wear bone ornaments and carry a skullstaff, etc., in the model of Shiva *Kapálin*, "Skull-bearer." *Kapálika* practice is relatively extreme. They are known as magicians, who drink from a skullcap and make offerings of human flesh into the fire.

13.137 By saluting the Áshmakan king, Víshruta implicates him, making him seem guilty.

13.153 The six qualities are the six ways of conducting foreign policy.

13.163 There are four tests of character: of loyalty, disinterestedness, continence and courage; or trials by religion, money, love and fear (ASh I.10).

13.164 An atheist, *nāstika*, is literally one who says "there is nothing," i.e., they are nihilists, non-believers and, at any rate, heretics.

13.165 But his story has not yet ended, and continues, still in Víshruta's voice, in the *Uttara/pīṭhikā*, the "Postscript Conclusion" attributed to Chakra·pani Dikshita.

CAST OF CHARACTERS

ACHÁRAVATI: wife of Chanda·ghosha, and mother of Mani·kárnika

AIRÁVATA: Indra's white elephant

AMBÁLIKA: "Little mother," princess of Anga, marries *Apahára·varman*

ÁMBIKA: "Mother," a name for the Goddess, and guardian of Tarávali

ANÁNTA·KIRTI: merchant of Ujjáyini, and husband of Nitámbavati

ANÁNTA·SIRA: village chief, and enemy of King Víkata·varman

ANÁNTA·VARMAN: king of Vidárbha, and not interested in politics

ANGÁRA·VARSHA: minister of Prince Simha·ghosha

Apahára·varman: "Protected by being taken away," son of Prahára·varman (king of Vidéha) and of Priyam·vada, and husband of Ambálika (princess of Anga)

ARHÁNTIKA: Buddhist nun

Artha·pala: "Protector of wealth," son of Kama·pala and of Kántimati, and husband of Mani·kárnika (princess of Kashi)

ARTHA·PATI: "Lord of wealth," rich merchant of Champa

ARYA·DASI: previous incarnation of Tarávali

ARYA·KETU: minister of Anánta·varman and then of Bháskara·varman

AVÁNTI·DEVA: king of Kúntala, and enemy of Anánta·varman

AVÁNTI·SÚNDARI: princess of Mágadha, daughter of King Mana·sara, and wife of *Raja·váhana*

BALA·BHADRA: husband of Ratnávati

BALA·CHÁNDRIKA: "The young moon," wife of *Pushpódbhava*, and girlfriend of Princess Avánti·súndari

BÁNDHUMATI: previous incarnation of Kántimati

BANDHU·PALA: merchant of Ujjáyini, and father of Chandra·pala

BHANU·VARMAN: king of Vana·vasa, and enemy of Anánta·varman

BHÁSKARA·VARMAN: prince of Vidárbha, rescued by *Víshruta*, his second cousin; reconquers the throne of his father Anánta·varman

BHIMA·VARMAN: prince of Suhma, and son of King Tunga·dhanvan *brahma·rákshasa*: demon who poses *Mitra·gupta* riddles

CHANDA·GHOSHA: prince, eldest son of Chanda·simha (king of Kashi), and brother-in-law of Kama·pala

CHANDA·SIMHA: king of Kashi, and father of Chanda·ghosha and Kántimati by Lilávati, of Simha·ghosha

CHANDA·VARMAN: "Viciously protected," nephew of King Mana·sara, and regent of Málava

CHANDRA·PALA: merchant of Ujjáyini, and friend of *Pushpódbhava*

CHANDRA·PÁLITA: courtier, son of Indra·pálita, and minister of the king of Áshmaka

CHANDRA·SENA: foster sister of Princess Kandukávati, and lover of Kosha·dasa

CHITRA·GUPTA: clerk of the City of the Dead

DARPA·SARA: crown prince of Málava, son of Mana·sara, practises asceticism on Mount Kailash

DARU·VARMAN: "Protected by cruelty," nephew of King Mana·sara, and regent of Málava

DHANA·MITRA: "Friend of wealth," AKA UDÁRAKA, "Generous," merchant of Champa, and fiancé of Kula·pálika

DHÁNYAKA: "Richard," husband of Dhúmini

DHARMA·PALA: "Protector of the Law," one of Raja·hamsa's three hereditary ministers, father of Sumántra, Sumítra and Kama·pala, and grandfather of *Mantra·gupta*, *Mitra·gupta* and *Artha·pala*

DHARMA·RÁKSHITA: "Protector of the Religion," Buddhist nun, and confidante of the courtesan Kama·máñjari

DHARMA·VÁRDHANA: "Increaser of Goodness," king of Shrávasti, and father of Princess Nava·málika

DHÚMINI: "Made of smoke" or "Dark as smoke," heroine of the first of *Mitra·gupta*'s stories

DURGA: AKA CHÁNDIKA DURGA, name of the Goddess in her fierce aspect

EKA·PINGA: "Having a single yellow mark in place of an eye," name of the god Kubéra

EKA·VIRA: king of Rishíka, and enemy of Anánta·varman

ENA·JANGHA: "Black antelope shank," courier of Darpa·sara

GANÉSHA: elephant-headed god, son of Shiva and Párvati, and the remover of obstacles

GANGES: river of the gods, incarnated in Kalpa·súndari

GAURI: "The auspicious aspect of the Goddess," wife of Satya·varman, and mother of *Soma·datta*

GÓMINI: heroine of *Mitra·gupta*'s second story

GRIHA·GUPTA: merchant of Válabhi, and father of Rátnavati (heroine of *Mitra·gupta*'s third story)

gúhyakas: demigods, like *yakshas*, who attend Kubéra and guard his treasure

INDRA·PÁLITA: minister of Vasánta·bhanu (king of Áshmaka)

JAYA·SINGHA: king of Andhra, carries off Princess Kánaka·lekha

KALA·GUPTA: merchant of Kala·yávana, father of Suvrítta (wife of Ratnódbhava), and grandfather of *Pushpódbhava*

KÁLAHA·KÁNTAKA: "A thorn in a fight," young man of Máthura, and in love with Nitámbavati (heroine of *Mitra·gupta*'s fourth story)

KALI: "The horrific aspect of the Goddess," first wife of Satya·varman

KALÍNDA·VARMAN: king of Kama·rupa, and father of Queen Kalpa·súndari

KALÍNDI: daughter of the king of the *ásuras*; marries Matánga

KALPA·SÚNDARI: queen of Vidéha, and wife of Víkata·varman; marries *Upahára·varman*

KAMA·MÁÑJARI: "Bouquet of love," courtesan, seductress of Maríchi, and sister of Raga·máñjari

KAMA·PALA: "The protector of love," son of Dharma·pala (minister of Raja·hamsa), marries Kántimati (princess of Kashi), and father of *Artha·pala*

KÁNAKA·LEKHA: princess of Kalínga, and daughter of King Kárdana; marries *Mantra·gupta*

KÁNAKAVATI: girlfriend of Rátnavati

KANDUKÁVATI: "Bearer of the ball," princess of Suhma, daughter of King Tunga·dhanvan; marries *Mitra·gupta*

KÁNTAKA: chief of the police of Champa

KÁNTIMATI: princess of Kashi, daughter of King Chanda·simha, wife of Kama·pala, and mother of *Artha·pala*

KÁRDANA: king of Kárdana, and father of Princess Kánaka·lekha

KHÁNATI: foreign merchant, described as "Greek," which probably makes him Persian or Arab, and accomplice of Míthilan notables

KOSHA·DASA: friend of *Mitra·gupta*, and lover of Chandra·sena

KSHMA·TALÓRVASHI: "The nymph Úrvashi on Earth," dancing girl of King Avánti·deva

KUBÉRA: god of wealth

KUBÉRA·DATTA: merchant of Champa, and father of Kula·pálika

KULA·PÁLIKA: "Her family's protector," young woman of Champa, promised to Dhana·mitra

KUMÁRA·GUPTA: king of Konkan, and enemy of Anánta·varman

KÚSUMA·DHANVAN: king of Kósala, father of Queen Vasum·dhara, and grandfather of Bháskara·varman

LAKSHMI: goddess of royal Majesty, of fortune, prosperity and beauty, and, like the Earth, a great king's ideal consort, as well as the wife of Vishnu

LILÁVATI: queen, and wife of Chanda·simha (king of Kashi)

LOPA·MUDRA: wife of the sage Agástya

MÁDHAVA·SENA: mother of the two courtesans Kama·máñjari and Raga·máñjari

MANA·PALA: "Protector of pride," minister of King Vira·ketu

MANA·SARA: "Whose essential strength is pride," king of Málava, conquers Raja·hamsa thanks to the assistance of Shiva

MÁNAVATI: wife of Kalínda·varman (king of Kama·rupa), and mother of Queen Kalpa·súndari

MANGÁLIKA: nurse of Princess Ambálika

MANI·BHADRA: prince of the *yakshas*, and father of Tarávali

MANI·KÁRNIKA: princess of Kashi, daughter of Chanda·simha and Achá-ravati, and wife of *Artha·pala*, her cousin

MAÑJU·VÁDINI: "Eloquent," princess of Vidárbha, daughter of Anánta·varman and Vasum·dhara, and wife of *Víshruta*

Mantra·gupta: son of Sumántra (minister of Raja·hamsa), marries Kána-ka·lekha (princess of Kalínga)

MARÍCHI: ascetic seduced by Kama·máñjari

MARKANDÉYA: ascetic whose curse transforms Súrata·máñjari into a silver chain

MATÁNGA: feral brahmin who becomes lord of the underworld

MATTA·KALA: king of the Latas, and suitor for the hand of Princess Vama·lóchana

MÉDINI: "Earth," queen of Suhma, and wife of King Tunga·dhanvan

Mitra·gupta: son of Sumítra (minister of Raja·hamsa); marries Kan-dukávati (princess of Suhma)

MITRA·VARMAN: king of Mahíshmati, and half-brother of Anánta·var-man

MRITYU·VÍJAYA: "Conqueror of death," elephant fought by Purna·bhadra

NAGA·PALA: king of Nasíkya, and enemy of Anánta·varman

NAGA·MÁLIKA: "Young jasmine," princess of Shravásti, daughter of King Dharma·várdhana, and wife of *Prámati*

NALI·JANGHA: "Reed shank" (the epithet for a crow or raven), guardian of Prince Bháskara·varman

NIDHI·PÁLITA: merchant of Champa, and father of Vasu·pálita

NIDHI·PATI·DATTA: father of Kánakavati

NÍMBAVATI: = RÁTNAVATI

NITÁMBAVATI: "Great hips," heroine of *Mitra·gupta*'s fourth story

PADMÓDBHAVA: one of the three hereditary ministers of King Raja·hamsa, father of Ratnódbhava and Súshruta, and grand-father of *Pushpódbhava* and *Víshruta*

PANCHÁLA·SHARMAN: a brahmin who helps *Prámati* to win Princess Nava·málika

PANCHÁLIKA: notable of Míthila, and friend of King Víkata·varman

PARITRÁTA: merchant of Míthila, and friend of King Víkata·varman

PRACHÁNDA·VARMAN: king of Útkala, brother of Chanda·varman, and suitor for the hand of Princess Mañju·vádini

PRAHÁRA·VARMAN: king of Vidéha, friend of Raja·hamsa, and father of *Apahára·varman* and *Upahára·varman*, banished from his kingdom by his nephews

Prámati: "Providence," son of Súmati, minister of King Raja·hamsa, according to the "Postscript Beginning," and son of Kama·pala according to the *Dasha·kumára·chárita*; marries Nava·málika (princess of Shravásti)

PUNYA·VARMAN: model king of Vidárbha, and father of Anánta·varman

PURNA·BHADRA: friend of Kama·pala

PUSHKÁRIKA: daughter of Upahára·varman's nurse, and attendant of Queen Kalpa·súndari

Pushpódbhava: "Born from a flower," son of Ratnódbhava and Suvrítta; marries Bala·chándrika

RAGA·MÁÑJARI: "Bouquet of love and melodies," courtesan, sister of Kama·máñjari, and wife of Apahára·varman

RAJA·HAMSA: "Best (swan) among kings," king of Mágadha, defeated by Mana·sara, forced into exile, and father of Prince *Raja·váhana*

Raja·váhana: "Bearer of royalty," son of Raja·hamsa, principal hero of the book; marries Avánti·súndari (princess of Málava)

RAMAYÁNTIKA: dancing-girl who dallies with Víkata·varman

RAMÉSHU: sea-captain of the Yávanas who pick *Mitra·gupta* up out of the sea

RÁTNAVATI: "Jewelled one," AKA NÍMBAVATI, "Tree of bitter fruits," heroine of the third of *Mitra·gupta*'s stories

RATNÓDBHAVA: "Jewel-born," son of Padmódbhava (minister of Raja·hamsa), marries Suvrítta on his voyages, and father of *Pushpódbhava*

RÍDDHIMATI: "Prospera," nurse to Princess Mani·kárnika

SÁGARA·DATTA: mother of Queen Vasum·dhara, daughter of Vaishrávana (merchant of Pátali·putra), and sister of Sindhu·datta

SATYA·VARMAN: "With truth as his armor," son of Sita·varman (minister of Raja·hamsa), marries the sisters Kali and Gauri, and father of *Soma·datta*

SHAKTI·KUMÁRA: marries Gómini, heroine of the third of *Mitra·gupta's* stories

SHAMBA: king, son of Krishna, and previous incarnation of *Raja·váhana*, who is thus biologically related to Vishnu in his manly avatar

SHASHÁNKA·SENA: girlfriend of Princess Kánaka·lekha

SHATA·HALI: friend of King Víkata·varman

SHÁUNAKA: previous incarnation of Kama·pala

SHIVA: bestows a divine mace on Mana·sara, and commands Matánga to become overlord of the underworld

SHIVA·NAGA: minister of King Simha·ghosha

SHRIGÁLIKA: nurse to the courtesan Raga·máñjari

SHÚDRAKA: earlier incarnation of Kama·pala

SIMHA·GHOSHA i.: notable of Champa, imprisoned by Kántaka, and liberated by Apahára·varman

SIMHA·GHOSHA ii.: prince of Kashi, and younger brother of King Chanda·simha

SIMHA·VARMAN: "Whose armor is a lion," king of Anga, and father of Princess Ambálika

SINDHU·DATTA: grandmother of *Víshruta*, and daughter of Vaishrávana (merchant of Pátali·putra)

SITA·VARMAN: one of Raja·hamsa's three hereditary ministers, father of Súmati and Satya·varman, and grandfather of *Prámati* and *Soma·datta*

Soma·datta: son of Satya·varman and Gauri, marries Vama·lóchana (princess of Pariyátra)

SOMA·DEVA·SHARMAN: ascetic, and disciple of Vama·deva

SOMA·PIDÁ: "Wife of Soma·pida, the presser of the Soma, with the moon as his diadem" name of the Goddess

STHUNA: minister of Prince Simha·ghosha

SULÁKSHANA: wife of Prince Simha·ghosha

SUMÁNTRA: son of Dharma·pala (minister of Raja·hamsa), and father of *Mantra·gupta*

SÚMATI: son of Sita·varman (minister of King Raja·hamsa), and father of *Prámati*

SUMÍTRA: son of Dharma·pala (minister of King Raja·hamsa), and father of *Mitra·gupta*

SUNDÁRAKA: inhabitant of Champa, and rival of Vasu·pálita

SÚRATA·MÁÑJARI: "Bouquet of erotic pleasures," divine nymph (*ápsaras*), cursed by Markandéya, and transformed into a silver chain

SÚSHRUTA: son of Padmódbhava (minister of King Raja·hamsa) and Sindhu·datta (daughter of Vaishrávana), and father of *Víshruta*

SUVRÍTTA: "Good news," wife of Ratnódbhava, and mother of *Pushpódbhava*

TARÁVALI: daughter of Mani·bhadra (prince of the *yakshas*), wife of Kama·pala, and mother of *Prámati*

TRY·ÁMBAKA: "Three-eyed" ("Three-mothered"), name of Shiva

UDÁRAKA: = DHANA·MITRA

Upahára·varman: son of Prahára·varman (king of Vidéha) and Priyam·vada, marries Kalpa·súndari (queen of Vidéha)

VAISHRÁVANA: merchant of Pátali·putra and grandfather of Vasum·dhara (queen of Vidárbha) and Súshruta (father of *Víshruta*)

VAMA·DEVA: ascetic who receives in his hermitage Raja·hamsa, in exile with his court

VAMA·LÓCHANA: "Lovely-eyed," princess of Pariyátra, and daughter of King Vira·ketu; marries *Soma·datta*

VASÁNTA·BHANU: king of Áshmaka, and enemy of Anánta·varman

VÁSUMATI: "Wealthy Earth," queen of Mágadha, and wife of King Raja·hamsa

VASUM·DHARA: "The Earth, bearer of treasure," queen of Vidárbha, and wife of King Anánta·varman

VASU·PÁLITA: "Protected by wealth," AKA VIRÚPAKA, "Ugly," merchant of Champa who becomes a Jain monk and is seduced by the courtesan Kama·máñjari

VASU·RÁKSHITA: "Protector of wealth," minister of King Anánta·varman

VIDYÉSHVARA: magician who marries *Raja·váhana* and Princess Avánti·súndari

VIHÁRA·BHADRA: courtier, and favorite of King Anánta·varman

VÍKATA·VARMAN: "Hideous," king of Vidéha, husband of Kalpa·súndari, and nephew of King Prahára·varman

VIMÁRDAKA: "Crusher," denizen of a gaming house in Champa

VÍNAYAVATI: prior incarnation of Kántimati

VINDHYA·VÁSINI: "She who dwells in the Vindhyas," name of the Goddess, and protector of Kandukávati

VIRA·KETU: king of Pariyátra, and father of Princess Vama·lóchana

VIRA·SENA: king of Múrala, and enemy of Anánta·varman

VISHÁLA·VARMAN: younger brother of King Víkata·varman

VIRA·SHÉKHARA: celestial spirit (*vidya·dhara*), who possesses Súrata·máñjari transformed into a silver chain

VISHNU: bestows a son on King Raja·hamsa

Víshruta: "The expert," son of Súshruta (minister of Raja·hamsa); marries Mañju·vádini (princess of Vidárbha)

YÁJÑAVATI: earlier incarnation of Avánti·súndari, and wife of King Shamba

yakshas: servants of Kubéra, the god of wealth, *yakshas* mix voluntarily with humans, on whom they can, if they are so minded, bestow wealth and good fortune

yakshis: female counterparts of *yakshas*

YAMA: god of Death, sends Matánga back to earth

INDEX

Sanskrit words are given according to the accented CSL pronuncuation aid in the English alphabetical order. They are followed by the conventional diacritics in brackets.

THE CLAY SANSKRIT LIBRARY

The volumes in the series are listed here in order of publication.
Titles marked with an asterisk* are also available in the
Digital Clay Sanskrit Library (eCSL).
For further information visit www.claysanskritlibrary.org

1. The Emperor of the Sorcerers (*Bṛhatkathāślokasaṃgraha*) (vol. 1 of 2) by *Budhasvāmin*. SIR JAMES MALLINSON
2. Heavenly Exploits (*Divyāvadāna*). JOEL TATELMAN
3. Maha·bhárata III: The Forest (*Vanaparvan*) (vol. 4 of 4)* WILLIAM J. JOHNSON
4. Much Ado about Religion (*Āgamaḍambara*) by *Bhaṭṭa Jayanta*. CSABA DEZSŐ
5. The Birth of Kumára (*Kumārasaṃbhava*) by *Kālidāsa*. DAVID SMITH
6. Ramáyana I: Boyhood (*Bālakāṇḍa*) by *Vālmīki*. ROBERT P. GOLDMAN
7. The Epitome of Queen Lilávati (*Līlāvatīsāra*) (vol. 1 of 2) by *Jinaratna*. R.C.C. FYNES
8. Ramáyana II: Ayódhya (*Ayodhyākāṇḍa*) by *Vālmīki*. SHELDON I. POLLOCK
9. Love Lyrics (*Amaruśataka, Śatakatraya & Caurapañcāśikā*) by *Amaru, Bhartṛhari & Bilhaṇa*. GREG BAILEY & RICHARD GOMBRICH
10. What Ten Young Men Did (*Daśakumāracarita*) by *Daṇḍin*. ISABELLE ONIANS
11. Three Satires (*Kaliviḍambana, Kalāvilāsa & Bhallaṭaśataka*) by *Nīlakaṇṭha, Kṣemendra & Bhallaṭa*. SOMADEVA VASUDEVA
12. Ramáyana IV: Kishkíndha (*Kiṣkindhākāṇḍa*) by *Vālmīki*. ROSALIND LEFEBER
13. The Emperor of the Sorcerers (*Bṛhatkathāślokasaṃgraha*) (vol. 2 of 2) by *Budhasvāmin*. SIR JAMES MALLINSON
14. Maha·bhárata IX: Shalya (*Śalyaparvan*) (vol. 1 of 2)* JUSTIN MEILAND

15. Rákshasa's Ring (*Mudrārākṣasa*)*
by *Viśākhadatta*. Michael Coulson
16. Messenger Poems (*Meghadūta, Pavanadūta & Haṃsadūta*)
by *Kālidāsa, Dhoyī & Rūpa Gosvāmin*. Sir James Mallinson
17. Ramáyana III: The Forest (*Araṇyakāṇḍa*)
by *Vālmīki*. Sheldon I. Pollock
18. The Epitome of Queen Lilávati (*Līlāvatīsāra*) (vol. 2 of 2)
by *Jinaratna*. R.C.C. Fynes
19. Five Discourses on Worldly Wisdom (*Pañcatantra*)*
by *Viṣṇuśarman*. Patrick Olivelle
20. Ramáyana V: Súndara (*Sundarakāṇḍa*) by *Vālmīki*.
Robert P. Goldman & Sally J. Sutherland Goldman
21. Maha·bhárata II: The Great Hall (*Sabhāparvan*)
Paul Wilmot
22. The Recognition of Shakúntala (*Abhijñānaśākuntala*) (Kashmir Recension) by *Kālidāsa*. Somadeva Vasudeva
23. Maha·bhárata VII: Drona (*Droṇaparvan*) (vol. 1 of 4)*
Vaughan Pilikian
24. Rama Beyond Price (*Anargharāghava*)
by *Murāri*. Judit Törzsök
25. Maha·bhárata IV: Viráta (*Virāṭaparvan*)
Kathleen Garbutt
26. Maha·bhárata VIII: Karna (*Karṇaparvan*) (vol. 1 of 2)
Adam Bowles
27. "The Lady of the Jewel Necklace" & "The Lady who Shows her Love" (*Ratnāvalī & Priyadarśikā*) by *Harṣa*.*
Wendy Doniger
28. The Ocean of the Rivers of Story (*Kathāsaritsāgara*) (vol. 1 of 7)
by *Somadeva*. Sir James Mallinson
29. Handsome Nanda (*Saundarananda*)*
by *Aśvaghoṣa*. Linda Covill
30. Maha·bhárata IX: Shalya (*Śalyaparvan*) (vol. 2 of 2)*
Justin Meiland
31. Rama's Last Act (*Uttararāmacarita*) by *Bhavabhūti*.
Sheldon Pollock. Foreword by Girish Karnad

32. "Friendly Advice" (*Hitopadeśa*) by *Nārāyaṇa* &
"King Víkrama's Adventures" (*Vikramacarita*). Judit Törzsök

33. Life of the Buddha (*Buddhacarita*)
by *Aśvaghoṣa*. Patrick Olivelle

34. Maha·bhárata V: Preparations for War (*Udyogaparvan*) (vol. 1 of 2)
Kathleen Garbutt. Foreword by Gurcharan Das

35. Maha·bhárata VIII: Karna (*Karṇaparvan*) (vol. 2 of 2)
Adam Bowles

36. Maha·bhárata V: Preparations for War (*Udyogaparvan*) (vol. 2 of 2)
Kathleen Garbutt

37. Maha·bhárata VI: Bhishma (*Bhīṣmaparvan*) (vol. 1 of 2)*
Including the "Bhagavad Gita" in Context
Alex Cherniak. Foreword by Ranajit Guha

38. The Ocean of the Rivers of Story (*Kathāsaritsāgara*) (vol. 2 of 7)
by *Somadeva*. Sir James Mallinson

39. "How the Nagas were Pleased" (*Nāgānanda*) by *Harṣa* &
"The Shattered Thighs" (*Ūrubhaṅga*) by *Bhāsa*.*
Andrew Skilton

40. Gita·govínda: Love Songs of Radha and Krishna (*Gītagovinda*)*
by *Jayadeva*. Lee Siegel. Foreword by Sudipta Kaviraj

41. "Bouquet of Rasa" & "River of Rasa" (*Rasamañjarī & Rasataraṅgiṇī*) by *Bhānudatta*. Sheldon Pollock

42. Garland of the Buddha's Past Lives (*Jātakamālā*) (vol. 1 of 2)*
by *Āryaśūra*. Justin Meiland

43. Maha·bhárata XII: Peace (*Śāntiparvan*) (vol. 3 of 5)*
"The Book of Liberation" (*Mokṣadharma*). Alexander Wynne

44. The Little Clay Cart (*Mṛcchakaṭikā*) by *Śūdraka*.
Diwakar Acharya. Foreword by Partha Chatterjee

45. Bhatti's Poem: The Death of Rávana (*Bhaṭṭikāvya*)*
by *Bhaṭṭi*. Oliver Fallon

46. "Self-Surrender," "Peace," "Compassion," and "The Mission of the Goose": Poems and Prayers from South India (*Ātmārpaṇastuti, Śāntivilāsa, Dayāśataka & Haṃsasaṃdeśa*) by *Appayya Dīkṣita, Nīlakaṇṭha Dīkṣita & Vedānta Deśika.* Yigal Bronner & David Shulman
Foreword by Gieve Patel
47. Maha·bhárata VI: Bhishma (*Bhīṣmaparvan*) (vol. 2 of 2)*
Alex Cherniak
48. How Úrvashi Was Won (*Vikramorvaśīya*) by *Kālidāsa*
Velcheru Narayana Rao & David Shulman
49. The Quartet of Causeries (*Caturbhāṇī*)
by *Śūdraka, Śyāmilaka, Vararuci & Īśvaradatta.*
Csaba Dezső & Somadeva Vasudeva
50. Garland of the Buddha's Past Lives (*Jātakamālā*) (vol. 2 of 2)*
by *Āryaśūra.* Justin Meiland
51. Princess Kadámbari (*Kādambarī*) (vol. 1 of 3)
by *Bāṇa.* David Smith
52. The Rise of Wisdom Moon (*Prabodhacandrodaya*)*
by *Kṛṣṇamiśra.* Matthew T. Kapstein
Foreword by J.N. Mohanty
53. Maha·bhárata VII: Drona (*Droṇaparvan*) (vol. 2 of 4)*
Vaughan Pilikian
54. Maha·bhárata X & XI: Dead of Night & The Women (*Sauptikaparvan & Strīparvan*).* Kate Crosby
55. Seven Hundred Elegant Verses (*Āryāsaptaśatī*)*
by *Govardhana.* Friedhelm Hardy
56. Málavika and Agni·mitra (*Mālavikāgnimitram*) by *Kālidāsa.*
Dániel Balogh & Eszter Somogyi

Permitted finals:							*(Except āḥ/aḥ)*			
k	ṭ	t	p	ṅ	n	m	ḥ/r	āḥ	aḥ	*Initial letters:*
k	ṭ	t	p	ṅ	n	ṃ	ḥ	āḥ	aḥ	k/kh
g	ḍ	d	b	ṅ	n	ṃ	r	ā	o	g/gh
k	ṭ	c	p	ṅ	ṃś	ṃ	ś	āś	aś	c/ch
g	ḍ	j	b	ṅ	ñ	ṃ	r	ā	o	j/jh
k	ṭ	ṭ	p	ṅ	ṃṣ	ṃ	ṣ	āṣ	aṣ	ṭ/ṭh
g	ḍ	ḍ	b	ṅ	ṇ	ṃ	r	ā	o	ḍ/ḍh
k	ṭ	t	p	ṅ	ṃs	ṃ	s	ās	as	t/th
g	ḍ	d	b	ṅ	n	ṃ	r	ā	o	d/dh
k	ṭ	t	p	ṅ	n	ṃ	ḥ	āḥ	aḥ	p/ph
g	ḍ	d	b	ṅ	n	ṃ	r	ā	o	b/bh
ṅ	ṇ	n	m	ṅ	n	ṃ	r	ā	o	*nasals* (n/m)
g	ḍ	d	b	ṅ	n	ṃ	r	ā	o	y/v
g	ḍ	d	b	ṅ	n	ṃ	*zero*[1]	ā	o	r
g	ḍ	l	b	ṅ	l̃[2]	ṃ	r	ā	o	l
k	ṭ	c ch	p	ṅ	ñ ś/ch	ṃ	ḥ	āḥ	aḥ	ś
k	ṭ	t	p	ṅ	n	ṃ	ḥ	āḥ	aḥ	ṣ/s
gg h	ḍḍ h	dd h	bb h	ṅ	n	ṃ	r	ā	o	h
g	ḍ	d	b	ṅ/ṅṅ[3]	n/nn[3]	m	r	ā	a[4]	*vowels*
k	ṭ	t	p	ṅ	n	m	ḥ	āḥ	aḥ	*zero*

[1]ḥ or r disappears, and if a/i/u precedes, this lengthens to ā/ī/ū. [2]e.g. tān+lokān=tāl̃ lokān.
[3]The doubling occurs if the preceding vowel is short. [4]Except: aḥ+a=o '.